Networking
Second Edition

Jeffrey S. Beasley
New Mexico State University

An Imprint of Pearson Education

Upper Saddle River, NJ • Boston • Indianapolis • San Francisco
New York • Toronto • Montreal • London • Munich • Paris • Madrid
Cape Town • Sydney • Tokyo • Singapore • Mexico City

PRENTICE
HALL

Networking, Second Edition

Jeffrey S. Beasley

The publisher offers excellent discounts on this book when ordered in quantity for bulk purchases or special sales, which may include electronic versions and/or custom covers and content particular to your business, training goals, marketing focus, and branding interests. For more information, please contact:

> U.S. Corporate and Government Sales
> (800) 382-3419
> corpsales@pearsontechgroup.com

For sales outside the United States please contact:

> International Sales
> international@pearson.com

Visit us on the Web: www.informit.com/ph

Library of Congress Cataloging-in-Publication Data

Beasley, Jeffrey S., 1955-

  Networking / Jeffrey S. Beasley. — 2nd ed.

    p. cm.

  ISBN-13: 978-0-13-135838-6 (hardcover w/cd)

  ISBN-10: 0-13-135838-3

  1. Computer networks—Design and construction. 2. TCP/IP (Computer network protocol) 3. Internetworking (Telecommunication) I. Title.

  TK5105.5.B39 2008

  004.6—dc22

                          2008032371

ISBN-13: 978-0-13-135838-6
ISBN-10: 0-13-135838-3
Text printed in the United States at Edwards Brothers in Ann Arbor, Michigan.
Eighth Printing, 2011

Associate Publisher
David Dusthimer

Senior Development Editor
Christopher Cleveland

Managing Editor
Patrick Kanouse

Senior Project Editor
Tonya Simpson

Copy Editor
Language Logistics, LLC

Indexer
Heather McNeil

Proofreader
Arle Writing and Editing

Technical Reviewers
Dan Bosch, Tami Day-Orsatti,
Jim Geier, Randy Ivener,
Steve McQuerry,
Shawn Merdinger,
Piyasat Nilkaew, Matt Peralta ,
Allan Reid, Holly Ricketts,
Able Sanchez, Lee Shombert,
Toby Skandier, Randy Zhang

Publishing Coordinator
Vanessa Evans

Multimedia Developer
Dan Scherf

This book is dedicated to my family Kim, Damon, and Dana

My Mom and Dad, Margaret and Harlan Beasley

My father-in-law, Chip Chippeaux

and to the memory of my mother-in-law, Jackie

Preface

This book provides a comprehensive look at computer networking from the point of view of the network administrator. It guides readers from an entry-level knowledge in computer networks to advanced concepts in Ethernet networks, router configuration, TCP/IP networks, routing protocols, local, campus, and wide area network configuration, network security, wireless networking, optical networks, Voice over IP, the network server, Linux networking, and industrial networks. After covering the entire text, readers will have gained a solid knowledge base in computer networks.

In my years of teaching, I have observed that technology students prefer to learn "how to swim" after they have gotten wet and taken in a little water. Then they are ready for more challenges. Show the students the technology, how it is used, and why, and they will take the applications of the technology to the next level. Allowing them to experiment with the technology helps them to develop a greater understanding. This book does just that.

ORGANIZATION OF THE TEXT

This text is designed to cover two semesters. The recommended chapters for the first semester are Chapters 1 to 8. Throughout the semester, the students will gain an appreciation of how basic computer networks and related hardware are interconnected to form a network. This involves understanding the concepts and issues of twisted-pair cable, interconnecting LANs, configuring TCP/IP, subnet masking, basic router configuration, and configuring routing protocols and wide area networking.

Chapters 9 to 16 are recommended for the second semester—configuring and managing the campus network, network security, wireless LANs, and optical networks. The instructor can choose from the following topics to complete the semester: installing and configuring Windows 2008/2003 network server, Voice over IP, Linux configuration, and industrial networks.

Key Pedagogical Features

- *Chapter Outline, Objectives, Key Terms,* and *Introduction* at the beginning of each chapter clearly outline specific goals for the reader. An example of these features is shown in Figure P-1.

Chapter Outline

Chapter Objectives

Introduction:
Chapter openers clearly outline specific goals

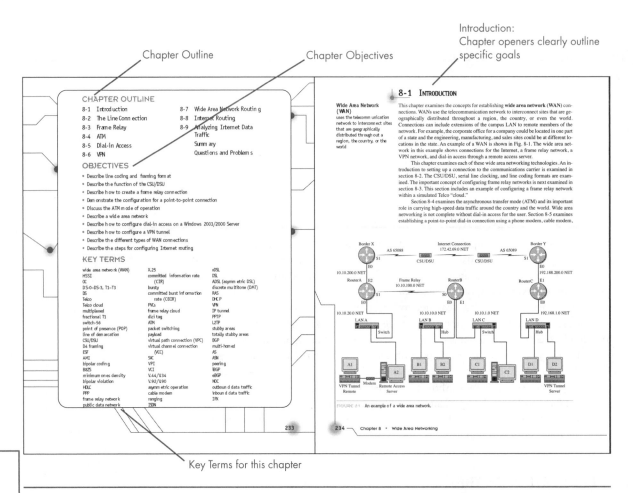

Key Terms for this chapter

FIGURE P-1

- *Net-Challenge Software* provides a simulated, hands-on experience in configuring routers. Exercises provided in the text (see Figure P-2) and on the CD challenge readers to undertake certain router/network configuration tasks. The challenges check the students' ability to enter basic networking commands and to set up router function, such as configuring the interface (Ethernet and Serial) and routing protocols (that is, OSPF, BGP, EIGRP, IGRP, RIP, and static). The software has the look and feel of actually being connected to the router's console port.
- *Protocol Analyzer Software* packaged with the text uses the Finisar Surveyor Demo. Examples of using the software to analyze data traffic are included throughout the text, as shown in Figure P-3.
- *Numerous worked-out examples* are included in every chapter to reinforce key concepts and aid in subject mastery, as shown in Figure P-3.

The Cisco uBR900 series cable access router. (Courtesy of Cisco System s)

A command used for displaying only the OSPF routes is *sh ip route ospf*. The results for this command from RouterA are shown:

```
RouterA#sh ip route ospf
     10.0.0.0/24 is subnetted, 6 subnets
O       10.10.5.0 [110/74] via 10.10.100.2, 00:10:03, Ethernet2
O       10.10.10.0 [110/74] via 10.10.200.2, 00:10:03, Ethernet1
O       10.10.150.0 [110/128] via 10.10.200.2, 00:10:03, Ethernet1
                    [110/128] via 10.10.100.2, 00:10:03, Ethernet2
```

Another command used for displaying protocol information for the router is *sh ip protocol*. The results for entering this command for RouterA are shown:

```
RouterA#sh ip protocol
Routing Protocol is "ospf 100"
  Sending updates every 0 seconds
  Invalid after 0 seconds, hold down 0, flushed after 0
  Outgoing update filter list for all interfaces is
  Incoming update filter list for all interfaces is
  Redistributing: ospf 100
  Routing for Networks:
    10.10.20.250/32
    10.10.100.1/32
    10.10.200.1/32
  Routing Information Sources:
    Gateway         Distance      Last Update
    10.10.100.1       110         00:06:01
    10.10.200.2       110         00:06:01
  Distance: (default is 110)
```

Networking Challenge—OSPF

Use the Net-Challenge simulator software included with the text's Companion CD-ROM to demonstrate that you can configure OSPF for RouterB in the campus LAN (the campus LAN is shown in Fig. 7-12 and is displayed on the computer screen once the software is started). Make sure that you have configured your computer's display to meet the 800 × 600 pixel display resolution requirement. Place the Net-Challenge

CD-ROM in your computer's drive. Open the **Net-Challenge** folder, click on *Net-Challenge.exe*. Once the software is running, click on the **Select Router Challenge** button. This opens a **Select Router Challenge** drop-down menu. Select *Chapter 7—OSPF*. This opens a check box that can be used to verify that you have completed all of the tasks.

1. Enter the privileged EXEC mode on the router.
2. Enter the router's terminal configuration mode, **Router(config)**.
3. Set the hostname to *RouterA*.
4. Configure the Ethernet0 interface with the following:
   IP address   10.10.20.250
   Subnet mask   255.255.255.0
5. Enable the E0 interface.
6. Configure the Ethernet1 interface with the following:
   IP address   10.10.200.1
   Subnet mask   255.255.255.0
7. Enable the E1 interface.
8. Configure the Ethernet2 interface with the following:
   IP address   10.10.100.1
   Subnet mask   255.255.255.0
9. Enable the E2 interface.
10. Enable OSPF with a network number of 100.
11. Use a single command line instruction to configure RouterA to run OSPF on all three of the Ethernet interfaces (use area 100).
12. Use the *sh ip int brief* command to check the interface status.
13. Use the *sh ip protocol* command to see if OSPF is running on RouterA.
14. Use the *sh ip route* command to verify that the three Ethernet ports are connected to RouterA.
15. Use the *sh run* command to view the running-configuration file on RouterA. Verify that OSPF is enabled and the proper network address is specified.

7-7 EIGRP—Enhanced Interior Gateway Routing Protocol

This section introduces techniques for configuring a router's interface to run EIGRP, the Enhanced Interior Gateway Routing Protocol. EIGRP is an enhanced version of the Interior Gateway Routing Protocol (IGRP). EIGRP is a Cisco proprietary link state protocol. EIGRP calculates route metrics in a similar way as IGRP but uses a technique to improve the detail on metrics.

EIGRP allows the use of variable length subnet masks, which is beneficial when trying to conserve the uses of IP addresses. EIGRP also uses "Hello" packets to verify that a link from one router to another is still active. This is similar to the OSPF "Hello" packet described in section 7-6. The routing table updates are exchanged when there is a change in the network. In other words, the routers don't exchange unnecessary information unless a route changes. This helps conserve the limited bandwidth of the network data link. When route information is exchanged, EIGRP quickly converges to the new route selection.

EIGRP
Enhanced Interior Gateway Routing Protocol

Exercises challenge readers to undertake certain tasks

Net-Challenges are found throughout the text

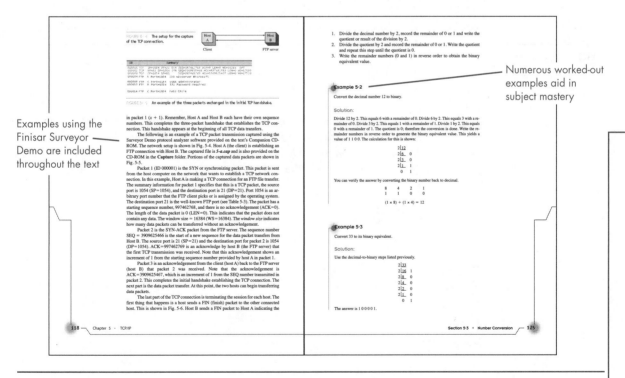

FIGURE 5-4 The setup for the capture of the TCP connection.

FIGURE 5-5 An example of the three packets exchanged in the initial TCP handshake.

Examples using the Finisar Surveyor Demo are included throughout the text

in packet 1 (*x* + 1). Remember, Host A and Host B each have their own sequence numbers. This completes the three-packet handshake that establishes the TCP connection. This handshake appears at the beginning of all TCP data transfers.

The following is an example of a TCP packet transmission captured using the Surveyor Demo protocol analyzer software provided on the text's Companion CD-ROM. The network setup is shown in Fig. 5-4. Host A (the client) is establishing an FTP connection with Host B. The captured file is *5-a.cap* and is also provided on the CD-ROM in the **Capture** folder. Portions of the captured data packets are shown in Fig. 5-5.

Packet 1 (ID 000001) is the SYN or synchronizing packet. This packet is sent from the host computer on the network that wants to establish a TCP network connection. In this example, Host A is making a TCP connection for an FTP file transfer. The summary information for packet 1 specifies that this is a TCP packet, the source port is 1054 (SP=1054), and the destination port is 21 (DP=21). Port 1054 is an arbitrary port number that the FTP client picks or is assigned by the operating system. The destination port 21 is the well-known FTP port (see Table 5-3). The packet has a starting sequence number, 997462768, and there is no acknowledgement (ACK=0). The length of the data packet is 0 (LEN=0). This indicates that the packet does not contain any data. The window size = 16384 (WS=16384). The *window size* indicates how many data packets can be transferred without an acknowledgement.

Packet 2 is the SYN-ACK packet from the FTP server. The sequence number SEQ = 3909625466 is the start of a new sequence for the data packet transfers from Host B. The source port is 21 (SP=21) and the destination port for packet 2 is 1054 (DP=1054). ACK=997462769 is an acknowledge by host B (the FTP server) that the first TCP transmission was received. Note that this acknowledgement shows an increment of 1 from the starting sequence number provided by host A in packet 1.

Packet 3 is an acknowledgement from the client (host A) back to the FTP server (host B) that packet 2 was received. Note that the acknowledgement is ACK=3909625467, which is an increment of 1 from the SEQ number transmitted in packet 2. This completes the initial handshake establishing the TCP connection. The next part is the data packet transfer. At this point, the two hosts can begin transferring data packets.

The last part of the TCP connection is terminating the session for each host. The first thing that happens is a host sends a FIN (finish) packet to the other connected host. This is shown in Fig. 5-6. Host B sends a FIN packet to Host A indicating the

1. Divide the decimal number by 2, record the remainder of 0 or 1 and write the quotient or result of the division by 2.
2. Divide the quotient by 2 and record the remainder of 0 or 1. Write the quotient and repeat this step until the quotient is 0.
3. Write the remainder numbers (0 and 1) in reverse order to obtain the binary equivalent value.

Example 5-2

Convert the decimal number 12 to binary.

Solution:

Divide 12 by 2. This equals 6 with a remainder of 0. Divide 6 by 2. This equals 3 with a remainder of 0. Divide 3 by 2. This equals 1 with a remainder of 1. Divide 1 by 2. This equals 0 with a remainder of 1. The quotient is 0; therefore the conversion is done. Write the remainder numbers in reverse order to generate the binary equivalent value. This yields a value of 1 1 0 0. The calculation for this is shown:

```
2|12
2|6   0
2|3   0
2|1   1
   0   1
```

You can verify the answer by converting the binary number back to decimal.

```
8    4    2    1
1    1    0    0
```

$(1 \times 8) + (1 \times 4) = 12$

Example 5-3

Convert 33 to its binary equivalent.

Solution:

Use the decimal-to-binary steps listed previously.

```
2|33
2|16   1
2|8    0
2|4    0
2|2    0
2|1    0
   0   1
```

The answer is 1 0 0 0 0 1.

Numerous worked-out examples aid in subject mastery

FIGURE P-3

- *Configuring, Analyzing, or Troubleshooting* sections, as shown in Figure P-4, are included with each chapter to guide the reader through advanced techniques in networking.

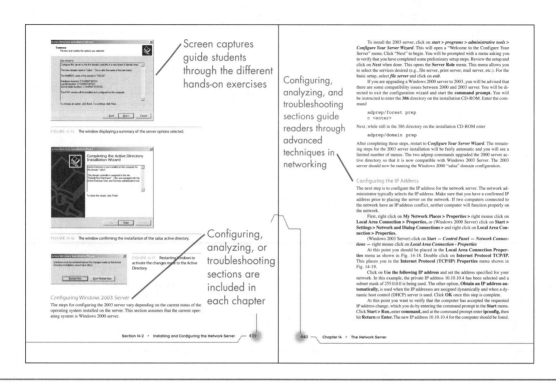

FIGURE P-4

- *Key Terms* and their definitions are highlighted in the margins to foster inquisitiveness and ensure retention. This is illustrated in Figure P-5.
- *Extensive Summaries, Questions,* and *Problems* as well as *Critical Thinking Questions* are found at the end of each chapter, as shown in Figure P-6.

Illustrations
and photos
enhance
the text

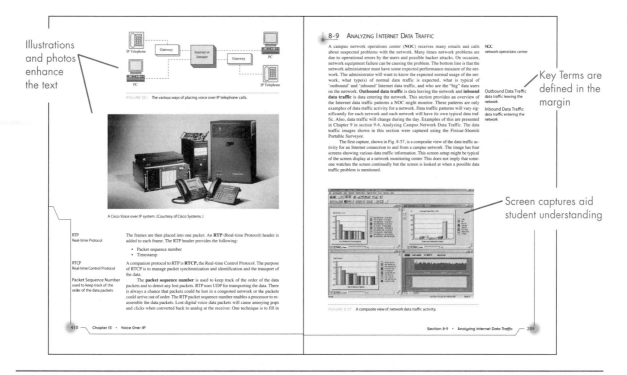

Key Terms are
defined in the
margin

Screen captures aid
student understanding

Summary of key concepts

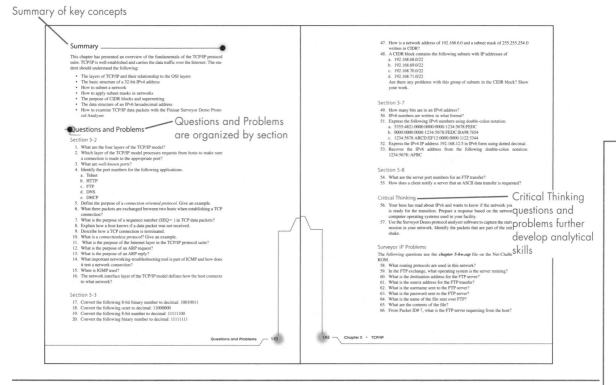

FIGURE P-5

FIGURE P-6

- An extensive *Glossary* is found at the end of the book and offers quick, accessible definitions to key terms and acronyms, as well as an exhaustive *Index* (Figure P-7).

Complete Glossary of terms and acronyms provide quick reference

Exhaustive Index provides quick reference

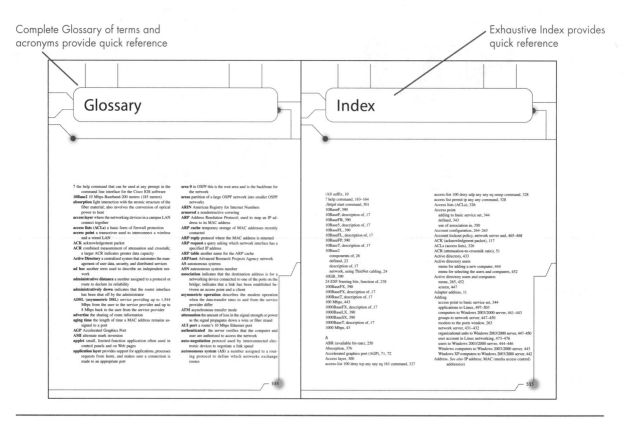

FIGURE P-7

Accompanying CD-ROM

The CD-ROM packaged with the text includes the Finisar Surveyor Demo software and captured data traffic used in the text. This software provides readers with the opportunity to capture data traffic on their own network. It also includes the Net-Challenge Software, which was developed specifically for this text.

Instructor Resources

The Instructor's Manual to accompany *Networking, Second Edition* (ISBN 0-13-135838-3) provides the entire book in PDF format along with instructor notes for each section within each chapter, recommending key concepts that should be covered in each chapter. Solutions to all chapter Questions and Problems sections are also included. In addition, the instructor will find a separate Solutions to the Net-Challenges Instructor's Edition PDF as well as a 18 laboratory exercises. Also a test bank with which to generate quizzes on the material found within the student edition of the book is provided.

ACKNOWLEDGMENTS

I am grateful to the many people who have helped with this text. My sincere thanks go to the following technical consultants:

- Holly Ricketts, for her help with the Windows 2008/2003 server and computer fundamentals, Piyasat Nilkew with his help with the router configuration and network security.
- Danny Bosch and Matthew Peralta for sharing their expertise with optical networks and unshielded twisted pair cabling, Abel Sanchez for sharing his extensive knowledge of Linux, and Don Yates for his help with the initial Net-Challenge software and his suggestions on industrial networking.
- Byron Hicks, for his helpful suggestions on the configuring, managing, and troubleshooting sections.
- Todd Bowman, CCIE#6316, for guiding me through the challenging routing protocols, wide area networking, managing a campus type network, and network security.

I would also like to thank my many past and present students for their help with this book.

- Jonathan Trejo and Nate Murillo for their work on the Net-Challenge software, Adam Segura for his help with taking pictures of the steps for CAT6 termination, Marc Montez, Carine George-Morris, Brian Morales, Michael Thomas, Jacob Ulibarri, Scott Leppelman, and Aarin Buskirk for their help with laboratory development. Your efforts are greatly appreciated.
- Aaron Shapiro and Aaron Jackson, for their help in testing the many network connections presented in the text.
- Paul Bueno and Anthony Bueno, for reading through the early draft of the text.
- Finisar Systems, for allowing me to include the Surveyor Demo Protocol Analyzer software with the text.

I appreciate the excellent feedback of the following reviewers: Phillip Davis, DelMar College, TX; Thomas D. Edwards, Carteret Community College, NC; William Hessmiller, Editors & Training Associates; Bill Liu, DeVry University, CA; and Timothy Staley, DeVry University, TX.

My thanks to the people at Prentice Hall for making this project possible: Dave Dusthimer, for providing me with the opportunity to work on the second edition of this text and Vanessa Evans, for helping make this process enjoyable. Thanks to Christopher Cleveland, and the all the people at Cisco Press, and also to the many technical editors for their help with editing the manuscript.

Special thanks to my family for their continued support and patience.

—*Jeffrey S. Beasley*

ABOUT THE AUTHOR

Jeff Beasley is a professor with the Department of Engineering Technology at New Mexico State University. He has been teaching with the department since 1988 and is the co-author of *Modern Electronic Communication and Electronic Devices and Circuits*.

http://web.nmsu.edu/~jbeasley/

Brief Contents

Chapter 1   Introduction to Computer Networks   2

Chapter 2   Physical Layer Cabling: Twisted Pair   48

Chapter 3   Computer Fundamentals   100

Chapter 4   Interconnecting the LANs   120

Chapter 5   TCP/IP   154

Chapter 6   Introduction to Router
             Configuration   192

Chapter 7   Routing Protocols   224

Chapter 8   Wide Area Networking   288

Chapter 9   Configuring and Managing the
             Campus Network   352

Chapter 10   Network Security   386

Chapter 11   Wireless Networking   412

Chapter 12   Optical Networking   446

Chapter 13   Voice over IP   486

Chapter 14   The Network Server   508

Chapter 15   Linux Networking   558

Chapter 16   Industrial Networks   616

Glossary   635

Index   651

Contents

Chapter 1   Introduction to Computer Networks   2

1-1	INTRODUCTION	5
1-2	NETWORK TOPOLOGIES	5
1-3	THE ETHERNET LAN	10
	IP (Internet Protocol) Addressing	15
1-4	ASSEMBLING A HOME NETWORK	16
	Securing the Home Network	27
	IP Addressing in the Home Network	29
1-5	ASSEMBLING AN OFFICE LAN	30
1-6	TESTING AND TROUBLESHOOTING A LAN	35
1-7	ANALYZING COMPUTER NETWORKS	37
Summary		43
Questions and Problems		43

Chapter 2   Physical Layer Cabling: Twisted Pair   48

2-1	INTRODUCTION	51
2-2	STRUCTURED CABLING	51
	Horizontal Cabling	54
2-3	UNSHIELDED TWISTED-PAIR CABLE	57
	Shielded Twisted-pair Cable	60
2-4	TERMINATING CAT6/5E/5 UTP CABLES	60
	Computer Communication	61
	Straight-through and Crossover Patch Cables	63
2-5	CABLE TESTING AND CERTIFICATION	71
	Testing the CAT6 Link	75
2-6	10 Gigabit Ethernet over Copper	83
	Overview	83
	Alien Crosstalk (AXT)	83
	Signal Transmission	85

2-7 TROUBLESHOOTING COMPUTER NETWORKS   86
    Installation   86
    Cable Stretching   87
    Cable Failing to Meet Manufacturer Specifications   87
    CAT5e Cable Test Examples   88
Summary   94
Questions and Problems   94

Chapter 3   Computer Fundamentals   100
3-1 INTRODUCTION   102
3-2 THE COMPUTER BUS CONNECTION   102
    Motherboard Bus Connections   103
3-3 DEVICE DRIVERS   107
    Verifying Device Drivers on Windows Vista/XP   108
    Verifying Device Drivers on Mac OS X   110
3-4 COMPUTER MEMORY   112
    Types of Memory   113
3-5 AN OVERVIEW OF FAT AND NTFS   114
    FAT   114
    FAT32   115
    NTFS   115
3-6 CONFIGURING THE BIOS BOOT SEQUENCE   116
Summary   117
Questions and Problems   117

Chapter 4   Interconnecting the LANs   120
4-1 INTRODUCTION   122
4-2 THE OSI MODEL   122
4-3 THE NETWORK BRIDGE   124
4-4 THE NETWORK SWITCH   128
    Hub–Switch Comparison   130
    Managed Switches   133
    Multilayer Switches   137
4-5 THE ROUTER   138
    The Router Interface: Cisco 2800 Series   139
    The Router Interface—Cisco 2600 Series   140
    The Router Interface—Cisco 2500 Series   140
4-6 INTERCONNECTING LANS WITH THE ROUTER   143
    Gateway Address   145
    Network Segments   145

4-7   CONFIGURING THE NETWORK INTERFACE—AUTO-
       NEGOTIATION   145
           Auto-Negotiation Steps   146
           Full Duplex/Half Duplex   146
Summary   149
Questions and Problems   149

Chapter 5   TCP/IP   154
5-1   INTRODUCTION   156
5-2   THE TCP/IP LAYERS   156
           The Application Layer   157
           The Transport Layer   158
           The Internet Layer   162
           The Network Interface Layer   164
5-3   NUMBER CONVERSION   165
           Binary-Decimal Conversion   165
           Decimal→Binary Conversion   166
           Hexadecimal Numbers   168
5-4   IPV4 ADDRESSING   170
           Private IP Addresses   173
           IP Address Assignment   173
5-5   SUBNET MASKS   173
5-6   CIDR BLOCKS   180
5-7   IPV6 ADDRESSING   182
5-8   ANALYZING COMPUTER NETWORKS—FTP DATA PACKETS   185
Summary   187
Questions and Problems   187

Chapter 6   Introduction to Router
                Configuration   192
6-1   INTRODUCTION   194
6-2   ROUTER FUNDAMENTALS   194
           Layer 3 Networks   195
6-3   THE CONSOLE PORT CONNECTION   201
           Configuring the HyperTerminal Software (Windows)   203
           Configuring the Z-Term Serial Communications
           Software (Mac)   205
6-4   THE ROUTER'S USER EXEC MODE (ROUTER>)   206
           The User EXEC Mode   206
           Router Configuration Challenge—The User EXEC Mode   209

6-5   THE ROUTER'S PRIVILEGED EXEC MODE (ROUTER#)   211

     Hostname   212

     Enable Secret   213

     Setting the Line Console Passwords   213

     Fast Ethernet Interface Configuration   214

     Serial Interface Configuration   214

     Router Configuration Challenge—The Privileged EXEC Mode   216

6-6   TROUBLESHOOTING THE ROUTER INTERFACE   217

Summary   221

Questions and Problems   221

Chapter 7   Routing Protocols   224

7-1   INTRODUCTION   227

7-2   STATIC ROUTING   227

     Gateway of Last Resort   233

     Configuring Static Routes   234

     Networking Challenge—Static Routes   236

7-3   DYNAMIC ROUTING PROTOCOLS   236

     Distance Vector Protocols   238

     Link State Protocols   239

7-4   RIP—ROUTING INFORMATION PROTOCOL   239

     Configuring Routes with RIP   242

     Networking Challenge—RIP   244

7-5   IGRP—INTERIOR GATEWAY ROUTING PROTOCOL   245

     Configuring Routes with IGRP   246

     Networking Challenge—IGRP   250

7-6   OSPF—OPEN SHORTEST PATH FIRST ROUTING PROTOCOL   250

     Configuring Routes with OSPF   252

     Networking Challenge—OSPF   256

7-7   EIGRP—ENHANCED INTERIOR GATEWAY ROUTING
PROTOCOL   257

     Configuring Routes with EIGRP   257

     Networking Challenge—EIGRP   262

7-8   CONFIGURING A JUNIPER ROUTER   262

     Operational Mode   263

     Router Configuration Mode   266

     Displaying the Router Interfaces   267

     Hostname Configuration   268

     Assigning an IP Address to an Interface   268

     Static Route   268

     RIP Configuration   269

     OSPF Configuration   270

7-9   TFTP—Trivial File Transfer Protocol   271

Configuring TFTP   271

Networking Challenge—TFTP   274

7-10   ANALYZING OSPF "HELLO" PACKETS   275

Summary   279

Questions and Problems   279

Chapter 8   Wide Area Networking   288

8-1   INTRODUCTION   291

8-2   THE LINE CONNECTION   292

Data Channels   292

Point of Presence   294

T1 Framing   294

Line Coding Formats   295

8-3   FRAME RELAY   298

Establishing a Frame Relay Connection   301

Configuring Frame Relay Point-to-Point on the Router   302

Networking Challenge—Frame Relay   305

8-4   ATM   305

Establishing the ATM Connection   308

8-5   DIAL-IN ACCESS   309

Analog Modem Technologies   309

Cable Modems   310

ISDN   310

xDSL Modems   312

The Remote Access Server   315

8-6   VPN   325

Configuring a VPN Virtual Interface (Router to Router)   327

Troubleshooting the VPN Tunnel Link   331

Configuring a VPN Server   331

Configuring a Remote Client's VPN Connection   332

8-7   WIDE AREA NETWORK ROUTING   337

8-8   INTERNET ROUTING   338

Configuring BGP   339

Networking Challenge—BGP   343

8-9   ANALYZING INTERNET DATA TRAFFIC   344

Utilization/Errors Strip Chart   344

Network Layer Matrix   345

Network Layer Host Table   346

Frame Size Distribution   347

Summary   348

Questions and Problems   348

**Chapter 9   Configuring and Managing the
Campus Network   352**

9-1   INTRODUCTION   354
9-2   DESIGNING THE CAMPUS NETWORK   354
       Core Layer   354
       Distribution Layer   355
       Access Layer   356
       Data Flow   356
       Selecting the Media   356
       Load Balancing   357
9-3   IP ASSIGNMENT AND DHCP   358
       The DHCP Data Packets   360
9-4   NETWORK SERVICES—DNS   361
       Campus DNS   363
9-5   NETWORK MANAGEMENT   364
       Configuring SNMP   365
       Power over Ethernet (PoE)   367
9-6   Switch/VLAN Configuration   369
       Virtual LAN (VLAN)   369
       Switch Configuration   370
       Hostname   371
       Enable Secret   372
       Setting the Line Console Passwords   372
       Static VLAN Configuration   373
       Networking Challenge—Static VLAN Configuration   376
       Spanning-Tree Protocol   377
9-7   ANALYZING CAMPUS NETWORK DATA TRAFFIC   378
Summary   381
Questions and Problems   381

Chapter 10   Network Security   386

10-1   INTRODUCTION   388
10-2   INTRUSION (HOW AN ATTACKER GAINS CONTROL OF A
       NETWORK)   388
       Social Engineering   389
       Password Cracking   389
       Packet Sniffing   390
       Vulnerable Software   391
       Viruses and Worms   393
       Wireless Vulnerabilities   394

10-3	DENIAL OF SERVICE	395
	Distributed Denial of Service Attacks (DDoS)	396
10-4	FIREWALLS AND ACCESS LISTS	396
	Attack Prevention	398
10-5	INTRUSION DETECTION	404
10-6	ANALYZING UNSECURED DATA PACKETS	405
Summary		409
Questions and Problems		409

Chapter 11	**Wireless Networking**	**412**
11-1	INTRODUCTION	414
11-2	THE IEEE 802.11 WIRELESS LAN STANDARD	414
11-3	802.11 WIRELESS NETWORKING	420
11-4	Bluetooth, WiMAX, and RFID	429
	Bluetooth	429
	WiMAX	432
	RFID (Radio Frequency Identification)	432
11-5	SECURING WIRELESS LANS	435
11-6	CONFIGURING A POINT-TO-MULTIPOINT WIRELESS LAN: A CASE STUDY	438
	1. Antenna Site Survey	439
	2. Establishing a Point-to-Point Wireless Link to the Home Network	439
	3–4. Configuring the Multipoint Distribution/Conducting an RF Site Survey	440
	5. Configuring the Remote Installations	442
Summary		443
Questions and Problems		443

Chapter 12	**Optical Networking**	**446**
12-1	INTRODUCTION	449
12-2	THE NATURE OF LIGHT	451
	Graded-Index Fiber	454
	Single-Mode Fibers	455
12-3	FIBER ATTENUATION AND DISPERSION	457
	Attenuation	457
	Dispersion	458
	Dispersion Compensation	460

12-4 OPTICAL COMPONENTS   461
          Intermediate Components   463
          Detectors   464
          Fiber Connectorization   466
12-5 OPTICAL NETWORKING ARCHITECTURES   468
          Defining Optical Networking   468
          Building Distribution   470
          Campus Distribution   472
12-6 SYSTEM DESIGN AND OPERATIONAL ISSUES   475
12-7 SAFETY   479
12-8 TROUBLESHOOTING COMPUTER NETWORKS (THE OTDR)   481
Summary   483
Questions and Problems   483

Chapter 13   Voice over IP   **486**
13-1 INTRODUCTION   488
13-2 THE BASICS OF VOICE OVER IP   488
13-3 VOICE OVER IP NETWORKS   490
          Replacing an Existing PBX Tie Line   491
          Upgrading Existing PBXs to Support IP Telephony   493
          Switching to a Complete IP Telephony Solution   494
13-4 QUALITY OF SERVICE   495
          Jitter   495
          Network Latency   496
          Queuing   496
13-5 ANALYZING VoIP DATA PACKETS   497
          Analyzing VoIP Telephone Call Data Packets   502
Summary   506
Questions and Problems   506

Chapter 14   The Network Server   **508**
14-1 INTRODUCTION   510
          Network Definitions   510
          Network Types   510
          Server Types   512
          Adding the Network Server   513
14-2 INSTALLING AND CONFIGURING THE NETWORK SERVER   514
          Creating a Server Domain (Windows 2003 Server)   514
          Configuring Windows 2008 Server   521
          Configuring the IP Address   521

14-3	ADDING COMPUTERS, USERS, AND GROUPS	522
	Adding Computers to the Windows 2008/2003 Server Domain	522
	Adding Users to the Windows 2008/2003 Server Domain	526
	Adding Organizational Units and Groups to the Windows 2008/2003 Server Domain	528
14-4	SETTING GROUP PERMISSIONS AND POLICIES	533
	2008 Server: Setting Domain Policies	534
	2003 Server: Setting Domain Policies	539
14-5	VERIFYING "NETWORK" AND "MY NETWORK PLACES" IN WINDOWS-BASED PCS	546
	"Network," Windows Vista	546
	"My Network Places" on Windows XP	546
	"My Network Places" on Windows 2000	550
	"Network Neighborhood" for Windows NT and 98	552
14-6	CONFIGURING THE NETWORK SERVER'S ACCOUNT LOCKOUT POLICY	552
Summary		556
Questions and Problems		556

Chapter 15	**Linux Networking**	**558**
15-1	INTRODUCTION	560
15-2	LOGGING ON TO LINUX	560
	Adding a User Account	561
15-3	LINUX FILE STRUCTURE AND FILE COMMANDS	565
	Listing Files	565
	Displaying File Contents	567
	Directory Operations	569
	File Operations	571
	Permissions and Ownership	573
15-4	LINUX ADMINISTRATION COMMANDS	577
	The *man* (manual) Command	577
	The *ps* (processes) Command	579
	The *su* (substitute user) Command	580
	The *mount* Command	581
	The *shutdown* Command	583
	Linux Tips	583
15-5	ADDING APPLICATIONS TO LINUX	584
15-6	LINUX NETWORKING	590
	Installing SSH	594
	The ftp Client	595
	The ftp Server	596

DNS Service on Linux 597
Changing the Hostname 597
15-7 TROUBLESHOOTING SYSTEM AND NETWORK PROBLEMS
WITH LINUX 598
Troubleshooting Boot Processes 598
Listing Users on the System 600
Network Security 601
Enabling and Disabling Boot Services 602
15-8 MANAGING THE LINUX SYSTEM 604
Summary 611
Questions and Problems 611

Chapter 16   Industrial Networks   616
16-1 INTRODUCTION 618
16-2 OVERVIEW OF INDUSTRIAL NETWORKS 618
Characteristics of Industrial Networks 619
16-3 INDUSTRIAL ETHERNET 625
Achieving Determinism 625
Topology 626
Switching 627
Cabling and Components 627
16-4 INDUSTRIAL ETHERNET PROTOCOLS 628
Ethernet/IP 629
Foundation Fieldbus High-Speed Ethernet (HSE) 629
Profinet 630
Interface for Distributed Automation (IDA) 630
Manufacturing Message Specification (MMS) 630
Modbus TCP 630
16-5 LEGACY DEVICE AND CONTROLLER LEVEL BUSES 630
Open Buses 630
Proprietary Buses 631
Summary 632
Questions and Problems 632

Glossary   635

Index   651

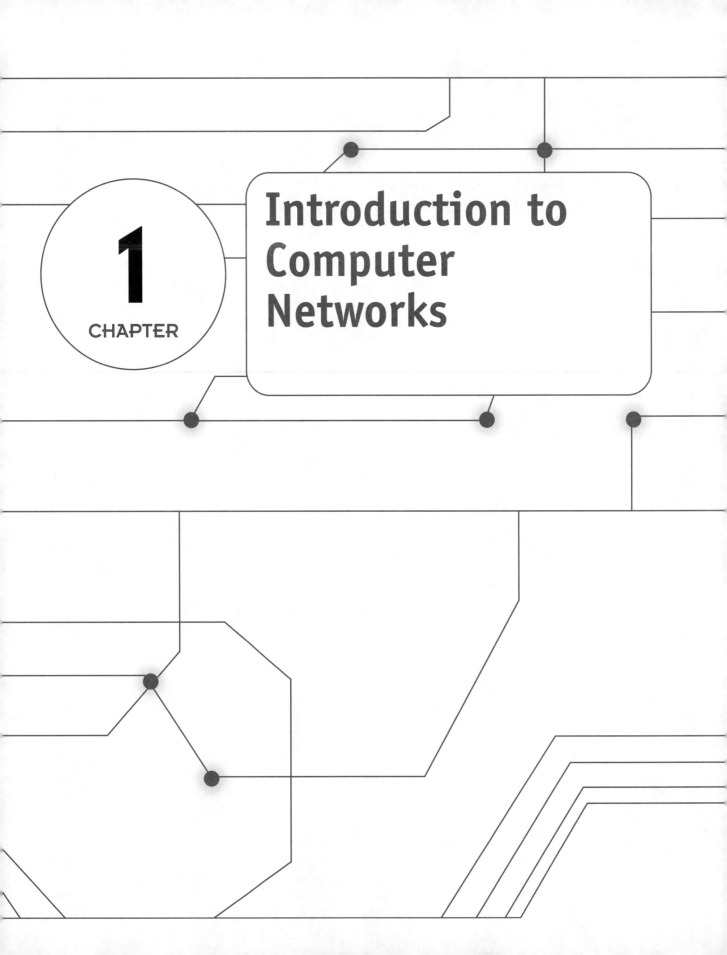

1

CHAPTER

Introduction to Computer Networks

CHAPTER OUTLINE

1-1   Introduction
1-2   Network Topologies
1-3   The Ethernet LAN
1-4   Assembling a Home Network
1-5   Assembling an Office LAN

1-6   Testing and Troubleshooting a LAN
1-7   Analyzing Computer Networks
Summary
Questions and Problems

OBJECTIVES

- Explain the various LAN topologies
- Define the function of a networking protocol
- Describe CSMA/CD for the Ethernet protocol
- Describe the structure of the Ethernet packet frame
- Define the function of the network interface card
- Describe the purpose of the MAC address on a networking device

- Discuss how to determine the MAC address for a computer
- Discuss the fundamentals of IP addressing
- Discuss the issues of configuring a home network
- Discuss the issue of assembling an office LAN
- Discuss the procedures for troubleshooting a LAN
- Describe how a protocol analyzer is used to examine network data packets

KEY TERMS

local area network (LAN)
protocol
topology
token-ring topology
token passing
IEEE
deterministic
token-ring hub
bus topology
ThinNet
star topology
hub
multiport repeater
broadcast
switch
ports

mesh topology
CSMA/CD
packet
network interface card (NIC)
MAC address
organizationally unique identifier (OUI)
Ethernet, physical, hardware, or adapter address
ipconfig /all
IANA
IP address
network number
host number
host address
ISP

private addresses
intranet
IP internetwork
TCP/IP
wired network
wireless network
Wi-Fi
wireless router
range extender
hotspots
Service Set Identifier (SSID)
firewall protection
Stateful Packet Inspection (SPI)
Virtual Private Network (VPN)

Network Address
Translation (NAT)

overloading

Port Address Trans-
lation (PAT)

CAT6 (category 6)

RJ-45

Mbps

numerics

ports

crossover

straight-through

uplink port

link light

link integrity test

link pulses

ping (packet Inter-
net groper)

ICMP

ipconfig

Address Resolution
Protocol (ARP)

ARP reply

echo request

1-1 INTRODUCTION

Each day computer users use their computer for sending and retrieving email, scheduling meetings, sharing files, preparing reports, exchanging images, and maybe checking the current price of an auction item on the Internet. All of this requires computers to access multiple networks and share their resources. The multiple networks required to accomplish this are the local area network (LAN), the campus area network (CAN), the metropolitan area network (MAN), and the wide area network (WAN).

This text introduces the reader to the techniques for implementing modern computer networks. Each chapter steps the student through the various modern networking technologies and methodologies and includes a section on configuring, analyzing, or troubleshooting computer networks. The accompanying CD-ROM comes with two software packages, the Finisar-Surveyor Demo protocol analyzer and the Net-Challenge simulator software developed specifically for this text. Each of these software enhancements provides the reader with invaluable insight into the inner workings of computer networking and with the experience of configuring and troubleshooting computer networks.

The ease of connecting to the Internet and the dramatic decrease in computer systems' cost have led to an explosion in their usage. Organizations such as corporations, colleges, and government agencies have acquired large numbers of single-user computer systems. These systems may be dedicated to word processing, scientific computation, process control, or may be general-purpose computers that perform many tasks. This has generated a need to interconnect these locally distributed computer networks. Interconnection allows users to exchange information (data) with other network members. It also allows resource sharing of expensive equipment such as file servers and high-quality graphics printers, or access to more powerful computers for tasks too complicated for the local computer to process. The network commonly used to accomplish this interconnection is called a **local area network (LAN)**, which is a network of users that share computer resources in a limited area.

Local Area Network (LAN)
Network of users that share computer resources in a limited area

1-2 NETWORK TOPOLOGIES

Local area networks are defined in terms of the **protocol** and the **topology** used for accessing the network. The networking protocol is the set of rules established for users to exchange information. The topology is the network architecture used to interconnect the networking equipment. The most common architectures for LANs are the star, ring, and bus. Examples are shown in Figure 1-1.

Protocol
Set of rules established for users to exchange information

Topology
Architecture of a network

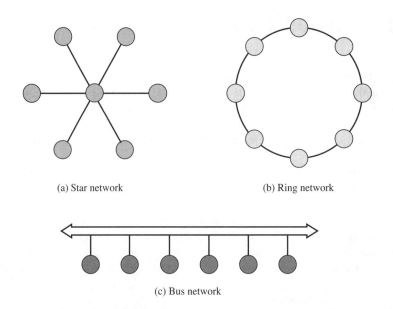

(a) Star network (b) Ring network

(c) Bus network

FIGURE 1-1   Network topologies. (From *Modern Electronic Communication* 9/e, by G. M. Miller & J. S. Beasley, 2008 Copyright © 2008 Pearson Education, Inc. Reprinted by permission of Pearson Education, Inc., Upper Saddle River, NJ.)

Token-ring Topology
A network topology configured in a logical ring that complements the token passing protocol

Token Passing
A technique where an electrical token circulates around a network—control of the token enables the user to gain access to the network

IEEE
Institute of Electrical and Electronics Engineers, one of the major standards-setting bodies for technological development

Deterministic
Access to the network is provided at fixed time intervals

Token-ring Hub
A hub that manages the passing of the token in a token-ring network

Bus Topology
The computers share the media (coaxial cable) for data transmission

ThinNet
A type of coaxial cable used to connect LANs configured with a bus topology

An example of a LAN configured using the **token-ring topology** is shown in Figure 1-2. In this topology, a "token" (shown as a T) is placed in the data channel and circulates around the ring, hence the name *token-ring*. If a user wants to transmit, the computer waits until it has control of the token. This technique is called **token passing** and is based on the **IEEE** 802.5 Token-Ring Network standard. A token-ring network is a **deterministic** network, meaning each station connected to the network is assured access for transmission of its messages at regular or fixed time intervals.

One disadvantage of the token-ring system is that if an error changes the token pattern, it can cause the token to stop circulating. Additionally, ring networks rely on each system to relay the data to the next user. A failed station can cause data traffic to cease. Another disadvantage of the token-ring network is from the troubleshooting and maintenance point of view. The token-ring path must be temporarily broken (path interrupted) if a computer or any device connected to the network is to be removed or added to the network. This results in downtime for the network. A fix to this is to attach all the computers to a central **token-ring hub**. Such a device manages the passing of the token rather than relying on individual computers to pass it, which improves the reliability of the network.

The **bus topology** is shown in Figure 1-3. In a bus system the computers share the media (coaxial cable) for data transmission. In this topology, a coaxial cable (called **ThinNet**) is looped through each networking device to facilitate data transfer.

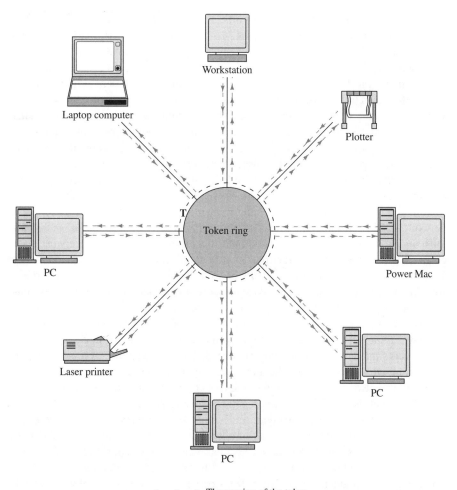

The passing of the token

FIGURE 1-2   The token-ring network topology.

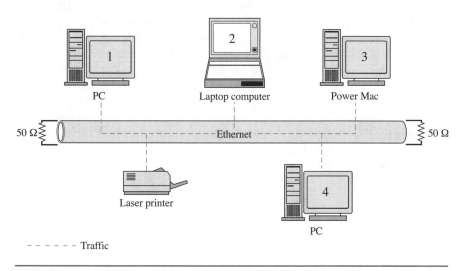

Traffic

FIGURE 1-3   The bus topology.

In a bus topology, all LAN data traffic is carried over a common coaxial cable link. Referring to Figure 1-3, if computer 1 is printing a large file, the line of communications will be between computer 1 and the printer. However, in a bus system, all networking devices will see computer 1's data traffic to the printer, and the other devices must wait for pauses in transmission or until it is complete before they can initiate their own transmission. If more than one computer's data is placed on the network at the same time, the data will be corrupted and must be retransmitted. This means that the use of a shared coaxial cable in a bus topology prevents data transmission from being very bandwidth-efficient. This is one reason, but not the only reason, why bus topologies are seldom used in modern computer networks.

The **star topology**, shown in Figure 1-4, is the most common networking topology in today's LANs. Twisted-pair cables (see Chapter 2) with modular plugs are used to connect the computers and other networking devices. At the center of a star network is either a switch or a hub. This connects the network devices and facilitates the transfer of data. For example, if computer 1 wants to send data to the network laser printer, the **hub** or switch provides the network connection. If a hub is used, computer 1's data is sent to the hub, which then forwards it to the printer. However, a hub is a **multiport repeater**, meaning the data it receives is **broadcast** to all devices connected to its ports. Therefore, the hub will broadcast computer 1's data traffic to all networking devices interconnected in the star network. The data traffic path for this is shown in the solid black arrowed lines going to all networking devices in Figure 1-4. This is similar to the bus topology in that all data traffic on the LAN is being seen by all computers. The fact that the hub broadcasts all data traffic to the devices connected to its network ports makes these devices of limited use in large networks, but hubs are sometimes still used in small, slower-speed LANs.

To minimize unnecessary data traffic and isolate sections of the network, a **switch** can be used at the center of a star network, as shown in Figure 1-4. Networking devices such as computers each have a hardware or physical address. (This concept is fully detailed in section 1-3.) A switch stores the hardware or physical address for each device connected to its ports. The storage of the address enables the switch to directly connect two communicating devices without broadcasting the data to all devices connected to its **ports**.

For example, if a switch is used instead of a hub, the data from computer 1 is transmitted directly to the printer, and the other computers do not see the data traffic. The traffic path for the switched network is shown in the dotted lines in Figure 1-4. The use of a switched connection greatly improves the efficiency of the available bandwidth. It also permits additional devices in the LAN to simultaneously communicate with each other without tying up network resources. For example, while computer 1 is printing a large file, computers 5 and 6 can communicate with each other, as shown in the dashed line in Figure 1-4. For troubleshooting and maintenance, individual computers can be removed without negatively affecting the network in a star topology. Also the upgrade from a hub to a switched topology can be accomplished without requiring a change in the cable infrastructure and therefore at minimal downtime and expense.

Star Topology
The most common networking topology in today's LANs where all networking devices connect to a central switch or hub

Hub
Broadcasts the data it receives to all devices connected to its ports

Multiport Repeater
Another name for a hub

Broadcast
Transmission of data by a hub to all devices connected to its ports

Switch
Forwards a frame it receives directly out the port associated with its destination address

Ports
The physical input/output interfaces to the networking hardware

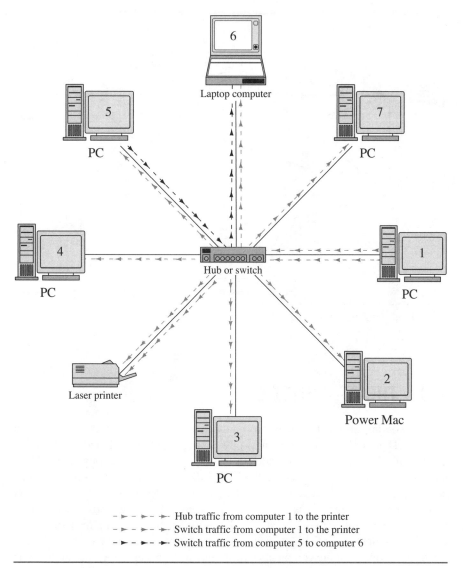

- ►- ►- ►- ►- Hub traffic from computer 1 to the printer
- ►- ►- ►- ►- Switch traffic from computer 1 to the printer
- ►- ►- ►- ►- Switch traffic from computer 5 to computer 6

FIGURE 1-4   The star topology.

Another topology is the **mesh topology**, shown in Figure 1-5. In this topology, all networking devices are directly connected to each other. This provides for full redundancy in the network data paths but at a cost. The additional data paths increase the cabling costs and an increase in the networking hardware cost (for example, expense of multiple network ports for each device connected to the network). This topology can be suitable for high-reliability applications but can be too costly for general networking applications.

Mesh Topology
All networking devices are directly connected to each other

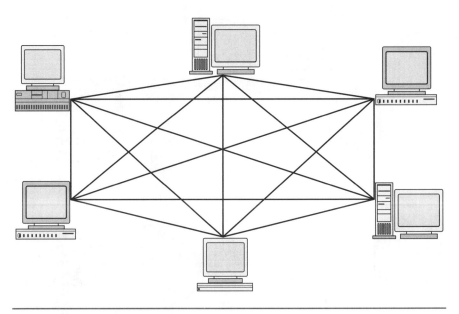

FIGURE 1-5   The mesh topology.

1-3   THE ETHERNET LAN

CSMA/CD
The Ethernet LAN media-access method, carrier sense multiple access with collision detection

The networking protocol used in most modern computer networks is Ethernet, a **CSMA/CD** protocol for local area networks. It originated in 1972, and the full specification for the protocol was provided in 1980 via a joint effort among Xerox, Digital Equipment Corporation, and Intel. *CSMA/CD* stands for "carrier sense multiple access with collision detection." Basically, for a computer to "talk" on the Ethernet network, it first "listens" to see whether there is any data traffic (carrier sense). This means that any computer connected to the LAN can be "listening" for data traffic, and any of the computers on the LAN can access the network (multiple access). There is a chance that two or more computers will attempt to broadcast a message at the same time; therefore, Ethernet systems must have the capability to detect data collisions (collision detection).

Packet
Provides grouping of the information for transmission

The information in an Ethernet network is exchanged in a **packet** format. The packet provides grouping of the information for transmission that includes the header, the data, and the trailer. The header consists of the preamble, the start frame delimiter, the destination and source addresses, and the length/type field. Next is the actual data being transmitted, followed by the pad that is used to bring the total number of bytes up to the minimum of 46 if the data field is less than 46 bytes. The last part of the frame is a 4-byte CRC (cyclic redundancy check) value used for error checking. The structure of the Ethernet packet frame is shown in Figure 1-6 and described in Table 1-1.

Preamble	Start frame delimiter	Destination MAC address	Source MAC address	Length type	Data	Pad	Frame check sequence

FIGURE 1-6 The data structure for the Ethernet frame. (From *Modern Electronic Communication 9/e*, by G. M. Miller & J. S. Beasley, 2008. Copyright © 2008 Pearson Education, Inc. Reprinted by permission of Pearson Education, Inc., Upper Saddle River, NJ.)

TABLE 1-1 Components of the Ethernet Packet Frame

Preamble	An alternating pattern of 1s and 0s used for synchronization.
Start frame delimiter	A binary 8-bit sequence of 1 0 1 0 1 0 1 1 that indicates the start of the frame.
Destination MAC address and Source MAC address	Each computer has an Ethernet network interface card (NIC) or network adapter that has a unique media access control (MAC) address associated with it. The MAC address is 6 bytes (12 hex characters) in length.
Length/type	An indication of the number of bytes in the data field if this value is less than 1500. If this number is greater than 1500, it indicates the type of data format; for example, IP and IPX.
Data	The variable length of data being transferred from the source to the destination.
Pad	A field used to bring the total number of bytes up to the minimum of 46 if the data field is less than 46 bytes.
Frame check sequence	A 4-byte CRC (cyclic redundancy check) value used for error detection. The CRC is performed on the bits from the destination MAC address through the Pad fields. If an error is detected, the frame is discarded.

The minimum length of the Ethernet frame is 64 bytes from the destination MAC address through the frame check sequence. The maximum Ethernet frame length is 1518 bytes, 6 bytes for the destination MAC address, 6 bytes for the source MAC address, 2 bytes for length/type, and 1500 bytes for the data.

Source: Adapted from *Modern Electronic Communication 9/e*, by G. M. Miller & J. S. Beasley, 2008. Copyright © 2008 Pearson Education, Inc. Adapted by permission of Pearson Education, Inc., Upper Saddle River, NJ.

How are the destination and source addresses for the data determined within a LAN? Networked devices, such as computers and network printers, each have an electronic hardware interface to the LAN called a **network interface card (NIC)** (see Figure 1-7) or integrated network port. The NIC contains a unique network address called the **MAC address**. MAC stands for "media access control." The MAC address is 6 bytes, or 48 bits, in length. The address is displayed in 12 hexadecimal digits. The first 6 digits are used to indicate the vendor of the network interface, also called the **organizationally unique identifier (OUI)**, and the last 6 numbers form a unique value for each NIC assigned by the vendor. IEEE is the worldwide source of registered OUIs.

Network Interface Card (NIC)
The electronic hardware used to interface the computer to the network

MAC Address
A unique 6-byte address assigned by the vendor of the network interface card

Organizationally Unique Identifier (OUI)
The first 3 bytes of the MAC address that identifies the manufacturer of the network hardware

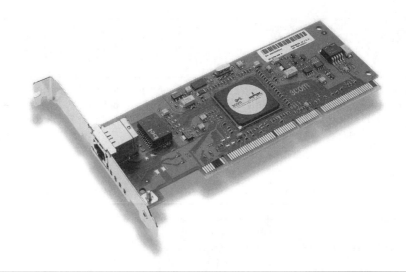

FIGURE 1-7   A 3COM network interface card (courtesy of 3Com Corporation).

The MAC address, also called the **Ethernet**, **physical**, **hardware**, or **adapter address**, can be obtained from computers operating under Microsoft Windows by typing the *ipconfig /all* command while in the command mode or at the MS-DOS prompt. The following is an example of obtaining the MAC address for a computer operating under Windows Vista or XP.

The first step is to enter the command window by selecting **Start** and then **Run**. You will obtain the Run window as shown in Figure 1-8. Enter **cmd** as shown and click **OK** to open the command prompt.

FIGURE 1-8   The Run window used to enter the command prompt in Windows XP.

In the command prompt, enter the *ipconfig /all* command as shown in Figure 1-9. The */all* switch on the command enables the MAC address information to be displayed—for this example, the information for computer 1. Note that the Host Name for the computer is Computer-1. This information is typically established when the computer's operating system is installed, but it can be changed as needed. This concept is presented in Chapter 14. The MAC address is listed under **Ethernet adapter Local Area Connection** as shown in Figure 1-9. The **Media State—Media**

disconnected text indicates that there is not an active Ethernet device, such as a hub or switch, connected to the computer. The **Description** lists the manufacturer and model of the network interface, and the **Physical Address** of **00-10-A4-13-99-2E** is the actual MAC address for the computer.

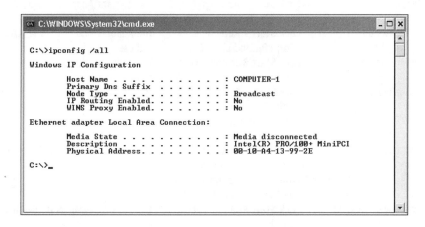

FIGURE 1-9   A typical text screen result when entering the *ipconfig /all* command in the command window.

In some Windows operating systems, the ***winipcfg*** command can be used to display the Ethernet adapter information (see Figure 1-10). In this example, the address is listed as the **Adapter Address**.

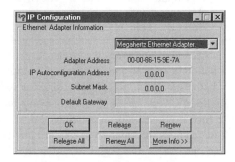

FIGURE 1-10   An example of the MAC address information obtained from a computer running under the Windows 98 operating system.

Table 1-2 lists how the MAC address can be obtained for different computer operating systems.

TABLE 1-2   Commands for Obtaining the MAC Address for Different Operating Systems

Operating System	Command Sequence	Comments
Windows 95	Click **Start—Run**, type **winipcfg**, and press **Enter**.	The Adapter Address is the MAC address.
Windows 98	Click **Start—Run**, type **winipcfg**, and press Enter.	The Adapter Address is the MAC address.
Windows ME	Click **Start Run**, type **cmd**, and then type **ipconfig/all**.	The Adapter Address is the MAC address.
Windows NT	Click **Start—Run** and type **winipcfg**. In the command prompt, type **ipconfig/all** and press **Enter**.	The Physical Address is the MAC address.
Windows 2000	Click **Start—Run** and type **cmd**. In the command prompt. type **ipconfig/all**, and then press **Enter**.	The Physical Address is the MAC address.
Windows Vista/XP	Click **Start Run** and type **cmd**. In the command prompt type **ipconfig/all**, and then press **Enter**.	The Physical Address is the MAC address.
Linux	At the command prompt type **ifconfig**.	The HWaddr line contains the MAC address.
Mac OS (9.x and older)	Click the **Apple**, and then select **Control Panels—AppleTalk** and click the **Info** button.	The Hardware Address is the MAC address.
Mac OS X	Click **Apple—About this MAC—more info— Network—Built-in Ethernet**.	The Hardware Address is the MAC address.

In summary, the MAC address provides the information that ultimately enables the data to reach a destination in a LAN. This is also how computer 1 and the printer communicated directly in the star topology example using the switch (refer to Figure 1-4). The switch stored the MAC addresses of all devices connected to its ports and used this information to forward the data from computer 1 directly to the printer. The switch also used the MAC address information to forward the data from computer 5 to computer 6 (refer to Figure 1-4).

MAC addresses are listed in hexadecimal (base-16). The complete MAC address consists of 12 hexadecimal digits. The first 6 digits identify the vendor. The last 6 form a serial number assigned by the manufacturer of the network interface card. A searchable database of IEEE OUI and company ID assignments is available at http://standards.ieee.org/regauth/oui/index.shtml. Table 1-3 lists a few examples of MAC addresses. Also large companies may have many OUI numbers assigned to them. For example, the OUI 00-AA-00 is only one of Intel's many OUIs.

TABLE 1-3 A Sample of MAC Addresses

Company ID-Vendor Serial #	Manufacturer (Company ID)
00-AA-00-B6-7A-57	Intel Corporation (00-AA-00)
00-00-86-15-9E-7A	Megahertz Corporation (00-00-86)
00-50-73-6C-32-11	Cisco Systems, Inc. (00-50-73)
00-04-76-B6-9D-06	3COM (00-04-76)
00-0A-27-B7-3E-F8	Apple Computer Inc. (00-0A-27)

IP (Internet Protocol) Addressing

The MAC address provides the physical address for the network interface card but provides no information as to its network location or even on what LAN, or in which building, city, or country the network resides. IP addressing provides a solution to worldwide addressing through incorporating a unique address that identifies the computer's local network. IP network numbers are assigned by **IANA (Internet Assigned Numbers Authority)**, the agency that assigns IP addresses to computer networks and makes sure no two different networks are assigned the same IP network address. The URL (Uniform Resource Locator) for IANA is http://www.iana.org/.

IP addresses are classified as either IPv4 or IPv6. IP version 4 (IPv4) is the current TCP/IP addressing technique being used on the Internet. Address space for IPv4 is quickly running out due to the rapid growth of the Internet and the development of new Internet-compatible technologies. However, both IPv4 and IPv6 are being supported by manufacturers of networking equipment and the latest computer operating systems. The details about IPv6 are addressed in Chapter 5. IPv4 is currently the most common method for assigning IP addresses. This text refers to IPv4 addressing as "IP addressing." The **IP address** is a 32-bit address that identifies on which network the computer is located and differentiates the computer from all other devices on the same network. The address is divided into four 8-bit parts. The format for the IP address is

A.B.C.D

where the A.B.C.D values are written as the decimal equivalent of the 8-bit binary value. The range for each of the decimal values is 0 to 255. IP addresses can be categorized by class. Examples of the classes of IP networks are provided in Table 1-4. The address range for each class is provided in Table 1-5.

IANA
The agency that assigns IP addresses to computer networks

IP Address
Unique 32-bit address that identifies on which network the computer is located as well as differentiates the computer from all other devices on the same network

TABLE 1-4 The Classes of IPv4 Networks

Class	Description	Example IP Numbers	Maximum Number of Hosts
Class A	Governments, very large networks	44.x.x.x.	$2^{24}=16,777,214$
Class B	Midsize companies, universities, and so on	128.123.x.x	$2^{16}=65,534$
Class C	Small networks	192.168.1.x	$2^{8}=254$
Class D	Reserved for multicast groups	224.x.x.x	not applicable

TABLE 1-5   The Address Range for Each Class of Network

Class A	0.0.0.0 to 127.255.255.255
Class B	128.0.0.0 to 191.255.255.255
Class C	192.0.0.0 to 223.255.255.255
Class D	224.0.0.0 to 239.255.255.255

Network Number
The portion of the IP address that defines which network the IP packet is originating from or being delivered to

Host Number
The portion of the IP address that defines the location of the networking device connected to the network; also called the host address

Host Address
Same as host number

ISP
Internet service provider

Private Addresses
IP addresses set aside for use in private intranets

Intranet
An internal network that provides file and resource sharing but is not accessed from the Internet

IP Internetwork
A network that uses IP addressing for identifying devices connected to the network

TCP/IP
Transmission Control Protocol/Internet Protocol, the protocol suite used for internetworks such as the Internet

Wired Network
Uses cables and connectors to establish the network connection

Wireless Network
Uses radio signals to establish the network connection

Examples of network addresses also are shown in Table 1-4. The decimal numbers indicate the **network number**, which is the portion of the IP address that defines which network the IP packet is originating from or being delivered to. The x entries for each class represent the **host number**, which is the portion of the IP address that defines the address of the networking device connected to the network. The host number is also called the **host address**. The network number provides sufficient information for routing the data to the appropriate destination network. A device on the destination network then uses the remaining information (the x portion) to direct the packet to the destination computer or host. The x portion of the address is typically assigned by the local network system administrator or is dynamically assigned when users need access outside their local networks. For example, your Internet service provider (**ISP**) dynamically assigns an IP address to your computer when you log on to the Internet. Remember, you can check the IP address assigned to your computer by your ISP using the ***ipconfig*** command in the command prompt.

For this chapter and the rest of the text, a group of IP addresses called **private addresses** will be used for assigning IP addresses to networks. Private addresses are IP addresses set aside for use in private **intranets**. An intranet is an internal internetwork that provides file and resource sharing. Private addresses are not valid addresses for Internet use because they have been reserved and are blocked by the ISP. However, these addresses can be used within a private LAN (intranet) to create an **IP internetwork**. An IP internetwork uses IP addressing for identifying devices connected to the network and is also the addressing scheme used in **TCP/IP** networks. TCP/IP stands for Transmission Control Protocol/Internet Protocol and is the protocol suite used for internetworks such as the Internet. The three address blocks for the private IP addresses are as follows:

> 10.0.0.0–10.255.255.255
> 172.16.0.0–172.31.255.255
> 192.168.0.0–192.168.255.255

The topic of IP addressing will be examined in greater detail throughout the text. For Chapter 1, the objective is to use the IP addresses for configuring the address of the computers for operation in a TCP/IP network.

1-4   ASSEMBLING A HOME NETWORK

Setting up a home network is probably one of the first networks that the student sets up. This is an exciting opportunity for the student to demonstrate their knowledge of computer networks, but setting up the home network can also be quite a challenge. One of the first questions asked is, "Do I want to set up a wired or wireless home network?" A **wired network** uses cabling and connectors to establish the network connections. A **wireless network** uses radio signals to establish the network connection.

The following are advantages of a wired network:

- Faster network data transfer speeds (within the LAN).
- Relatively inexpensive to setup.
- The network is not susceptible to outside interference.

The following are disadvantages of the wired network:

- The cable connections typically require the use of specialized tools.
- The cable installation can be labor-intensive and expensive.

Section 1-5 introduces setting up wired networks for both office and home networks; however, the home networking technologies are presented in this section.

A wireless home network is probably the most common home network configuration in use today. The advantages of a wireless network are many including the following:

- User mobility
- Simple installations
- No cables

Disadvantages of a wireless network can include

- Security issues.
- The data transfer speed within the LAN can be slower than wired networks.

Wireless networks also go by the name **Wi-Fi**, which is the abbreviated name for the Wi-Fi Alliance (Wi-Fi stands for wireless fidelity). The Wi-Fi Alliance is an organization whose function is to test and certify wireless equipment for compliance with the 802.11x standards, which is the group of wireless standards developed under IEEE 802.11. The most common wireless standards include

- 802.11a (Wireless-A)—This standard can provide data transfer rates up to 54 Mbps and an operating range up to 75 feet. It operates at 5GHz.
- 802.11b (Wireless-B)—This standard can provide data transfer rates up to 11 Mbps with ranges of 100 to 150 feet. It operates at 2.4 GHz.
- 802.11g (Wireless-G)—This standard can provide data transfer rates up to 54 Mbps up to 150 feet. It operates at 2.4 GHz.
- 802.11n (Wireless-N)—This is the next generation of high-speed wireless connectivity promising data transfer rates up to $4 \times 802.11g$ speeds (200+Mbps). It operates at 2.4 GHz.

Figure 1-11 illustrates the placement and type of equipment found in a typical wired or wireless home network. Figure 1-11 (a) shows a wired LAN that is using cabling to interconnect the networking devices. A router is being used to make the connection to the ISP. The router can also contain a switch and a broadband modem. The switch is used to interconnect other networking devices, and the broadband modem is used to make the data connection to the ISP. The most common broadband connections to the ISP are via a cable modem and DSL. In some cases the router, switch, and broadband modem will be separate devices, but most often they will be integrated into one device. One of the computers may also have the configuration settings for managing the router, which can include the settings for connecting to the ISP.

Figure 1-11 (b) shows a wireless LAN that is being used to interconnect the networking devices. A **wireless router** is being used to make the data connection to the

Wi-Fi
Wi-Fi Alliance—an organization that tests and certifies wireless equipment for compliance with the 802.11x standards

Wireless Router
Device used to interconnect wireless networking devices and to give access to wired devices and establish the broadband Internet connection to the ISP

ISP, which is typically via a cable or DSL modem. The wireless router also has a wireless access point and will typically have a switch to facilitate wired network connections. Sometimes the broadband modem is integrated into the wireless router. The access point is used to establish the wireless network connection to each of the wireless computers. Access points and specifics relative to their operation in wireless networks are discussed in greater detail in Chapter 11.

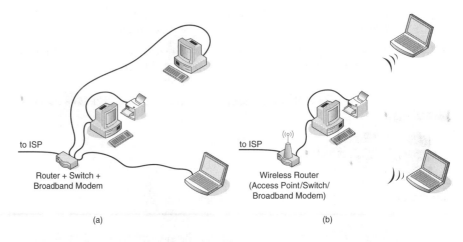

to ISP

Router + Switch +
Broadband Modem

(a)

to ISP

Wireless Router
(Access Point/Switch/
Broadband Modem)

(b)

FIGURE 1-11   An example of a (a) wired and (b) wireless WiFi home network.

The components of a home network can include the following:

- **Hub**—This is used to interconnect networking devices. A drawback to the hub is that it broadcasts the data it receives to all devices connected to its ports. The hub has been replaced by the network switch in most modern networks. Figure 1-12 provides an image of a hub.

FIGURE 1-12   Linksys EtherFast ® 8-Port 10/100 Auto-Sensing Hub (courtesy of Linksys).

- **Switch**—This is the best choice for interconnecting networking devices. It can establish a direct connection from the sender to the destination without passing the data traffic to other networking devices. Figure 1-13 provides an image of a switch.

FIGURE 1-13   Linksys 24-Port 10/100/1000 Gigabit Switch (courtesy of Linksys).

- **Network Adapter**—Wired and wireless network adapters are available. The type of network adapter used in desktop computers is called the Network Interface Card (NIC). Figure 1-14 provides an image of a wired network adapter. This type of NIC is inserted into an expansion slot on the computer's motherboard and is a wired-only adapter.

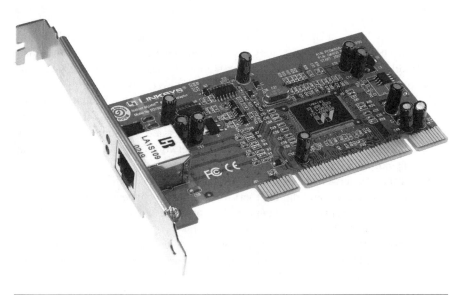

FIGURE 1-14   Linksys Instant Gigabit Network Adapter (courtesy of Linksys).

The PC Card adapter connects to notebook computers and provides an RJ-45 jack for connecting to wired networks. RJ stands for registered jack. This device supports connections to both 10 and 100 Mbps networks. Figure 1-15 provides an image of a PC card adapter

FIGURE 1-15   Linksys EtherFast® 10/100 32-Bit Integrated CardBus PC Card (courtesy of Linksys).

The Wireless-N adapter inserts into a notebook or laptop computer PC Card slot. The Wireless-N technology offers a data transfer speed that is faster than Wireless-G and is also compatible with both Wireless-B and Wireless-G technologies. Figure 1-16 provides an image of a Wireless-N adapter.

Another option for connecting to networks is to use a network adapter that attaches to a USB port on the computer. This device has the USB type A connector on one end and an RJ-45 jack on the other and will support connections to both 10, 100 Mbps, and 1000 Mbps data networks. Figure 1-17 provides an image of a USB network adapter.

- **Router**—A networking device used to connect two or more networks (for example, your LAN and the Internet) using a single connection to your ISP. A modern home networking router can also contain a switch and a broadband modem. Figure 1-18 provides an image of a router.
- **Access Point**—Used to interconnect wireless devices and provide a connection to the wired LAN. The data transfer speeds for access points are dictated by the choice of wireless technology for the clients, but this device will support Wireless-N. Figure 1-19 provides an image of an access point.

FIGURE 1-16   Linksys Wireless-N Notebook Adapter (courtesy of Linksys).

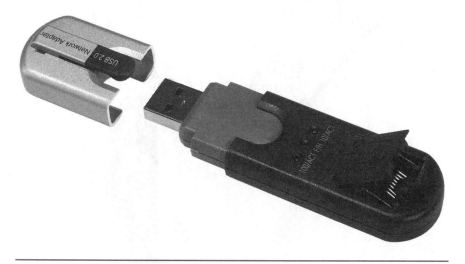

FIGURE 1-17   Linksys Compact USB 2.0 10/100 Network Adapter (courtesy of Linksys).

- **Wireless router**—This device uses RF to connect to the networking devices. A wireless router typically contains a router, switch, and a wireless access point and is probably the most common way to interconnect wireless LANs to the ISP's access device. Note that these devices also have wired network connections available on the system. Figure 1-20 provides an image of a wireless router.

FIGURE 1-18   Linksys EtherFast® Cable/DSL Firewall Router with 4-Port Switch (courtesy of Linksys).

FIGURE 1-19   The Linksys Wireless-N access point.

FIGURE 1-20   Linksys Wireless-G Broadband Router (courtesy of Linksys).

- **Broadband Modem/Gateway**—This describes the device used to provide high-speed data access via your cable connection or via a telephone company's DSL connection. A gateway combines a modem and a router into one network box. Figure 1-21 provides an image of a broadband modem/gateway.
- **Cable Modem**—This device is used to make a broadband network connection from your home network to the ISP using your cable connection. This setup requires a splitter to separate the cable TV from the home network. Access to the Internet is typically provided by the cable TV service provider. Figure 1-22 provides an image of a cable modem.

FIGURE 1-21 Linksys Wireless-G Cable Gateway (courtesy of Linksys).

FIGURE 1-22 Linksys Cable Modem with USB and Ethernet Connections (courtesy of Linksys).

- **DSL Modem**—This device is used to make a broadband network connection from your home network to the ISP using the telephone line. Broadband access to the Internet is provided via the phone company or a separate ISP. The DSL connection requires the placement of filters on all telephone lines to prevent interference. Figure 1-23 provides an image of a DSL modem.

FIGURE 1-23   Linksys ADSL2 Modem (courtesy of Linksys).

Several issues should be considered when planning for a home network, including the following:

- **Data speed**—This will be determined by whether you chose to implement a wired or wireless home network. Wired networks offer the best data transfer rate inside the home network, up to 10Gbps. The best data transfer rates for a wireless home network can be obtained using 802.11n (Wireless-N) technology. This is the next generation of high-speed wireless connectivity promising data transfer rates up to $4 \times 802.11g$ speeds (200+ Mbps).
- **Cost**—Implementing a high-speed wired network can be quite expensive. With the networking hardware, cabling, and related hardware, you can incur an unexpected additional cost for implementing the high-speed wired home network. The cost of switching to or implementing an 802.11n Wireless-N network is minimal and is a suitable alternative to a wired network. But remember, the maximum data rate for a Wireless-N network is still much lower than that possible with a wired LAN.
- **Ease of implementation**—A wireless home network is probably the easiest to implement if the cabling and connectors for a wired network are not already installed. The time required to install the wireless home network is usually minimal as long as unexpected problems do not surface.
- **Appearance**—A wireless home network offers the best choice in regards to appearance because there won't be cables and networking hardware scattered

around the house. The wireless home network will require a wireless router and an external wired connection to the ISP (refer to Figure 1-11(b)).

- **Home access**—The choice of wired or wireless technology will not affect home access. However, the wired network will offer the best data transfer speed internal to the network, but the wireless network offers the best choice for mobility.
- **Public access**—The choice of wired or wireless technology will not impact public access. The data rate for the connection to/from the ISP will be the limiting factor for the data transfer rate for public access.

It is not uncommon for a wired or wireless home network to stop functioning, although the downtime is usually minimal. The steps for troubleshooting wired and wireless home networks include the following:

Step 1   Check to make sure the proper lights for your networking device that connects you to your ISP are properly displayed. Incorrect lights can indicate a connection problem with your cable modem, DSL modem, or telephone connection. Your ISP might also be having a problem, and you might need to call them to verify your connection.

Step 2   One of the first steps usually used to fix basic connection problems to the ISP is to reboot the host computer (the computer connected to the router) and to reboot the router. This usually will fix the problem, and the correct lights should be displayed. In some cases, you might also have to power down/up your broadband modem. (Note that the broadband modem might be integrated with the router.) Once again, check to see whether the correct lights are being displayed.

Step 3   You should always verify your hardware cable or phone connection is in place and has not been pulled loose. Make corrections as needed. You should also verify that all wireless units have a network connection. The following are steps to verify wireless connectivity for Windows Vista, Windows XP, and MAC OS X:

- **Windows Vista:** Click **Start—Network Connections** or click **Start—Control Panel—Network and Sharing Center**. The wireless connection will show enabled if there is a wireless connection.
- **Windows XP:** Right-click **My Network Places**. The computer will indicate whether there is a wireless network connection.
- **MAC OS X:** Click the **Apple icon—System Preferences—Network**. If you are connected:
  - A green AirPort icon is displayed, and the words "airport is connected to network" appear.
  - A yellow icon indicates that AirPort is turned on but is not connected to a network.
  - A red icon indicates AirPort is turned off.

Also note that if you are connected to a wireless network, a radio wave icon will appear at the top of the screen in the menu bar to indicate you are connected to a wireless network.

Step 4   Sometimes you might need to verify your network settings. This can happen if your computer has lost the data for the settings. In this case, follow the steps provided by the manufacturer of your broadband modem or your ISP.

The following are the basic steps for establishing the wireless connection for a wireless notebook computer running Windows Vista, XP, and MAC OS X:

- **Windows Vista:** Click **Start—Settings—Network Connections** and then right-click **Wireless Network Connection**. You might need to click **Enable** and/or **Connect/Disconnect** to establish a wireless connection. A red X indicates a wireless connection is not established.
- **Windows XP:** This can vary depending on your wireless card. Click **Start—Programs** and select the setup program for your wireless card. Follow the steps displayed on the screen to establish a wireless network connection. You will need to know the name of the network you want to join as well as the SSID. The SSID is the Service Set Identifier and is used to identify what wireless devices are allowed to connect to the network.
- **MAC OS X:** Click the **Apple icon—System Preferences—Network**, and then click **Show—Network Status—Connect—Turn AirPort on**. Close the AirPort window and click **Configure—By default join a specific network**. Enter the wireless network name (SSID) and password (WEP code), and then click **Apply Now**. A radio wave should now appear at the top of the screen in the menu bar, which indicates the network is connected.

There are many choices of wireless technologies for configuring a wireless network. The 802.11b, g, and n (Wireless-B, -G, and -N) technologies are compatible even though they offer different data speeds. If compatible but different wireless technologies are being used, the data transfer speeds will be negotiated at the rate specified by the slowest technology. For example, the 802.11n (Wireless-N) standard offers a faster data rate (comparable to Wireless-G), but when devices of both technologies are present, the data transfer rate will be negotiated at the Wireless-G data rate.

In some cases, the wireless signal might not be reaching all the areas that need coverage. In this case, a device called a **range extender** can be used. This device relays the wireless signals from an access point or wireless router into areas with a weak signal or no signal at all. This improves the wireless remote access from all points in the home. This same technology can also be used to improve connectivity in stores and warehouses and can also be used to provide excellent connectivity in public places such as **hotspots**. Hotspots are defined as a limited geographic area that provides wireless access for the public. Hotspots are typically found in airports, restaurants, libraries, and schools.

Range Extender
Device that relays the wireless signals from an access point or wireless router into areas with a weak signal or no signal at all

Hotspots
A limited geographic area that provides wireless access for the public

Securing the Home Network

There are many potential security issues associated with a wireless network. Securing the home wireless network is extremely important because a wireless signal can be intercepted by the wrong person, and they can possibly connect to your network. The following are some basic steps that can be used to help protect the home network.

1. **Change the default factory passwords.** Wireless equipment is shipped with default passwords that are set at the factory. These default settings are known by the public, including people who would like to gain access into your network and possibly change your settings. It is best that you select your own password that is a combination of alphanumeric characters.

Service Set Identifier (SSID)
Name that is used to identify your wireless network and is used by your access point or wireless router to establish an association

2. **Change the default SSID.** The SSID is the name used to identify your network and is used by your access point or wireless router to establish an association. Establishing an association means that a wireless client can join the network. The SSID can be up to 32 characters and should be changed often so hackers who have figured out your SSID will no longer have access to your home network.

3. **Turn encryption on.** Probably the most important thing to do is turn on the security features that include data encryption. These options include Wired Equivalent Privacy (WEP) and Wi-Fi Protected Access (WPA) and WPA2. WPA2 is a product certification issued by the Wi-Fi Alliance. It uses a stronger encryption than WPA and is also backward compatible with adapters using WPA.

4. **Turn off the SSID broadcast.** Wireless systems broadcast the SSID so that the network can be easily identified as an available network. Hackers can use this information to possibly gain access to your network, so it is a good idea to turn off the SSID broadcast. The exception to this is in hotspots where public access is available. Please note, hotspots make it easy for the user to gain wireless access but hackers can also be on the same network, so it is very important to have encryption turned on.

5. **Enable MAC address filtering.** All computer devices use a unique MAC address for identifying the device. This can be used to select what devices can be allowed access to the network. When MAC address filtering is turned on, only wireless devices that have specific MAC addresses will be allowed access to the network.

Another important security concern is limiting outside access to your home network via your connection to the ISP. The following are some things that can be done to protect the home network from outside threats:

- **Network Address Translation:** The outsider sees only the router IP address because the IP addresses of the internal networking devices are not provided on the Internet. Only the ISP-assigned IP address of the router is provided. The home network typically uses a private address that is not routable on the Internet. (Private IP addresses are blocked by the ISP).

Firewall Protection
Used to prevent unauthorized access to your network

Stateful Packet Inspection (SPI)
Type of firewall that inspects incoming data packets to make sure they correspond to an outgoing request

Virtual Private Network (VPN)
Establishes a secure network connection and is a way to protect your LAN's data from being observed by outsiders

- **Firewall protection:** A common practice is to turn on the **firewall protection**. The purpose of a firewall is to prevent unauthorized access to your network. Firewall protection is available in both the Windows and MAC operating environments. A type of firewall protection is **Stateful Packet Inspection (SPI)**. This type of firewall inspects incoming data packets to make sure they correspond to an outgoing request. For example, you may be exchanging information with a website. Data packets that are not requested are rejected. The topic of firewalls is covered in more detail in Chapter 10, "Network Security."

- **Establish a VPN connection when transferring sensitive information:** A **Virtual Private Network (VPN)** establishes a secure network connection and is a way to protect your LAN's data from being observed by outsiders. The VPN connection capability is available with Windows Vista, Windows XP, and MAC OS X. A VPN connection enables a remote or mobile user to access the network as if they were actually physically at the network. Additionally, the VPN connection is encrypted, providing privacy for the data packets being transmitted.

IP Addressing in the Home Network

A common question asked about home networks is, "How is IP addressing handled for all the computers connected to the Internet?" The home network typically has only one connection to the ISP, but multiple computers can be connected to the Internet at the same time. The answer is that IP addressing for the home network is managed by the router or wireless router that connects to the ISP. The ISP will issue an IP address to the router from an available pool of IP addresses managed by the ISP. The computers in the home network should be issued private IP addresses (applicable ranges are 10.0.0.0–10.255.255.255; 172.16.0.0–172.31.255.255; 192.168.0.0–192.168.255.255) using a technique called **Network Address Translation (NAT)**.

An example is provided in Figure 1-24. A routable public IP address is issued by the ISP for the wireless router. This public IP address enables all computers in the home network access to the Internet. The wireless router issues private addresses to all computers connected to the network.

Network Address Translation (NAT)
Translates the private IP address to a public address for routing over the Internet

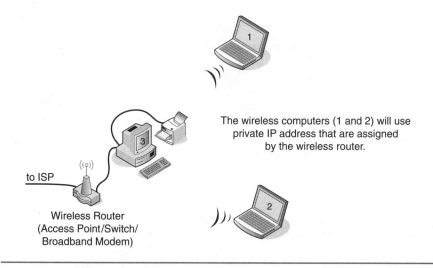

The wireless computers (1 and 2) will use private IP address that are assigned by the wireless router.

to ISP

Wireless Router
(Access Point/Switch/
Broadband Modem)

FIGURE 1-24   A home network using a wireless router connected to the ISP.

NAT translates the private IP address to a public address for routing over the Internet. For example, computer 1 in the home network (see Figure 1-24) might establish a connection to an Internet website. The wireless router uses NAT to translate computer 1's private IP address to the public IP address assigned to the router. The router uses a technique called **overloading**, where NAT translates the home network's private IP addresses to the single public IP address assigned by the ISP. In addition, the NAT process tracks a port number for the connection. This technique is called **Port Address Translation (PAT)**. The router stores the home network's IP address and port number in a NAT lookup table. The port number differentiates the computer that is establishing a connection to the Internet because the router uses the same address for all computers. This port number is used when a data packet is returned to the home network. The port number identifies the computer that established the Internet connection, and the router can deliver the data packet to the correct computer.

Overloading
Where NAT translates the home network's private IP addresses to a single public IP address

Port Address Translation (PAT)
A port number is tracked with the client computer's private address when translating to a public address

For example, if computer 1 establishes a connection to a website on the Internet, the data packets from the website are sent back to computer 1 using the home network's routable public IP address. This first step enables the data packet to be routed back to the home network. Next, the router uses the NAT lookup table and port number to translate the destination for the data packet back to the computer 1 private IP address and original port number, which might be different. Figure 1-25 demonstrates an example of the NAT translation process for a home network. The home network has been assigned Class C private IP addresses (192.168.0.x) by the router. The x is a unique number (from 1–254) assigned to each computer. The router translates the private IP addresses to the public routable IP address assigned by the ISP. Additionally, the router tracks a port number with the public IP address to identify the computer. For example, the computer with the private IP address of 192.168.0.64 is assigned the public IP address 128.123.246.55:1962, where 1962 is the port number tracked by the router.

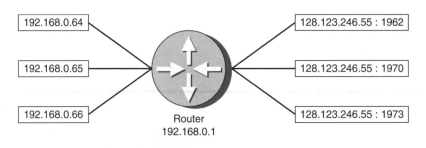

FIGURE 1-25   The NAT translation using PAT.

1-5   ASSEMBLING AN OFFICE LAN

An example of assembling an office-type LAN is presented in this section. The Ethernet protocol will be used for managing the exchange of data in the network. The networking devices will be interconnected in a star topology. There are many options for assembling and configuring a LAN, but this example presents a networking approach that is simple and consistent with modern computer networking. It will also provide a good introduction to the networking topics presented in the text.

For this example, three computers and one printer are to be configured in the star topology. Each device in the network will be assigned an IP address from the private address space. The following step-by-step discussion guides you through the process of assembling, configuring, and testing an office LAN:

Step 1   The first step in assembling an office LAN is to document the devices to be connected in the network and prepare a simple sketch of the proposed network. Each device's MAC and IP addresses should be included in the network drawing documentation.

Figure 1-26 provides an example of a small office LAN. The desired IP addresses and the actual MAC addresses for each computer and printer are listed. Remember, each NIC contains a unique MAC address and the IP addresses are locally assigned by the network administrator. The MAC addresses were obtained by entering the ***ipconfig /all*** command from the command prompt in Windows XP. Repeat this step for all computing devices connected to the LAN. The results of the MAC address inquiries are provided in Table 1-6. Each networking device will be assigned an IP address. Table 1-6 also lists the planned IP addresses of the devices used in this office LAN.

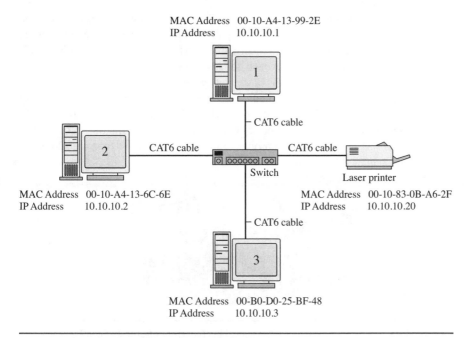

FIGURE 1-26   An example of a small office LAN star topology.

TABLE 1-6   The MAC and Assigned IP Address for the Devices in the Office LAN

Device (Hostname)	MAC Address	IP Address
Computer 1	00-10-A4-13-99-2E	10.10.10.1
Computer 2	00-10-A4-13-6C-6E	10.10.10.2
Computer 3	00-B0-D0-25-BF-48	10.10.10.3
Laser Printer	00-10-83-0B-A6-2F	10.10.10.20

Note

In this text, you will function as the network administrator. The network administrator must know how to obtain all IP and MAC address information for devices connected to the network. This requires that the network administrator keep *good documentation* of the network.

Step 2   Connect all the networking devices using the star topology shown in Figure 1-26.

At the center of this star topology network will be a switch or a hub. Recall that either can be used to connect the networking devices. The switch is the best choice because the hub broadcasts data it receives to all devices connected to its ports, and the switch enables the devices to communicate directly. Although hubs are not as sophisticated as switches and are not reflective of modern computer networking, the hub is still suitable for use in small networks.

The connections from the switch to the computers and the printer will be made using premade twisted-pair patch cables. The cable type used here is **CAT6 (category 6)** twisted-pair cable. CAT6 twisted-pair cables have **RJ-45** modular connectors on each end, as shown in Figure 1-27, and are capable of carrying 1000 **Mbps** (1 gigabit) *or more* of data up to a length of 100 meters. The twisted-pair media and its various category specifications are discussed in Chapter 2. If the network hardware and software are properly set up, all computers will be able to access the printer and other computers. Issues associated with the proper cabling including CAT 6/5e are addressed in Chapter 2.

CAT6 (category 6)
Twisted-pair cables capable of carrying up to 1000 Mbps (1 gigabit) of data up to a length of 100 meters

RJ-45
The 8-pin modular connector used with CAT6/5e/5 cable

Mbps
Megabits per second

FIGURE 1-27   The RJ-45 twisted-pair patch cables (courtesy of StarTech.com).

Numerics
A numerical representation

The media used for transporting data in a modern computer network are either twisted-pair or fiber optic cables. The principles behind selecting, installing, and testing twisted-pair cabling are presented in Chapter 2. Table 1-7 lists the common **numerics** used to describe the data rates for the twisted-pair media and the older style copper coaxial cable used in a LAN. Common numerics for fiber optic LANs are also listed. Numerics are an alphanumeric description of a technology. For example, *100BaseT* means that this is a 100-Mbps, baseband, twisted-pair technology.

TABLE 1-7   Common Numerics for Ethernet LAN Cabling

Numeric	Description
10Base2	10 Mbps over coaxial cable up to 185 m, also called ThinNet (seldom used anymore)
10Base5	10 Mbps over coaxial cable up to 500 m, also called ThickNet (seldom used anymore)
10BaseT	10 Mbps over twisted pair
10BaseF	10 Mbps over multimode fiber optic cable
10BaseFL	10 Mbps over 850 nm multimode fiber optic cable
100BaseT	100 Mbps over twisted pair (also called Fast Ethernet)
100BaseFX	100 Mbps over fiber

Numeric	Description
1000BaseT	1000 Mbps over twisted pair
1000BaseFX	1000 Mbps over fiber
10GE	10 Gigabit Ethernet

Source: Adapted from Modem Electronic Communication 9/e, by G. M. Miller & J. S. Beasley, 2008. Copyright© 2008 Pearson Education, Inc. Adapted by permission of Pearson Education, Inc., Upper Saddle River, NJ.

The RJ-45 plugs connect to the switch inputs via the RJ-45 jacks. Figure 1-28 shows a simple 8-port switch. The inputs to the switch are also called the input **ports**, which are the interfaces for the networking devices. The switch inputs that are marked with an "x" [Figure 1-28(b)] indicate that these devices are cross-connected, meaning the transmit and receive pairs on the twisted-pair cable are crossed to properly align each for data communication. The term for a cable that has cross-connected TX/RX data lines is **crossover**.

Ports
The interface for the networking devices

Crossover
Transmit and receive signal pairs are crossed to properly align the transmit signal on one device with the receive signal on the other device

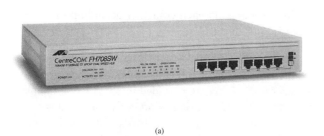

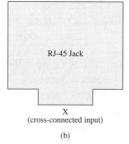

RJ-45 Jack

X
(cross-connected input)

(a)   (b)

FIGURE 1-28   (a) The switch used to connect the networking devices; (b) closeup view of "x" input (courtesy of Anixter Inc.).

Figure 1-29(a) provides an example of this cross-connected concept. Switches usually have at least one port that can be switched or selected for use as either a cross-connected or **straight-through** input. A straight-through port is also called an **uplink port**. The uplink port allows for the connection of a switch to a switch or a hub without having to use a special cable. Devices requiring the cross-connected input port are computers, printers, and routers. Devices requiring a straight-through connection are uplink connections to other switches or hubs. Figure 1-29(b) provides a block diagram explaining the concept of a straight-through input.

A networking connection can be verified by examining the **link light** on the switch or hub. The presence of a link light indicates that the transmit and receive pairs are properly aligned and the connected devices are communicating. Absence of the light indicates a possible cabling or hardware problem. The Ethernet protocol can use the **link integrity test** to verify that a communication link between two Ethernet devices has been established. The link light remains lit when communication is established and remains lit as long as there is a periodic exchange of link pulses from the attached devices.

Straight-through
Transmit and receive signal pairs are aligned end-to-end

Uplink Port
Allows the connection of a hub or switch to another hub or switch without having to use a crossover cable

Link Light
Indicates that the transmit and receive pairs are properly aligned

Link Integrity Test
Protocol used to verify that a communication link between two Ethernet devices has been established

Link Pulses
Sent by each of the connected devices via the twisted-pair cables when data is not being transmitted to indicate that the link is still up

Link pulses are sent by each of the connected devices via the twisted-pair cables to indicate that the link is up, but the link pulses are not part of the Ethernet packet and are sent at regular intervals when data is not being transmitted.

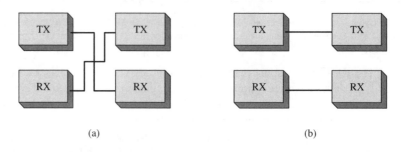

(a)   (b)

FIGURE 1-29 (a) An example of the wiring on an "x" type input on a hub; (b) an example of straight-through wiring.

Step 3 Configure the IP address settings on each computer according to the assigned addresses provided in Table 1-6.

The following describes how the network administrator configures the computers to operate on the LAN. This requires that each computing device be assigned an IP address. The assigned IP addresses for this LAN are provided in Table 1-6. Examples of configuring the computers in the office LAN using Windows Vista, Windows XP, and MAC OS X follow. A printer is also attached to the network and setup for printers is discussed later in the text.

- **Windows Vista:** Click **Start—Network Connection** or click **Start—Control Panel—Network and Sharing Center**. Right-click **Local Area Connection** and select **Properties**, and then click **Continue**. This opens the Local Area Connection Properties menu. Double-click **Internet Protocol Version 4 (TCP/IPv4)**. This opens the Properties menu. Now select **Use the following IP address**, enter the IP address and subnet mask, and click **OK**.
- **Windows XP:** To set the IP address in Windows XP, click **Start—Settings—Control Panel** and click **Network Connections**. Right-click **Local Area Connection**, and then click **Properties**. You should see the Local Area Connection Properties menu. Make sure the **TCP/IP** box is checked and the words *Internet Protocol TCP/IP* are highlighted (selected). Click the **Properties** button. You should now see the **Internet Protocol (TCP/IP) Properties** menu. At this point you must specify whether the IP address is to be obtained automatically or if you are to use a specified (static) address. For this example click **Use the following IP address**. Type the desired IP address and subnet mask and select **OK**.
- **MAC OS X:** Click **Apple—System Preferences—Network**, and then click **Network Status** and select **Built-In Ethernet**. A new screen should appear and with the option **Configure IPv4**; select **Manually**. This option lets you manually set the IP address and subnet mask. Fields should now be displayed for inputting both the IP address and subnet mask. Enter the desired IP address and subnet mask and select **Apply Now**.

The IP addresses and subnet mask being used in the office LAN example are listed in Table 1-6. The IP address for computer 1 is 10.10.10.1, and in this example, a subnet mask of 255.255.0.0 is being used. Subnet masking is examined in detail in Chapter 5. For now, leave the remaining fields empty; their purpose will be discussed later in the text. Your network configuration for computer 1 should now be complete. These steps are repeated for computers 2 and 3 in this LAN example.

1-6   TESTING AND TROUBLESHOOTING A LAN

When the network configurations on the computers are completed and the cable connections are in place, you will need to test and possibly troubleshoot the network. First, verify that the computers are properly connected on the network. Do this by verifying that you have link lights on each switch port that is connected to a computer or other networking device. Link verification will typically appear as a lit link light. An example of a switch with the link light activated is shown in Figure 1-30.

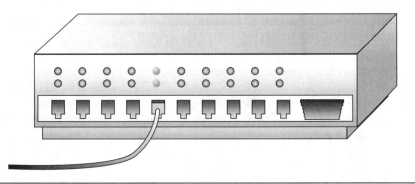

FIGURE 1-30   An example of the link light on a hub.

Once you have verified that the networking devices are physically connected together, use the **ping** command to verify that the networking devices are communicating. **Ping** stands for **Packet Internet Groper** that uses **ICMP (Internet Control Message Protocol)** echo requests and replies to test that a device on the network is reachable. The ICMP protocol verifies that messages are being delivered. The **ping** command is available in the command window of Windows to verify the networking devices are communicating. The command structure for the **ping** command is as follows:

```
Usage ping[-t][-a][-n count)[-1 size][-f -i TTL][-v TOS] [-r count][-s
    count]
[[-j host-list]:[-k host-list][-w timeout] destination-list
Options
-t              Ping the specified host until stopped
                    To see statistics and continue, type Control-Break
                    To stop, type Control-C
-a              Resolve addresses to host-names
-n count        Number of echo requests to send
-1 size         Send buffer size
-f              Set Don't Fragment flag in packet
-I              TTL  Time To Live v  TOS    Type Of Service
r count         Record route for count hops
```

Ping (Packet Internet Groper)
Command used to test that a device on the network is reachable

ICMP
Internet Control Message Protocol

```
s count      Timestamp for count hops
j host-list  Loose source route along host-list
k host-list  Strict source route along host-list
w timeout    Timeout in milliseconds to wait for each reply
```

For example, the command ***ping 10.10.10.1*** is used to ping the IP address for computer 1. The IP address 10.10.10.1 is the destination address. Another example would be the destination IP address for computer 3; in this case ***ping 10.10.10.3*** would be used. (Refer to Table 1-6 and Figure 1-26 for the IP addresses of the computers in our sample network.)

The following is an example of pinging another computer on the network to verify that the computers are communicating. In this example, computer 1 is used to ping computer 2. Remember, the ***ping*** command is executed from the command window.

```
ping 10.10.10.2
Pinging 10.10.10.2 with 32 bytes of data:
Reply from 10.10.10.2: bytes 32 time<1ms TTL 128
Reply from 10.10.10.2: bytes 32 time<1ms TTL 128
Reply from 10.10.10.2: bytes 32 time<1ms TTL 128
Reply from 10.10.10.2: bytes 32 time<1ms TTL 128
Ping statistics for 10.10.10.2:
        Packets: Sent = 4, Received = 4, Lost = 0 (0% loss),
Approximate round trip times in milli-seconds:
        Minimum = 0ms, Maximum = 0ms, Average = 0ms
```

The text shows that 32 bytes of data are being sent to the computer with the IP address of 10.10.10.2. The "Reply from 10.10.10.2" indicates that computer 2 received the message. The type of data packets being sent are explained in section 1-7. If the computer at IP address 10.10.10.2 did not respond, the message **"Request timed out."** is displayed:

```
ping 10.10.10.2
Pinging 10.10.10.2 with 32 bytes of data:
Request timed out.
Request timed out.
Request timed out.
Request timed out.

Ping statistics for 10.10.10.2:
        Packets: Sent = 4, Received = 0, Lost= 4
(100% loss),
```

ipconfig
Command used to display
the computer's address

At times you may want to verify the IP address of the computer you are working on. Remember, a method of obtaining the IP address is to enter the command ***ipconfig*** at the command prompt. It is not necessary to include the ***/all switch*** after the ***ipconfig*** command unless you also want the MAC address information displayed. Figure 1-31 shows an example of displaying the IP address for computer 1.

Windows IP Configuration
Ethernet adapter Local Area Connection:
    Connection-specific DNS Suffix .:
    IP Address............: 10.10.10.1
    Subnet Mask...........: 255.255.0.0
    Default Gateway ....:

(a)

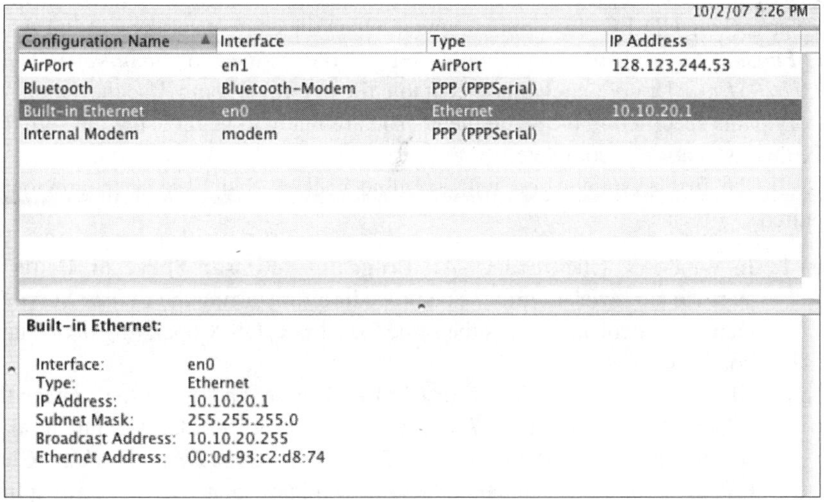

Configuration Name ▲	Interface	Type	IP Address
AirPort	en1	AirPort	128.123.244.53
Bluetooth	Bluetooth-Modem	PPP (PPPSerial)	
Built-in Ethernet	en0	Ethernet	10.10.20.1
Internal Modem	modem	PPP (PPPSerial)	

10/2/07 2:26 PM

Built-in Ethernet:

Interface:	en0
Type:	Ethernet
IP Address:	10.10.20.1
Subnet Mask:	255.255.255.0
Broadcast Address:	10.10.20.255
Ethernet Address:	00:0d:93:c2:d8:74

(b)

FIGURE 1-31   (a) An example of displaying the IP address for computer 1 using the *ipconfig* command in Windows and (b) an example of the displayed IP address in MAC OS X for the Built-in Ethernet connection.

1-7 ANALYZING COMPUTER NETWORKS

Each chapter in this text includes a section on configuring, analyzing, or troubleshooting computer networks. The purpose of these additions to each chapter is to provide a thorough examination of networking concepts. The objective of this section in Chapter 1 is to introduce the techniques for using a protocol analyzer to examine how networking packets are exchanged in a TCP/IP network. The TCP/IP protocol is examined in detail in Chapter 5, "TCP/IP." You will actually be able to develop an understanding of the protocols being used and packets being transferred prior to studying the theory behind the protocols.

    The CD-ROM included with the text contains the Finisar Surveyor Demo v9.0 protocol analyzer. The Surveyor Demo software includes many advanced features for packet capture and analysis. The capabilities of this software will help you gain a thorough understanding of packet transfers and networking protocols. Additionally, you will gain an introductory understanding of the capabilities and techniques for using a sophisticated software protocol analyzer. The protocol analyzer has the capability to capture and decode data packets and allows the user to inspect the packet contents. This enables the user to investigate how information is being transferred in the network. Additionally, the information provided by the protocol analyzer enables the user to detect, identify, and correct network problems. You are guided through the steps of using the Surveyor protocol analyzer.

In this section, the packets transferred in the process of pinging a computer are examined. This exercise is based on the exercise presented in section 1-6 and uses the IP and MAC addresses specified in Table 1-6. The following steps guide you through installing and using the Surveyor Demo software on a Windows computer or a MAC with a dual-core Intel processor and a Windows emulator. Place the text's Companion Networking CD-ROM in your computer. Open the contents of the CD-ROM and the *Finisar* file folder. You should see a file named *SetupSurveyorDemo-9.0.0.62051.exe*. Double-click this executable file to initiate setup. Use the default directory paths specified in the setup menu. You are ready to begin using the software once the installation is complete.

In the first example, you will examine packets that have been previously captured.

Step 1 In Windows, Click **Start—All Programs—Finisar Surveyor Demo** to start the surveyor program. The procedure for starting the Finisar Surveyor Demo protocol analyzer is the same for a MAC OS X operating in the dual-boot mode with XP.

Step 2 Click **File—Open**, select your CD-ROM drive, and select the *Finisar* file folder. Double-click the *Ch1-6.cap* file to open the file. You might see a screen that says, "***You can see only 250 frames in the Demo version.***" Click **OK** to begin. This statement is letting you know that you are seeing a limited number of data packets on your network. This is a suitable limitation relative to the concepts presented in the text.

Note

Click the **Capture View** button at the bottom of the **Surveyor Demo—Detail View** screen. The button is shown in Figure 1-32.

◄ ▶ ▌ Capture View ⟩ **Overview** ⟨ Servers ⟨ Transactions ⟨ Issues ⟨ Clients ⟩

FIGURE 1-32   The Capture View button on the Surveyor Demo Detail View screen.

Once you click the **Capture View** button, you should see the captured packets on your screen. Figure 1-33 shows the detail view screen. In this example, the information on the screen is showing the transfer of packets that occurs when one computer pings another. In this case, computer 1 pinged computer 2. Recall that the MAC addresses and assigned IP addresses for computer 1 and computer 2 are listed in Table 1-6 and in Figure 1-26. The MAC and IP addresses are listed again for your reference:

Name	MAC Address	IP Address
Computer 1	00-10-A4-13-99-2E	10.10.10.1
Computer 2	00-10-A4-13-6C-6E	10.10.10.2

The Bounce Chart displayed on the right side of the Detail View screen is showing that an ARP request broadcast was sent from computer 10.10.10.1, and computer 10.10.10.2 replied back with its IP address. You can click **Capture Views—Application Bounce Chart** to close the bounce chart.

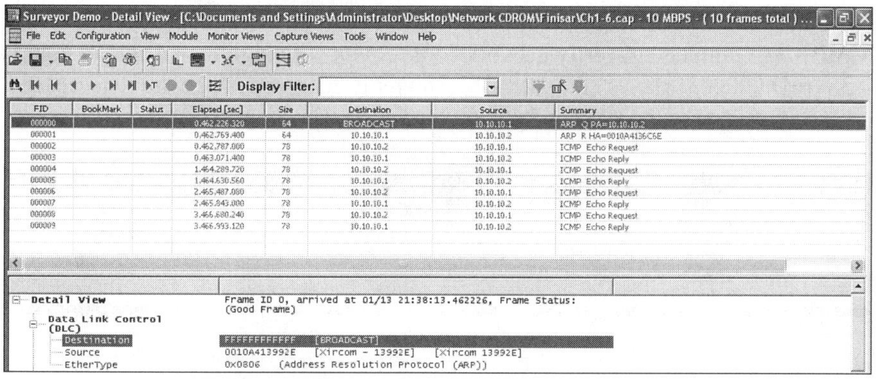

FIGURE 1-33   The captured packets showing the ping from computer 1 to computer 2.

In this example, a ***ping*** command is issued from computer 1 to computer 2. The structure of the command issued by computer 1 at the command prompt is

```
ping 10.10.10.2
```

As shown in Frame ID (FID) 000000 in Figure 1-33, computer 1 issues an **ARP** request on the LAN. ARP stands for "Address Resolution Protocol," which is a protocol used to map an IP address to its MAC address. The source of the packet is 00-10-A4-13-99-2E (computer 1). The destination address on the local area network shown is BROADCAST, which means this message is being sent to all computers on the network. A query (Q) being asked is who has the IP address 10.10.10.2 (PA).

The highlighted area (FID 000001) in Figure 1-34 shows computer 2 replying with its MAC address back to computer 1. This is called an **ARP reply**, which is a protocol where the MAC address is returned. The source of the ARP reply is from 00-10-A4-13-6C-6E (computer 2), which is replying that the MAC address for 10.10.10.2 is 00-10-A4-13-6C-6E (HA). In this case, the owner of the IP address replied to the message.

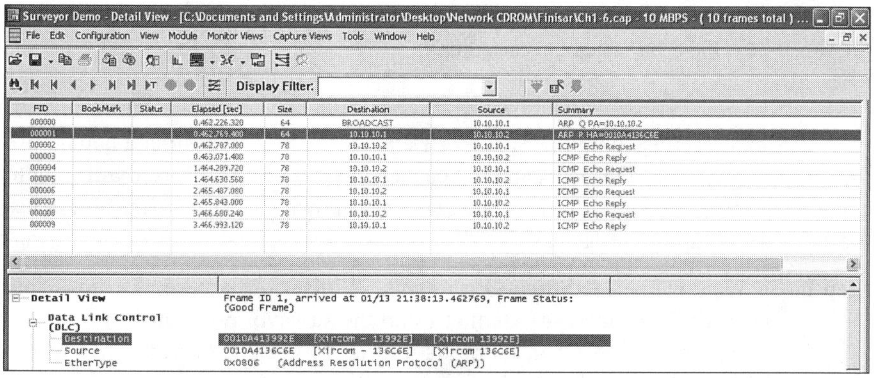

Address Resolution Protocol (ARP)
Used to map an IP address to its MAC address

ARP Reply
A network protocol where the MAC address is returned

FIGURE 1-34   Computer 2 replying with its MAC address back to computer 1.

Echo Request
Part of the ICMP protocol that requests a reply from a computer

Figure 1-35 shows computer 1 sending an **echo request** directly to computer 2. An echo request is the part of the ICMP protocol that requests a reply from a computer. Notice in the echo request that the destination address is 00-10-A4-13-6C-6E (computer 2's MAC address), and the source is 00-10-A4-13-99-2E (computer 1's MAC address). Recall that computer 1 now knows the MAC address for IP address 10.10.10.2 so the *ping* request can be sent directly. In this step, computer 1 uses the ICMP *ping* command to verify network connectivity. The highlighted area in Figure 1-36 (FID 000003) shows computer 2's echo reply. This series of echo requests and replies repeats three more times for a total of four cycles.

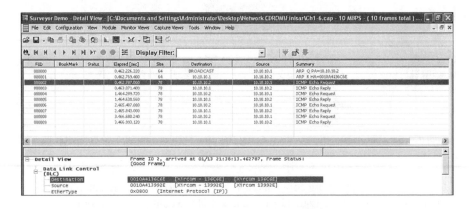

FIGURE 1-35 Computer 1 is sending an echo request to computer 2.

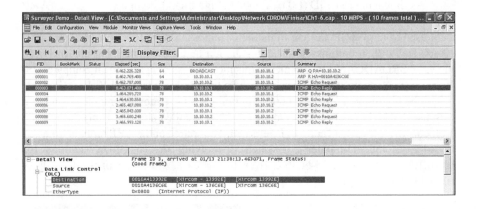

FIGURE 1-36 The echo reply from computer 2.

The first exercise with the Surveyor Demo software demonstrated how to use the protocol analyzer to inspect captured packets. In most cases the user will want to capture data packets from their own network. The following steps describe how to use the software to capture packets.

Step 1 In Windows, click **Start—Programs—Finisar—Surveyor Demo—** and select **Finisar Surveyor Demo** to start the surveyor program.

To capture packets on an operating network, you can either click **Module—Start** as shown in Figure 1-37 or click the green arrow under the **Monitor**

Views button as shown in Figure 1-38. You should see activity on your Cap+Mon screen as shown in Figure 1-39. The lines in the Cap+Mon window show the network utilization and the network errors, of which there are currently none.

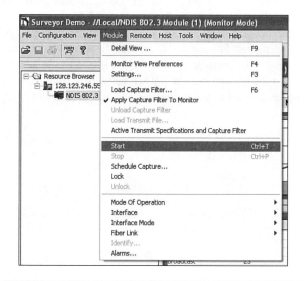

FIGURE 1-37 Initializing the Surveyor Demo to capture data packets from your network.

FIGURE 1-38 Starting the capture.

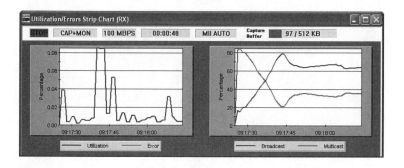

FIGURE 1-39 An example of network activity as displayed on the Surveyor Demo screen

Step 2 To examine the packets, stop the simulation by clicking the red **Stop** button or by clicking **Module—Stop**. The overview screen will be displayed after the capture is stopped. You might see a screen that says, **"You can see only 250 frames in the DEMO version. All but the last 250 packets will be blocked without the full release version of Finisar Surveyor."** Click **OK** to begin. Click the **Capture View** tab at the bottom left of the overview screen to view the captured data packets. The captured data packets should now be displayed. Remember, there must be some activity on your network for packets to be transferred. You may see little traffic activity if your network is in the lab and there is limited network activity. You can always use the *ping* command to generate some network data activity if needed.

SUMMARY

Chapter 1 introduced the basic concepts of computer networking. The technologies and techniques for assembling a computer network using the Ethernet protocol have been presented. The student should now understand the following major topics:

- The various LAN topologies
- The concept of CSMA/CD in the Ethernet protocol
- The structure of the Ethernet frame
- The purpose of the network interface card
- The purpose of the MAC address
- How to determine the MAC address for a computer
- The purpose and structure of the IP address
- The concept of private IP addresses
- The network topologies and technologies used to implement twisted-pair computer networks
- How to configure and verify a computer's IP address
- How to configure a home network and an office LAN
- The purpose of the link light
- The purpose of using *ping* to test a network connection
- Using a protocol analyzer to examine simple network data traffic

QUESTIONS AND PROBLEMS

Section 1-1

1. State whether the following network descriptions are describing a MAN, WAN, or LAN:
   a. A network of users that share computer resources in a limited area
   b. A network of users that share computer resources across a metropolitan area
   c. A network that connects local area networks across a large geographic area
2. Expand the acronym *NIC*.
3. Expand the acronym *MAC*.
4. Expand the acronym *LAN*.
5. Expand the acronym *WAN*.

Section 1-2

6. Define the term *protocol*.
7. Define the term *topology*.
8. Define the term *deterministic*.

9. A disadvantage of the token-ring system is that if an error changes the token pattern, it can cause the token to stop circulating. This can be eliminated by adding a
    a. Router
    b. Multiport repeater
    c. Token passer
    d. Token-ring hub
10. State the network topology being used in the following figure (Bus, Star, Ring, or Mesh).

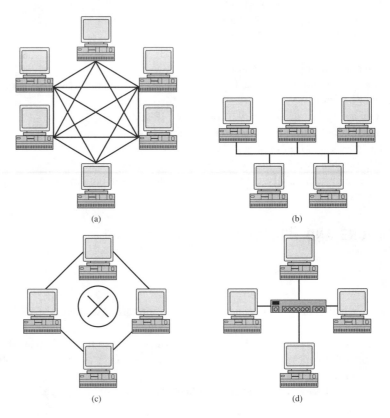

(a)

(b)

(c)

(d)

    a.
    b.
    c.
    d.
11. What is the difference between a *hub* and a *switch*?

Section 1-3

12. Define the acronym *CSMA/CD* and the protocol that uses CSMA/CD.
13. What information is not included in an Ethernet frame?
    a. Frame size
    b. Source MAC address
    c. Pad
    d. Frame check sequence

14. What is the minimum size of the data payload in an Ethernet frame?
15. What is the minimum and maximum size of an Ethernet frame?
16. Define the acronym *OUI*. Where is the OUI used?
17. What does the *OUI* represent?
18. In Windows Vista or Windows XP, how would you find the Ethernet (MAC) address?
19. INTERNET SEARCH: Find the device manufacturer for the following Ethernet devices:
    a. 00-C0-4F-49-68-AB—
    b. 00-0A-27-B7-3E-F8—
    c. 00-04-76-B6-9D-06—
    d. 00-00-36-69-42-27—
20. State the class of address (A, B, or C) for the following IP addresses:
    a. 46.39.42.05— *a*
    b. 220.244.38.168—*c*
    c. 198.1.0.4— *c*
    d. 126.87.12.34—*a*
    e. 99.150.200.251—*a*
    f. 128.64.32.16— *B*
21. Expand the acronym *TCP/IP*.

Section 1-4

22. Cite the three advantages of a wired network.
23. Cite three advantages of a wireless network.
24. What does it mean for a wireless networking device to be Wi-Fi compliant?
25. What are the most common types of equipment that are used to establish a broadband connection to the ISP?
26. Name six issues that should be considered when planning a home network?
27. Why is checking the lights of the networking device that connects to the ISP important?
28. What is the purpose of a range expander?
29. What is a hotspot?
30. List five steps that can be used to protect the home network.
31. You have the choice of selecting a networking device with WEP and another with WPA. Which offers better security and why?
32. What are the potential problems of using the default factory passwords?
33. What is the purpose of the SSID, and what can the network administrator do to protect the network from hackers who might have learned the SSID?
34. What is the purpose of MAC filtering on a wireless network?
35. How does NAT (Network Address Translation) help protect outsider access to computers in the home network?
36. What is Stateful Packet Inspection?
37. What is a VPN, and how does it protect the data transferred over a wireless network?
38. How is IP addressing typically handled in a home network?

39. What is Port Address Translation (PAT)?

40. A router on a home network is assigned an IP address of 128.123.45.67. A computer in the home network is assigned a private IP address of 192.168.10.62. This computer is assigned the public IP address 128.123.45.67:1922. Which IP address is used for routing data packets on the Internet? Is overloading being used?

Section 1-5

41. Which of the following is not a step in building an office LAN?
    a. Obtaining proper government permits
    b. Configuring the network settings
    c. Connecting the devices together
    d. Network documentation

42. What does *RJ-45* represent?
    a. A 45-pin connector for CAT6
    b. An IEEE standard for data speed
    c. An 8-pin modular connector for twisted pair Ethernet
    d. Protocol used to verify a communications link

43. What is an *uplink port*?

44. What is the maximum speed and length for Category 6 cabling?

45. What do the link lights on a hub represent?

46. What does *cross-connected* mean?

47. Documentation: Draw a network diagram similar to Figure 1-26 consisting of 3 computers, a switch, and a printer. Use the MAC addresses given in Table 1-6. Assign each network device an IP address from the private address space 192.168.5.x network. You are the network administrator and may choose the host address for each device.

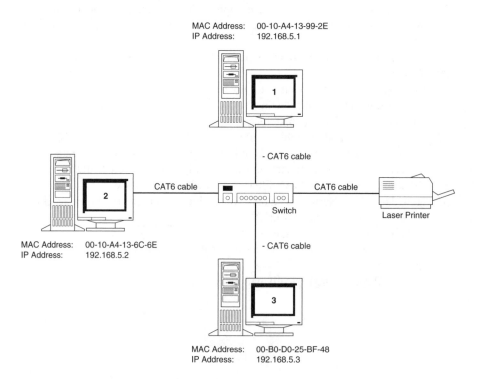

Section 1-6

48. What command would you use to ping 10.3.9.42 indefinitely?
49. What command would you use to ping 192.168.5.36 20 times with 1024 bytes of data?
50. Expand the acronym *TTL*.

Section 1-7

51. Expand the acronym *ARP.*
52. What is the purpose of an ARP request?
53. Expand the acronym *ICMP.*
54. What is an *echo request*?
55. What is the purpose of a protocol analyzer?

Critical Thinking

56. In terms of computer security, a switch offers better security than a hub. Why is this?

Included on the Companion CD-ROM in the Finisar capture file folder is a network packet capture file called *Packet1a.cap.* Open this file in the Finisar-Shomiti Surveyor Demo program. The following five questions refer to this file.

57. What are the MAC addresses of the computers involved?
58. Which IP addresses correspond to each MAC address?
59. Which packet IDs correspond to ARP requests?
60. Which packet IDs correspond to ARP replies?
61. Which computers are pinging which computers?

2 CHAPTER

Physical Layer Cabling: Twisted Pair

CHAPTER OUTLINE

2-1 Introduction
2-2 Structured Cabling
2-3 Unshielded Twisted-Pair Cable
2-4 Terminating CAT6/5e/5 UTP Cables
2-5 Cable Testing and Certification

2-6 10 Gigabit Ethernet over Copper
2-7 Troubleshooting Computer
Networks
Summary
Questions and Problems

OBJECTIVES

- Describe the six subsystems of a structured cabling system

- Define horizontal cabling

- Define UTP and STP

- Define the categories of UTP cable

- Describe the difference in the T568A and T568B wire color order

- Describe the procedure for placing RJ-45 plugs and jacks on twisted-pair cable

- Describe how to terminate twisted-pair cable for computer networks

- Define the basic concepts for planning a cable installation for an office LAN

- Describe the procedure for certifying a twisted-pair cable for CAT6 and CAT5e

- Describe the issues of running 10 gigabit Ethernet over copper

- Describe the basic steps for troubleshooting cable problems

KEY TERMS

physical layer
EIA
TIA
campus network
EIA/TIA 568-B
building entrance
entrance facilities (EF)
equipment room (ER)
telecommunications closet
TR
backbone cabling
horizontal cabling
TCO
work area
main cross-connect (MC)

intermediate cross-connect (IC)
Cross-connect
horizontal cross-connect (HC)
MDF (Main Distribution Frame or Main Equipment Room)
CD (Campus Distributor)
BD (Building Distributor)
FD (Floor Distributors)
WO (workstation or work area outlet)
TO (telecommunications outlet)
terminated
8P8C

patch cable
UTP
CAT6/6a
CAT5/e
balanced mode
FastEthernet
network congestion
bottlenecking
full duplex
gigabit Ethernet
CAT7/7a and CAT6a
10GBASE-T
STP
EMI
T568A

continues

T568B
color map
TX
RX
straight-through cable
wire-map
crossover cable
link
full channel
attenuation (insertion loss)
near-end crosstalk (NEXT)
crosstalk

power sum NEXT (PSNEXT)
equal level FEXT (ELFEXT)
PSELFEXT
ACR
PSACR
return loss
propagation delay
nominal velocity of propagation (NVP)
delay skew
pair data
IEEE 802.3an-2006
10GBASE-T

10GBASE-T
Alien Crosstalk (AXT)
PSANEXT
PSAACRF
F/UTP
TCL
ELTCTL
LCL
TCTL
PSANEXT
PSAACRF
multilevel encoding
hybrid echo cancellation circuit

2-1   INTRODUCTION

This chapter examines the twisted-pair media used to link computers together to form a local area network (LAN). This is called **physical layer** cabling. The term *physical layer* describes the media that interconnects networking devices. The objective of this chapter is for the reader to gain an introductory understanding of the cable media including the category types, the steps for terminating cables, cable testing, certification, and troubleshooting. The main focus will be on the use of unshielded twisted-pair (UTP) cable in computer networks, although an overview of shielded twisted-pair (STP) is presented. Fiber optic cables are playing a very important role in modern computer networks and are not overlooked in this text. This media is thoroughly examined in Chapter 12.

This chapter begins with an overview of the concept of structured cabling. This section defines the six subsystems of a structured cabling system and focuses on the basic issues associated with horizontal cabling or wiring a LAN. Next, the basic operational characteristics of unshielded twisted-pair (UTP) cable are examined. The discussion includes an examination of the various categories of UTP cable currently available. Next is an overview of constructing twisted-pair patch and horizontal link cabling. The tools and techniques for properly terminating UTP cabling for both CAT6 and CAT5e are presented. An introduction to testing and certifying CAT6 and CAT5e cables follows. This section includes several examples of cable test data and how to interpret the test results. The chapter concludes with a section on troubleshooting computer networks, with a focus on the cable or physical layer failures.

Physical Layer
Describes the media that interconnects networking devices

2-2   STRUCTURED CABLING

The first major standard describing a structured cabling system for computer networks was the TIA/EIA 568-A in 1995. **EIA** is the Electronics Industries Alliance, a trade organization that lobbies for the interests of manufacturers of electronics-related equipment. **TIA** stands for the Telecommunications Industry Association, which is a trade organization that represents the interests of the telecommunications industry. The most important addendum to the EIA/TIA 568-A standard was Addendum 5, published in 1999. This addendum defined the transmission performance specifications for 4-pair 100-ohm category 5e twisted-pair cabling. TIA/EIA adopted new category 6 (CAT6) cable specifications in June 2002. This is the type of cabling recommended for use in today's computer networks, although CAT7 twisted-pair cabling may soon become the recommended standard.

The EIA/TIA 568-A standard defined the minimum requirements for the internal telecommunications wiring in buildings and between structures in a **campus network**. A campus network consists of interconnected LANs within a limited geographic area such as a college campus, a military base, or a group of commercial buildings. The EIA/TIA 568-A was revised and updated many times, and in 2000 a new standard, the **EIA/TIA 568-B** was published. The three parts of the EIA/TIA 568-B are as follows:

- **EIA/TIA-568-B.1:** Commercial Cabling Standard, Master Document
- **EIA/TIA-568-B.2:** Twisted-pair Media
- **EIA/TIA-568-B.3:** Optical Fiber Cabling Standard

EIA
Electronic Industries Alliance

TIA
Telecommunications Industry Association

Campus Network
Interconnected LANs within a limited geographic area

EIA/TIA 568-B
The standard that defines the six subsystems of a structured cabling system

Within the EIA/TIA 569B Commercial Standard for Telecommunication Pathways and Spaces are guidelines defining the six subsystems of a structured cabling system:

Building Entrance
Entrance Facilities (EF)
Equipment Room (ER)
Backbone Cabling
Telecommunications Closet
TR
Horizontal Cabling
TCO
Work Area

1. **Building Entrance:** The point where the external cabling and wireless services interconnects with the internal building cabling in the equipment room. This is used by both public and/or private access (for example, Telco, satellite, cable TV, security, and so on). The building entrance is also called the **entrance facilities (EF)**. Both public and private network cables enter the building at this point, and typically each has separate facilities for the different access providers.
2. **Equipment Room (ER):** A room set aside for complex electronic equipment such as the network servers and telephone equipment.
3. **Telecommunications Closet:** The location of the cabling termination points that includes the mechanical terminations and the distribution frames. The connection of the horizontal cabling to the backbone wiring is made at this point. This is also called the telecommunications room (**TR**) or telecommunications enclosure (**TE**).

Note

One room can serve as the entrance facility, equipment room, and the telecommunications closet.

---

4. **Backbone Cabling:** Cabling that interconnects telecommunication closets, equipment rooms, and cabling entrances in the same building and between buildings.
5. **Horizontal Cabling:** Cabling that extends out from the telecommunications closet into the LAN work area. Typically, the horizontal wiring is structured in a star configuration running to each area telecommunications outlet (**TCO**). This is the wall plate where the fiber or twisted-pair cable terminates in the room. In some cases, the TCO terminates telephone, fiber, and video in addition to data into the same wall plate.
6. **Work Area:** The location of the computers and printers, patch cables, jacks, computer adapter cables, and fiber jumpers.

Main Cross-connect (MC)
Usually connects two or more buildings and is typically the central telecommunications connection point for a campus or building. It is also called the **Main Distribution Frame (MDF)** or **Main Equipment Room**. The MC connects to telco, an ISP, and so on. Another term for the MC is the campus distributor (**CD**).

Intermediate Cross-connect (IC)
Also called the building distributor (BD) and is the building's connection point to the campus backbone. The IC links the MC to the horizontal cross-connect (HC).

Figure 2-1 provides a drawing of the structure for a telecommunications cabling system. In the figure, it shows the connection of the carriers (Telco, ISP, and so on) coming into the equipment room (ER). The ER is the space set aside for the carrier's equipment contained in the **main cross-connect (MC)** or **intermediate cross-connect (IC)**. The entrance facility (EF) consists of the cabling, connector hardware, protection devices that are used as the interface between any external building cabling, and wireless services with the equipment room. This area is used by both public and private access providers (for example, Telco, satellite, cable TV, security, and so on). The ER and EF space is typically combined with the MC equipment room.

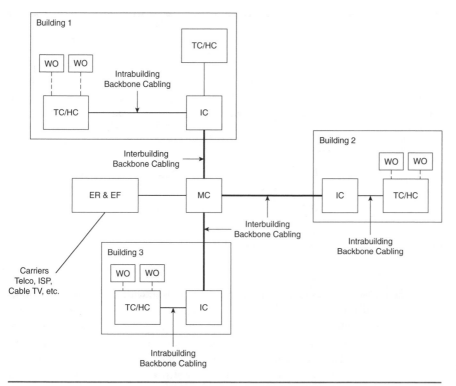

FIGURE 2-1 The telecommunications Cabling System Architecture.

Between the main cross-connect (MC) and the intermediate cross-connect (IC) are the campus backbone cabling (listed as the interbuilding backbone cabling). This defines the connections between the MC and IC. A definition of a **cross-connect** is a space where you are going to take one or multiple cables and connect them to one or more cables or equipment. For example, you could be bringing in 60 UTP cables, 50 could be cross-connected to a switch and 10 cross-connected to a backbone cable going to another location. Typical connections between the MC and IC are single-mode and multimode fibers and possibly coax for cable TV, although most installations are migrating to fiber. The building backbone cabling (intrabuilding backbone cabling) makes the connection between the IC and the TC/HC. TC is the telecommunications closet and HC is the **horizontal cross-connect (HC)**. Usually this connection is CAT5 UTP or better, or possibly single- or multimode fiber or some combination. Fiber is the best choice for making these connections, although copper is sometimes used. The horizontal cabling is the cabling between the HC and the work area. It is usually CAT5 UTP or better or fiber. The standard currently specifies CAT6. Fiber is gaining acceptance for connecting to the **work area outlets (WO)**.

Figure 2-2 provides a more detailed view of the cabling from the main cross-connect (MC) to the intermediate cross-connect (IC) and the horizontal cross-connect (HC). This drawing shows the three layers of the recommended backbone hierarchy cabling for a computer network. The first level of the hierarchy is the MC. The MC connects to the second level of the hierarchy, the IC. The backbone cabling connects the MC to the IC and the IC to the telecommunications closet (TC)/HC. The HC connects the horizontal cabling to the work area and to the workstation outlets (WO).

Cross-connect
A space where you are going to take one or multiple cables and connect them to one or more cables or equipment

Horizontal Cross-connect (HC)
The connection between the building distributors and the horizontal cabling to the work area or workstation outlet—another term used for the HC is the floor distributors (FD)

Workstation or Work Area Outlet (WO)
Also called the TO (telecommunications outlet), it's used to connect devices to the cable plant. The cable type typically used is CAT3, CAT5, CAT5e, CAT6, CAT6A, and various coaxial cables. Devices typically connected to these outlets are PCs, printers, servers, phones, televisions, and wireless access points.

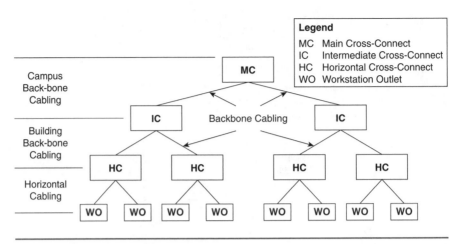

Legend

MC   Main Cross-Connect
IC   Intermediate Cross-Connect
HC   Horizontal Cross-Connect
WO   Workstation Outlet

FIGURE 2-2   The Campus Network Hierarchical topology

The focus of this chapter is on the issues associated with the horizontal cabling and the work area (LAN) subsystems. The text addresses all six subsystems of a structured cabling system, but at the point when the networking concepts and related hardware are introduced. Many of the concepts covered in each structured cabling subsystem require that the reader have a firm grasp of basic networking to gain a full appreciation of how each network piece fits into a structured cabled system.

Horizontal Cabling

Permanent network cabling within a building is considered to be *horizontal cabling,* defined as the cabling that extends out from the telecommunications closet into the LAN work area. Take time to plan for your horizontal cabling installation because this is where your network interfaces with the users. There is always a substantial installation cost associated with horizontal cabling, and there is an even greater cost of having to replace or upgrade a cable installation. You don't want to have to recable your system very often. Careful attention should be given to planning for the horizontal cabling of a LAN. Make sure you fully understand your current networking needs and that your proposed plan meets the needs. Also make sure your plan addresses future needs and growth of your network.

Figure 2-3 illustrates the basic blocks of a horizontal cabling system from the telecommunications closet to the computer in the LAN. The following components are typically found in the telecommunications closet:

A. Backbone cabling interconnecting this closet with other closets
B. Switch or hub
C. Patch panels
D. Patch cables
E. Cabling to the LAN (horizontal cabling)
F. Wall plate
G. Patch cable connecting the computer to the wall plate

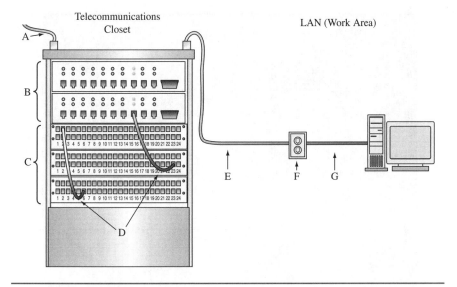

FIGURE 2-3   Block diagram of a horizontal cabling system.

Item E in Figure 2-3 shows the cabling leaving the telecommunications closet. The cable extends to where it is **terminated** at the wall plate (item F) in the LAN or work area. The term *terminated* describes where the cable connects to a jack in a wall plate, a patch panel, or an RJ-45 modular plug. In this case, the cable terminates into an RJ-45 jack in the wall plate. Figure 2-4 provides an example of the RJ-45 wall plate and patch panel.

Terminated
Describes where the cable connects to a jack or a patch panel

Note

The proper term for the RJ-45 modular plug used in computer systems is actually *8P8C* for both male and female connectors. 8P8C stands for 8-pin 8-conductors and is defined by ANSI/TIA-968-A and B but is commonly called RJ-45 by both professionals and end users.

8P8C
The correct name for the modular 8-pin, 8-connector computer connectors—the common term is RJ-45

An individual cable is used to connect each connector in the outlet to the patch panel in the telecommunications closet (F to E). RJ-45 (8P8C) plugs and jacks are defined in section 2-4.

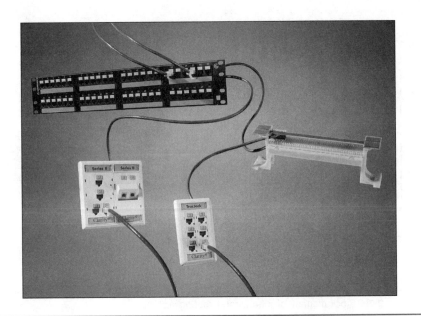

FIGURE 2-4   The Ortronics clarity twisted-pair system (courtesy of Ortronics).

Patch Cable
Cabling (often twisted-pair) used to make the physical connection between networking equipment

In a star topology, there is an individual cable run for each outlet in the wall plate. This means that you assign one computer to each terminated outlet. A **patch cable** (item G) is used to make the physical connection from the computer to the wall plate as shown in Figure 2-3. A patch cable is a short cable used to make the physical connection between networking equipment. There is a 100-meter overall length limitation of the cable run from the telecommunications closet to the networking device in the work area. This includes the length of the patch cables at each end (items D and G) plus the cable run (item E). A general rule of thumb is to allow 90 meters for the cable run from the telecommunications closet to the work area (item E). This allows 5 meters of cable length for the work area and 5 meters for the patch cables in the telecommunications closet (item D) and the work area (item G). Figure 2-5 shows an example of the insides of a telecommunications closet.

FIGURE 2-5   Inside a telecommunications closet.

2-3   UNSHIELDED TWISTED-PAIR CABLE

Unshielded twisted-pair (**UTP**) cable plays an important role in computer networking. The most common twisted-pair standards used for computer networking today are category 6 (**CAT6**), category 6a (**CAT6a**), and category 5e (**CAT5e**). CAT6 cable is tested to provide the transmission of data rates up to 1000 Mbps for a maximum length of 100 meters. CAT6a is an improved version of CAT6 and will support 10 gigabit Ethernet.

CAT5e cable is an enhanced version of CAT5 and provides improved performance requirements of the cable. CAT6 provides improved performance and a bandwidth of 250 MHz. CAT5/5e twisted-pair cable contains four color-coded pairs of 24-gauge wires terminated with an RJ-45 (8P8C) connector. Figure 2-6 provides an example of a CAT5e cable terminated with an RJ-45 (8P8C) modular plug. CAT6 twisted-pair cable also contains four color-coded wires, but the wire gauge is 23AWG. CAT6 cable has a stiffer feel compared to CAT5e.

UTP
Unshielded twisted-pair

CAT6/6a
The current standard in high performance twisted-pair cable

CAT5e
Enhanced version of CAT5

FIGURE 2-6   An example of an RJ-45 modular plug (courtesy of Cyberguys.com).

The precise manner in which the twist of CAT6/5e/5 cable is maintained, even at the terminations, provides a significant increase in signal transmission performance. CAT5/5e standards allow 0.5 inches of untwisted cable pair at the termination. CAT6 has an even tighter requirement that allows for only 3/8-inch of untwisted cable at the termination. The termination is the point where the cable is connected to terminals in a modular plug, jack, or patch panel.

Balanced Mode
Neither wire in the wire pairs connects to ground

CAT6/5e/5 twisted-pair cable contains four twisted wire pairs for a total of eight wires. In twisted-pair cable, none of the wires in the wire pairs are connected to ground. The signals on the wires are set up for a high (+) and low (-) signal line. The (+) indicates that the phase relationship of the signal on the wire is positive and the (-) indicates that the phase of the signal on the wire is negative; both signals are relative to a virtual ground. This is called a **balanced mode** of operation—the balance of the two wire pairs helps maintain the required level of performance in terms of crosstalk and noise rejection.

Table 2-1 lists the different categories of twisted-pair cable defined by the EIA/TIA 568B standard. The table includes an application description and minimum bandwidth for each category. Notice that there is not a listing for CAT1 and CAT2.

TABLE 2-1   Different Categories for Twisted-pair Cable, Based on TIA568B

Category	Description	Bandwidth/Data Rate
Category 3 (CAT3)	Telephone installations Class C	Up to 16 Mbps
Category 5 (CAT5)	Computer networks Class D	Up to 100 MHz/100 Mbps 100-m length
Enhanced CAT5 (CAT5e)	Computer networks	100 MHz/1000 Mbps applications with improved noise performance in a full duplex mode

Category	Description	Bandwidth/Data Rate
Category 6 (CAT6)	Higher-speed computer	Up to 250 MHz networks Class E/1000Mbps CAT6 supports 10 Gbps but at distances less than 100 meters
Category 6a (CAT6a)	Increased bandwidth	Up to 500 MHz networks Class Ea/10 Gbps
Category 7 (CAT7)	Proposed standard	Up to 600 MHz speed computer networks Class F/10 Gbps
Category 7a (CAT7a)		

CAT1 and CAT2 cable specifications are not defined in the EIA/TIA 568B standard. The first CAT or category specification is for CAT3. CAT3 is being replaced with CAT5e or better. CAT4 is not listed in the table because the category was removed from the TIA568B standard as its data capacity specification was outdated. The category 5 cable standard was established in 1991, and many computer networks are still using the older CAT5 cables. Certified CAT5 cabling works well in both Ethernet and FastEthernet networking environments that run 10 Mbps Ethernet and 100 Mbps FastEthernet data rates. Note that the term **FastEthernet** is used to describe the 100 Mbps data rate for FastEthernet networks.

In some cases, users on networks are experiencing **network congestion** or **bottlenecking** of the data due to the increased file transfer sizes and the limited bandwidth of their network. These terms describe excessive data traffic that is slowing down computer communications even in FastEthernet networks. Basically, the demands on the network exceeded the performance capabilities of the CAT5 cable. The slowdown of the data is of major concern in computer networks. File access time is delayed, productivity is affected, and the time required to complete a task is increased. A slowdown in your network could be costing your company money. Can you imagine the consequences if a slowdown in your network causes a delay in the company's billing?

TIA/EIA ratified the CAT5e cabling specification in 1999 to address this continuing need for greater data handling capacity in the computer networks. The enhanced CAT5 cable (CAT5e) provides an improvement in cable performance, and if all components of the cable installation are done according to specification, then CAT5e will support **full duplex gigabit Ethernet** (1000 Mbps Ethernet) using all four wire pairs. Full duplex means that the computer system can transmit and receive at the same time. TIA/EIA ratified the CAT6 cabling specification in June 2002. This cable provides an even better performance specification and 250 MHz of bandwidth, and maintains backward compatibility with CAT5/5e. CAT6 can support 10-Gbps data rates but over a distance less than 55 meters. The **CAT6a** standard supports 10-gigabit data rates up to 100 meters, and **CAT7** will also support 10 Gbps up to 100 meters with improved bandwidth. The 10-gigabit standard over copper is called **10GBASE-T**.

FastEthernet
An Ethernet system operating at 100 Mbps

Network Congestion
A slowdown on network data traffic movement

Bottlenecking
Another term for network congestion

Full Duplex
Computer system can transmit and receive at the same time

Gigabit Ethernet
1000 Mbps Ethernet

CAT7/7a and CAT6a
UTP cable standards that support 10 gigabit date rates for a length of 100 meters

10GBASE-T
10-gigabit over twisted-pair copper

Shielded Twisted-pair Cable

In some applications, a wire screen or metal foil shield is placed around the twisted-pair cable. Cable with the addition of a shield is called shielded twisted-pair (**STP**) cable. The addition of this shield reduces the potential for electromagnetic interference (**EMI**) as long as the shield is grounded. EMI originates from devices such as motors and power lines, and from some lighting devices such as fluorescent lights.

The shield on the twisted-pair cable does not reject all potentially interfering noise (EMI), but it does greatly reduce noise interference. There is an active debate in the networking community as to which product is superior, UTP or STP. It is important to note that the objective of both cables is to successfully transport data from the telecommunications closet to the work area. Industry testing on STP cable has shown that the addition of a shield does increase the usable bandwidth of the cable by increasing the noise rejection between each of the wire pairs. However, the tests have shown that there is not a significant advantage of placing a shield over a properly installed 4pair 100-ohm UTP cable. Additionally, STP is more expensive, and the increased costs may not justify the benefits. For now, most manufacturers are recommending the use of UTP cable for cabling computer networks except for very noisy environments.

2-4   TERMINATING CAT6/5E/5 UTP CABLES

This section introduces the techniques for terminating high-performance UTP cables. Terminating the RJ-45 (8P8C) connector for CAT6/5e/5 cable is defined by the EIA/TIA standard EIA/TIA568-B.2 and B.2-1. This portion of the standard defines the specifications of the copper cabling hardware. The standard specifies cabling components, transmission, system models, and the measurement procedures needed for verification of the balanced twisted-pair cabling.

Within the EIA/TIA568B standard are the wiring guidelines **T568A** and **T568B**. These wiring guidelines specify the color of wire that connects to what pin on the connector. The specification of the wire color that connects to what pin is called a **color map**. Table 2-2 provides the color maps specified by the T568A and T568B wiring guidelines.

TABLE 2-2   The Wiring Color Schemes for T568A and T568B

Pin #	568A Wire Color	568B Wire Color
1	White-Green	White-Orange
2	Green	Orange
3	White-Orange	White-Green
4	Blue	Blue
5	White-Blue	White-Blue
6	Orange	Green
7	White-Brown	White-Brown
8	Brown	Brown

Figure 2-7 (a) shows the placement of the wire pairs in the RJ-45 (8P8C) modular plug and Figure 2-7 (b) for the T568A and T568B standards. The pin numbers for the RJ-45 (8P8C) modular plug are shown at the top of the figure and a wire color table is also provided for reference. In the T568A wire color scheme (Figure 2-7 [a]), a white-green wire connects to pin 1, the wire color green connects to pin 2, and the wire color connected to pin 3 is white-orange, and so on. Similar information is provided in Figure 2-7 (b) for the T568B wiring standard. The color of the wire connected to pin 1 is white-orange, pin 2 is orange, pin 3 is white-green, and so on. This information also agrees with Table 2-2.

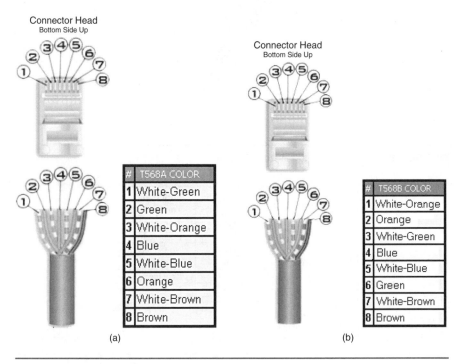

#	T568A COLOR
1	White-Green
2	Green
3	White-Orange
4	Blue
5	White-Blue
6	Orange
7	White-Brown
8	Brown

#	T568B COLOR
1	White-Orange
2	Orange
3	White-Green
4	Blue
5	White-Blue
6	Green
7	White-Brown
8	Brown

(a)   (b)

FIGURE 2-7   (a) The wiring of the RJ-45 (8P8C) connector and the wire color codes for the T568A standard; (b) the wiring of the RJ-45 connector for the T568B standard (courtesy of StarTech.com).

A common question is, "What is the difference between T568A and T568B?" Basically, these are just two different manufacturer standards used to wire the modular connector hardware. There is not a performance improvement with either, just a color order choice. Industry tends to favor the T568A wiring order; however, either order can be used as long as the order is maintained throughout the network.

This material has defined the wire color order for terminating the RJ-45 (8P8C) plugs and jacks onto the CAT6/5e twisted-pair cables. Be able to describe the difference between the T568A and T568B wire color order and make sure you know what wire color configuration you are using in a network, T568A or T568B, and that you specify hardware that is compatible with your selected color scheme.

Computer Communication

As mentioned in section 2-2, the CAT6/5e cable contains four twisted wire pairs. Figure 2-8 provides a picture of the four wire pairs. Figure 2-9 shows the signals and pin number assignments for the RJ-45 (8P8C) plug for CAT5e. Notice in Figure 2-9 that the Transmit Out signals are marked with a (+) and (-). The Receive In (+) and (-) signals are also marked in the same way. The (+) and (-) symbols are typical ways of indicating the positive and negative sides of a balanced wire pair. Recall from section 2-3 that in a balanced mode of operation, neither signal line is at ground.

FIGURE 2-8   The four wire pairs of the CAT6/CAT5e.

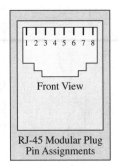

Front View

RJ-45 Modular Plug
Pin Assignments

Pin No.	Function
Pin 1	Transmit Out +
Pin 2	Transmit Out –
Pin 3	Receive In +
Pin 4	No Connection
Pin 5	No Connection
Pin 6	Receive In –
Pin 7	No Connection
Pin 8	No Connection

FIGURE 2-9   The pin assignments and signal names for the RJ-45 (8P8C) modular plug (CAT5e).

TX
Abbreviation for transmit

RX
Abbreviation for receive

For computers to communicate in a LAN, the transmit and receive pairs must be properly aligned. This means the transmit (**TX**) (+) and (-) signals must connect to the receive (**RX**) (+) and (-) as shown in Figure 2-10. Notice in Figure 2-10 that pins 1–2 of device A connect to pins 3–6 of device B. Pins 1–2 of device B connect to pins 3–6 of device A. This configuration is always valid when the data rates are 10 or 100 Mbps.

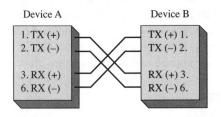

Device A

1. TX (+)
2. TX (−)
3. RX (+)
6. RX (−)

Device B

TX (+) 1.
TX (−) 2.
RX (+) 3.
RX (−) 6.

FIGURE 2-10   The proper alignment of the transmit and receive pairs in a CAT6/5e data link operating 10 or 100 Mbps.

In a LAN, the proper alignment of the transmit and receive pairs is managed by a switch or hub, not typically in the cable. Remember, in a star topology, all network communication travels through a switch or hub. You will see an "X" on many of the switch and hub input ports, indicating that this is a cross-connected input. This means that transmit and receive pairs are internally swapped to maintain proper signal alignment of the TX and RX pairs. Even if the "X" is missing, the switch or hub still properly aligns the TX and RX wire pairs. There is an exception to this on many switches and hubs. Some switches and hubs have an input port that can be selected to be "straight" or "crossed." These ports are typically used in uplink applications when you connect a switch or hub to another switch or hub. Just remember, proper alignment of the transmit and receive pair must be maintained for the computers to communicate. And a final note, if the wires are not properly connected, there won't be a link light.

There is a difference with the signal names for the UTP cable when operating at 1 Gbps and 10 Gbps. At these higher data rates, the use of all four wire pairs is required and the data is bidirectional, which means the same wire pairs are being used for both transmitting and receiving data. Figure 2.11 shows the pin assignments and signal names.

Pin	1000 Mbps and 10 Gbps Color (T568A)	10/100 Mbps	1000 Mbps and 10 Gbps
1	green/white	TX+	BI_DA+
2	Green	TX–	BI_DA–
3	orange/white	RX+	
4	blue	–	BI_DC+
5	blue/white	–	BI_DC–
6	orange	RX–	BI_DB–
7	brown/white	–	BI_DD+
8	brown	–	BI_DD–

(a) The pin assignments and signal names for 1 Gbps and 10 Gbps (T568A).

Pin	1000 Mbps and 10 Gbps Color (T568B)	10/100 Mbps Signal	1000 Mbps Signal
1	orange/white	TX+	BI_DA+
2	Orange	TX–	BI_DA–
3	green/white	RX+	BI_DB+
4	blue	–	BI_DC+
5	blue/white	–	BI_DC–
6	green	RX–	BI_DB–
7	brown/white	–	BI_DD+
8	brown	–	BI_DD–

(b) The pin assignments and signal names for 1 Gbps and 10 Gbps (T568B).

FIGURE 2-11   The pin assignments and signal names for 1 Gbps and 10 Gbps (T568A and T568B).

Straight-through and Crossover Patch Cables

Category 6/5e twisted-pair cables are used to connect networking components to each other in the network. These cables are commonly called *patch cables*. In this section a technique for terminating CAT6/5e cables with RJ-45 (8P8C) modular

Straight-through Cable
The wire pairs in the cable connect to the same pin numbers on each end

Wire-map
A graphical or text description of the wire connections from pin to pin

plugs is demonstrated for two different configurations of patch cables, a straight-through and a crossover cable. In a **straight-through cable** the four wire pairs connect to the same pin numbers on each end of the cable. For example, pin 1 on one end connects to pin 1 on the other end. Figure 2-12 shows an example of the **wire-map** for a straight-through cable. A wire-map is a graphical or text description of the wire connections from pin to pin for a cable under test. Notice that in Figure 2-12 the transmit and receive pairs connect to the same connector pin numbers at each end of the cable, hence the name *straight* or *straight-through* cable.

```
        A                    B
        1 ─────────────── 1
        2 ─────────────── 2
        3 ─────────────── 3
        4 ─────────────── 4
        5 ─────────────── 5
        6 ─────────────── 6
        7 ─────────────── 7
        8 ─────────────── 8
```

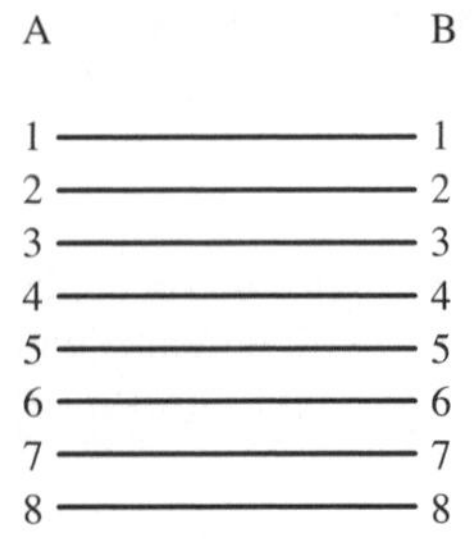

FIGURE 2-12   The wire-map for a straight-through cable.

Crossover Cable
Transmit and receiver wire pairs are crossed

In some applications in 10/100 Mbps data links, it is necessary to construct a cable where the transmit and receive wire pairs are reversed in the cable rather than by the switch or the hub. This cable configuration is called a **crossover cable**, which means the transmit pair of device A connects to the receive pair of device B, and the transmit pair of B connects to the receive pair of A. Figure 2-13 shows the wire-map for a crossover cable.

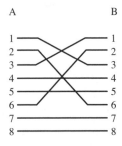

FIGURE 2-13   The wire-map for crossover cable 10/100 Mbps links.

Note

The crossover cable diagram shown in Figure 2-13 is for 10/100 Mbps. A gigabit crossover cable requires that all four wire-pairs be crossed. Although this is possible, it is not practical to make a gigabit crossover cable because of the limit on untwisted wire.

Terminating the CAT6 Horizontal Link Cable This section presents the steps required for terminating a CAT6 cable using the AMP SL series termination procedure, the AMP SL tool, CAT6 cable, and the AMP SL Series AMP-TWIST-6S Category 6 modular jacks. In this example, an RJ-45 (8P8C) jack is used to terminate each end of the cable. One end connects to a wall plate in the network work area. The other end will terminate into a CAT6 RJ-45 (8P8C) patch panel, which is typically located in the LAN network closet.

The technical specifications and assembly requirements are more stringent with CAT6. This means that more care must be taken when terminating a CAT6 cable. However, advancements in the tools and connectors have actually made it easier to terminate CAT6 than it was with the old punch-down tools. The steps for terminating the CAT6 horizontal link cables are as follows:

1. Before terminating the cable, inspect the cable for any damage that might have occurred in installation. Examples of damage to look for include nicked or cut wires and possible stretching of the cable.
2. At the work area outlet end, add about one foot extra and cut the wire. Then coil the extra cable and insert it in the receptacle box. It is good to leave a little extra in case you make an error in installation and have to redo the termination. Remember, you can't splice a CAT6 cable. At the distribution end, you will route the cable and create a slack loop. A slack loop is simply extra cable looped at the distribution end that is used if the equipment must be moved. In cases where you are having the cable pulled through duct-work or conduit by an installer, make sure you specify that extra cable length will be run. This will vary for each installation. Remember to allow for 5 meters in the telecommunications closet and allow for 5 meters in the work area.
3. Place a bend limiting strain relief boot on the cable, as shown in Figure 2-14 (a). This is used in the last step to secure the RJ-45 (8P8C) jack. After placing the boot on the cable, you will need to strip approximately three inches of cable jacket from the UTP cable as shown in Figure 2-14 (b). Be careful not to nick or cut the wires.

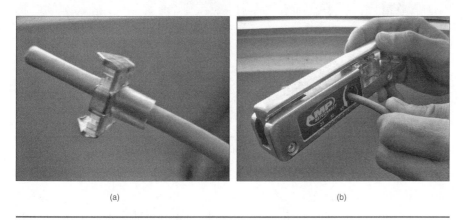

(a)   (b)

FIGURE 2-14 (a) Placing the bend-limiting strain relief boot on the cable and (b) stripping off three inches of jacket from the UTP cable.

4. Remove the jacket from the UTP cable. Bend the cable at the cut, as shown in Figure 2-15 (a) and remove the jacket and expose the four wire pairs as shown in Figure 2-15 (b).

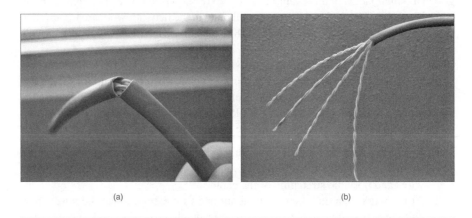

(a)   (b)

FIGURE 2-15   (a) Separating the cut jacket from the wire pairs and (b) removing of the jacket and exposing the four wire pairs.

5. Cut the plastic pull line and the string as shown in Figure 2-16 (a). The plastic line adds strength to cable for pulling, and the string is used to remove extra cable jacket as needed. Place a lacing fixture on the cable, as shown in Figure 2-16 (b), and sort the wires in either T568A or T668B color order.

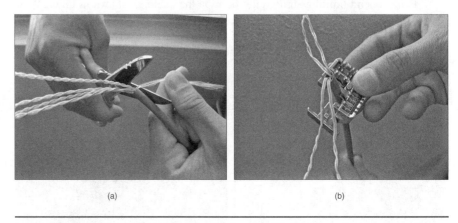

(a)   (b)

FIGURE 2-16   (a) Removing the plastic pull line and (b) placing the lacing tool on the cable with the color sorted cable pairs.

The sorted wire pairs are matched up with colors provided on the lacing fixture for 568A and 568B as shown in Figure 2-17.

6. Place the wires in the slots of the lacing tool as shown in Figure 2-18. The wire colors are matched to the proper order (T568A/T568B) displayed on the sides of the lacing tool.

FIGURE 2-17   The sides of the lacing tool showing the T568A and T568B wire color connections.

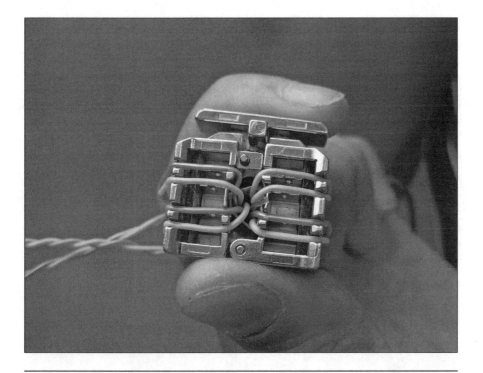

FIGURE 2-18   The routed cable wires on the lacing tool. The wire order shown is T568B.

7. Align an RJ-45 (8P8C) jack with the lacing fixture as shown in Figure 2-19 (a). The RJ-45 jack must be properly aligned with the wires on the lacing fixture to maintain proper color order. Figure 2-19 (b) provides a close-up picture of the AMP SL series AMP-TWIST-6S modular jack. This picture shows the locations of the displacement connectors on the modulator jack.

8. Insert the RJ-45 (8P8C) modular jack into the AMP SL tool as shown in Figure 2-20 (a), and then insert the RJ-45 (8P8C) jack into the AMP SL tool as shown in Figure 2-20 (b). Press the wires into the eight displacement connectors on the RJ-45 (8P8C) jack using the AMP SL tool as shown in Figure 2-20 (c). This technique enables the pair twist to be maintained right up to the point of termination. In fact, the untwisted-pair length is less than or equal to one-quarter inch.

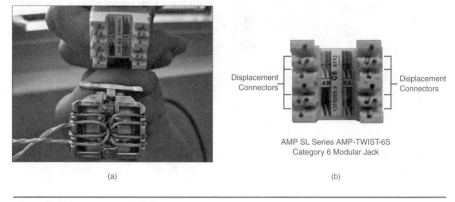

(a)	(b)

AMP SL Series AMP-TWIST-6S
Category 6 Modular Jack

FIGURE 2-19   (a) Aligning the RJ-45 (8P8C) jack and the lacing fixture; (b) a close-up view of the AMP-TWIST-6S CAT6 modular jack.

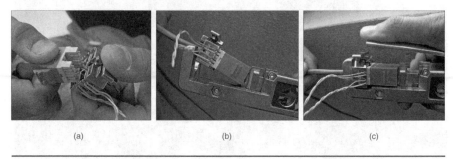

(a)	(b)	(c)

FIGURE 2-20   (a) Aligning the RJ-45 (8P8C) jack with the lacing tool; (b) inserting the RJ-45 (8P8C) jack and the lacing tool into the AMP SL tool; and (c) using the AMP SL tool to crimp the RJ-45 (8P8C) jack onto the eight displacement connectors and to cut the wires.

9. Connect the bend-limiting strain relief boot to the RJ-45 (8P8C) jack as shown in Figure 2-21 (a). Figure 2-21 (b) shows the completed termination.

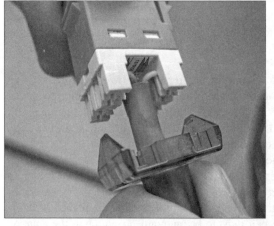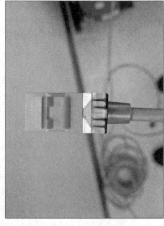

(a) Connecting the bend-limiting strain relief boot to the RJ-45 jack.   (b) The finished RJ-45 jack termination.

FIGURE 2-21   Connecting the bend-limiting strain relief boot to the RJ-45 (8P8C) jack.

Assembling the Straight-through CAT5e/5 Patch Cable This section presents a technique for assembling a straight-through CAT5e/5 patch cable. In a straight-through patch cable, the wire pairs in the cable connect to the same pin numbers on each end of the CAT5e/5 patch cable. Figure 2-22 shows a CAT5e patch cable with RJ-45 (8P8C) modular plugs.

FIGURE 2-22   CAT5e patch cable with RJ-45 (8P8C) modular plugs (courtesy of StarTech.com).

The steps for making straight-through patch cables are as follows:

1. Before terminating the cable, inspect the cable for any damage that might have occurred in installation, such as nicked or cut wires and possible stretching of the cable.
2. Measure the cable to length, add about six inches extra, and cut the wire. It is good to have a little extra in case you make an error in installation and have to redo the termination. You can't splice CAT5e/5 twisted-pair cable!
3. Strip approximately three-fourths of an inch of the cable jacket from the end of the cable using a cable stripper. Figure 2-23 illustrates how to use a cable stripper. Notice that the stripper is positioned about three-fourths of an inch from the end of the cable. The cable insulation is removed by rotating the insulation stripper around the wire until the wire jacket is loose and easily removable. (Note: These tools must be periodically adjusted so that the blade cuts through the outer insulation only. If the blades are set too deep, they will nick the wires, and the process must be repeated. The damaged portion of the cable must be cut away. Nicking the insulation of the twisted-pair wires is *not permitted*!)

FIGURE 2-23   An example of using the cable jacket stripper to remove the insulation.

4. Sort the wire pairs so that they fit into the connector and orient the wire in the proper order for either T568A or T568B as shown in Figures 2-24 (a) and 2-24 (b).

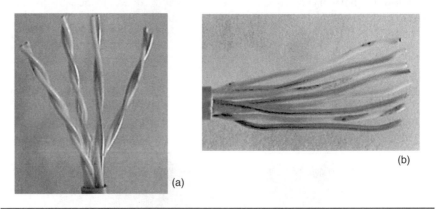

(a)

(b)

FIGURE 2-24   (a) Separating wire pairs; (b) orienting the wires.

5. Clip the wires so that they are even and insert the wires onto the RJ-45 (8P8C) modular plug as shown in Figure 2-25.

FIGURE 2-25   The clipped wires ready for insertion into the RJ-45 (8P8C) plug.

6. Push the wires into the connector until the ends of each wire can be seen through the clear end of the connector. (Note: Now is the time to verify that the wire order is correct.) The wires are visible through the plastic connector, as shown in Figure 2-26.

FIGURE 2-26   Wires pushed into the RJ-45 (8P8C) plug.

7. Use a crimping tool to crimp the wires onto the RJ-45 (8P8C) plug. The RJ-45 plug is inserted into the crimping tool until it stops as shown in Figure 2-27 (a). Next, squeeze the handle on the crimping tool all the way until it clicks and releases (see Figure 2-27 [b]). This step crimps the wire onto the insulation displacement connector pins on the RJ-45 (8P8C) jack.

 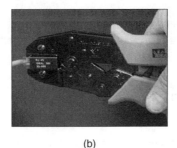

(a)   (b)

FIGURE 2-27   (a) Inserting the connector; (b) crimping the connector.

8. Repeat these steps for the other end of the twisted-pair cable.

The next step is to test the cable. These techniques and procedures are discussed in section 2-5.

2-5 CABLE TESTING AND CERTIFICATION

The need for increased data rates is pushing the technology of twisted-pair cable to even greater performance requirements and placing even greater demands on accurate testing of the cable infrastructure. The data speeds over twisted-pair copper cable are now at 10 Gbps. The EIA/TIA 568B standard defines the minimum cable specifications for twisted-pair categories operating over bandwidths of 100 MHz and at data rates up to 10 Gbps.

The CAT6/5e designations are simply minimum performance measurements of the cables, and the attached terminating hardware such as RJ-45 (8P8C) plugs, jacks, and patch panels. The **link** (the point from one cable termination to another) and the **full channel** (which consists of all the link elements from the hub or switch to the wall plate) must satisfy minimum **attenuation** loss and **near-end crosstalk (NEXT)** for a minimum frequency of 100 MHz. Figure 2-28 shows a graphical representation of the link and the full channel. Table 2-3 lists the CAT5e, CAT6, CAT6A, CAT7, and CAT7A EIA/TIA 568B channel specifications.

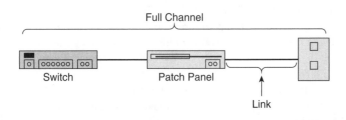

FIGURE 2-28   The link and channel areas for cable testing.

Link
Point from one cable termination to another

Full Channel
Consists of all the link elements from the wall plate to the hub or switch

Attenuation (Insertion Loss)
The amount of loss in the signal strength as it propagates down a wire or fiber strand

Near-end Crosstalk (NEXT)
A measure of the level of crosstalk or signal coupling within the cable, with a high NEXT (dB) value being desirable

TABLE 2-3   EIA/TIA 568B CAT5e, CAT6, CAT6A, CAT7 and CAT7A Channel Specifications

Parameter	Category 5e	Category 6	Category 6A	Category 7/7A
Class	Class D	Class E	Class E$_A$	Class F/F$_A$
Bandwidth	100 MHz	250 Mhz	500 MHz	600 MHz/ 1000 MHz
Insertion Loss (dB)	24.0	21.3	20.9	20.8/20.3
NEXT Loss (dB)	30.1	39.9	39.9	62.9/65.0
PSNEXT Loss (dB)	27.1	37.1	37.1	59.9/62.0
ACR (dB)	6.1	18.6	18.6	42.1/46.1
PSACR (dB)	3.1	15.8	15.8	39.1/41.7
ACRF1 (ELFEXT) (dB)	17.4	23.3	23.3	44.4/47.4
PSACRF2 (PSELFEXT) (dB)	14.4	20.3	20.3	41.1/44.4
Return Loss (dB)	10.0	12.0	12.0	12.0/12.0
* PANEXT Loss (dB)	n/s	n/s	60.0	n/s / 67.0
* PSAACRF (dB)	n/s	n/s	37.0	n/s / 52.0
* TCL (dB)	n/s	n/s	20.3	20.3/20.3
*ELTCTL (dB)	n/s	n/s	0.5	0/0
Propagation Delat (ns)	548	548	548	548/548
Delay Skew (ns)	50	50	50	30/30

*These parameters are discussed in section 2-7, "10 Gigabit Ethernet over Copper."

The list that follows describes some of the parameters listed in Table 2-3:

- **Attenuation (Insertion Loss):** This parameter defines the amount of loss in signal strength as it propagates down the wire. This is caused by the resistance of the twisted-pair cable, the connectors, and leakage of the electrical signal through the cable insulation. Attenuation also will increase with an increase in frequencies due to the inductance and capacitance of the cable. The cable test results will report a margin. Margin for attenuation (insertion loss) is defined as the difference between the measured value and the limit for the test. If the margin shows a negative value, the test has failed. A negative value is produced when the measured value is less than the limit. The limit for attenuation (insertion loss) for CAT6 is 21.3dB, CAT6A is 20.9, CAT7 is 20.8, and CAT7a is 20.3. It is also important to note that UTP cables have a limit on how much the cable can be bent (bend radius). The limit on the bend radius is four times the outer jacket diameter. The reason for this is bends exceeding the limit can introduce attenuation loss.

- **NEXT:** When current travels in a wire, an electromagnetic field is created. This field can induce a voltage in adjacent wires resulting in crosstalk. **Crosstalk** is what you occasionally hear on the telephone when you can faintly hear another conversation. Near-end crosstalk, or NEXT, is a measure of the level of crosstalk, or signal coupling within the cable. The measurement is called *near-end testing* because the receiver is more likely to pick up the crosstalk from the transmit to the receiver wire pairs at the ends. The transmit signal levels at each end are strong, and the cable is more susceptible to crosstalk at this point. Additionally, the receive signal levels have been attenuated due to normal cable path loss and are significantly weaker than the transmit signal. A high NEXT (dB) value is desirable.

Crosstalk
Signal coupling in a cable

Figure 2-29 graphically depicts NEXT. The dark gray area shows where the near-end crosstalk occurs. The margin is the difference between the measured value and the limit. A negative number means the measured value is less than the limit, and therefore the measurement fails. Crosstalk is more problematic at higher data rates (for example, 1 Gbps, 10 Gbps). Figure 2-30 shows how CAT6 cable has a built-in separator to help minimize crosstalk among wire pairs. This separator is used to keep each wire pair at a minimum distance from other wire pairs. This addition reduces crosstalk at higher frequencies and helps provide improved signal bandwidth, and therefore it will support faster data rates. This addition also helps improve the far-end cross-talk. Note that not all cable manufacturers use the separator.

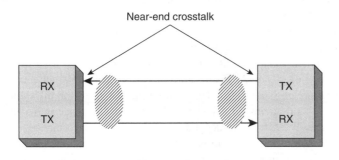

FIGURE 2-29   A graphical depiction of near-end crosstalk.

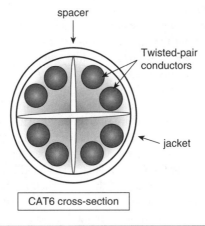

FIGURE 2-30   The cross section of a CAT6 cable showing the separator used to minimize crosstalk problems.

- **Power Sum NEXT (PSNEXT):** The enhanced twisted-pair cable must meet four-pair NEXT requirements, called PSNEXT testing. Basically, power sum testing measures the total crosstalk of all cable pairs. This test ensures that the cable can carry data traffic on all four pairs at the same time with minimal interference. A higher PSNEXT value is desirable because it indicates better cable performance.

Power Sum NEXT (PSNEXT)

Equal Level FEXT (ELFEXT)
FEXT
PSELFEXT

- **Equal Level FEXT (ELFEXT):** This measurement differs from NEXT in that the measurement is for the far end of the cable. Additionally, the ELFEXT measurement does not depend on the length of the cable. This is because ELFEXT is obtained by subtracting the attenuation value from the far-end crosstalk (**FEXT**) loss. Higher ELFEXT values (dB) indicate the signals at the far end of the cable are larger than the cross-talk measured at the far end. A larger ELFEXT (dB) value is desirable. A poor ELFEXT can result in data loss.
- **PSELFEXT:** Power sum ELFEXT that uses all four wire pairs to obtain a combined ELFEXT performance measurement. This value is the difference the test signal level and the cross-talk measured at the far end of the cable. A higher PSELFEXT value indicates better cable performance.

ACR
PSACR
Return Loss
Propagation Delay
Nominal Velocity of Propagation (NVP)
Delay Skew

- **ACR:** This measurement compares the signal level from a transmitter at the far end to the crosstalk measured at the near end. A larger ACR indicates that the cable has a greater data capacity and also indicates the cable's ability to handle a greater bandwidth. Essentially, it is a combined measurement of the quality of the cable. A higher ACR value (dB) is desirable.
- **PSACR:** Power sum ACR uses all four wire pairs to obtain the measure of the attenuation–crosstalk ratio. This is a measurement of the difference between PSNEXT and attenuation (insertion loss). The difference is measured in dB, and higher PSACR dB values indicate better cable performance.
- **Return Loss:** An equally important twisted-pair cable measurement is return loss. This measurement provides a measure of the ratio of power transmitted into a cable to the amount of power returned or reflected. The signal reflection is due to impedance changes in the cable link and the impedance changes contributing to cable loss. Cables are not perfect, so there will always be some reflection. Examples of the causes for impedance changes are non-uniformity in impedance throughout the cable, the diameter of the copper, cable handling, and dielectric differences. A low return loss value (dB) is desirable.
- **Propagation Delay:** This is a measure of the amount of time it takes for a signal to propagate from one end of the cable to the other. The delay of the signal is affected by the **nominal velocity of propagation (NVP)** of the cable. NVP is some percentage of the velocity of light and is dependent on the type of cable being tested. The typical delay value for CAT5/5e UTP cable is about 5.7 nsec per meter. The EIA/TIA specification allows for 548 nsec for the maximum 100-meter run for CAT5e, CAT6, CAT6a, CAT7, and CAT7A
- **Delay Skew:** This is a measure of the difference in arrival time between the fastest and the slowest signal in a UTP wire pair. It is critical in high-speed data transmission that the data on the wire pair arrive at the other end at the same time. If the wire lengths of different wire pairs are significantly different, then the data on one wire will take longer to propagate along the wire, hence arriving at the receiver at a different time and potentially creating distortion of the data and data packet loss. The wire pair with the shortest length will typically have the least delay skew.

Testing the CAT6 Link

Tests on a CAT6 link were conducted using a Fluke Networks DTX-1800 CableAnalyzer. The tests required the use of an injector unit (main/master) and a remote as shown in Figure 2-31. The test set conducts all required EIA/TIA568B tests to meet CAT6 certification for both channel and link tests. The following discussion describes the tests conducted for certifying a CAT6 UTP terminated cable link. *Testing a link* means that the test was conducted on the cable from one cable termination to the other terminated end. The tests were conducted using a DTX-1800 CableAnalyzer (master) and a DTX-1800 smart remote *(slave)*. The test results are displayed using the Fluke Networks LinkWare software.

FIGURE 2-31 The test setup for the CAT6 cable tests.

The first menu, shown in Figure 2-32, shows the summary test information for the cable test. This summary list is for the Cable ID-Chamisa 2092 test. The summary list is shown to underscore the importance of documenting the tests and the certification process. The test results provide a record of the cable performance on that day. The name is Chamisa 2092, which is the building (Chamisa) and cable number (2092), and these are used to keep track of the location and cable being tested. The menu also includes the type of test, TIA Cat6 Perm Link, and it also lists the model and serial numbers for the DTX-1800 cable testers. When conducting Permanent Link testing, the master unit should be at the distribution end (Telecommunications Closet), and the slave should be connected to the outlet in the work area. All this information is useful if problems occur with the cabling and also serves as a way to certify your cable installation before switching your network over to a new cable plant. Notice the result entered for the test result: **Pass**. This quickly tells us that the cable passed *all* CAT6 performance specifications.

The next menu, shown in Figure 2-33, lists the wire-map results for the test. This menu shows that this is a straight-through cable, as depicted by the picture of the wire-map. The wire-map menu shows that this cable is wired T568B.

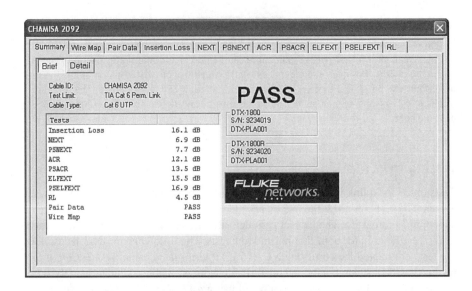

FIGURE 2-32   The summary menu for the UTP cable test.

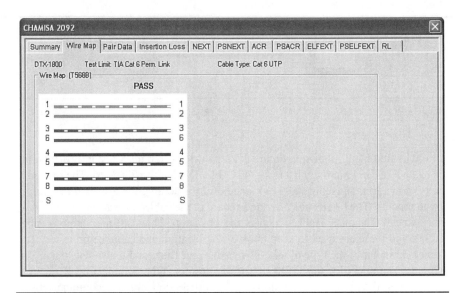

FIGURE 2-33   The wire-map test results.

Pair Data
Data collected on the UTP

Figure 2-34 shows the menu for the **pair data**, which are the tests on the four wire pairs in the UTP cable. This menu is showing the test data for the following wire pairs; 1–2, 3–6, 4–5, and 7–8. The menu first shows that cable passed length, propagation delay, and delay skew. The test results show that wire pair 7/8 has a delay skew test result of 18 ns. Recall that delay skew is a measure of the difference in arrival times between the fastest and slowest signal in a UTP wire pair. The maximum delay skew allowed for the test is 45 ns. The maximum delay skew allowed under EIA/TIA 568B is 50 ns; however, the Permanent Link test has a maximum delay skew limit of 44 ns. Also note that the maximum length for the test is set to be 295 feet, which is less than the 100-meter (328-feet) limit. Once again, the Permanent Link test is allowing for extra cable in the telecommunication room and the work area. The pair data menu also displays the length and delay of each wire pair. The wire pair lengths for the cable are as follows:

    1–2: 158 ft.
    3–6: 166 ft.
    4–5: 168 ft.
    7–8: 156 ft.

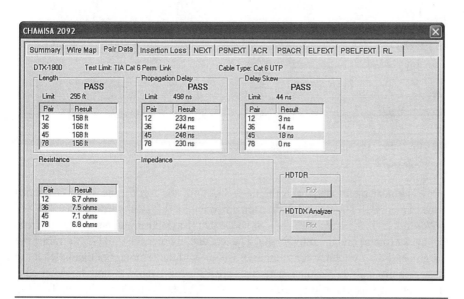

FIGURE 2-34 The pair data test results.

Notice the difference in the wire pair lengths. This is due to the different twists used in the UTP cable. This also underscores the importance of properly grouping wire pairs when terminating a UTP cable. A mismatched pair will result in wires of different lengths. For long cables, this is of major concern. The maximum length of the cable in a Permanent Link test is 308 ft. (~93.8 m.). Remember, this is a CAT6 link test, and some length must be left at the ends for connecting to the computer and the equipment in the telecommunications room. The full channel test would have a maximum of 100 meters (~328 ft.). The expected delays for the wire pairs are also provided. As expected, the delays differ for each wire pair.

The next test menu, shown in Figure 2-35, is for insertion loss. This test is conducted for each wire pair. The test reports the maximum insertion loss and the frequency at which the measurement is made. The tester frequency sweeps the cable and records the measurements as the cable is tested. For pair 3–6, the worst-case insertion loss (attenuation) is 15.0 dB at 250 MHz. Overall margins for the insertion loss measurements are displayed in the center of the Insertion Loss menu. The *margin* (16.1 dB) is the difference between the limit (31.1 dB) and the measured value (15.0 dB). This is showing that the test exceeds the minimum performance specification.

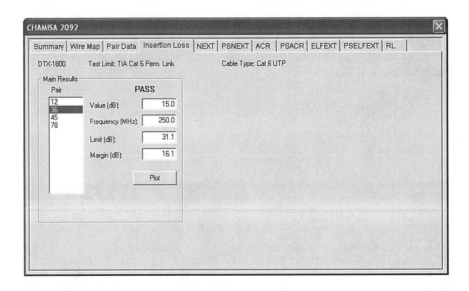

FIGURE 2-35   The insertion loss test results.

The next menu, shown in Figure 2-36, is for the NEXT (near-end crosstalk) measurements. Tests are conducted on all combinations of wire pairs (1–2/3–6, 1–2/4–5, 1–2/7–8, 3–6/4–5, 3–6/7–8, and 4–5/7–8). Measurements are taken from the master (main) and the remote unit. The test data includes the dB NEXT value, the margin, and the frequency for the master (main) and the remote. For example, at the master (main), pair 1–2/3–6 has a 48.5 dB NEXT, a margin of 7.8, and the worst-case measurement was made at a frequency of 117.5 MHz. At the remote, pair 1–2/3–6 has a 42.6 dB NEXT, a margin of 6.9, and the worst-case measurement was made at a frequency of 237 MHz.

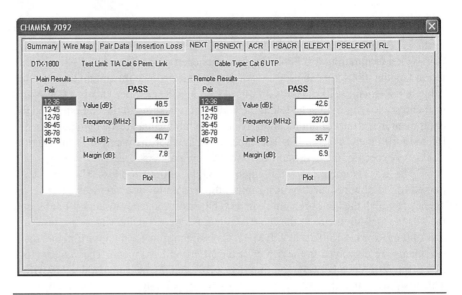

FIGURE 2-36   The NEXT test results.

Figure 3-37 shows the Power Sum NEXT test results. Recall that power sum measurements provide a measure of the total crosstalk of all cable pairs, ensuring that the cable can simultaneously carry data traffic on all four wire pairs with minimal interference. The measurements are made from both ends of the cable link. EIA/TIA568B allows a PSNEXT measurement of 30.2 dB. The data shows that the worst-case test results of 46.6 dB are well within specifications.

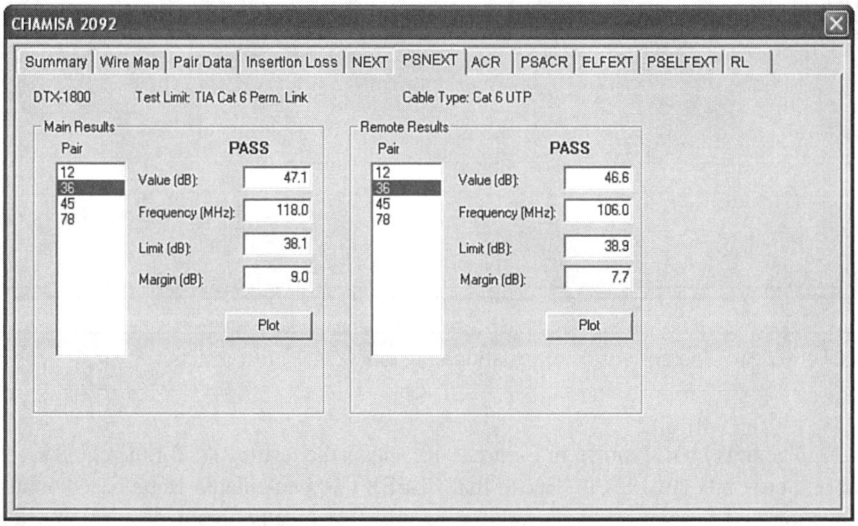

FIGURE 2-37 The power sum NEXT test results.

Figure 2-38 provides the ACR test results. The tests show that the worst case is at the remote for pair 3–6/4–5 with a measurement of 69.3 dB at 5.9 MHz. The test limit is 57.2 dB, and there is a 12.1 dB margin. Figure 2-39 provides the power-sum ACR measurements. Pair 3–6 at the main measures 59dB with a margin of 14 dB. Pair 3–6 at the remote measures 68.4 dB with a margin of 13.5 dB.

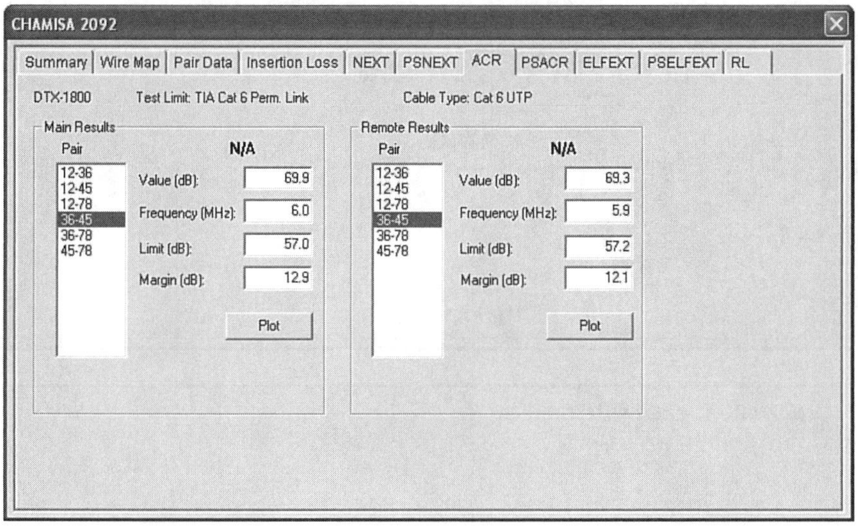

FIGURE 2-38 The attenuation-crosstalk (ACR) test results.

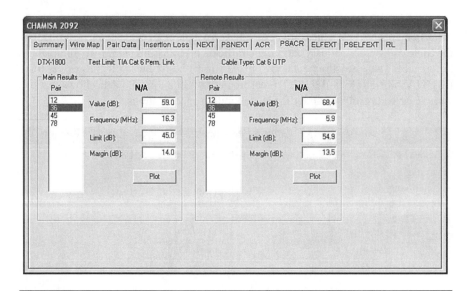

FIGURE 2-39   The power-sum attenuation-crosstalk (PSACR) test results.

The next menu, shown in Figure 2-40, shows the test results for the equal level far-end crosstalk (ELFEXT). Recall that ELFEXT is a calculated value based on attenuation and far-end crosstalk measurements. Test results obtained by the master (main) and the remote are displayed for all wire pair combinations of the cable link. The next menu is for the power sum measurements. The results are provided in Figure 2-41. Both the ELFEXT and PSELFEXT tests indicate that each passed.

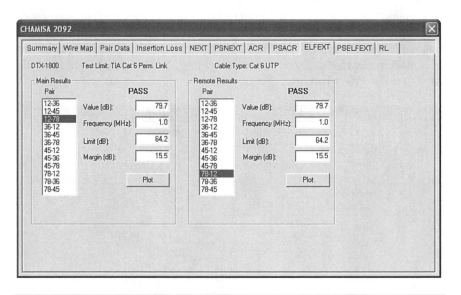

FIGURE 2-40   The ELFEXT test results.

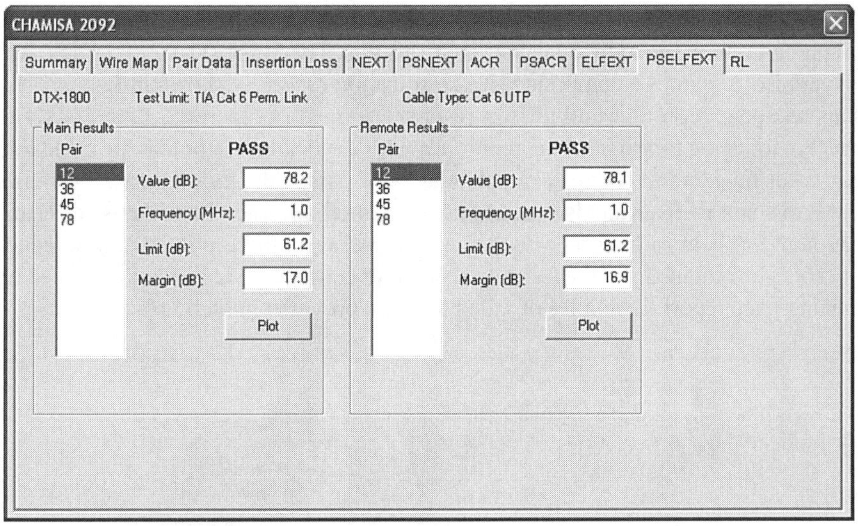

FIGURE 2-41   The power-sum ELFEXT test results.

The last menu, shown in Figure 2-42, is for return loss. The test reports the maximum attenuation and the frequency at which the measurement is made. The return loss is measured from both the main and remote units. The return-loss measurements are displayed in dB and are made for different frequencies as the cable analyzer frequency sweeps the cable. The worst return-loss measurement (greatest dB value) is highlighted. The return loss for wire pair 4–5 is 14.7 dB at 241.5 MHz from the main and 16.2 dB at 235 MHz from the remote. The overall limits and margins for the return-loss measurements are also displayed.

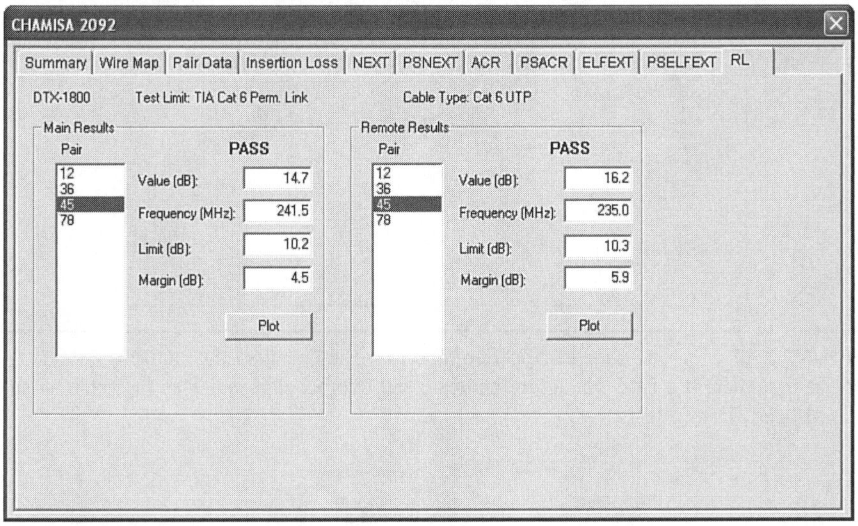

FIGURE 2-42   The return loss test results.

Recall that the first menu (summary) showed that the cable passed all tests. Stepping through the individual tests confirms this. The Fluke DTX-1800 Cable Analyzer also generates a comprehensive certification report, as shown in Figure 2-43. This one-page report lists all the test results described in Figures 2-32 to 2-42. The checkmark at the top right of the report provides a quick indicator that the cable link passed or failed a test. In this example, the cable passed the test. Figure 2-44 shows the PASS and FAIL symbols for the certification report. The comprehensive certification report is most likely the document you will want to keep in a file as a record of cable performance. All the test data needed for certifying a CAT6 link are listed on the one-page report. Examples of failed tests are provided in section 2-7.

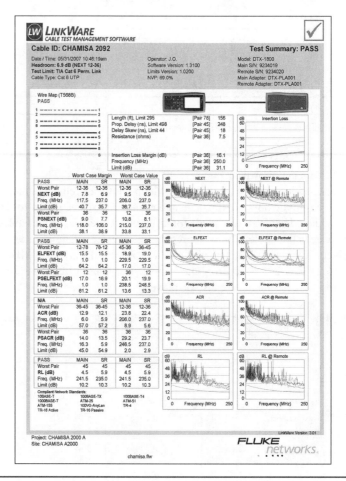

FIGURE 2-43 The one-page certification report for the Chamissa-2092 CAT6 cable test. Notice that there is a PASS symbol in the upper-right corner that indicates the cable passed all CAT6 certification tests.

PASS   FAIL

FIGURE 2-44 The PASS and FAIL symbols used on a Fluke DTX certification reports.

82   Chapter 2 • Physical Layer Cabling: Twisted Pair

2-6 10 GIGABIT ETHERNET OVER COPPER

Ethernet over copper is available for 10 Mbps (Ethernet), 100 Mbps (FastEthernet), 1000 Mbps (gigabit Ethernet), and now 10 Gbps (ten gigabit Ethernet). (Note that Mbps is "megabits per second." Some literature writes this as Mb/s). The increase in the required bandwidth for transporting a ten gigabit data transfer rate is placing increased demands on the copper cable as well as the hardware used for terminating the cable ends and for connecting to the networking equipment. There are three improvements required for transmitting the higher data bit rates over the copper cabling:

1. Improve the cable so it can carry greater bandwidth.
2. Improve the electronics used to transmit and receive (recover) the data.
3. Utilize improvements in both the cable and electronics to facilitate greater bandwidths and distance.

This section examines the changes in technology that are required to enable the transportation of ten-gigabit data (**10GBASE-T**) over copper. The first part presents an overview of ten-gigabit Ethernet over copper. The second part examines the modifications that were required to the technical specs (CAT6A and CAT7/7A) that are necessary for testing and certifying twisted-pair copper cable that is transporting ten-gigabit data rates. The last section examines the issues of how the ten-gigabit data is actually transmitted.

10GBASE-T
10 Gbps over twisted-pair copper cable

Overview

The standard for 10 Gbps is **IEEE 802.3an-2006 10GBASE-T**. This standard was developed to support running 10 Gbps data over twisted-pair cabling. The newer standard requires the bandwidth to be increased from 250 MHz to 500 MHz. Additionally, the new standard supports 10G Ethernet up to 100 meters in cable length. At one time, most people assumed that higher data rates would be limited to fiber optics. While this is still true for lengthy runs (more than 100 meters) twisted-pair copper is finding its place in the horizontal runs from the telecommunications closet to the work area.

IEEE 802.3an-2006 10GBASE-T
The standard for 10 Gbps

Alien Crosstalk (AXT)

Alien Crosstalk is an important issue at higher data rates such as with 10GBASE-T. **Alien Crosstalk (AXT)** is unwanted signal coupling from one permanent link to another. Basically, this is the coupling of a signal from one 4-pair cable to another 4-pair cable. An example is shown in Figure 2-45. This figure depicts the Alien Crosstalk (AXT) from one 4-pair cable to another 4-pair cable. The other key measurements for 10GBASE-T are **NEXT (PSANEXT)**, **FEXT (PSAACRF)**, and **Return Loss**. PSANEXT (Power Sum Alien Near-End Crosstalk) and PSAACRF (Power Sum Alien Attenuation to Crosstalk Ratio) are new measurements for NEXT and FEXT that incorporate measures for Alien Crosstalk. Alien Crosstalk is considered to be the main electrical limiting parameter for 10G Ethernet. Alien Crosstalk causes disturbances in the neighboring cable. It is difficult for the electronics to cancel the AXT noise created; therefore, new cables have been developed to support the 10 Gbps data rates. The newer cables have improved the cable separation, and new connectors have also been developed to help meet the required specifications to support 10G. An example of the change in the cable construction was shown in the CAT6 cross-section, Figure 2-30.

Alien Crosstalk (AXT)
Unwanted signal coupling from one permanent link to another

PSANEXT
Power Sum Alien Near-End Cross-Talk

PSAACRF
Power Sum Alien Attenuation to Crosstalk Ratio

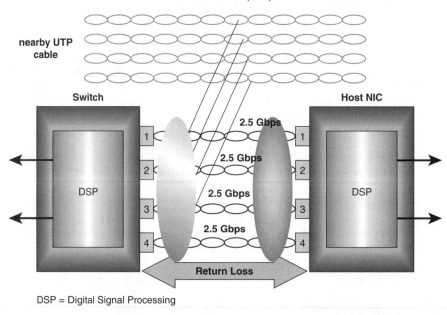

Alien Crosstalk (AXT)

nearby UTP
cable

Switch

Host NIC

2.5 Gbps

2.5 Gbps

2.5 Gbps

2.5 Gbps

DSP

DSP

Return Loss

DSP = Digital Signal Processing

FIGURE 2-45   Alien Crosstalk from a neighboring 4-pair cable.

F/UTP
Foil over twisted-pair
cabling

TCL
Transverse Conversion Loss

ELTCTL
Equal Level Transverse
Conversion Transfer Loss

LCL
Longitudinal Conversion Loss

TCTL
Transverse Conversion
Transfer Loss

PSANEXT
Power-Sum Alien Near-End
Crosstalk

PSAACRF
Power-Sum Alien Attenuation
Cross-talk Ratio Far-End

Cable manufacturers are starting to offer CAT6 and higher grades of twisted-pair cable with foil over each of the four wire-pairs. The designation for this type of cable is foil twisted-pair (**F/UTP**). There are several advantages to using a shielded cable. The first is that a shielded cable offers better security because there is less chance that the data will radiate outside the cable. Additionally, the foil shield helps improve noise immunity from Electro-Magnetic Interference (EMI), Radio Frequency Interference (RFI), and most importantly, AXT.

Transmission of data over twisted-pair cabling relies on the signals being "balanced" over the wire pairs. The balance or symmetry of the signal over the wire pairs helps minimize unwanted leakage of the signal. There are two parameters now defined for CAT6 and better cabling that address the issue of balanced data. The first is **TCL (Transverse Conversion Loss)**, and the other is **ELTCTL (Equal Level Transverse Conversion Loss)**. The TCL measurement is obtained by applying a common-mode signal to the input and measuring the differential signal level on the output. TCL is sometimes called **LCL (Longitudinal Conversion Loss)**. The ELTCLT value (expressed in dB) is the difference between the TCTL and the differential mode insertion loss of the pair being measured. TCTL is the loss from a balanced signal at the near-end to the unbalanced signal at the far end.

The newer tests also require additional Power-Sum tests. These are **PSANEXT (Power-Sum Alien Near-End Cross-Talk)** and **PSAACRF (Power-Sum Alien Attenuation Cross-talk Ratio Far-end)**. These tests have been developed to help ensure cable compatibility with data transmission and reception that requires the use of all four wire-pairs. Both gigabit and ten gigabit require the use of all four wire pairs.

Signal Transmission

The 10GBASE-T system requires the use of all four wire pairs as shown in Figure 2-46. This system splits the 10 Gbps of data into four 2.5-Gbps data channels. This same technique is also used for 1000 Mbps (1-gigabit) data rates, except the 1000 Mbps signal is split into four 250 Mbps data channels. The system requires the use of signal conditioners and Digital Signal Processing (DSP) circuits for both transmission and reception. The data transmission for ten gigabit uses a **multilevel encoding** technique as shown in Figure 2-47. The advantage of this type of encoding is the reduction in the required bandwidth required to transport the data.

Multilevel Encoding
Technique used to reduce in the required bandwidth required to transport the data

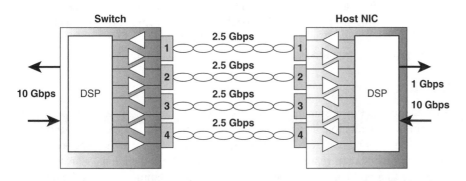

FIGURE 2-46   The four wire-pairs in UTP cabling required for transporting 10GBASE-T data. This same technique is used for 1000 Mbps except the data rate for each of the four channels is 250 Mbps.

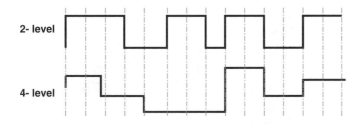

FIGURE 2-47   An example of multilevel encoding of the data streams to reduce the required bandwidth.

10GBASE-T data transmission also requires the use of Digital Signal Processing (DSP) Compensation Techniques. The DSP circuitry provides many functions, such as signal conditioning and echo cancellation. Anytime a signal is transmitted down a cable, part of the signal will be reflected. This reflection adds to overall signal degradation and limits the performance of the system. In 10GBASE-T, the transmit and receive signals are sharing the same wire pair. This is called full duplex transmission and requires the use of a device called a **hybrid echo cancellation circuit**. The hybrid circuit removes the transmitted signal from the receive signal.

Hybrid Echo Cancellation Circuit
Removes the transmitted signal from the receive signal

The final issue with 10GBASE-T signal transmission is the performance of the cable. As mentioned previously, return loss, insertion loss, and crosstalk are all key limiting issues for 10GBASE-T. Crosstalk is the most important factor. The types of crosstalk observed are AXT (Alien Crosstalk), NEXT (near-end crosstalk), FEXT (far-end cosstalk), and ELFEXT (equal level far-end crosstalk). The cabling systems that will support 10GBASE-T operation with links up to 100 meters are CAT6 with the foil screen (FTP), augmented CAT6 (CAT6a), CAT7, and CAT7a.

2-7 TROUBLESHOOTING COMPUTER NETWORKS

This section examines some of the issues that the network administrator can have with both CAT6 and CAT5e cables tests. It is important that the network administrator monitor all parts of the cable installation, from pulling to terminating the cable ends. The reasons why a cable fails a certification test can be due to multiple types of problems, such as with installation, cable stretching, and the cable failing to meet manufacturer specifications. These types of problems are discussed next, followed by a look at the certification reports for failures of both CAT6 and CAT5e.

Installation

If you obtain bad PowerSum measurements or NEXT or FEXT, there might be a problem with the installation. The certification report provided in Figure 2-48 indicates this cable does not pass CAT6 certification, as shown by the X in the upper-right corner of the certification report. This test indicates a "NEXT" failure, which is most likely due to a problem at the terminations. The most common error is the installer has allowed too much untwisted cable at the termination point. Remember, the twist on UTP cable must be maintained to less than 3/8-inch. At this point, the best thing is to go and inspect the terminations to see if any terminations have too much untwisted cable and verify whether there is a procedure problem with the installation.

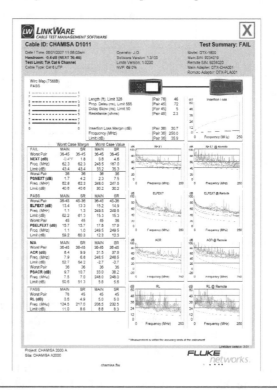

FIGURE 2-48   The DTX-1800 certification report: Failure due to termination problem.

Cable Stretching

It is important to avoid stretching of the UTP cable. Stretching of the cable is bad because it changes the electrical characteristics of the cable, increasing the attenuation and crosstalk. The maximum pulling tension is specified by the manufacturer data sheets, and the datasheet will list the maximum pulling tension put on a cable. The units for the pulling tension are expressed in lb-ft.

Cable Failing to Meet Manufacturer Specifications

Occasionally, manufacturers do experience problems with the cable failing to meet specifications. This could be due to a bad production run, and the result is that the cable does not meet minimum specifications. Repeated test failures with no apparent reason for the failure could indicate that the problem is with the cable. This rarely happens, but there is a possibility that there was a bad cable production run. As the manager you want to isolate the source of the problem.

Figure 2-49 provides another CAT6 certification report, which indicates that the cable failed due to excessive insertion loss. Examination of the certification report shows that the cable length for pairs 7–8 is 311 ft. The maximum cable length for a permanent link is 295 ft. This cable run is too long for it to be certifiable.

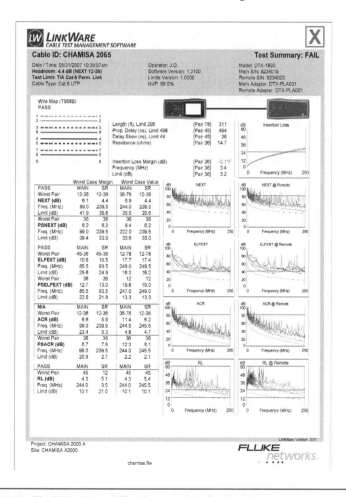

FIGURE 2-49   The DTX-1800 certification report: Failure due to excessive insertion loss.

CAT5e Cable Test Examples

The next section presents some test results for several CAT5e cable tests. There are still many CAT5e horizontal cable runs already in place, and these runs support 100-Mbps data rates. Therefore, it is important for the network administrator to have a good understanding of certifying CAT5e links. The objective of this section is to acquaint the reader with possible CAT5e test results and problems they might encounter on the job. The procedures presented are the same for CAT6 except that the test mode of the cable analyzer must be set to CAT5e performance specifications. The testers used for conducting the CAT5e certification reports are the Fluke OMNIscanner and OMNIremote.

Test 1   The first example presented is the test on a short patch cable. This shows that short patch cables can and should be tested. UTP cable testing is not restricted to long cables. The length of the wire pairs is about 3 feet. You also have a record that this cable meets CAT5e requirements. The test was conducted using the OMNIscanner. The OMNIscanner certification report verifies that the cable passes the CAT5e link test. Figure 2-50 shows the certification report, which indicates that the cable passed the test. This report shows that the cable length is 3 feet.

Test 2   This shows the test on the same 3-foot cable used in Test 1; however, the cable no longer meets CAT5e requirements, as shown in Figure 2-51. The test results indicate FAIL. In fact, careful inspection of the cable showed that it had been cut or nicked. This underscores the importance of documenting the network installation and having a record that the cable link was certified. Test 1 showed that the cable met specifications, but damage to the cable no longer enables it to meet CAT5e link specifications.

Inspection of the wire-map test results (see Figure 2-51) shows the cable failed, highlighted by the FAIL symbol in the upper-right corner of the certification report. In this test, the cable has failed a wire-map test. Not only is the text highlighted, but there is an exclamation preceding the text that indicates a failure. A quick check of the wire-map test shows that the number 4 wire was not detected at the remote.

Test 3   This cable test (Figure 2-52) also generated a test result of FAIL. Examination of the attenuation and return-loss menu shows that the cable failed to meet CAT5e attenuation and return-loss specifications. The permitted attenuation in CAT5e cable is 24 dB. However, the 1–2 and 3–6 pairs have attenuation losses of 38.0 dB and 41.1 dB. Both cases greatly exceed the permitted maximum. An arrow points to these attenuation loss scores.

This cable also fails return loss for pairs 1–2 and 3–6. CAT5e cable permits 10 dB of return-loss. The tests show that the pairs fail the return-loss test at both the OMNIscanner and the remote test unit. This cable will fail a CAT5e certification based solely on attenuation or return loss. In fact, this cable also fails NEXT, ELFEXT, and PSELFEXT tests. Any of these failures are sufficient to not certify this cable.

PASS

OMNIScanner2 Certification Report

Circuit ID:	Pre-cut	**OMNIScanner**		**OMNIRemote**
Project:	TIA Project	50D99L00377	SW: V06.00	50E99L00037
Owner:	OMNISCANNER 2	**Adapter**		**Adapter**
Autotest:	*Cat 5E Link*	CHAN 5/5E/6		CHAN 5/5E/6
Cable:	Cat 5E UTP			
NVP:	72			
Site:	Las Cruces			
Building:	Manufacturing			
Floor:	3rd			
Closet:	315A			

	Limit	12	36	45	78
Length ft	(308)	3	3	3	3
Delay (ns):	(518)	4	4	4	4
Resistance (Ohms):	(—)	—	—	—	—

Wiremap	Expected	Actual		
OMNI:	12345678	12345678	Skew (ns):	(45) 0
Remote:	12345678	12345678	Bandwidth (MHz):	—

Attenuation
Overall Margin (dB)¹ 19.9

Pairs	dB	Margin	MHz
12	0.3	21.0	97.4
36	0.4	20.1	90.7
45	0.4	21.0	97.4
78	0.3	19.9	88.4

Return Loss
Overall Margin (dB)¹ —

	OMNIScanner			OMNIRemote		
Pairs	dB	Margin	MHz	dB	Margin	MHz
12	23.8	11.4	90.7	23.4	11.2	99.0
36	23.2	10.4	80.8	22.5	10.0	88.9
45	23.1	10.1	74.7	24.2	11.0	70.7
78	23.9	11.5	91.3	24.1	12.0	99.0

NEXT
Overall Margin (dB)¹ 3.0

	OMNIScanner			OMNIRemote		
Pairs	dB	Margin	MHz	dB	Margin	MHz
12/36	62.5	18.7	19.6	61.7	14.0	11.3
12/45	59.2	21.8	48.6	46.6	14.3	99.9
12/78	93.1	33.1	1.2	52.4	20.0	99.2
36/45	50.5	8.6	25.9	45.9	3.0	22.6
36/78	56.0	13.3	23.2	53.5	9.0	18.1
45/78	51.6	14.6	51.6	47.3	14.9	99.0

ACR
Overall Margin (dB)¹ —

	OMNIScanner			OMNIRemote		
Pairs	dB	Margin	MHz	dB	Margin	MHz
12/36	—	—	—	—	—	—
12/45	—	—	—	—	—	—
12/78	—	—	—	—	—	—
36/45	—	—	—	—	—	—
36/78	—	—	—	—	—	—
45/78	—	—	—	—	—	—

ELFEXT
Overall Margin (dB)¹ 15.3

	OMNIScanner			OMNIRemote		
Pairs	dB	Margin	MHz	dB	Margin	MHz
12/36	60.0	22.0	12.7	60.1	22.1	12.7
12/45	55.3	16.9	12.0	74.6	16.9	1.4
12/78	69.8	30.6	10.9	85.3	30.4	1.9
36/12	60.1	22.1	12.7	60.0	22.0	12.7
36/45	46.1	20.0	49.5	76.8	20.4	1.6
36/78	64.2	28.2	16.0	48.9	28.6	97.4
45/12	74.6	16.8	1.4	73.3	16.9	1.6
45/36	76.7	20.3	1.6	45.9	20.0	51.1
45/78	71.9	15.5	1.6	73.0	15.3	1.4
78/12	85.3	30.4	1.9	69.9	30.6	10.9
78/36	48.8	28.6	97.4	64.2	28.2	16.0
78/45	73.0	15.3	1.4	53.7	15.5	12.4

PSNEXT
Overall Margin (dB)¹ 4.9

	OMNIScanner			OMNIRemote		
Pairs	dB	Margin	MHz	dB	Margin	MHz
12	65.7	20.4	10.4	44.8	15.5	99.9
36	49.1	10.3	25.9	44.7	4.9	22.6
45	49.8	11.0	25.9	46.1	6.0	21.9
78	50.4	14.6	39.6	50.6	11.8	26.2

PSELFEXT
Overall Margin (dB)¹ 15.5

	OMNIScanner			OMNIRemote		
Pairs	dB	Margin	MHz	dB	Margin	MHz
12	73.6	18.8	1.4	54.2	18.7	12.0
36	75.9	21.2	1.4	75.8	21.1	1.4
45	68.9	15.5	1.6	69.0	15.6	1.6
78	71.7	18.2	1.6	72.8	18.0	1.4

PSACR
Overall Margin (dB)¹ —

	OMNIScanner			OMNIRemote		
Pairs	dB	Margin	MHz	dB	Margin	MHz
12	—	—	—	—	—	—
36	—	—	—	—	—	—
45	—	—	—	—	—	—
78	—	—	—	—	—	—

¹ Overall margin value is the worst margin for OMNI and Remote.

MICROTEST®

Date: 2/15/2002   2:35:00 PM   Page 1

FIGURE 2-50   The certification report for Test 1 showing that the short jumper cable passes CAT5e link test.

FAIL

OMNIScanner2 Certification Report

Circuit ID:	Cut	**OMNIScanner**			**OMNIRemote**	
Project:	TIA Project	50D99L00377	SW: V06.00		50E99L00037	
Owner:	OMNISCANNER 2	**Adapter**			**Adapter**	
Autotest:	*Cat 5E Link*	CHAN 5/5E/6			CHAN 5/5E/6	
Cable:	Cat 5E UTP					
NVP:	72					

			Limit	12	36	45	78
Site:	Las Cruces	Length ft	(308)	3	3	!1	3
Building:	Manufacturing	Delay (ns):	(518)	4	4	1	4
Floor:	3rd	Resistance (Ohms):	(---)	---	---	---	---
Closet:	315						

Wiremap	Expected	Actual		
OMNI:	12345678	! 12345678	Skew (ns):	(45) 3
Remote:	12345678	! 123 5678	Bandwidth (MHz):	---

Attenuation — Overall Margin (dB)¹ 20.0

Pairs	dB	Margin	MHz
12	0.3	20.4	92.5
36	0.4	20.0	89.3
45	---	---	---
78	0.3	20.8	95.8

Return Loss — Overall Margin (dB)¹ ---

	OMNIScanner			OMNIRemote		
Pairs	dB	Margin	MHz	dB	Margin	MHz
12	23.8	11.4	91.6	23.3	11.1	97.6
36	23.4	10.9	87.5	22.6	10.1	88.6
45	---	---	---	---	---	---
78	23.4	11.3	99.0	23.7	11.6	97.9

NEXT — Overall Margin (dB)¹ 11.2

	OMNIScanner			OMNIRemote		
Pairs	dB	Margin	MHz	dB	Margin	MHz
12/36	62.7	16.8	14.5	59.2	14.1	16.3
12/45	---	---	---	---	---	---
12/78	69.6	32.7	52.5	51.4	19.1	99.7
36/45	---	---	---	---	---	---
36/78	57.9	14.6	21.2	55.0	11.2	19.6
45/78	---	---	---	---	---	---

ACR — Overall Margin (dB)¹ ---

	OMNIScanner			OMNIRemote		
Pairs	dB	Margin	MHz	dB	Margin	MHz
12/36	---	---	---	---	---	---
12/45	---	---	---	---	---	---
12/78	---	---	---	---	---	---
36/45	---	---	---	---	---	---
36/78	---	---	---	---	---	---
45/78	---	---	---	---	---	---

ELFEXT — Overall Margin (dB)¹ 22.0

	OMNIScanner			OMNIRemote		
Pairs	dB	Margin	MHz	dB	Margin	MHz
12/36	61.0	22.0	11.3	60.3	22.0	12.2
12/45	---	---	---	---	---	---
12/78	68.0	29.7	12.2	85.3	28.9	1.6
36/12	60.3	22.0	12.2	60.9	22.0	11.3
36/45	---	---	---	---	---	---
36/78	67.0	27.9	11.1	66.3	28.5	12.9
45/12	---	---	---	---	---	---
45/36	---	---	---	---	---	---
45/78	---	---	---	---	---	---
78/12	85.3	28.9	1.6	68.0	29.7	12.2
78/36	66.3	28.5	12.9	67.0	27.9	11.1
78/45	---	---	---	---	---	---

PSNEXT — Overall Margin (dB)¹ 11.6

	OMNIScanner			OMNIRemote		
Pairs	dB	Margin	MHz	dB	Margin	MHz
12	---	---	---	---	---	---
36	---	---	---	---	---	---
45	---	---	---	---	---	---
78	---	---	---	---	---	---

PSELFEXT — Overall Margin (dB)¹ 9.9

	OMNIScanner			OMNIRemote		
Pairs	dB	Margin	MHz	dB	Margin	MHz
12	---	---	---	---	---	---
36	---	---	---	---	---	---
45	---	---	---	---	---	---
78	---	---	---	---	---	---

PSACR — Overall Margin (dB)¹ ---

	OMNIScanner			OMNIRemote		
Pairs	dB	Margin	MHz	dB	Margin	MHz
12	---	---	---	---	---	---
36	---	---	---	---	---	---
45	---	---	---	---	---	---
78	---	---	---	---	---	---

¹ Overall margin value is the worst margin for OMNI and Remote.

MICROTEST®

Date: 2/15/2002   2:39:00 PM   Page 1

FIGURE 2-51   The results for Test 2 showing that the cable failed the CAT5e link test.

FAIL

OMNIScanner2 Certification Report

Circuit ID:	Split Pairs		**OMNIScanner**			**OMNIRemote**
Project:	TIA Project		50D99L00377	**SW:** V06.00		50E99L00037
Owner:	OMNISCANNER 2		**Adapter**			**Adapter**
			CHAN 5/5E/6			CHAN 5/5E/6
Autotest:	*Cat 5E Link*					
Cable:	Cat 5E UTP					
NVP:	72					

			Limit	**12**	**36**	**45**	**78**
Site:	Las Cruces						
Building:	Manufacturing						
Floor:	3rd	**Length** ft	(308)	45	45	47	47
Closet:	315A	**Delay (ns):**	(518)	64	64	66	67
		Resistance (Ohms):	(—)	—	—	—	—

	Wiremap	**Expected**	**Actual**			
OMNI:		12345678	! 12345678	**Skew (ns):**	(45)	3
Remote:		12345678	! 12345678	**Bandwidth (MHz):**		----

Attenuation — Overall Margin (dB)¹ -19.5

Pairs	dB	Margin	MHz
12	! 38.0	-16.4	99.4
36	! 41.1	-19.5	99.9
45	2.9	18.6	99.2
78	2.9	18.7	99.9

Return Loss — Overall Margin (dB)¹ -5.4

	OMNIScanner			OMNIRemote		
Pairs	dB	Margin	MHz	dB	Margin	MHz
12	! 10.6	-5.3	29.3	! 10.5	-5.3	29.5
36	! 10.4	-5.4	29.8	! 10.6	-5.2	29.3
45	19.4	6.1	68.0	20.8	3.8	1.4
78	20.3	3.3	1.4	21.3	4.3	1.6

NEXT — Overall Margin (dB)¹ -37.7

	OMNIScanner			OMNIRemote		
Pairs	dB	Margin	MHz	dB	Margin	MHz
12/36	! 22.3	-37.7	1.6	! 11.0	-36.4	11.8
12/45	56.6	5.4	6.8	54.2	3.5	7.3
12/78	69.8	9.9	1.9	70.2	10.9	2.1
36/45	39.4	4.9	74.1	56.1	3.9	5.9
36/78	68.2	9.6	2.3	68.7	9.4	2.1
45/78	59.5	15.5	19.0	57.3	13.2	19.0

ACR — Overall Margin (dB)¹

	OMNIScanner			OMNIRemote		
Pairs	dB	Margin	MHz	dB	Margin	MHz
12/36	----	----	----	—	—	—
12/45	----	----	----	—	—	—
12/78	----	----	----	—	—	—
36/45	----	----	----	—	—	----
36/78	----	----	----	—	—	—
45/78	----	----	----	—	—	—

ELFEXT — Overall Margin (dB)¹ -30.1

	OMNIScanner			OMNIRemote		
Pairs	dB	Margin	MHz	dB	Margin	MHz
12/36	! 26.4	-30.1	1.6	! 26.6	-29.9	1.6
12/45	67.8	16.6	2.8	37.2	16.6	93.8
12/78	80.0	22.3	1.4	80.1	22.3	1.4
36/12	! 26.6	-29.9	1.6	! 26.4	-30.1	1.6
36/45	60.8	14.7	5.0	35.4	13.0	76.3
36/78	79.9	22.2	1.4	57.9	21.2	14.7
45/12	! 8.6	-11.4	99.4	! 10.4	-9.6	99.4
45/36	! 1.9	-18.2	99.4	! 5.8	-14.2	99.9
45/78	50.3	15.5	18.3	49.8	15.2	18.7
78/12	! 14.4	-5.6	99.4	! 9.2	-10.9	99.4
78/36	! 10.4	-9.7	99.9	23.3	3.3	99.9
78/45	49.9	15.3	18.7	50.4	15.6	18.3

PSNEXT — Overall Margin (dB)¹ -34.7

	OMNIScanner			OMNIRemote		
Pairs	dB	Margin	MHz	dB	Margin	MHz
12	! 22.2	-34.7	2.1	! 11.0	-33.4	11.8
36	! 22.2	-34.7	2.1	! 11.0	-33.4	11.8
45	53.1	5.3	7.3	52.0	3.7	6.8
78	66.1	9.2	2.1	66.3	9.4	2.1

PSELFEXT — Overall Margin (dB)¹ -27.1

	OMNIScanner			OMNIRemote		
Pairs	dB	Margin	MHz	dB	Margin	MHz
12	! 26.6	-26.8	1.6	! 26.4	-27.0	1.6
36	! 26.4	-27.1	1.6	! 26.6	-26.9	1.6
45	68.9	14.2	1.4	33.6	14.2	76.3
78	72.0	17.3	1.4	72.1	17.4	1.4

PSACR — Overall Margin (dB)¹ ----

	OMNIScanner			OMNIRemote		
Pairs	dB	Margin	MHz	dB	Margin	MHz
12	----	----	----	----	----	----
36	----	----	----	—	----	—
45	----	----	----	—	----	—
78	----	----	----	—	—	—

¹ Overall margin value is the worst margin for OMNI and Remote.

MICROTEST®

Date: 2/15/2002   2:07:00 PM   Page 1

FIGURE 2-52 The Test 3 CAT5e link test showing failures with attenuation.

Test 4 Figure 2-53 shows the certification report for the cable tested in Test 4. This cable test generated a test result of FAIL. Examination of the certification report shows the cable failed the delay skew. This cable exceeds the maximum allowed by EIA/TIA 568B. Additionally, this cable fails attenuation, ELFEXT, and PSELFEXT tests. No, the cable should not be certified.

The measured delay skew of 47 ns exceeds the tester setting of 45 ns. The EIA/TIA 568B standard permits a delay skew of 50 ns, so actually this cable meets delay skew requirements for CAT5e cable. The specification set on the tester actually exceeds the CAT5e requirements. Should the cable have been certified? Look at the length measurement for the 3–6 pair length. The cable is 1040 feet in length. Remember, the maximum cable length for a CAT5e cable run is 100 meters

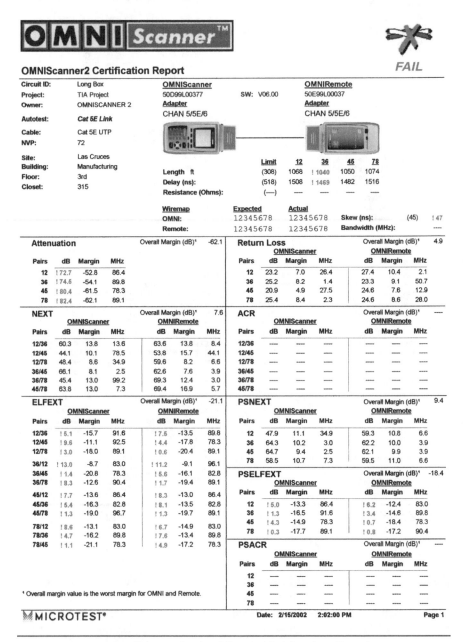

FIGURE 2-53 A CAT5e link test showing failures with delay skew (Test 4).

Summary of CAT5e Cable Test Examples   This section has provided a few examples of CAT5e link tests. The objective has been to provide actual test data for different cable problems that might occur on the job. In the tests where a failure was detected, the tester displayed a failed screen, and the certification report identified the problem. The following is a summary of the tests:

- **Test 1:** The certification report shows a test result of PASS.
- **Test 2:** The certification report shows a test result of FAIL. The report shows the cable failed the wire-map test.
- **Test 3:** This cable test generated a test result of FAIL. Examination of the attenuation and return-loss shows that the cable failed to meet CAT5e attenuation and return-loss specifications. The cable also failed NEXT, ELFEXT, PSNEXT, and PSELFEXT tests.
- **Test 4:** The certification report shows the cable fails the CAT5e link test. Examination of the report shows the cable failed the delay skew measurement because the cable length exceeded the 100-meter maximum. The cable also fails attenuation, ELFEXT, and PSELFEXT tests.

The reasons for examining the test results is to find out why a cable fails a test. You need to know whether the problem is with your terminations, cable layout, or the way the cable is installed. Keeping a record of the cable tests will help you isolate recurring problems.

Tests 1 and 2 demonstrate the importance of keeping a record of tests. In this case, the cable was certified but later failed. The documentation provided by the certification report provides evidence that the cable was functioning properly and did meet CAT5e specifications.

Summary

This chapter introduced the basics of horizontal cabling and unshielded twisted-pair cable. The major topics the student should now understand include the following:

- Six subsystems of a structured cabling system
- The purpose of the telecommunication closet and the LAN work area
- The performance capabilities of CAT6/5e UTP
- The wiring color schemes for T568A and T568B
- The pin assignments for the RJ-45 (8P8C) modular plug
- The technical issues of copper over 10G Ethernet
- The procedures for testing a CAT6/5e link
- The procedures for troubleshooting a CAT6/5e link
- How to examine and use the test results provided by a CAT6/5e link certification report

Questions and Problems

Section 2-2

1. When was the first major standard describing a structured cabling system released?
   a. 1999
   b. 1989
   c. 1995
   d. 1998
2. What doe EIA and TIA stand for?
3. What are the three parts of the EIA/TIA 568-B standard?
4. Identify the six subsystems of a structured cabling system.
5. Which subsystem does permanent networking cabling within a building belong to?
6. What is a cross-connect?
7. What is the main cross-connect?
8. The Telco and the ISP usually connect to what room in the campus network hierarchy?
9. What is the WO, and what is its purpose?
10. The patch cable from a computer typically terminates into which of the following?
    a. Jack in a wall plate
    b. BNC connector
    c. Thin net
    d. RJ-11 modular plug
    e. RG-59
11. What is the over all length limitation of an individual cable run from the telecommunications closet to a networking device in the work area.
12. A general rule of thumb is to allow how many meters for the cable run from the telecommunications closet to the work area?

Section 2-3

13. How many pins does an RJ-45 modular plug have?
14. What is the difference in CAT 5 and CAT 5e?
15. What is the data rate for Ethernet?
16. What is the data rate for FastEthernet?
17. What improvements will CAT6 and CAT7 cable provide?
18. What is the data rate for gigabit Ethernet?
19. What is a benefit of using shielded twisted-pair cabling?
20. Which cable, UTP or STP, is preferred by the industry?

Section 2-4

21. What are the color maps and pin # assignments for T568A and T568B?
22. What is the difference between T568A and T568B?
23. How many wires are in a CAT6 twisted-pair cable?
24. How many wire pairs are in a CAT6 twisted-pair cable?
25. In regards to a CAT6 cable, what pin numbers in an RJ-45 connecter are used to carry data in a FastEthernet network?
26. What does an "X" on the input to a hub represent?
27. Define the term cross-connected input.
28. Draw a picture of properly aligned transmit and receive signal of a computer's data link that is running Ethernet data rates.
29. What is the difference between "straight" and "cross-connected" input ports?
30. Draw the wire-map for a "cross over" CAT6 UTP cable running FastEthernet.
31. Define a UTP link test.
32. Define a UTP full channel test.
33. Define the term NEXT and what it measures.
34. A NEXT measurement of 59.5 dB is made on wire pairs 1–2/3–6. A next measurement of 51.8db is made on wire pairs 3–6/7–8. Which cable pairs have the best measure NEXT performance?
35. Define Power-Sum measurements.
36. Define propagation delay.
37. Signals travel in a cable at some percentage of the velocity of light. The term of this is?
38. Why is delay skew critical?
39. Why are power-sum measurements critical for high-speed data communication over UTP?
40. The expected attenuation loss of a 20m UTP cable should be (greater or less than) a 90m UTP cable?
41. What is 8P8C, and what connector type is most associated with this?
42. What are the pin assignments for 1/10 Gbps?
43. What is the purpose of a lacing tool?

Section 2-5

44. What is the limit on the bend radius for a UTP cable, and why is this important?
45. Is a high PSNEXT measurement desirable?
46. Define margin (dB) relative to cable measurements. What does it mean if the margin lists a negative value?

Section 2-6

47. Define Alien Crosstalk and draw a picture of how this can happen.
48. What is F/UTP, and what is its purpose?
49. Why is balance an issue in UTP cables, and what is TCL?

Critical Thinking

50. Answer the following questions for the certification report shown in Figure 2-54.
    a. What is the length of pair 7–8?
    b. What is the length of pair 4–5?
    c. Why did this cable fail the test?

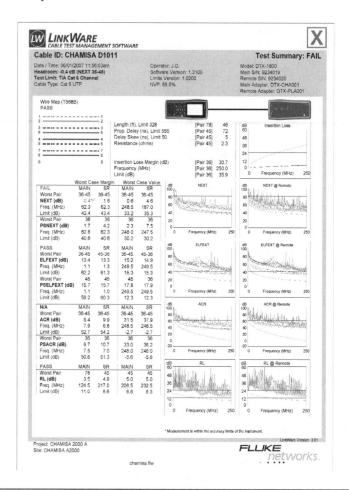

FIGURE 2-54 The certification report for problem 50.

51. Answer the following questions for the certification report shown in Figure 2-55.
    a. What is the length of wire pair 7–8?
    b. What is the delay skew for pair 4–5?
    c. Why did this cable fail the wire-map test?

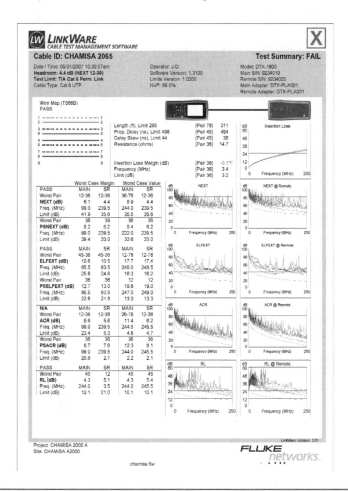

FIGURE 2-55 The certification report for problem 51.

52. Answer the following questions for the certification report shown in Figure 2-56.
    a. Why did the cable fail the test?
    b. Draw the wire-map diagram for this cable.

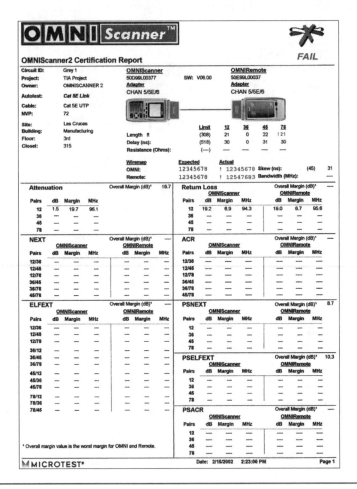

FIGURE 2-56   The certification report for problem 52.

3
CHAPTER

Computer Fundamentals

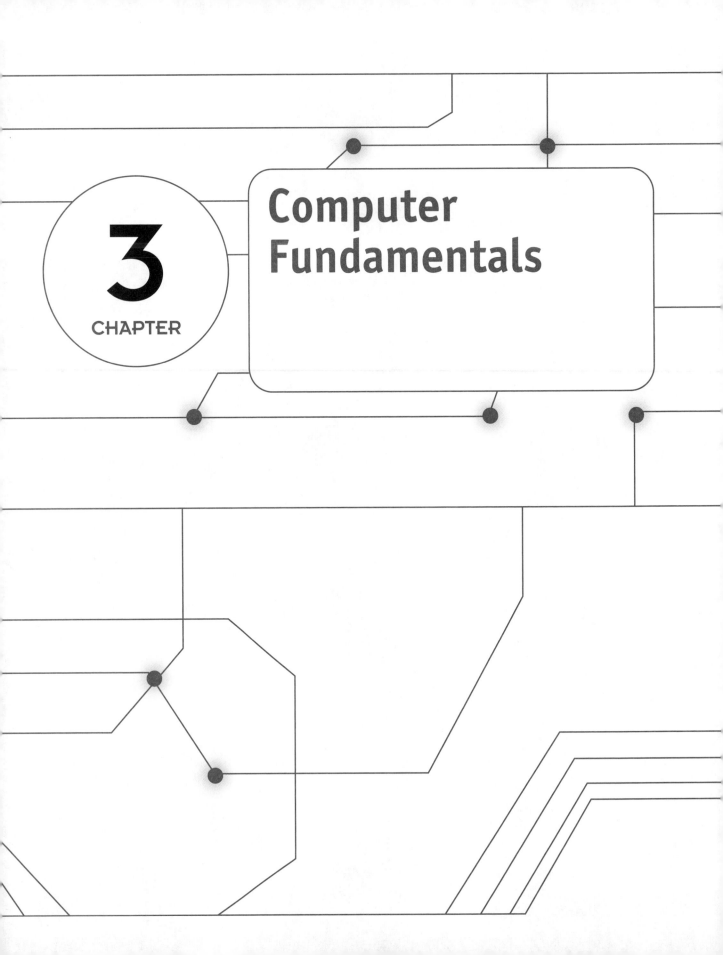

CHAPTER OUTLINE

3-1 Introduction
3-2 The Computer Bus Connection
3-3 Device Drivers
3-4 Computer Memory

3-5 An Overview of FAT and NTFS
3-6 Configuring the BIOS Boot Sequence
Summary
Questions and Problems

OBJECTIVES

- Identify the different motherboard bus connections used with network interface cards
- Verify the computer's device drivers
- Identify the different computer memory modules available

- Check for the amount of installed computer memory
- Be able to discuss the differences between NTFS and FAT
- Be able to configure the computer's boot sequence

KEY TERMS

combo terminations
PCI
ISA
EISA
USB 1.1
USB 2.0
IEEE 1394 (Firewire, i-Link)
SCSI
IDE (PATA)

SATA
AGP
interrupt request (IRQ)
device drivers
DIMM
DRAM
ECC RAM
EDO RAM
SDRAM
DDR SDRAM

DDR RAM (RDRAM)
DDR2 SDRAM
FAT
clusters
FAT16
FAT32
NTFS
boot sequence
BIOS (Basic Input Output System)

3-1   INTRODUCTION

This chapter presents an overview of the basic computer knowledge the LAN network administrator must have to work with today's networks. It is important for the network administrator to have an excellent understanding of the computer hardware he or she will be working with prior to learning how to configure the network. Questions concerning the computer's hardware will surface during network installation or during everyday network troubleshooting, and the better acquainted the administrator is with the computer hardware terminology, the easier his or her job will be.

The motherboard connections and adapters for the network interface card are examined in section 3-2. This section reviews the many types of motherboard connections and adapters available for network interface cards and other computer cards. The purpose of device drivers is examined in section 3-3. This section includes steps for verifying device drivers in the Windows Vista/XP and Mac OS X operating systems. It is not uncommon for a device driver to fail, requiring that the computer either be restarted or the device driver to be reloaded.

Each computer operating system has a different suggested minimum memory requirement. Section 3-4 provides an overview of the suggested memory requirements for the Windows and Mac operating systems. This section examines the different types of memory modules currently available and how to check for the amount of installed memory.

The network LAN administrator is typically responsible for upgrading the operating systems for the computers used in the LAN. A query asked when installing the newer operating systems is if the hard drive is to be formatted FAT or NTFS. Section 3-5 provides an overview of the FAT and NTFS file systems and discusses the advantages and disadvantages of each. The chapter concludes with a section on configuring the BIOS boot sequence. An example of configuring the boot sequence is offered.

3-2   THE COMPUTER BUS CONNECTION

Combo Terminations
The interface supports multiple types of media connections

The purpose of the network interface card (NIC) is to provide an electrical interface for the computer to the network. The NIC must have the proper termination for connecting to the LAN media and the proper motherboard or adapter connection for connecting to the computer. In the small office LAN example shown in Figure 3-1, CAT6 cabling is used to connect the networking devices to the network. CAT6 cable is terminated with an RJ-45 modular plug; therefore, the NIC must have an RJ-45 modular jack for connecting the patch cable from the wall plate to the computer. The NIC can also have **combo terminations** for supporting multiple types of network media such as UTP, fiber, or possibly a USB port. An example of a NIC card with a combo input supporting both RJ-45 and USB 2.0 connections is provided in Figure 3-2.

The NIC also provides the proper protocol interface to the network. In the examples presented in the text, the NIC provides the interface to an Ethernet network. This requires that the NIC be an Ethernet type running at 10/100/1000 Mbps or possibly 10 Gbps. The speed choice depends on the capability and configuration for your LAN. The NIC also contains the Mac address, which provides the source or destination address of packets (refer to Chapter 1 for a complete discussion on NICs).

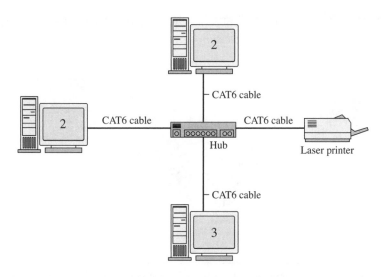

FIGURE 3-1   A small office LAN.

FIGURE 3-2   A combo network interface card with both an RJ-45 and two USB type A female adapters (courtesy of StarTech.com).

Motherboard Bus Connections

The objective of this section is to help acquaint the reader with the different types of motherboard bus connections available for NICs. Some of the bus connections mentioned also support other hardware technologies such as hard drives, USB connections, video cards, sound cards, and so on. It is important for the network administrator to be familiar with the type of bus interconnects that are available. You don't know for certain which computer bus connection you will need until you have opened the computer chassis and examined the motherboard. A discussion of the most common computer bus technologies follows.

- **PCI**—Peripheral Component Interconnect. PCI is the best bus choice for current computers. PCI supports 32- and 64-bit implementations (see Figure 3-3).

PCI

- **ISA**—Industry Standard Architecture. Allows for 16-bit data transfers between the motherboard and the expansion board (see Figure 3-4).

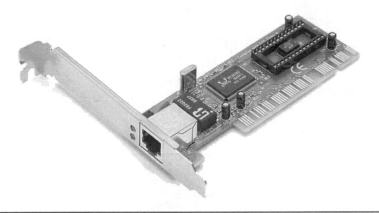

FIGURE 3-3   A network interface card using a PCI bus connection (courtesy of StarTech.com).

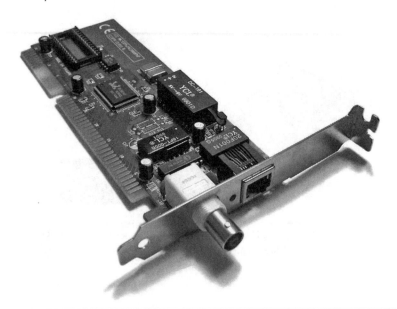

FIGURE 3-4   A network interface card with an ISA motherboard connection (courtesy of Cyberguys.com).

- **EISA**—Extended Industry Standard Architecture. EISA extends the ISA bus to 32-bit data transfers.
- **USB 1.1**—Universal Serial Bus. This interface supports data rates up to 12 Mbps. The USB interface does not require that the computer be turned off or rebooted to activate the connection.
- **USB 2.0**—Universal Serial Bus. This USB interface supports data rates up to 480 Mbps and is used when connecting a USB adapter to a 100 Mbps network.

The original specification for the USB connection provided for two types of connectors, Type A and Type B, shown in Figure 3-5 (a and b). Currently, five types of USB connectors are available for use with a variety of devices including smartphones, PDAs, and cameras. A picture of the five types of USB connectors is provided in Figure 3-5(c). The USB cable length is limited to 5 meters (approximately 16 feet).

- **IEEE 1394 (Firewire, i-Link)**—A high-speed, low-cost interconnection standard that supports data speeds of 100 to 400 Mbps. [Figure 3-6(a) and (b)]

- **SCSI**—Small Computer System Interface. Consists of a SCSI host adapter, SCSI devices such as hard drives, DVD, CD-ROM, and internal or external SCSI cables, terminators, and adapters. There are several benefits of using the **SCSI interface**. It is a fairly fast interface, up to 320 megabytes per second (MBps), and an additional benefit is that the SCSI interface has been around for more than 20 years. It has been thoroughly tested and is known to be very reliable (see Figure 3-7[a] and [b]).

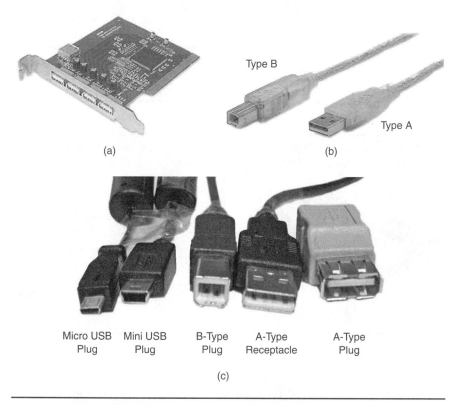

(a)

Type B

Type A

(b)

Micro USB Plug   Mini USB Plug   B-Type Plug   A-Type Receptacle   A-Type Plug

(c)

FIGURE 3-5   (a) USB card (courtesy of Cyberguys.com). (b) Type A and B USB cables (courtesy of StarTech.com). (c) A group picture of the five types of USB connectors: micro USB plug, mini USB plug, B-type plug, A-type plug, and A-type receptacle.

- **IDE**—Integrated Drive Electronics. Standard electronic interface between the computer's motherboard and storage devices such as hard drives. The IDE interface is now known as **PATA**, the **P**arallel **A**dvanced **T**echnology **A**ttachment. The data transfer speeds for IDE (PATA) are slower than SCSI (see Figure 3-7 [a] and [b]).

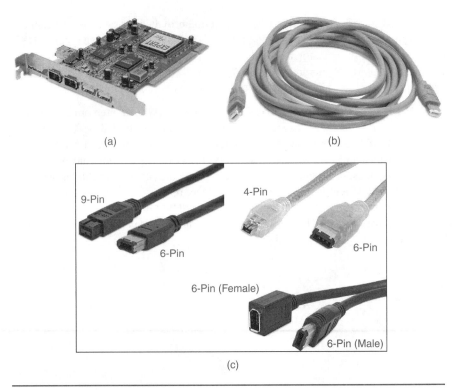

FIGURE 3-6   (a) Firewire interface card. (b) Firewire cable. (c) A composite view of 4-, 6-, and 9-pin Firewire connectors (Courtesy of StarTech.com).

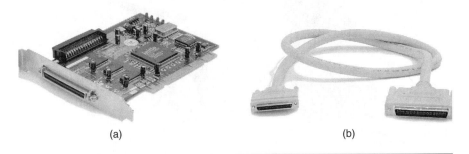

FIGURE 3-7   (a) SCSI interface card; (b) SCSI cable (courtesy of StarTech.com).

SATA
AGP
Interrupt Request (IRQ)

- **SATA**—**S**erial **A**dvanced **T**echnology **A**ttachment. This technology was developed to replace IDE (PATA) technology. SATA devices provide data transfer speeds of 3 Gbps, and new versions of SATA devices are expected to support 6-Gbps data transfers (see Figure 3-8).
- **AGP**—Accelerated Graphics Port. For use in high-speed 3D graphics applications (see Figure 3-9).
- **Interrupt Request (IRQ)**—The IRQ number determines where a computer's CPU should look for an interrupt request from a hardware device such as the network interface card. Today most NICs are plug and play, which means the computer operating system will select the proper IRQ for your NIC. In older or legacy systems the IRQ had to be manually set, or you had to contact the vendor to obtain the proper IRQ number.

(a)   (b)

FIGURE 3-8   (a) 2-port Serial ATA and 1-port ATA/133 IDE PCI card (b) SATA cable
(courtesy of StarTech.com).

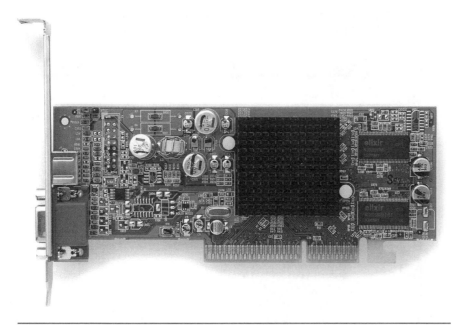

FIGURE 3-9   AGP video card (courtesy of Cyberguys.com).

3-3   DEVICE DRIVERS

The **device drivers** are the software installed on the computer that interfaces the operating system with the hardware or to the network. The new computer operating systems come preloaded with device drivers for the most common hardware. The computer detects the hardware and automatically installs the proper driver. This is a feature of "plug and play" architecture. However, the drivers for newly developed hardware will not come with the operating system CD-ROM. In this case, the software device driver must be installed. The device driver typically comes preloaded on a CD-ROM. It is always best to use the driver that comes with the hardware if you aren't sure about the driver. If you can't find the driver disk that came with the hardware or you

Device Drivers
Interface the operating
system to the hardware

can't find the proper driver preloaded in the operating system, go to the manufacturer's website and search for and download the driver. If this doesn't work, do a generic search on the Web for the device driver you need. Use caution and make sure you are using a reliable site to download the device driver. The steps for displaying and verifying the device drivers for Windows Vista, XP, and the Mac OS X are listed next.

Verifying Device Drivers on Windows Vista/XP

To verify the device drivers for Windows Vista/XP, follow these steps:

1. In Vista, right-click **Computer** and select **Properties**. This opens the **System Properties Window**. Click **Continue**. The Device Manager window will be displayed as shown in Figure 3-10.

    To enter the device manager in Windows XP, right-click **My Computer** and select **Properties—Hardware—Device Manager**. The Device Manager window will be displayed.

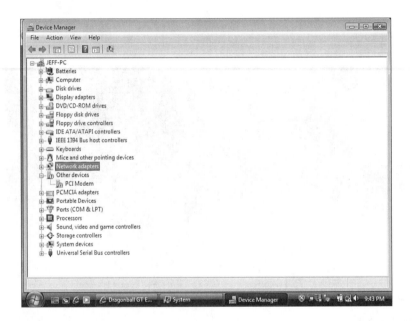

FIGURE 3-10   The System Properties menu in Vista.

2. To display the hardware connected to your system, click the plus (+) sign next to the device. Double-click the device name. This opens the Properties window for the selected device. Figure 3-11 provides an example.
    Figure 3-12 shows an arrow pointing to the yellow exclamation point next to the PCI modem device. This denotes a nonworking driver for the PCI modem.
3. Double-click the failed device to check the status of the driver for the PCI modem. This opens the Properties window for the PCI modem (see Figure 3-13).

FIGURE 3-11   The Device Properties menu in Vista.

The exclamation point indicates a driver error.

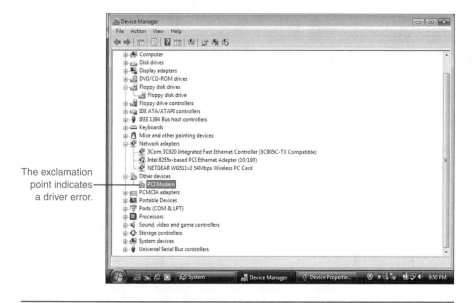

FIGURE 3-12   The Device Manager window.

4. To check the driver details, click the **Driver** tab in the Properties window (Figure 3-13). In this window you have the option of getting more driver details or of updating, rolling back, disabling, or uninstalling the driver. Figure 3-14 shows the window for the driver tab.

FIGURE 3-13   An example of a failed device driver for the PCI modem.

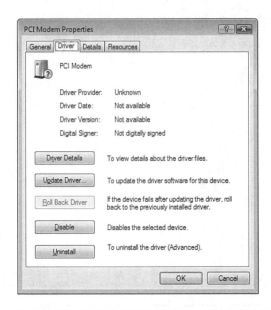

FIGURE 3-14   The Driver tab menu for the failed driver.

Verifying Device Drivers on Mac OS X

To view and verify the device drivers installed on a Mac OS X computer, click the **Apple** icon—**About this Mac**. This opens the About this Mac window. Click **More Info...**. This opens the System Profile window as shown in Figure 3-15. Click Extensions under the Software contents located on the left side of the window. This opens up a list of drivers in the System Profile window (Figure 3-16). The state of a driver can be viewed by selecting the driver and examining the comments at the bottom of the System Profile window. Figure 3-17 shows an example. In this example, the IODVDStorageFamily driver has been selected. The status of the driver shows that it is not currently loaded as indicated by the arrow.

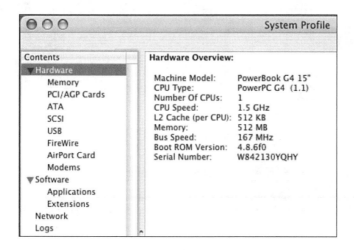

FIGURE 3-15   The System Profile window for Mac OS X.

Extension Name		Version	Last Modified
IOPCIFamily		1.4	3/22/04 10:59 PM
IOPlatformFunction		1.6.1	1/12/05 11:22 AM
IOPlatformPluginFamily		1.5.5	3/30/05 9:48 PM
IOSCSIArchitectureModelFamily		1.3.9	3/30/05 9:19 PM
IOSCSIBlockCommandsDevice		1.3.9	3/30/05 9:19 PM
IOSCSIFamily		1.3.7	11/7/04 5:22 PM
IOSCSIParallelFamily		1.3.7	11/7/04 5:22 PM
IOSCSIReducedBlockCommandsDevice		1.3.9	3/30/05 9:19 PM
IOSerialFamily		6.0	3/30/05 9:28 PM
IOStorageFamily		1.3.4	11/7/04 5:10 PM
IOSystemManagement		7.9.0	3/30/05 9:12 PM
IOUSBFamily		2.1.5	3/30/05 9:21 PM
IOUSBHIDDriver		2.1.4	1/27/05 7:11 AM
IOUSBHIDDriverSafeBoot		2.0.5	1/27/05 7:11 AM
IOUSBMassStorageClass		1.3.2	3/30/05 9:23 PM
IOUSBUserClient		2.1.4	1/27/05 7:11 AM
IPFirewall		1.3	3/22/04 10:56 PM
iPodDriver		1.0.0	11/7/04 5:16 PM
iPodFireWireTransportSupport		1.1.1	11/7/04 5:16 PM
iPodSBCDriver		1.1.1	11/7/04 5:16 PM

FIGURE 3-16   A list of the drivers for Mac OS X.

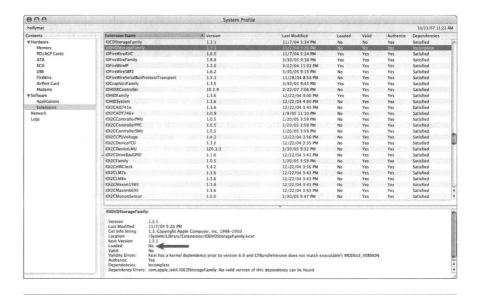

FIGURE 3-17   An example of a driver that is not currently loaded for Mac OS X computer.

3-4   COMPUTER MEMORY

Each operating system has a suggested minimum memory, or random access memory (RAM), requirement. Table 3-1 lists the suggested memory requirements for eight different Windows operating systems. The bottom line is, install as much memory as the motherboard of your server can support. Client computers can typically operate without having the maximum amount of memory available. (Of course, this depends on the application software running on the client computer.) The selection of memory for your computer depends on the motherboard.

TABLE 3-1   Suggested Memory Requirements for Windows and Mac
Operating Systems

Operating System	Recommended Memory
Windows 98	64 MB to 128 MB
Windows XP	256 MB or more
Windows Vista	512 MB or more
Windows 2000 (Professional)	128 MB or more
Windows 2000 (Server)	512 MB or more
Windows 2003 (Server)	1 GB or more
Windows 2008 (Server)	2 GB or more
Mac OS X	256 MB or more
Mac OS X (Leopard)	512 MB or more
Mac OS X (Server)	1 GB or more

Types of Memory

Computer memory comes in many types. The selection for your computer depends on what type can be mounted on your computer's motherboard. Table 3-2 lists the different types of memory used in today's computer motherboards.

TABLE 3-2   Different Types of Memory

Memory Type	Definition
DIMM	Dual in-line memory module. Supports 64-bit data transfers; 168 pins on the memory module.
DRAM	Dynamic random access memory. Each bit is stored in a cell, and the cell must be periodically refreshed to retain the stored information; replaced by SDRAM.
ECC RAM	Error-Correcting Code Random Access Memory. This type of memory checks the data for errors as it passes through the memory device.
EDO RAM	Extended data-out RAM. Better speed performance than DRAM; replaced by SDRAM.
SDRAM	Synchronous DRAM. Synchronizes memory access with the CPU for faster data transfers; a block of data can be transferred to the CPU while another block is being set up for transfer.
DDR SDRAM	Double-data-rate SDRAM. Transfers data on the edges of the system clock, speeding up the data transfer.
DRD RAM (RDRAM)	Direct RAMBUS DRAM. Used with high-end Intel computers; also called PC800, based on doubling the bus rate of the Pentium 4.
DDR2 SDRAM	Double-Data-Rate two Synchronous Dynamic Random Access Memory is used in high-speed computer and digital electronic devices.

The quickest way to check for the amount of RAM installed on a Windows computer is to simultaneously press the **Windows** and **Pause/Break** keys on the computer's keyboard. The keys are shown in Figure 3-18. The amount of memory installed on a Mac OS X computer can be display by clicking **Apple—About This Mac**. This opens the About This Mac window, and the type of memory and amount are displayed as shown in Figure 3-19.

FIGURE 3-18   The Windows and Pause/Break keys used to check the computer's installed memory.

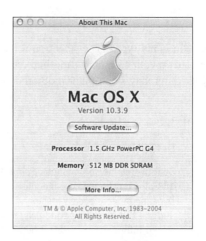

FIGURE 3-19   The About This Mac window showing the type and amount of memory installed.

3-5   AN OVERVIEW OF FAT AND NTFS

The local network administrator is responsible for maintaining the network and the computers in the LAN. This same person spends a lot of time upgrading the operating system and programs. When a new operating system is installed, the hard drive will need to be reformatted. The installer will have to make a choice for the type of format used: FAT or NTFS. The following discussion outlines these file formats and lists the advantages and disadvantages of each.

FAT

FAT
File allocation table

Clusters
Storage area for files and directories

FAT16
Uses a 16-bit file allocation table

FAT stands for "file allocation table." The purpose of the file allocation table is to keep track of where the file information is located on the media (for example, hard drive, Zip disks, 3.5" disks, and so on). A disk that is formatted using FAT allocates **clusters** on the disk for storing information such as the file and directory data. This is called the *data area* of the partition. The FAT keeps a record of the cluster location for the file. For large files, this requires that multiple clusters be used and a record kept of each. Files are given the first available space on the drive.

The FAT system is also called **FAT16**. The 16 indicates the number of bits for the file allocation table. The FAT16 system creates 2^{16} clusters. The FAT16 file system works best for hard drives or partitions that are 200 MB or smaller in size. The overhead for a FAT file system degrades the performance of the file access, but most importantly it isn't possible to set file permissions in FAT16 partitions. Table 3-3 provides a summary of the advantages and disadvantages of the FAT16 system.

TABLE 3-3 Advantages and Disadvantages of the FAT16 File System

Advantages	Disadvantages
FAT16 works best for hard drives or partitions that are 200 MB or less in size FAT16 uses very little overhead	200 MB hard drive or partition size limitation for optimal performance Not possible to set file permissions in the FAT partitions Filename size is limited to 8.3 characters (eight characters plus three more after the decimal) FAT partitions are limited to a maximum of 4 GB in Windows NT and 2 GB in DOS

FAT32

FAT32 is an improvement over the FAT16 system. FAT32 uses a 32-bit file allocation table but four bits are reserved; therefore, FAT32 produces 2^{28} clusters. FAT32 supports hard drives up to 2 terabytes in size. It uses variable cluster sizes to more efficiently use the disk space. The FAT32 system is less susceptible to disk data failures. Table 3-4 provides a summary of the advantages and disadvantages of FAT 32.

FAT32
Uses a 32-bit file allocation table

TABLE 3-4 Advantages and Disadvantages of the FAT32 File System

Advantages	Disadvantages
Supports up to 2 terabytes of disk space Less susceptible to disk data failures A better use of disk space	No built-in file security system No built-in data compression scheme Cannot be used with Windows NT

NTFS

NTFS is the New Technology File System developed by Microsoft Corporation. NTFS was developed to address the need for improved reliability, security and access control, size barriers, storage efficiency, and the use of long filenames in an operating system. Table 3-5 provides a summary of the advantages and disadvantages of the NTFS system.

NTFS
New Technology File System

TABLE 3-5 Summary of NTFS Advantages and Disadvantages

Advantages	Disadvantages
Reliability—the ability to recover from problems without the loss of data Security and access control—control access to files and file folders Size barriers—allow for very large disk partitions Storage efficiency—improvement in the method for allocating space to files Long filenames—allow filenames up to 255 characters	The overhead for NTFS is approximately 4 MB of disk space on a 100-MB partition

3-6 CONFIGURING THE BIOS BOOT SEQUENCE

Boot Sequence
The order in which the computer selects a drive for loading the computer's boot instructions

BIOS (Basic Input Output System)
Contains the basic instructions needed by the computer to operate

The network LAN administrator is responsible for maintaining all aspects of the LAN, including tasks such as performing hardware and software upgrades. In some cases, the administrator must make changes to the computer's boot sequence, especially when reloading or upgrading a computer's operating system. For example, a software upgrade might require the use of a CD-ROM boot disk. The boot sequence might be set to first look for the information in a 3.5 disk and then the hard drive. This requires the network administrator to enter the computer's BIOS and change the **boot sequence**. The computer's **BIOS (Basic Input Output System)** contains the basic instructions needed by the computer to initialize. The boot sequence is the order in which the computer selects the drive for loading the computer's boot (initialization) instructions.

Entering the boot sequence on the computer varies for each manufacturer of computer motherboards. You might press **F2** or the **Delete (del)** key when instructed, or in some cases you might not even receive a prompt saying "press this key" to enter the BIOS. Entering the BIOS setup mode for the computer allows the user to modify parameters such as setting the boot sequence and interrupt requests.

When the computer boots, it looks for instructions in the BIOS for where to search for a disk containing the operating system it needs to load. The boot sequence defined in the BIOS instructs the computer in what order and where to look for the operating system. The operating system could be on the CD-ROM, the hard drive, or the 3.5 disk. Additionally, each disk is assigned a drive letter (A, B, C, and so on) by the connection to the disk controller.

In the BIOS, you can specify the order of the boot sequence by selecting the **Boot Sequence** menu and then selecting where your computer should look first. For example, the boot sequence order listed could be as follows:

1. On Board or USB Floppy Drive
2. On Board SATA Hard Drive
3. On Board PATA Hard Drive
4. On Board or USB CDROM Drive
5. On Board Network Controller
6. USB Device

In this example, the boot sequence is set so that the computer looks first at the On Board or USB Floppy Drive.

Typical instructions are:

1. Select the device you want to change the order.
2. Press (+) or (-) to move the device up or down.

For example, to make the On Board or USB CD-ROM drive the boot drive, select **On Board or USB CDROM Drive (#5)** and then press the plus (+) key three times. This changes the order for the boot sequence to the following:

1. On Board or USB CDROM Drive
2. On Board or USB Floppy Drive
3. On Board SATA Hard Drive
4. On Board PATA Hard Drive
5. On Board Network Controller
6. USB Device

The computer is now set to boot from the On Board or USB CD-ROM drive. This boot sequence is the preferred order in today's computers.

SUMMARY

This chapter has presented an overview of the introductory computer knowledge needed for a network LAN administrator to function in today's Windows-based computer systems. The student should understand the following:

- The different types of motherboard connections
- How to verify device drivers
- How to check for installed computer memory and the minimum requirements needed for different operating systems
- The advantages and disadvantages of FAT and NTFS
- How to configure a computer's BIOS boot sequence

QUESTIONS AND PROBLEMS

Section 3-2

1. What is the purpose of the network interface card?
2. What is currently the best computer bus technology?
3. What is an advantage of USB?
4. What is the other name for the IDE interface?
5. If transfer speed is the issue, which interface should be selected, SCSI or SATA?
6. What is the limit on cable length for USB cables? (hint: Search the Internet for the answer.)

Section 3-3

7. What does a computer use to interface the computer hardware to the computer?
8. What symbol is used to indicate a failed device driver in Windows XP?

Section 3-4

9. What is the command sequence for checking the amount of installed memory (a) on a Windows computer (b) on a Mac OS X computer?
10. What is the suggested memory requirement for the following:
    a. Windows Vista workstation?
    b. Windows 2008 server?
    c. Windows 2003 Server?
11. A user in the network is running Windows 95 on his computer. A software package he wants to run requires 128 MB. What is your recommendation regarding the operating system and memory requirements? Justify your answer.
12. What is SDRAM?
13. What is DDR2 SDRAM?

Section 3-5

14. What is a cluster?
15. Which of the following are advantages of the FAT16 file system?
    a. A better use of disk space
    b. Uses little overhead
    c. 2^{16} clusters
    d. Setting file permissions
16. Which of the following are advantages of the FAT32 file system?
    a. A better use of disk space
    b. Setting file permissions
    c. Supports up to 2 terabytes of disk space
    d. Less susceptible to point data failures
17. Which of the following are true about NTFS?
    a. Improved security access control
    b. Recommended for use with 3.5? disks
    c. More reliable than FAT32
    d. Allows the use of long file names
    e. Developed by IBM for Microsoft

Section 3-6

18. Why is boot sequence order important?
19. What is the procedure for entering the boot sequence on the computer?

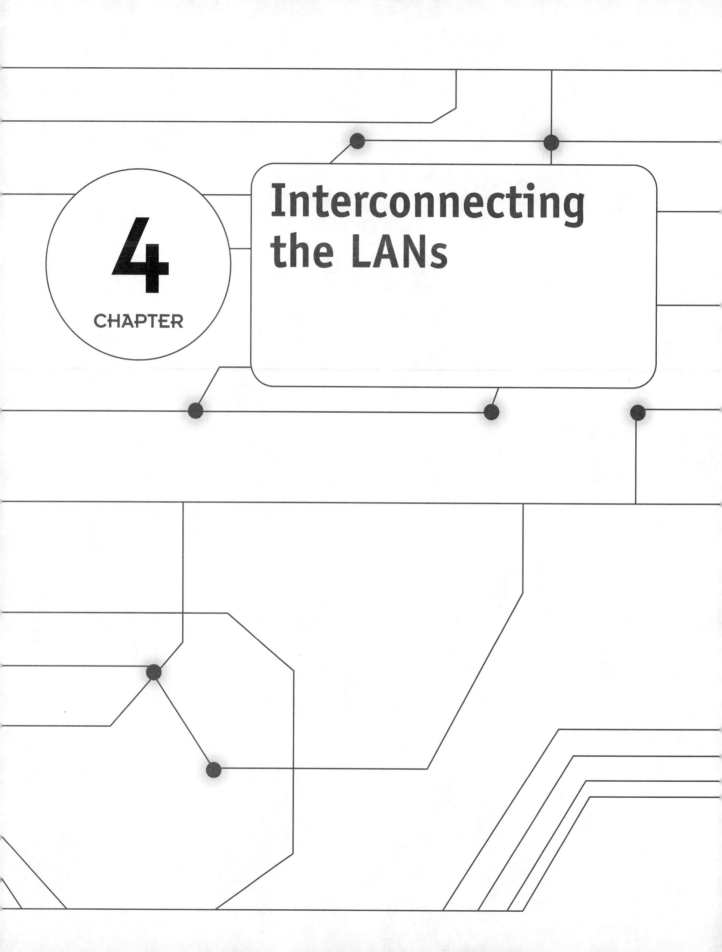

4

CHAPTER

Interconnecting the LANs

CHAPTER OUTLINE

4-1   Introduction
4-2   The OSI Model
4-3   The Network Bridge
4-4   The Network Switch
4-5   The Router

4-6   Interconnecting LANs with the Router
4-7   Configuring the Network Interface—
       Auto-negotiation
Summary
Questions and Problems

OBJECTIVES

- Define the OSI model and its application to computer networks
- Describe how a bridge is used to interconnect LANs
- Describe how a switch is used to interconnect LANs
- Discuss the advantages of using a switch instead of a hub

- Describe the function of a router when used to interconnect LANs
- Describe the interface associated with a router
- Describe the function of a gateway in a computer network
- Describe the concept of a network segment
- Describe the concept of auto-negotiation

KEY TERMS

campus network
OSI
OSI model
physical layer
data link layer
network layer
transport layer
session layer
presentation layer
application layer
bridge
bridging table
association
broadcast storm
network slowdown
ARP cache
ARP table
transparent bridge
translation bridge
layer 2 switch

multiport bridge
multicast
managed switch
Cisco Network Assistant
(CNA)
dynamic assignment
static assignment
secure addresses
aging time
isolating the collision
domain
CAM (content addressable
memory)
flooding
broadcast domain
store-and-forward
cut-through
switch latency
error threshold
multilayer switch (MLS)
wire speed routing

network address
logical address
router interface
power on/off
auxiliary input
console input
serial ports
AUI port
media converter
enterprise network
FastEthernet port (FA0/0,
FA0/1, FA0/2, …)
serial port (S0/0, S0/1,
S0/2, …)
routing table
gateway
auto-negotiation
fast link pulse (FLP)
half duplex

4-1   INTRODUCTION

Campus Network
A collection of two or more interconnected LANs in a limited geographic area

The utility of LANs led to the desire to connect two (or more) networks together. For example, a large corporation may have had separate networks for research and engineering and another for its manufacturing units. It was probable that these network systems used totally different networking technologies and specifications for communicating and were located in different cities, states, or even countries, but it was deemed necessary to "tie" them together. The objective of this and subsequent chapters is to introduce the concepts and issues behind interconnecting LANs. Interconnecting LANs in a **campus network** or even interconnecting LANs in wide-area networks (WANs) incorporate similar concepts and issues. The campus network is a collection of two or more interconnected LANs, either within a building or housed externally in multiple buildings.

The framework defining the network layers for linking networks together is defined by the OSI model, introduced in section 4-2. The OSI model provides a framework for networking that ensures compatibility in the network hardware and software. The concepts behind the hardware technologies used to interconnect LANs are presented in sections 4.3 to 4.5. The properties of a networking bridge are defined in section 4-3. The layer 2 switch is examined in section 4-4, and the router is introduced in section 4-5. An example of interconnecting LANs is provided in section 4-6. The chapter concludes with a section on the concept of auto-negotiation, examining the advantages and disadvantages of this network configuration option.

4-2   THE OSI MODEL

OSI
Open system interconnect

OSI Model
The seven layers describing network functions

An open systems interconnect (**OSI**) reference model was developed by the International Organization for Standardization in 1984 to enable different types of networks to be linked together. The model contains seven layers, as shown in Figure 4-1. These layers describe networking functions from the physical network interface to the software applications interfaces. The intent of the **OSI model** is to provide a framework for networking that ensures compatibility in the network hardware and software and to accelerate the development of new networking technologies. A discussion of the OSI model follows and a summary of the seven layers appears in Table 4-1.

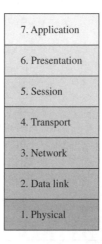

FIGURE 4-1   The seven layers of the OSI reference model.

TABLE 4-1 Summary of the OSI Layers

Layer	Function	Examples
7. Application	support for applications	HTTP, FTP, SMTP (email)
6. Presentation	protocol conversion, data translation	ASCII, JPEG
5. Session	establishes, manages, and terminates sessions	NFS, SQL
4. Transport	ensures error-free packets	TCP, UDP
3. Network	provides routing decisions	IP, IPX
2. Data link	provides for the flow of data	MAC addresses
1. Physical	signals and media	NICs, twisted-pair cable, fiber

1. **Physical layer:** Provides the electrical and mechanical connection to the network. Examples of technologies working in this layer are EIA/TIA related technologies, UTP, fiber, and NICs.
2. **Data link layer:** Handles error recovery, flow control (synchronization), and sequencing (which terminals are sending and which are receiving). It is considered the "media access control layer" and is where MAC addressing is defined. The Ethernet 802.3 standard is defined in this area, which is why the MAC address is sometimes called the Ethernet address.
3. **Network layer:** Accepts outgoing messages and combines messages or segments into packets, adding a header that includes routing information. It acts as the network controller. Examples are IP and IPX.
4. **Transport layer:** Is concerned with message integrity between source and destination. It also segments/reassembles (the packets) and handles flow control. Examples are TCP and UDP.
5. **Session layer:** Provides the control functions necessary to establish, manage, and terminate the connections as required to satisfy the user request. Examples are NFS and SQL.
6. **Presentation layer:** Accepts and structures the messages for the application. It translates the message from one code to another if necessary. This layer is responsible for data compression and encryption. Examples are ASCII and JPEG.
7. **Application layer:** Interacts with application programs that incorporate a communication component such as your Internet browser and email. This layer is responsible for logging the message in, interpreting the request, and determining what information is needed to support the request. Examples are HTTP, FTP, and SMTP.

Physical Layer
Data Link Layer
Network Layer
Transport Layer
Session Layer
Presentation Layer
Application Layer

Note

Network administrators often describe networking problems by layer number. For example, a physical link problem is described as a layer 1 problem; a router problem is layer 3.

The network administrator uses the OSI model to troubleshoot network problems by verifying functionality of each layer. In many cases, troubleshooting the network problem requires the network administrator to isolate at what layer the network problem occurs.

For example, assume that a network is having problems accessing an email server that uses SMTP, a layer 7 application. The first troubleshooting step for the network administrator is to ping the IP address of the email server (layer 3 test). A "ping" to an IP address can be used to check quickly that there is a network connection. A "reply from" response for the ping indicates the connection to the server is up. A "request timed out" response indicates the network connection is down. This could be due to a cabling problem (layer 1) or a problem with a switch (layer 2) or a router (layer 3), or the email server could be completely down (layer 7). In the case of "request timed out" the network administrator will have to go directly to the telecommunications closet or the machine to troubleshoot the problem. In this case, the administrator should first check for layer 1 (physical layer) problems. Many times this just requires verifying that a network cable is connected. Remember the concept of checking for a link light? Cables do get knocked loose or break.

The network administrator needs to have a good understanding of all seven layers of the OSI model. Knowledge of the layers can help to isolate the network problem. There are three basic steps in the process of isolating the network problem:

- Is the connection to the machine down? (layer 1)
- Is the network down? (layer 3)
- Is a service on a specific machine down? (layer 7)

This chapter continues with an introduction to the concepts behind assembling LANs together in a campus network. A campus network consists of interconnecting multiple LANs in multiple buildings together in a limited geographic area. The hardware used to interconnect the LANs in a campus network is presented in sections 4-3, 4-4, and 4-5. This discussion introduces bridges, switches, and routers.

By this time the need for good networking documentation becomes apparent. A centralized database for the campus network becomes essential. The database should include network documentation and network address assignments. The need for careful documentation is discussed throughout the text.

4-3 THE NETWORK BRIDGE

Bridge
A networking device that uses the MAC address to forward data and interconnect two LANs

A bridge is used in computer networks to interconnect two LANs together and separate network segments. Recall that a *segment* is a section of a network separated by bridges, switches, and routers. The **bridge** is a layer 2 device in the OSI model, meaning that it uses the MAC address information to make decisions regarding forwarding data packets. Only the data that needs to be sent across the bridge to the adjacent network segment is forwarded. This makes it possible to isolate or segment the network data traffic. An example of using a bridge to segment two Ethernet LANs is shown in Figure 4-2. The picture shows that LAN A connects to port 1 of the bridge, and LAN B connects to port 2 on the bridge, creating two segments, as shown. There are four computers in LAN A and three computers in LAN B.

Bridging Table
List of MAC addresses and port locations for hosts connected to the bridge ports

Bridges monitor all data traffic in each of the LAN segments connected to its ports. Recall that a *port* is an input/output connection on a networking device. The bridges use the MAC addresses to build a **bridging table** of MAC addresses and port locations for hosts connected to the bridge ports. A sample bridging table is provided in Table 4-2. The table shows the stored MAC address and the port where the address was obtained.

The source MAC address is stored in the bridge table as soon as a host talks (transmits a data packet) on the LAN. For example, if computer 1 in LAN A sends a message to computer 2 (see Figure 4-2), the bridge will store the MAC addresses of both computers and record that both of these computers are connected to port 1. If computers 5 or 6 are placing data packets on the network, then the source MAC addresses for 5 and 6 are stored in the bridge table, and it is recorded that these computers connect to port 2 on the bridge. The MAC addresses for computers 3 and 4 will not be added to the bridging table until each transmits a data packet.

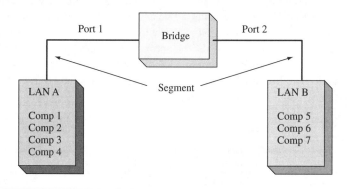

FIGURE 4-2   Using a bridge to interconnect two Ethernet LANs.

TABLE 4-2   Bridging Table

MAC Address	Port
00-40-96-25-85-BB	1
00-40-96-25-8E-BC	1
00-60-97-61-78-5B	2
00-C0-4F-27-20-C7	2

The bridge monitors the data on its ports to check for an **association** between the destination MAC address of the Ethernet frames to any of the hosts connected to its ports. An association indicates that the destination MAC address for a host is connected to one of the ports on the bridge. If an association is found, the data is forwarded to that port. For example, assume that computer 1 sends a message to computer 5 (see Figure 4-2). The bridge detects an association between the destination MAC address for computer 5 and port 2. The bridge then forwards the data from computer 1 to computer 5 in LAN B via port 2.

The capability of a bridge to forward data packets only when there is an association is used to isolate data traffic in each segment. For example, assume that computer 1 and computer 2 in LAN A generate a lot of data traffic. The computers in LAN B will not see any of the data traffic as long as there is not an association between the destination MAC addresses of the Ethernet packets and any of the hosts in LAN B (computers 5, 6, and 7).

A potential problem with bridges has to do with the way broadcasts are handled. All broadcasts in a LAN will be forwarded to all hosts connected within the bridged LANs. For example, the broadcast associated with an ARP will appear on all

Association
Indicates that the destination address is for a networking device connected to one of the ports on the bridge

hosts. In the address resolution protocol (ARP—see Chapter 1), a broadcast is sent to all hosts in a LAN connected to the bridge. This is graphically shown in Figure 4-3. The bridge forwards all broadcasts; therefore, an ARP request broadcasting the message "Who has this IP address?" is sent to all hosts on the LAN. The data packets associated with ARP requests are small, but it requires computer time to process each request. Excessive amounts of broadcasts being forwarded by the bridge can lead to a **broadcast storm**, resulting in degraded network performance, called a **network slowdown.**

The MAC address entries stored in a bridge table are temporary. Each MAC address entry to the bridge table remains active as long as there is periodic data traffic activity from that host on its port. However, an entry into the table is deleted if the port becomes inactive. In other words, the entries stored into the table have a limited lifetime. An expiration timer will commence once the MAC address is entered into the bridge table. The lifetime for the entry is renewed by new data traffic by the computer, and the MAC address is reentered.

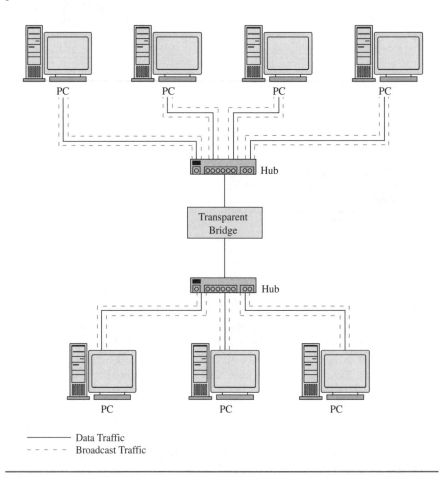

Data Traffic
- - - - - Broadcast Traffic

FIGURE 4-3   An example of using a bridge to isolate data traffic.

In a similar manner, all networking devices (for example, computers) contain an **ARP cache**, a temporary storage of MAC addresses recently contacted. This is also called the **ARP table**. The ARP cache holds the MAC address of a host, and this enables the message to be sent directly to the destination MAC address without the computer having to issue an ARP request for a MAC address. The ARP cache contents on a Windows computer can be viewed using the *arp -a* command while in the command prompt, as shown here:

Windows			Mac OS X
C:\arp -a			
Interface: 10.10.20.2 on Interface x1000002			jmac:~mymac$ arp –a
Internet Address	Physical Address	Type	C1.salsa.org (192.168.12.1) at
10.10.20.3	00-08-a3-a7-78-0c	dynamic	00-08-a3-a7-78-0c on en1
10.10.20.4	00-03-ba-04-ba-ef	dynamic	[ethernet]
			C3.salsa.org (192.168.12.1) at
			00-08-a3-a7-78-0c on en1
			[ethernet]

The ARP cache contents on a Mac OS X computer can be viewed using the *arp -a* command while in the terminal mode.

The following message is generated if all the ARP entries have expired:

```
c:\arp -a
No ARP Entries Found
```

The name for the type of bridge used to interconnect two LANs running the same type of protocol (for example, Ethernet) is a **transparent bridge**. Bridges are also used to interconnect two LANs that are operating two different networking protocols. For example, LAN A could be an Ethernet LAN and LAN B could be a token ring. This type of bridge is called a **translation bridge**. An example is provided in Figure 4-4. The bridge allows data from one LAN to be transferred to another. Also the MAC addressing information is standardized so the same address information is used regardless of the protocol.

Transparent Bridge
Interconnects two LANs running the same type of protocol

Translation Bridge
Used to interconnect two LANs that are operating two different networking protocols

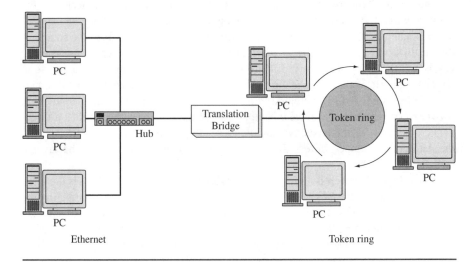

FIGURE 4-4 Using a translation bridge to interconnect an Ethernet and token-ring LAN.

A common application today using a bridge is interconnecting LANs using wireless technology. The use of wireless bridges in LANs is a popular choice for interconnecting the LANs when the cost of physically connecting them is prohibitive. Wireless technology and its LAN applications are presented in Chapter 11.

The use of a bridge is not as common as it used to be except for wireless network applications. There are new networking technologies available that provide similar capabilities to the bridge but that are much more powerful. However, the bridge still is useful and has several advantages. Table 4-3 provides a summary of the advantages and disadvantages of a networking bridge.

TABLE 4-3   Summary of the Advantages and Disadvantages of a Bridge for Interconnecting LANs

Advantages	Disadvantages
Easy to install	Works best in low-traffic areas
Does an excellent job of isolating the data traffic in two segments	Forwards broadcasts and is susceptible to broadcast storms
Relatively inexpensive	
Can be used to interconnect two LANs with different protocols and hardware	
Reduces collision domains (remember how the CSMA/CD protocol works)	

4-4   THE NETWORK SWITCH

The bridge provides a method for isolating the collision domains for interconnected LANs but lacks the capability to provide a direct data connection for the hosts. The bridge forwards the data traffic to all computers connected to its port. This was shown in Figure 4-3. The networking hub provides a technology for sharing access to the network with all computers connected to its ports in the LAN but lacks the capability to isolate the data traffic and provide a direct data connection from the source to the destination computer. The increase in the number of computers being used in LANs and the increased data traffic are making bridges and hubs of limited use in larger LANs. Basically, there is too much data traffic to be shared by the entire network. What is needed is a networking device that provides a direct data connection between communicating devices. Neither the bridge nor the hub provides a direct data connection for the hosts. A technology developed to improve the efficiency of the data networks and address the need for direct data connections is the layer 2 switch.

Layer 2 Switch
An improved network technology that provides a direct data connection for network devices in a LAN

The **layer 2 switch** is an improved network technology that addresses the issue of providing direct data connections, minimizing data collisions, and maximizing the use of a LAN's bandwidth; in other words, that improves the efficiency of the data transfer in the network. The switch operates at layer 2 of the OSI model and therefore uses the MAC or Ethernet address for making decisions for forwarding data packets. The switch monitors data traffic on its ports and collects MAC address information in the same way the bridge does to build a table of MAC addresses for the devices connected to its ports. The switch has multiple ports similar to the hub and can switch in a data connection from any port to any other port, similar to the bridge. This is why the switch is sometimes called a **multiport bridge**. The switch minimizes traffic congestion and isolates data traffic in the LAN. An example of a switch being used in a LAN is provided in Figure 4-5.

Multiport Bridge
Another name for a layer 2 switch

Figure 4-5 shows a switch being used in the LAN to interconnect the hosts. In this figure, the hub has been replaced with a switch. The change from a hub to a switch is relatively easy. The port connections are the same (RJ-45), and once the connections are changed and the device is powered on, the switch begins to make the direct data connections for multiple ports using layer 2 switching.

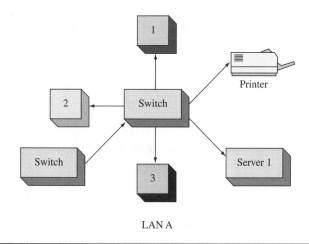

LAN A

FIGURE 4-5   A switch used to interconnect hosts in a LAN.

The LAN shown in Figure 4-6 contains 14 computers and 2 printers connected to 16 ports on the switch, configured in a star topology. If the computer connected to port 1 is printing a file on the laser printer (port 12), the switch will set up a direct connection between ports 1 and 12. The computer at port 14 could also be communicating with the computer at port 7 and the computer at port 6 could be printing a file on the color printer at port 16. The use of the switch enables simultaneous direct data connections for multiple pairs of hosts connected to the network. Each switch connection provides a link with minimal collisions and therefore maximum use of the LAN's bandwidth. A link with minimal collisions is possible since only the two computers that established the link will be communicating over the channel. Recall that in the star topology each host has a direct connection to the switch. Therefore, when the link is established between the two hosts, their link is isolated from any other data traffic. However, the exception to this is when broadcast or **multicast** messages are sent in the LAN. In the case of a broadcast message, the message is sent to all devices connected to the LAN. A multicast message is sent to a specific group of hosts on the network.

Multicast
Messages are sent to a specific group of hosts on the network

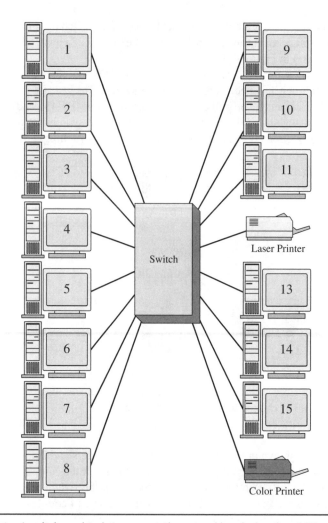

FIGURE 4-6   A switch used to interconnect the networking devices in a LAN.

Hub–Switch Comparison

An experiment was set up to test the data handling characteristics of a hub and a switch given the same input instructions. The objective of this experiment was to show that data traffic is isolated with a switch but not with a hub. For this experiment, a LAN using a hub and a LAN using a switch were assembled. The LANs are shown in Figs. 4-7 (a) and (b). Each LAN contains four computers connected in a star topology. The computers are marked 1–4 for reference. The IP addresses are listed for each host.

The Hub Experimental Results In this experiment, computer 1 pinged computer 3. Computer 2 was used to capture the LAN data traffic using the Finisar Surveyor Demo protocol analyzer software. What are the expected results? Remember, a hub is a multiport repeater, and all data traffic input to the hub is passed on to all hosts connected to its ports. See the Ping Command Review box for a brief review of the use of the ***ping*** command.

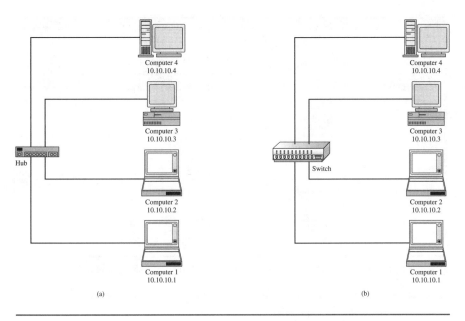

FIGURE 4-7   (a) The LAN experiment with a HUB; (b) the LAN experiment with a switch.

PING COMMAND REVIEW   The ***ping*** command is used to verify that a network connection exists between two computers. The command format for ***ping*** is

```
ping [ip address] {for this example ping 10.10.10.3}
```

Once a link is established between the two computers, a series of echo requests and echo replies are issued by the networking devices to test the time it takes for data to pass through the link. The protocol used by the ***ping*** command is ICMP, the Internet Connection Message Protocol.

The ***ping*** command is issued to an IP address; however, delivery of this command to the computer designated by the IP address requires that a MAC address be identified for final delivery. The computer issuing the ***ping*** may not know the MAC address of the computer holding the identified IP address (no entry in the ARP cache table); therefore, an ARP request is issued. An ARP request is broadcast to all computers connected in the LAN. The computer that holds the IP address replies with its MAC address, and a direct line of communications is then established.

The data traffic collected by computer 2 when computer 1 pinged computer 3 is provided in Figure 4-8. The first line of the captured data shows the ARP request asking who has the IP address 10.10.10.3. The second line of the captured data shows the reply from 10.10.10.3 with the MAC address of 00-B0-D0-25-BF-48. The next eight lines in the captured data are the series of four echo requests and replies associated with a ping request. Even though computer 2 was not being pinged or replying to the ARP request, the data traffic was still present on computer 2's hub port. The echo reply is from a Dell network interface card with the last six characters of the MAC address of 25-BF-48. The echo request is coming from a computer with 13-99-2E as the last six hex characters of its MAC address.

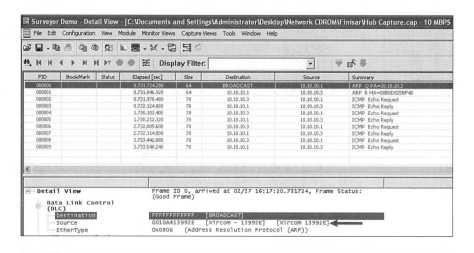

FIGURE 4-8 The captured data traffic by computer 2 for the LAN [Figure 4-7 (a)] using a hub.

The Switch Experimental Results The same experiment was repeated for the LAN shown in Figure 4-7 (b), this time using a switch to interconnect the computers instead of a hub. This network consists of four computers connected in a star topology using a switch at the center of the network. The ***ping*** command was sent from computer 1 to computer 3, ***ping 10.10.10.3***. The ARP cache for computer 1 is empty; therefore, the MAC address for computer 3 is not known by computer 1. An ARP request is issued by computer 1, and computer 3 replies. The series of echo requests and echo replies follow; however, the data traffic captured by computer 2 (Figure 4-9), shows the ARP request asking who has the IP address 10.10.10.3. This is the last of the data communications between computers 1 and 3 seen by computer 2. A direct line of communication between computers 1 and 3 is established by the switch that prevents computer 2 from seeing the data traffic from computers 1 and 3. The only data traffic seen by computer 2 in this process was the broadcast of the ARP request. This is true for any other hosts in the LAN. The results of this experiment show that the use of the switch substantially reduces data traffic in the LAN, particularly unnecessary data traffic. The experiment shows that the broadcast associated with an ARP request is seen by all computers but not the ARP replies in a LAN using a switch. This is because a direct data connection is established between the two hosts. This experiment used pings and ARPs; however, this same advantage of using a switch is true when transferring files, image downloads, file printing, and so on. The data traffic is isolated from other computers on the LAN. Remember, the switch uses MAC addresses to establish what computers are connected to its ports. The switch then extracts the destination MAC address from the Ethernet data packets to determine what port to switch the data to.

FIGURE 4-9 The data traffic captured by computer 2 for the LAN [Figure 4-7 (b)] using a switch.

Managed Switches

A **managed switch** is simply a network switch that allows the network administrator to monitor, configure, and manage certain network features such as what computers are allowed to access the LAN via the switch. Access to the management features for the switch is password protected so that only the network administrators can gain entry. The following information describes some of the features of the managed interface for a Cisco Catalyst 2900 series switch established using the **Cisco Network Assistant (CNA)**. This software can be downloaded from Cisco and provides an easy way to manage the features of the Cisco switches. *(Note:* The download requires that you have set-up a Cisco user account and password. The Cisco Network Assistant provides for a centralized mode for completing various network administration tasks for switches, routers, and wireless networking equipment.)

The start-up menu for a Cisco Catalyst 2960 switch obtained via the Cisco Network Assistant (CNA) is provided in Figure 4-10. The image is showing the current setup for the switch. The assigned IP address for the switch is 192.168.1.1, and a router and a switch are interconnected with the switch. The steps for setting the IP address for an interface on the switch are presented later in this section.

Managed Switch
Allows the network administrator to monitor, configure, and manage select network features

Cisco Network Assistant (CNA)
A management software tool from Cisco that simplifies switch configuration and troubleshooting.

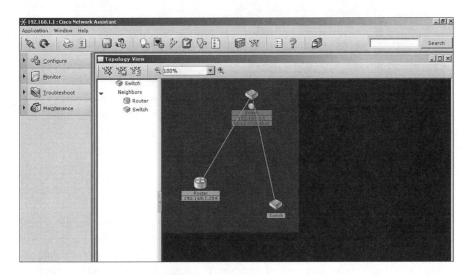

FIGURE 4-10 The start-up menu of a Cisco Catalyst switch using the Cisco Network Administrator software.

The current connections to the ports on the switch can be viewed by clicking the stacked switch icon at the top of the screen as shown in Figure 4-11. The image of the switch port connections shows ports 1, 2, and 3 are brighter, indicating that there are networking devices connected to the ports. The MAC addresses of the devices connected to the switch ports can be displayed by clicking the MAC address button under the Configure button as shown in Figure 4-12. There are four MAC addresses assigned to port 1, one MAC address assigned to port 2, and one MAC address assigned to port 3. Multiple networking devices can be connected to a port if the devices are first connected to another switch or hub and the output of the switch or hub is connected to one switch port. An example showing four devices connected through a hub to port 1 on the switch is shown in Figure 4-13. The output interface information for the MAC Addresses table shows the following information in Figure 4-12:

> FastEthernet 0/1
> FastEthernet 0/2
> FastEthernet 0/3

Notice that the Dynamic Address tab is highlighted. This indicates that this is a listing of the MAC addresses that have been assigned dynamically. **Dynamic assignment** means that the MAC address was assigned to a port when a host was connected. There is also a tab for Static Addresses. A static MAC address indicates that the MAC address has been manually assigned to an interface, and the port assignment does not expire. The Secure tab shows what switch ports have been secured. This means that a MAC address has been assigned to a port, and the port will automatically disable itself if a device with a different MAC address connects to the secured port.

FIGURE 4-11 The highlighted ports showing the current connections and the location of the stacked switches icon.

The FastEthernet 0/1, FastEthernet 0/2, FastEthernet 0/3 notation indicates the [Interface Type Slot#/Interface#] on the switch, and FastEthernet indicates that this interface supports 100 Mbps and 10 Mbps data rate connections.

The "Aging Time" is listed to be 300 seconds. **Aging time** is the length of time a MAC address remains assigned to a port. The assignment of the MAC address will be removed if there is no data activity within this time. If the computer with the assigned MAC address initiates new data activity, the aging time counter is restarted, and the MAC address remains assigned to the port. The management window shows a switch setting for enabling "Aging." This switch is used to turn off the aging counter so that a MAC address assignment on a port never expires.

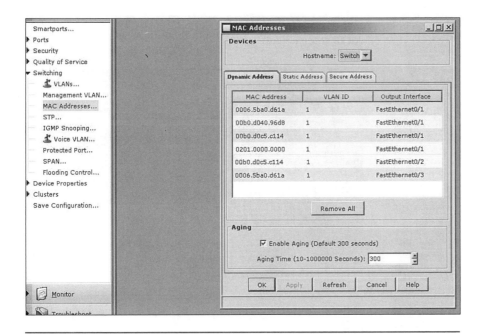

FIGURE 4-12   The menu listing the MAC addresses currently connected to the switch.

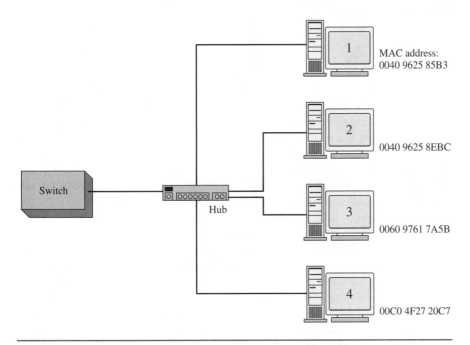

FIGURE 4-13   An example of a hub connected to a switch port, with four computers connected to the hub.

The IP address on a switch interface can be configured using the Cisco Network Assistant software by clicking **Configure—Device Properties—IP Addresses**. This opens the IP Addresses menu shown in Figure 4-14. Click the area where the IP address should be entered. This opens a text box for entering the IP address. Enter the IP address and click **OK** to save the IP address.

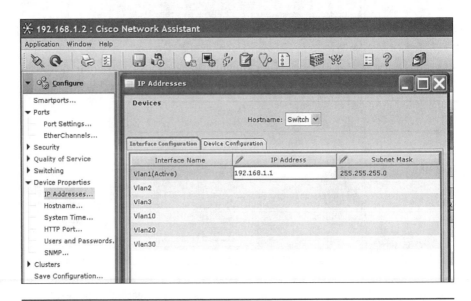

FIGURE 4-14 Configuring an IP address on an interface.

Isolating the Collision Domains
Breaking the network into segments where a segment is a portion of the network where the data traffic from one part of the network is isolated from the other networking devices

The benefits of a using a network switch are many in a modern computer network. These benefits include less network congestion, faster data transfers, and excellent manageability. It has been shown that a network switch can be used to replace the network hub, and the advantage is data traffic within a LAN is isolated. The term for this is **isolating the collision domains**, which is breaking the network into segments. A segment is a portion of the network where the data traffic from one part of the network is isolated from the other networking devices. A direct benefit of isolating collision domains is there will be an increase in the data transfer speed and throughput. This is due to the fact that the LAN bandwidth is not being shared, and chances of data collisions are minimized. As a result, the LAN will exhibit faster data transfers, and latency within the LAN will be significantly reduced. Reduced latency means that the data packets will arrive at the destination more quickly.

Content Addressable Memory (CAM)
A table of MAC addresses and port mapping used by the switch to identify connected networking devices

Switches learn the MAC addresses of the connected networking by extracting the MAC address information from the headers of Ethernet data packet headers of transmitted data packets (refer back to Figure 1-6). The switch will map the extracted MAC address to the port where the data packet came in. This information is stored in **Content Addressable Memory (CAM)**. CAM is a table of MAC address and port mapping used by the switch to identify connected networking devices. The extracted MAC addresses are then used by the switch to map a direct communication between two network devices connected to its ports. The MAC address and port information remain in CAM as long as the device connected to the switch port remains active. A time-stamp establishes the time when the mapping of the MAC address to a switch port is established. However, switches limit the amount of time address and port information are stored in CAM. This is called aging time. The mapping information will be deleted from the switch's CAM if there is no activity during this set time. This technique keeps the mapping information stored in CAM up to date.

What happens if the destination MAC address is not stored in CAM? In this case, the packet is transmitted out all switch ports except for the port where the packet was received. This is called **flooding**.

It has been shown that switches minimize the collision domain due to the fact that a direct switch connection is made between networking devices. However, it is important to remember that switches do not reduce the broadcast domain. In a **broadcast domain**, any network broadcast sent over the network will be seen by all networking devices in the same network. Broadcasts within a LAN will be passed by switches. Refer back to the discussion of Figure 4-8 and 4-9 for an example.

There are two modes used in a switch to forward frames. These are **store-and-forward** and **cut-through**.

- **Store-and-Forward:** In this mode, the entire frame of data is received before any decision is made regarding forwarding the data packet to its destination. There is **switch latency** in this mode because the destination and source MAC addresses must be extracted from the packet, and the entire packet must be received before it is sent to the destination. The term **switch latency** is the length of time a data packet takes from the time it enters a switch until it exits. An advantage of the store-and-forward mode is that the switch checks the data packet for errors before it is sent on to the destination. A disadvantage is lengthy data packets will take a longer time before they exit the switch and are sent to the destination.
- **Cut-Through:** In this mode, the data packet is forwarded to the destination as soon as the destination MAC address has been read. This minimizes the switch latency; however, no error detection is provided by the switch. There are two forms of cut-through switching—Fast-Forward and Fragment Free.
    - **Fast-Forward:** This mode offers the minimum switch latency. The received data packet is sent to the destination as soon as the destination MAC address is extracted.
    - **Fragment-Free:** In this mode, fragment collisions are filtered out by the switch. **Fragment-collisions** are collisions that occur within the first 64 bytes of the data packet. Recall from Chapter 1, Table 1-1 that the minimum Ethernet data packet size is 64 bytes. The collisions create packets smaller than 64 bytes, which are discarded. Latency is measured from the time the first bit is received until it is transmitted.
- **Adaptive Cut-Through:** This is a combination of the store-and-forward mode and cut-through. The cut-through mode is used until an **error threshold** (errors in the data packets) has been exceeded. The switch mode changes from cut-through to store-and-forward after the error threshold has been exceeded.

Multilayer Switches

Newer switch technologies are available to help further improve the performance of computer networks. The term used to describe these switches is **multilayer switches** (**MLS**). An example is a layer 3 switch. Layer 3 switches still work at layer 2 but additionally work at the network layer (layer 3) of the OSI model and use IP addressing for making decisions to route a data packet in the best direction. The major difference is that the packet switching in basic routers is handled by a programmed microprocessor. The layer 3 switch uses ASICs (application specific integrated circuits) hardware to handle the packet switching. The advantage of using hardware to

Flooding
The term used to describe what happens when a switch doesn't have the destination MAC address stored in CAM

Broadcast Domain
Any network broadcast sent over the network will be seen by all networking devices in this domain

Store-and-Forward
The entire frame of data is received before any decision is made regarding forwarding the data packet to its destination

Cut-Through
The data packet is forwarded to the destination as soon as the destination MAC address has been read

Switch Latency
The length of time a data packet takes from the time it enters a switch until it exits

Error Threshold
The point where the number of errors in the data packets has reached a threshold and the switch changes from the cut-through to the store-and-forward mode

Multilayer Switch (MLS)
Operates at layer 2 but functions at the higher layers

Wire Speed Routing
Data packets are processed
as fast as they arrive

handle the packet switching is a significant reduction in processing time (software versus hardware). In fact, the processing time of layer 3 switches can be as fast as the input data rate. This is called **wire speed routing**, where the data packets are processed as fast as they are arriving. Multilayer switches can also work at the upper layers of the OSI model. An example is a layer 4 switch that processes data packets at the transport layer of the OSI model.

4-5 THE ROUTER

Network Address
Another name for the layer 3
address

Logical Address
Describes the IP address
location of the network and
the address location of the
host in the network

The router is the most powerful networking device used today to interconnect LANs. The router is a layer 3 device in the OSI model, which means the router uses the **network address** (layer 3 addressing) to make routing decisions regarding forwarding data packets. Remember, the OSI model separates network responsibilities into different layers. In the OSI model, the layer 3 or network layer responsibilities include handling of the network address. The network address is also called a *logical address,* rather than being a physical address such as the MAC address. The *physical address* is the hardware or MAC address embedded into the network interface card. The **logical address** describes the IP address location of the network and the address location of the host in the network.

Essentially, the router is configured to know how to route data packets entering or exiting the LAN. This differs from the bridge and the layer 2 switch, which use the Ethernet address for making decisions regarding forwarding data packets and only know how to forward data to hosts physically connected to their ports.

Routers are used to interconnect LANs in a campus network. Routers can be used to interconnect networks that use the same protocol (e.g., Ethernet), or they can be used to interconnect LANs that are using different layer 2 technologies such as an Ethernet and token ring. Routers also make it possible to interconnect to LANs around the country and the world and interconnect to many different networking protocols.

Router Interface
The physical connection
where the router connects to
the network

Routers have multiple port connections for connecting to the LANs, and by definition a router must have a minimum of three ports. The common symbol used to represent a router in a networking drawing is provided in Figure 4-15. The arrows pointing in and out indicate that data enters and exits the routers through multiple ports. The router ports are *bidirectional,* meaning that data can enter and exit the same router port. Often the router ports are called the **router interface**, the physical connection where the router connects to the network.

FIGURE 4-15   The network symbol for a router.

The Router Interface: Cisco 2800 Series

Figure 4-16 shows the rear panel view (interface side) of a Cisco 2800 series router.

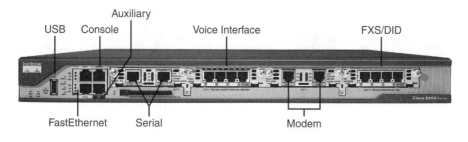

FIGURE 4-16 The rear panel view of a Cisco 2800 series router.

The following describes the function of each interface.

- **USB Interface:** The USB ports are used for storage and security support.
- **FastEthernet Ports:** FE0/0: Fast Ethernet (10/100 Mbps) and FE0/1: Fast Ethernet (10/100 Mbps).
- **Console Input:** This input provides an RS-232 serial communications link into the router for initial router configuration. A special cable, called a *console cable,* is used to connect the console input to the serial port on a computer. The console cable can have RJ-45 plugs on each end and requires the use of an RJ-45 to DB9 adapter for connecting to the computer's COM1 or COM2 serial port. The console cable can also have an RJ-45 connector on one end and an integrated DB9 connector on the other end.
- **Auxiliary Input:** This input is used to connect a dial-in modem into the router. The auxiliary port provides an alternate way to remotely log into the router if the network is down. This port also uses an RJ-45 connection.
- **Serial Interface:** CTRLR T1 1 and CTRLR T1 0
  This is a serial connection and it has a built-in CSU/DSU. This interface is used to provide a T1 connection to the communications carrier. (*Note:* The CSU/DSU function is presented in Chapter 8.) This type of connection (RJ-45) replaces the older cabling using V.35 cable (shown later in Figure 4-19). There are three LEDs on this interface:
    - **AL**—alarm
    - **LP**—loop
    - **CD**—Carrier Detect
- **Voice Interface Card (VIC2-4FXO):** This interface shows four phone line connections. This router can be programmed as a small PBX (Private Branch Exchange) for use in a small office. The PBX function is presented in Chapter 8.
- **WAN Interface Card (WIC2AM):** This interface has two RJ-11 jacks and has two V.90 analog internal modems. These modems can be used to handle both incoming and outgoing modem calls. This interface is listed as modem in Figure 4-16.
- **VIC-4FXS/DID:** This interface is a four-port FXS and DID voice/fax interface card. FXS is a Foreign Exchange Interface that connects directly to a standard telephone. DID is Direct Inward Dialing and is a feature that enables callers to directly call an extension on a PBX. This interface is listed as FXS/DID in Figure 4-16.

The Router Interface—Cisco 2600 Series

Figure 4-17 shows the rear panel view (interface side) of a Cisco 2600 series router.

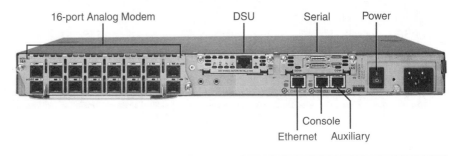

FIGURE 4-17 The rear panel view of a Cisco 2600 series router.

The following describes the function of each interface to the network:

- **Power On/Off:** Turns on/off electrical power to the router.
- **Auxiliary Input:** Used to connect a dial-in modem into the router. The auxiliary port provides an alternate way to remotely log into the router if the network is down. This port also uses an RJ-45 connection.
- **Console Input:** Provides an RS-232 serial communications link into the router for initial router configuration. A special cable, called a *console cable*, is used to connect the console input to the serial port on a computer. The console cable uses RJ-45 plugs on each end and requires the use of an RJ-45 to DB9 adapter for connecting to the COM1 or COM2 serial port.
- **Serial Ports:** Provides a serial data communication link into and out of the router, using V.35 serial interface cables.
- **DSU Port:** This T1 controller port connection is used to make the serial connection to Telco. This module has a built-in CSU/DSU module. There are five LEDs next to the RJ45 jack. These LEDs are for the following:

    TD—Transmit Data

    LP—Loop

    RD—Receive Data

    CD—Carrier Detect

    AL—Alarm

- **Ethernet Port:** This connection provides a 10/100 Mbps Ethernet data link.
- **Analog Modem Ports:** This router has a 16-port analog network module.

The Router Interface—Cisco 2500 Series

Figure 4-18 shows the rear panel view (interface side) of a Cisco 2500 series router.

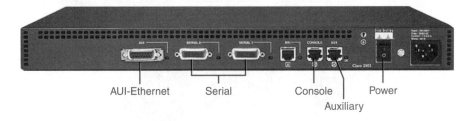

AUI-Ethernet   Serial   Console   Power
                          Auxiliary

FIGURE 4-18   The rear panel view of a Cisco 2500 series router.

The following describes the function of each interface to the network.

- **Power On/Off:** Turns on/off electrical power to the router.
- **Auxiliary Input:** Used to connect a dial-in modem into the router. The auxiliary port provides an alternate way to remotely log into the router if the network is down. This port also uses an RJ-45 connection.
- **Console Input:** Provides an RS-232 serial communications link into the router for initial router configuration. A special cable, called a *console cable,* is used to connect the console input to the serial port on a computer. The console cable uses RJ-45 plugs on each end and requires the use of an RJ-45 to DB9 adapter for connecting to the COM1 or COM2 serial port.
- **Serial Ports:** Provides a serial data communication link into and out of the router, using V.35 serial interface cables. An example of a V.35 cable is shown in Figure 4-19.
- **AUI Port:** This is a 10 Mbps Ethernet port. AUI stands for "attachment unit interface."

A **media converter** is used to convert the 15-pin AUI port to the 8-pin RJ-45 connector. An example of an AUI to RJ-45 media converter is shown in Figure 4-20. Media converters are commonly used in computer networks to adapt layer 1 or physical layer technologies from one technology to another. For example:

AUI to twisted pair (RJ-45) AUI to fiber
RJ-45 to fiber

Power On/Off
Auxiliary Input
Console Input
Serial Ports
AUI Port

Media Converter
Used to adapt a layer 1
(physical layer) technology
to another layer 1
technology

FIGURE 4-19   An example of a Cisco V.35 DTE cable (courtesy of StarTech.com).

FIGURE 4-20   A CentreCom™ 210TS AUI to RJ-45 media converter.

Figure 4-21 shows a Cisco 7200 series router, which provides adaptable interfaces for connecting to many physical layer technologies such as FastEthernet, gigabit Ethernet, ATM, and FDDI.

FIGURE 4-21   A Cisco 7200 series router (courtesy of Cisco Systems).

4-6 INTERCONNECTING LANS WITH THE ROUTER

The previous section introduced the function of a router in a network. A router routes data based on the destination network address or logical address rather than the physical address used by layer 2 devices, such as the switch and the bridge. Information exchanged with bridges and layer 2 switches requires that the MAC address for the hosts be known. Routed networks such as most enterprise and campus networks use IP addressing for managing the data movement. **Enterprise network** is a term used to describe the network used by a large company. The use of the network or logical address on computers allows the information to be sent from a LAN to a destination without requiring that the computer know the MAC address of the destination computer. Remember, delivery of data packets is based on knowing the MAC address of the destination.

An overview of the router interface was presented in section 4-5. The router interface provides a way to access the router for configuration either locally or remotely. Interfaces are provided for making serial connections to the router and to other devices that require a serial communications link. For example, interfaces to wide area networking devices require a serial interface. RJ-45 ports are provided on the router interface for connecting the router to a LAN. Older routers can require the use of an AUI port to establish an Ethernet connection to a UTP cable. This port provides a 10 Mbps data connection to Ethernet (10 Mbps) networks. The RJ-45 connection is used to connect both Ethernet (10 Mbps), FastEthernet (100 Mbps), Gigabit Ethernet (1000 Mbps), and 10 Gigabit Ethernet (10G) to a LAN. The RJ-45 connection can also support gigabit and 10G Ethernet, but high-speed data networks can also use a fiber connection.

This section introduces the information needed to design, manage, and configure campus networks. An example of a small interconnected LAN is provided in Figure 4-22. This example shows four Ethernet LANs interconnected using three routers. The LANs are configured in a star topology using switches at the center of the LAN. The LANs are labeled LAN A, LAN B, LAN C, and LAN D. The routers are labeled RouterA, RouterB, and RouterC (router naming protocols are discussed in Chapter 6). Connection of the routers to the LANs is provided by the router's **FastEthernet port (FA0/0, FA0/1, FA0/2, . . .)**. Look for the FA label in Figure 4-22.

The interconnections for the routers and the LANs are summarized as follows:

- **RouterA** connects directly to the LAN A switch via FastEthernet port FA0/0. RouterA also connects directly to RouterB via the FastEthernet port FA0/1 and connects to RouterC via FastEthernet port FA0/2.
- **RouterB** connects directly to the LAN B switch via FastEthernet port FA0/0. RouterB connects to the LAN C switch via FastEthernet port FA0/1. RouterB connects directly to RouterA via FastEthernet port FA0/2 and connects to RouterC via FastEthernet port FA0/3.
- **RouterC** connects directly to the LAN D switch via the FastEthernet port FA0/0. Connection to RouterB is provided via Ethernet port FA0/1. RouterC connects to RouterA via FastEthernet port FA0/2.

The **serial ports (S0/0, S0/1, S0/2, . . .)** are not being used to interconnect the routers in this example campus network. The serial interfaces are typically used to interconnect LANs that connect through a data communications carrier such as a telephone company (Telco).

Enterprise Network
Term used to describe the network used by a large company

FastEthernet Port (FA0/0, FA0/1, FA0/2, . . .)
Naming of the FastEthernet ports on the router

Serial Port (S0/0, S0/1, S0/2, . . .)
Naming of the serial ports on the router

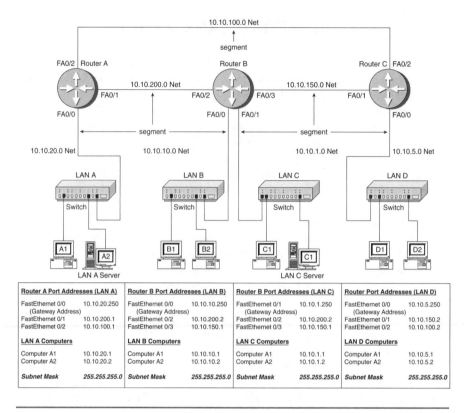

Router A Port Addresses (LAN A)		Router B Port Addresses (LAN B)		Router B Port Addresses (LAN C)		Router Port Addresses (LAN D)	
FastEthernet 0/0 (Gateway Address)	10.10.20.250	FastEthernet 0/0 (Gateway Address)	10.10.10.250	FastEthernet 0/1 (Gateway Address)	10.10.1.250	FastEthernet 0/0 (Gateway Address)	10.10.5.250
FastEthernet 0/1	10.10.200.1	FastEthernet 0/2	10.10.200.2	FastEthernet 0/2	10.10.200.2	FastEthernet 0/1	10.10.150.2
FastEthernet 0/2	10.10.100.1	FastEthernet 0/3	10.10.150.1	FastEthernet 0/3	10.10.150.1	FastEthernet 0/2	10.10.100.2
LAN A Computers		**LAN B Computers**		**LAN C Computers**		**LAN D Computers**	
Computer A1	10.10.20.1	Computer A1	10.10.10.1	Computer A1	10.10.1.1	Computer A1	10.10.5.1
Computer A2	10.10.20.2	Computer A2	10.10.10.2	Computer A2	10.10.1.2	Computer A2	10.10.5.2
Subnet Mask	*255.255.255.0*	*Subnet Mask*	*255.255.255.0*	*Subnet Mask*	*255.255.255.0*	*Subnet Mask*	*255.255.255.0*

FIGURE 4-22 A small interconnected LAN.

The network configuration provided in Figure 4-22 enables data packets to be sent and received from any host on the network once the routers in the network have been properly configured. For example, computer A1 in LAN A could be sending data to computer D1 in LAN D. This requires that the IP address for computer D1 is known by the user sending the data from computer A1. The data from computer A1 will first travel to the switch where the data is passed to RouterA via the FA0/0 FastEthernet data port. RouterA will examine the network address of the data packet and use configured routing instructions stored in routing tables to decide where to forward the data. RouterA determines that an available path to RouterC is via the FA0/2 FastEthernet port connection. The data is then sent directly to RouterC. RouterC determines that the data packet should be forwarded to the FA0/0 port to reach computer D1 in LAN D. The data is then sent to D1. Alternately, RouterA could have sent the data to RouterC through RouterB via Router A's FA0/1 FastEthernet port. Path selection for data packets is examined in Chapter 7.

Routing Table
Keeps track of the routes to use for forwarding data to its destination

Delivery of the information over the network was made possible by the use of an IP address and **routing tables**. Routing tables keep track of the routes used for forwarding data to its destination. RouterA used its routing table to determine a network data path so computer A1's data could reach computer D1 in LAN D. RouterA determines that a path to the network where computer D1 is located can be obtained via RouterA's FA0/2 FastEthernet port to the FA0/2 FastEthernet port on RouterC. RouterC determines that computer D1 is on LAN D, which connects to RouterC's FA0/0 FastEthernet port. An ARP request is issued by RouterC to determine the MAC address of computer D1. The MAC address is then used for final delivery of the data to computer D1.

If RouterA determines that the network path to RouterC is down, RouterA can route the data packet to RouterC through RouterB. After RouterB receives the data packet from RouterA, it uses its routing tables to determine where to forward the data packet. RouterB determines that the data needs to be sent to RouterC, and it uses the FA0/3 FastEthernet port to forward the data.

Gateway Address

The term **gateway** is used to describe the address of the networking device that enables the hosts in a LAN to connect to networks and hosts outside the LAN. For example, for all hosts in LAN A, the gateway address will be 10.10.10.250. This address is configured on the host computer. Any IP packets with a destination outside the LAN will be sent to the gateway address.

Network Segments

The *network segment* defines the networking link between two LANs. There is a segment associated with each connection of an internetworking device (e.g., router–hub, router–switch, router–router). For example, the IP address for the network segment connecting LAN A to the router is 10.10.20.0. All hosts connected to this segment must contain a 10.10.20.x because a subnet mask of 255.255.255.0 is being used. Subnet masking is fully explained in Chapter 5.

Routers use the information about the network segments to determine where to forward data packets. For example, the network segments that connect to RouterA include

> 10.10.20.0
> 10.10.200.0
> 10.10.100.0

The computers in LAN A will have a 10.10.20.x address. All the computers in this network must contain a 10.10.20.x IP address. For example, computer A1 in LAN A will have the assigned IP address of 10.10.20.1 and a gateway address of 10.10.20.250. The computers in LAN B are located in the 10.10.10.0 network. This means that all the computers in this network must contain a 10.10.10.x IP address. The *x* part of the IP address is assigned for each host. The gateway address for the hosts in LAN B is 10.10.10.250.

4-7 CONFIGURING THE NETWORK INTERFACE— AUTO-NEGOTIATION

Most modern networking internetworking technologies (for example, hubs, switches, bridges, routers) now incorporate the **auto-negotiation** protocol. The protocol enables the Ethernet equipment to automate many of the installation steps. This includes automatically configuring the operating speeds (e.g., 10/100/1000 Mbps) and the selection of full or half duplex operation for the data link. The auto-negotiation protocol is defined in the IEEE Ethernet standard 802.3x for FastEthernet.

The auto-negotiation protocol uses a **fast link pulse (FLP)** to carry the information between each end of a data link. A data link is shown in Figure 4-23. The data rate for the fast link pulses is 10 Mbps, the same as for 10BaseT. The link pulses were designed to operate over the limited bandwidth supported by CAT3 cabling. Therefore, even if a link is negotiated, there is no guarantee that the negotiated data rate will work over the link. Other tests on the cable link must be used to certify the cable can carry the negotiated data link configuration (see Chapter 2).

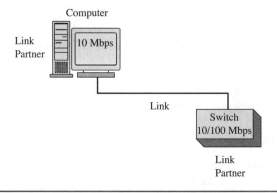

FIGURE 4-23   The two ends of a data link negotiating the operating parameters.

Auto-Negotiation Steps

Each link partner shares or advertises its data link capabilities with the other link partner. The two link partners then use the advertised capabilities to establish the fastest possible data link rate for both links. In the example of the link partners shown in Figure 4-23, computer 1 advertises that its interface supports 10 Mbps. The switch advertises that it supports both 10 and 100 Mbps. The network interfaces on each link partner are set for auto-negotiation; therefore, the 10 Mbps operating mode is selected. This is the fastest data rate that can be used in this data link. The data rate is limited by the 10 Mbps capabilities of the computer's network interface.

Note: Auto-negotiation is established when an Ethernet link is established. The link information is only sent one time, when the link is established. The negotiated link configuration will remain until the link is broken or the interfaces are reconfigured.

Full Duplex/Half Duplex

Modern network interfaces for computer networks have the capability of running the data over the links in either full or half duplex mode. As noted previously, *full duplex* means that the communications device can transmit and receive at the same time. **Half duplex** means the communications device can transmit or receive but not at the same time.

In full duplex operation (10/100 Mbps), the media must have separate transmit and receive data paths. This is provided for in CAT6/5e/5 cable with pairs 1–2 (transmit) and pairs 3–6 (receive). Full duplex with gigabit and 10 gigabit data rates require the use of all four wire pairs (1–2, 3–6, 4–5, 7–8). An important note is that the full duplex mode in computer network links is only for point-to-point links. This means that there can only be two end stations on the link. The CSMA/CD protocol is turned off; therefore, there can't be another networking device competing for use of the link. An example of networking devices that can run full duplex are computers connected to a switch. The switch can be configured to run the full duplex mode. This also requires that each end station on the link must be configurable to run full duplex mode.

In half duplex operation, the link uses the CSMA/CD protocol. This means only one device talks at a time, and while the one device is talking, the other networking devices "listen" to the network traffic. Examples of networks configured for full and half duplex mode are shown in Figure 4-24 (a) and (b). In full duplex operation [Figure 4-24 (a)], CSMA/CD is turned off, and computers 1, 2, and the switch are transmitting and receiving at the same time. In half duplex mode [Figure 4-24 (b)], CSMA/CD is turned on, computer 1 is transmitting, and computer 2 is "listening" or receiving the data transmission.

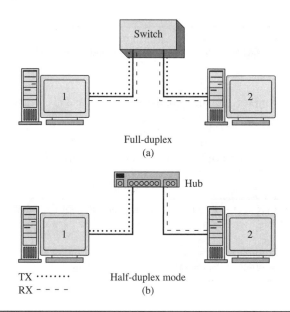

FIGURE 4-24   (a) Computer 1 transmits and receives at the same time; (b) computer 1 transmits; others listen.

An example of the port management features available with the Cisco switch using the Cisco Network Administrator software is provided in Figure 4-25 (a) and (b). The settings for the speed are shown in Figure 4-25 (a). An example of setting the switch for auto, half, and full-duplex are shown in Figure 4-25 (b). The auto setting is for auto-negotiate.

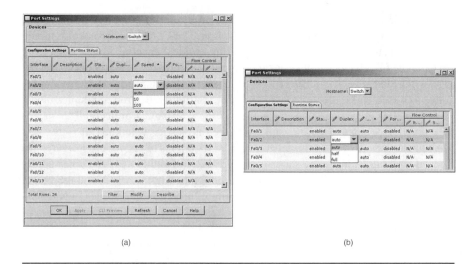

(a)   (b)

FIGURE 4-25   An example of the port management options available with a Cisco switch:
(a) 100 Mbps auto-negotiation; (b) 10 Mbps half/full duplex option.

Table 4-4 provides a summary of the advantages and disadvantages of the auto-negotiation protocol.

TABLE 4-4   Summary of the Auto-negotiation Protocol

Advantages	Disadvantages
Useful in LANs that have multiple users with multiple connection capabilities	Not recommended for fixed data links such as the backbone in a network
The auto-negotiation feature can maximize the data links' throughput	A failed negotiation on a functioning link can cause a link failure

Summary

This chapter has established how LANs are interconnected. The layers of the OSI model were presented. Examples of layer 1 (physical layer), layer 2 (data link layer) and layer 3 (network layer) were presented. The need for careful documentation was addressed in this chapter. The importance of this will become more relevant as the complexity in network topics increases from chapter to chapter. Internetworking hardware such as bridges, switches, and routers were discussed and examples of using these technologies presented.

A technique for internetworking the LANs using routers has been presented. In addition, the purpose of a router and its hardware interface has been defined. And the use of switches and hubs to connect to the routers has been demonstrated. The purpose of a gateway has been explained and demonstrated. The concept of a network segment has been examined.

The concepts the student should understand from Chapter 4 are the following:

- The layers of the OSI model and how a network administrator uses the layers to troubleshoot network problems
- How bridges are used to interconnect separate LANs
- How a switch is used in a network and why the switch improves network performance
- Understand and be able to identify the various connections on a the router interface
- How a router is used to interconnect LANs
- The purpose of a gateway in a computer network
- The concept of a network segment
- The concept of auto-negotiation

Questions and Problems

Section 4-2

1. What are the seven layers of the OSI model?
2. Which OSI layer is responsible for adding a header that includes routing information?
3. Which OSI layer is considered the media access control layer?
4. Which OSI layer combines messages or segments into packets?
5. Which OSI layer is responsible for the mechanical connection to the network?
6. The OSI layer responsible for data compression and encryption is which layer?
7. TCP functions at what layer of the OSI model?
8. HTTP functions at what layer of the OSI model?
9. IP and IPX are examples of protocols that operate in what layer of the OSI model?
10. The network interface card operates at what layer of the OSI model?
11. Why are the layers of the OSI model important to the network administrator?

Section 4-3

12. What is a *bridge*?
13. Define a *segment*.
14. What information is stored in a bridge table?
15. What is an *association* on a bridge, and how is it used?
16. Excessive amounts of broadcasts on a network are called a _____.
17. What command is used on a computer to view the contents of the ARP cache?
18. An empty ARP cache indicates what?
19. Why do entries into the bridging table have a limited lifetime?
20. Which of the following are advantages of using a bridge to interconnect LANs?
    a. Works best in low traffic areas
    b. Relatively inexpensive
    c. Can be used to route data traffic
    d. Easy to install
    e. Reduces collision domains

Section 4-4

21. The network switch operates at what layer of the OSI model?
22. Another name for a switch is
    a. Multiport repeater
    b. Multiport bridge
    c. Multiport router
    d. Multiport hub
23. How does a switch provide a link with minimal collisions?
24. The link for a switch connection is isolated from other data traffic except for what type of messages?
25. Explain what data traffic is sent across a network when a computer pings another computer. A hub is used to interconnect the computers.
26. Explain what data traffic is seen by computer 3 when computer 1 pings computer 2 in a LAN. A switch is used to interconnect the computers.
27. Explain the concept of *dynamic assignment* on a switch.
28. Define *aging time* on a switch.
29. Explain how a switch learns MAC addresses, and where does a switch store the address?
30. What happens if a MAC address is not stored in CAM on a switch?
31. What two modes are used by a switch to forward frames?
32. What switch mode offers minimum latency?
33. What is error threshold, and what mode is it associated with?
34. Explain the difference in store-and-forward and the cut-through mode on a switch.
35. How does a layer 3 switch differ from a layer 2 switch?
36. What is meant by the term wire-speed routing?

Section 4-5

37. A router uses the network address on a data packet for what purpose?
38. What is the *logical address*?

39. The physical connection where a router connects to the network is called the
    a. Router port
    b. Network port
    c. Network interface
    d. Router interface
40. The connection to the router's console input is typically which of the following?
    a. RS-232
    b. RJ-45
    c. DB9
    d. RJ-11
41. AUI stands for
    a. Auxiliary Unit Input
    b. Attachment Unit Interconnect
    c. Auxiliary Unit Interface
    d. Attachment Unit Interface
42. The AUI port on a router connects to what networking protocol?
    a. 100BaseT
    b. 10BaseT
    c. Token ring
    d. Ethernet

Section 4-6

43. Define enterprise network.
44. The router interface most commonly used to interconnect LANs in a campus network is
    a. Serial
    b. Console port
    c. Ethernet
    d. ATM
45. Serial interfaces on a router are typically used to
    a. Interconnect routers
    b. Interconnect hubs
    c. Connect to communication carriers
    d. Connect to auxiliary ports
46. The designation E0 indicates
    a. Ethernet port 0
    b. Ethernet input
    c. External port 0
    d. Exit port 0
47. Routing tables on a router keep track of
    a. Port assignments
    b. MAC address assignments
    c. Gateway addresses of LANs
    d. Routes to use for forwarding data to its destination

48. The convention used for naming of the serial port 0 on a router is
    a. S0
    b. System 0
    c. Serial interface 0
    d. Serial AUI 0
49. Define the term gateway.

Section 4-7

50. What is the purpose of the fast link pulse?
51. Define *full duplex.*
52. Define *half duplex.*
53. Which of the following is a disadvantage of the auto-negotiation protocol?
    a. Only useful in LANs that have multiple connection capabilities
    b. A failed negotiation on a functioning link can cause a link failure
    c. Recommended for use in critical network data paths
    d. Works at 10 Mbps

Critical Thinking

54. Describe how a network administrator uses the OSI model to isolate a network problem.
55. Why is auto-negotiation not recommended for use in critical network data paths?

5

CHAPTER

TCP/IP

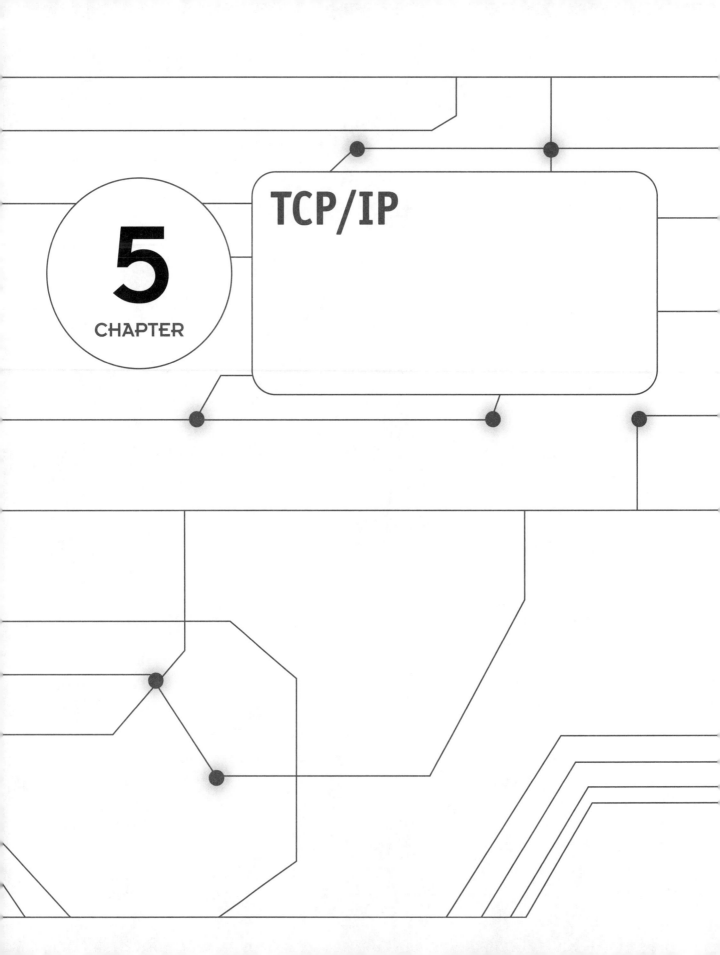

5-1   Introduction
5-2   The TCP/IP Layers
5-3   Number Conversion
5-4   IPv4 Addressing
5-5   Subnet Masks
5-6   CIDR Blocks

5-7   IPv6 Addressing
5-8   Analyzing Computer Networks—FTP
      Data Packets
Summary
Questions and Problems

OBJECTIVES

- Develop an understanding of the four layers of the TCP/IP model
- Define how a TCP connection is established, maintained, and terminated
- Investigate the properties of the UDP connectionless protocol
- Define the five classes of IPv4 addresses
- Investigate the properties of basic number conversion

- Define the purpose of subnet masking
- Investigate the implementation of CIDR blocks and supernetting
- Apply subnet masking concepts to allocate space for hosts in a subnet
- Use a protocol analyzer to analyze TCP data packets
- Define the structure of IPv6
- Analyze TCP data packets

KEY TERMS

NCP
ARPAnet
well-known ports
ICANN
transport layer protocols
TCP
connection-oriented
protocol
SYN, SYN ACK, ACK
UDP
Internet layer
IP (Internet Protocol)
ARP

IGMP
multicasting
multicast address
network interface layer
hex
IPv4
class A, B, C, D, and E
non-Internet routable IP
addresses
ARIN
subnet mask
classful
supernetting

CIDR
prefix length notation
CIDR block
supernets
IPv6
IPng
full IPv6 address
unicast address
multicast address
anycast address
6to4 prefix

FTP

5-1 INTRODUCTION

Transmission Control Protocol/Internet Protocol (TCP/IP) is the protocol suite used for communications between hosts in most local networks and on the Internet. TCP/IP can be used to enable network communications in LANs, campus networks, and wide area networks as long as the hosts support the protocol. TCP/IP is widely supported and is included in operating systems such as Windows 9x, NT, 2K, XP, Vista, Mac OS, Linux, and Unix.

TCP/IP was developed by the Defense Advanced Research Projects Agency (DARPA) to provide a way to network the computers of government researchers. The DARPA-funded initiative forced the use of a standard networking protocol by all defense contractors.

NCP
Network Control Protocol

ARPAnet
Advanced Research Projects
Agency network

The transmission control protocol was first proposed in 1974 in a paper by Vint Cerf and Bob Kahn. The suite of protocols called TCP/IP was introduced in 1978. In 1983, TCP/IP replaced the network control protocol (**NCP**) as the standard networking protocol used by the Advanced Research Projects Agency network (**ARPAnet**), considered the predecessor to today's Internet.

This chapter examines the fundamentals of the TCP/IP protocol suite. The relationship of the TCP/IP model to the OSI model is presented in section 5-2. The layers of the TCP/IP protocol are examined: the application layer, the transport layer, the Internet layer, and the network interface layer. Section 5-3 contains a discussion on numbering systems used in TCP/IP networks, including examples of converting decimal, hexadecimal, and binary numbers. The fundamentals of IP addressing are reintroduced in section 5-4. (The concept of IP addressing was first introduced in Chapter 1, "Introduction to Computer Networks.") This section examines the 32-bit structure of IPv4 addressing, the current version used in the Internet. This section goes into detail about the role and features of IP addressing in computer networks.

The concept of subnet masking is examined in section 5-5. This section presents many examples of calculating and applying subnet masks to networks. The material presented provides the student with the knowledge base to master subnet masking–related concepts that are presented later in the text. The fundamentals of CIDR blocks and supernetting are examined in section 5-6. An overview of the new IP addressing standard, IPv6, appears in section 5-7. The chapter concludes with examples of using the Surveyor Demo software to capture and analyze TCP/IP data traffic.

5-2 THE TCP/IP LAYERS

In this section we examine the four layers of the TCP/IP model: application, transport, Internet, and network interface. Each of these layers and their purpose are defined in Table 5-1. The TCP/IP protocol was established in 1978, prior to the final release of the OSI model (see Chapter 4); however, the four layers of the TCP/IP model do correlate with the seven layers of the OSI model, as shown in Figure 5-1.

TABLE 5-1   The Four Layers of the TCP/IP Model

Layer	Purpose of the Layer
Application layer	Defines the applications used to process requests and what ports and sockets are used
Transport layer	Defines the type of connection established between hosts and how acknowledgements are sent
Internet layer	Defines the protocols used for addressing and routing the data packets
Network interface layer	Defines how the host connects to the network

OSI Model	TCP/IP Model	TCP/IP Protocol Suite
Application Presentation Session	Application	Telnet, FTP, SMTP, DNS, SNMP
Transport	Transport	TCP, UDP
Network	Internet	IP, ICMP, ARP
Data Link Physical	Network Interface	Ethernet, ATM, Token Ring, Frame Relay

FIGURE 5-1   The layers of the TCP/IP model and their relationship to the OSI model.

The Application Layer

The top level of the TCP/IP stack is the *application* layer. This layer is used to process requests from hosts and to make sure a connection is made to an appropriate port. A *port* is basically an address used to direct data to the proper destination application.

There are 65,536 possible TCP ports. Ports 1 to 1023 are called **well-known ports** or *reserved* ports. These ports are reserved by **ICANN** (Internet Corporation for Assigned Names and Numbers). Ports 1024–49151 are called *registered* ports and are registered with ICANN. Ports 49152–65535 are called *dynamic* or *private* ports. Table 5-2 summarizes port numbers.

Well-known Ports
Ports reserved by ICANN

ICANN
Internet Corporation for Assigned Names and Numbers

TABLE 5-2   Port Number Assignments

Port Numbers	Description
1 to 1023	The "well-known" ports
1024 to 49,151	Registered ports
49,152 to 65,535	Private ports

Examples of well-known ports include HTTP (port 80), HTTPS (port 443), and SSH (port 22). Applications use these port numbers when communicating with another application. An example of this is shown in Figure 5-2. Host B is passing to Host A data that is destined for port 80 (HTTP). HTTP is the HyperText Transfer Protocol, used for transferring nonsecure Web-based documents to a Web browser such as Netscape or Internet Explorer. Host A receives the packet and passes the application up to the port 80 application. Table 5-3 lists some popular applications and their port numbers for TCP/IP. This list includes FTP, SSH, SMTP, DNS, DHCP, HTTP, and HTTPS.

FIGURE 5-2   An example of two hosts connected for a TCP transmission.

TABLE 5-3   Common Applications and Their Port Numbers

Port Number	Application	Description
20, 21	FTP	File Transfer Protocol
22	SSH	Secure Shell
23	Telnet	Virtual terminal connection
25	SMTP	Simple Mail Transfer Protocol
53	DNS	Domain name server
67, 68	DHCP (BOOTP-Client) (BOOTP-Server)	Dynamic Host Control Protocol
69	TFTP	Trivial File Transfer protocol
80	HTTP	Hypertext Transfer protocol
110	POP3	Post Office Protocol
161	SNMP	Simple Network Management Protocol
443	HTTPS	Secure HTTP
445	SMB	Server message block
1701	L2TP	Layer 2 Tunneling Protocol
1720	H.323/Q.931	Voice over IP
1723	PPTP	Point-to-point Tunneling Protocol

You can find a complete list of ports at http://www.iana.org/assignments/port-numbers.

The Transport Layer

Transport Layer Protocols
Define the type of connection established between hosts and how acknowledgements are sent

TCP
Transport Control Protocol

Connection-Oriented Protocol
Establishes a network connection, manages the delivery of data, and terminates the connection

The **transport layer protocols** in TCP/IP are very important in establishing a network connection, managing the delivery of data between a source and destination host, and terminating the data connection. There are two transport protocols within the TCP/IP transport layer, TCP and UDP. **TCP**, the Transport Control Protocol, is a **connection-oriented protocol**, which means it establishes the network connection, manages the data transfer, and terminates the connection. The TCP protocol establishes a set of rules or guidelines for establishing the connection. TCP verifies the delivery of the data packets through the network and includes support for error checking and recovering lost data. TCP then specifies a procedure for terminating the network connection.

A unique sequence of three data packets is exchanged at the beginning of a TCP connection between two hosts, as shown in Figure 5-3. This is a virtual connection that is made over the network. This sequence is as follows:

1. The **SYN** (Synchronizing) packet
2. The **SYN ACK** (Synchronizing Acknowledgement) packet
3. The **ACK** (Acknowledgement) packet

SYN
SYN ACK
ACK

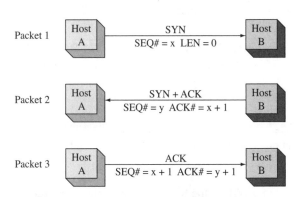

FIGURE 5-3   The three-packet initial TCP handshake.

The host initiating the connection will send a synchronizing packet (SYN) (see Figure 5-3). In this example, Host A issues a SYN packet to initiate the TCP handshake. The SYN will have a sequence number (SEQ) associated with it. In the example shown in Figure 5-3, the sequence number is x. The sequence number is used to keep track of the data packets being transferred from Host A to Host B. The length of the packet being sent by Host A is 0 (LEN 0), which indicates that the packet contains no data.

In packet 2, Host B replies with a SYN ACK packet. The ACK is an acknowledgement that Host B received the packet from Host A. There is a number attached to the ACK with a value of $(x + 1)$ that should be the sum of the SEQ# from packet 1 plus the length (LEN) of packet 1. Recall that the length of packet 1 is 0 (LEN 0), but packet 1 counts as one packet; therefore, Host B replies with an acknowledgement of packet 1 sequence number plus 1 $(x + 1)$. This acknowledgement notifies Host A that the packet (packet 1) was received. Packet 2 from Host B will also have a sequence number issued by Host B. In this packet, the sequence number has a value of y. This sequence number is used to keep track of packets transferred by Host B.

In packet 3, Host A acknowledges the reception of Host B's packet. The ACK number is an increment of one higher than the SEQ# sent by Host B in packet 2 $(y + 1)$. Host A also sends an updated SEQ# that is one larger than the SEQ# Host A sent in packet 1 $(x + 1)$. Remember, Host A and Host B each have their own sequence numbers. This completes the three-packet handshake that establishes the TCP connection. This handshake appears at the beginning of all TCP data transfers.

The following is an example of a TCP packet transmission captured using the Surveyor Demo protocol analyzer software provided on the text's companion

CD-ROM. The network setup is shown in Figure 5-4. Host A (the client) is establishing an FTP connection with Host B. The captured file is *5-a.cap* and is also provided on the CD-ROM in the *Capture* folder. Portions of the captured data packets are shown in Figure 5-5.

Host
A

Client

Host
B

FTP server

FIGURE 5-4   The setup for the capture of the TCP connection.

ID		Summary
000001 TCP	SP=1054 DP=21 SYN	SEQ=997462768 ACK=0 LEN=0 WS=16384 OPT
000002 TCP	SP=21 DP=1054 SYN	SEQ=3909625466 ACK=997462769 LEN=0 WS=17520
000003 TCP	SP=1054 DP=21	SEQ=997462769 ACK=3909625467 LEN=0 WS=17520
000004 FTP	R Port=1054	220 w2kserver Microsoft
000009 FTP	C Port=1054	USER administrator
000010 FTP	R Port=1054	331 Password required
000014 FTP	C Port=1054	PASS Chile

FIGURE 5-5   An example of the three packets exchanged in the initial TCP handshake.

Packet 1 (ID 000001) is the SYN or synchronizing packet. This packet is sent from the host computer on the network that wants to establish a TCP network connection. In this example, Host A is making a TCP connection for an FTP file transfer. The summary information for packet 1 specifies that this is a TCP packet, the source port is 1054 (SP=1054), and the destination port is 21 (DP=21). Port 1054 is an arbitrary port number that the FTP client picks or is assigned by the operating system. The destination port 21 is the well-known FTP port (see Table 5-3). The packet has a starting sequence number, 997462768, and there is no acknowledgement (ACK=0). The length of the data packet is 0 (LEN=0). This indicates that the packet does not contain any data. The window size = 16384 (WS=16384). The *window size* indicates how many data packets can be transferred without an acknowledgement.

Packet 2 is the SYN-ACK packet from the FTP server. The sequence number SEQ=3909625466 is the start of a new sequence for the data packet transfers from Host B. The source port is 21 (SP=21) and the destination port for packet 2 is 1054 (DP=1054). ACK=997462769 is an acknowledge by host B (the FTP server) that the first TCP transmission was received. Note that this acknowledgement shows an increment of 1 from the starting sequence number provided by host A in packet 1.

Packet 3 is an acknowledgement from the client (host A) back to the FTP server (host B) that packet 2 was received. Note that the acknowledgement is ACK=3909625467, which is an increment of 1 from the SEQ number transmitted in packet 2. This completes the initial handshake establishing the TCP connection. The next part is the data packet transfer. At this point, the two hosts can begin transferring data packets.

The last part of the TCP connection is terminating the session for each host. The first thing that happens is a host sends a FIN (finish) packet to the other connected host. This is shown in Figure 5-6. Host B sends a FIN packet to Host A indicating the data transmission is complete. Host A responds with an ACK packet acknowledging the reception of the FIN packet. Host A then sends Host B a FIN packet indicating that the connection is being terminated. Host B replies with an ACK packet.

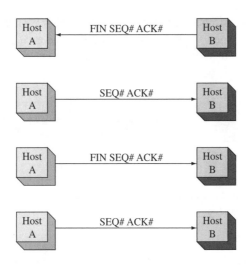

FIGURE 5-6 Terminating the TCP

Figure 5-7 shows an example of terminating a TCP connection. This example was captured with the Surveyor Demo protocol analyzer software. The captured file is *5-a.cap* and it is provided on the companion CD-ROM in the *Finisar* folder.

ID		Summary
000048 TCP	SP=21 DP=1054 FIN	SEQ=3909625742 ACK=997462851 LEN=0 WS=17438
000049 TCP	SP=1054 DP=21	SEQ=997462851 ACK=3909625743 LEN=0 WS=17245
000050 TCP	SP=1054 DP=21 FIN	SEQ=997462851 ACK=3909625743 LEN=0 WS=17245
000051 TCP	SP=21 DP=1054	SEQ=3909625743 ACK=997462852 LEN=0 WS=17438

FIGURE 5-7 An example of the four-packet TCP connection termination.

Packet 48 (see Figure 5-7) is a TCP packet with a source port of 21 (SP=21) and a destination port of 1054 (DP=1054). The FIN statement is shown, followed by a SEQ# and an ACK#. Remember, the SEQ and ACK numbers are used to keep track of the number of packets transmitted and an acknowledgement of the number received. The LEN of packet 48 is 0, which means the packet does not contain any data. Packet 49 is an acknowledgement from the host, at port 1054, of the FIN packet. Remember, the FIN packet was sent by the host at the source port 21. In packet 50 the host at port 1054 sends a FIN packet to the host at the destination port 21. In packet 51, the host at port 21 acknowledges the reception of the FIN packet and the four-packet sequence closes the TCP connection.

UDP, the User Datagram Protocol, is a *connectionless* protocol. This means UDP packets are transported over the network without a connection being established and without any acknowledgement that the data packets arrived at the destination. UDP is useful in applications such as videoconferencing and audio feeds, where such acknowledgements are not necessary.

UDP
User Datagram Protocol

Figure 5-8 provides an example of a UDP packet transfer. Packet 136 is the start of a UDP packet transfer of an Internet audio feed. A TCP connection to the Internet was made first, and then the feed was started. At that time, the UDP connectionless packets started. Packets 138, 139, and 140 are the same types of packets with a length of 789. No acknowledgements are sent back from the client. All the packets are coming from the Internet source. UDP does not have a procedure for terminating the data transfer; the source either stops delivery of the data packets or the client terminates the connection.

FIGURE 5-8   An example of a UDP packet transfer.

The Internet Layer

The TCP/IP **Internet layer** defines the protocols used for addressing and routing the data packets. Protocols that are part of the TCP/IP Internet layer include IP, ARP, ICMP, and IGMP. We examine these protocols next.

IP   The **IP (Internet Protocol)** defines the addressing used to identify the source and destination addresses of data packets being delivered over an IP network. The IP address is a logical address that consists of a network and a host address portion. The network portion is used to direct the data to the proper network. The host address identifies the address locally assigned to the host. The network portion of the address is similar to the area code for a telephone number. The host address is similar to the local exchange number. The network and host portions of the IP address are then used to route the data packets to the destination. (IP addressing and subnet masking are examined in detail in sections 5-4 and 5-5.)

ARP   ARP, the Address Resolution Protocol, is used to resolve an IP address to a hardware address for final delivery of data packets to the destination. ARP issues a query in a network called an *ARP request*, asking which network interface has this IP address. The host assigned the IP address replies with an *ARP reply*, the protocol that contains the hardware address for the destination host. An example of an ARP request captured with the Surveyor Demo Protocol Analyzer software is provided in Figure 5-9. As shown highlighted in Figure 5-9 (a), an ARP request is issued on the LAN. The source MAC address of the packet is 00-10-A4-13-99-2E. The destination address on the local area network shown is BROADCAST, which means this message is being sent to all computers in the local area network. A query (Q) is being asked who has the IP address 10.10.10.1 (PA=). *PA* is an abbreviation for *protocol address*.

The highlighted area in Figure 5-9 (b) shows the destination computer's ARP reply, sending its MAC address back to the source that issued the ARP request. (The *R* after the ARP indicates this is an ARP reply.) The source of the ARP reply is 00-10A4-13-6C-6E, which is replying that the MAC address for 10.10.10.1 is 00-10-A4-13-6C-6E (HA=). HA is an abbreviation for Hardware Address. In this case, the owner of the IP address replied to the message, but this is not always the case. Sometimes another networking device, such as a router, can provide the MAC address information. In that case, the MAC address being returned is for the next networking device in the route to the destination.

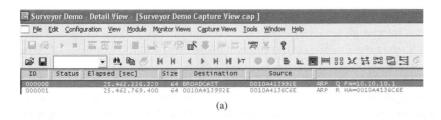

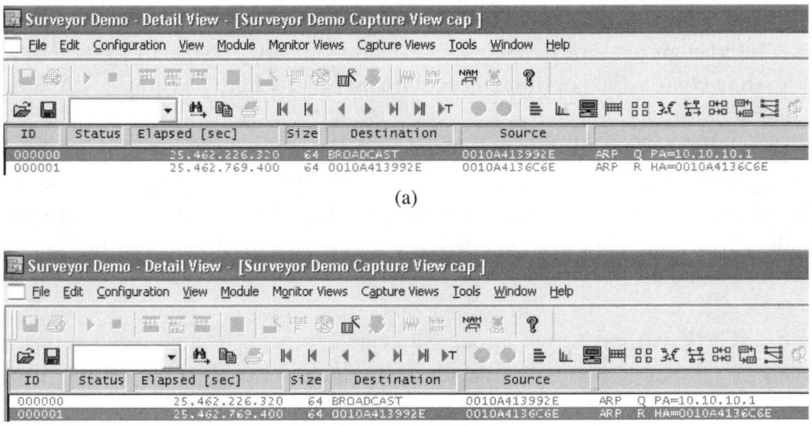

FIGURE 5-9   (a) The captured packets showing the ARP request; (b) the ARP reply.

A breakdown of the packet details of the ARP request is provided in Figure 5-10. The description of the ARP request is a broadcast that is the uppercase F. This means that all binary data bits are set to a logical 1. The data packet with all Fs is highlighted at the bottom of the image. Can you find the source address for the ARP request? The source address of 00-10-A4-13-99-2E immediately follows the destination address. The four hexadecimal characters (0x0806) identify this as an ARP packet. The 0x indicates that the 0806 is a hexadecimal number. We discuss hexadecimal numbers in section 5-3.

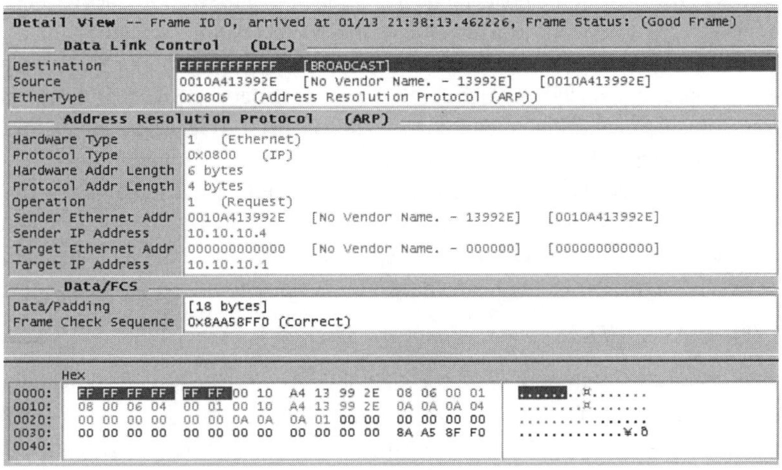

```
Detail View -- Frame ID 0, arrived at 01/13 21:38:13.462226, Frame Status: (Good Frame)
      Data Link Control    (DLC)
Destination       FFFFFFFFFFFF    [BROADCAST]
Source            0010A413992E    [No Vendor Name. - 13992E]    [0010A413992E]
EtherType         0x0806    (Address Resolution Protocol (ARP))
      Address Resolution Protocol    (ARP)
Hardware Type         1    (Ethernet)
Protocol Type         0x0800    (IP)
Hardware Addr Length  6 bytes
Protocol Addr Length  4 bytes
Operation             1    (Request)
Sender Ethernet Addr  0010A413992E    [No Vendor Name. - 13992E]    [0010A413992E]
Sender IP Address     10.10.10.4
Target Ethernet Addr  000000000000    [No Vendor Name. - 000000]    [000000000000]
Target IP Address     10.10.10.1
      Data/FCS
Data/Padding          [18 bytes]
Frame Check Sequence  0x8AA58FF0 (Correct)


      Hex
0000:  FF FF FF FF  FF FF 00 10  A4 13 99 2E  08 06 00 01    ..........¤.......
0010:  08 00 06 04  00 01 00 10  A4 13 99 2E  0A 0A 0A 04    ........¤.......
0020:  00 00 00 00  00 00 0A 0A  0A 01 00 00  00 00 00 00    ................
0030:  00 00 00 00  00 00 00 00  00 00 00 00  8A A5 8F F0    ..............¥.ð
0040:
```

FIGURE 5-10   The details of the ARP broadcast packet.

ICMP   The Internet Control Message Protocol (ICMP) is used to control the flow of data in the network, for reporting errors, and for performing diagnostics. A networking device, such as a router, sends an ICMP *source-quench* packet to a host that requests a slowdown in the data transfer.

A very important troubleshooting tool within the ICMP protocol is *ping,* the packet Internet groper. The *ping* command is used to verify connectivity with another host in the network. The destination host could be in a LAN, a campus LAN, or on the Internet.

The *ping* command was introduced in Chapter 1 and used in Chapter 4 to test the data packet deliveries in a LAN using a hub or switch. The *ping* command uses a series of echo requests, and the networking device receiving the echo requests responds with a series of echo replies to test a network connection. Refer to Chapters 1 and 4 for examples.

IGMP **IGMP** is the Internet Group Message Protocol. It is used when one host needs to send data to many destination hosts. This is called **multicasting**. The addresses used to send a multicast data packet are called **multicast addresses** and are reserved addresses not assigned to hosts in a network. An example of an application that uses IGMP packets is when a router uses multicasting to share routing tables. This is explained in Chapter 7, when routing protocols are examined.

Another application of IGMP packets is when a host wants to stream data to multiple hosts. *Streaming* means the data is sent without waiting for any acknowledgement that the data packets were delivered. In fact, in the IGMP protocol, the source doesn't care whether the destination receives a packet. Streaming is an important application in the transfer of audio and video files over the Internet. Another feature of IGMP is that the data is handed off to the application layer as it arrives. This enables the appropriate application to begin processing the data for playback.

The Network Interface Layer

The **network interface layer** of the TCP/IP model defines how the host connects to the network. Recall that the host can be a computer or a networking device such as a router. The type of network to which the host connects is not dictated by the TCP/IP protocol. The host could be a computer connected to an Ethernet or token-ring network or a router connected to a frame relay wide area network. TCP/IP is not dependent on a specific networking technology; therefore, TCP/IP can be adapted to run on newer networking technologies such as ATM (asynchronous transfer mode).

In the network interface layer every TCP/IP data packet must have a destination and a source MAC address in the TCP/IP header. The MAC or hardware address is found on the host's network interface card or connection, and it is 12 hexadecimal characters in length. For example, the network interface could have a MAC address of

00-10-A4-13-99-2E

The hardware address is used for final delivery of data packets to the next destination in a network. The first six hexadecimal numbers represent the organization that manufactured the card. This is called the *OUI* (organizational unit identifier). The last six digits are unique numbers assigned by the manufacturer of the network interface. The concept of the MAC address was fully explained in Chapter 1 and you are encouraged to refer to this material for a thorough review.

5-3 NUMBER CONVERSION

This section reviews the numbering systems used in computer networking, with a focus on converting binary, decimal, and hexadecimal numbers.

Binary-Decimal Conversion

Binary numbers are represented as a logical 0 or logical 1 in base 2 format. This means that each number has a place value of 2^n, where n is the place value position of the binary digit. The place values start at 2^0 with the least significant bit (LSB) position. For example, the binary number 1 0 1 1 has the place values of 2^0 for the LSB position to 2^3 for the most significant bit (MSB) position.

Place value	2^3	2^2	2^1	2^0
Binary digit	1	0	1	1
MSB→LSB	MSB			LSB

The 1 and 0 are used as a multiplier times the place value. For example, the conversion of 1 0 1 1 to decimal is as follows:

$$1 \times 2^3 = 8$$
$$0 \times 2^2 = 0$$
$$1 \times 2^1 = 2$$
$$\underline{1 \times 2^0 = 1}$$
$$\text{sum} = 11$$

Note that the place value was multiplied by the value of the binary digit.

Instead of writing $2^0, 2^1, 2^2, \ldots$, it is easier to write the decimal equivalent for each place value (for example, 1, 2, 4, 8, 16, 32, 64, 128). The calculations for determining each place value are as follows:

$2^0 = 1$	$2^1 = 2$	$2^2 = 4$	$2^3 = 8$
$2^4 = 16$	$2^5 = 32$	$2^6 = 64$	$2^7 = 128$

This is shown in Table 5-4.

TABLE 5-4   Place Values for Eight Binary Numbers (an Octet)

Place value (decimal)	128	64	32	16	8	4	2	1
Place value	2^7	2^6	2^5	2^4	2^3	2^2	2^1	2^0
MSB—LSB	MSB							LSB

For example, the place values for the binary number 1 0 0 1 0 0 can be set up as follows:

Place value (decimal)	32	16	8	4	2	1
Place value	2^5	2^4	2^3	2^2	2^1	2^0
Binary digit	1	0	0	1	0	0
MSB→LSB	MSB					LSB

Every place value that has a binary digit of 1 is used to sum a total for determining the decimal equivalent for the binary number. In this example, the decimal equivalent is $32 + 4 = 36$. After working a few examples it becomes obvious that the base 2 place values can be written by inspection in their decimal equivalence. The rightmost place value is 1, the next place value is 2, the next is 4, and so on.

The 8-bit octet numbers used in IP addressing are converted from binary to decimal in the same manner. The following example demonstrates this.

Example 5-1

Given a 32-bit IP address number expressed in binary format, convert the number to a dotted-decimal format.

1 1 0 0 0 0 0 0	1 0 1 0 1 0 0 0	0 0 1 0 0 0 0 0	0 0 0 0 1 1 0 0
octet-4	octet-3	octet-2	octet-1

Solution:

First, assign the place value for each binary position.

	128	64	32	16	8	4	2	1
octet-1	0	0	0	0	1	1	0	0

$$(1 \times 8) + (1 \times 4) = 8 + 4 = 12$$

	128	64	32	16	8	4	2	1
octet-2	0	0	1	0	0	0	0	0

$$(1 \times 32) = 32$$

	128	64	32	16	8	4	2	1
octet-3	1	0	1	0	1	0	0	0

$$(1 \times 128) + (1 \times 32) (1 \times 8) = 128 + 32 + 8 = 168$$

	128	64	32	16	8	4	2	1
octet-4	1	1	0	0	0	0	0	0

$$(1 \times 128) + (1 \times 64) = 128 + 64 = 192$$

Therefore, the dotted decimal equivalent is 192.168.32.12.

Decimal→Binary Conversion

The simplest way to convert a decimal number to binary is using division, repeatedly dividing the decimal number by 2 until the quotient is 0. The division steps for converting decimal numbers to binary are as follows:

1. Divide the decimal number by 2, record the remainder of 0 or 1, and write the quotient or result of the division by 2.

2. Divide the quotient by 2 and record the remainder of 0 or 1. Write the quotient and repeat this step until the quotient is 0.
3. Write the remainder numbers (0 and 1) in reverse order to obtain the binary equivalent value.

Example 5-2

Convert the decimal number 12 to binary.

Solution:

Divide 12 by 2. This equals 6 with a remainder of 0. Divide 6 by 2. This equals 3 with a remainder of 0. Divide 3 by 2. This equals 1 with a remainder of 1. Divide 1 by 2. This equals 0 with a remainder of 1. The quotient is 0; therefore, the conversion is done. Write the remainder numbers in reverse order to generate the binary equivalent value. This yields a value of 1 1 0 0. The calculation for this is shown:

$$
\begin{array}{ll}
2\underline{|12} & \\
2\underline{|6} & 0 \\
2\underline{|3} & 0 \\
2\underline{|1} & 1 \\
0 & 1
\end{array}
$$

You can verify the answer by converting the binary number back to decimal.

$$
\begin{array}{cccc}
8 & 4 & 2 & 1 \\
1 & 1 & 0 & 0
\end{array}
$$

$$(1 \times 8) + (1 \times 4) = 12$$

Example 5-3

Convert 33 to its binary equivalent.

Solution:

Use the decimal-to-binary steps listed previously.

$$
\begin{array}{ll}
2\underline{|33} & \\
2\underline{|16} & 1 \\
2\underline{|8} & 0 \\
2\underline{|4} & 0 \\
2\underline{|2} & 0 \\
2\underline{|1} & 0 \\
0 & 1
\end{array}
$$

The answer is 1 0 0 0 0 1.

Example 5-4

Convert the decimal number 254 to binary.

Solution

Use the decimal-to-binary steps listed previously.

$$
\begin{array}{ll}
2\underline{|254} & \\
2\underline{|127} & 0 \\
2\underline{|63} & 1 \\
2\underline{|31} & 1 \\
2\underline{|15} & 1 \\
2\underline{|7} & 1 \\
2\underline{|3} & 1 \\
2\underline{|1} & 1 \\
0 & 1
\end{array}
$$

The answer is 1 1 1 1 1 1 1 0.

Hexadecimal Numbers

Hex
Hexadecimal, base 16

Hexadecimal numbers (**hex**) are base 16 numbers. A conversion lookup table for hexadecimal is provided in Table 5-5. It takes four binary numbers to represent a hexadecimal number. Notice that the letters A to F are used to represent the decimal numbers 10 to 15.

Converting Hexadecimal The simplest way to convert hexadecimal numbers to binary is through the use of either a calculator or a lookup table such as Table 5-5.

TABLE 5-5   Hexadecimal Conversion Table

Decimal	Hexadecimal	Binary
0	0	0 0 0 0
1	1	0 0 0 1
2	2	0 0 1 0
3	3	0 0 1 1
4	4	0 1 0 0
5	5	0 1 0 1
6	6	0 1 1 0
7	7	0 1 1 1
8	8	1 0 0 0
9	9	1 0 0 1
10	A	1 0 1 0
11	B	1 0 1 1
12	C	1 1 0 0
13	D	1 1 0 1
14	E	1 1 1 0
15	F	1 1 1 1

Hexadecimal numbers are used in computer networks to represent the computer's 12-hex character MAC address and are used to display the packet details in a protocol analyzer, as shown in Figure 5-11. Hex numbers are also used in IPv6 addressing (discussed in section 5-7).

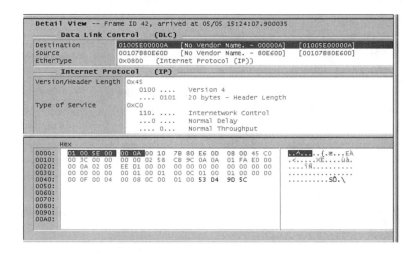

FIGURE 5-11 An example of the use of hex numbers in data packets.

The highlighted region in Figure 5-11 shows the destination MAC address of 01005E00000A, which is a 12-digit hexadecimal code. Notice that the EtherType number is 0x0800, defining that this an Internet protocol packet. Also note that the numbers at the bottom of the screen are expressed in hex format. These numbers are the values in the data packets.

0x800—The 0x indicates this is a hexadecimal number.

$0x800_H$—The subscript H is sometimes used to indicate that this is a hexadecimal number. The subscript notation is not always practical to display in a text format, so this style is of limited use.

The following are examples of converting hexadecimal numbers to binary.

Example 5-5

Convert the hexadecimal number 0x48AF to binary.

Solution:

Use Table 5-5 to convert the hex numbers.

Hex:	4	8	A	F
Binary:	0 1 0 0	1 0 0 0	1 0 1 0	1 1 1 1

Example 5-6

Convert the hexadecimal number 0x0800 to binary.

Solution:

Use Table 5-5 to convert the hex numbers.

Hex:	0	8	0	0
Binary:	0 0 0 0	1 0 0 0	0 0 0 0	0 0 0 0

Converting binary numbers to hexadecimal requires that the binary numbers be separated into groups of four beginning with the LSB position. If the binary sequence doesn't have 4 bits use leading 0s to pad the number. The binary numbers used in computer networks are always a multiple of four in length; therefore, you won't have to pad any of the numbers with leading 0s.

Example 5-7

Convert the binary number 0 1 0 0 1 1 0 0 1 0 1 0 to hexadecimal.

Solution:

Separate the binary numbers into groups of four beginning with the LSB position. Next use the conversion lookup table (Table 5-5) to convert each 4-bit binary group to hexadecimal.

0 1 0 0	1 1 0 0	1 0 1 0
4	C	A

The answer is 0x4CA.

5-4   IPV4 ADDRESSING

IP addressing provides a standardized format for assigning a unique routable address for every host in a TCP/IP network. You may ask, "The host in a TCP/IP network already has a hardware (MAC) address, so why the need for the IP address?"

The answer is that internetworking devices need a routable network address to deliver data packets outside the LAN. The IP address is similar to a telephone number. The network portion of the IP address is similar to the telephone's area code. The host portion of the IP address is similar to the telephone's 7-bit local exchange number. This section identifies the network and host portion of an IP address and describes how IP addressing is used to identify the address for a host in a network.

The IP addressing version currently being used on the Internet and for TCP/IP data traffic is **IPv4**. There are five classes of IPv4 addresses: **class A, B, C, D, and E**. The address breakdown for each class is provided in Table 5-6. Classes A, B, and C are the primary addresses used over the Internet and for TCP/IP data traffic. Class D is used for multicasting (explained in Chapter 7). The class E range is experimental

IPv4
The IP version currently being used on the Internet

Class A, B, C, D, and E
The five classes of IPv4

and is not used on the Internet. A new IP addressing scheme called IPv6 has been developed for use on the Internet. This address scheme is examined in section 5-7.

TABLE 5-6   IPv4 Address Classes and Address Range

Class	IP Address Range
A	0.0.0.0 to 127.255.255.255
B	128.0.0.0 to 191.255.255.255
C	192.0.0.0 to 223.255.255.255
D	224.0.0.0 to 239.255.255.255
E	240.0.0.0 to 254.255.255.255

Note

The 0.0.0.0 and 127.x.x.x addresses are special-purpose addresses. The 0.0.0.0 IP address refers to the source host on this network. The 127.x.x.x addresses are used as the Internet loopback address. A datagram sent by a higher-level protocol to an address anywhere within this block should loop back inside the host. The most common loopback address used is 127.0.0.1. The 127.x.x.x addresses should never appear on the network.

Each IP address consists of four 8-bit octets, providing a total binary data length of 32 bits. Figure 5-12 shows the 32-bit structure for the IP address. Each octet in the IP address is expressed in terms of its decimal equivalent. The decimal equivalent representation of the four octets shown in Figure 5-12 is 10.10.20.1. The breakdown for determining each octet in decimal and binary is provided in Table 5-7.

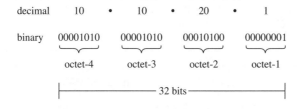

FIGURE 5-12   The structure of the 32-bit IPv4 address.

TABLE 5-7   Decimal→Binary Octet Breakdown for the 10.10.20.1 IPv4 Address

Octet	Decimal	Binary
4	10	0 0 0 0 1 0 1 0
3	10	0 0 0 0 1 0 1 0
2	20	0 0 0 1 0 1 0 0
1	1	0 0 0 0 0 0 0 1

Representing the binary data in decimal form simplifies the user interface. TCP/IP uses the binary form (represented as 32 1/0 bits) for transporting the IP address, but the user interface is typically expressed in a *dotted-decimal* format. The 10.10.20.1 IP address is an example of dotted-decimal.

Each of the four octets of the IPv4 address represents either a network or a host portion of the IP address. The breakdown in each of the address classes for network and host bits is shown in Figure 5-13 and in Table 5-8. Class A has 8 bits assigned for the network address and 24 bits for the host. Class B has 16 bits for the network address and 16 bits for the host. Class C has 24 bits assigned for the network address and 8 bits for the host.

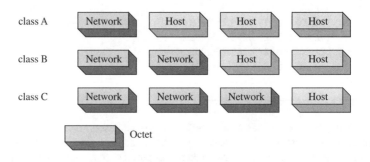

FIGURE 5-13 The octets making up the network and host portions of the IPv4 address for classes A, B, and C.

TABLE 5-8 Breakdown of the Network and Host Bits by Class

Class	Network Bits	Host Bits
A	8	24
B	16	16
C	24	8

The number of host bits in the IP address classes determines how many hosts can be created for each class of address. The equation

$2^n - 2$, where n = number of host bits

is used to calculate the number of host IP addresses that can be created for a network. For example, a class C address has 8 host bits; therefore $2^8 - 2 = 254$ host IP addresses can be assigned to a class C network. The reason for the " – 2" value in the equation when calculating the number of host addresses is the host IP address cannot be all 1s or all 0s. The all 1s state is reserved for network broadcasts and the all 0s state is reserved for the network address. Table 5-9 lists the total number of available host IP addresses for each class of network. (A technique called *subnetting* is introduced in this chapter in section 5-5. This section shows how host bits are borrowed and added to the network address bit to create subnets in a network.)

TABLE 5-9 Number of Host IP Addresses by Class

Class	Number of Host Bits	Number of Hosts
A	24	16,777,214
B	16	65,534
C	8	254

Private IP Addresses

Address ranges in class A, B, and C have been set aside for private use. These addresses, called *private addresses*, are not used for Internet data traffic but are intended to be used specifically on internal networks called *intranets*. Table 5-10 lists the private address ranges.

TABLE 5-10   Private IP Addresses

Class	Address Range
A	10.0.0.0 to 10.255.255.255
B	172.16.0.0 to 172.31.255.255
C	192.168.0.0 to 192.168.255.255

The IP addresses used in this text are in the private address range. Functionally, private addresses work the same as public addresses except they are not routed on the Internet. These are called **non-internet routable IP addresses** and are blocked by Internet service providers.

IP Address Assignment

IP addresses are assigned by **ARIN,** the American Registry for Internet Numbers. Their Web address is http://www.arin.net. ARIN assigns IP address space to Internet service providers (ISPs) and end users, but only to those who qualify. This requires that the ISP or end user be large enough to merit a block of addresses. When blocks of addresses are allocated by ARIN to ISPs, the ISPs issue addresses to their customers. For example, a Telco could be the ISP that has a large block of IP addresses and issues an IP address to a user. A local ISP could also be assigned a block of IP addresses from ARIN, but the local ISP must have a large number of users.

ARIN also assigns end users IP addresses. Once again, the end user must qualify to receive a block of addresses from ARIN. This usually means that the end user must be large. For example, many universities and large businesses can receive a block of IP addresses from ARIN. However, most end users will get their IP addresses from an ISP (for example, Telco) or have IP addresses assigned dynamically when they connect to the ISP.

5-5   SUBNET MASKS

The objective of this section is to demonstrate how to establish subnet masks for use in computer networks. *Subnetting* is a technique used to break down (or partition) networks into subnets. The subnets are created through the use of subnet masks. The **subnet mask** identifies what bits in the IP address are to be used to represent the network/subnet portion of an IP address.

Subnets are created by borrowing bits from the host portion of the IP address. This is shown in Figure 5-14. The network portion of the IP address and the new subnet bits are used to define the new subnet. Routers use this information to properly forward data packets to the proper subnet. The class C network shown in Figure 5-15 is partitioned into four subnets. It takes 2 bits to provide four possible subnets; therefore, 2 bits are borrowed from the host bits. This means the process of creating the four subnets reduces the number of bits available for host IP addresses.

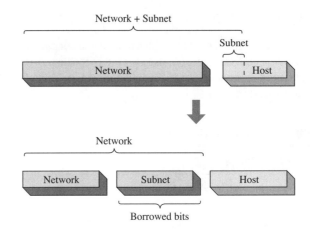

FIGURE 5-14 Borrowing bits from the host to create subnets.

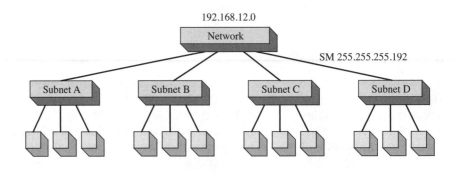

FIGURE 5-15 Partitioning a network into subnets.

Assume that the network has an IP address of 192.168.12.0. The 2 bits are borrowed from the host portion of the IP address to create the four subnets. A class C network has 24 network bits and 8 host bits. Two bits are borrowed from the host address to create the 4 subnets. The network plus subnet portion of the IP address is now 24 + 2, or 26 bits in length, and the host portion is now 6 bits. The breakdown of the 32-bit IP address is shown in Figure 5-16.

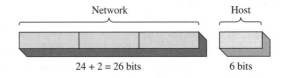

FIGURE 5-16 The breakdown of the IP address to allow for the creation of four subnets.

The equations for calculating the number of subnets created and the number of hosts/subnet are provided in Equations 5-1 and 5-2.

| # of subnets created | 2^x | [Equation 5-1] |
| # of hosts/subnet | $2^{(y-x)}$ | [Equation 5-2] |

where x = # of bits borrowed from the host bits
y = # host bits for the class of network
(A = 24, B = 16, C = 8)

Breaking down the 192.168.12.0 network into four subnets required borrowing two host bits. Therefore, $x = 2$ and because this is a class C network, $y = 8$.

$x = 2$ (the number of bits used from the host)
$y = 8$ (number of bits for a class C network)

Applying these values to equation 5-2 yields

The number of subnets created = $2^x = 2^{(2)} = 4$
The number of hosts/subnet = $2^{(y-x)} = 2^{(8-2)} = 64$

When creating subnets, it is important to note that each subnet will have both a network and a broadcast address. Taking this into consideration, the equations for calculating the number of hosts/subnet are modified to account for the number of usable hosts/subnet. The modified equations are as follows:

The number of usable hosts/subnet = $2^{(y-x)} - 2$ [Equation 5-3]

The next step is to determine the subnet mask required for creating the four subnets. Recall that creating the four subnets required borrowing 2 host bits. The two MSB (most significant bit) positions, borrowed from the host and network portion of the IP address, must be included in the subnet mask selection. The purpose of the subnet mask is to specify the bit positions used to identify the network and subnet bits. Applying the subnet mask is basically a logical AND operation. Setting the subnet mask bit position to a 1 enables the bit value from the IP address to pass. Setting the subnet mask bit value to 0 disables the IP address from appearing on the output. This is shown in the truth table for a logical AND operation:

Subnet Mask Bit	IP Address Bit	Output
0	0	0
0	1	0
1	0	0
1	1	1

Notice that when the subnet mask bit is set to 0, the output is forced to 0. When the subnet mask bit is set to 1, the output follows the IP address bit.

The subnet mask consists of bit position values set to either a 1 or a 0. A bit position set to a 1 indicates that the bit position is used to identify a network or subnet bit. The subnet mask for identifying the class C network 192.168.12.0 will be 255.255.255.x. This conversion is shown next.

| **Binary** | 1 1 1 1 1 1 1 1 | 1 1 1 1 1 1 1 1 | 1 1 1 1 1 1 1 1 | x x x x x x x x |
| **Decimal** | 255 | 255 | 255 | x |

The subnet mask also identifies the subnet bits. The two MSBs were borrowed from the host bits; therefore, the last octet of the subnet mask will be

		—Subnet—			——— Host Addresses ———				
Place value	128	64	32	16	8	4	2	1
	1	1	x	x	x	x	x	x

where the 1 indicates this place is used for the subnet mask and the *x* means that the place value is left for the host address. Summing the two bit position values that have a 1 yields 128 + 64 = 192. The 192 is placed in the last octet of the subnet mask. The complete subnet mask is 255.255.255.192.

The two subnet bits create four subnets, and each subnet has its own network address. The network addresses are used to route data packets to the correct subnet. Table 5-11 shows the four subnet addresses listed in both binary and decimal format.

(*Note:* The six host bits are all set at 0 in a subnet's network address.)

TABLE 5-11   Binary and Decimal Equivalents for the Subnet's Network Address

Place Value		Host Bits	Subnet Address
128	**64**		
0	0	0 0 0 0 0 0	0
0	1	0 0 0 0 0 0	64
1	0	0 0 0 0 0 0	128
1	1	0 0 0 0 0 0	192

Each subnet will also have its own broadcast address. The broadcast address for the subnet is used to broadcast packets to all hosts in the subnet. (*Note:* All host bits are set to 1 for a broadcast.) Table 5-12 shows the binary and decimal equivalents for the subnet's broadcast address.

TABLE 5-12   Binary and Decimal Equivalents for the Subnet's Broadcast Address

	|— Subnet —|	|——— Host Bits ———|					Decimal Equivalent
Place Value	128	64	32	16	8	4	2	1	
	0	0	1	1	1	1	1	1	63
	0	1	1	1	1	1	1	1	127
	1	0	1	1	1	1	1	1	191
	1	1	1	1	1	1	1	1	255
Place Value	128	64	32	16	8	4	2	1	

Given this information, the network and broadcast address can be defined for the four subnets of the 192.168.12.0 network. These addresses for the four subnets are provided in Table 5-13.

TABLE 5-13 Network and Broadcast Addresses for the Four Subnets of the 192.168.12.0 Network

Subnet	Network Address	Broadcast Address
1st subnet (0)	192.168.12.0	192.168.12.63
2nd subnet (64)	192.168.12.64	192.168.12.127
3rd subnet (128)	192.168.12.128	192.168.12.191
4th subnet (192)	192.168.12.192	192.168.12.255

The same technique for subnet masking can be applied to class A, B, or C addresses. The following examples demonstrate subnet mask selection in a network.

Example 5-8

Given a network address of 10.0.0.0, divide the network into 8 subnets. Specify the subnet mask, the network and broadcast addresses, and the number of usable hosts/subnet.

Solution:

Creating 8 subnets requires borrowing 3 host bits; therefore $x = 3$. This is a class A network; therefore $y = 24$.

Using equation 5-1, the number of subnets $= 2^3 = 8$.
Using equation 5-3, the number of usable hosts $= 2^{(24-3)} - 2 = 2097150$.
The 8 subnets will be

128	64	32	Host Bits	Subnet
0	0	0	x x x x x	0
0	0	1	x x x x x	32
0	1	0	x x x x x	64
0	1	1	x x x x x	96
1	0	0	x x x x x	128
1	0	1	x x x x x	160
1	1	0	x x x x x	192
1	1	1	x x x x x	224

Therefore, the network and broadcast addresses for the 8 subnets will be

Subnet		Network Address	Broadcast Address
0 subnet	(0 0 0)	10.0.0.0	10.31.255.255
32 subnet	(0 0 1)	10.32.0.0	10.63.255.255
64 subnet	(0 1 0)	10.64.0.0	10.95.255.255
96 subnet	(0 1 1)	10.96.0.0	10.127.255.255
128 subnet	(1 0 0)	10.128.0.0	10.159.255.255
160 subnet	(1 0 1)	10.160.0.0	10.191.255.255
192 subnet	(1 1 0)	10.192.0.0	10.223.255.255
224 subnet	(1 1 1)	10.224.0.0	10.255.255.255

The subnet mask for creating the 8 subnets will be 255.224.0.0.

The 224 in Example 5-8 comes from setting the subnet mask to select the three MSB positions in the host portion of the address, as shown in Figure 5-17.

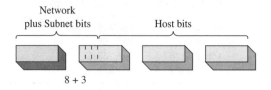

Network
plus Subnet bits   Host bits

8 + 3

FIGURE 5-17 The network, subnet, and host bit positions for creating the eight subnets in Example 5-8.

Another way to look at selecting a subnet mask is by specifying how many usable hosts are available to be assigned in a subnet. For example, assume that 62 usable host addresses are to be available in a subnet. Assume this is for a class C network. Using Equation 5-2,

$$62 = 2^{(8-x)} - 2$$
$$64 = 2^{(8-x)}$$

Using logarithms to solve for x:

$$\log 64 = (8-x)\,(\log 2)$$
$$\log 64/(\log 2) = 8-x$$
$$6 = 8-x \text{ therefore, } x = 2$$

Instead of using logarithms, a table such as that shown in Table 5-14 can be used. Example 5-9 shows how the table can be used to determine the subnet mask.

TABLE 5-14 Number of Bits Borrowed to Create a Specific Number of Usable Hosts

	# of Host Bits Needed		
# of Usable Hosts	Class A	Class B	Class C
1022	14	6	–
510	15	7	–
254	16	8	–
126	17	9	–
62	18	10	2
30	19	11	3
14	20	12	4
6	21	13	5
2	22	14	6

Example 5-9

Determine the subnet mask required for the router-to-router link shown in Figure 5-18 if only two host addresses are required for this link.

FIGURE 5-18 Setting a subnet mask for a router-to-router link that provides two host addresses.

Solution:

Using Table 5-14 to determine the number of host bits borrowed for creating a subnet with two usable hosts, we find that 14 host bits are borrowed for this class B network. This means the first three octets plus the 6 MSB positions of the fourth octet will be used to create the subnet mask. The decimal equivalent for the six MSB bit positions is $128 + 64 + 32 + 16 + 8 + 4 = 252$.

Binary	1 1 1 1 1 1 1 1	1 1 1 1 1 1 1 1	1 1 1 1 1 1 1 1	1 1 1 1 1 1 x x
Decimal	255	255	255	252

Therefore, the subnet mask is going to be 255.255.255.252.

Computers use the subnet mask to control data flow within networks. Computers in a LAN use a subnet mask to determine whether the destination IP address is intended for a host in the same LAN or if the data packet should be sent to the gateway IP address of the LAN. The gateway IP address is typically the physical network interface on a layer 3 switch or a router.

For example, assume that the IP address of the computer in the LAN is 172.16.35.3. A subnet mask of 255.255.255.0 is being used. This means that all data packets with an IP address between 172.16.35.0 and 172.16.35.255 stay in the LAN. A data packet with a destination IP address of 172.16.34.15 is sent to the LAN gateway. The 255.255.255.0 subnet mask indicates that all bits in the first three octets must match each other to stay in this LAN.

This can be verified by "ANDing" the subnet mask with the destination address as shown:

172.16.35.3
<u>255.255.255.0</u>
172.16.35.0 is in the same LAN subnet, sent to the gateway

172.16.34.15
<u>255.255.255.0</u>
176.16.34.0 not in the same subnet as the LAN

This section has demonstrated techniques for establishing subnets and subnet masks in computer networks. Examples have been presented that guide the reader through the process of borrowing bits to determining the number of available hosts in the subnet. The next section examines the concepts of expanding the subnet IP address range past the class boundaries using CIDR blocks.

5-6 CIDR BLOCKS

Classful
The IP and subnet addresses are within the same network

Supernetting
Allows multiple networks to be specified by one subnet mask

CIDR
Classless interdomain routing

Up to this point, this chapter has focused on the issues of **classful** networks. *Classful* means that the IP addresses and subnets are within the same network. The problem with classful addressing is there is a lot of unused IP address space. For example, a class A IP network has more than 16 million possible host addresses. A class B network has more than 65,000 host addresses. The fact is only a limited number of class A and B address space has been allocated for Internet use.

A technique called **supernetting** was proposed in 1992 to eliminate the class boundaries and to make available the unused IP address space. Supernetting allows multiple networks to be specified by one subnet mask. In other words, the class boundary could be overcome.

Supernetting required a simpler way to indicate the subnet mask. The technique developed is called **CIDR,** classless interdomain routing. CIDR (pronounced "cider") notation specifies the number of bits set to a 1 that make up the subnet mask. For example, the class C size subnet mask 255.255.255.0 is listed in CIDR notation as /24. This indicates the 24 bits are set to a 1. A class B size subnet is written as /16 and a class A subnet is written as /8. CIDR can also be used to represent subnets that identify only part of the octet bits in an IP address. For example, a subnet mask of 255.255.192.0 is written in CIDR as /18. The /18 comes from the 18 bits that are set to a 1 as shown:

255	255	192	0
1 1 1 1 1 1 1 1	1 1 1 1 1 1 1 1	1 1 0 0 0 0 0 0	0 0 0 0 0 0 0 0

Prefix length notation
Another shorthand technique for writing the subnet mask except class boundaries are not being crossed

An alternative to the CIDR notation is the **prefix length notation**. This is another shorthand technique for writing the subnet mask. For example, the subnet mask 255.255.255.192 is written as /26. This notation shows the number of network and host bits being used to create the subnet mask. In the case of a /26 subnet mask, 24 network bits and 2 host bits are being used. Yes, this is basically the same as the CIDR except class boundaries are not being crossed and network bits are not being borrowed.

A network address and the subnet mask of 192.168.12.0 255.255.252.0 can be written in CIDR notation as 192.168.12.0/22. Table 5-15 provides the CIDR for the most common subnet masks.

TABLE 5-15   CIDR–Subnet Mask Conversion

CIDR	Subnet Mask	CIDR	Subnet Mask
/8	255.0.0.0	/21	255.255.248.0
/9	255.128.0.0	/22	255.255.252.0
/10	255.192.0.0	/23	255.255.254.0
/11	255.224.0.0	/24	255.255.255.0

CIDR	Subnet Mask	CIDR	Subnet Mask
/12	255.240.0.0	/25	255.255.255.128
/13	255.248.0.0	/26	255.255.255.192
/14	255.252.0.0	/27	255.255.255.224
/15	255.254.0.0	/28	255.255.255.240
/16	255.255.0.0	/29	255.255.255.248
/17	255.255.128.0	/30	255.255.255.252
/18	255.255.192.0	/31	255.255.255.254
/19	255.255.224.0	/32	255.255.255.255
/20	255.255.240.0		

CIDR blocks are used to break down the class barriers in IP addressing. For example, two class C networks (192.168.78.0/24 and 192.168.79.0/24) can be grouped together as one big subnet. These two networks can be grouped together by modifying the /24 CIDR number to /23. This means that one bit has been borrowed from the network address bits to combine the two networks into one supernet. Writing these two networks in CIDR notation provides 192.168.78.0/23. This reduces the two class C subnets to one larger network. The group of networks defined by CIDR notation is called a **CIDR block**. When you group two or more classful networks together they are called **supernets**. This term is synonymous with CIDR blocks. The group of four IP addresses from 192.168.76.0 to 192.168.79.0 with a CIDR of /22 is a supernet. The supernet uses a CIDR subnet mask (/22) that is shorter than the number of network bits for class C network (/24). Another example of a supernet is 172.16.0.0/12. 172.16.0.0 is a class B address and the CIDR subnet mask (/12) is less than the 16 bits for the network portion of a class B address.

The problem with randomly applying CIDR blocks to class A, B, and C addresses is that there are boundaries in each class, and these boundaries can't be crossed. If a boundary is crossed, the IP address maps to another subnet. For example, the CIDR block is expanded to include four class C networks. This means that all four class C networks need to be specified by the same CIDR subnet mask to avoid crossing boundaries. The new subnet mask is 255.255.252.0. The following example demonstrates what happens if a boundary is crossed.

CIDR Block
The grouping of two or more class networks together; also called *supernetting*

Supernets
The grouping of two or more class networks together; also called *CIDR blocks*

Example 5-10

Explore what happens if the boundary in IP addresses for class C subnets is crossed. For this example, the subnets have IP addresses of

    192.168.78.0/22
    192.168.79.0/22
    192.168.80.0/22
    192.168.81.0/22

Solution:

Applying the /22 subnet mask to 192.168.78.0 and 192.168.80.0 provides the following. (*Note:* The binary values of the affected octet are shown, and applying the subnet mask means that the binary values of the IP address and the subnet mask are ANDed together.)

Place Value	128	64	32	16	8	4	2	1
192.168.78.0 IP	0	1	0	0	1	1	1	1
255.255.252.0 SM	1	1	1	1	1	1	0	0
192.168.76.0	0	1	0	0	1	1	0	0 (76)

$$64 + 8 + 4 = 76$$

Now the same subnet mask is applied to the 192.168.80.0 subnet.

Place Value	128	64	32	16	8	4	2	1
192.168.80.0 IP	0	1	0	1	0	0	0	0
255.255.252.0 SM	1	1	1	1	1	1	0	0
192.168.80.0	0	1	0	1	0	0	0	0 (80)

$$64 + 16 = 80$$

IP = IP Address   SM = subnet mask

Applying the /22 subnet mask places these two IP addresses in different subnets. The first IP address is placed in the "76" subnet while the second IP address is placed in the "80" subnet. The boundary line has been crossed, placing the IP addresses in different subnets when the /22 is applied.

This example shows what will happen if a boundary is crossed in IP addressing. If four class C subnets need to be grouped into one CIDR block, IP addresses from the ranges shown could be used:

192.168.76.0 to 192.168.79.0 (all will be in the "76" subnet), or

192.168.80.0 to 192.168.83.0 (all will be in the "80" subnet)

Careful planning is required to make sure the IP addresses can all be specified by the same subnet mask. The goal of this section has been to develop an understanding of supernets, classless routing, and CIDR blocks. The reader should also understand the CIDR notation and be able to determine whether a group of IP addresses is in the same subnet.

5-7 IPV6 ADDRESSING

IPv6
IP version 6

IPng
The next generation IP

IP version 4 (IPv4) is the current TCP/IP addressing technique being used on the Internet. Address space for IPv4 is quickly running out due to the rapid growth of the Internet and the development of new Internet-compatible technologies such as the IP addressable telephone. IP version 6 (**IPv6**) is the proposed solution for expanding the possible number of users on the Internet. IPv6 is also called **IPng,** the next generation IP.

IPv6 uses a 128-bit address technique, compared to IPv4's 32-bit address structure. IPv6 provides for a large number of IP addresses (2^{128}). IPv6 numbers are written in hexadecimal rather than dotted decimal. For example, the following is a 32 hexadecimal digit IPv6 address (*Note:* 32 hex digits × 4 bits/hex digit = 128 bits):

6789:ABCD:1234:EF98:7654:321F:EDCB:AF21

Full IPv6 Address
All 32 hexadecimal positions contain a value other than 0

This is classified as a **full IPv6 address**. The *full* means that all 32 hexadecimal positions contain a value other than 0.

Why doesn't IPv6 use the dotted decimal format of IPv4? It would take many decimal numbers to represent the IPv6 address. Each decimal number takes at least 7 binary bits in ASCII (American Standard Code for Information Interchange) code. For example, the decimal equivalent of the first eight hexadecimal characters in the previous full IPv6 address is

6	7	8	9	:A	B	C	D
103		.137		.171		.205	

The completed decimal equivalent number for the full IPv6 address is

103.137.171.205.18.52.239.152.118.84.50.31.237.203.175.33

The equivalent decimal number is 42 characters in length. In fact, the decimal equivalent number could be 48 decimal numbers long.

In terms of bits, one 4 hex bit group requires $4 \times 4 = 16$ bits. Assuming that 8 bits are used to represent the decimal numbers, it will take $12 \times 8 = 72$ bits to express one hex bit group in a decimal format. There is a significant bit savings obtained by expressing the IPv6 address in a hexadecimal format.

IPv6 uses seven colons (:) as separators to group the 32 hex characters into eight groups of four. Some IPv6 numbers will have a 0 within the address. In this case, IPv6 allows the number to be compressed to make it easier to write the number. For example, assume that an IPv6 number is as follows:

6789:0000:0000:EF98:7654:321F:EDCB:AF21

Consecutive 0s can be dropped and a double-colon notation can be used:

6789::EF98:7654:321F:EDCB:AF21

Recovering the compressed number in double-colon notation simply requires that all numbers left of the double notation be entered beginning with the leftmost slot of the IPv6 address. Next, start with the numbers to the right of the double colon.

Begin with the rightmost slot of the IPv6 address slots and enter the numbers from right to left until the double colon is reached. Zeros are entered into any empty slots.

<u>6789</u> :0 :0 :EF98 :7654 :321F :EDCB :AF21

IPv4 numbers can be written in the new IPv6 form by writing the IPv4 number in hexadecimal and placing the number to the right of a double colon. Example 5-11 demonstrates how a dotted-decimal IP number can be converted to IPv6 hexadecimal.

Example 5-11

Convert the IPv4 address of 192.168.5.20 to an IPv6 hexadecimal address.

Solution:

First convert each dotted-decimal number to hexadecimal.

Decimal	Hex
192	C0
168	A8
5	05
20	14

(*Hint:* use a calculator or a lookup table to convert the decimal numbers to hexadecimal.) The IPv6 address will have many leading 0s; therefore, the IPv6 hex address can be written in double-colon notation as

:: C0A8:0514

IPv4 numbers can also be written in IPv6 form by writing the IPv4 number in dotted-decimal format as shown. Note that the number is preceded by 24 hexadecimal 0s.

0000: 0000: 0000: 0000: 0000: 0000:192.168.5.20

This number can be reduced as follows:

::192.168.5.20

Unicast Address
Used to identify a single network interface address, and data packets are sent directly to the computer with the specified IPv6 address

Multicast Address
Data packets sent to a multicast address are sent to the entire group of networking devices, such as a group of routers running the same routing protocol

Anycast Address
Is obtained from a list of addresses

6to4 Prefix
A technique that enables IPv6 hosts to communicate over the IPv4 Internet.

There are three types of IPv6 addresses: **unicast**, **multicast**, and **anycast.** The unicast IPv6 address is used to identify a single network interface address and data packets are sent directly to the computer with the specified IPv6 address. Multicast IPv6 addresses are defined for a group of networking devices. Data packets sent to a multicast address are sent to the entire group of networking devices, such as a group of routers running the same routing protocol. Multicast addresses all start with the prefix FF00::/8. The next group of characters in the IPv6 multicast address (the second octet) are called the scope. The scope bits are used to identify which ISP should carry the data traffic. The anycast IPv6 address is obtained from a list of addresses but is only delivered to the nearest node.

IPv6 addressing is being used in a limited number of network sites (for example, www.6bone.com and the federal government) however, the Internet is still running IPv4 and will be for some time. However, there are transition strategies in place to help with the IPv4-to-IPv6 transition.

One possible transition to IPv6 is called the **6to4 Prefix**, which is essentially a technique that enables IPv6 sites to communicate over the IPv4 Internet. This requires the use of a 6to4-enabled router, which means that 6to4 tunneling has been enabled. This also requires the use of a 6to4 Relay router that forwards 6to4 data traffic to other 6to4 routers on the Internet.

Figure 5-19 illustrates the structure of the 6to4 prefix for hosts. The 32 bits of the IPv4 address fit into the first 48 bits of the IPv6 address.

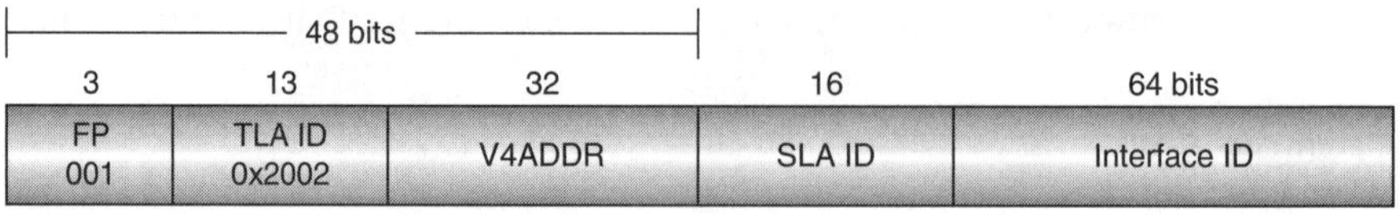

3	13	32	16	64 bits
FP 001	TLA ID 0x2002	V4ADDR	SLA ID	Interface ID

FIGURE 5-19   The 6to4 Prefix Format

Note the following in Figure 5-19:

- **FP** is the format prefix, which is made up of the higher order bits. The **001** indicates that this is a global unicast address. The current list of the IPv6 address allocation can be viewed at http://www.iana.org/assignments/ipv6-unicast-address-assignments.

- **TLA ID (0x2002)** is the top-level identifiers issued to local Internet registries. These IDs are administered by IANA (http://www.iana.org/). The TLA is used to identify the highest level in the routing hierarchy. The TLA ID is 13 bits long.
- **V4ADDR** is the IPv4 address of the 6to4 endpoint and is 32 bits long.
- **SLA ID** is the site level aggregation identifier that is used by individual organizations to identify subnets within their sites. The SLA ID is 16 bits long.
- **Interface ID** is the link-level host identifier, used to indicate an interface on a specific subnet. The interface ID is equivalent to the host IP address in IPv4.

The 6to4 prefix format enables IPv6 domains to communicate with each other even if they don't have an IPv6 ISP. Additionally, IPv6 can be used within the intranet but access to the Internet is still available. The 6to4 provides unicast IPv6 connectivity between IPv6 host and via the IPv4 Internet.

When will the Internet switch to IPv6? The answer is not clear, but the networking community recognizes that something must be done to address the limited availability of current IP address space. Manufacturers have already incorporated IPv6 capabilities in their routers and operating systems. What about IPv4? The bottom line is that the switch to IPv6 will not come without providing some way for IPv4 networks to still function. Additionally, techniques such as Network Address Translation (NAT—see Chapter 1) have made it possible for intranets to use the private address space and still be able to connect to the Internet. This has significantly reduced the number of IP addresses required for each network.

5-8   ANALYZING COMPUTER NETWORKS—FTP DATA PACKETS

This section explores the data packet contents of an FTP data transfer. **FTP** is the File Transfer Protocol defined in the TCP/IP model. The captured file is available on the companion CD-ROM in the *Capture* folder. The filename is *5-d.cap*. This file contains several TCP transactions. This discussion will identify the packet IP for reference.

FTP
File Transfer Protocol

Figure 5-20 provides the setup for this data capture. The MAC addresses for the client and server are provided as reference. The beginning of the FTP is shown in packet 4 in Figure 5-21 (a). The packet shows that a connection is being made from a Windows server to port 1054 on a client computer. In packet 7, the client is responding with a username of *administrator*. In packet 8 the server is telling the client that a password is required. The client responds with the password *Chile* in packet 10. In packet 13 the server acknowledges that the user *administrator* is connected to the server.

In packet 17 [Figure 5-21 (b)] the client is notifying the server that an ASCII data transfer is requested. This is indicated in the Type A statement. In packet 18, the server acknowledges that an ASCII transfer is requested (*Type set to A*). Packet 23 is a request from the client to start the data packet transfer from the server. The text *STOR text.txt* signifies this. In packet 24 the server indicates that it is opening the ASCII mode for the transfer. When the FTP connection is established, the port numbers change to handle the data transfer as shown in packet 30, SP = 20 DP = 1055. Packets 37, 39, and 40 are the closing of the FTP transfer [Figure 5-21 (c)]. The FTP data packets examined are part of a TCP connection. This required that a TCP connection was both established and closed. In fact, the TCP initial handshake and the connection closing for this FTP session were presented in section 5-2.

Dell 271F6B

00107B7F8147

1054

Client

Server

FIGURE 5-20   The computer setup for the FTP packet transfer.

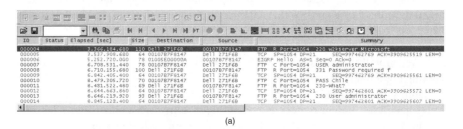

(a)

(b)

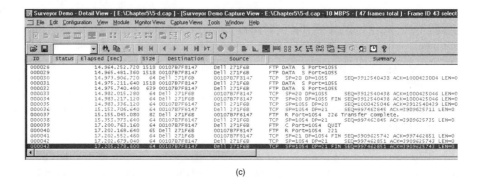

(c)

FIGURE 5-21   (a) The beginning of the FTP data packet transfer; (b) the request for an ASCII data transfer by the client; (c) the closing of the FTP transfer.

Summary

This chapter has presented an overview of the fundamentals of the TCP/IP protocol suite. TCP/IP is well established and carries the data traffic over the Internet. The student should understand the following:

- The layers of TCP/IP and their relationship to the OSI layers
- The basic structure of a 32-bit IPv4 address
- How to subnet a network
- How to apply subnet masks in networks
- The purpose of CIDR blocks and supernetting
- The data structure of an IPv6 hexadecimal address
- The structure and purpose of the 6to4 protocol
- How to examine TCP/IP data packets with the Finisar Surveyor Demo Protocol Analyzer

Questions and Problems

Section 5-2

1. What are the four layers of the TCP/IP model?
2. Which layer of the TCP/IP model processes requests from hosts to make sure a connection is made to the appropriate port?
3. What are *well-known ports*?
4. Identify the port numbers for the following applications.
    a. Telnet
    b. HTTP
    c. FTP
    d. DNS
    e. DHCP
5. Define the purpose of a *connection oriented protocol*. Give an example.
6. What three packets are exchanged between two hosts when establishing a TCP connection?
7. What is the purpose of a sequence number (SEQ=) in TCP data packets?
8. Explain how a host knows whether a data packet was not received.
9. Describe how a TCP connection is terminated.
10. What is a *connectionless protocol*? Give an example.
11. What is the purpose of the Internet layer in the TCP/IP protocol suite?
12. What is the purpose of an ARP request?
13. What is the purpose of an ARP reply?
14. What important networking-troubleshooting tool is part of ICMP, and how does it test a network connection?
15. When is IGMP used?
16. The network interface layer of the TCP/IP model defines how the host connects to what network?

Section 5-3

17. Convert the following 8-bit binary number to decimal: 10010011
18. Convert the following octet to decimal: 11000000
19. Convert the following 8-bit number to decimal: 11111100
20. Convert the following binary number to decimal: 11111111
21. Convert the number 192 to its binary equivalent.
22. Convert the number 65 to its binary equivalent.
23. Convert the number 96 to its binary equivalent.
24. What is the equivalent hexadecimal number for 13?
25. Convert 0x5AF3 to binary. Use Table 5-5.
26. Convert 1011011011110001 to hexadecimal.

Section 5-4

27. What is the IP address range for class C addresses?
28. What is the purpose of class D IP addresses?
29. How many bits are in an IPv4 address? How many octets?
30. The IP address is typically expressed in what format for the user?
31. The IP address 192.168.12.2 is an example of what format?
32. How many network bits are in each of the following classes?
    a. Class A
    b. Class B
33. How many network and host bits are in a class C network address?
34. What is the purpose of a private IP address?
35. Can private IP addresses be routed?
36. How are private IP addresses handled on the Internet?
37. What organization assigns IP addresses?

Section 5-5

38. How many host bits are borrowed if four subnets are created? 2
39. What is the purpose of a subnet mask? Tells what network on.
40. A host computer is assigned the IP address 192.168.12.8 and a subnet mask of 255.255.255.192. The host sends a packet to another host with an IP address of 192.168.12.65. Is the destination IP address in the same subnet as 192.168.12.8? Show why or why not.
41. The subnet mask 255.255.255.224 is applied to a packet with a destination IP address of 192.168.12.135. What subnet is the packet sent to?
42. The subnet mask 255.255.255.0 is applied to a packet with the following IP addresses. What subnet is the packet sent to?
    a. 10.20.35.12
    b. 10.20.35.3
    c. 10.50.35.6
    d. 192.168.12.8

43. Given an IP address of 193.10.10.0, answer the following questions if the number of subnets created is 4.
   a. Determine the network address and the broadcast address for each subnet.

	Network Address	Broadcast Address
1st subnet		
2nd subnet		
3rd subnet		
4th subnet		

   b. Determine the subnet mask:
   c. Determine the number of usable hosts per subnet:

44. Given a network IP address of 211.123.83.0, answer the following questions if 8 subnets are to be created. The 8 subnets include the network and broadcast address.
   a. Determine the network address and the broadcast address for each subnet.

	Network Address	Broadcast Address
1st subnet	211 123 83. 0	211 . 123 .83. 31
2nd subnet	211 123 83. 32	211 . 123 . 83 . 63
3rd subnet	211 .123 .83 .64	211 . 123 . 83 . 95
4th subnet	211 .123 .83 .96	211 . 123 . 83 . 127
5th subnet	211.123 .83 . 128	211 .123 . 83 . 159
6th subnet	211 .123 ,83 .160	211 . 123 .83 ,191
7th subnet	211.123 .83 . 192	211 .123 ,83 ,223
8th subnet	211 .123 .83 ,224	211 .123 . 83 . 255

   b. Determine the subnet mask:
   c. Determine the number of hosts per subnet

45. Complete the following table, given class C subnetting.

# Mask Bits	Subnet Mask	# Subnets	# Hosts/Subnet
2	255.255.255.192	4	62
3			
4			
5			
6			

Section 5-6

46. Complete the following table.

Network Address	Class	Classless Interdomain Routing (CIDR)	Subnet Mask	# Subnets	# Hosts/ Subnet
128.123.0.0	B	/30	255.255.255.252	16384	2
135.45.0.0		/25			
193.10.10.0		/28			
211.123.83.0		/26			
10.0.0.0		/13			
32.0.0.0		/20			
204.204.5.0		/28			
223.201.65.0		/27			
156.35.0.0		/21			
116.0.0.0		/14			
145.23.0.0		/29			
199.12.1.0		/30			
15.0.0.0		/29			

47. How is a network address of 192.168.6.0 and a subnet mask of 255.255.254.0 written in CIDR?

48. A CIDR block contains the following subnets with IP addresses of
    a. 192.168.68.0/22
    b. 192.168.69.0/22
    c. 192.168.70.0/22
    d. 192.168.71.0/22

    Are there any problems with this group of subnets in the CIDR block? Show your work.

Section 5-7

49. How many bits are in an IPv6 address?
50. IPv6 numbers are written in what format?
51. Express the following IPv6 numbers using double-colon notation:
    a. 5355:4821:0000:0000:0000:1234:5678:FEDC
    b. 0000:0000:0000:1234:5678:FEDC:BA98:7654
    c. 1234:5678:ABCD:EF12:0000:0000:1122:3344
52. Express the IPv4 IP address 192.168.12.5 in IPv6 form using dotted decimal.
53. Recover the IPv6 address from the following double-colon notation:

    1234:5678::AFBC

54. Define the structure of the 6to4 prefix.
55. What is the purpose of the 6to4 relay router?

Section 5-8

56. What are the server port numbers for an FTP transfer?
57. How does a client notify a server that an ASCII data transfer is requested?

Critical Thinking

58. Your boss has read about IPv6 and wants to know if the network you oversee is ready for the transition. Prepare a response based on the networking and computer operating systems used in your facility.
59. Use the Surveyor Demo protocol analyzer software to capture the start of a TCP session in your network. Identify the packets that are part of the initial handshake.

Surveyor IP Problems

The following questions use the *chapter 5-hw.cap* file on the Net-Challenge CD-ROM.

60. What routing protocols are used in this network?
61. In the FTP exchange, what operating system is the server running?
62. What is the destination address for the FTP server?
63. What is the source address for the FTP transfer?
64. What is the username sent to the FTP server?
65. What is the password sent to the FTP server?
66. What is the name of the file sent over FTP?
67. What are the contents of the file?
68. From Packet ID# 7, what is the FTP server requesting from the host?

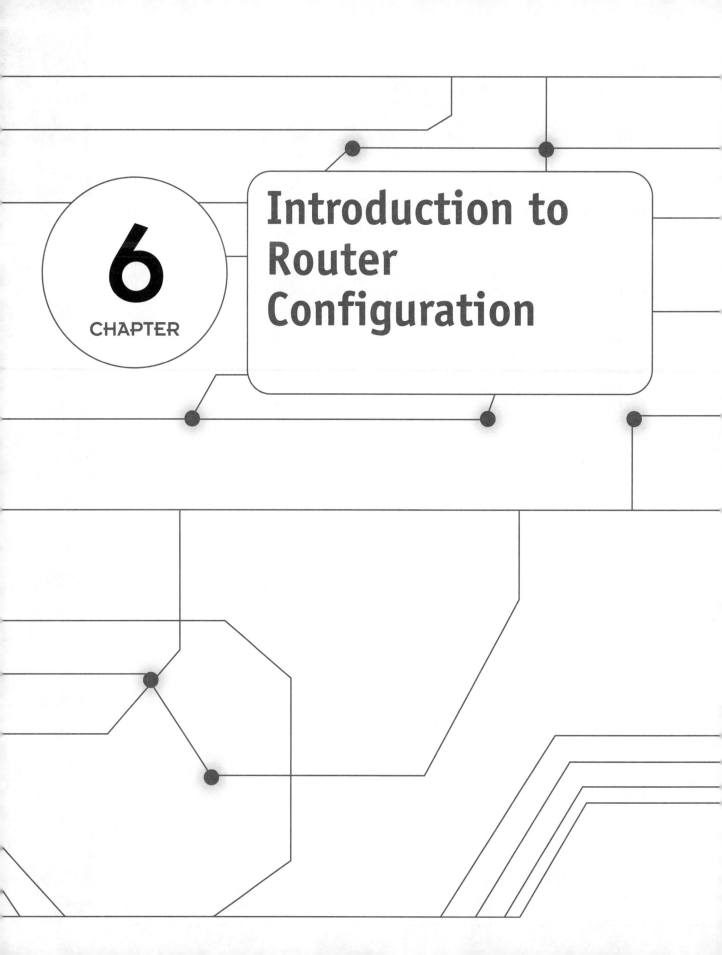

6
CHAPTER

Introduction to
Router
Configuration

CHAPTER OUTLINE

6-1   Introduction
6-2   Router Fundamentals
6-3   The Console Port Connection
6-4   The Router's User EXEC Mode
      (Router>)

6-5   The Router's Privileged EXEC Mode
      (Router#)
6-6   Troubleshooting the Router Interface
Summary
Questions and Problems

OBJECTIVES

- Describe the purpose of a router
- Describe the purpose of a gateway
- Describe the steps (software and hardware) for connecting to a router's console port
- Describe the Cisco IOS command structure
- Define the function of the command-line interface
- Define the functional difference with the router's user and privileged EXEC modes

- Be able to enter basic router configuration modes
- Demonstrate that you can enable and disable certain router interfaces
- Demonstrate that you can perform basic router troubleshooting
- Describe what information is contained in the running-configuration file
- Define what it means for an interface to be administratively up or down

KEY TERMS

Cisco IOS
command line interface (CLI)
CCNA
CCNP
CCIE
broadcast domain
flat network
routed network
layer 3 network
default gateway address
next hop address
subnet, NET
RS-232

DB-9
DB-25
console cable
COM1, COM2, . . .
rollover cable
hostname
user EXEC mode
user mode
?
show flash
show version
router uptime
privileged mode

enable
Router#
configure terminal (conf t)
Router(config)#
Router(config-line)#
Router(config-if)#
no shutdown (no shut)
show ip interface brief (sh ip int brief)
DCE
DTE
Keepalive packet
administratively down

6-1   INTRODUCTION

Cisco IOS
Cisco Internet Operating
System, the operating
software used in all Cisco
routers

**Command Line Interface
(CLI)**
The interface type used for
inputting commands and
configuring devices such as
routers

CCNA
Cisco Certified Network
Associate

CCNP
Cisco Certified Network
Professional

CCIE
Cisco Certified Internet
Expert

The main objective of this chapter is to introduce the use of the **Cisco IOS** (Internet Operating System) software for configuring routers. Cisco IOS is the operating software used to configure all Cisco routers. It includes a **command line interface (CLI)** for inputting instructions to configure the Cisco router interface. There are many choices for routers in the market; however, Cisco routers have set the standard. Also, Cisco certifications such as the **CCNA** (Cisco Certified Network Associate), the **CCNP** (Cisco Certified Network Professional), and the professional benchmark for internetworking expertise, the **CCIE** (Cisco Certified Internet Expert), base their testing on the applicant's ability to configure, troubleshoot, and analyze LANs that incorporate Cisco routers and switches.

An overview of router fundamentals is presented in section 6-2. Some of the router concepts and terminology presented in Chapter 4 are reexamined, in particular the following:

- The concepts of interconnecting LANs with routers
- The concept of a network segment
- Data flow through a routed network

The procedure for configuring a router through the router's console port is presented in section 6-3. The discussion includes an overview of configuring a computer's serial communication software and selecting the proper cable and hardware for connecting the console port to a computer. Sections 6-4 and 6-5 introduce the steps for accessing and programming the router interface. The user EXEC mode is examined in section 6-4, the privileged EXEC mode in section 6-5. These sections teach the reader how to work with the Cisco IOS command structure and how to access many of the configuration layers in the Cisco IOS. Sections 6-4 and 6-5 also include networking challenges using the Net-Challenge software included with the accompanying companion CD-ROM. These challenges enable students to test their ability to access and program a router's interface. The simulator software was developed specifically for this text and emulates programming the interface of a Cisco router. The console port connection is emulated with the software, and although the simulator doesn't emulate all the router programming modes or operational features, it does emulate the functions presented in the text. The chapter concludes with a section on troubleshooting the router interface. This section introduces a commonly used router command and how the command is used to troubleshoot and isolate router configuration problems.

6-2   ROUTER FUNDAMENTALS

This section further defines the function of a router in a network and describes how data packets travel through a layer 3 network. A layer 3 network uses IP addressing for routing data packets to the final destination. Delivery of the data packets is made possible by the use of a destination MAC address, IP address, network addresses, and routing tables. Each of these concepts is examined in this section.

LANs are not necessarily restricted in size. A LAN can have 20 computers, 200 computers, or even more. Multiple LANs also may be interconnected to essentially create one large LAN. For example, the first floor of a building could be set up as one

LAN, the second floor as another LAN, and the third floor another. The three LANs in the building can be interconnected into essentially one large LAN using switches, with the switches interconnected as shown in Figure 6-1.

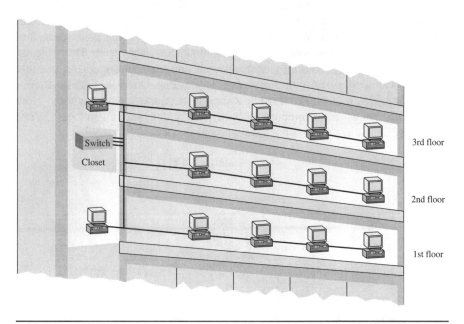

Switch

Closet

3rd floor

2nd floor

1st floor

FIGURE 6-1   Three floors of a building interconnected using switches to form one large LAN.

Is it bad to interconnect LANs this way? As long as switches are being used to interconnect the computers, the impact of the interconnected LANs has minimal impact on network performance. This is true as long as there are not too many computers in the LAN. The number of computers in the LAN is an issue because layer 2 switches do not separate **broadcast domains**. This means that any broadcast sent out on the network (for example, the broadcast associated with an ARP request) will be sent to all computers in the LAN. Excessive broadcasts are a problem because each computer must process the broadcast to determine whether it needs to respond, and this essentially slows down the computer and the network. Virtual LANs are now being used to interconnect LANs. This concept is examined in Chapter 9.

A network with multiple LANs interconnected together at the layer 2 level is called a **flat network**. A flat network is where the LANs share the same broadcast domain. The use of a flat network should be avoided if possible for the simple reason that the network response time is greatly affected. Flat networks can be avoided by the use of layer 3 networks. This topic is discussed next.

Broadcast Domain
Any broadcast sent out on the network is seen by all hosts in this domain

Flat Network
A network where the LANs share the same broadcast domain

Layer 3 Networks

In both the simple office type LAN introduced in Chapter 1 and the building LAN just discussed, the hosts are interconnected with a switch or a hub. This allows data to be exchanged within the LAN; however, data cannot be routed to other networks. Also, the broadcast domain of one LAN is not isolated from another LAN's broadcast domain. The solution for breaking up the broadcast domains and to provide network routing is to incorporate routing hardware into the network design to create a **routed network**. A routed network uses layer 3 addressing for selecting routes to forward data packets, so a better name for this network is a **layer 3 network**.

In layer 3 networks, routers and layer 3 switches are used to interconnect the networks and LANs, isolating broadcast domains and enabling hosts from different LANs and networks to exchange data. Data packet delivery is achieved by handing off data to adjacent routers until the packet reaches its final destination. This typically involves passing data packets through many routers and many networks. An example of a layer 3 network is shown in Figure 6-2. This example has four LANs interconnected using three routers. The IP address for each networking device is listed. How does information get from computer A1 in LAN A to computer C1 in LAN C? The following discussion describes the travel of the data packets.

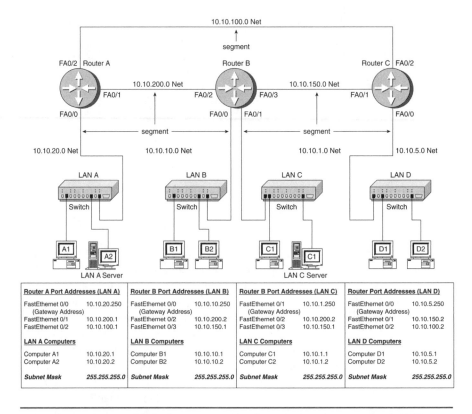

Router A Port Addresses (LAN A)		Router B Port Addresses (LAN B)		Router B Port Addresses (LAN C)		Router Port Addresses (LAN D)	
FastEthernet 0/0 (Gateway Address)	10.10.20.250	FastEthernet 0/0 (Gateway Address)	10.10.10.250	FastEthernet 0/1 (Gateway Address)	10.10.1.250	FastEthernet 0/0 (Gateway Address)	10.10.5.250
FastEthernet 0/1	10.10.200.1	FastEthernet 0/2	10.10.200.2	FastEthernet 0/2	10.10.200.2	FastEthernet 0/1	10.10.150.2
FastEthernet 0/2	10.10.100.1	FastEthernet 0/3	10.10.150.1	FastEthernet 0/3	10.10.150.1	FastEthernet 0/2	10.10.100.2
LAN A Computers		**LAN B Computers**		**LAN C Computers**		**LAN D Computers**	
Computer A1	10.10.20.1	Computer B1	10.10.10.1	Computer C1	10.10.1.1	Computer D1	10.10.5.1
Computer A2	10.10.20.2	Computer B2	10.10.10.2	Computer C2	10.10.1.2	Computer D2	10.10.5.2
Subnet Mask	*255.255.255.0*	*Subnet Mask*	*255.255.255.0*	*Subnet Mask*	*255.255.255.0*	*Subnet Mask*	*255.255.255.0*

FIGURE 6-2   An example of a layer 3 network using routers to interconnect the LANs.

Computer A1 (IP address 10.10.20.1) sends a data packet to computer C1 (IP address 10.10.1.1). First, computer A1 uses the assigned subnet mask (255.255.255.0) to determine whether the destination IP address 10.10.1.1 is in the same subnet or network as itself. Applying the subnet mask to the destination address shows the final destination of the data packet is the 10.10.1.0 network (10.10.1.0 NET). This is not the same subnet or network in which computer A1 resides (10.10.20.0 NET). Therefore, the data packet is forwarded to the **default gateway address** defined by the computer. The default gateway address is the IP address of a networking device (for example, a router) used to forward data that needs to exit the

LAN. An example of setting a computer's default gateway is provided in Figure 6-3. The default gateway address for computer A1 is 10.10.20.250. This is the IP address of Router A's FastEthernet0/0 port. Figure 6-2 shows that Router A's FastEthernet FA0/0 port connects directly to the switch in LAN A.

FIGURE 6-3   The TCP/IP menu for setting the default gateway address for computer A1.

Recall that the term *gateway* describes the networking device that enables data to enter and exit a LAN, and is where the host computers forward data packets that need to exit the LAN. In most networks, the gateway is typically a router or switch port address. An example of a gateway is provided in the block diagram shown in Figure 6-4. An important concept is that the IP address of the gateway must be in the same subnet as the LAN that connects to the gateway, and this same gateway enables data traffic to enter and exit the LAN. An example of using the subnet mask to determine the destination network is provided in Example 6-1.

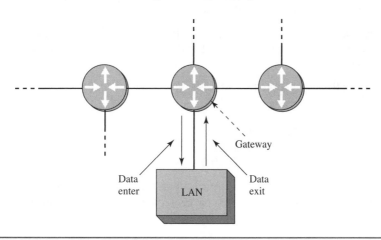

FIGURE 6-4   Data flow to and from the gateway.

Example 6-1

Problem:

A computer host sends two data packets out on the network. Each packet has a different IP destination address. Determine whether the data packets are to be forwarded to the default gateway or should remain in the same LAN as the host. The source host IP address is 10.10.20.2, and a subnet mask of 255.255.255.0 is being used. The destination IP addresses for the data packets are 10.10.1.1 and 10.10.20.3.

Solution:

First determine the network or subnet where the source host resides. This can be determined by "ANDing" the subnet mask with the source host IP address as shown. Subnet masks and subnets were presented in Chapter 5, section 5-5, and should be reviewed if this concept is difficult to follow. Remember, subnet masking is a binary AND operation. The decimal numbers are the equivalent of the 8-bit binary number. For example:

255	1 1 1 1 1 1 1 1
20	0 0 0 1 0 1 0 0
10	0 0 0 0 1 0 1 0
2	0 0 0 0 0 0 1 0

Source IP address	10. 10. 20. 2
Subnet mask	255.255. 255. 0
Subnet	10. 10. 20. 0

Therefore, the source host is in the 10.10.20.0 subnet (10.10.20.0 NET).

a. Determine the destination network for a data packet given the following information:

Destination IP address	10. 10. 1. 1
Subnet mask	255.255.255. 0
Subnet	10. 10. 1. 0

Answer: The destination subnet address for Part a is 10.10.1.0. This is not in the same subnet as the 10.10.20.2 host (10.10.20.0 NET). Therefore, the data packet is forwarded to the default gateway.

b. Determine the destination network for a data packet given the following information:

Destination IP address	10. 10. 20. 3
Subnet mask	255.255.255. 0
Subnet	10. 10. 20. 0

Answer: The destination subnet address for Part b is 10.10.20.0, which is the same subnet as the host. Therefore, the data packet remains in the 10.10.20.0 subnet.

The IP address of the data packet sent from the source computer to the gateway is examined by the router and a next hop address is selected. The gateway examines the destination IP address of all data packets arriving at its interface. The router uses a routing table to determine a network data path and the next hop address. As noted previously, a *routing table* is a list of the possible networks that can be used to route the data packets. Alternative data paths are usually provided so that a new route can be selected and data delivery maintained even if a network route is down. The **next hop address** is the IP address of the next networking device that can be used to forward the data packet to its destination.

Next Hop Address
The IP address of the next networking device that can be used to forward the data packet to its destination

For example, assume that a data packet is to be delivered from a host in LAN A to a destination address in LAN C (see Figure 6-2). The data packet is forwarded to the LAN A gateway, which is the FastEthernet 0/0 (FA0/0) port on Router A. The router examines the data packet and determines that the data can be sent to the host in LAN C via Router A's FastEthernet 0/2 (FA0/2) interface over the 10.10.100.0 NET to Router C, then to Router B, and finally to LAN C. The routing table also shows that there is a route to LAN C via Router A's FastEthernet 0/1 (FA0/1) interface over the 10.10.200.0 NET. The next hop off Router A's FastEthernet 0/1 (FA0/1) interface is the FA0/2 FastEthernet interface on Router B. Which is the better route?

In terms of hops, data from LAN A will have to travel over two hops (Router C and Router B) to reach LAN C. The route to LAN C via Router B requires only one hop; therefore, Router A will select the 10.10. 200.0 NET to route the data to LAN C because its has fewer router hops. The IP address of the FastEthernet 0/2 (FA0/2) port on Router B is called the next hop address. In each case, the next hop address is the IP address of the next networking device. For example, if the data travels to LAN C via Router B, the next hop address off Router A is the IP address of the FastEthernet 0/2 (FA0/2) port on Router B (10.10.200.2).

The MAC addresses are used to define the hardware address of the next hop in the network. When the next hop is defined, its MAC address is determined and the data packet is relayed.

When the routes are fully configured, data packets can be exchanged between any LANs in the interconnected routed network. For example, data can be exchanged between any of the hosts in any of the LANs shown in Figure 6-2. Computer A2 in LAN A can exchange data with computer D1 in LAN D, and computer C1 in LAN C can exchange data with computer B2 in LAN B. This differs from the simple office LAN that has restricted data packet delivery: The data packets can be exchanged only within the LAN. Using IP addressing and routers enables the data to be delivered outside the LAN. Recall that a *segment* in a network defines the physical link between two internetworking devices (for example, router-hub, router-switch, or router-router). For example, in an interconnected network, a segment is the name of the link between a router and another router. Another example is the segment that connects a router to a LAN via a hub or a switch. Each network segment has its own network address. For the small campus network shown in Figure 6-2, the network IP address for the segment connecting LAN A to the router is 10.10.20.0. All hosts connected to this segment must contain a 10.10.20.#. For example, Computer A1 is assigned the IP address 10.10.20.1.

The segment is sometimes called the **subnet** or **NET**. These terms are associated with a network segment address, such as 10.10.20.0. In this case, the network is called the 10.10.20.0 NET. All hosts in the 10.10.20.0 NET will have a 10.10.20.# IP address. The network addresses are used when configuring the routers and defining

Subnet, NET
Other terms for the segment

what networks are connected to the router. For example, the networks attached to Router A in Figure 6-2 are listed in Table 6-1.

The physical layer interface on the router provides a way to connect the router to other networking devices on the network. For example, the FastEthernet ports on the router are used to connect to other FastEthernet ports on other routers. Gigabit and 10 gigabit Ethernet ports are also available on routers to connect to other high-speed Ethernet ports. (The sample network shown in Figure 6-2 includes only FastEthernet ports.) Routers also contain serial interfaces that are used to interconnect the router and the network to other serial communication devices. For example, connection to wide area networks requires the use of a serial interface to connect to a communications carrier such as Sprint, MCI, AT&T, and so on. The data speeds for the serial communication ports on routers can vary from slow (56 kbps) up to high-speed DS3 data rates (47+ Mbps), OC3 (155 Mbps), OC12 (622 Mbps), or even OC192 (9953 Mbps).

The following is a summary of the discussion on layer 3 networks. The components of a layer 3 network are shown in Figure 6-5. The source host computer has an installed network interface card (NIC) and an assigned IP address and subnet mask.

TABLE 6-1   The Networks (Subnets) Attached to Router A in Figure 6-2

Router Port	Subnet
FA0/0	10.10.20.0
FA0/1	10.10.200.0
FA0/2	10.10.100.0

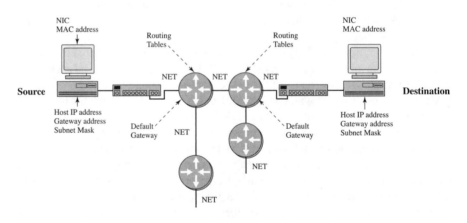

FIGURE 6-5   The components of a layer 3 network.

The subnet mask is used to determine whether the data is to stay in the LAN or is to be forwarded to the default gateway provided by the router. The router uses its subnet mask to determine the destination network address. The destination network address is checked with the router's routing table to select the best route to the destination. The data is then forwarded to the next router, which is the next hop address. The next router examines the data packet, determines the destination network address, checks its routing table, and then forwards the data to the next hop. If the destination network is directly connected to the router, it issues an ARP request to determine the MAC address of the destination host. Final delivery is then accomplished by forwarding the data using the destination host computer's MAC address. Routing of the data through the networks is at layer 3 and the final delivery of data in the network is at layer 2.

6-3   THE CONSOLE PORT CONNECTION

The router's console port is used as the initial interface for configuring the router. It is a slow-speed serial communications link (9600 bps) and is the only way to communicate with the router until the router interfaces have been configured. Specifically, the console connection is an **RS-232** serial communications port that uses an RJ-45 jack to connect to its interface. The RS-232 protocol running on the console port is the same communications protocol format used on a computer's (COM1, COM2) port; however, the connector for the serial communications port on the computer is either a **DB-9** or **DB-25** type connector. (*Note:* DB25 connectors are seldom used.) Figure 6-6 (a) and (b) shows drawings of the DB-9 and DB-25 connector ends. The DB-9 connection uses nine pins and the DB-25 connection uses 25 pins.

RS-232
Serial communications port

DB-9
9-pin connector

DB-25
25-pin connector

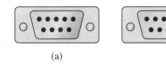

(a)   (b)

FIGURE 6-6   (a) DB-9 connector; (b) DB-25 connector (courtesy of StarTech.com).

The connection from the router to the serial port on the computer requires a cable run from the computer's serial port to the RJ-45 console jack input on the router. This can be accomplished using a cable with the DB-9 and RJ-45 plug ends, as shown in Figure 6-7 (a), or using an RJ-45 rollover cable and a DB-9 to RJ-45 adapter as shown in Figure 6-7 (b). Another option is to use a USB to 9-pin RS-232 adapter as shown in Figure 6-7 (c). A cable that connects the router's console port to the computer's serial port is called a **console cable**.

Connect the DB-9 end of the console cable to any of the available serial ports (**COM1, COM2, . . .**) on the computer. The router's console input uses an RJ-45 jack and the console cable must have an RJ-45 plug. The cable used to connect the RJ-45 plug to the computer is called a **rollover cable**, which is a flat cable that reverses signals on each cable end; for example, pins 1–8, 2–7, 3–6, and so on. Table 6-2 shows the signal assignments and pin number for each end of the rollover cable. Note that the pin numbers for the cables are swapped at each end.

Console Cable
A cable that connects a router's console port to a computer's serial port

COM1, COM2, . . .
The computer's serial communication ports

Rollover Cable
A cable with the signals reversed at each end

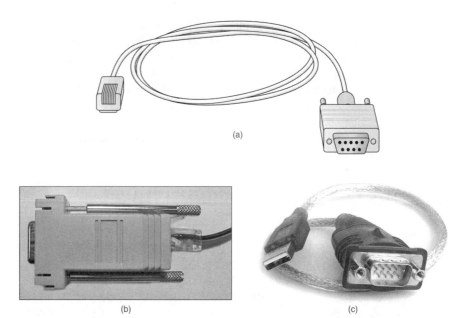

FIGURE 6-7 (a) A console cable with an integrated DB-9 connector; (b) a console cable using an RJ-45 rollover cable and a DB-9 to an RJ-45 adapter; (c) a USB to RS-232 adapter (courtesy of StarTech.com).

TABLE 6-2 Signal and Pin Assignments for the Console Rollover Cable

Signal	Function	RJ-45 end A	RJ-45 end B
RTS	Ready-to-Send	1	8
DTR	Data Terminal Ready	2	7
TXD	Transmit Data	3	6
GND	Ground	4	5
GND	Ground	5	4
RXD	Receive Data	6	3
DSR	Data Send Ready	7	2
CTS	Clear-to-Send	8	1

A serial communications software package such as HyperTerminal can be used to establish the communications link to the router's console input. The settings for the serial interface on a Cisco router's console port are provided in Table 6-3.

TABLE 6-3 Settings for Connecting to the Router Console Port

Bits per second	9600
Data bits	8
Parity	None
Stop bits	1
Flow control	none

The next step is to set up the console connection from a computer to the router. This requires that one RJ-45 end of a rollover cable be connected to the console port in the back of the router. The other end of the cable connects to one of the 9-pin serial communication ports (COM ports) of the computer. Note which serial port you connect to. You will have to specify the serial port (for example, COM1, COM2, and so on) when configuring the HyperTerminal serial communications software.

Configuring the HyperTerminal Software (Windows)

The HyperTerminal software is available on Windows XP but must be purchased separately for Windows Vista. After HyperTerminal is installed, click **Start—Programs—Accessories—Communications** and click **HyperTerminal** to start the HyperTerminal software on your computer. Click **Start—Programs—Hyperterminal** on Windows Vista. The **Connection Description** menu shown in Figure 6-8 will appear. Enter a name for your connection, such as *CiscoRouter*, and select an icon to be associated with the connection. Click **OK** when done.

FIGURE 6-8   The HyperTerminal Connection Description menu.

The next menu displayed is shown in Figure 6-9. This is the **Connect To** menu, which lets you specify how you are making the serial connection to the router. This example shows the connection is configured to use the computer's COM2 serial port. Change the Connect Using parameter to match the connection (COM1, COM2, . . .) you have made on your computer. Click **OK** when done.

FIGURE 6-9   The HyperTerminal Connect To menu.

The next menu is the **Properties** menu for your serial connection. This menu is labeled **COM2 Properties** because the Connect Using COM2 parameter was specified in the previous menu. Recall that the settings for connecting to the router's serial console port were provided in Table 6-3. The COM2 properties will have to be set to match these settings. Figure 6-10 shows the **COM2 Properties** menu with the settings entered. Click **OK** when done, and the **CiscoRouter—HyperTeminal** screen will be displayed. Press Enter to start the terminal communications. You should see the image shown in Figure 6-11 when a connection has been established. If the text does not display **Press RETURN to get started**, press Enter to see whether the router resets itself. Another possible screen you might see might have only the **Router>** prompt. Press Enter, and if the **Router>** prompt remains, you are connected. If this doesn't correct the displayed text, the router might need to be restarted.

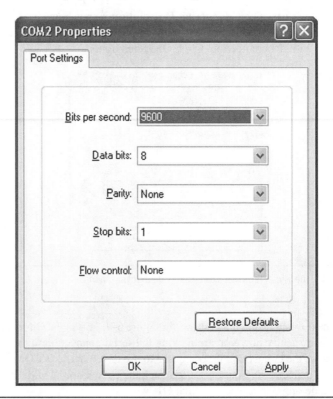

FIGURE 6-10   The Properties menu for configuring the serial port connection.

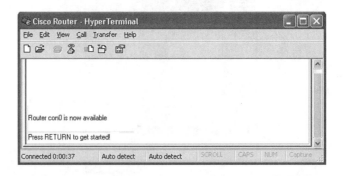

FIGURE 6-11   The Cisco router console port—HyperTerminal screen.

Configuring the Z-Term Serial Communications Software (Mac)

The following are the steps for establishing a console port via the USB serial connection on the Mac computer. This requires the following:

- A serial communication software such as ZTerm. ZTerm is a shareware program for the Mac that can be downloaded from the Internet.
- A USB to a 9-pin RS-232 male serial adapter, such as the USB to 9-pin adapter cable shown in Figure 6-7 (c). (*Note:* The USB-serial adapter can require that an additional driver be installed.)

Install the serial communications software and the driver. Start the serial communications software. Click **Setting—Modem Preferences** as shown in Figure 6-12. This opens the window shown in Figure 6-13. You will need to change the serial port so that it is set to **usbserial0**, and click **OK** when the change to usbserial0 has been made. Next, click **Settings—Connection** to open the menu shown in Figure 6-14. The following settings need to be set for the serial console connection. Click **OK** when done.

Data Rate: 9600
Data Bits: 8
Parity: N
Stop Bits: 1
Hardware Handshake

FIGURE 6-12   The Mac OS X menu for configuring the settings for the serial interface.

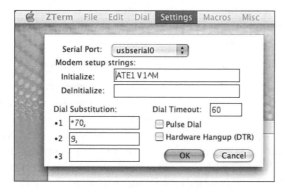

FIGURE 6-13   The Mac OS X menu for setting the serial port to usbserial0.

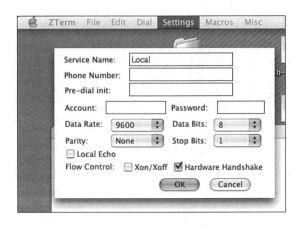

FIGURE 6-14   The Mac OS X window listing the serial communication link settings.

6-4   THE ROUTER'S USER EXEC MODE (ROUTER>)

This section introduces the use of the Cisco Internetwork Operating System (Cisco IOS) used for configuring Cisco routers. Cisco IOS, the standard interface software available on all Cisco routers, is regularly updated, thus providing improved configuration, management, and monitoring capabilities.

The Cisco IOS structure is fairly easy to navigate after you learn a few basic commands. Cisco IOS uses a command line interface (CLI) for inputting commands when configuring Cisco routers. This section explains some simple concepts, such as how to access the Help menu, using the *show* commands, and configuration options. The text comes with the Net-Challenge Companion CD-ROM that includes a router simulator specifically developed for this text. The simulator enables you to practice accessing various router modes and gain practice configuring a router for use in a network. The networking challenges presented in the text are available with the Companion CD-ROM for testing your knowledge.

The User EXEC Mode

The first text you see on the terminal screen after a console connection is made to the router is **Router con0 is now available**. This text confirms that you have connected to the router's console port.

```
Router con0 is now available Press RETURN to get started! Router>
```

Hostname
The name assigned to a networking device

User EXEC Mode
Used by a user to check to router status

User Mode
Same as the user EXEC mode

You are prompted to **Press RETURN to get started!** Press **Return** (the **Enter** key on the keyboard) to connect to the router. The prompt **Router>** indicates that you have connected to a router with the **hostname** Router, and the **>** symbol indicates that you have entered the **user EXEC mode** on the router. The user EXEC mode, also called the **user mode**, is the unsecured first level of entry passed through when accessing the router's interface. It does not allow the user any access to the router's configuration options. However, some of the router parameters, such as the version of the Cisco IOS software running on the machine, memory, flash, and the available commands, can be viewed.

You can view the commands that are recognized at the user level by entering a **?** after the **Router>** prompt. The **?** is the universal help command in Cisco IOS that allows you to view the available commands from any prompt. The following shows an example of using the **?** command to display the available commands from the **Router>** prompt:

? The help command that can be used at any prompt in the command line interface for the Cisco IOS software

```
Router>?
Exec commands:
access-enable     Create a temporary Access-List entry

clear             Reset functions

connect           Open a terminal connection disable Turn off privileged
  commands

disconnect        Disconnect an existing network connection
enable            Turn on privileged commands
exit              Exit from the EXEC
help              Description of the interactive help system lock Lock
  the terminal
login             Log in as a particular user logout Exit from the EXEC
mrinfo            Request neighbor and version information from a multi-
  cast router
mstat             Show statistics after multiple multicast traceroutes
mtrace            Trace reverse
multicast         path from destination to source
name-connection   Name an existing network connection
pad               Open a X.29 PAD connection ping Send echo messages
ppp               Start IETF Point-to-Point Protocol (PPP)
resume            Resume an active network connection
rlogin            Open an rlogin connection
set               Set system parameter (not config) show
Show              running system information
slip              Start Serial-line IP (SLIP)
systat            Display information about terminal lines
telnet            Open a telnet connection
terminal          Set terminal line parameters
traceroute        Trace route to destination
tunnel            Open a tunnel connection
where             List active connections
x28               Become an X.28 PAD
x3                Set X.3 parameters on PAD
```

It's obvious from the **Router>** help listing that the command options are quite extensive, and it takes some time to master them all. The objective of this chapter is to introduce the fundamental commands required for navigating the Cisco IOS and for configuring the router's interface. In particular, this section concentrates on the commands and procedures for configuring the router's FastEthernet and serial ports.

Another way to display commands or features is to place a **?** after the command. For example, placing a **?** after the *show* command lists all the options available for the *show* command.

```
Router>show ?
```

The **?** following a command can be used after any command from any prompt in the command line interface in the Cisco IOS software. An example of placing the **?** after the *show* command at the **Router>** prompt lists the available options in the user mode for the *show* command:

```
Router>show ?
backup       Backup status
clock        Display the system clock
dialer       Dialer parameters and statistics
```

```
flash:          display information about flash: file system
history         Display the session command history
hosts           IP domain-name, lookup style, nameservers, and host table
   location        Display the system location
modemcap        Show Modem Capabilities database
ppp             PPP parameters and statistics
rmon            rmon statistics
rtr             Response Time Reporter (RTR)
sessions        Information about Telnet connections
snmp            snmp statistics
tacacs          Shows tacacs + server statistics
terminal        Display terminal configuration parameters
traffic-shape   Traffic rate shaping configuration
users           Display information about terminal lines

version         System hardware and software status
```

show flash
Lists the details of the router's flash memory

Two key options for *show* in the user (**Router>**) mode are *show flash* and *show version*. *Show flash* lists the details of the router's flash memory, while *show version* lists the version of the Cisco IOS software running on the router. Examples of each are provided.

The *show flash* command displays the flash memory available and the amount of flash memory used. This command is typically used to verify whether there is sufficient memory available to load a new version of the Cisco IOS software. In this example, the IOS software is already installed, the file length is 6788464, and the name of the file is *c2500-d-1.120-4*.

```
Router>show flash
System flash directory: File Length Name/status
1 6788464 c2800-d-1.120-4
[6788528 bytes used, 1600080 available, 8388608 total]
8192K bytes of processor board System flash (Read ONLY)
```

show version
Lists the version of the Cisco IOS software running on the router

Router Uptime
The amount of time the router has been running

The following listing for *show version* indicates that the router is operating version 12.4. Notice that the *show version* command also lists the amount of time that the router has been running. This is listed as the **Router uptime**. In this example the router has been running 41 minutes, and it indicates that the system was restarted by power-on. This is a good place to check when troubleshooting intermittent problems with a router. Recurring statements that the router was restarted by power-on could indicate that the router has an intermittent power supply problem or that the power to the router is intermittent. Another possibility is that someone is resetting the router. This is not common because access to the router is typically password protected.

```
Router>show version
Cisco Internetwork Operating System Software
IOS (tm) 2800 Software (C2800-D-L), Version 12.4, RELEASE SOFTWARE (fc1)
   Copyright (c) 1986-2006 by Cisco Systems, Inc.
Compiled Wed 14-Apr-06 21:21 by prod_rel_team
Image text-base: 0x03037C88, data-base: 0x00001000

ROM: System Bootstrap, Version 12.04(10c), SOFTWARE
BOOTFLASH: 3000 Bootstrap Software (IGS-BOOT-R), Version 12.2(10c),
   RELEASE SOFTWARE (fc1)

Router uptime is 41 minutes
System restarted by power-on
System image file is "flash:c2800-d-1.120-4"

cisco 2800 (68030) processor (revision N) with 2048K/2048K bytes of mem-
   ory. Processor board ID 14733315, with hardware revision 00000000
```

```
Bridging software.
X.25 software, Version 3.0.0.
1 FastEthernet/IEEE 802.3 interface(s)
2 Serial network interface(s)
32K bytes of non-volatile configuration memory.
8192K bytes of processor board System flash (Read ONLY)

Configuration register is 0x42
```

Router Configuration Challenge—The User EXEC Mode

Use the Net-Challenge software included with the companion CD-ROM to complete this exercise. Place the disk in your computer's CD-ROM drive. The Net-Challenge software is located in the *Net-Challenge* folder on the CD-ROM. Open the folder and click the *Net-Challenge.exe* file. The program will open on your desktop with the screen shown in Figure 6-15. The Net-Challenge software is based on a three-router campus network setting. The software allows the user to configure each of the three routers and to configure the network interface for computers in the LANs attached to each router. Connection to each router is provided by clicking one of the three router buttons shown in Figure 6-15. Clicking a router button connects the selected router to a console session, thus enabling the simulated console terminal access to all three routers. The routers are marked with their default hostnames of Router A, Router B, and Router C. This challenge tests your ability to use router commands in the user EXEC mode. Click the *Net-Challenge.exe* file to start the software. Then click the **Select Challenge** button to open a list of challenges available with the software. Select the **User EXEC Mode** challenge. Selecting a challenge will open a checkbox window, as shown in Figure 6-16. The tasks in each challenge will be checked as completed, as appropriate.

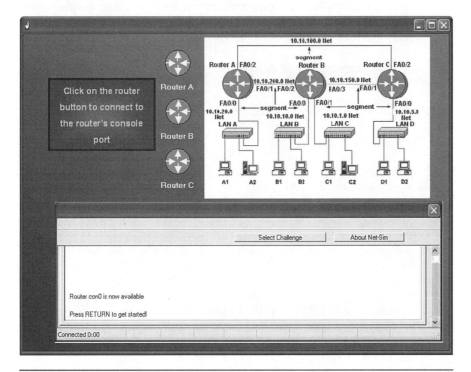

FIGURE 6-15   The Net-Challenge screen.

FIGURE 6-16   The checkbox for the User EXEC Net-Challenge software.

1. Make sure you are connected to Router A by clicking the appropriate selection button.
2. Demonstrate that you can enter the router's user EXEC mode. The router screen will display **Router>** when you are in the user EXEC mode.
3. Use the **?** for help to see the available command options in the Net-Challenge simulation software. You should see that the *enable*, *exit*, and *show* commands are available from the **Router>** prompt. The Net-Challenge software displays only the available commands and options within the software. The text provides examples of what the full command and help options look like.
4. Enter *exit* from the Router> prompt (*Router>exit*). Where does this place you? You should be back at the **Press RETURN** screen, as shown in Figure 6-17.
5. Reenter the user EXEC mode by pressing **Return**.

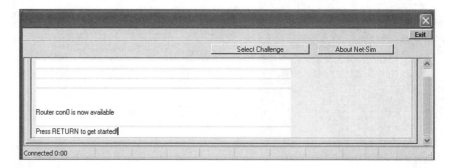

FIGURE 6-17   The screen that should be displayed in Step 4 after entering the *exit* command.

6. Enter the command *show* after the **Router>** prompt (*Router>show*). This step generates an "error unknown command" message. Include a **?** after the *show* command to see what options are available for *show*. The text displayed on the terminal screen should look like Figure 6-18.

FIGURE 6-18   The display for Step 6 using the *show* command.

7. Enter the command ***show flash*** at the **Router>** prompt on the command line interface. Describe the information displayed.
8. Enter the command ***show version*** at the **Router>** prompt on the command line interface. Describe the information displayed.
9. Enter the command ***show history*** at the **Router>** prompt on the command line interface. Describe the information displayed.

6-5   THE ROUTER'S PRIVILEGED EXEC MODE (ROUTER#)

Configuring a router interface requires you to enter **privileged mode** on the router. The privileged EXEC mode allows full access for configuring the router interfaces and configuring a routing protocol. This section focuses on general configuration steps for the router and configuring the router's interfaces, FastEthernet, and serial ports. Configuring routing protocols is examined in Chapter 7.

You enter the privileged mode using the command *enable* at the **Router>** prompt as shown. The # sign after the router name indicates you are in the privileged EXEC mode (**Router#**).

```
Router> enable
Password:
Router#
```

Entry into the router's privileged mode is typically password protected. The exception to this is when a router has not been configured and a password has not been assigned to it. In this case, pressing Enter on the keyboard from the **Router>** prompt will place you in the router's privileged mode (**Router#**). The two different steps for entering the router's privileged mode are shown in Figure 6-19: (a) no password protection and (b) password required.

Use caution when you have entered the privileged mode in a router. It is easy to make mistakes, and incorrectly entered router configurations will adversely affect your network. This text comes with the Net-Challenge router simulator on the companion CD-ROM to help you gain experience with router configuration. In fact, most of the router configuration commands presented in the text can be implemented in the router simulator on the companion CD-ROM. Many options are available for configuring the router and the router's interfaces from the **Router#** prompt. This section presents the key options needed to configure the router.

Privileged Mode
Allows the router ports and routing features to be configured

enable
The command used to enter the router's privileged mode

Router#
The pound sign indicates that the user is in the router's privileged EXEC mode

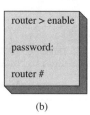

(a)

(b)

FIGURE 6-19   The steps for entering the router's privileged EXEC mode: (a) no password; (b) password required.

Hostname

The next commands examined require that the router's terminal configuration mode be entered. To do this, enter the command *configure terminal* (abbreviated *conf t*) at the **RouterA#** prompt to enter the router's configuration mode.

```
RouterA#conf t
Enter configuration commands, one per line. End with CNTL/Z.
RouterA(config)#

Or

RouterA#configure terminal
Enter configuration commands, one per line. End with CNTL/Z.
RouterA(config)#
```

Note the change in the prompt to **RouterA(config)#.** This indicates that the router is in terminal configuration mode.

The first router configuration option examined enables the user to assign a hostname to the router. The generic name or the name of an unconfigured Cisco router is *router*, and the **hostname** command enables the user to change the name to specifically identify the router. For example, valid hostname structures include RouterA, Router-A, or Router_A, while Router A is not valid. Valid router hostnames may not have any spaces. The word *router* does not have to be used in the hostname. The hostname can reflect the manner in which the router is being used. For example, a router can serve as the network gateway for the LANs in a building; for example, for a building named Goddard the router could be called *Goddard_gate.* This tells the network administrator the location and purpose of the router.

In the privileged mode (**Router#**) enter the command ***hostname [router-name] <enter>***. This sets the hostname for the router to *router-name*. The following example demonstrates how the router's hostname is changed to *RouterA*. Notice the change with the router's name from the first to the second line after the ***hostname*** command is entered.

```
Router(config)# hostname RouterA
RouterA#(config)
```

Enable Secret

Password protection for the privileged (enable) mode is configured by setting **enable secret**. The steps are as follows: Enter the router's configure terminal mode by entering *configure terminal* or *conf t* at the **Router#** prompt. Enter the command *enable secret [your-password] <enter>*. The following is an example:

```
Router# conf t
Router(config)#
Router(config)# enable secret my-secret
```

This example sets the password for entering the router's privileged EXEC mode to *my-secret*. The password for entering the router's privileged mode must now be entered to gain access to the mode.

Setting the Line Console Passwords

The router has three line connections through which a user may gain access to the router. The line connections available on a router can be displayed using the *line ?* command at the **Router(config)#** prompt. The available line connections are as follows:

aux	Auxiliary line
console	Primary terminal line (console port)
vty	Virtual terminal (for a telnet connection)

Router(config)#
The prompt for the router's terminal configuration mode

The *console* (primary terminal line) is the console port, *vty* is the virtual terminal used for telnet connections, and *aux* is used to establish an external modem connection. The following steps demonstrate how to configure password protection for the console port and the virtual terminal.

The console port configuration is as follows. Enter the command *line console 0 <enter>*. Next, enter the command *login*, press Enter, and then type the command *password [my-secret2]*, where *my-secret2* is the console port password. The following is an example of using these commands:

```
Router(config)# line console 0
Router(config-line)# login
Router(config-line)# password [my-secret2]
```

Note the change in the router prompt to **Router(config-line)#**, indicating you are in the router's line configuration mode.

Password protection for the virtual terminal (line vty) is set from the router's configuration mode. The virtual terminal is the method for entering the router via a Telnet connection. First enter the command *line vty 0 4*. This places the router in the line configuration mode (config-line). The 0 4 represents the number of vty lines to which the following configuration parameters will be applied. The five virtual terminal connections are identified as 0, 1, 2, 3, and 4. Next enter the command *password [my-secret3]*. The entry *my-secret3* is the password for the virtual terminal connection. The last step is to enter *login*, and press Enter.

Router(config-line)#
The prompt indicating you are in the router's line configuration mode

```
Router(config)# line vty 0 4
Router(config-line)# password [my-secret3]
Router(config-line)# login
```

Fast Ethernet Interface Configuration

Routers can have Ethernet (10 Mbps), Fast Ethernet (100 Mbps), gigabit Ethernet (1000 Mbps), and ten gigabit (10G) interfaces. These routers can have multiple interfaces supporting 10/100/1000 Mbps and 10 Gbps connections, and the steps for configuring each interface are basically the same. Each interface is assigned a numerical number. For example, a router could have three FastEthernet interfaces identified as

FastEthernet 0/0

FastEthernet 0/1

FastEthernet 0/2

Router(config-if)#

Indicates that you are in the router's interface configuration mode

no shutdown (no shut)

Enables a router's interface

The following steps describe how to configure a router's FastEthernet 0/0 port (FastEthernet 0/0, also listed as fa0/0 and FA0/0). In the router's configuration mode [**Router(config)#**], enter *interface fa0/0* and press Enter. This changes the router's prompt to **Router(config-if)#**, indicating you are in the router's interface configuration mode. The router keeps track of the interface you are configuring. The abbreviated command *int fa0/0* is used to access the FastEthernet0/0 interface. The router prompt will still show **Router(config-if)#**. Next enter the assigned IP address for the FastEthernet 0/0 port—for example, *ip address 10.10.20.250 255.255.255.0*—and press Enter. Next the router interface must be enabled. This is accomplished using the *no shutdown (no shut)* command. The following are the steps for configuring a FastEthernet interface.

```
Router(config)# int fa0/0
Router(config-if)# ip address 10.10.20.250 255.255.255.0
Router(config-if)#no shut
2w0d: %LINEPROTO-5-UPDOWN: Line protocol on Interface FastEthernet0/0,
    changed state to up
```

show ip interface brief (sh ip int brief)

The command used to verify the status of the router's interfaces

Notice that the router prompts you that the line protocol on interface FastEthernet 0/0 changed state to up. Repeat the previous steps for each of the FastEthernet interfaces. The command *show ip interface brief (sh ip int brief)* entered at the enable prompt (**Router#**) can be used to verify the status of the router interfaces. The following is an example:

```
Router# sh ip int brief
Interface      IP-Address    OK?  Method  Status  Protocol
FastEthernet0  10.10.20.250  YES  manual  up      up
FastEthernet1  10.10.200.1   YES  manual  up      up
FastEthernet2  10.10.100.1   YES  manual  up      up
```

Serial Interface Configuration

DCE

Data Communications Equipment (the serial interface responsible for clocking)

DTE

Data Terminal Equipment (the serial interface designed for connecting to a CSU/DSU to outside digital communication services)

The router's serial ports are used to interface to other serial communication devices. The serial communications link is often used in campus networks to connect to wide area networks or the Internet. Configuring the serial port requires that the following questions be answered:

- What is the IP address of the interface?
- What is the subnet mask for the interface?
- What interfaces are responsible for providing clocking?

In the router's serial communication links, there will be a **DCE** and a **DTE** end. The serial cables on older routers are called *V.35* cables. Examples are shown in

Figure 6-20. DCE stands for Data Communication Equipment and DTE stands for Data Terminal Equipment. The DTE interface on the V.35 cable is designed for connecting the router to a CSU/DSU and outside digital communication services. In regards to clocking, the serial interface that is defined to be the DCE is responsible for providing clocking. (The serial communications link is examined in detail in Chapters 8 and 9.) This section shows how to check to see whether your serial connection is DCE or DTE. Modern routers have a built-in CSU/DSU and use an RJ-45 cable to establish the wide area network or Internet connection.

(a)   (b)

FIGURE 6-20   The (a) DCE and (b) DTE ends of V.35 serial cable (courtesy of StarTech.com).

From the router's **config** prompt, enter the command *int s0/0* to access the Serial0/0 interface. The router's prompt changes to **Router(config-if)#** to indicate that the interface configuration has been entered. Notice this is the same prompt as when configuring the FastEthernet interfaces. Next configure the IP address and subnet mask for the serial interface by entering the command *ip address 10.10.50.30 255.255.255.0*. These steps are shown as follows:

```
Router(config)# int s0/0
Router(config-if)# ip address 10.10.50.30 255.255.255.0
```

If this is a serial DCE connection, you must set the clock rate. The serial connection can have either a DCE or DTE end. Routers use RJ-45 and V.35 connections to connect to the serial interface. In the case of V.35 cables, the DCE end of the serial connection is defined to be the female end of the V.35 cable. The DTE end of the cable is defined to be the male end of the V.35 cable. The female and male ends of V.35 cables are shown in Figure 6-20 (a) and (b). There are three ways to check the cable to see if the connection is DCE or DTE.

1. The command *show controllers serial [interface number]* can be used to determine whether your serial interface is a DCE or DTE interface. An abbreviated listing of the displayed results for the *show controllers serial 0* command is shown. The Serial0/0 interface is a V.35 DCE cable. This command should be used when you have an RJ-45 connection.
2. The V.35 cables are typically labeled to indicate whether they are a DTE or DCE cable.
3. Inspect the end of the V.35 cable to determine whether it is male (DTE) or female (DCE).

The customer is usually the DTE end, and the clock rate will be set by the communications carrier. The exception to this is when the customer is setting up a back-to-back serial connection within their own network. In this case, the customer sets the clock rate. The following is an example of using the ***show controllers*** command for a DCE interface:

```
Router# sh controllers serial 0/0
HD unit 0, idb     0xCF958, driver structure at 0xD4DC8
buffer size 1524 HD unit 0, V.35 DCE cable
cpb    0x21, eda    0x4940, cda    0x4800
.
.
.
```

The next example shows the results of the ***show controllers serial [interface number]*** for a DTE interface. This example shows that the Serial0/1 interface is being checked.

```
RouterA#sh controllers serial 0/1
HD unit 1, idb     0xD9050, driver structure at 0xDE4C0
buffer size 1524 HD unit 1, V.35 DTE cable
cpb    0x22, eda    0x30A0, cda    0x30B4
.
.
.
```

The clocking for the serial interface is set using the ***clock rate*** command followed by a data rate. The clock rate for the serial interface on the router can be set from 1200 bps to 4 Mbps. The following is the command for setting the clock rate to 56000:

```
Router(config-if)# clock rate 56000
```

Next the serial interface must be enabled using the ***no shut*** command. The router prompts the console port that interface Serial 0/0 changed state to up. These steps are repeated for all the serial interfaces.

```
Router(config-if)# no shut
2w0d: %LINK-3-UPDOWN: Interface Serial0/0, changed state to up
2w0d: %LINEPROTO-5-UPDOWN: Line protocol on Interface Serial0/0, changed
      state to up
```

The status of the serial interfaces can be checked using the ***sh ip int brief*** command as shown. Section 6-6 explains the meaning of all the information displayed using the ***sh ip int brief*** command.

```
Router# sh ip int brief
Interface      IP-Address     OK?   Method   Status   Protocol
FastEthernet0  10.10.20.250   YES   manual     up       up
FastEthernet1  10.10.200.1    YES   manual     up       up
FastEthernet2  10.10.100.1    YES   manual     up       up
Serial0        10.10.128.1    YES   manual     up       up
Serial1        10.10.64.1     YES   manual     up       up
```

Router Configuration Challenge—The Privileged EXEC Mode

Use the Net-Challenge software included with the companion CD-ROM to complete this exercise. Place the CD-ROM in your computer's drive. The software is located in the *NetChallenge* folder on the CD-ROM. Open the folder and click the *NetChallenge.exe* file. The program will open on your desktop with the screen shown in Figure 6-15. The Net-Challenge software is based on a three-router campus network setting. The software allows the user to configure each of the three routers and to configure the network interface for computers in the LANs attached to each router.

Connection to each router is provided by clicking one of the three router buttons shown in Figure 6-15. Clicking a button connects the selected router to a terminal console session, enabling the simulated console terminal access to all three routers. The routers are marked with their default hostnames of Router A, Router B, and Router C. This challenge tests your ability to use router commands in the privileged EXEC mode, also called the enable mode. Click the *Net-Challenge.exe* file to start the software. Next, click the **Select Challenge** button to open a list of challenges available with the software. Select the **Chapter 6 Privileged EXEC Mode** challenge to open a checkbox screen. Each challenge will be checked when the task has been successfully completed.

1. Make sure you are connected to Router A by clicking the appropriate selection button.
2. Demonstrate that you can enter the router's privileged EXEC mode. The router screen should display **Router#**. The password is **Chile**.
3. Place the router in the terminal configuration mode [**Router(config)#**].
4. Use the *hostname* command to change the router hostname to RouterA.
5. Set the **enable secret** for the router to **Chile**.
6. Set the **vty password** to **ConCarne**.
7. Configure the three FastEthernet interfaces on RouterA as follows:

   FastEthernet0/0   (fa0/0)   10.10.20.250   255.255.255.0

   FastEthernet0/1   (fa0/1)   10.10.200.1   255.255.255.0

   FastEthernet0/2   (fa0/2)   10.10.100.1   255.255.255.0

8. Enable each of the router FastEthernet interfaces using the *no shut* command.
9. Use the *sh ip int brief* command to verify that the interfaces have been configured and are functioning. For this challenge, the interfaces on Router B and Router C have already been configured.
10. Configure the serial interfaces on the router. Serial interface 0/0 is the DCE. The clock rate should be set to 56000. The IP addresses and subnet masks are as follows: (*Note:* Use clock rate.)

    Serial 0/0   10.10.128.1   255.255.255.0

    Serial 0/1   10.10.64.1   255.255.255.0

11. Use the *sh ip int brief* command to verify that the serial interfaces are properly configured. For this challenge, the interfaces on Router B and Router C have already been configured.
12. Use the *ping* command to verify that you have a network connection for the following interfaces:

    RouterA FA0/1 (10.10.200.1) to RouterB FA0/2 (10.10.200.2)

    RouterA FA0/2 (10.10.100.1) to RouterC FA0/2 (10.10.100.2)

6-6   TROUBLESHOOTING THE ROUTER INTERFACE

This section examines one of the most commonly used router commands for troubleshooting and isolating problems that might be related to the router configuration and router interfaces. The command is ***show ip interface brief (sh ip int brief)***. Typically, the network administrator will be able to telnet into the router to establish a virtual terminal connection. The virtual terminal enables the administrator to connect to the router without physically plugging in to it. The onscreen appearance of the virtual terminal connection will appear the same as the console port connection. Remember, the virtual interface is password protected and only authorized users can access the router through this interface.

The first step is to check the status of the interfaces and verify that the interfaces are attached to another networking device using the ***sh ip int brief*** command. The command provides a quick look at information about the interfaces, such as the following:

Interface	The type of interface:
	Ethernet: 10 Mbps
	Fast Ethernet: 100 Mbps
	Gigabit Ethernet: 1000 Mbps
	Serial: 2500 bps to 4 Mbps and higher for high-speed serial interfaces
IP-Address	The IP address assigned to the interface
OK?	Indicates whether the interface is functioning
Method	"How the interface was brought up" (for example, manual, tftp)
Status	{current router status "up", "down" or "administratively down"}
	Line Protocol displayed results differ for FastEthernet and the Serial interfaces. For FastEthernet, status "up" indicates that the FastEthernet interface has been administratively brought up.
Protocol	The protocol "up" indicates that you are seeing the **Keepalive packet**. Keepalive indicates that the FastEthernet interface is connected to another networking device such as a hub, switch, or router. A protocol status of "down" indicates that the Ethernet port is not physically connected to another network device. This is not the same as the link integrity pulse that activates the link light. The link integrity pulse does not send out a small Ethernet packet; Keepalive sends out such a packet.

Keepalive Packet
Indicates that the Ethernet interface is connected to another networking device such as a hub, switch, or router

The following demonstrates how ***sh ip int brief*** can be used to check the status of the interfaces for different conditions such as status down, status up/protocol down, and status/protocol down**.** This includes examples of how to interpret the results displayed by the ***sh ip int brief*** command. This is of particular importance when troubleshooting a possible cable or link failure. When a FastEthernet interface cable is not attached or the link is broken, the protocol shows "down." If a serial interface cable is not attached or the link is broken, the status and the protocol both show "down."

The following are text outputs from a Cisco router that demonstrate how the router status and protocol settings change based on the interface configuration and setup. The first text displays that the three Ethernet interfaces and two serial interfaces are properly configured. The status "up" means that the interface has been administratively turned on by the network administrator.

```
sh ip int brief
Interface       IP-Address      OK?    Method   Status   Protocol
FastEthernet0/0 10.10.20.250    YES    manual   up       up
FastEthernet0/1 10.10.200.1     YES    manual   up       up
FastEthernet0/2 10.10.100.1     YES    manual   up       up
Serial0/0       10.10.128.1     YES    manual   up       up
Serial0/1       10.10.64.1      YES    manual   up       up
```

The next example demonstrates that the router provides a prompt if the link between the router's FastEthernet0/0 interface and another networking device is lost. Within a few seconds of losing the link, the prompt shown appears:

```
2w0d: %LINEPROTO-5-UPDOWN: Line protocol on Interface
FastEthernet0/0, changed state to down
```

The **sh ip int brief** command shows that the protocol for FastEthernet0/0 is "down" and the status is still "up," meaning the interface is still enabled but the router is not communicating with another networking device such as a hub, switch, or router. Therefore, the protocol "down" condition for the FastEthernet interface, as viewed by the **sh ip int brief** command, indicates that there is a loss of communications between the router and a connected networking device. You might have to physically check the router's FastEthernet interface for a link light. In this example, a link light check on the router showed that there was not a link and in fact, the RJ-45 plug connected to the router had come loose.

```
RouterA#sh ip int brief
Interface       IP-Address      OK?    Method   Status   Protocol
FastEthernet0/0 10.10.20.250    YES    manual   up       down
FastEthernet0/1 10.10.200.1     YES    manual   up       up
FastEthernet0/2 10.10.100.1     YES    manual   up       up
Serial0/0       10.10.128.1     YES    manual   up       up
Serial0/1       10.10.64.1      YES    manual   up       up
```

Reconnecting the RF-45 cable reestablishes the link for the FastEthernet0/0 interface and the networking device. The router provides a prompt that the FastEthernet0/0 line protocol has changed state to "up." The **sh ip int brief** command now shows that all interface status is "up" and protocol is "up."

```
2w0d: %LINEPROTO-5-UPDOWN: Line protocol on Interface FastEthernet0/0,
    changed state to up
RouterA#sh ip int brief
Interface       IP-Address      OK?    Method   Status   Protocol
FastEthernet0/0 10.10.20.250    YES    manual   up       up
FastEthernet0/1 10.10.200.1     YES    manual   up       up
FastEthernet0/2 10.10.100.1     YES    manual   up       up
Serial0/0       10.10.128.1     YES    manual   up       up
Serial0/1       10.10.64.1      YES    manual   up       up
```

The router's serial ports behave differently than the FastEthernet interfaces, as shown with the following examples. The previous router text display using the **sh ip int brief** command shows that the Serial0/0 interface status is "up" and the protocol is "up." If the serial link is lost or disconnected, the interface goes down and a prompt is sent to the console screen as shown. The prompt advises the administrator that the Serial0/0 interface has changed state to "down" and the line protocol for Serial0/0 is also "down." The **sh ip int brief** command now shows that the status and line protocol for Serial0/0 are "down."

```
2w0d: %LINK-3-UPDOWN: Interface Serial0/0, changed state to down
2w0d: %LINEPROTO-5-UPDOWN: Line protocol on Interface Serial0/0, changed
    state to down
```

```
RouterA#sh ip int brief
Interface        IP-Address     OK?    Method     Status     Protocol
FastEthernet0/0  10.10.20.250   YES    manual     up         up
FastEthernet0/1  10.10.200.1    YES    manual     up         up
FastEthernet0/2  10.10.100.1    YES    manual     up         up
Serial0/0        10.10.128.1    YES    manual     down       down
Serial1/1        10.10.64.1     YES    manual     up         up
```

Reestablishing the serial connection will change the status back to "up" and the protocol back to "up" as shown. Note that the prompt includes a statement that communication to 10.10.128.2 has been resumed. This is the IP address of the serial interface attached to the router's Serial0 interface.

```
2w0d: %LINK-3-UPDOWN: Interface Serial0, changed state to up
2w0d: %LINEPROTO-5-UPDOWN: Line protocol on Interface Serial0, changed
   state to up
[Resuming connection 1 to 10.10.128.2 ... ]
RouterA#sh ip int brief
Interface        IP-Address     OK?    Method     Status     Protocol
FastEthernet0/0  10.10.20.250   YES    manual     up         up
FastEthernet0/1  10.10.200.1    YES    manual     up         up
FastEthernet0/2  10.10.100.1    YES    manual     up         up
Serial0/0        10.10.128.1    YES    manual     up         up
Serial10/1       10.10.64.1     YES    manual     up         up
```

Administratively Down
Indicates that the router interface has been shut off by the administrator

This screen shows that the Serial0 interface is "administratively down." The term **administratively down** indicates that the router interface has been shut off by the administrator. Note the difference with the terms *down* and *administratively down*. Reissuing the command ***no shut*** for the Serial0/0 interface should correct the problem.

```
RouterA#sh ip int brief
Interface        IP-Address     OK?  Method  Status                  Protocol
FastEthernet0/0  10.10.20.250   YES  manual  up                      up
FastEthernet0/1  10.10.200.1    YES  manual  up                      up
FastEthernet0/2  10.10.100.1    YES  manual  up                      up
Serial0/0        10.10.128.1    YES  manual  administratively down   up
Serial0/1        10.10.64.1     YES  manual  up                      up
```

This section has presented the ***sh ip int brief*** command and how it can be used to troubleshoot and isolate router interface problems. The status differs for the Ethernet and serial interfaces. This is an important concept and something you will encounter when working with routers.

Summary

This chapter presented an overview of routers, a technique for establishing a console port connection, and the basic steps for configuring the router's interface. The student should understand the difference in the router's user and privileged EXEC modes. A list of the router prompts encountered in this chapter appears in Table 6-4.

TABLE 6-4   Router Prompts and Their Definitions

Prompt	Definition
Router>	User EXEC mode
Router#	Privileged EXEC
mode Router(config)#	Configuration mode
Router(config-if)#	Interface configuration mode
Router(config-line)#	Line terminal configuration mode

The student should understand and be able to demonstrate the steps for configuring the Ethernet and serial interfaces. These concepts are used repeatedly in the next chapters. A new router troubleshooting command (***sh ip int brief***) was added to the list of networking troubleshooting steps. The student should make sure the concepts discussed in section 6-6 are well understood. This command is very useful for troubleshooting and isolating router problems.

Questions and Problems

Section 6-1

1. What is the command line interface used for on a Cisco router?
2. Define *Cisco IOS.*

Section 6-2

3. Define a broadcast domain.
4. What is a flat network?
5. What is a layer 3 network?
6. Define the purpose of a gateway.
7. Where is the default gateway address assigned on Windows?
8. A computer with a host IP address of 10.10.5.1 sends a data packet with a destination IP address of 10.10.5.2. A subnet mask of 255.255.255.0 is being used. Determine whether the packet stays in the LAN or is sent to the gateway. Show your work.
9. Repeat problem 8 if the destination IP address for the data packet is 10.5.10.2. The subnet mask is still the same. Show your work.
10. Repeat problem 9 if the subnet mask is changed to 255.0.0.0. Show your work.
11. Repeat problem 9 if the subnet mask is changed to 255.255.0.0. Show your work.

12. The IP address for computer C2 is 10.10.1.2. The IP address for computer B1 is 10.10.10.1. A subnet mask of 255.255.0.0 is being used. Are the computers in the same network? Show your work.

13. Determine the router hop count from Router A to Router D in the network shown in Figure 6-21 for the route with the fewest hops.

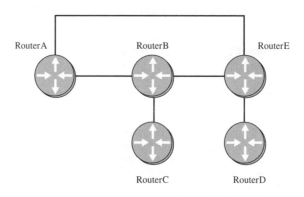

FIGURE 6-21   Network Topology for Problem 13.

14. List all the possible routes from Router B to Router D in the network shown in problem 13.

15. What subnets are attached to Router B in Figure 6-21?

16. List the subnets attached to Router C in Figure 6-21.

17. What is the next hop address for FastEthernet port 1, Router A in Figure 6-21?

18. What is the next hop address for the FastEthernet port 2, Router C in Figure 6-21?

Section 6-3

19. What is a rollover cable?

20. What values are used when configuring HyperTerminal for connecting to a Cisco router's console port?

Section 6-4

21. What command is used to find out the version of the IOS running on a Cisco router? Show the prompt and the command.

22. What is the help command in Cisco IOS?

23. What command can be used to see the uptime for a router?

24. What command is used to verify that there is sufficient memory available to load a new version of the Cisco IOS software?

25. What is the router prompt for the user EXEC mode?

26. If you enter *exit* from the **Router>** prompt, where does it place you?

Section 6-5

27. What is the router prompt for the privileged EXEC mode?

28. What command is used to enter the router's privileged mode?

29. What command is used to configure a router's hostname to *Tech-router*?
30. What command is used to enter the router's terminal configuration mode?
31. What is the router prompt for the terminal configuration mode?
32. What is the command for setting password protection for the privileged mode? The password is *Tech*.
33. What does the command *line vty 0 4* mean?
34. Describe the steps to configure and enable a FastEthernet0/1 router interface with the IP address 10.10.20.250 and a subnet mask of 255.255.0.0.
35. What is the best command to view the router interface status and protocol?
36. Is clocking of a router's serial interface set by the DCE or the DTE?
37. What are the three ways to see if your router's serial port is a DCE or DTE end?
38. What command is used to set the data speed on a router's serial port to 56 kbps?
39. What is the router prompt for the interface configuration mode?

Section 6-6

40. What is the purpose of the Keepalive packet?
41. The *sh ip int brief* command indicated that the protocol for a FastEthernet interface is "down." What does this mean?
42. What is the difference in a serial interface with a status of *down* and a status of *administratively down*?

Critical Thinking

43. What does the command line *vty 0 1* mean?
44. How can you check to see if the FastEthernet interface on a router is connected to the FastEthernet interface on another networking device?
45. You suspect that a router's LAN gateway is down. Describe how you would troubleshoot the problem.

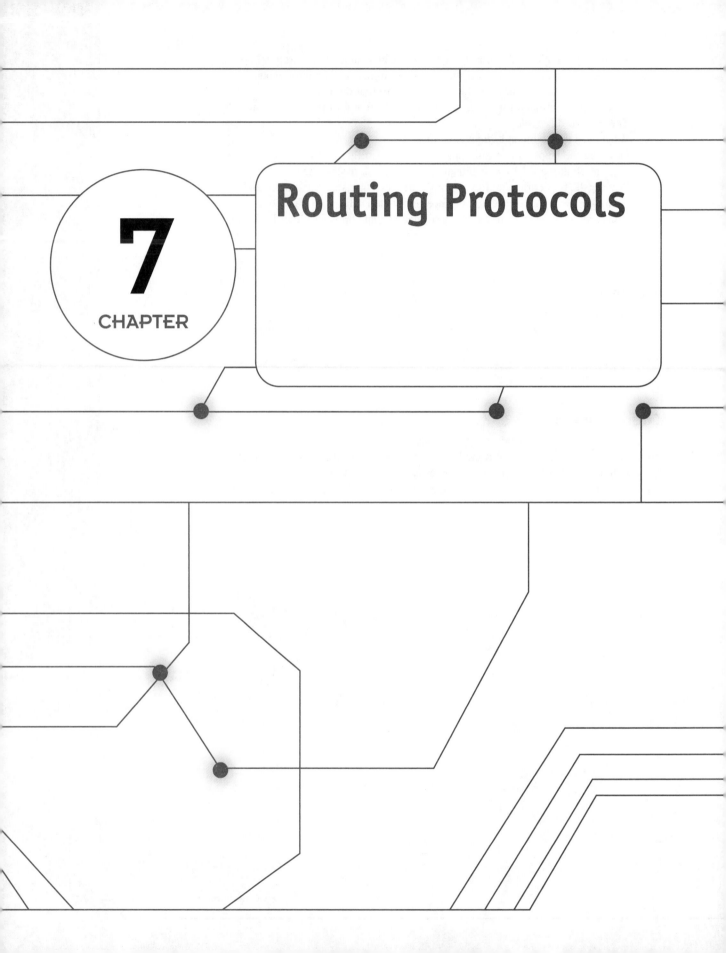

7 CHAPTER

Routing Protocols

CHAPTER OUTLINE

7-1   Introduction
7-2   Static Routing
7-3   Dynamic Routing Protocols
7-4   RIP—Routing Information Protocol
7-5   IGRP—Interior Gateway Routing Protocol
7-6   OSPF—Open Shortest Path First Routing Protocol

7-7   EIGRP—Enhanced Interior Gateway Routing Protocol
7-8   Configuring a Juniper Router
7-9   TFTP—Trivial File Transfer Protocol
7-10 Analyzing OSPF "Hello" Packets
Summary
Questions and Problems

OBJECTIVES

- Describe the difference between static and dynamic routing protocols
- Describe the difference in distance vector and link state protocols
- Be able to configure a basic setup for static, RIP, IGRP, OSPF, and EIGRP routing protocols
- Understand the relative amount of traffic generated by each protocol

- Understand the basics of configuring a Juniper router
- Understand the purpose of and be able to configure a TFTP sever
- Use the Surveyor Demo software to capture and analyze the OSPF "Hello" packets
- Describe the purpose of the "Hello" packet

KEY TERMS

static route
netstat -r
route print
loopback
ip route
variable length subnet masking
show ip route (sh ip route)
routing table code S
routing table code C
gateway of last resort
show ip route static (sh ip route static)
show running-config (sh run)

show startup-config (sh start)
copy run start
write memory (wr m)
dynamic routing protocols
path determination
metric
convergence
load balancing
hop count
reliability
bandwidth
delay
cost
load

ticks
distance vector protocol
link state protocol
RIP
routing loop
advertise
class network address
classful addressing
show ip protocol (sh ip protocol)
IGRP
holddowns
split horizons
administrative distance
router igrp [AS number]

continues

225

autonomous system (AS)

classful network

Router(config-router)#

show ip route igrp (sh ip route igrp)

OSPF

IETF

link state advertisement (LSA)

"Hello" packets

areas

backbone

variable length sub-masks (VLSM)

route flapping

router ospf [number]

network number

wild card bits

area 0

EIGRP

JUNOS

{master}

re0 { and re1 { ...

PIC

Permanent interfaces

Management Ethernet interfaces

Internal Internet interfaces

Transient interfaces

commit

commit and- quit

TFTP

network mask

hello interval

router dead interval

RID

OSPFIGP

IGP

7-1   INTRODUCTION

This chapter introduces the basic concepts of routing protocols. *Routing protocols* provide a standardized format for route management including route selection, sharing route status with neighbor routers, and calculating alternative routes if the best-path route is down. The focus of this chapter is on the use of routing protocols in a campus network environment.

   Static routing protocols are presented in section 7-2. This section includes examples of how to configure static routes and view the routes in a routing table. The material includes a discussion of when and where static protocols are used and also when and why it is not advantageous to use a static routing protocol. An overview of the concept of dynamic protocols is presented in section 7-3. Dynamic protocols are divided into two areas, distance vector and link state. Examples of configuring the distance vector protocols RIP and IGRP are presented in sections 7-4 and 7-5. Configuring the link state protocol OSPF is examined in section 7-6, and the steps for configuring the distance vector protocol EIGRP are examined in section 7-7. Section 7-8 examines the steps for configuring a Juniper router. The configuration commands are similar but there are some distinct differences with the JUNOS operating system. It is important to periodically back up the router configuration files. A procedure for doing this is by using a Trivial File Transfer Protocol (TFTP) server, and this topic is examined in section 7-9. Section 7-10 examines the OSPF "Hello" packets used by routers to initiate and maintain communication with neighbor routers. The parameters of the "Hello" packet are examined using the Surveyor Demo protocol analyzer.

   Each routing protocol section in this chapter contains a networking challenge that is included with the Net-Challenge companion CD-ROM. These challenges enable you to configure each routing protocol on a virtual router.

7-2   STATIC ROUTING

The objective of this section is to demonstrate how data packets are routed in a network using a static routing protocol. The techniques for configuring static routes so that data packets can be forwarded are presented. A **static route** is a list of IP addresses to which data traffic can be forwarded and has been manually entered into either a router's or computer's routing table. A static route is specified in a PC computer in terms of the computer's default gateway, and routers sometimes use a static route when specifying where the network data traffic is to be forwarded. Examples of specifying the static route(s) for a computer are first examined.

   The most common static route used in a host computer is the default gateway. The *default gateway* specifies where the data traffic is to be sent when the destination address for the data is not in the same LAN or is unknown. If you don't have a route specified for a subnet in your network, the default route is used. For example, if your PC is on the 10.10.0.0 network and it wants to send data to 100.100.20.1, the data is sent to the default gateway as specified by the TCP/IP setup on your PC. An example of setting the host computer's default gateway is shown in Figure 7-1 for both (a) Windows Vista and (b) Mac OS X. In this example, the default IP address is 10.10.20.250 with a subnet mask of 255.255.255.0 for the computer in LAN A with the IP address of 10.10.20.1.

Static Route
A data traffic route that has been manually entered into either a router's or a computer's routing table

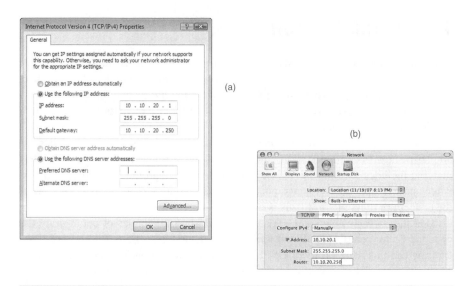

FIGURE 7-1   Setting the default gateway address or default static route on the host computer (PC and Mac OS X).

netstat -r
The command used to obtain the routing table for a host PC computer

route print
Produces same displayed result as *netstat -r*

Loopback
The data is routed directly back to the source

The routing tables for the host PC computer can be obtained by entering the command *netstat -r* at the PC's command prompt and from the Mac OS X terminal screen. An example is shown in Figure 7-2 (a). The command *route print* can also be used to view the active routes from the host PC, as shown in Figure 7-2 (b).

The default route is specified in the routing table by a 0.0.0.0 network address entry with a subnet mask of 0.0.0.0. The gateway address of 10.10.20.250 is the IP address of the FastEthernet port of the router connected to the LAN. The IP address of 10.10.20.1 for the interface is the IP address for the host computer's network interface card (NIC). The network destination of 10.10.20.0 is returned to the computer's NIC at IP address 10.10.20.1. The gateway for the network destination of 10.10.20.1 is 127.0.0.1, which is a **loopback** to the host computer. A loopback means the data is routed directly back to the source. In this case, the source is the computer's NIC. The loopback can be used to check whether the network interface is working; if it is, pinging IP address 127.0.0.1 will generate a reply.

What about setting static routes for a router in a small campus network? First, let's examine how data packets travel from one LAN to another in the three-router campus network shown in Figure 7-3. Specifically, how is information sent from a host computer in LAN A (10.10.20.0 subnet) to a host computer in LAN B (10.10.10.0 subnet)? The data packets must travel from LAN A to the RouterA gateway (FA0/0 interface), from RouterA to RouterB via the 10.10.200.0 subnet, and then to LAN B via the RouterB gateway (FA0/0 interface). This requires that a physical communications link be established between the routers and a routing protocol defined for Routers A and B before data packets can be exchanged. The physical connection will typically be CAT6/5e UTP or a fiber connection.

```
C:\netstat -r

Route Table
---------------------------------------------------------------------------------
Interface List
0x1 ........................... MS TCP Loopback interface
0x2 ...00 b0 d0 25 bf 48 ...... 3Com 3C920 Integrated Fast Ethernet Controller
3C905C-TX Compatible) — Packet Scheduler Miniport
---------------------------------------------------------------------------------
---------------------------------------------------------------------------------
Active Routes:
Network Destination        Netmask          Gateway       Interface    Metric
          0.0.0.0          0.0.0.0      10.10.20.250      10.10.20.1      20
       10.10.20.0    255.255.255.0       10.10.20.1      10.10.20.1      20
       10.10.20.1  255.255.255.255        127.0.0.1       127.0.0.1      20
   10.255.255.255  255.255.255.255       10.10.20.1      10.10.20.1      20
        127.0.0.0        255.0.0.0        127.0.0.1       127.0.0.1       1
        224.0.0.0        240.0.0.0       10.10.20.1      10.10.20.1      20
  255.255.255.255  255.255.255.255       10.10.20.1      10.10.20.1       1
Default Gateway:       10.10.20.250
---------------------------------------------------------------------------------
Persistent Routes:
  None
```
                                     (a)


```
C:\route print
---------------------------------------------------------------------------------
Interface List
0x1 ........................... MS TCP Loopback interface
0x2 ...00 b0 d0 25 bf 48 ...... 3Com 3C920 Integrated Fast Ethernet Controller
3C905C-TX Compatible) — Packet Scheduler Miniport
---------------------------------------------------------------------------------
---------------------------------------------------------------------------------
Active Routes:
Network Destination        Netmask          Gateway       Interface    Metric
          0.0.0.0          0.0.0.0      10.10.20.250      10.10.20.1      20
       10.10.20.0    255.255.255.0       10.10.20.1      10.10.20.1      20
       10.10.20.1  255.255.255.255        127.0.0.1       127.0.0.1      20
   10.255.255.255  255.255.255.255       10.10.20.1      10.10.20.1      20
        127.0.0.0        255.0.0.0        127.0.0.1       127.0.0.1       1
        224.0.0.0        240.0.0.0       10.10.20.1      10.10.20.1      20
  255.255.255.255  255.255.255.255       10.10.20.1      10.10.20.1       1
Default Gateway:       10.10.20.250
---------------------------------------------------------------------------------
Persistent Routes:
  None
```
                                     (b)

FIGURE 7-2   (a) A host computer's static route listing obtained using the netstat -r
command; (b) a host computer's static route listing obtained using the route print
command.

   A simplified network can be used to demonstrate what is required to develop
static routes in a multiple-router network. For this example, two routers from the campus network are used. The two routers, RouterA and RouterB, connect to LANs A
and B as shown in Figure 7-4. This simplified network will be used to describe how
data packets travel from LAN A—RouterA—RouterB—LAN B and what is required
to define the static routes.

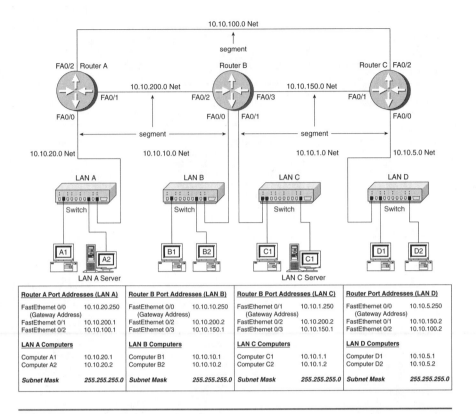

Router A Port Addresses (LAN A) | Router B Port Addresses (LAN B) | Router B Port Addresses (LAN C) | Router Port Addresses (LAN D)

Router A Port Addresses (LAN A)		Router B Port Addresses (LAN B)		Router B Port Addresses (LAN C)		Router Port Addresses (LAN D)	
FastEthernet 0/0 (Gateway Address)	10.10.20.250	FastEthernet 0/0 (Gateway Address)	10.10.10.250	FastEthernet 0/1 (Gateway Address)	10.10.1.250	FastEthernet 0/0 (Gateway Address)	10.10.5.250
FastEthernet 0/1	10.10.200.1	FastEthernet 0/2	10.10.200.2	FastEthernet 0/2	10.10.200.2	FastEthernet 0/1	10.10.150.2
FastEthernet 0/2	10.10.100.1	FastEthernet 0/3	10.10.150.1	FastEthernet 0/3	10.10.150.1	FastEthernet 0/2	10.10.100.2
LAN A Computers		**LAN B Computers**		**LAN C Computers**		**LAN D Computers**	
Computer A1	10.10.20.1	Computer B1	10.10.10.1	Computer C1	10.10.1.1	Computer D1	10.10.5.1
Computer A2	10.10.20.2	Computer B2	10.10.10.2	Computer C2	10.10.1.2	Computer D2	10.10.5.2
Subnet Mask	*255.255.255.0*	*Subnet Mask*	*255.255.255.0*	*Subnet Mask*	*255.255.255.0*	*Subnet Mask*	*255.255.255.0*

FIGURE 7-3   A three-router campus network.

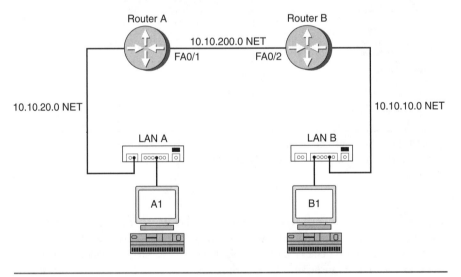

FIGURE 7-4   A simplified two-router network.

The data packets pass through three subnets (indicated by *NET*) when traveling from LAN A to LAN B. The IP subnets for each network are as follows:

10.10.20.0 NET	LAN A
10.10.200.0 NET	RouterA connection to RouterB
10.10.10.0 NET	LAN B

In this network, there are only two routers, with RouterA directly connected to RouterB. This means that the only route between the routers is via the 10.10.200.0 NET, which is the connection between Routers A and B. The static route information is entered from the router's configure terminal prompt **(config)#** using the *ip route* command. The command structure for ***ip route*** is

```
Router(config)#ip route <destination> <subnet mask> <next hop>
```

ip route
The router configuration command for manually setting the next hop IP address

where the *destination* is the network's destination IP address (NET), the *subnet mask* is what has been defined for the subnets, and the *next hop* is the IP address of the next router in the link. The command for routing the data to the 10.10.10.0 subnet is as follows:

```
RouterA(config)#ip route 10.10.10.0 255.255.255.0 10.10.200.2
```

The following configuration information is entered into RouterA:

Destination Subnet IP Address	Subnet Mask	Next Hop IP Address
10.10.10.0	255.255.255.0	10.10.200.2

The next hop IP address is the IP address of the Ethernet2 port on RouterB. Now the router knows how to deliver data packets from host computers in the 10.10.20.0 NET (LAN A) to destination computers in the 10.10.10.0 NET (LAN B). (*Note:* Each static route can use a different subnet mask. This is called **variable length subnet masking**. For example, one static route could have a subnet mask of 255.255.255.0 and another could have a subnet mask of 255.255.255.252.)

Variable Length Subnet Masking
Routes can be configured using different subnet masks

The routing address entry into the routing table can be verified by entering the command *show ip route (sh ip route)* from the router's **(config)#** prompt. An example of this is shown:

```
RouterA#show ip route
Codes: C connected, S static, I IGRP, R RIP, M mobile, B BGP D EIGRP, EX
    EIGRP external, O OSPF, IA OSPF inter area
N1 OSPF NSSA external type 1, N2 OSPF NSSA external type 2
E1 OSPF external type 1, E2 OSPF external type 2, E EGP
i IS-IS, L1 IS-IS level-1, L2 IS-IS level-2, * candidate default
U per-user static route, o ODR T traffic engineered route
Gateway of last resort is not set
10.0.0.0/24 is subnetted, 2 subnets
S 10.10.10.0 [1/0] via 10.10.200.2
C 10.10.200.0 is directly connected, FastEthernet1
```

show ip route (sh ip route)
The command that displays the routes and the routing address entry into the routing table

What about data traffic flow from the 10.10.10.0 NET (LAN B) to the 10.10.20.0 NET (LAN A)? Once again, the data packets pass through three subnets (indicated by NET) when traveling from LAN B to LAN A. The IP addresses for each subnet are as follows:

10.10.10.0 NET	LAN B
10.10.200.0 NET	RouterB connection to RouterA
10.10.20.0 NET	LAN A

In this scenario, LAN B connects directly to RouterB and the only route to LAN A from RouterB is via the 10.10.200.0 NET, which is the connection between Routers B and A. The destination network IP address is 10.10.20.0. The command input to RouterB for routing the data to the 10.10.20.0 subnet is as follows:

```
RouterB(config)#ip route 10.10.20.0 255.255.255.0 10.10.200.1
```

The following information is entered into the router:

Destination Subnet IP Address	Subnet Mask	Next Hop IP Address
10.10.20.0	255.255.255.0	10.10.200.1

The next hop IP address is the IP address of the FastEthernet0/1 port on RouterA. Now a static route has been configured on RouterB to route data packets from host computers in the 10.10.10.0 NET (LAN B) to destination computers in the 10.10.20.0 NET (LAN A). The entries into RouterB's routing table can be confirmed by using the command *sh ip route* at the **Router#** prompt, as shown:

```
RouterB#sh ip route
Codes: C connected, S static, I IGRP, R RIP, M mobile, B BGP D EIGRP, EX
    EIGRP external, O OSPF, IA OSPF inter area
N1 OSPF NSSA external type 1, N2 OSPF NSSA external type 2
E1 OSPF external type 1, E2 OSPF external type 2, E EGP
i IS-IS, L1 IS-IS level-1, L2 IS-IS level-2, * candidate default
U per-user static route, o ODR T traffic engineered route
Gateway of last resort is not set
10.0.0.0/24 is subnetted, 2 subnets
S 10.10.20.0 [1/0] via 10.10.200.1
C 10.10.200.0 is directly connected, FastEthernet0/2
```

routing table code S
The router code for a static route

routing table code C
The router code for specifying a directly connected network

The *sh ip route* command lists a table of codes first, followed by the routes. This listing shows a static route (S) 10.10.20.0 via 10.10.200.1, which indicates that a static route to the destination 10.10.20.0 subnet can be reached via the next hop of 10.10.200.1. The C indicates that the 10.10.200.0 network is directly connected to the FastEthernet02 port.

This simplified network has only one route; therefore, the entries for the static routes using the *ip route* command are limited but were required for each router. Static routes are sometimes used when configuring the routers for routing in a small network. Static routing is not the best choice, as we will learn, but it can be suitable if the network is small (for example, the two-router network). It can be suitable for situations in which there is only one route to the destination, such as a wide area network or Internet feed. This concept is examined in Chapter 8.

What about using static routes in the three-router campus network shown in Figure 7-3? A computer in LAN A (10.10.20.0 NET) sends data to a computer in LAN B (10.10.10.0 NET). This is the same requirement specified in the two-router network example. Once again, a static route must be entered into RouterA's routing table telling the router how to forward data to the 10.10.10.0 NET. However, in this example there are two possible choices for a data packet to travel to the 10.10.10.0 NET from RouterA. The IP addresses for the two possible next hops are 10.10.200.2 and 10.10.100.2. The following are the router commands:

```
RouterA(config)#ip route 10.10.10.0 255.255.255.0 10.10.200.2
RouterA(config)#ip route 10.10.10.0 255.255.255.0 10.10.100.2
```

What about sending information from LAN A to LAN C or to LAN D? This requires four more additional *ip route* entries into the router's routing table, as shown:

```
RouterA(config)#ip route 10.10.1.0 255.255.255.0 10.10.200.2
RouterA(config)#ip route 10.10.1.0 255.255.255.0 10.10.100.2
RouterA(config)#ip route 10.10.5.0 255.255.255.0 10.10.200.2
RouterA(config)#ip route 10.10.5.0 255.255.255.0 10.10.100.2
```

But wait, we aren't done. We must enter return static routes for all the LANs back to LAN A, and then enter the static routes for the other three LANs. For troubleshooting purposes, we want to be able to ping all the Ethernet interfaces on the subnets, so we need to add static IP routes to each subnet (NET). For example, defining a route to the 10.10.150.0 NET, the following are the static IP route entries:

```
RouterA(config)#ip route 10.10.150.0 255.255.255.0 10.10.200.2
RouterA(config)#ip route 10.10.150.0 255.255.255.0 10.10.100.2
```

This means that many static route entries must be made for the routes in this network to be completely defined. This requires a lot of time and if routes change in the network, new static entries must be made and old static routes must be deleted. The problem with using a static routing protocol in your network is the amount of maintenance required by the network administrator just to keep the route selections up to date in a large network. Assume that the network connection uses five router hops. The entries for the static routes on each router are numerous, and if the routes change, the routing tables in all routers must be manually updated to account for the data path changes.

When static routes are used, the network administrator in essence becomes the routing protocol. In other words, the network administrator is making all the decisions regarding data traffic routing. This requires the administrator to know all network data routes, set up the routes to each subnet, and be constantly aware of any route changes. This is in contrast to dynamic routing protocols that communicate routing information between the routers to determine the best route to use to forward the data packets. The concept of a dynamic routing protocol is introduced in section 7-3, and in subsequent sections we examine examples of the dynamic routing protocols RIP, IGRP, OSPF, and EIGRP.

Gateway of Last Resort

One of the most important applications for using a static route is for configuring the **gateway of last resort** on a router. The gateway of last resort is the IP address of the router in your network where data packets with unknown routes should be forwarded. The purpose of this is to configure a route for data packets that do not have a destination route configured in the routing table. In this case, a default route can be configured that instructs the router to forward the data packet(s) with an unknown route to another router. The command for doing this is

Gateway of last resort
The IP address of the router in your network where data packets with unknown routes should be forwarded

```
ip route 0.0.0.0   0.0.0.0   <next hop address>
```

If this static route has not been configured, the router will display the following message when the *show ip route* command is entered:

```
Gateway of last resort is not set
```

This means the router does not know how to route a data packet with a destination IP address that differs from the routes stored in the routing table.

Configuring Static Routes

The following discussion describes how to configure static routes on a Cisco router. The topology being used is the three-router campus network shown in Figure 7-3. This demonstration is for configuring the static routes for RouterA only.

The first step is to connect to the router via a console or virtual terminal connection. Next, enter the privileged EXEC mode as shown:

```
Router con0 is now available Press RETURN to get started!
RouterA>en
RouterA#
```

Next, enter the configure terminal mode on the router [**RouterA(config)#**] using the *configure terminal (conf t)* command. Before configuring the static routes, make sure the interfaces are configured. The FastEthernet0/1 interface is configured with the assigned IP address of 10.10.200.1 and a subnet mask of 255.255.255.0, and the FastEthernet0/2 interface is assigned the 10.10.100.1 IP address and a subnet mask of 255.255.255.0. The *no shut* command is used to enable the FastEthernet ports.

```
Router#conf t
Enter configuration commands, one per line. End with CNTL/Z.
Router(config)#int fa0/1
Router(config-if)#ip address 10.10.200.1 255.255.255.0
Router(config-if)#no shut
00:19:07: %LINK-3-UPDOWN: Interface FastEthernet0/1, changed state to up
Router(config)#int fa0/2
Router(config-if)#ip address 10.10.100.1 255.255.255.0
Router(config-if)#no shut
00:21:05: %LINK-3-UPDOWN: Interface FastEthernet0/2, changed state to up
```

Notice that the FastEthernet0/1 and FastEthernet0/2 interfaces change state to *up* after the *no shut* command is issued. It is good to verify the interface status using the *show ip interface brief (sh ip int brief)* command as shown.

```
RouterA#sh ip int brief
00:22:18: %SYS-5-CONFIG_I: Configured from console
Interface        IP-Address  OK? Method Status  Protocol
FastEthernet0/1  10.10.200.1 YES manual up      down
FastEthernet0/2  10.10.100.1 YES manual up      down
```

The status for both FastEthernet ports show that they are *up*; however, the line protocol *down* tells us there is not a physical connection established between the routers. Refer to section 6-6 for a review of the results displayed by status and protocol. This problem with the "protocol down" is fixed by reestablishing the physical connection between the routers.

The static routes are entered using the *ip route* command after the interfaces are configured. You don't have to enter all routes at once, but all routes must be properly entered for the network to work. Only the routes to the 10.10.10.0 NET have been listed to shorten the example.

```
RouterA(config)#ip route 10.10.10.0 255.255.255.0 10.10.200.2
RouterA(config)#ip route 10.10.10.0 255.255.255.0 10.10.100.2
```

show ip route static (sh ip route static)
Limits the routes displayed to only static

There are two places to verify whether the static routes are properly configured. First, verify that the routes are in the routing table using either the *show ip route* or the *show ip route static (sh ip route static)* command. Adding the word *static* after *show ip route* limits the routes displayed to only *static*. An important note is that the routes are displayed using the *show ip route* command only if the line protocol is *up*.

```
RouterA#sh ip route
Codes: C connected, S static, I IGRP, R RIP, M mobile, B BGP D EIGRP, EX
    EIGRP external, O OSPF, IA OSPF inter area
N1 OSPF NSSA external type 1, N2 OSPF NSSA external type 2
E1 OSPF external type 1, E2 OSPF external type 2, E EGP
i IS-IS, L1 IS-IS level-1, L2 IS-IS level-2, * candidate default
U per-user static route, o ODR T traffic engineered route
Gateway of last resort is not set
10.0.0.0/24 is subnetted, 2 subnets
S 10.10.10.0 [1/0] via 10.10.200.2
S 10.10.10.0 [1/0] via 10.10.100.2
C 10.10.200.0 is directly connected, FastEthernet0/1
C 10.10.100.0 is directly connected, FastEthernet0/2
```

The command for showing only the static routes is

```
RouterA#sh ip route static
```

The other place to check the routing configuration is by examining the router's running-configuration file using the command *show running-config (sh run)* as shown. The command displays the current configuration of the router but it does not show what is currently saved in the router's nonvolatile memory (NVRAM). The command *show startup-config (sh start)* displays the router's configuration saved in NVRAM.

```
RouterA#sh run
Using 519 out of 32762 bytes
!
version 12.0
service timestamps debug uptime service timestamps log uptime no service
    password-encryption
!
hostname Router
!
!
ip subnet-zero
!
interface FastEthernet0/1
ip address 10.10.200.1 255.255.255.0
 no ip directed-broadcast no keepalive
!
interface FastEthernet0/2
 ip address 10.10.100.1 255.255.255.0
 no ip directed-broadcast no keepalive
!
ip classless
ip route 10.10.10.0 255.255.255.0 10.10.200.2
ip route 10.10.10.0 255.255.255.0 10.10.100.2
!
line con 0
transport input none line aux 0
line vty 0 4
!
end
```

It is important that you save your configuration changes to the router as you go. Save changes to the router configuration using the *copy running-configuration startup-configuration* command (*copy run start*) or *write memory (wr m)* as shown:

```
RouterA#copy run start
RouterA#wr m
```

Table 7-1 in the section that follows shows a summary of the commands used when configuring the static routes.

show running-config (sh run)
The command that displays the router's running-configuration

show startup-config (sh start)
The command that displays the router's startup-configuration

copy run start
The command for copying the running-configuration to the startup-configuration

write memory (wr m)
The command that saves your configuration changes to memory

Networking Challenge—Static Routes

TABLE 7-1   Summary of Commands Used to Configure the Static Routing Protocol

Command	Use
ip route	Used to specify the destination IP address, the subnet mask, and the next hop IP address
show ip route	Shows the IP routes listed in the routing table
show ip route static	Shows only the static IP routes listed in the routing table
show running-configuration	Shows the router's running-configuration
show startup-configuration	Shows the router's saved configuration in NVRAM
write memory	Copies the current router changes to memory (NVRAM)
copy run start	Copies the current router changes to memory (NVRAM)

Use the Network Challenge software included with the text's companion CD-ROM to demonstrate that you can configure static routes for a router. Place the CD-ROM in your computer's drive. Open the Net-Challenge folder and double click the *Net-Challenge.exe* file. Select the **Chapter 7—Static Routes** challenge. Use the software to demonstrate that you can complete the following tasks.

This challenge requires you to configure the static routes for RouterA.

1. Click the RouterA select button and press Return to get started.
2. Configure the default gateway address for computerA1 in LAN A (10.10.20.250). To do so, click the computer A1 icon in LAN A to bring up the **TCP/IP Properties** menu. Click OK on the menu, and press Enter to see the check.
3. Configure the IP addresses for the FastEthernet0/0 and FastEthernet0/1 ports. *Note:* Click the RouterA symbol in the topology to display the IP addresses and subnet mask for the router.
4. Use the *no shut* command to enable both FastEthernet ports.
5. Use the *show ip int brief* command to view the current interface status.
6. Use the *ip route* command to configure two routes to the 10.10.10.0 subnet (NET). *Note:* Click the RouterB and RouterC symbols in the network topology to display the IP addresses for the router interfaces. (Use a 255.255.255.0 subnet mask.)
7. Use the *show ip route* command to view whether the routes are entered into the router's routing table.
8. Use the *show run* command to verify whether the static routes are listed in the router's running-configuration.

7-3   DYNAMIC ROUTING PROTOCOLS

The concept of configuring a network using a static routing protocol was presented in section 7-2. It became obvious that the time required for entering and maintaining the static routes was a problem. Therefore, a static routing protocol is of limited use for campuswide network routing but is essential when configuring the default route (gateway of last resort) on routers. However, static routes are used in situations such as configuring small networks with few routes.

This section introduces an improvement over static routing through the use of **dynamic routing protocols**. Dynamic routing protocols enable the router's routing tables to be dynamically updated to account for loss or changes in routes or changes in data traffic. The routers update their routing tables using information obtained from adjacent routers. The features of dynamic routing protocol are defined in Table 7-2. The routing protocol is responsible for managing the exchange of routing information between the routers, and the choice of protocol defines how the routing information is exchanged and used.

TABLE 7-2 Features of Dynamic Routing Protocols

Feature	Description
1	What information is exchanged between routers
2	When updated routing information is exchanged
3	Steps for reacting to changes in the network
4	Criteria for establishing the best route selection

Four key issues are associated with dynamic routing protocols: **path determination, metric, convergence,** and **load balancing**. These issues are defined in Table 7-3.

TABLE 7-3 The Four Key Issues in Dynamic Routing Protocols

Item	Issue	Purpose
1	Path determination	A procedure in the protocol that is used to determine the best route.
2	Metric	A numeric measure assigned to routes for ranking the routes best to worst; the smaller the number, the better.
3	Convergence	This happens when a router obtains a clear view of the routes in a network. The time it takes for the router to obtain a clear view is called the *convergence time*.
4	Load balancing	A procedure in the protocol that enables routers to use any of the multiple data paths available from multiple routers to reach the destination.

Examples of route metrics are as follows:

- **Hop count:** The number of routers the data packet must pass through to reach the destination network
- **Reliability:** A measure of the reliability of the link, typically in terms of the amount of errors
- **Bandwidth:** Having to do with the data capacity of the networking link; a Fast-Ethernet 100 Mbps link has greater data capacity than a 10 Mbps Ethernet link
- **Delay:** The time it takes for a data packet to travel from source to destination
- **Cost:** A value typically assigned by the network administrator that takes into account bandwidth and expense
- **Load:** Having to do with the network activity on a link or router
- **Ticks:** The measured delay time in terms of clock ticks, where each tick is approximately 55 milliseconds (1/18 second)

There are two types of dynamic routing protocols: distance vector and link state. These protocols are briefly introduced in this section. The procedures for configuring a router to use dynamic routing protocols are examined in sections 7-4 to 7-7.

Distance Vector Protocols

Distance Vector Protocol
A routing algorithm that periodically sends the entire routing table to its neighboring or adjacent router

A **distance vector protocol** is a routing algorithm that periodically sends the entire routing table to its neighboring or adjacent router. When the neighboring router receives the table, it assigns a distance vector number to each route. The distance vector number is typically specified by some metric such as hop count.

In a distance vector protocol, the router first determines its neighbors or adjacent routers. All the connected routes will have a distance or hop count of 0. An example is shown in Figure 7-5. Routers use the hop count metric to determine the best route to forward a data packet. An example of determining the hop count to a destination subnet is provided in Figure 7-6.

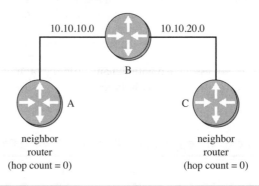

FIGURE 7-5 An example of router neighbors (hop count = 0).

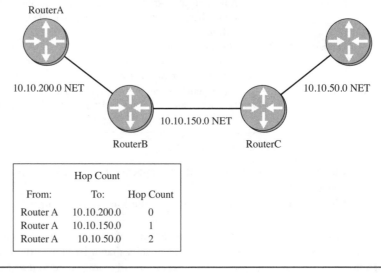

Hop Count		
From:	To:	Hop Count
Router A	10.10.200.0	0
Router A	10.10.150.0	1
Router A	10.10.50.0	2

FIGURE 7-6 An example of determining the router hops.

The hop count from RouterA to the 10.10.200.0, 10.10.150.0, and 10.10.50.0 subnets are as follows:

From	To	Hop Count
RouterA	10.10.200.0	0
RouterA	10.10.150.0	1
RouterA	10.10.50.0	2

In a distance vector protocol, each router determines its neighbors, builds its list of neighboring routers, and sends its routing table to its neighbors. The neighboring routers update their routing table based on the received information. When complete, each router's routing table provides a list of known routes within the network.

Link State Protocols

Link state protocols establish a relationship with a neighboring router. The routers exchange link state advertisements to update neighbors regarding route status. The link state advertisements are sent only if there is a change or loss in the network routes and the link state protocols converge to route selection quickly. This is a distinct advantage over distance vector protocols that exchange updated routing tables at fixed time intervals and are slow to converge. In fact, link state routing protocols are replacing distance vector protocols. Link state protocols are also called *shortest-path first protocols*, based on the algorithm developed by E. W. Dijkstra. An example of a link state protocol is OSPF, examined in section 7-6. Link state protocols use "Hello" packets to verify that communication is still established with neighbor routers. The key issues of link state protocols are summarized in Table 7-4.

Link State Protocol
Establishes a relationship with a neighboring router and uses route advertisements to build routing tables

TABLE 7-4   Key Issues of Link State Protocols

- Finds neighbors/adjacencies
- Uses route advertisements to build routing table
- Sends "Hello" packets
- Sends updates when routing changes

7-4   RIP—ROUTING INFORMATION PROTOCOL

Routing Information Protocol (**RIP**) is a dynamic routing protocol, meaning the routers periodically exchange routes. RIP is classified as a distance vector protocol using router hop count as the metric. RIP permits a maximum of 15 hops to prevent **routing loops**. Routing loops occur when a router forwards packets back to the router that sent them, as graphically shown in Figure 7-7. RIP and other distance vector routing protocols send the entire routing table to neighbor routers at regular time intervals. Sometimes the routing tables can be quite large and the transfer can consume network bandwidth. This is of great concern in networks with limited bandwidth because the periodic exchange can lead to slowdowns in data traffic. The default time interval for RIP for exchanging routing tables is 30 seconds. This results in slow route convergence, and if there are multiple routers sharing RIP routes, there will be even longer convergence time.

RIP
Routing Information Protocol

Routing Loop
Data is forwarded back to the router that sent the data packets

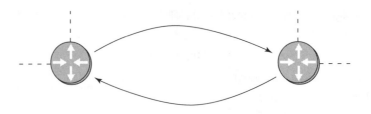

FIGURE 7-7   An example of data packet travel in a routing loop. Note that the packets never leave the routes between the two routers.

Advertise
The sharing of route information

Class Network Address
The network portion of the IP address based on the class of the network

Classful Addressing
The network portion of a particular network address

The RIP routing protocol is enabled on the router by entering the command *router RIP* at the **Router(config)#** prompt in the privileged EXEC mode. Next, network statements are required to declare what networks will be advertised by the RIP routing protocol. To **advertise** the network means the routing table containing the network is shared with its neighbors. The network command requires the use of a **class network address** (class A, class B, class C) after the *network* command. This is called **classful addressing**. A class network address or classful address is the network portion of the address for the particular class of the network. For example, LAN A in our campus network is on the 10.10.20.0 NET, as shown in Figure 7-8. This is a class A network and the network portion of the address is 10.0.0.0. The structure of the network command is *network [network address]*, where the *network address* is the network where RIP is to be advertised; therefore, the command in RIP will be *network 10.0.0.0*.

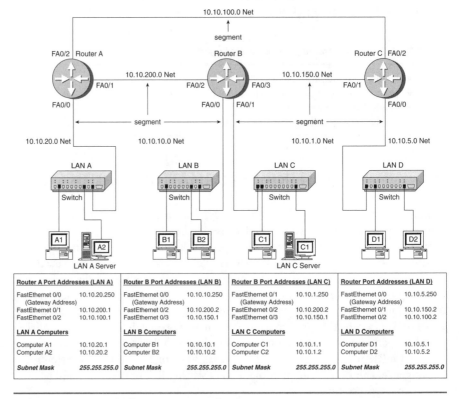

FIGURE 7-8   LAN A in the campus network.

The following discussion explains how to initialize RIP and how to set the networks attached to the router. After these commands are entered, any interfaces that are part of the 10.0.0.0 network will run the RIP routing protocol. Note that subnets or subnet masks are not specified in the RIP network command because the class network address is used and all IP addresses in the network (for example, 10.0.0.0) are enabled to use RIP.

```
Router(config)#router rip
Router(config-router)#network 10.0.0.0
```

RIP can be used only in *contiguous* networks, meaning the networks and routes must have the same class network address. This means the router addresses for the network connecting the routers must be the same class as the LAN connected to the router. This is shown in Figure 7-9 (a) and (b). LAN A and B have a 10.#.#.# address (also called a *10 network* address). The network address connecting the two routers must also be a "10" network address. The IP address for the network connecting the two routers in Figure 7-9 (a) is 10.10.200.0. This is a "10" network address. The network shown in Figure 7-9 (b) uses the IP address of 192.168.10.0 for the network connecting the two routers. An address of 192.168.10.0 is in the 192.168.10.0 network. This is not part of the 10.0.0.0 network; therefore, the 192.168.10.0 address is not suitable for use in RIP.

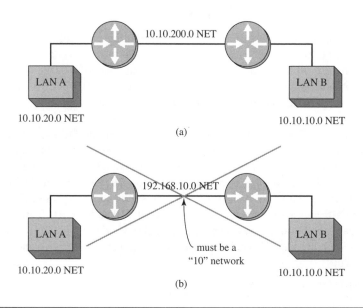

FIGURE 7-9   An example of (a) a contiguous network and (b) a discontiguous network.

RIP is a relatively simple routing protocol to configure. However, RIP is good only for very small networks that have a limited staff size to manage the network and is not suited for networks that need fast convergence. RIP is a standard protocol, not a proprietary protocol, meaning the use of the protocol is not limited to certain equipment manufacturers.

Configuring Routes with RIP

The first step in configuring the router for RIP is to set up the interfaces. This includes assigning an IP address and a subnet mask to the interface using the command *ip address A.B.C.D. subnet-mask*. Next the interface is enabled using the *no shut* command. The following are the steps for configuring the FastEthernet0/1 interface on RouterA in the campus network shown previously in Figure 7-8:

```
Router con0 is now available
Press RETURN to get started.
RouterA>en
Password:
RouterA# conf t
Enter configuration commands, one per line. End with CNTL/Z.
Router(config)#int fa0/1
Router(config-if)#ip address 10.10.200.1 255.255.255.0
Router(config-if)#no shut
00:59:03: %LINEPROTO-5-UPDOWN: Line protocol on Interface FastEthernet1,
    changed state to up
```

Next, enter the router's configuration mode [**Router(config)#**] and input the command *router rip* to use the RIP routing protocol. The next step is to specify the network that uses RIP for routing. These two steps are shown next:

```
Router(config)#router rip
Router(config-router)#network 10.0.0.0
```

The command *router rip* enables the RIP routing protocol and the command *network 10.0.0.0* instructs the router to use RIP on the "10" network. Remember, RIP requires the use of a class network address (for example, 10.0.0.0). Notice that the *router rip* command places the router in the **(config-router)** mode, as shown in the prompt. This indicates that the router is in the state for specifying the networks using RIP.

It's a good idea to periodically check that the router interfaces are properly configured. The command *show ip interface brief (sh ip int brief)* is used to check the interfaces. This is an important troubleshooting command when looking for reasons why the router is not working. Use this command to check to see if the IP address has been assigned to the interface and to check the status and protocol settings. In this case, the FastEthernet0/1 port has been assigned the IP address 10.10.200.1, the status is *up*, and the protocol is *up*. The FastEthernet 0/0 and 0/2 ports for RouterA have not been configured, as shown, and the staus is administratively down and the protocol is down:

```
Router#sh ip int brief
Interface       IP-Address    OK?  Method  Status                  Proto-
                                                                    col
FastEthernet0/0  unassigned   YES  manual  administratively down   down
FastEthernet0/1  10.10.200.1  YES  manual  up                      up
FastEthernet0/2  unassigned   YES  unset   administratively down   down
```

show ip protocol (sh ip protocol)
Displays the routing protocol running on the router

The command *show ip protocol (sh ip protocol)* is used to display the routing protocols running on the router, as shown. This command will display protocol information only after the routing protocol has been enabled and the network addresses are specified. Notice that there are no values specified for the FastEthernet0/0 and FastEthernet0/2 ports. Neither of these interfaces has been configured. The *show ip protocol* command also shows that router updates are being sent every 30 seconds and indicates that the next update is due in five seconds.

```
RouterA#sh ip protocol
Routing Protocol is "rip"
Sending updates every 30 seconds, next due in 5 seconds
Invalid after 180 seconds, hold down 180, flushed after 240
Outgoing update filter list for all interfaces is Incoming update filter
   list for all interfaces is Redistributing: rip
Default version control: send version 1, receive any version
Interface         Send Recv Key-chain
FastEthernet0/0    0    0    0
FastEthernet0/1    1    1    2
FastEthernet0/2    0    0    0
Routing for Networks:
10.0.0.0
Routing Information Sources:
Gateway Distance Last Update
10.10.200.1 120 00:00:14
Distance: (default is 120)
```

The routes configured for the router can be displayed using the ***show ip route
(sh ip route)*** command as shown. In this example, the FastEthernet0/0 and FastEth-
ernet0/2 ports for RouterA have been configured and are displayed:

```
Router#sh ip route
Codes: C - connected, S - static, I - IGRP, R - RIP, M - mobile, B - BGP
    D - EIGRP, EX - EIGRP external, O - OSPF, IA - OSPF inter area
N1 - OSPF NSSA external type 1, N2 - OSPF NSSA external type 2
E1 - OSPF external type 1, E2 - OSPF external type 2, E - EGP
I - IS-IS, L1 - IS-IS level-1, L2 - IS-IS level-2, * candidate default
U - per-user static route, o - ODR T - traffic engineered route
Gateway of last resort is not set
10.0.0.0/24 is subnetted, 1 subnets
C 10.10.20.0 is directly connected, FastEthernet0/0
C 10.10.200.0 is directly connected, FastEthernet0/1
C 10.10.100.0 is directly connected, FastEthernet0/2
```

Verify the settings in the running-configuration file by using the ***sh run*** command. Recall that this is the abbreviated command for ***show running-configuration***.
The configuration list should show that the interfaces have been assigned an IP address and that RIP has been configured.

```
RouterA#sh run                    ! 1. sh run command
Building configuration...         ! 2. assembling the data file
!                                 ! 3. ! is used for spaces or comments
Current configuration:
!
version 12.0                      ! 6. displays the Cisco IOS version ser-
   vice timestamps debug uptime
service timestamps log uptime
no service password-encryption    ! 9. the enable (line 14) and vty
   (line 42)
                                  ! passwords appear as plaintext
!
hostname RouterA                  11. the name of the router
!
enable secret 5 $1$6EWO$kWlakDz89zac.koh/pyG4.    ! 13. the encrypted
   enable
                                          !secret
enable password Salsa             !14. the enable password
!
ip subnet-zero                    ! 16. enables subnet zero routing
!
interface FastEthernet0/0              ! 18. FastEthernet0/0 settings
ip address 10.10.20.0 255.255.255.0
 no ip directed-broadcast
!
```

```
interface FastEthernet0/1            ! 22. FastEthernet0/1 settings
 ip address 10.10.200.1 255.255.255.0
 no ip directed-broadcast
 no mop enabled
!
interface FastEthernet0/2            ! 27. FastEthernet0/2 settings
 ip address 10.10.100.1 255.255.255.0
 no ip directed-broadcast no mop enabled
!
router rip                   ! 33. enable RIP
network 10.0.0.0                     ! 34. specify a network class address
!
ip classless
!
line con 0
transport input none
line aux 0
line vty 0 4                         ! 41. virtual terminal settings for tel-
    net
password ConCarne                    ! 42. telnet password
login
!
end
```

Lines 18, 22, and 27 list the assigned IP addresses for the interface. Lines 33 and 34 show that RIP has been configured for the router. The *sh run* command displays the router's running configuration. The *copy run start* command must be entered to save to NVRAM the changes made to the router's configuration.

Networking Challenge—RIP

Use the router simulator software included with the text's companion CD-ROM to demonstrate that you can configure RIP for RouterA in the campus LAN. (*Note:* The campus LAN is shown in Figure 7-8 and is displayed on the computer screen after the software is started.) Place the CD-ROM in your computer's drive. Open the *Net-Challenge* folder, and click *NetChallenge.exe*. When the software is running, click the **Select Router Challenge** button to open a **Select Router Challenge** drop-down menu. Select *Chapter 7—RIP*. This opens a checkbox that can be used to verify that you have completed all the tasks.

1. Enter the privileged EXEC mode on the router.
2. Enter the router configuration mode, **Router(config)**.
3. Configure the FastEthernet0/0 interface with the following:
   IP address 10.10.20.250
   Subnet mask 255.255.255.0
4. Enable the FA0/0 interface.
5. Configure the FastEthernet0/1 interface with the following:
   IP address 10.10.200.1
   Subnet mask 255.255.255.0
6. Enable the FA0/1 interface.
7. Configure the FastEthernet0/2 interface with the following:
   IP address 10.10.100.1
   Subnet mask 255.255.255.0
8. Enable the FA0/2 interface.
9. Enable RIP.
10. Use the *network* command to specify the class network address to be used by RIP (10.0.0.0).

11. Use the *sh ip int brief* command to check the interface status.
12. Use the *sh ip protocol* command to see whether RIP is running. (*Note:* This requires that Steps 9 and 10 are complete or the response will be "no protocol."
13. Use the *show ip route* command to verify whether the three FastEthernet ports are connected to the router.
14. Display the contents of the *running-configuration* file. Verify that RIP is enabled and the proper network address is specified.
15. Copy the router's running-configuration to the startup-configuration.
16. Display the contents of the startup-configuration.

7-5 IGRP—INTERIOR GATEWAY ROUTING PROTOCOL

Interior Gateway Routing Protocol (**IGRP**) is a Cisco proprietary distance vector dynamic routing protocol. IGRP is similar to RIP in that it is simple to configure. IGRP has some of the same limitations as RIP in that the networks must have contiguous network addresses, and IGRP can't have variable length subnet masks. However, IGRP has a maximum hop count of 255 compared to RIP, which has a 16-router hop limitation. The time interval for exchanging the routing tables with IGRP is 90 seconds. This limits the effect routing table exchanges can have on data traffic compared to RIP, which updates tables every 30 seconds.

IGRP uses a composite metric (set of metrics) consisting of internetwork delay, reliability, bandwidth, and load for determining the best route. The router provides default settings or the network administrator can customize route selection to better meet the needs of routing in and out of its network.

IGRP includes two features that improve its stability in routing data packets:

- **Holddowns:** Prevent a bad route from being reinstated
- **Split horizons:** Prevent information about a route from being sent back the same way it came, thus preventing routing loops

If you have the same route to a destination configured with IGRP and RIP, the preferred route is with IGRP. This preference is accomplished with a parameter called **administrative distance**. The administrative distance is a number assigned to a protocol or a route to declare its reliability. The lower the administrative distance number, the better the protocol or route. Each routing protocol has a default administrative distance.

A router uses the administrative distance to resolve which routing protocol is chosen when there are conflicts. For example, a router might learn a route to a 10.0.0.0 network using RIP. The same router might also learn of a route to the 10.0.0.0 network using IGRP. RIP has an administrative distance of 120 and IGRP has an administrative distance of 100. IGRP has the lower administrative distance number; therefore, the router will select the IGRP route. A summary of administrative distances for selected routing protocols is provided in Table 7-5.

IGRP
Interior Gateway Routing Protocol

Holddowns
Split Horizons

Administrative Distance
A number assigned to a protocol or route to declare its reliability

TABLE 7-5 Administrative Distances and Routing Protocols

Protocol	Administrative Distance
Connected	0
Static route	1
EIGRP	90
IGRP	100
OSPF	110
RIP	120

router igrp [*AS number*]
The router command for specifying IGRP

Autonomous System (AS)
A number assigned to a routing protocol to define which networks exchange routes

Classful Network
Same as a class network

The command for specifying the IGRP routing protocol is ***router igrp*** *[AS number]* where the AS number is an **autonomous system (AS)** number assigned to the protocol. An autonomous system number is similar to a server's domain in that the router looks for another connected router using IGRP that has the same AS number. If the networks have the same AS number, IGRP routes will be exchanged.

```
RouterA(config)# router igrp 200
RouterA(config)# network 10.0.0.0
```

IGRP can be used only in contiguous networks, which means the subnets in the network must belong to the same **classful network**. A classful network is the same as a class network. This means the router addresses for the network connecting the routers must be the same class network as the LAN connected to the router. This was shown in Figure 7-9 (a) and (b). LAN A and B have a 10.#.#.# address (as noted, also called a *10 network* address). The network address connecting the two routers must also be a "10" network address. The IP address for the network connecting the two routers in Figure 7-9 (a) is 10.10.200.0. This is a "10" network address. The network shown in Figure 7-9 (b) uses the IP address of 192.168.10.0 for the network connecting the two routers. An address of 192.168.10.0 is in the 192.168.10.0 network. This is not part of the "10" network; therefore, the 192.168.10.0 address cannot be used in this position.

Configuring Routes with IGRP

This section demonstrates how to configure the routers to use the IGRP routing protocol for the three-router campus network shown in Figure 7-10.

The first step in configuring RouterA to use IGRP is to set up the IP address and subnet masks for the interfaces on the three routers. Make sure you use the ***no shut*** command to enable the interface. Next, at the **RouterA(config)#** prompt, enter the command ***router igrp*** *[AS number]* to use the IGRP routing protocol. You must also specify the network that will be using IGRP for routing. These two steps are as follows:

```
RouterA(config)#router igrp 200
RouterA(config-router)#network 10.0.0.0
```

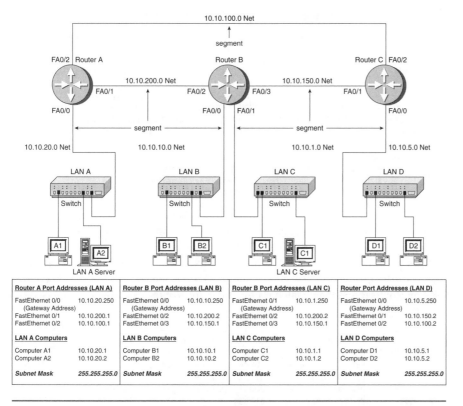

FIGURE 7-10   Routers A, B, and C in the three-router campus network.

The command ***router igrp 200*** enables the IGRP routing protocol and specifies an autonomous number of 200. The command ***network 10.0.0.0*** instructs the router to use IGRP on the "10" network. Notice that the ***router igrp*** command places the router in the **RouterA(config-router)#** mode as shown in the prompt. This indicates that the router is in the state for specifying the IGRP-specific commands. You can verify that IGRP is running on RouterA by entering the command ***sh ip protocol*** as shown at the enable prompt (**RouterA#**):

Router(config-router)#
The prompt indicating the router is in the mode to accept routing commands

```
RouterA# sh ip protocol
Routing Protocol is "igrp 200"
Sending updates every 90 seconds, next due in 53 seconds
Invalid after 270 seconds, hold down 280, flushed after 630
Outgoing update filter list for all interfaces is Incoming update filter
    list for all interfaces is Default networks flagged in outgoing
    updates Default networks accepted from incoming updates IGRP metric
    weight K1 1, K2 0, K3 1, K4 0, K5 0
IGRP maximum hopcount 100
IGRP maximum metric variance 1
Redistributing: igrp 10
Routing for Networks:
10.0.0.0
Routing Information Sources:
Gateway Distance Last Update
Distance: (default is 100)
```

The text shows that the routing protocol is "igrp 200", updates are being sent every 90 seconds, and it states that the next update is due in 53 seconds.

Next, the command ***show ip route (sh ip route)*** can be used to examine the contents of RouterA's routing table to see if any IGRP routes have been received:

```
RouterA# sh ip route
Codes: C connected, S static, I IGRP, R RIP, M mobile, B BGP D EIGRP, EX
    EIGRP external, O OSPF, IA OSPF inter area
N1 OSPF NSSA external type 1, N2 OSPF NSSA external type 2
E1 OSPF external type 1, E2 OSPF external type 2, E EGP
i IS-IS, L1 IS-IS level-1, L2 IS-IS level-2, * candidate default
U per-user static route, o ODR T traffic engineered route
Gateway of last resort is not set
10.0.0.0/24 is subnetted, 3 subnets
C 10.10.20.0 is directly connected, FastEthernet0/0
C 10.10.100.0 is directly connected, FastEthernet0/1
C 10.10.200.0 is directly connected, FastEthernet0/2
```

The command ***sh ip protocol*** indicates whether IGRP has been enabled on the router. This table shows the connected (C) networks but IGRP (I) is not enabled for any networks. Why? At this point, IGRP has been enabled only on RouterA in the campus network. Routers B and C also need to have IGRP enabled. Use the commands ***router igrp*** and ***network*** to enable IGRP on RouterB. IGRP was next configured on RouterB and the updated routing table for RouterA is provided:

```
RouterA# sh ip route
Codes: C connected, S static, I IGRP, R RIP, M mobile, B BGP D EIGRP, EX
    EIGRP external, O OSPF, IA OSPF inter area
N1 OSPF NSSA external type 1, N2 OSPF NSSA external type 2
E1 OSPF external type 1, E2 OSPF external type 2, E EGP
i IS-IS, L1 IS-IS level-1, L2 IS-IS level-2, * candidate default
U per-user static route, o ODR T traffic engineered route
Gateway of last resort is not set
10.0.0.0/24 is subnetted, 6 subnets
I 10.10.1.0 [100/8576] via 10.10.200.2, 00:00:54, FastEthernet0/1
I 10.10.10.0 [100/8576] via 10.10.200.2, 00:00:54, FastEthernet0/1
C 10.10.20.0 is directly connected, FastEthernet0/0
C 10.10.100.0 is directly connected, FastEthernet0/2
I 10.10.150.0 [100/10476] via 10.10.200.2, 00:00:54, FastEthernet0/1
C 10.10.200.0 is directly connected, FastEthernet0/1
```

Examination of the routing table shows IGRP is being used for routing to three subnets, 10.10.1.0, 10.10.10.0, and 10.10.150.0, and that three subnets are directly connected to RouterA, 10.10.20.0, 10.10.100.0, and 10.10.200.0. There are seven subnets in the campus LAN shown in Figure 7-10. IGRP has been configured on Routers A and B but routes using IGRP have not been defined in the campus network for the 10.10.5.0 NET. This requires that IGRP be enabled on RouterC. The commands ***router igrp*** and ***network*** are used to enable IGRP on RouterC. After configuring IGRP on RouterC, examination of RouterA's routing table shows the following:

```
RouterA# sh ip route
Codes: C connected, S static, I IGRP, R RIP, M mobile, B BGP D EIGRP, EX
    EIGRP external, O OSPF, IA OSPF inter area
N1 OSPF NSSA external type 1, N2 OSPF NSSA external type 2
E1 OSPF external type 1, E2 OSPF external type 2, E EGP
i IS-IS, L1 IS-IS level-1, L2 IS-IS level-2, * candidate default
U per-user static route, o ODR T traffic engineered route
Gateway of last resort is not set
10.0.0.0/24 is subnetted, 7 subnets
I 10.10.1.0 [100/8576] via 10.10.200.2, 00:01:11, FastEthernet0/1
I 10.10.5.0 [100/8576] via 10.10.100.2, 00:01:03, FastEthernet0/2
I 10.10.10.0 [100/8576] via 10.10.200.2, 00:01:11, FastEthernet0/1
C 10.10.20.0 is directly connected, FastEthernet0/0
C 10.10.100.0 is directly connected, FastEthernet0/2
```

```
I 10.10.150.0 [100/10476] via 10.10.200.2, 00:01:11, FastEthernet0/1
[100/10476] via 10.10.100.2, 00:01:03, FastEthernet0/2
C 10.10.200.0 is directly connected, FastEthernet0/1
```

IGRP has now been configured for the three routers in the campus network and routes have been defined for all seven subnets.

The command *show ip route igrp (sh ip route igrp)* can be used to view the routing table for one protocol, such as IGRP, as shown:

show ip route igrp (sh ip route igrp)
Displays only the IGRP routes

```
RouterA#sh ip route igrp
10.0.0.0/24 is subnetted, 7 subnets
I 10.10.1.0 [100/8576] via 10.10.200.2, 00:00:02, FastEthernet0/1
I 10.10.5.0 [100/8576] via 10.10.100.2, 00:00:03, FastEthernet0/2
I 10.10.10.0 [100/8576] via 10.10.200.2, 00:00:02, FastEthernet0/1
I 10.10.150.0 [100/10476] via 10.10.200.2, 00:00:02, FastEthernet0/1
```

The final step is to view the running-configuration in each router using the *sh run* command. The running-configuration for RouterA is provided. Notice the entries for *router igrp 200* and *network 10.0.0.0* in the running-configuration file.

```
RouterA#sh run
Building configuration...
Current configuration:
!
version 12.0
service timestamps debug uptime service timestamps log uptime no service
   password-encryption
!
hostname RouterA
!
enable secret 5 $1$6M4r$dleo7h1WP0AYu0K/cM6M91
enable password Salsa
!
ip subnet-zero
!
interface FastEthernet0/0
 ip address 10.10.20.250 255.255.255.0
 no ip directed-broadcast
!
interface FastEthernet0/1
 ip address 10.10.200.1 255.255.255.0
 no ip directed-broadcast
!
interface FastEthernet0/2
 ip address 10.10.100.1 255.255.255.0
 no ip directed-broadcast
!
router igrp 200
network 10.0.0.0
!
ip classless
!
line con 0
transport input none line aux 0
line vty 0 4 password chile login
!
end
```

Remember to use the *copy run start* command to save the changes made to NVRAM.

Networking Challenge—IGRP

Use the Net-Challenge simulator software included with the text's companion CD-ROM to demonstrate that you can configure IGRP for RouterB in the campus LAN (the campus LAN is shown in Figure 7-10 and is displayed on the computer screen after the software is started). Place the Net-Challenge CD-ROM in your computer's drive. Open the *Net-Challenge* folder, and click *NetChallenge.exe*. When the software is running, click the **Select Router Challenge** button to open a **Select Router Challenge** drop-down menu. Select *Chapter 7— IGRP*. This opens a checkbox that can be used to verify that you have completed all the tasks. A check next to a task indicates that the task has been successfully completed.

1. Click the RouterA button.
2. Enter the privileged EXEC mode on the router.
3. Enter the router configuration mode, **Router(config)**.
4. Set the hostname to *RouterA*.
5. Configure the FastEthernet0/0 interface with the following:
   IP address 10.10.20.250
   Subnet mask 255.255.255.0
6. Enable the FA0/0 interface.
7. Configure the FastEthernet0/1 interface with the following:
   IP address 10.10.200.1
   Subnet mask 255.255.255.0
8. Enable the FA0/1 interface.
9. Configure the FastEthernet0/2 interface with the following:
   IP address 10.10.100.1
   Subnet mask 255.255.255.0
10. Enable the FA0/2 interface.
11. Enable IGRP on RouterA, using an AS of 200.
12. Use the *network* command to specify the class network address to be used by IGRP.
13. Use the *sh ip int brief* command to check the interface status.
14. Use the *sh ip protocol* to see whether IGRP is running.
15. Use the *sh ip route* command to verify that the four FastEthernet ports are connected to the router.
16. Use the *sh run* command to view the running-configuration file. Verify that IGRP is enabled and the proper network address is specified.
17. Copy the running-configuration to the startup-configuration.
18. Display the contents of the startup configuration.

7-6   OSPF—OPEN SHORTEST PATH FIRST ROUTING PROTOCOL

OSPF
Open Shortest Path First routing protocol

IETF
Internet Engineering Task Force

Open Shortest Path First (**OSPF**) is a dynamic routing protocol, classified as a link state protocol. It was developed by the Interior Gateway Protocol (IGP) working group for the Internet Engineering Task Force (**IETF**) specifically for use in TCP/IP networks. OSPF is an open, not proprietary, protocol and is supported by many vendors. The main advantages of OSPF are rapid convergence and the consumption of very little bandwidth. When a network is completely *converged*, all the routers in the network agree on the best routes. After the initial flooding of routes in the form of **link state advertisements** or **LSAs**, OSPF sends route updates only when there is a change in the network. Every time LSAs are sent, each router must recalculate the routing table.

This is a distinct advantage over RIP and IGRP. Recall that RIP and IGRP exchange the entire routing table at fixed time intervals. RIP updates every 30 seconds, IGRP every 90 seconds. Also, in RIP and IGRP, the routing table update is propagated through the network at regular timer intervals, and therefore the convergence to final routes is slow. In OSPF, an LSA is sent as soon as the loss of a route has been detected. The loss is immediately reported to neighbor routers and new routes are calculated much faster than with RIP and IGRP.

OSPF sends small **"Hello" packets** at regular time intervals to adjacent routers to verify that the link between two routers is active and the routers are communicating. If a router fails to respond to a "Hello," it is assumed that the link or possibly the router is down. The OSPF "Hello" packet captured with the Surveyor Demo protocol analyzer is discussed in section 7-10.

OSPF uses the concept of **areas** to partition a large network into smaller networks. The advantage of this is that the routers have to calculate routes only for their area. If a route goes down in a given area, only the routers in that area have to calculate new routes. Any number between 0 and 4294967295 ($2^{32} - 1$) can be used; however, area 0 is reserved for the root area, which is the **backbone** for the network. The backbone is the primary path for data traffic to and from destinations and sources in the campus network. All areas must connect to area 0, and area 0 cannot be split. The area numbers can also be expressed in IP notation—for example, area 0 could be 0.0.0.0—or you can specify an area as 192.168.25.0 or in subnet notation. Hence the need for the large upper area number. ($2^{32} - 1$) = 255.255.255.255 when converted to a decimal number.

OSPF allows the use of **variable length subnet masks (VLSMs)**, which enable different size subnets in the network to better meet the needs of the network and more efficiently use the network's limited IP address space. For example, point-to-point inter-router links don't need a large block of addresses assigned to them. An example of an inter-router link is shown in Figure 7-11. A subnet of size 4 is sufficient for the inter-router link that includes the IP addresses for the router interfaces, the network address, and the broadcast address. A subnet mask of 255.255.255.252 meets this requirement of a subnet size 4 and is permissible in OSPF. This subnet mask provides for the addressing of the two host addresses (the router interfaces on each end), and the network and broadcast addresses, which provides the total subnet size of 4. (Refer to Chapter 5 to review subnet masking if needed.) This is an important advantage of OSPF because using variable length subnet masks minimizes the waste of IP addresses when interconnecting subnets. A summary of OSPF's advantages and disadvantages is presented in Table 7-6.

Link State Advertisement (LSA)
The exchange of updated link state information when routes change

"Hello" Packets
Used in the OSPF protocol to verify that the links are still communicating

Areas
The partition of a large OSPF network into smaller OSPF networks

Backbone
The primary path for data traffic to and from destinations and sources in the campus network

Variable Length Subnet Masks (VLSM)
Allows the use of subnet masks to better fit the needs of the network, thereby minimizing the waste of IP addresses when interconnecting subnets

FA0/0   FA0/1
10.10.250.1   10.10.250.2

10.10.250.0 Network address
10.10.250.3 Broadcast address
10.10.25.0 Subnet

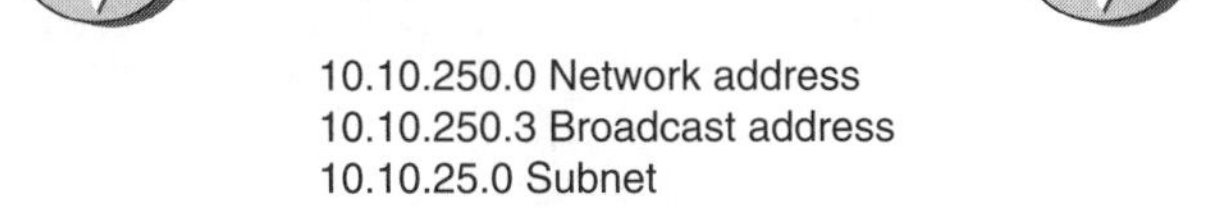

FIGURE 7-11   An inter-router link subnetted to provide for two host IP address, a network address and a broadcast address.

TABLE 7-6   Summary of Advantages and Disadvantages of OSPF

Advantages	Disadvantages
Not proprietary—available for use by all vendors	Can be very complicated to implement
Link state changes are immediately reported, which enables rapid convergence	Is process intensive due to routing table calculations
Consumes very little network bandwidth	Intermittent routes that are going up and down will create excessive LSA updates—this is called **route flapping**
Uses VLSM (variable length subnet masking)	
Uses areas to partition the network into smaller networks, minimizing the number of route calculations	

Route Flapping
Intermittent routes going up and down creating excessive LSA updates

Configuring Routes with OSPF

This section describes a procedure for configuring OSPF on a router. The first example is for configuring the three routers in the campus LAN shown in Figure 7-12. The routers will be configured to run OSPF on each of the router's three Ethernet interfaces. The example begins with configuring RouterA. RouterA must first be placed in the router's configuration mode [**Router(config)#**] as shown:

```
RouterA#conf t
Enter configuration commands, one per line. End with CNTL/Z.
RouterA(config)#
```

The next step is to enter the information about the IP address for each of the Ethernet interfaces. The IP addresses for RouterA are as follows:

FastEthernet0/0	10.10.20.250
FastEthernet0/1	10.10.200.1
FastEthernet0/2	10.10.100.1

A subnet mask of 255.255.255.0 is assigned to each of the FastEthernet interfaces. After the FastEthernet interfaces are configured, verify the configuration settings using the *sh ip int brief* command as shown. Make sure the status for the FastEthernet interfaces are *up*. This indicates that the interfaces are turned on and an Ethernet networking device is connected. The protocol will show *down* until the Ethernet cable is connected and the connecting interface is enabled. In this case, the connecting interfaces to FA0/1 and FA0/2 are not enabled and therefore show a status of *down*.

```
RouterA#sh ip int brief
Interface       IP-Address    OK?  Method  Status  Protocol
FastEthernet0/0 10.10.20.250  YES  manual  up      up
FastEthernet0/1 10.10.200.1   YES  manual  up      down
FastEthernet0/2 10.10.100.1   YES  manual  up      down
```

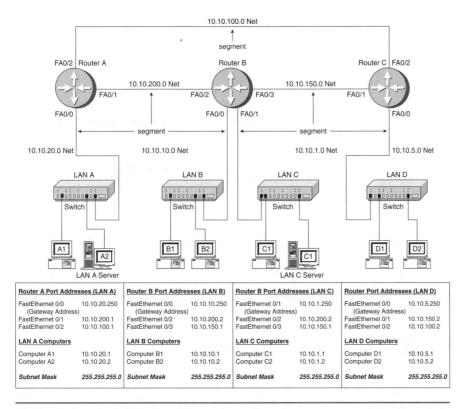

FIGURE 7-12   The three-router campus LAN.

Router A Port Addresses (LAN A)		Router B Port Addresses (LAN B)		Router B Port Addresses (LAN C)		Router Port Addresses (LAN D)	
FastEthernet 0/0 (Gateway Address)	10.10.20.250	FastEthernet 0/0 (Gateway Address)	10.10.10.250	FastEthernet 0/1 (Gateway Address)	10.10.1.250	FastEthernet 0/0 (Gateway Address)	10.10.5.250
FastEthernet 0/1	10.10.200.1	FastEthernet 0/2	10.10.200.2	FastEthernet 0/2	10.10.200.2	FastEthernet 0/1	10.10.150.2
FastEthernet 0/2	10.10.100.1	FastEthernet 0/3	10.10.150.1	FastEthernet 0/3	10.10.150.1	FastEthernet 0/2	10.10.100.2
LAN A Computers		**LAN B Computers**		**LAN C Computers**		**LAN D Computers**	
Computer A1	10.10.20.1	Computer B1	10.10.10.1	Computer C1	10.10.1.1	Computer D1	10.10.5.1
Computer A2	10.10.20.2	Computer B2	10.10.10.2	Computer C2	10.10.1.2	Computer D2	10.10.5.2
Subnet Mask	**255.255.255.0**	**Subnet Mask**	**255.255.255.0**	**Subnet Mask**	**255.255.255.0**	**Subnet Mask**	**255.255.255.0**

Next, the command *router ospf <process id>* is used to enable OSPF routing. In this case, the command *router ospf 100* is entered. The 100 is the *process id number*. This number must be the same on each router for OSPF to exchange routes. The process id number is selected by the network administrator and is not used for routing outside the network. It is customary to use the same process id throughout the network for ease of management but it is not required. Entering the *router ospf 100* command places the router in the **RouterA(config-router)#** prompt:

> **router ospf [number]**
> The command used to enable OSPF routing

```
RouterA(config)#router ospf 100
RouterA(config-router)#
```

The next step is to define the network running OSPF by entering the *network* command followed by the IP address of the interface, the OSPF wild card bits, and then an area number. The following text shows each step and lists the results of entering a question mark as the command is entered. When entering the command *network ?* the router prompts you to enter the IP address of the interface.

```
RouterA(config-router)#network ?
A.B.C.D Network number
```

A.B.C.D is the IP address or **network number** for the Ethernet interface. Next, entering *network 10.10.20.250 ?* prompts you to enter the OSPF wild card bits in the form of A.B.C.D. The **wild card bits**, also called the *inverse mask bits,* are used to match the network IP address (A.B.C.D format) to interface IPs. If there is a match, the subnet on the interface is advertised out OSPF and OSPF packets are sent out the

> **Network Number**
> Another name for the IP subnet

> **Wild Card Bits**
> Used to match network IP addresses to interface IPs

interface. A 0 wild card bit is used to indicate a "must" match. A 255 is a "don't care," hence the name *inverse mask*.

Area 0
In OSPF this is the root area
and is the backbone for the
network

The last entry when defining an OSPF route is for the area. Remember, areas are used to partition a large network into smaller networks. **Area 0** is the root area and is the backbone for the network. All other areas must connect to area 0. Area 0 cannot be split. Other area numbers are specified by the network administrator.

Assume that the router command ***network 10.10.20.250 0.0.0.0 area 0*** is entered. The wild card bits indicate that any interface with an address of 10.10.20.250 must run OSPF on the interface and will be assigned to area 0 (the network backbone). Assume that the router command ***network 10.10.20.250 0.255.255.255 area 0*** is entered. The wild card bits indicate that any interface with an IP address of 10.x.x.x must run OSPF on the interface and will be assigned to area 0.

```
RouterA(config-router)#network 10.10.20.250 ?
  A.B.C.D OSPF wild card bits
RouterA(config-router)#network 10.10.20.250 0.0.0.0 ?
area Set the OSPF area ID
RouterA(config-router)#network 10.10.20.250 0.0.0.0 area 0
```

The following text details the three OSPF network entries needed to configure OSPF routing for RouterA:

```
RouterA(config-router)#network 10.10.20.250 0.0.0.0 area 0
RouterA(config-router)#network 10.10.200.1 0.0.0.0 area 0
RouterA(config-router)#network 10.10.100.1 0.0.0.0 area 0
```

Note that the RouterA interface to LAN A (10.10.20.250 NET) is listed when configuring OSPF. This is used in OSPF to advertise the LAN to the other routers. Also note that the network has been assigned to area 0 (the backbone). The command ***sh ip int brief*** is used to check the status of the interfaces. The text protocol *down* indicates that the cable to the interface is either unplugged or the interface is shut down.

```
RouterA#show int brief
Interface        IP-Address      OK?   Method   Status   Protocol
FastEthernet0/0  10.10.20.250    YES   NVRAM    up       up
FastEthernet0/1  10.10.200.1     YES   manual   up       down
FastEthernet0/2  10.10.100.1     YES   manual   up       down
```

This problem with the "protocol down" is fixed by reestablishing the physical connection between the routers.

The next step is to configure RouterB. First configure the four FastEthernet interfaces on RouterB. Next, the OSPF routing protocol for RouterB is set. In this example, one command line instruction is used to configure RouterB to run OSPF on all four of its interfaces. This is done with a subnet mask or wild card in OSPF. First enter RouterB's configuration mode using the ***conf t*** command. The command ***router ospf 100*** is entered. Note that the same process id number of 100 is being used. The next step is to enter ***network 10.0.0.0 0.255.255.255 area 0***. This command tells the router that any address that starts with a "10" belongs to area 0 on RouterB.

```
RouterB#conf t
Enter configuration commands, one per line. End with CNTL/Z.
RouterB(config)#router ospf 100
RouterB(config-router)#network 10.0.0.0 0.255.255.255 area 0
```

Verify that the interfaces are properly configured using the ***sh ip int brief*** command, as shown:

```
RouterB#sh ip int brief
Interface        IP-Address     OK?   Method   Status   Protocol
FastEthernet0/0  10.10.10.250   YES   manual   up       up
FastEthernet0/1  10.10.1.250    YES   manual   up       up
FastEthernet0/2  10.10.200.2    YES   manual   up       up
FastEthernet0/3  10.10.150.1    YES   manual   up       down
```

The FastEthernet0/3 interface shows the protocol is *down* because the connecting interface is shut down on RouterC.

The next step is to configure RouterC. The OSPF routing protocol for RouterC is set using the command ***router OSPF 100*** followed by ***network 10.0.0.0 0.255.255.255 area 0***, as shown.

```
RouterC(config)#router ospf 100
RouterC(config-router)#network 10.0.0.0 0.255.255.255 area 0
```

The interfaces on RouterC are checked using the ***sh ip int brief*** command, as shown:

```
RouterC#sh ip int brief
Interface        IP-Address   OK? Method Status Protocol
FastEthernet0/0  10.10.5.250  YES manual up     up
FastEthernet0/1  10.10.150.2  YES manual up     up
FastEthernet0/2  10.10.100.2  YES manual up     up
```

Notice that protocol shows *up* for all interfaces. This is because all interfaces are connected and the interfaces are enabled.

The following is a partial listing of the running-configuration file on RouterA that shows the router OSPF network configuration. Similar information will appear on Routers B and C.

```
.
.
.
router ospf 100
 network 10.10.200.1 0.0.0.0 area 0 network 10.10.20.250 0.0.0.0 area 0
 network 10.10.100.1 0.0.0.0 area 0
.
.
.
```

The routing table for RouterA can be checked using the command ***sh ip route***, as shown. The routing table indicates there are seven subnets in the campus network shown in Figure 7-12. The "Os" indicate the subnets running OSPF and "C" indicates the subnets directly connected to the router:

```
RouterA#sh ip route
Codes: C connected, S static, I IGRP, R RIP, M mobile, B BGP D EIGRP, EX
   EIGRP external, O OSPF, IA OSPF inter area
N1 OSPF NSSA external type 1, N2 OSPF NSSA external type 2
E1 OSPF external type 1, E2 OSPF external type 2, E EGP
i IS-IS, L1 IS-IS level-1, L2 IS-IS level-2, * candidate default
U per-user static route, o ODR T traffic engineered route
Gateway of last resort is not set
10.0.0.0/24 is subnetted, 7 subnets
O 10.10.5.0 [110/74] via 10.10.100.2, 00:03:28, FastEthernet0/2
O 10.10.10.0 [110/74] via 10.10.200.2, 00:03:28, FastEthernet0/1
O 10.10.1.0 [110/74] via 10.10.200.2, 00:03:28, FastEthernet0/1
C 10.10.20.0 is directly connected, FastEthernet0/0
C 10.10.100.0 is directly connected, FastEthernet0/2
O 10.10.150.0 [110/128] via 10.10.200.2, 00:03:28, FastEthernet0/1
[110/128] via 10.10.100.2, 00:03:28, FastEthernet0/2
C 10.10.200.0 is directly connected, FastEthernet0/1
```

A command used to display only the OSPF routes is **sh ip route ospf**. The following are the results for this command from RouterA:

```
RouterA#sh ip route ospf
10.0.0.0/24 is subnetted, 6 subnets
O 10.10.5.0 [110/74] via 10.10.100.2, 00:10:03, FastEthernet0/2
O 10.10.10.0 [110/74] via 10.10.200.2, 00:10:03, FastEthernet0/1
O 10.10.150.0 [110/128] via 10.10.200.2, 00:10:03, FastEthernet0/1
  [110/128] via 10.10.100.2, 00:10:03, FastEthernet0/2
```

Another command used for displaying protocol information for the router is **sh ip protocol**. The following are the results for entering this command for RouterA:

```
RouterA#sh ip protocol
Routing Protocol is "ospf 100" Sending updates every 0 seconds
Invalid after 0 seconds, hold down 0, flushed after 0
Outgoing update filter list for all interfaces is Incoming update filter
  list for all interfaces is Redistributing: ospf 100
Routing for Networks:
10.10.20.250/32
10.10.100.1/32
10.10.200.1/32
Routing Information Sources:
Gateway Distance Last Update
10.10.100.1 110 00:06:01
10.10.200.2 110 00:06:01
Distance: (default is 110)
```

Networking Challenge—OSPF

Use the Net-Challenge simulator software included with the text's companion CD-ROM to demonstrate that you can configure OSPF for RouterB in the campus LAN (the campus LAN is shown in Figure 7-12 and is displayed on the computer screen when the software is started). Place the Net-Challenge CD-ROM in your computer's drive. Open the *Net-Challenge* folder and click *NetChallenge.exe.* When the software is running, click the **Select Router Challenge** button to open a **Select Router Challenge** drop-down menu. Select *Chapter 7— OSPF*. This opens a checkbox that can be used to verify that you have completed all the tasks.

1. Enter the privileged EXEC mode on the router.
2. Enter the router's terminal configuration mode, **Router(config)**.
3. Set the hostname to *RouterA*.
4. Configure the FastEthernet0/0 interface with the following:
   IP address 10.10.20.250
   Subnet mask 255.255.255.0
5. Enable the FA0/0 interface.
6. Configure the FastEthernet0/1 interface with the following:
   IP address 10.10.200.1
   Subnet mask 255.255.255.0
7. Enable the FA0/1 interface.
8. Configure the FastEthernet0/2 interface with the following:
   IP address 10.10.100.1
   Subnet mask 255.255.255.0
9. Enable the FA0/2 interface.
10. Enable OSPF with a network number of 100.
11. Use a single command-line instruction to configure RouterA to run OSPF on all three of the FastEthernet interfaces (use area 100).

12. Use the **sh ip int brief** command to check the interface status.
13. Use the **sh ip protocol** command to see whether OSPF is running on RouterA.
14. Use the **sh ip route** command to verify that the three FastEthernet ports are connected to RouterA.
15. Use the **sh run** command to view the running-configuration file on RouterA. Verify that OSPF is enabled and the proper network address is specified.

7-7 EIGRP—ENHANCED INTERIOR GATEWAY ROUTING PROTOCOL

This section introduces techniques for configuring a router's interface to run **EIGRP**, the Enhanced Interior Gateway Routing Protocol. EIGRP is an enhanced version of the Interior Gateway Routing Protocol (IGRP). EIGRP is a Cisco proprietary protocol and is often called a hybrid routing protocol that incorporates the best of the distance vector and link-state algorithms. EIGRP calculates route metrics in a similar way as IGRP but uses a technique to improve the detail on metrics.

> **EIGRP**
> Enhanced Interior Gateway
> Routing Protocol

EIGRP allows the use of variable length subnet masks, which is beneficial when you're trying to conserve the uses of IP addresses. EIGRP also uses "Hello" packets to verify that a link from one router to another is still active. This is similar to the OSPF "Hello" packet described in section 7-10. The routing table updates are exchanged when there is a change in the network. In other words, the routers don't exchange unnecessary information unless a route changes. This helps conserve the limited bandwidth of the network data link. When route information is exchanged, EIGRP quickly converges to the new route selection.

The four components of EIGRP are as follows:

- **Neighbor Discovery Recovery:** Used to learn about other routers on directly attached networks. This is also used to discover whether neighbor routers are unreachable. This discovery is accomplished by periodically sending "Hello" packets. The "Hello" packets are used to verify that a neighbor router is functioning.
- **Reliable Transport Protocol:** Used to guarantee delivery of EIGRP packets to neighbor routers. Both unicast and multicast packet transmission are supported.
- **DUAL Finite State Machine:** Used to track all routes advertised by its neighbors and is used for route computation to obtain loop-free routing.
- **Protocol Dependent Modules:** Responsible for handling network layer, protocol-specific requirements. For example, the IP-EIGRP module is responsible for extracting information from the EIGRP packets and passing this information to DUAL. DUAL uses this information to make routing decisions, and IP-EIGRP then redistributes the learned routes.

Configuring Routes with EIGRP

This section describes a procedure for configuring EIGRP on a router. The first example is for configuring RouterA in the campus LAN shown in Figure 7-13.

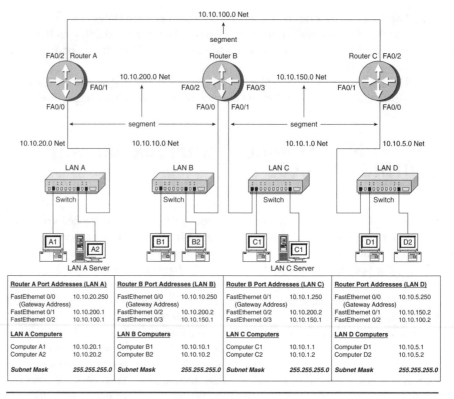

FIGURE 7-13 The three-router campus LAN.

Router A Port Addresses (LAN A)		Router B Port Addresses (LAN B)		Router B Port Addresses (LAN C)		Router Port Addresses (LAN D)	
FastEthernet 0/0 (Gateway Address)	10.10.20.250	FastEthernet 0/0 (Gateway Address)	10.10.10.250	FastEthernet 0/1 (Gateway Address)	10.10.1.250	FastEthernet 0/0 (Gateway Address)	10.10.5.250
FastEthernet 0/1	10.10.200.1	FastEthernet 0/2	10.10.200.2	FastEthernet 0/2	10.10.200.2	FastEthernet 0/1	10.10.150.2
FastEthernet 0/2	10.10.100.1	FastEthernet 0/3	10.10.150.1	FastEthernet 0/3	10.10.150.1	FastEthernet 0/2	10.10.100.2
LAN A Computers		**LAN B Computers**		**LAN C Computers**		**LAN D Computers**	
Computer A1	10.10.20.1	Computer B1	10.10.10.1	Computer C1	10.10.1.1	Computer D1	10.10.5.1
Computer A2	10.10.20.2	Computer B2	10.10.10.2	Computer C2	10.10.1.2	Computer D2	10.10.5.2
Subnet Mask	*255.255.255.0*	*Subnet Mask*	*255.255.255.0*	*Subnet Mask*	*255.255.255.0*	*Subnet Mask*	*255.255.255.0*

The three routers in the campus LAN will be configured to run EIGRP. The first step is to configure the interfaces on each of the three routers. The IP addresses and the subnet masks for the router interfaces are as follows:

RouterA

FA0/0	10.10.20.250	255.255.255.0
FA0/1	10.10.200.1	255.255.255.0
FA0/2	10.10.100.1	255.255.255.0

RouterB

FA0/0	10.10.10.250	255.255.255.0
FA0/1	10.10.1.250	255.255.255.0
FA0/2	10.10.200.2	255.255.255.0
FA0/3	10.10.150.1	255.255.255.0

RouterC

FA0/0	10.10.5.250	255.255.255.0
FA0/1	10.10.150.2	255.255.255.0
FA0/2	10.10.100.2	255.255.255.0

After configuring the router interfaces, the EIGRP routing protocol for RouterA will be configured. Use the ***conf t*** command to enter the router's configuration mode. Next enter the command ***router eigrp [AS number]***. The AS number is the same as that for the IGRP routing protocol: Any AS number can be used. The router uses the AS numbers to determine which routers share routing tables. Only routers with the same AS number will share routing updates The command ***router eigrp 150*** is entered as shown. The prompt changes to (**config-router**) and the next command entered sets the network to run EIGRP. In this example, the command ***network 10.0.0.0*** is entered. This instructs the router to run EIGRP on any of the router's interfaces that have an IP address that begins with 10. A different network command will be used on RouterB to show how the command can be used to specify a limited IP address range.

```
RouterA(config)#router eigrp 150
RouterA(config-router)#network 10.0.0.0
```

Now the 10.x.x.x interfaces on RouterA are configured to run EIGRP. The command ***sh ip protocol*** is entered to verify that the EIGRP routing protocol is enabled on RouterA.

```
RouterA# sh ip protocol
Routing Protocol is "eigrp 150"
Outgoing update filter list for all interfaces is Incoming update filter
   list for all interfaces is Default networks flagged in outgoing
   updates Default networks accepted from incoming updates EIGRP metric
   weight K1 1, K2 0, K3 1, K4 0, K5 0
EIGRP maximum hopcount 100
EIGRP maximum metric variance 1
Redistributing: eigrp 150
Automatic network summarization is in effect
Routing for Networks:
10.0.0.0
Routing Information Sources:
Gateway Distance Last Update
10.10.200.2 90 00:00:09
Distance: internal 90 external 170
```

The top line states that the routing protocol is "eigrp 150" and indicates that it has been nine seconds since the last update to the routing table. In EIGRP, updates to the routing table are made when there are changes in the network.

Another useful command is ***sh ip route***. The following are the results of entering the command. In this case, the router does not show any EIGRP routes to the subnets in the network because EIGRP has not been configured on RouterB or RouterC.

```
RouterA#sh ip route
Codes: C connected, S static, I IGRP, R RIP, M mobile, B BGP D EIGRP, EX
    EIGRP external, O OSPF, IA OSPF inter area
N1 OSPF NSSA external type 1, N2 OSPF NSSA external type 2
E1 OSPF external type 1, E2 OSPF external type 2, E EGP
i IS-IS, L1 IS-IS level-1, L2 IS-IS level-2, * candidate default
U per-user static route, o ODR T traffic engineered route
Gateway of last resort is not set
10.0.0.0/24 is subnetted, 3 subnets
C 10.10.20.0 is directly connected, FastEthernet0/0
C 10.10.200.0 is directly connected, FastEthernet0/1
C 10.10.100.0 is directly connected, FastEthernet0/2
```

The command ***sh ip int brief*** is entered and the status and protocols for the Ethernet interfaces are *up*. These will show *up* as long as there is a network connection to the interfaces.

```
RouterA#sh ip int brief
Interface        IP-Address    OK?  Method  Status  Protocol
FastEthernet0/0  10.10.20.250  YES  NVRAM   up      up
FastEthernet0/1  10.10.200.1   YES  manual  up      up
FastEthernet0/2  10.10.100.1   YES  manual  up      up
```

The ***sh run*** command is used to view the contents of the router's running-configuration file. The following shows the part of the configuration file that shows the entries for EIGRP. Notice that these entries are the same as the commands entered earlier when configuring EIGRP.

```
!
router eigrp 150
 network 10.0.0.0
!
```

The next step is to configure RouterB. The configuration mode **(config)#** for RouterB is entered and the command ***router eigrp 150*** is entered. Remember, 150 is the AS number, which is the same number used when configuring RouterA. The next command is used to set the network that is running EIGRP. In this case, the command ***network 10.10.0.0*** is entered. This means that on RouterB, all interfaces with a 10.10.x.x address will run the EIGRP protocol. In this case, all interfaces on RouterB have a 10.10.x.x address and will run EIGRP.

```
RouterB#conf t
Enter configuration commands, one per line. End with CNTL/Z.
RouterB(config)#router eigrp 150
RouterB(config-router)#network 10.10.0.0
```

The command ***sh ip protocol*** is used to verify that EIGRP is running on RouterB. The text shows that eigrp 150 is running on RouterB and it has been 27 seconds since the last update to the routing table.

```
RouterB#sh ip protocol
Routing Protocol is "eigrp 150"
Outgoing update filter list for all interfaces is Incoming update filter
    list for all interfaces is Default networks flagged in outgoing
    updates Default networks accepted from incoming updates EIGRP metric
    weight K1 1, K2 0, K3 1, K4 0, K5 0
EIGRP maximum hopcount 100
EIGRP maximum metric variance 1
Redistributing: eigrp 150
Automatic network summarization is in effect
Routing for Networks:
10.0.0.0
Routing Information Sources:
Gateway Distance Last Update
10.10.200.1 90 00:00:27
Distance: internal 90 external 170
```

The ***sh ip route*** command for RouterB shows that six routes are on RouterB and there are EIGRP routes to the 10.10.20.0 and 10.10.100.0 subnets. The code for the EIGRP routes is "D." Remember, the "C" code is for the subnets directly connected to the router.

```
RouterB#sh ip route
Codes: C connected, S static, I IGRP, R RIP, M mobile, B BGP D EIGRP, EX
    EIGRP external, O OSPF, IA OSPF inter area
```

```
N1 OSPF NSSA external type 1, N2 OSPF NSSA external type 2
E1 OSPF external type 1, E2 OSPF external type 2, E EGP
i IS-IS, L1 IS-IS level-1, L2 IS-IS level-2, * candidate default
U per-user static route, o ODR T traffic engineered route
Gateway of last resort is not set
10.0.0.0/24 is subnetted, 6 subnets
C 10.10.10.0 is directly connected, FastEthernet0/0
C 10.10.1.0 is directly connected, FastEthernet0/1
D 10.10.20.0 [90/2195456] via 10.10.200.1, 00:00:09, FastEthernet0/2
D 10.10.100.0 [90/2681856] via 10.10.200.1, 00:00:09, FastEthernet0/2
C 10.10.150.0 is directly connected, FastEthernet0/3
C 10.10.200.0 is directly connected, FastEthernet0/2
```

A check of the IP routes on RouterA also shows that RouterA and RouterB are exchanging routes with each other. RouterA now shows six subnets. Once again, the "D" indicates the EIGRP routes and the "C" indicates the directly connected subnets.

```
RouterA#sh ip route
Codes: C connected, S static, I IGRP, R RIP, M mobile, B BGP D EIGRP, EX
   EIGRP external, O OSPF, IA OSPF inter area
N1 OSPF NSSA external type 1, N2 OSPF NSSA external type 2
E1 OSPF external type 1, E2 OSPF external type 2, E EGP
i IS-IS, L1 IS-IS level-1, L2 IS-IS level-2, * candidate default
U per-user static route, o ODR T traffic engineered route
Gateway of last resort is not set
10.0.0.0/24 is subnetted, 6 subnets
D 10.10.10.0 [90/2195456] via 10.10.200.2, 00:00:50, FastEthernet0/1
D 10.10.1.0 [90/2195456] via 10.10.200.2, 00:00:50, FastEthernet0/1
C 10.10.20.0 is directly connected, FastEthernet0/0
C 10.10.100.0 is directly connected, FastEthernet0/2
D 10.10.150.0 [90/2681856] via 10.10.200.2, 00:00:50, FastEthernet0/1
C 10.10.200.0 is directly connected, FastEthernet0/1
```

The last step is to configure EIGRP for RouterC using the *router eigrp 150* command. The command *network 10.10.0.0* is used to instruct the router to assign EIGRP to all interfaces that are under the 10.10.0.0 network. In this case, all interfaces on RouterC have a 10.10.x.x address and therefore will run EIGRP.

```
RouterC(config)#router eigrp 150
RouterC(config-router)#network 10.10.0.0
```

The *sh ip route* command is used to display the IP routes for RouterC. RouterC shows seven subnets. In fact, there are seven subnets in the campus LAN shown in Figure 7-13. This completes the setup for running EIGRP on the campus LAN.

```
RouterC#sh ip route
Codes: C connected, S static, I IGRP, R RIP, M mobile, B BGP D EIGRP, EX
   EIGRP external, O OSPF, IA OSPF inter area
E1 OSPF external type 1, E2 OSPF external type 2, E EGP
i IS-IS, L1 IS-IS level-1, L2 IS-IS level-2, * candidate default
Gateway of last resort is not set
10.0.0.0 255.255.255.0 is subnetted, 7 subnets
C 10.10.5.0 is directly connected, FastEthernet0/0
D 10.10.10.0 [90/2195456] via 10.10.150.1, 00:00:01, FastEthernet0/1
D 10.10.1.0 [90/2195456] via 10.10.150.1, 00:00:01, FastEthernet0/1
D 10.10.20.0 [90/2195456] via 10.10.100.1, 00:00:01, FastEthernet0/2
C 10.10.100.0 is directly connected, FastEthernet0/2
C 10.10.150.0 is directly connected, FastEthernet0/1
D 10.10.200.0 [90/2681856] via 10.10.150.1, 00:00:01, FastEthernet0/1
         [90/2681856] via 10.10.100.1, 00:00:01, FastEthernet0/2
```

Networking Challenge—EIGRP

Use the router simulator software included with the text's companion CD-ROM to demonstrate that you can configure EIGRP for RouterA in the campus LAN (the campus LAN is shown in Figure 7-13 and is displayed on the computer screen when the software is started). EIGRP has already been configured for RouterB and RouterC. Place the CD-ROM in your computer's drive. Open the *Net-Challenge* folder and click *Net-Challenge.exe*. When the software is running, click the **Select Router Challenge** button to open a **Select Router Challenge** drop-down menu. Select *Chapter 7—EIGRP*. This opens a checkbox that can be used to verify that you have completed all the tasks.

1. Enter the privileged EXEC mode on the router.
2. Enter the router configuration mode, **Router(config)**.
3. Set the hostname to *RouterA*.
4. Configure the FastEthernet0/0 interface with the following:
   IP address 10.10.20.250
   Subnet mask 255.255.255.0
5. Enable the FA0/0 interface.
6. Configure the FastEthernet0/1 interface with the following:
   IP address 10.10.200.1
   Subnet mask 255.255.255.0
7. Enable the FA0/1 interface.
8. Configure the FastEthernet0/2 interface with the following:
   IP address 10.10.100.1
   Subnet mask 255.255.255.0
9. Enable the FA0/2 interface.
10. Enable EIGRP with an AS number of 200.
11. Enter the network command that enables EIGRP on the router.
12. Use the *sh ip int brief* command to check the interface status.
13. Use the *sh ip protocol* command to see whether EIGRP is running on RouterA.
14. Use the *sh ip route* command to verify that the three FastEthernet ports are connected to RouterA.
15. Use the *sh run* command to view the running-configuration file on RouterA. Verify that EIGRP is enabled and the proper network address is specified.
16. Use the *ping* command to verify connection to the following interfaces:
    10.10.5.250
    10.10.150.1
    10.10.200.2
    10.10.100.2

7-8   CONFIGURING A JUNIPER ROUTER

JUNOS
The operating system used by Juniper routers

This section demonstrates the steps for basic configuration of a Juniper router. There are distinct differences between the Juniper router configuration compared to Cisco IOS; however, many of the steps and prompts are similar to Cisco router configuration, as you'll learn. The operating system (OS) used by Juniper routers is called **JUNOS**. The JUNOS software has two different command modes:

- Operational mode
- Configuration mode

Operational Mode

This is the first mode encountered after logging in to the Juniper router. This mode allows for the following:

1. Monitoring network connectivity (for example, using the *ping* command)
2. Troubleshooting the router interface and network connections
3. Entry point for router configuration

The following examples demonstrate the basic commands used in the operational mode of the JUNOS command line interface (CLI). The connection to the Juniper router demonstrated in this section is being made via an ssh session (secure telnet); however, a console serial connection can also be made directly with the Juniper router, and this connection is used to make the initial router interface configurations.

The first prompt displayed after connecting to the router asks for a password. After you correctly enter the password, you enter the router's **{master}** mode and the **router>** prompt is displayed. The prompt for the CLI is the >, and the text preceding the > lists the names of the user and the router. In this case, the username is **net-admin** and the router name is **noc**. Juniper routers use the {master} prompt to indicate that you are in the master routing engine mode This prompt appears only when the Juniper router is equipped with two routing engines and the two engines are running in a graceful switchover redundancy mode.

{master}
The prompt indicating you are in the master routing engine mode on a Juniper router

The following shows an example of the prompts displayed after establishing the router connection. In this example the connection is made by net-admin and this user has superuser privileges.

```
Password:

{master}
net-admin@noc>
```

The question mark (**?**) is used for the universal help command in the Juniper OS (operating system). For example, the **?** can be entered to see what options are available. It is not necessary to press Enter after typing the question mark. The following is a list of the available commands available at the > prompt.

```
net-admin@noc> ?

Possible completions:
    clear        Clear information in the system
    configure    Manipulate software configuration information
    file         Perform file operations
    help         Provide help information
    mtrace       Trace mtrace packets from source to receiver.
    monitor      Real-time debugging
    ping         Ping a remote target
    quit         Exit the management session
    request      Make system-level requests
    restart      Restart a software process
    set          Set CLI properties, date, time, craft display text
    show         Show information about the system
    ssh          Open a secure shell to another host
    start        Start a software process
    telnet       Telnet to another host
    test         Diagnostic debugging commands
    traceroute   Trace the route to a remote host
net-admin@noc>
```

The question mark can also be added only after part of a command is entered. For example, the following is a partial listing of the options with the **show ?** command.

```
{master}

net-admin@noc> show ?
Possible completions:
  Accounting      Show accounting profiles and records
  aps             Show Automatic Protection Switching information
  arp                 Show system Address Resolution Protocol table
   entries
  as-path         Show table of known autonomous system paths
  bfd             Show Bidirectional Forwarding Detection information
  bgp             Show Border Gateway Protocol information
  chassis         Show chassis information
  class-of-service    Show class-of-service (CoS) information
  cli             Show command-line interface settings
  configuration   Show current configuration
  connections     Show circuit cross-connect connections
   .
   .
   .
```

The JUNOS operating system has another option that enables the user to enter only part of a command. With this feature, the incomplete command will be completed by JUNOS if the user is still in the CLI mode. This means the user doesn't have to remember the full command. JUNOS will fill in the expected text given the information obtained from the entered keystrokes. This is accomplished by entering a partial command then and pressing the spacebar or the tab key. For example, entering **show in <spacebar>** lists the remaining text of a possible matching command, **nterfaces**. Press Enter to accept the displayed text. The following is an example:

```
net-admin@noc>show in <spacebar>terfaces <Enter>

Physical interface: at-0/1/0, Enabled, Physical link is Up
  Interface index: 11, SNMP ifIndex: 65
  Link-level type: ATM-PVC, MTU: 4482, Clocking: Internal, SONET mode
  Speed: OC12, Loopback: None, Payload scrambler: Enabled
  Device flags   : Present Running
  Link flags     : 0x01
[...Output truncated...]
```

The following shows another example of entering an incomplete command where an ambiguous result can occur. For example, entering **show c <spacebar>** results in an ambiguous result because there are three possible matching commands. In this case, the user must type more characters for JUNOS to recognize the desired command, or the user must type the complete command.

```
net-admin@noc> show c<Space>
'c' is ambiguous.
Possible completions:
  chassis             Show chassis information
  class-of-service    Show class-of-service (CoS) information
  cli                     Show command-line interface settings
  configuration       Show current configuration
  connections         Show circuit cross-connect connections
```

The next example demonstrates the results of entering the **show version** at the **>** prompt. This command can be used to show which version of the Juniper software is running on the router, and it also lists all the software suites installed on the router.

```
--- JUNOS 7.6R2.6 built 2006-07-08 09:43:10 UTC

{master}
net-admin@noc> show version

Hostname: noc
Model: m10i
JUNOS Base OS boot [7.6R2.6]
JUNOS Base OS Software Suite [7.6R2.6]
JUNOS Kernel Software Suite [7.6R2.6]
JUNOS Packet Forwarding Engine Support (M7i/M10i) [7.6R2.6]
JUNOS Routing Software Suite [7.6R2.6]
JUNOS Online Documentation [7.6R2.6]
JUNOS Crypto Software Suite [7.6R2.6]
```

In this case, the router is running the Model: m10i software. The Juniper system is based on the Unix OS platform. It has a Free BSD Unix–based kernel with different software systems handling different functions. For example, this listing shows that there is a JUNOS routing software suite, a packet forwarding engine, a crypto software suite, and other software. This individual software suite setup allows one feature to be updated (for example, router updates) without having to update the entire router box.

The next example uses the ***show configuration*** command to display the Juniper router current configuration. This is analogous to entering the ***show running-configuration*** command on a Cisco router.

```
{master}
net-admin@noc>show configuration

version 7.6R2.6;
groups {
    re0 {
        system {
            host-name checs-atm-re0;
            backup-router 10.10.20.250 destination 10.10.10.5/24;
        }
        interfaces {
            fxp0 {
                description "Out of Band Management interface re0";
                unit 0 {
                    family inet;
                }
            }
        }
    \   }

        re1 {
            system {
            .
            .
            .
```

The **re0 {** and **re1 {** .. notations identify the system configuration for the routing engines 0 and 1. (The location of the routing engines on a Juniper router are shown in Figure 7-14.) The statement Out of Band Management indicates that the FastEthernet0 (fxp0) interface is an additional interface that can be used to connect to the router if the main network is down. The term *in band* refers to the primary network connection.

re0 { and re1 { ...
This identifies the location of the system configuration text for the routing engines

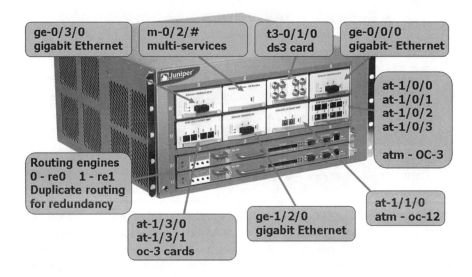

FIGURE 7-14   The physical interfaces on a Juniper router.

PIC
Physical interface card

The Juniper router shown in Figure 7-14 shows several types of physical inter-face cards (**PIC**). Each interface plus its name are listed. The ge interfaces are giga-bit Ethernet. The multi-services card enables expanded services such as stateful firewall protection, network address translation, and other functions. The t3/ds3 card provides for a 44.736 Mbps data rate connection. The at is for Asynchronous Trans-mission Mode (ATM), and this example also shows oc-3 (155.52 Mbps) and oc-12 (622.08 Mbps) connections. This router also has two routing engines; the duplicate engines are for redundancy.

Network connectivity with other networking devices can be verified with the Juniper router by using the ***ping*** command as shown next. This command is being is-sued at the {master} mode.

```
{master}
net-admin@noc> ping 192.168.32.5
{master}
net-admin@noc-atm-re1> ping 172.16.83.3
PING 172.16.83.3 (172.16.83.3): 56 data bytes
64 bytes from 172.16.83.3: icmp_seq=0 ttl=62 time=1.493 ms
64 bytes from 172.16.83.3: icmp_seq=1 ttl=62 time=1.000 ms
64 bytes from 172.16.83.3: icmp_seq=2 ttl=62 time=1.096 ms
64 bytes from 172.16.83.3: icmp_seq=3 ttl=62 time=1.082 ms
64 bytes from 172.16.83.3: icmp_seq=4 ttl=62 time=1.417 ms
64 bytes from 172.16.83.3: icmp_seq=5 ttl=62 time=1.159 ms
^C
--- 172.16.83.3 ping statistics ---
6 packets transmitted, 6 packets received, 0% packet loss
round-trip min/avg/max/stddev = 1.000/1.208/1.493/0.182 ms
```

Router Configuration Mode

Permanent Interfaces
Defined to be either Management or Internal Ethernet interfaces

There are two types of interfaces for the Juniper routers:

Management Ethernet Interfaces
This enables the router to establish both ssh and telnet connections

- **Permanent interfaces:** Two types of permanent interfaces exist:
  - **Management Ethernet Interface:** This interface enables the router to establish both ssh and telnet connections.

- **Internal Ethernet interface:** This interface is the main communications link between the JUNOS software and the router's packet forwarding engines.
- **Transient interfaces:** These interfaces receive and transmit the data packets to and from the network. They are located on the physical interface card and can be inserted and removed at any time. These interfaces must be configured before they can be used.

The Juniper routers also have both a console and auxiliary serial port. The console port is used to establish a serial terminal connection and is used for initial router configuration. The auxiliary port is used to connect to a modem and for remote access when there is a failure with the regular network connection.

Displaying the Router Interfaces

The command for displaying the router interfaces and their status is *show interfaces brief*. The following shows an example of using this command.

```
{master}
net-admin@noc> show interfaces brief
Physical interface: ge-0/0/0, Enabled, Physical link is Up
  Description: Feed to Network-Backup
  Link-level type: Ethernet, MTU: 1514, Speed: 1000mbps, Loopback: Dis-
   abled,
  Source filtering: Disabled, Flow control: Enabled, Auto-negotiation:
   Enabled,
  Remote fault: Online
  Device flags   : Present Running
  Interface flags: SNMP-Traps Internal: 0x4000
  Link flags     : None

  Logical interface ge-0/0/0.0
    Description: Feed to Network-Backup
    Flags: SNMP-Traps Encapsulation: ENET2
    inet  172.16.35.12/30


Physical interface: ge-0/1/0, Enabled, Physical link is Down
  Link-level type: Ethernet, MTU: 1514, Speed: 1000mbps, Loopback: Dis-
   abled,
  Source filtering: Disabled, Flow control: Enabled, Auto-negotiation:
   Enabled,
  Remote fault: Online
  Device flags   : Present Running Down
  Interface flags: Hardware-Down SNMP-Traps Internal: 0x4000
  Link flags     : None

Logical interface ge-0/1/0.0
    Description: Feed to Network-Backup
    Flags: SNMP-Traps Encapsulation: ENET2
    inet  192.168.12.7/30
    .
    .
    .
```

The ge-0/0/0 physical interface shows that it is enabled and the physical link is up. This indicates that the link can pass data packets. The ge-0/1/0 physical interface shows that it is down and the interface is disabled. This listing also shows logical interfaces for ge-0/0/0.0 and 0/1/0.0, which are defined by the IP addresses (inet) set for each interface. Notice that each of the two gigabit Ethernet interfaces (ge-0/1/0

Internal Ethernet Interfaces
The main communications link between the JUNOS software and the router's packet forwarding engines.

Transient Interfaces
These interfaces both receive and transmit data to/from the network

and ge-0/0/0) have both a physical and a logical interface setting. The ge-#/#/# notation for the physical interfaces is defined as follows:

- **Media type:** ge (gigabit Ethernet). Other options for media type are Sonet (so), ATM (at), FastEthernet(fxp)
- **Slot number:** 0
- **Slot number on the interface:** 0
- **Port**: 0

The notation for the logical interface lists the media type, slot number, slot number for the interface, and port. It also shows a description, a flag for SNMP, and the IP address.

Hostname Configuration

The hostname on a Juniper router can be change by entering the configuration mode. First enter the *configure* command, which places you in the [edit] mode. Notice that the prompt now has a **#** after it, indicating you are in the configuration mode. Next, enter *edit system* which places you in the [edit system] mode. You change the hostname of the router using the *set host-name* < *name* > command. The following is an example where the hostname of the router is changed from router to Juniper. (*Note:* This change will not be implemented until the configuration is saved using the *commit* command.)

```
net-admin@noc> configure
[edit]
net-admin@noc>#edit system
[edit system]
net-admin@noc># set host-name Juniper
[edit system]
net-admin@noc>#commit
[edit system]
net-admin@Juniper>#
```

Assigning an IP Address to an Interface

The next example shows how an IP address is assigned to an interface. In this case, the interface is ge-0/0/0.

```
net-admin@noc> configure
[edit]
net-admin@noc>#edit interfaces ge-0/0/0
[edit interfaces ge-0/0/0]
net-admin@noc>#edit unit 0
[edit interfaces ge-0/0/0 unit 0]
net-admin@noc>#edit family inet
[edit interfaces ge-0/0/0 unit 0 family inet]
net-admin@noc>#set address 192.168.1.1/24
[edit interfaces ge-0/0/0 unit 0 family inet]
net-admin@noc>#
```

Static Route

You can configure a static route on a Juniper router by entering the edit mode. The {master}[edit] prompts should be displayed after you enter this mode. The command *edit routing-options static* places you in the mode to configure the static route. The prompt changes to **{master}[edit routing-options static]**. The following shows an example:

```
{master}[edit]
net-admin@noc# edit routing-options static

{master}[edit routing-options static]
net-admin@noc#
```

The next step is to configure the static router. This simply requires you to enter *destination IP address / {subnet – CIDR}* and *next-hop address*. The following shows an example:

```
{master}[edit routing-options static]
net-admin@noc# # set route 172.16.32.81/32  next-hop 172.16.64.161

{master}[edit routing-options static]
net-admin@noc#
```

RIP Configuration

The following steps demonstrate the procedure for configuring the RIP routing protocol on a Juniper router. The first step is to enter the configuration mode using the *configure* command as shown. The prompt then changes to [edit].

```
net-admin@noc>configure
[edit]
```

The next step is to enter the *edit protocols* command, which places the router in the [edit protocols] mode. Then, enter the command *edit rip*. The prompt changes to [edit protocols rip], which places the router in the mode for configuring the RIP routing protocol.

```
net-admin@noc>edit protocols
[edit protocols]

net-admin@noc>#edit rip
[edit protocols rip]
```

The next steps are used to enable the advertising of RIP routing via specific interfaces.

```
net-admin@noc>edit group neighbors
[edit protocols rip group neighbors]

user@host#set neighbor ge-0/0/0
[edit protocols rip group neighbors]

user@host#set neighbor ge-0/0/1
[edit protocols rip group neighbors]
user@host#
```

The *commit* command is used to save software configuration changes to the configuration database, and it also activates the configuration on the router. Changes to the configuration are not saved unless you issue the *commit* command.

```
net-admin@noc# commit
commit complete
```

commit
The command used to save changes to the configuration file

Or do this to quit the commit the configuration and exit the configuration mode:

```
[edit]
net-admin@noc# commit and- quit

commit complete
exiting configuration mode
net-admin@noc>
```

OSPF Configuration

The next example examines configuring the OSPF routing protocol for the Juniper router. In this case, the current system configuration file is edited with the required information. The commands in the following OSPF script are set off with brackets ({}). There is an open bracket at the beginning of each command level and a closing brace at the end for each open brace. The following is an example of how to configure an OSPF backbone that has two gigabit Ethernet interfaces. You must be in the [edit] mode, so enter the *configure* command. You enter the script after entering the configure mode, which has the [edit] prompt displayed.

```
net-admin@noc> configure
[edit]
protocols {
    ospf {
        area 0.0.0.0 {
            interface ge-0/0/0 {
                hello-interval 5;
                dead-interval 20;
            }
            interface ge-0/0/1 {
            hello-interval 5;
            dead-interval 20;
            }
        }
    }
}
```

This configuration is for the backbone (area 0.0.0.0). The two gigabit interfaces are ge-0/0/0 and ge-0/0/1. The "Hello" interval is being set to 5 seconds and the dead interval is being set to 20 seconds. The "Hello" interval is how often OSPF "Hello" packets are sent to other routers in the same area, and the dead interval is how much time can expire before the other routers in the area assume the router is dead or the link has failed.

Another way to configure the same information for OSPF is shown next. This example produces the same result as previously presented for the OSPF routing, except everything is entered at the command line. Enter the [edit] mode using the *configure* command. Next, enter the *set protocols* command followed by the desired settings for the interface. The *set protocols* command and desired settings must be repeated for each interface. Enter the command sequence *commit and- quit* to save the configuration and exit the configuration mode.

```
net-admin@noc> configure
[edit]
user@host# set protocols ospf area 0.0.0.0 interface ge-0/0/0 hello-
    interval 5 dead-interval 20
[edit]
user@host# set protocols ospf area 0.0.0.0 interface ge-0/0/1 hello-
    interval 5 dead-interval 20
```

```
[edit]
net-admin@noc# commit and- quit

commit complete
exiting configuration mode
net-admin@noc>
```

This section has provided a brief introduction to the steps for configuring Juniper routers and using the JUNOS CLI. More information on configuring Juniper routers can be obtained at the following Juniper Networks site. This site has a lot of support information for the various versions of the *JUNOS CLI User Guide*.

http://www.juniper.net/techpubs/software/junos/

7-9   TFTP—TRIVIAL FILE TRANSFER PROTOCOL

Trivial File Transfer Protocol (**TFTP**) is a simple file transfer protocol often used with routers and switches to save and reload the configuration files to and from a remote server. The files are saved in case of equipment failure, for rebooting, or for upgrading or archiving the configuration files. It is not uncommon for the configuration files to be backed up daily. The backup is typically done automatically. Changes to router and switch configuration files can occur on a daily basis, and an automatic or regularly scheduled backup is a safe way to ensure the configuration files are archived. Isn't it true that the configuration files can be saved to NVRAM? The answer is yes, but if there is a complete equipment failure the current router or switch configuration will be lost. Saving the configuration files to another machine is a safer way to prevent loss. The TFTP server is also used for updating and saving the Internetwork Operating System (IOS) files stored in flash. Examples of how to save and reload files stored on the TFTP server are demonstrated later in this section.

TFTP uses port 69 to establish the network connection and the User Datagram Protocol (UDP) to transport the files. TFTP has no authentication or encryption capabilities and is not a secure transfer; therefore, it is recommended that file transfers should be limited to private networks. The IP addresses for private networks are as follows:

> 10.0.0.0–10.255.255.255
> 172.16.00–172.31.255.255
> 192.168..0.0–192.168.255.255)

Configuring TFTP

Before you can save the router or switch configuration files you must install the TFTP server software on your computer. Many freeware and shareware TFTP software packages are available on the Internet. The available software can be found by searching for "tftp server" using your Internet search engine. (Note: You must have the TFTP software running on your computer for the file transfer to work.) Newer versions of the router and switch IOS now support FTP in addition to TFTP for the file transfer. The advantage of FTP is that a secure file transfer can be established using, for example, SSH File Transfer Protocol (SFTP), while TFTP is not secure. Additionally, FTP overcomes the 16 megabyte file transfer limit of some IOS versions. FTP file transfer sizes are not limited.

TFTP
Trivial File Transfer Protocol

When you first set up the router or switch you must make sure it is on the same subnet as the TFTP server because you don't have routing set up yet; therefore, the destination IPs for the router/switch and the TFTP server must be on the same subnet. An example of this is provided in Figure 7-15. The IP address for RouterC has been configured to 192.168.10.1/28. The TFTP server software has been installed on computer, D2 and the IP address for computer D2 has been configured to 192.168.10.5/28. This places RouterC and computer D2 (TFTP server) on the same subnet in the 192.168.10.0 network. Also note that both RouterC and computer D2 are connected to the same switch.

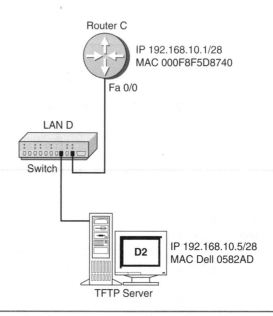

FIGURE 7-15   An example of placing the router and the TFTP server on the same network.

The following are the basic commands used to save and load files to and from the TFTP server. Abbreviated commands that are recognized by the Net-Challenge software are provided in brackets [ ]. Your first requirement is that you place the router in the privileged EXEC mode as shown.

1. Enter the enable mode on your router.

```
RouterC>enable
Password:
```

The router's running-configuration file can be saved to the TFTP server using the following command.

2. Save to the TFTP server.

```
RouterC#copy running-config tftp [copy run tftp]
Address or name of remote host []?192.168.10.5
Destination filename [running-config]? <enter the filename to be saved>
!!
872 bytes copied in 5.176 secs (174 bytes/sec)
```

The router's running-configuration file stored on the TFTP server can be re-loaded using the following command.

3. Load from the TFTP server.

```
RouterC#copy tftp running-config [copy tftp run]
Address or name of remote host [   ]? 192.168.10.5
Source filename [   ]? <enter the saved file name>
Destination filename [running-config]?
Accessing tftp://192.168.10.5/network-name...
Loading network-name from 192.168.10.5 (via Ethernet0): !
[OK - 872/1024 bytes]

872 bytes copied in 4.400 secs (218 bytes/sec)
router#
```

Figures 7-16 to 7-18 are captured data files of the TFTP write process using the Finisar Surveyor demo protocol analyzer. Figure 7-16 shows the capture for packet 2. The source is the router with an IP address of 192.168.10.1 and the destination is the TFTP server with an IP address of 192.168.10.5. The middle of Figure 7-16 shows that the User Datagram Protocol (UDP) is being used with a source port of 56401 and a destination port 69 (the Trivial File Transfer port). The bottom of Figure 7-16 shows that a write request has been requested. The filename is config, which is the destination filename. The data is being transferred in the octet mode (also called the binary image transfer mode). In this mode, the data is transferred in one-byte units.

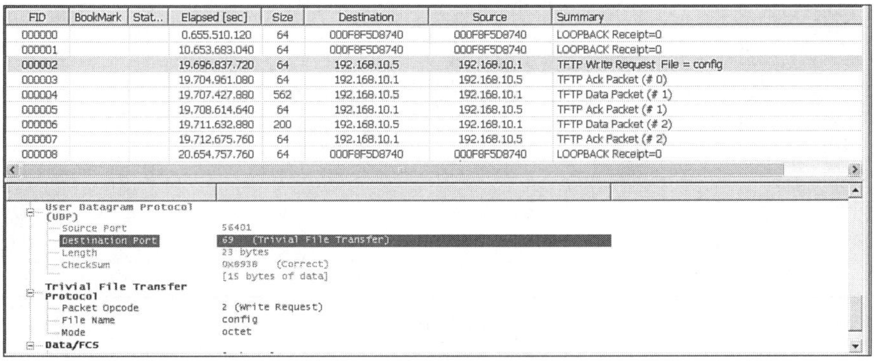

FID	BookMark	Stat...	Elapsed [sec]	Size	Destination	Source	Summary
000000			0.655.510.120	64	000F8F5D8740	000F8F5D8740	LOOPBACK Receipt=0
000001			10.653.683.040	64	000F8F5D8740	000F8F5D8740	LOOPBACK Receipt=0
000002			19.696.837.720	64	192.168.10.5	192.168.10.1	TFTP Write Request File = config
000003			19.704.961.080	64	192.168.10.1	192.168.10.5	TFTP Ack Packet (# 0)
000004			19.707.427.880	562	192.168.10.5	192.168.10.1	TFTP Data Packet (# 1)
000005			19.708.614.640	64	192.168.10.1	192.168.10.5	TFTP Ack Packet (# 1)
000006			19.711.632.880	200	192.168.10.5	192.168.10.1	TFTP Data Packet (# 2)
000007			19.712.675.760	64	192.168.10.1	192.168.10.5	TFTP Ack Packet (# 2)
000008			20.654.757.760	64	000F8F5D8740	000F8F5D8740	LOOPBACK Receipt=0

```
User Datagram Protocol
(UDP)
    Source Port         56401
    Destination Port    69  (Trivial File Transfer)
    Length              23 bytes
    CheckSum            0x8938  (Correct)
                        [15 bytes of data]
Trivial File Transfer
Protocol
    Packet Opcode       2 (Write Request)
    File Name           config
    Mode                octet
Data/FCS
```

FIGURE 7-16   A TFTP write request to port 69.

Figure 7-17 (packet 3) shows that the TFTP server computer at source port (SP) 1102 replies back to the router (destination port DP 56401). Note that the TFTP server is now using port 1102. Port 69 is used initially to establish the TFTP connection but the server will select an available port for the data transfer.

The beginning of the data transfer is shown in Figure 7-18 in packet 4 (FID 000004). The source port is 56401 (router) and the destination port is 1102 (TFTP server). The packet size of the initial data transfer is 562 bytes. The actual text of the data transfer is displayed at the bottom of Figure 7-18. Notice that the data transfer text is readable, which introduces security issues if the configuration data is being transferred over a network.

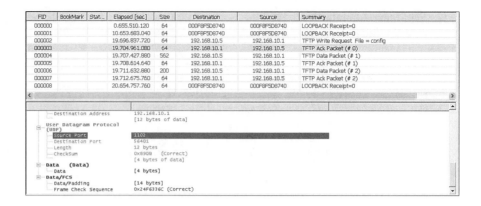

FIGURE 7-17 A TFTP write request—port assignments.

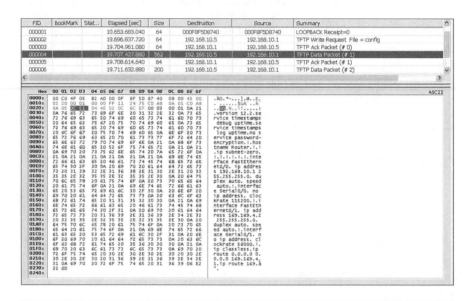

FIGURE 7-18 A TFTP write request—data transfer.

Networking Challenge—TFTP

Use the Network Challenge V2.0 simulator software included with the text's companion CD-ROM to demonstrate that you can configure TFTP from RouterC in the campus LAN to computer D2 in LAN D. Place the Network Challenge CD-ROM in your computer's CD drive. Open the *Networking Challenge* folder and click *NetChallenge.exe*. When the software is running, click the **Select Challenge** button to open a **Select Challenge** drop-down menu. Select **Chapter 7—TFTP**. This opens a checkbox that can be used to verify that you have completed all the tasks.

1. Enter the privileged EXEC mode on RouterC. Use the password Chile. (*Note:* Chile is pronounced "chill-a.")
2. Enter the router configuration mode, **RouterC(config)**.

3. Set the hostname to RouterC.
4. Configure RouterC's FastEthernet port 0/1 with an IP address of 192.168.12.5 and a subnet mask of /28.
5. Enable RouterC's FastEthernet port 0/1.
6. Verify that RouterC's FastEthernet port 0/1 interface is properly configured.
7. Configure the IP address of the TFTP server, located on computer D2 in LAN D, to 192.168.12.1 with a /28 subnet mask. The gateway IP address is 192.168.12.5.
8. Verify that the TFTP server (computer D1) and RouterC have network connectivity.
9. Use the proper command to copy the running-configuration on RouterC to the TFTP server (computer D1—LAN D). Use a filename of *RC-tftp-12-5-06*. If the command is not successful, check your configurations.
10. Use the proper command to copy the *RC-tftp-12-5-06* file from the TFTP server to the running-configuration on RouterC.
11. Use the proper command to verify that the TFTP file has been copied onto RouterC.
12. RouterC's Cisco IOS must be updated to a newer version called c2600-d-l-12.5(3), which is located on the FTP server on computer D1 in LAN D. (*Note:* the character l is the letter l.) Enter the proper command to install the newer IOS version stored on the TFTP server onto RouterC.
13. Use the proper command to verify that RouterC's IOS has been updated.
14. RouterC's Cisco IOS needs to be saved on the TFTP server on computer D1 in LAN D. Enter the proper command to save RouterC's current IOS onto the TFTP server (Computer D1—LAND).

7-10   ANALYZING OSPF "HELLO" PACKETS

"Hello" packets are periodically sent in OSPF networks to initiate and maintain communications with neighbor routers. The "Hello" packets contain parameters including specifications for the following:

- **Network Mask:** The mask contains 32 bits in four octets (8-bit groups). The masking is a logical "AND" operation, and the bits that are set high allow the address data to pass. For example, a network mask of 255.255.255.0 has the first 24 bits set high in the first three octets. The hexadecimal equivalent (base 16) for this network mask is 0xffffff00.
- **Hello Interval:** The time between "Hello" packets.
- **Router Dead Interval:** The length of time a router neighbor is quiet (no "Hello" packets) before assuming the neighbor is dead.

OSPF uses a class D multicast IP address to send out the "Hello" packets to the neighbors. OSPF networks have been assigned the multicast IP address of 224.0.0.5 for sending "Hello" packets. Multicast IP addresses for use with multicast protocols are in the range of 224.0.0.0 to 239.255.255.255. This is called the *class D IP address range.* The IP address range above class D is called class E and addresses range from 240.0.0.0 to 254.255.255.255. Class E is called the *IP address experimental range.*

Network Mask
Hello Interval
Router Dead Interval

RID
Router ID

The test network shown in Figure 7-19 was set up so that the transmission of OSPF "Hello" packets could be viewed. The Surveyor Demo protocol analyzer was installed on computer D1 in LAN D (192.168.1.0 NET). LAN D has been configured to be an OSPF advertised route; therefore, computers in LAN D will receive the OSPF multicasts used to capture the data packets. OSPF broadcasts the LAN address as part of the routed addresses. The multicast is sent to all neighbor OSPF router connections. The captured data packets for the network are shown in Figure 7-20. The highlighted line, beginning with the ID of "000001" in the first column, is the first detected occurrence of a data packet on the network. The elapsed time is 5.278.530.840 seconds (column 2). The size of the packet is 82 bytes (column 3). The destination (specified in column 4) is an OSPFIGP_Router multicast. The source IP address is 192.168.1.250, which is the IP address for the router interface. The packet summary (column 6) indicates this is an OSPF Hello from **RID** (router ID) 192.168.200.11.

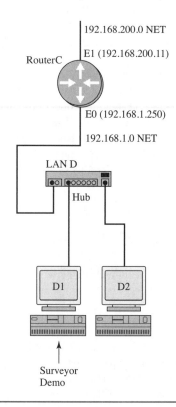

FIGURE 7-19   The test network for capturing the OSPF "Hello" packets.

OSPFIGP
Open Shortest Path First
Interior Gateway Protocol

One of the complex things about OSPF is the assignment of the router ID (RID). The router ID is an IP address chosen from all interfaces on the router. Cisco IOS first examines the loopback address for the router's ID IP address. If a loopback address is not being used, the highest IP address for a router interface is selected as the router ID. In this case, the highest loopback IP address is 192.168.200.11, the IP address for the E1 Ethernet interface. The middle panel in Figure 7-20 shows that the destination address is 224.0.0.5 and defines this as OSPFIGP_Router. **OSPFIGP** stands for Open Shortest Path First Interior Gateway Protocol, which is a concatenated form of OSPF and IGP. The OSPF protocol is classified as an Interior Gateway Protocol (IGP). **IGP** represents entities under the same autonomous domain (administrative and security policies). Remember, when you specify the OSPF protocol, a process id number is entered; for example, *router ospf 100*.

IGP
Interior Gateway Protocol

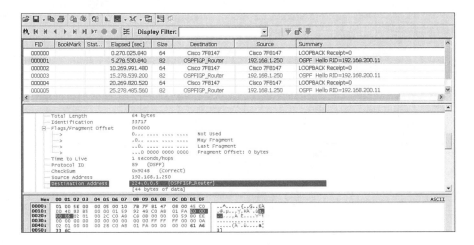

FIGURE 7-20   The captured OSPF multicasts.

The bottom panel in Figure 7-20 is the actual data packet displayed in hexadecimal (base 16) code. The highlighted hex code is

E 0 0 0 0 0 0 5

This is the hexadecimal value for 224.0.0.5, the destination IP address of the multicast.

Hexadecimal Value   E 0   0 0   0 0   0 5
Decimal Equivalent 224   0   0   5

Note: The decimal equivalent of E0 is 14, and (14 × 16 + 0) = 224.

A detailed view of the OSPF packet information is provided in Figure 7-21. This information is available in the Open Shortest Path First (OSPF) window as shown in Figure 7-21.

In addition to the version number, the router ID is listed (192.168.200.11), and the hello interval is specified to be 10 seconds. Looking again at Figure 7-21, the OSPF "Hello" packets are approximately 10 seconds apart. The router dead interval is 40 seconds.

This section has demonstrated how to use the Surveyor Demo Protocol Analyzer to capture OSPF "Hello" packets. Figures 7-20 and 7-21 and the accompanying text explained how to extract information from the captured packets.

```
⊟ Open Shortest Path First
  (OSPF)
   ─ Version                    2
   ─ Type                       1    (Hello)
   ─ Length                     44 bytes
   ─ Router ID                  192.168.200.11
   ─ Area ID                    0.0.0.89
   ─ Checksum                   0xB0EE
   ─ AuType                     0    (Null Authentication)
   ─ Authentication             0000000000000000
   ─ Network Mask               255.255.255.0
   ─ Hello Interval             10 seconds
  ⊟ Optional Capabilities       0x02
        ─ >                      0... ....    Not Used (MBZ)
        ─ >                      .0.. ....    Opaque-LSAs NOT Forwarded
        ─ >                      ..0. ....    Demand Circuit Bit
        ─ >                      ...0 ....    External Attributes Bit
        ─ >                      .... 0...    No NSSA Capability
        ─ >                      .... .0..    No Multicast Capability
        ─ >                      .... ..1.    External Routing Capability
        ─ >                      .... ...0    No Type of Service Routing Capability
   ─ Router Priority            1
   ─ Router Dead Interval       40 seconds
   ─ Designated Router          192.168.1.250
   ⋯ Backup Designated Router   0.0.0.0
```

FIGURE 7-21   A detailed view of the OSPF packet information.

SUMMARY

This chapter presented examples of configuring routing protocols. The network challenge exercises provided the opportunity for the student to test her or his configuration skill prior to actually configuring a real router. The student should be able to configure and verify operation of the following protocols:

Static
RIP
IGRP
OSPF
EIGRP

Additionally, this chapter examined the steps for configuring a Juniper router and how to set up and communicate with a TFTP server. The last section examined the OSPF "Hello" packets.

QUESTIONS AND PROBLEMS

Section 7-2

1. What is a routing table?
2. What is the most common static route used in a host computer?
3. What command is used to view a PC computer's routing table?
4. What is meant by a 0.0.0.0 network address entry with a subnet mask of 0.0.0.0 in a PC's routing table?
5. What is the 127.0.0.1 IP address and what is it used for?
6. What is the router command to configure a static route from LAN A to LAN B for the network shown in Figure 7-22?

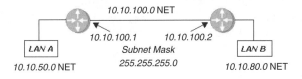

FIGURE 7-22   The network for problem 6.

7. What is the difference between a router's running-configuration and startup-configuration?
8. What is the router command used to view the routes entered into the router's routing table?
9. What is the router command used to configure a static route for a router?

10. List two static routes to route data from LAN A to LAN C. The network is shown in Figure 7-23. Assume a subnet mask of 255.255.255.0.

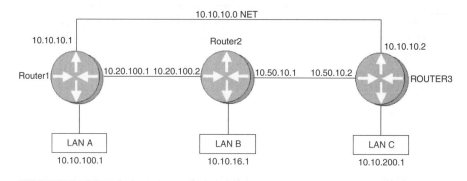

10.10.10.0 NET

10.10.10.1

Router2

10.10.10.2

Router1 10.20.100.1 10.20.100.2 10.50.10.1 10.50.10.2 ROUTER3

LAN A
10.10.100.1

LAN B
10.10.16.1

LAN C
10.10.200.1

FIGURE 7-23 The network for problems 10 through 13.

11. List two static routes to route data from LAN B to LAN C in Figure 7-23. Assume a subnet mask of 255.255.255.0.
12. Which of the following are suitable subnet masks for use in configuring static routes for the network shown in Figure 7-23?
    a. 255.255.0.0
    b. 255.0.0.0
    c. 255.255.255.224
    d. All the above
    e. None of the above
13. A static route is configured to route data from LAN A to LAN B on Router1 in Figure 7-23. Which of the following are appropriate static routes to achieve this goal?
    a. ip route 10.10.16.0 255.255.255.255 10.20.100.2
    b. ip route 10.10.16.0 255.255.255.0 10.20.100.2
    c. ip route 10.10.16.0 255.255.255.255 10.10.10.2
    d. ip route 10.10.16.0 255.255.0.0 10.10.10.2
    Subnet masks on A and C are not appropriate

Section 7-3

14. What is the difference between a *static* and a *dynamic* routing protocol?
15. What are the four key issues in dynamic routing protocols?
16. Define *hop count*.
17. Which of the following is *not* a metric used in dynamic routing protocols?
    a. Hop count
    b. Cost
    c. Runs
    d. Ticks
18. A distance vector protocol typically uses what as the metric?

19. Determine the hop count for Router2 to subnet B in Figure 7-24.

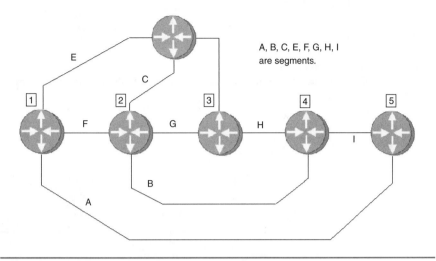

A, B, C, E, F, G, H, I
are segments.

FIGURE 7-24   The network for problems 19 through 21.

20. For Figure 7-24, what is the hop count from Router5 to subnet G?
21. For Figure 7-24, what is the hop count from Router3 to subnet A?
22. Link state protocols issue what to update neighbor routers regarding route status?
    a. Hop status
    b. Link state advertisements
    c. "Hello" packets
    d. Adjacencies
23. Which of the following are key issues of link state protocols?
    a. Send updates every 90 seconds
    b. Send update when routing changes
    c. Use link lights to establish adjacencies
    d. Use a hop count metric to determine the best route to a destination

Section 7-4

24. RIP is classified as a
    a. Distance vector protocol
    b. Dynamic routing protocol
    c. Link state protocol
    d. a and c
    e. a and b
    f. b and c
25. Define *routing loops*.
26. Which of the following are examples of classful addresses?
    a. 10.10.0.0
    b. 192.168.0.0
    c. 10.1.0.0
    d. 10.0.0.0

27. What is the router command to enable the RIP routing protocol on a router?
    a. *config router RIP*
    b. *router rip*
    c. *rip 10.0.0.0*
    d. *network 10.0.0.0*
28. What does it mean to *advertise* a network?
29. The network shown in Figure 7-25 is an example of which of the following?
    a. Contiguous network
    b. Discontiguous network

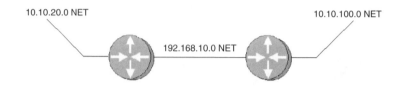

10.10.20.0 NET   10.10.100.0 NET

192.168.10.0 NET

FIGURE 7-25   The network for problem 29.

30. Write the commands to enable RIP on an interface with an IP address of 192.168.10.0.
31. The command *show ip protocol* is used on a router to
    a. Display the routing protocol that can run on the router
    b. Display the IP address of the routers running an IP protocol
    c. Display the routing protocols running on the router
    d. None of the above
32. The command *show ip interface brief* is used on a router to
    a. Check the current configuration of the interfaces
    b. Check the assigned IP addresses for the interface
    c. Check the status of the interfaces
    d. All the above
    e. None of the above
33. The command *show ip route* is used on a router to
    a. Set a static route
    b. Configure a static route
    c. Display the configured routes on a router
    d. Display how often routing updates are sent
    e. C and D
    f. B and D
34. The command used to display the router's current running-configuration is
    a. *show run*
    b. *show routing*
    c. *show interface*
    d. *show controller*

Section 7-5

35. How is the IGRP similar to RIP?
36. What improvements does IGRP provide relative to RIP?

37. The command for specifying the IGRP routing protocol on a router is
    a. *router igrp [0#]*
    b. *router igrp [as number]*
    c. *router igrp*
    d. *router igrp [FF]*
38. You can verify that the IGRP routing protocol is running on a router by using the command
    a. *show run*
    b. *show ip int brief*
    c. *show flash*
    d. *show ip protocol*
39. The router command used to copy the running-configuration to NVRAM is
    a. *copy run tftp*
    b. *copy run start*
    c. *copy run flash*
    d. *copy run show*
40. What information does *show ip route igrp* provide?
    a. View the routing table for only the IGRP protocol
    b. View the routing table for all protocols except IGRP
    c. Enable IP routing with IGRP
    d. Instruct the router to use IP routing
41. What is the router command for displaying the startup-configuration?
    a. *show run*
    b. *show flash*
    c. *show history*
    d. *show start*

Section 7-6

42. OSPF is (select all that apply)
    a. Open Shortest Path First routing protocol
    b. An open protocol
    c. Developed specifically for TCP/IP networks
    d. Developed specifically for IPX networks
    e. A distance vector protocol
    f. A dynamic routing protocol
    g. A link state protocol
    h. A high consumer of bandwidth
43. In OSPF, route updates are sent in the form of
    a. Link state advertisements
    b. Exchanging routing tables every 30 seconds
    c. Exchanging routing tables every 90 seconds
    d. IETF packets
44. The OSPF routing protocol uses these to verify that a link between two routers is active and the routers are communicating:
    a. LSAs
    b. "Hello" packets
    c. ARP messages
    d. Ping

45. Areas in the OSPF protocol are
    a. Not used
    b. Used to partition a large network into small networks
    c. Used to combine small networks into one large network
    d. An inefficient use of bandwidth
46. Variable length subnet masks
    a. Minimize wasted IP address space when interconnecting subnets
    b. Are not recommended in modern computer networks
    c. Reduce the number of bits required in a subnet mask from 32 to 24
    d. Are the same as classful addressing
47. Which is *not* an advantage of OSPF?
    a. Very easy to implement
    b. Uses VLSM
    c. Link state changes are immediately reported
    d. Not a proprietary protocol
48. Define *router flapping*.
49. The command structure for enabling OSPF routing on a router is
    a. ***router ospf***
    b. ***router ospf [area]***
    c. ***routing protocol ospf***
    d. ***router ospf [number]***
50. Another name for wild card bits is
    a. OSPF pass-through bits
    b. Area 0 selection bits
    c. Inverse mask bits
    d. Route selection bits
51. Area 0 is
    a. Used to hide data packets
    b. Root or backbone for the network
    c. Inverse mask bits
    d. Route selection bits
52. Which of the following is *not* a correct statement for configuring a route to run over OSPF? Assume that the OSPF protocol has been enabled.
    a. *network 10.10.20.1 1.1.1.1 area 0*
    b. *network 10.10.20.1 1.0.0.0 area 0*
    c. *network 10.0.0.0 1.0.0.0*
    d. *network 10.10.100.1 0.0.0.0 area 0*
53. The command ***show ip route ospf***
    a. Is not valid in OSPF
    b. Displays only the IP routes
    c. Displays only the OSPF routes
    d. Enables OSPF routing
54. The ***sh ip route*** command is entered on RouterB in the campus LAN shown in Figure 7-12. The LAN has been fully configured to run the OSPF protocol.
    a. How many OSPF subnets are running on the network?
    b. Identify the connected C and OSPF O subnets.
55. The ***sh ip route*** command is entered on RouterC in the campus LAN shown in Figure 7-12. The LAN has been fully configured to run the OSPF protocol.
    a. How many OSPF subnets are running on the network?
    b. Identify the connected C and OSPF O subnets.

Section 7-7

56. *EIGRP* stands for
    a. Enhanced Interior Routing Protocol
    b. Enhanced Interior Gateway Routing Protocol
    c. Enhanced Internet Gateway Routing Protocol
    d. None of the above
57. The command for enabling EIGRP on a router is
    a. *router igrp [as number]*
    b. *router eigrp*
    c. *router eigrp [as number]*
    d. *router eigrp enable*
58. The command *network 10.10.0.0* is entered on a router after EIGRP has been enabled. Define what this means.
59. What router command can be used to verify EIGRP is running on the router?
    a. *show run*
    b. *show ip int brief*
    c. *show history*
    d. *show ip protocol*
60. What router command will show how many subnets are configured?
    a. *show run*
    b. *show ip int brief*
    c. *show list*
    d. *show ip route*
61. What router command will show whether the router is exchanging routes?
    a. *show run*
    b. *show ip int brief*
    c. *show list*
    d. *show ip route*
62. The *sh ip route* command is entered on RouterA in the campus LAN shown in Figure 7-13. The LAN has been fully configured to run the EIGRP protocol.
    a. How many EIGRP subnets are running on the network?
    b. Identify the connected C and EIGRP D subnets.
63. The *sh ip route* command is entered on RouterB in the campus LAN shown in Figure 7-13. The LAN has been fully configured to run the EIGRP protocol.
    a. How many EIGRP subnets are running on the network?
    b. Identify the connected C and EIGRP D subnets.

Section 7-8

64. What are the two command modes for the JUNOS operating system?
65. What does the {**master**} prompt indicate in JUNOS?
66. What does the net-admin@noc> prompt indicate in JUNOS?
67. What is the help command in JUNOS?
68. What does it mean if the following is displayed after entering the *show interfaces* command?
    Physical interface: at-0/1/0, Enabled, Physical link is Up
69. What is the command used to display the Juniper router current configuration? Show the proper prompt for the command.

70. The following is displayed after entering the show configuration command. What does **re0 {** represent?

```
{master}
net-admin@noc>show configuration
version 7.6R2.6;
groups {
    re0 {
        system {
            host-name checs-atm-re0;
            backup-router 10.10.20.250 destination 10.10.10.5/24;
            }
    }

            }
```

71. What is meant by out of band management ?
72. What is a management Ethernet interface?
73. What is an internal Ethernet interface?
74. What are transient interfaces?
75. What is the command for displaying the router interfaces and their status?
76. What is the command sequence to change the hostname on a Juniper router to Piyasat?
77. Can the following command sequence be used to change the IP address on an interface? Why or why not?

```
net-admin@noc> configure
[edit]
net-admin@noc>#edit interfaces ge-0/0/0
[edit interfaces ge-0/0/0]
net-admin@noc>#edit unit 0
[edit interfaces ge-0/0/0 unit 0]
net-admin@noc>#edit family inet
[edit interfaces ge-0/0/0 unit 0 family inet]
net-admin@noc>#set address 192.168.1.1/24
[edit interfaces ge-0/0/0 unit 0 family inet]
net-admin@noc>#
```

78. What is the correct command for configuring a static route on a Juniper router given a destination of 216.234.214.82 with a subnet mask of 255.255.255.255 and the next hop is 216.31.32.161?
79. (a) What command is used to save a configuration in JUNOS? (b) What command sequence saves the JUNOS configuration and exits the configuration mode?
80. Write the script (with braces {) for the following command sequence for OSPF:

```
net-admin@noc> configure
 [edit]
user@host# set protocols ospf area 10.0.0.0 interface at-0/0/0 hello-
interval 10 dead-interval 40
[edit]
user@host# set protocols ospf area 10.0.0.0 interface ge-0/0/1 hello-
interval 10 dead-interval 40
```

Section 7-9

81. What port does TFTP use?
82. List the command and prompt used to save a router configuration file to the TFTP server.
83. List the command and prompt used to load a save configuration file from the TFTP server.
84. Use the Finisar Surveyor demo software to capture a file transfer to a TFTP server. Prepare a report on your findings. Identify the port used to establish the TFTP transfer and the source and destination ports used for the TFTP file transfer.
85. Repeat problem 84 for loading a file from a TFTP server.

Section 7-10

86. The hello interval is
    a. The time between "Hello" packets
    b. The timing of the "Hello" header
    c. The timing of the router dead interval
    d. None of the above
87. OSPF multicasts are sent out as what class of address?
    a. Class A
    b. Class B
    c. Class C
    d. Class D
    e. Class E
88. OSPF "Hello" packets are sent out every
    a. 30 seconds
    b. 90 seconds
    c. 10 seconds
    d. None of the above
89. The Router ID (RID) in OSPF "Hello" packets is chosen from
    a. Loopback addresses
    b. OSPF 16P_Router
    c. Highest IP address on an interface
    d. a and c
    e. b and c

Critical Thinking

90. You are configuring a router connection to a remote network. What protocol would you select if there is only one network route to the remote network? Explain why you selected the protocol.
91. You are configuring the routing protocols for a small network. What routing protocol would you select and why?

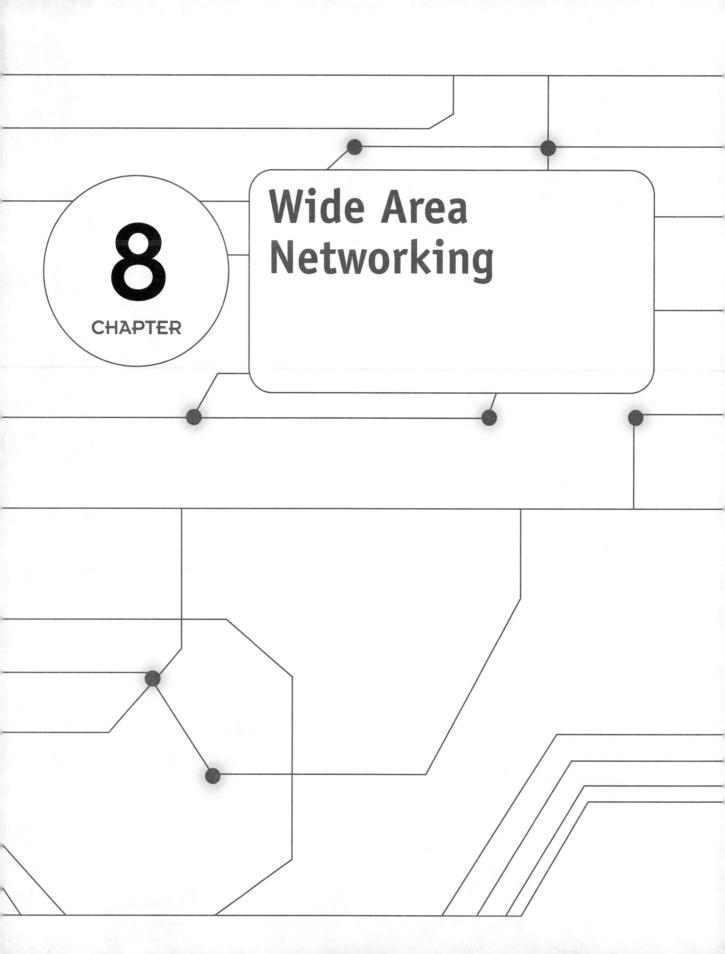

8

CHAPTER

Wide Area
Networking

CHAPTER OUTLINE

8-1   Introduction
8-2   The Line Connection
8-3   Frame Relay
8-4   ATM
8-5   Dial-in Access
8-6   VPN

8-7   Wide Area Network Routing
8-8   Internet Routing
8-9   Analyzing Internet Data Traffic
Summary
Questions and Problems

OBJECTIVES

- Describe line coding and framing format
- Describe the function of the CSU/DSU
- Describe how to create a Frame Relay connection
- Demonstrate the configuration for a point-to-point connection
- Discuss the ATM mode of operation
- Describe a wide area network

- Describe how to configure dial-in access
- Describe how to configure a VPN tunnel
- Describe how to establish computer-to-server VPN connections
- Describe the different types of WAN connections
- Describe the steps for configuring Internet routing

KEY TERMS

wide area network (WAN)
HSSI
OC
DS-0 to DS-3, T1 to T3
DS
telco
telco cloud
multiplexed
fractional T1
switch-56
point of presence (POP)
line of demarcation
CSU/DSU
D4 framing
ESF
AMI
bipolar coding
B8ZS

minimum ones density
bipolar violation
HDLC
PPP
Frame Relay network
public data network
X.25
committed information rate (CIR)
bursty
committed burst information rate (CBIR)
PVCs
Frame Relay cloud
dlci tag
ATM
packet switching
payload

virtual path connection (VPC)
virtual channel connection (VCC)
SVC
VPI
VCI
V.44/V.34
V.92/V.90
asymmetric operation
cable modem
ranging
ISDN
xDSL
DSL
ADSL (asymmetric DSL)
discrete multitone (DMT)
RAS

continues

KEY TERMS   continued

DHCP	totally stubby areas	eBGP
VPN	BGP	NOC
IP tunnel	multi-homed	outbound data
PPTP	AS	traffic
L2TP	ASN	inbound data traffic
IPsec	peering	IPX
stubby areas	iBGP	

8-1 INTRODUCTION

This chapter examines the concepts for establishing **wide area network (WAN)** connections. WANs use the telecommunication network to interconnect sites that are geographically distributed throughout a region, the country, or even the world. Connections can include extensions of the campus LAN to remote members of the network. For example, the corporate office for a company could be located in one part of a state and the engineering, manufacturing, and sales sites could be at different locations in the state. An example of a WAN is shown in Figure 8-1. The wide area network in this example shows connections for the Internet, a Frame Relay network, a Virtual Private Network (VPN), and dial-in access through a remote access server.

Wide Area Network (WAN)
Uses the telecommunication network to interconnect sites that are geographically distributed throughout a region, the country, or the world

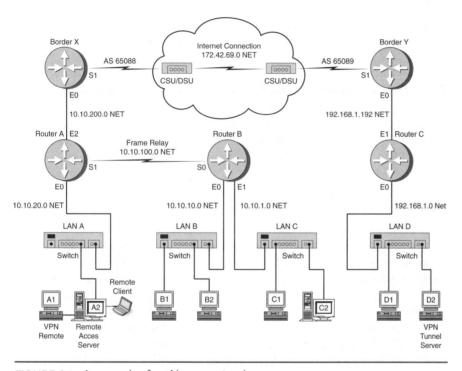

FIGURE 8-1   An example of a wide area network.

This chapter examines each of these wide area networking technologies. An introduction to setting up a connection to the communications carrier is examined in section 8-2. The Channel Service Unit/Data Service Unit (CSU/DSU), serial line clocking, and line coding formats are examined. The important concept of configuring Frame Relay networks is next examined in section 8-3. This section includes an example of configuring a Frame Relay network within a simulated Telco "cloud."

Section 8-4 examines the asynchronous transfer mode (ATM) and its important role in carrying high-speed data traffic around the country and the world. Wide area networking is not complete without dial-in access for the user. Section 8-5 examines establishing a point-to-point dial-in connection using a phone modem, cable modem, Digital Subscriber Line (DSL) service, and other technologies. Section 8-5 concludes with an example of configuring a remote access server to accept dial-in connections.

Section 8-1 • INTRODUCTION   291

Creating virtual private networks (VPNs) is examined in section 8-6. The steps for creating a VPN tunnel are examined and the section concludes with steps for configuring a VPN connection on a router-to-router tunnel and configuring a VPN remote client. An overview of the issues of wide area network routing is presented in section 8-7. The protocols used for routing Internet data traffic are examined in section 8-8. The chapter concludes with an example of using the Surveyor Demo protocol analyzer to examine Internet data traffic entering and exiting a campus LAN.

8-2 THE LINE CONNECTION

HSSI
High-speed serial interface

OC
Optical carrier

This section introduces the basic knowledge needed for configuring the high-speed serial data transmission interfaces used to connect LANs together and to connect the campus network to the outside world. The term "high speed" is relative. For large networks, a high-speed connection could be a DS-3 (44.7+ Mbps) or a connection to an **HSSI** (high-speed serial interface) that supports data rates from 300 kbps to 52 Mbps. For small networks, the high-speed serial connection out of the network could be a T1 (1.544 Mbps). The T1 data rate is fast relative to the connection speed provided by a dial-up phone modem, so some users would call this a "high-speed" connection. Topics in this section include an introduction to the data standards currently being used in data communications and the data formats being used. These data standards include T1 to T3, DS-1 to DS-3, E1, E3, and the **OC** (optical carrier) data rates of OC-1 to OC-192.

Data Channels

DS-0 to DS-3; T1 to T3
Common telecommunication
data rates

DS
Digital signal

Telco
The local telephone company

The most common communications data rates for end users are **DS-0 to DS-3** and **T1 to T3**. The T1/DS-1 and T3/DS-3 designations are actually the same data rates and the terms are used interchangeably. The Bell system "T" carriers were established in the 1960s primarily for transporting digitized telephone conversations. In the early 1980s, the digital signal (**DS**) subscriber lines became available. The data rates for the T/DS carriers are listed in Table 8-1. The DS0 designation is for the base rate of the digital signal lines, basically the data rate of a digitized telephone call.

The T1 line is capable of carrying 24 DS-0 transmissions or 24 voice channels. Each DS-0 line uses 64 kbps (56 kbps) of data, but the data rate of 56 kbps in parentheses after 64 kbps indicates the rate actually available to the user in some cases. In other words, the DS-0 line does not guarantee that the full 64 kbps line is available. This depends on the connection provided by the communications carrier (**telco**—the local telephone company) and the equipment used to make the connection. When a 56-kbps connection is used, the other part of the data is for the overhead (synchronization and framing) required for the digital transmission.

TABLE 8-1 Data Rates for the T and DS Carriers

Designation	Data Rate
DS-0	64 kbps (56 kbps)
T1 (DS-1)	1.544 Mbps
T2 (DS-2)	6.312 Mbps
T3 (DS-3)	44.736 Mbps
T4 (DS-4)	274.176 Mbps

The data lines are leased from a communications carrier for carrying any type of data, including voice, data, and video. It is important to note that when you lease a T1 (DS-1) line from the communications carrier to provide a data connection from point A to point B, the communications carrier does not provide you with your own point-to-point private physical connection. The communications carrier provides you with sufficient data bandwidth and a switched connection in its system to carry your data traffic to the destination. Most likely, your data will be multiplexed with hundreds of other T1/DS-1 data channels. An example of this is shown in Figure 8-2. Networks A and B each have established and configured a T1 data connection to the **telco cloud**. The Telco cloud is the switched network the telecommunications carrier uses to get the data to its destination. The data from network A enters the telco cloud and is routed to the destination, network B. The term *cloud* is often used to describe the interconnection of networks via the Internet.

Telco Cloud
The telecommunications carrier's switched network used to transport data to its destination; also used to describe the interconnected networks on the Internet

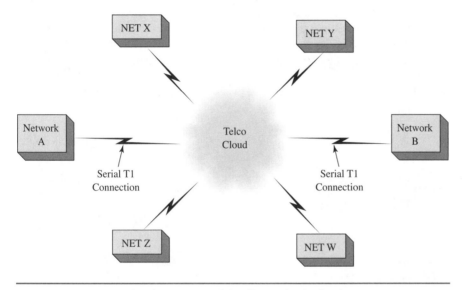

FIGURE 8-2 Transporting data over a T1/DS-1 line to the destination.

Note that networks W, X, Y, and Z also interconnect to the telco cloud. These networks can also be exchanging data packets, possibly over the same lines carrying data to and from networks A and B. In other words, the data from each network is being **multiplexed** together to reach the destination.

Sometimes, a wide area network connection might only require that a portion of the data capacity of the T1 bandwidth be leased or used. This is called **fractional T1**. Fractional T1 data rates up to 772 kbps are available. The most common fractional T1 data rate is 56 kbps. This is called a *DS-0 line*. The 56 kbps lines are provided either as dedicated 24-hour leased lines or through a dial-up connection called **switch-56**. In the case of a dial-up connection, the user only pays for the data bandwidth when the service is needed.

Two other designations for data rates are E1 and E3. These designations are used throughout the world where the T-carrier designation is not used. For example, these designations are primarily used in Europe. The data rates for E1 and E3 are listed in Table 8-2.

Multiplexed
Combining data packets for transport

Fractional T1
Indicates that only a portion of the T1 bandwidth is being used

Switch-56
A 56 kbps dial-up data connection

TABLE 8-2   E1 and E3 Data Transmission Rates

Designation	Data Rate
E1	2.048 Mbps
E3	34.368 Mbps

Point of Presence

Point of Presence (POP)
The point where the customer connects the network data traffic to the communications carrier

Line of Demarcation
The point where ownership of the communications equipment changes from the communications carrier to the user

CSU/DSU
The channel service unit/data service unit

The place where the communications carrier brings in service to a facility is called the **point of presence (POP)**. This is where users connect their network to the communications carrier. The link to the communications carrier can be copper, fiber, digital microwave, or digital satellite. Another term related to this is the **line of demarcation**, which is the point where ownership of the communications equipment changes from the communications carrier to the customer.

The communications carrier will require the data connection be made through a **CSU/DSU** (channel service unit/data service unit). The CSU/DSU provides the hardware data interface to the carrier. This includes adding the framing information for maintaining the data flow, storing performance data, and providing line management. Figure 8-3 illustrates an example of inserting the CSU/DSU in the connection to the Telco cloud.

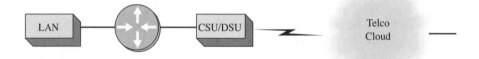

FIGURE 8-3   The placement of the CSU/DSU in the connection to the Telco cloud.

The CSU/DSU also has three alarm modes for advising the user of problems on the link: red, yellow, and blue. The conditions for each alarm are defined in Table 8-3.

TABLE 8-3   CSU/DSU Alarms

Red Alarm	A local equipment alarm that indicates that the incoming signal has been corrupted.
Yellow Alarm	Indicates that a failure in the link has been detected.
Blue Alarm	Indicates a total loss of incoming signal.

T1 Framing

D4 Framing
The original data framing used in T1 circuits

The original framing for the data in T1 circuits is based on **D4 framing**. The D4 frame consists of 24 voice channels (8 kbps)—8 bits per channel plus one framing bit, for a total of 193 bits. The D4 system uses a 12-bit framing sequence to maintain synchronization of the receiving equipment. The D4 12-bit framing sequence is generated from 12 D4 frames.

1 0 0 0 1 1 0 1 1 1 0 0

ESF (extended superframe framing) is an improvement in data performance over D4 framing. ESF extends the frame length to 24 frames, compared to D4's 12. The extended frame length creates 24 ESF framing bits. Table 8-4 shows how the 24 bits are used. ESF uses only 6 bits for frame synchronization, compared to the 12 synchronizing bits used in D4 framing. ESF uses 6 bits for computing an error check code. The code is used to verify that data transmission was received without errors. Twelve bits of the ESF frame are used for maintenance and control of the communications link. Examples of the use of the maintenance and control bits include obtaining performance data from the link and configuring loopbacks for testing the link. As you will recall, a *loopback* is when the data is routed back to the sender. Three loopback tests are graphically shown in Figure 8-4. Loopback test A is used to test the cable connecting the router to the CSU/DSU. Test B is used to test the link through the CSU/DSU. Loopback test C tests the CSU and the link to Telco.

ESF
Extended superframe framing

TABLE 8-4   Function of the 24 ESF Framing Bits

6 bits	Frame synchronization
6 bits	Error detection
12 bits	Communications link control and maintenance

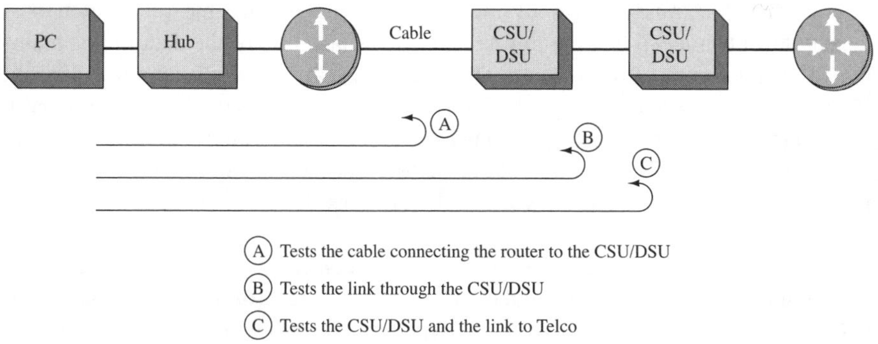

Ⓐ Tests the cable connecting the router to the CSU/DSU

Ⓑ Tests the link through the CSU/DSU

Ⓒ Tests the CSU/DSU and the link to Telco

FIGURE 8-4   Three loopback configurations used to test a communications link.

Line Coding Formats

The data connection to the communications carrier requires that the proper data encoding format be selected for the CSU/DSU. Data are encoded in such a way that timing information of the binary stream is maintained and the logical 1s and 0s can still be detected.

A fundamental coding scheme that was developed for transmission over T1 circuits is **AMI** (alternate mark inversion). The AMI code provides for alternating voltage level pulses V(+) and V(-) to represent the 1s. This technique virtually removes

AMI
Alternate mark inversion

Bipolar Coding
Successive 1s are represented by pulses in the opposite voltage direction

the DC component of the data stream. Figure 8-5 shows an example of the AMI coded wave form. Notice that successive 1s are represented by pulses in the opposite direction (V+ and V-). This is called **bipolar coding**.

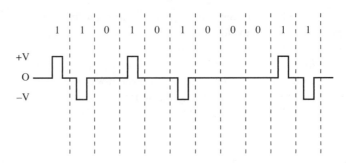

FIGURE 8-5   An example of the AMI data encoding format.

The 0s have a voltage level of zero volts; notice that when there are successive 0s a straight line at zero volts is generated. A flat line generated by a long string of 0s can produce a loss of timing and synchronization. This deficiency can be overcome by the transmission of the appropriate start, stop, and synchronizing bits, but this comes at the price of adding overhead bits to the data transmission and consuming a portion of the data communication channel's bandwidth.

B8ZS
Bipolar 8 zero substitution

Minimum Ones Density
A pulse is intentionally sent in the data stream even if the data being transmitted is a series of all 0s

The **B8ZS** (bipolar 8 zero substitution) data encoding format was developed to improve data transmission over T1 circuits. T1 circuits require that a minimum ones density level be met so that the timing and synchronization of the data link is maintained. Maintaining a **minimum ones density** means that a pulse is intentionally sent in the data stream even if the data being transmitted is a series of all 0s. Intentionally inserting the pulses in the data stream helps maintain the timing and synchronization of the data stream. The inserted data pulses include two **bipolar violations**, which means the pulse is in the same voltage direction as the previous pulse in the data stream.

Bipolar Violation
The pulse is in the same voltage direction as the previous pulse

In B8ZS encoding, eight consecutive 0s are replaced with an eight-bit sequence that contains two intentional bipolar violations. Figure 8-6 shows an example of B8ZS encoding. The receiver detects the bipolar violations in the data stream and replaces the inserted byte (8 bits) with all 0s to recover the original data stream. Thus the timing is maintained without corrupting the data. The advantage of using the B8ZS encoded format is that the bipolar violations enable the timing of the data transmission to remain synchronized without the need for overhead bits. This allows the use of the full data capacity of the channel.

HDLC
High-level data link control, a synchronous proprietary protocol

PPP
Point-to-Point Protocol

Two other serial line protocols commonly used in wide area networking are **HDLC** (high-level data link control) and **PPP** (Point-to-Point Protocol). Both of these protocols are used by routers to carry data over a serial line connection, typically over direct connections such as with T1. PPP is used for serial interface connections such as that provided by modems. PPP is a full duplex protocol and is a subset of the HDLC data encapsulation. Examples of direct connections using HDLC and PPP are shown in Figure 8-7.

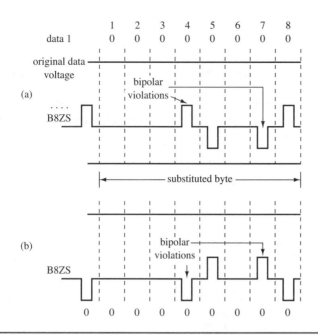

FIGURE 8-6   Intentional bipolar violations in B8ZS Encoding.

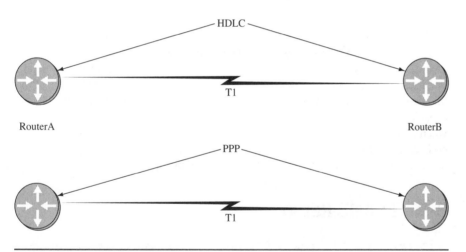

FIGURE 8-7   An example of a direct connection.

The routers at each end must be configured with the proper data encapsulation. *Data encapsulation* means the data is properly packaged for transport over a serial communications line. The type of encapsulation depends on the hardware being used to make the connection. The command for setting the data encapsulation is ***encapsulation (encap)***. The options for the data encapsulation on the router can be viewed by entering ***encap ?*** at the router's **(config-if)#** prompt. The following shows an example of using the ***encap ?*** command:

```
Router(config-if)#encap ?
atm-dxi ATM-DXI encapsulation frame-relay Frame Relay networks hdlc Ser-
    ial HDLC synchronous lapb LAPB (X.25 Level 2)
```

```
ppp Point-to-Point protocol
smds Switched Megabit Data Service (SMDS)
x2 X.25
```

The serial interface can be configured to run HDLC from the **(config-if)#** prompt.

(*Note:* The **(config-if)#** prompt is the prompt for the interface currently being configured and is the same for all interfaces. Examples for setting the data encapsulation to HDLC and PPP on the Serial0 interface are shown.)

```
Router# conf t
Router(config)# int s0
Router(config-if)#encap hdlc
Router# conf t
Router(config)# int s0
Router(config-if)#encap ppp
```

The data encapsulation can be verified by using the *sh int s0* command. The seventh line in this example shows that the encapsulation is HDLC:

```
RouterB#sh int s0
Serial0 is up, line protocol is up
Hardware is HD64570
Description: ISP Connection
Internet address is 192.168.1.2/24
MTU 1500 bytes, BW 1544 Kbit, DLY 20000 usec, rely 255/255, load 1/255
Encapsulation HDLC, loopback not set, keepalive set (10 sec)
.
.
.
```

The type of network being configured and the equipment being used to make the direct connection determines the selection of the format for data encapsulation. For example, Cisco routers automatically configure the serial interfaces to run HDLC but the Cisco routers support many data encapsulation formats. The HDLC data encapsulation formats are implemented differently by some vendors, and there are times when some equipment is not interoperable with other equipment even though they both have specified the HDLC encapsulation. In that case, another encapsulation format such as PPP can be used to make the direct connection.

8-3   FRAME RELAY

Frame Relay Network
A packet switching network designed to carry data traffic over a public data network

Public Data Network
A local telephone company or a communications carrier

X.25
A packet-switched protocol designed for data transmission over analog lines

Committed Information Rate (CIR)
Guaranteed data rate or bandwidth to be used in the Frame Relay connection

A **Frame Relay network** is designed to carry data traffic over a **public data network** (PDN) (for example, telco). Frame Relay evolved from the **X.25** packet switching systems. The X.25 protocol was designed for data transmission over analog lines and incorporated the error checking and flow control required to maintain a reliable data link over these lines. Frame Relay is designed to operate over higher-quality, more reliable digital data lines and therefore does not require the error checking and data flow control of X.25. Frame Relay operates on the premise that the data channels will introduce no bit errors or, in the worst case, minimal bit errors. Without the overhead bits for error checking and data-flow control, the data capacity of a Frame Relay system is greatly improved. Frame Relay does provide error detection at the receivers. If an error is detected, the receiver system corrects the error.

The commercial carrier (telco) provides the switch for the Frame Relay network. The telco provides a guaranteed data rate, or **committed information rate** (**CIR**), based on the service and bandwidth requested by the user. For example, the user may request a T1 data service with a CIR of 768 kbps. A T1 connection allows a maximum data rate of 1.544 Mbps. The network (telco) allows for **bursty** data transmissions and will allow the data transfer to go up to the T1 connection carrier bandwidth even though the CIR is 768 kbps. *Bursty* means the data rates can momentarily exceed the leased CIR data rate of the service. Communication carriers use what is called a **committed burst information rate (CBIR)** that enables subscribers to exceed the committed information rate (CIR) during times of heavy traffic. (*Note:* The bursty data transmission rate can never exceed the data rate of the physical connection. For example, because the maximum data rate for a T1 data service is 1.544 Mbps, the bursty data rate can never exceed this rate.)

The focus of this section is on establishing point-to-point Frame Relay connections. Topics covered include establishing Frame Relay **PVCs** (permanent virtual connections) inside the **Frame Relay cloud**. Your telco has a Frame Relay cloud that provides all the required data switches for routing the data to the destination network and establishing the PVC or a virtual direct connection. The permanent virtual connections are made through the Frame Relay cloud to the other end. There can be multiple virtual circuits within the cloud.

There are two basic setups for Frame Relay. The hub and spoke shown in Figure 8-8 is one, where all the end nodes connect to one main hub. The hub serves as a central station for the end nodes or spokes. The downside of the hub and spoke is that two sites, such as B and C shown in Figure 8-8, must send their data traffic through the hub (A) to get to the other spoke. The other setup for Frame Relay is full mesh, which is a network with all sites connected via a PVC as illustrated in Figure 8-9. Adding another connection to make a full mesh requires only a software change within the Frame Relay cloud. Nodes B and C can communicate directly in a full mesh Frame Relay network using a PVC.

Bursty
Data rates can momentarily exceed the leased data rate of the service

Committed Burst Information Rate (CBIR)
Enables subscribers to exceed the committed information rate (CIR) during times of heavy traffic

PVCs
Permanent virtual connections

Frame Relay Cloud
Provides all the required switches for routing the data to the destination network, usually provided by your local telco

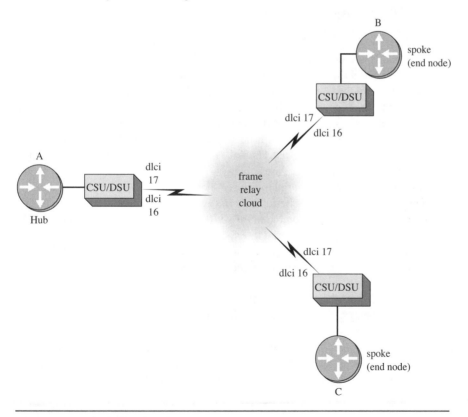

FIGURE 8-8   The hub and spoke Frame Relay connection.

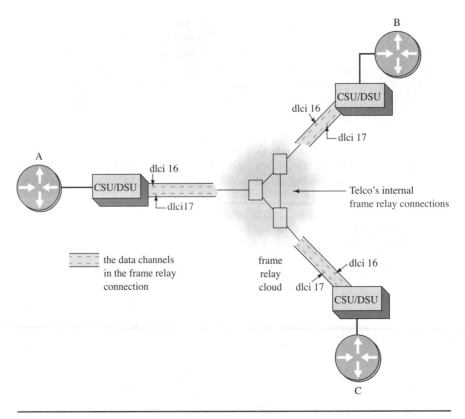

FIGURE 8-9   The full mesh Frame Relay connection.

dlci Tag
The data link connection identifier assigned by a telco for use within the telco cloud; the tag associates which PVC is coming through and where it is coming from

Each PVC is identified by a dlci tag. (*Note:* The acronym *dlci* is pronounced "del-see.") The **dlci tag** is the data link connection identifier assigned by telco for use within the telco cloud. The tag associates which PVC is coming through and where it is coming from. Dlcis have only local relevance to the connection to telco and the router. The telco maps the dlcis from one interface to a dlci on another interface.

Sometimes a subinterface is used to configure Frame Relay networks on a Cisco router. The subinterfaces used to make the Frame Relay connection act and behave like physical interfaces but are actually software connections. The subinterface is part of one of the router's serial interfaces. For example, *s0.1* indicates that this is a subinterface on the router's Serial0 interface. The subinterfaces on the router are configured using the router command ***int ser 0.1***. This example indicates this is the subinterface for the 0.1 virtual serial interface. Note that subinterfaces can be configured on most router physical interfaces and are not limited to the serial interfaces.

In Frame Relay, subinterfaces are how the router handles the PVC connection. *Point-to-point* means you have only one PVC or dlci on one subinterface. This also means each subinterface will have different IP subnets. The previous way to set up a Frame Relay connection was point-to-multipoint. All PVCs or dlcis were assigned to one interface.

The term *point-to-point* describes the connection of the user to the Frame Relay cloud provided by telco. The user is connected to only one end of the virtual interface, as shown in Figure 8-10. The user's router connects through a CSU/DSU to the telco Frame Relay cloud. Point-to-point is the preferred way to handle Frame Relay: The setup is simple to follow and the connection acts like a regular physical serial interface. A *point-to-point physical interface* is a serial T1 interface that connects directly from one end user to the other through telco, not through a Frame Relay cloud.

FIGURE 8-10   The point-to-point connection to the Frame Relay cloud.

Frame Relay can be run on any serial interface of a Cisco router. An IP address is not assigned to a physical interface in Frame Relay because the physical interface is always a point-to-multipoint interface. In contrast, subinterfaces can be made point-to-point or point-to-multipoint.

The physical setup for Frame Relay will be similar to the setup for a point-to-point T1 setup. You must have a CSU/DSU, and the framing, line coding, and clocking must be set up for it.

Establishing a Frame Relay Connection

The following steps describe how to establish a Frame Relay connection:

1. Identify the location of the end sites that are to be interconnected with the Frame Relay cloud. Determine whether the remote sites are within or external to your telco service area. If the Frame Relay connection involves more than one telco—for example, site A is in New Mexico (telco is Qwest) and site B is in Texas (telco is Southwestern Bell)—the connection would have to be provided by a national telco such as AT&T, MCI, or Sprint, except for the last mile, which must be provided by the local telco. If both sites are in the same telco service area, that telco can provide the full Frame Relay network connection.
2. Determine the data bandwidth needed for the Frame Relay network. The typical connection for Frame Relay is T1.
3. Order your data lines for the Frame Relay connection from the telco.
4. The telco makes the connection for the Frame Relay network within the telco Frame Relay cloud. This includes the PVCs between the ends requested. The PVCs are programmed within the telco's Frame Relay network.
5. The telco then provides deliverables for establishing the Frame Relay connections. This includes the physical connection to telco. Typically this is an RJ-45 connection that connects to the CSU/DSU.
6. Next, make a serial connection from your router to the CSU/DSU.
7. The telco will provide you with a dlci number. You will program the dlci into the router to match the subnets with the hubs when configuring the subinterfaces.

8. For management purposes, obtain the circuit number from the telco. This number is used when calling telco to obtain help when reporting Frame Relay network problems.

Configuring Frame Relay Point-to-Point on the Router

The following is an example of configuring a Frame Relay network using two routers, as shown in Figure 8-11. Routers B and C are the end nodes of the network. At the center is the telco Frame Relay cloud. This example demonstrates the commands used for configuring a point-to-point virtual connection on a router. In this example, the connection is established on the router's subinterfaces or virtual serial interfaces.

The first step is to configure one of the end nodes. The interface that connects to the telco should already be connected through a CSU/DSU and configured according to the guidelines provided by the telco. The telco will also have provided dlci numbers for the Frame Relay links; in this example they are 200 and 100, as shown in Figure 8-11.

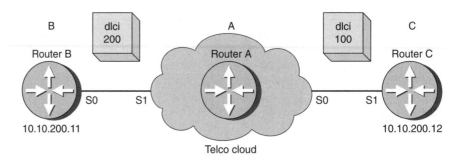

FIGURE 8-11 The Frame Relay network.

RouterB will be configured first. Enter the router's configuration mode using the ***conf t*** command. Next, select the Serial0/0 interface using the ***int s0/ 0*** command. Enter the command ***encapsulation frame-relay*** to instruct the interface to encapsulate the data for Frame Relay. Next, configure the Frame Relay subinterface using the command ***int s0/0.1 point-to-point***. This instructs the router to configure a subinterface and configure the interface for point to point. Notice that the prompt has changed to **RouterB(config-subif)#**, indicating to the user that the subinterface configuration mode has been entered.

```
RouterB#conf t
Enter configuration commands, one per line. End with CNTL/Z.
RouterB(config)#int s0/0
RouterB(config-if)#encapsulation frame-relay
RouterB(config-if)#no shut
RouterB(config)#int s0/0.1 point-to-point
RouterB(config-subif)#
```

The next step is to configure the IP address for the subinterface. In this case, the IP address of 10.10.200.11 has been assigned to RouterB's subinterface. The last step on RouterB is to configure the assigned dlci number (200) to the subinterface using the command ***frame-relay interface-dlci 200***. This is the number assigned to the connection by telco. Notice that the prompt changes to **RouterB(config-fr-dlci)#**.

```
RouterB(config-subif)#ip address 10.10.200.11 255.255.255.0
RouterB(config-subif)#frame-relay interface-dlci 200
RouterB(config-fr-dlci)#
```

Use the *sh run* command to view the running configuration. Save the updated router configuration using the *copy run start* command. The portion of the running configuration that shows the changes to the Serial0 interface is provided.

```
!
interface Serial0.0
 no ip address
 no ip directed-broadcast encapsulation frame-relay
!
interface Serial0/0.1 point-to-point
ip address 10.10.200.11 255.255.255.0
 no ip directed-broadcast
 frame-relay interface-dlci 200
!
```

The command *sh ip int brief* is used to view the status of the interfaces as shown. Notice that the Serial0/0 and Serial0/1 interfaces are both *administratively down*. This means the interfaces have not been enabled using the *no shut* command.

```
RouterB#sh ip int br
Interface        IP-Address   OK? Method Status                 Protocol
FastEthernet0/0  unassigned   YES unset  administratively down  down
FastEthernet0/1  unassigned   YES unset  administratively down  down
Serial0/0        unassigned   YES unset  administratively down  down
Serial0/0.1      10.10.200.11 YES manual administratively down  down
Serial0/1        unassigned   YES unset  administratively down  down
```

The steps for enabling the Serial0/0 interface are shown in the following:

```
RouterB#conf t
Enter configuration commands, one per line. End with CNTL/Z.
RouterB(config)#int s0/0
RouterB(config-if)#no shut
RouterB#
5d13h: %SYS-5-CONFIG_I: Configured from console by console
5d13h: %LINK-3-UPDOWN: Interface Serial0/0, changed state to up
5d13h: %FR-5-DLCICHANGE: Interface Serial0/0  DLCI 200 state changed to
    INACTIVE
5d13h: %LINEPROTO-5-UPDOWN: Line protocol on Interface Serial0/0,
    changed state to up
```

The *sh ip int brief* command for RouterB now shows that the Serial0/0 interface is *up* but the subinterface 0/0.1 is still *administratively down*. The command *no shut* must be issued on the subinterface to turn it on, as shown:

```
RouterB#sh ip int br
Interface        IP-Address   OK? Method Status                 Protocol
FastEthernet0/0  unassigned   YES unset  administratively down  down
FastEthernet0/1  unassigned   YES unset  administratively down  down
Serial0/0        unassigned   YES unset  up                     up
Serial0/0.1      10.10.200.11 YES manual administratively down  down
Serial0/1        unassigned   YES unset  administratively down  down

RouterB#conf t
Enter configuration commands, one per line. End with CNTL/Z.
RouterB(config)#int s0/0.1
RouterB(config-subif)#no shut
RouterB(config-subif)#
5d13h: %FR-5-DLCICHANGE: Interface Serial0/0  DLCI 200 state changed to
    ACTIVE
5d13h: %FR-5-DLCICHANGE: Interface Serial0/0  DLCI 200 state changed to
    INACTIVE
5d13h: %LINEPROTO-5-UPDOWN: Line protocol on Interface Serial0/0.1,
    changed state to down
```

Notice that when the subinterface is enabled using the ***no shut*** command, the subinterface attempts to become ACTIVE but changes state back to INACTIVE because the other end of the Frame Relay point-to-point connection has not been configured. The next step is to configure the other end on RouterC.

RouterC's Serial0/1 interface connects to the telco Frame Relay cloud as shown in Figure 8-11. The dlci assigned by the telco to this connection is 100. The commands for configuring RouterC are the same as for RouterB. The steps for configuring the serial interface and subinterface are shown next:

```
RouterC#conf t
Enter configuration commands, one per line. End with CNTL/Z.
RouterC(config)#int s0/1
RouterC(config-if)#encap frame-relay
RouterC(config-if)#no shut
RouterC(config-if)#int s0/1.1 point-to-point
RouterC(config-subif)#ip address 10.10.200.12 255.255.255.0
RouterC(config-subif)#no shut
RouterC(config-subif)#frame-relay interface-dlci 100
RouterC(config-fr-dlci)#
```

The running-configuration for the Serial1 interface on RouterC now shows the following. Don't forget to save the updates to NVRAM using the ***copy run start*** command.

```
!
interface Serial0/1
no ip address
!
interface Serial0/1.1 point-to-point
ip address 10.10.200.12 255.255.255.0
no arp frame-relay
frame-relay interface-dlci 100
!
```

Use the ***sh ip int br*** command to view the status of the interfaces as shown. The Serial0/1 interface is *up*, indicating there is a connection to the interface and the subinterface (serial 0/1.1) is also *up*, indicating the Frame Relay connection is up.

```
RouterC#sh ip int br
Interface          IP-Address     OK? Method Status                 Protocol
FastEthernet0/0    unassigned     YES unset  administratively down  down
Serial0/0          unassigned     YES unset  administratively down  down
Serial0/1          unassigned     YES unset  up                     up
Serial0/1.1        10.10.200.12   YES manual up                     up
```

The Frame Relay connection can be checked by pinging the IP address of the other subinterface (10.10.200.11) as shown here:

```
RouterC#ping 10.10.200.11
Type escape sequence to abort.
Sending 5, 100-byte ICMP Echos to 10.10.200.11, timeout is 2 seconds:
!!!!!
Success rate is 100 percent (5/5), round-trip min/avg/max    68/68/68 ms
```

The ping is successful, indicating that the Frame Relay connection has been properly configured. The command ***show frame-relay PVC*** is used to check packet delivery over the Frame Relay network.

```
RouterC#sh frame-relay pvc
PVC Statistics for interface Serial0/0 (Frame Relay DTE)
PVC Statistics for interface Serial0/1 (Frame Relay DTE)
DLCI = 100, DLCI USAGE = LOCAL, PVC STATUS = ACTIVE, INTERFACE = Ser-
   ial0/1.1
```

```
input pkts 206      output pkts 207      in bytes 16768
out bytes 16642     dropped pkts 0       in FECN pkts 0
in BECN pkts 0      out FECN pkts 0      out BECN pkts 0
in DE pkts 0        out DE pkts 0
out bcast pkts 190  out bcast bytes 14994
pvc create time 2d21h, last time pvc status changed 00:13:39
```

Networking Challenge—Frame Relay

Use the Network Challenge software to demonstrate that you can configure Frame Relay for RouterB and RouterC in the Frame Relay Network provided in Figure 8-11. Place the Networking CD-ROM in your computer's CD drive. Open the *Network Challenge* folder and click ***Net-Challenge.exe***. When the software is running, click the **Select Challenge** button to open a Select Challenge drop-down menu. Select **Chapter 8—Frame Relay**. This opens a checkbox that can be used to verify that you have completed all the tasks.

1. Enter the privileged EXEC mode on RouterB. Use the password Chile.
2. Enter the router configuration mode, Router(config).
3. Set the hostname to RouterB.
4. Enter the configuration mode for the serial 0/0 interface (Router B).
5. Set the encapsulation mode for the serial 0/0 interface to frame-relay.
6. Configure a point-to-point subinterface (0/0.1) on RouterB.
7. Configure the IP address for the subinterface on the serial 0/0 to 10.10.200.11 with a subnet mask of 255.255.255.0.
8. Configure RouterB's S0/0.1 frame-relay subinterface to use dlci 200.
9. Use the proper command to verify that RouterB is properly configured.
10. Enable the RouterB frame-relay subinterface.
11. Select Router C and enter RouterC's privileged EXEC mode. Use the password Chile.
12. Enter the router configuration mode, RouterC(config).
13. Set the hostname to RouterC.
14. Enter the configuration mode for the serial 0/1 interface (Router C).
15. Set the encapsulation mode for the serial 0/1 interface to frame-relay.
16. Configure a 0/1.1 subinterface point-to-point for the serial 1 interface on RouterB.
17. Configure the IP address for the RouterC subinterface on serial 0/1.1 to 10.10.200.12 with a subnet mask of 255.255.255.0.
18. Configure RouterC's S0/1.1 frame-relay subinterface to use dlci 100.
19. Use the proper command to verify that RouterC is properly configured.
20. Enable the RouterC frame-relay subinterface.
21. Use the *ping* command to verify that RouterB sees the 10.10.200.12 interface on RouterC.
22. Use the proper command to verify packet delivery over the Frame Relay network.

8-4   ATM

Asynchronous Transfer Mode (**ATM**) is a cell relay technique designed for voice, data, and video traffic. Cell relay is considered to be an evolution of **packet switching** in that packets or cells are processed at switching centers and directed to the best

ATM
Asynchronous transfer mode

Packet Switching
Packets are processed at switching centers and directed to the best network for delivery

network for delivery. The stations connected to an ATM network transmit octets (8 bits of data) in a cell that is 53 octets (bytes) long. Forty-eight bytes of the cell are for data (or **payload**) and five bytes are for the cell header. The ATM cell header contains the data bits used for error checking, virtual circuit identification, and payload type. All ATM stations are always transmitting cells, but the empty cells are discarded at the ATM switch. This provides more efficient use of the available bandwidth and allows for bursty traffic. Also, the station is guaranteed access to the network with a specified data frame size. This is not true for IP networks, where heavy traffic can bring the system to a crawl. The ATM protocol was designed for use in high-speed multimedia networking, including operation in high-speed data transmission from T1 up to T3, E3, and SONET. (SONET stands for synchronous optical network and is covered in Chapter 12.) The standard data rate for ATM is 155 Mbps, although the rates are continually evolving.

ATM is connection oriented, using two different types of connections, a **virtual path connection** (**VPC**) and a **virtual channel connection** (**VCC**). A virtual channel connection is used to carry the ATM cell data from user to user. The virtual channels are combined to create a virtual path connection, which is used to connect the end users. Virtual circuits can be configured as permanent virtual connections (PVCs) or they can be configured as switched virtual circuits (**SVCs**).

Five classes of services are available with ATM, based on the needs of the user. In some applications, users need a constant bit rate for applications such as teleconferencing. In another application, users might need only limited periods of higher bandwidth to handle bursty data traffic. The five ATM service classes are described in Table 8-5.

TABLE 8-5   The Five ATM Service Classes

ATM Service Class	Acronym	Description	Typical Use
constant bit-rate	CBR	Cell rate is constant	Telephone, video-conferencing television
Variable bit-rate/ non–real time	VBR-NRT	Cell rate is variable	Email
Variable bit-rate real time	VBR-RT	Cell rate is variable but can be constant on demand	Voice traffic
Available bit-rate	ABR	Users are allowed to specify a minimum cell rate	File transfers/ email
Unspecified bit-rate	UBR		TCP/IP

ATM uses an 8-bit virtual path identifier (**VPI**) to identify the virtual circuits used to deliver cells in the ATM network. A 16-bit virtual circuit identifier (**VCI**) is used to identify the connection between the two ATM stations. The VPI and VCI numbers are provided by the telco. Together the numbers are used to create an ATM PVC (permanent virtual circuit) through the ATM cloud as demonstrated in Figure 8-12.

The VPI/VCI numbers (1/33) shown in Figure 8-12 are for the ATM PVC interface. RouterA connects to the ATM cloud via an ATM physical interface on the router. RouterB also connects to the ATM cloud via an ATM physical interface on the router. In this example, the name for the physical interface on RouterA is ATM 4/0. This is comparable to the E0 name for the router's Ethernet0 interface.

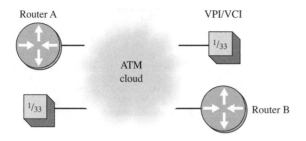

FIGURE 8-12 An example of a connection to an ATM cloud.

The following listing is from a router configured to run ATM:

```
Interface ATM 4/0
description net atm (1 2 3 4 5 6 7 8 9)
no ip address
atm scrambling cell-payload atm framing cbitplcp
no atm ilmi-keepalive
```

The first line, ***Interface ATM 4/0***, identifies the physical interface being configured, in this case ATM interface 4. The second line, ***description net atm (1 2 3 4 5 6 7 8 9)***, is a description of the ATM connection. The name of the connection is net; it is an ATM connection and the telco circuit number is 1 2 3 4 5 6 7 8 9. The third line, ***no ip address***, indicates that no IP address is specified for the ATM interface. The physical interface on an ATM connection is not assigned an IP address. The two commands ***atm scrambling cell-payload*** and ***atm framing cbitplcp*** are entries required to make the connection to the telco interface. Telco specifies the format for these commands. The entry ***no atm ilmi-keepalive*** is used to disable the generation of keepalive messages.

The next group of commands are used to configure the router's subinterface:

```
interface ATM4/0.33 point-to-point
description PVC to CityB (1 2 3 4 5 4 3 2 1)
ip address 192.168.23.1 255.255.255.0
pvc netB 1/33
vbr-nrt 3000 3000 1 broadcast encapsulation aal5snap
```

The entry ***interface ATM 4/0.33 point-to-point*** indicates that the VCI number for the subinterface is 33 and it is on the ATM 4 physical interface. It also indicates that this is a point-to-point connection. The second line is for the description of the subinterface. It indicates that this is a PVC for connecting to CityB's network, and the telco circuit number is 1 2 3 4 5 4 3 2 1. The third line specifies the IP address for the subinterface.

The entry ***pvc netB 1/33*** creates a PVC with a VPI of 1 and a VCI of 33.

The entry ***vdr-nrt 3000 3000 1*** is used to configure the peak, average, and burst options for voice traffic over the PVC. This parameter is typically specified by telco. The output pcr (peak cell rate) is 3000 kbps and the output scr (sustained cell rate) is 3000 kbps. The 1 indicates an output mbs (maximum burst size) of 1.

The entry ***broadcast*** enables broadcasts to be forwarded across the ATM PVC. The entry ***encapsulation aal5snap*** indicates that the ATM adaptation layer 5 is to be used to prepare the data for transmission over ATM. AAL5 encapsulation is typically specified to transport TCP/IP data traffic over ATM.

To display the ATM interfaces, enter the *show atm vc* router command as demonstrated in the following ouput:

```
router#sh atm vc
VCD/                                          Peak  Avg/Min Burst
Interface  Name      VPI  VCI  Type  Encaps  SC  Kbps  Kbps    Cells Sts
1/0.32     atmnorth  1    32   PVC   SNAP    UBR 100000               UP
1/0.33     2         1    33   PVC   SNAP    UBR 3000                 UP
1/0.34     6         1    34   PVC   SNAP    CBR 5000                 UP
salsa-backup#
```

The 1/0.32 indicates the this is the 1/0 physical interface and the .32 is the PVC. The type is a PVC (permanent virtual connection), the encapsulation is SNAP (the Subnetwork Access Protocol), the service class is UBR, which is an unspecified bit rate running TCP/IP. The bit rate is 100000 kbps and the status (Sts) is up.

The next command shows how to display only a specific atm virtual channel (vc); the command is *show atm vc interface atm1/0.33*. This command only displays the atm1/0.33 virtual channel. The types of atm interfaces typically listsed are DS3 (44.736 Mbps), OC-3 (155.52 Mbps) OC-12 (622.08 Mbps), and OC-192 (9953.28 Mbps).

```
router#sh atm vc interface atm1/0.33
VCD/                                          Peak  Avg/Min Burst
Interface  Name   VPI  VCI  Type Encaps SC  Kbps  Kbps   Cells  Sts
1/0.33     2      1    33   PVC  SNAP   UBR 3000                 UP
router#
```

The last command examined is used to display information on the interface. The command used is *show controller atm<slot/port>*. In this case, the information on the **atm1/0** interface is displayed. Part of the display for the **atm1/0** interface is listed.

```
router#sh controller atm1/0
Interface ATM1/0 is up
Hardware is ENHANCED ATM PA Plus - OC3 (155000Kbps)
Framer is PMC PM5346 S/UNI-155-LITE, SAR is LSI ATMIZER II
Firmware rev: X102, Framer rev: 0, ATMIZER II rev: 4
  idb=0x638A43E0, ds=0x638AC000, vc=0x638F76E0
  slot 1, unit 1, subunit 0, fci_type 0x03A9, ticks 226930
  2400 rx buffers: size=512, encap=64, trailer=28, magic=4
Curr Stats:
  VCC count: current=6, peak=6
  AAL2 VCC count: 0
  AAL2 TX no buffer count: 0
.
.
.
.
```

Establishing the ATM Connection

The previous discussion has defined what ATM is and how to display information about the interface on your router. The last discussion describes the steps required for establishing an ATM connection with the telco.

1. Determine the speed required for the ATM data connection. This will be based on the budget available for making the connection and the data bandwidth needs of the network.
2. Select the hardware to be used for making the ATM connection. This also depends on the budget available for the network connection and the data connection speed selected.

3. Order the ATM connection from the telco.
4. Telco will set up the ATM switch connection within the telco cloud and provide you with the circuit number. This includes the VPI# and the VCI#.
5. The next step is to configure the local hardware with the information provided by telco.
6. After completing the local ATM configuration, contact the telco and they will verify your settings and test the connection. After the telco completes their testing, the ATM connection is ready to use.

8-5   DIAL-IN ACCESS

This section addresses the technologies used to facilitate dial-in access to a network. This includes an overview of analog, digital, and hybrid techniques used for establishing a remote network connection via the telephone connection.

The limitations of a modem connection are first examined, followed by an overview of the V.92/V.90 standard (hybrid connection). Next, high-speed access is examined using cable modems, ISDN, and the latest in high-speed remote digital access, xDSL. This section concludes with the last piece needed for remote access, the remote access server. This includes the steps for setting up a Windows 2003 remote access server to accept dial-in access via a modem connection.

Analog Modem Technologies

The voice frequency (analog) channels of the public switched telephone network are used extensively for the transmission of digital data. Transporting data over analog channels requires that the data be converted to an analog form that can be sent over the bandwidth-limited line voice-grade channels. In voice-grade telephone lines, the bandwidth is limited by transformers, carrier systems, and line loading. Each of these factors contributes to attenuation of all signals below 300 Hz and above 3400 Hz. While the bandwidth from 300 to 3400 Hz is suitable for voice transmission, it is not appropriate for digital data transmission because the digital pulse contains *harmonics* (higher frequencies) well outside this range. To transmit data via a phone requires the conversion of a signal to fit totally within the 300 to 3400-Hz range. This conversion is provided by a modem.

There are currently two major modem standards for providing high-speed modem connections to an analog telephone line. These standards are **V.44/V.34**, which is totally analog and supports data rates up to 33.6 kbps, and **V.92/V.90**, which is a combination of digital and analog and supports data rates up to 56 kbps. The V.92/V.90 modem connection requires a V.92 or V.90-compatible modem and an Internet service provider (ISP) that has a digital line service back to the phone company. The data transfer with V.92/V.90 is called **asymmetric operation** because the data rate connection to the service provider is typically at V.34 speeds, whereas the data rate connection from the service provider is at the V.92/V.90 speed (56 kbps). The difference in the data rates in asymmetric operation is due to the noise introduced by the analog-to-digital conversion.

The modem link from your computer to the PSTN (your telephone connection) is typically analog. This analog signal is converted to digital at the phone company's central office. If the ISP has a digital connection to the phone company, an analog-to-digital conversion is not required. However, the signal from the ISP through the phone

V.44/V.34
The standard for all analog modem connections with a maximum data rate of up to 34 kbps; V.44 provides improved data compression, smaller file sizes that provide faster file transfers and improved Web browsing

V.92/V.90
The standard for a combination analog and digital modem connection with a maximum data rate of 56 kbps; V.92 provides a quick connect feature that cuts down on negotiation and handshake time compared to V.90

Asymmetric Operation
Describes the modem operation when the data transfer rates to and from the service provider differ

company is converted back to analog for reception by your modem. The digital-to-analog process does not typically introduce enough noise to affect the data rate. Figure 8-13 shows the digital–analog path for V.92/V.90.

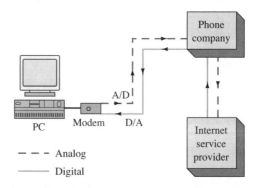

FIGURE 8-13   The digital-analog data path for V.92/V.90.

Cable Modems

Cable Modem
A modem that can use the high bandwidth of a cable television system to deliver high-speed data to and from the service provider

Ranging
A technique used by cable modems to determine the time it takes for data to travel to the cable head end

Cable modems provide an alternative way to access a service provider. Cable modems capitalize on their high-bandwidth network to deliver high-speed, two-way data. Data rates range from 128 kbps to 10 Mbps upstream (computer to the cable head end) and 10 to 30 Mbps downstream (cable head end back to the computer). The cable modem connections can also be one-way when the television service implemented on the cable system precludes two-way communications. In this case, the subscriber connects to the service provider via the traditional telephone and receives the return data via the cable modem. The data service does not impair the delivery of the cable television programming. Currently cable systems are using the Ethernet protocol to transfer the data over the network. Many subscribers use the same upstream connection. This leads to a potential collision problem, so a technique called **ranging** is used. With ranging, each cable modem determines the amount of time needed for its data to travel to the cable head end. This technique minimizes the collision rate, keeping it to less than 25 percent.

ISDN

ISDN
Integrated services digital network

The integrated services digital network (**ISDN**) is an established data communication link for both voice and data using a set of standardized interfaces. For businesses, the primary attractions are increased capability, flexibility, and decreasing cost. If one type of service—say, facsimile—is required in the morning and another in the afternoon—perhaps teleconferencing or computer links—it can easily shift back and forth. At present, the hookup for a given service might take a substantial time to complete. With ISDN, new capacities will be available just by asking for them through a terminal.

The ISDN contains four major interface points, as shown in Figure 8-14. The R, S, T, and U partitions allow for a variety of equipment to be connected into the system. Type 1, or TE1, equipment includes digital telephones and terminals that comply with ISDN recommendations. Type 2, or TE2, gear is not compatible with ISDN specifications. It needs a terminal adapter to change the data to channel rate. The TE2 equipment interfaces the network via the R interface point.

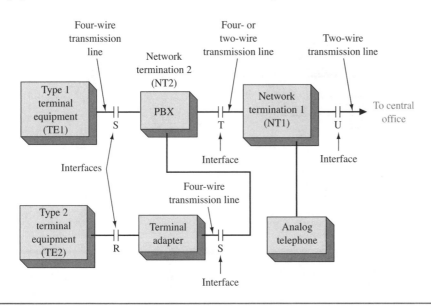

FIGURE 8-14 ISDN setup illustration of R, S, T, and U interfaces. (Source: *Modern Electronic Communication* 9/e, by G. M. Miller & J. S. Beasley, 2008, p. 499. Copyright © 2008 Pearson Education, Inc. Reprinted by permission of Pearson Education, Inc., Upper Saddle River, NJ.)

The ISDN standards also define two network termination (NT) points. NT1 represents the telephone company's network termination as viewed by the customer. NT2 represents the termination of such things as local area networks and private branch exchanges.

The customer ties in with the ISDN's NT1 point with the S interface. If an NT2 termination also exists, an additional T reference point linking both NT2 and NT1 will act as an interface; otherwise, the S and T reference points are identical. The CCITT recommendations call for both S and T reference points to be four-wire synchronous interfaces that operate at a basic access rate of 192 kbps. They are called the *local loop*.

Reference point U links NT1 points on either side of a pair of users over a two-wire 192-kbps span. The two termination points are essentially the central office switches. The ISDN specifications spell out a basic system as two B channels and one D channel (2B + D). The two B channels operate at 64 kbps each while the D channel is at 16 kbps, for a total of 144 kbps. The 48-kbps difference between the basic 192 kbps access rate and the 2B + D rate of 144 kbps is mainly for protocol signaling. The 2B + D channels are what the S and T four-wire reference points see. The B channels carry voice and data, while the D channel handles signaling, low-rate packet data, and low-speed telemetry transmissions.

The CCITT defines two types of communication channels from the ISDN central office to the user, the basic access and the primary access, as illustrated in Figure 8-15. The basic access service is the 192-kbps channel already discussed and serves small installations. The primary access channel has a total overall data rate of 1.544

Mbps and will serve installations with larger data rates. The channel contains 23 64-kbps B channels plus a 64-kbps D channel.

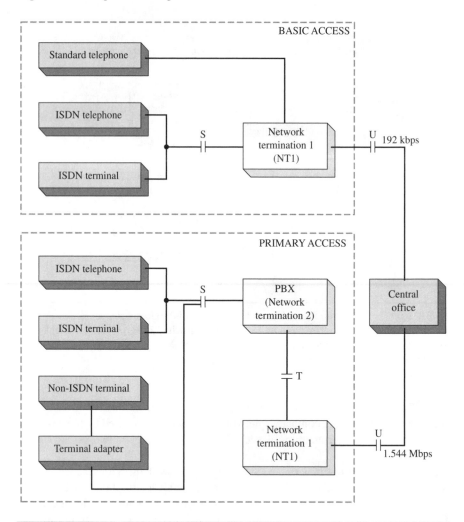

FIGURE 8-15 A basic and primary access ISDN system. (Source: *Modern Electronic Communication* 9/e, by G. M. Miller & J. S. Beasley, 2008, p. 500. Copyright © 2008 Pearson Education, Inc. Reprinted by permission of Pearson Education, Inc., Upper Saddle River, NJ.)

xDSL Modems

xDSL
A generic representation of the various DSL technologies that are available

DSL
Digital subscriber line

The **xDSL** modem is considered to be the next generation of high-speed Internet access technology. **DSL** stands for *digital subscriber line*, and the "x" generically represents the various types of DSL technologies that are currently available. The DSL technology uses existing copper telephone lines to carry data. Copper telephone lines can carry high-speed data over limited distances, and the DSL technologies use this trait to provide a high data rate connection. However, the actual data rate depends on the quality of the copper cable, the wire gauge, the amount of crosstalk, the presence of load coils, the bridge taps, and the distance of the phone service's central office.

DSL is the base technology in xDSL services. It is somewhat related to the ISDN service; however, the DSL technologies provide a significant increase in bandwidth and DSL is a point-to-point technology. ISDN is a switch technology and can experience traffic congestion at the phone service's central office. The available xDSL services and their projected data rates are provided in Table 8-6.

TABLE 8-6   xDSL Services and Data Rates

Technology	Data Rate	Distance Limitation
ADSL	1.5–8 Mbps downstream	18,000 ft
	Up to 1.544 Mbps upstream	
IDSL	Up to 144 kbps full duplex	18,000 ft
HDSL	1.544 Mbps full duplex	12,000 to 15,000 ft
SDSL	1.544 Mbps full duplex	10,000 ft
VDSL	13–52 Mbps downstream	1,000 to 4,500 ft
	1.5–2.3 Mbps upstream	

DSL services use filtering techniques to enable the transport of data and voice traffic on the same cable. Figure 8-16 shows an example of the ADSL frequency spectrum. Note that the voice channel, the upstream data connection (from the home computer), and the downstream data connection (from the service provider) each occupy their own portion of the frequency spectrum. **ADSL (asymmetric DSL)** is based on the assumption that the user needs more bandwidth to receive transmissions (down stream link) than for transmission (upstream link). ADSL can provide data rates up to 1.544 Mbps upstream 1.5 to 8 Mbps downstream.

ADSL (Asymmetric DSL)
A service providing up to 1.544 Mbps from the user to the service provider and up to 8 Mbps back to the user from the service provider

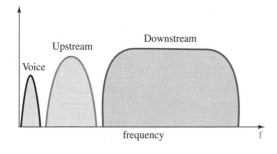

FIGURE 8-16   The ADSL frequency spectrum. (Source: *Modern Electronic Communication* 9/e, by G. M. Miller & J. S. Beasley, 2008, p. 502. Copyright ©2008 Pearson Education, Inc. Reprinted by permission of Pearson Education, Inc., Upper Saddle River, NJ.)

The bandwidth of a copper telephone line is limited to 300 to 3400 Hz. The xDSL services use special signal-processing techniques for recovering received data and a unique modulation technique for inserting the data on the line. For ADSL, a multicarrier technique called **discrete multitone (DMT)** modulation is used to carry the data over the copper lines. It is well understood that the performance of copper lines can vary from site to site. DMT uses a technique to optimize the performance of each site's copper telephone lines. The DMT modem can use up to 256 subchannel frequencies to carry the data over copper lines. A test is initiated at startup to determine which of the 256 subchannel frequencies should be used to carry the digital

Discrete Multitone (DMT)
A multicarrier technique used to transport digital data over copper telephone lines

data. The system then selects the best subchannels and splits the data over those available for transmission.

ADSL is receiving the most attention because its data modulation technique, DMT, is already an industry standard. Figure 8-17 provides an example of an xDSL network. The ADSL system requires an ADSL modem, which must be compatible with the service provider. Additionally, a POTS (Plain Old Telephone Service) splitter is required to separate the voice and data connection. The filter is placed inline with the phone connection to remove any of the high-frequency upstream data noise that gets into the voice frequency spectrum (refer to Figure 8-16). A filter is required for all telephone connections to eliminate noise interference any time a computer is in use on the connection.

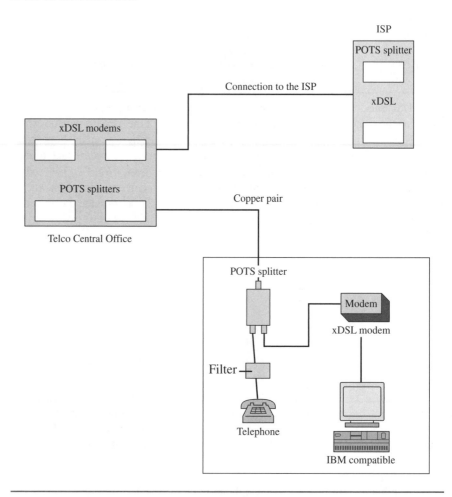

FIGURE 8-17   An xDSL connection to an ISP. *(Source: Modern Electronic Communication 9/e, by G. M. Miller & J. S. Beasley, 2008, p. 503. Copyright ©2008 Pearson Education, Inc. Reprinted by permission of Pearson Education, Inc., Upper Saddle River, NJ.)*

The Remote Access Server

The remote access server (**RAS**) is the last piece needed for completing a dial-up connection to the network. The remote access server provides a way for the outside user to gain access to a network. The connection to a RAS is typically provided through a telephone line provided by the PSTN (public switched telephone network); in other words, the basic telephone service. The dial-up connection could also be via cable modem, ISDN, or DSL technology.

The protocol typically used for connecting to a RAS is PPP (Point-to-Point Protocol), introduced in section 8-2. PPP helps establish the dial-up connection, manages data exchanges between the user and the RAS, and manages the data packets for delivery over TCP/IP.

The following steps describe how to configure RAS for a Windows 2003 server. The server connects to the PSTN through a modem (analog, cable, ISDN, DSL) to the telephone connection. The outside client also connects his or her PC to the PSTN through a modem. This is shown in Figure 8-18. The steps for the client-side configuration of a computer running Windows Vista, XP and Mac OS X are also provided.

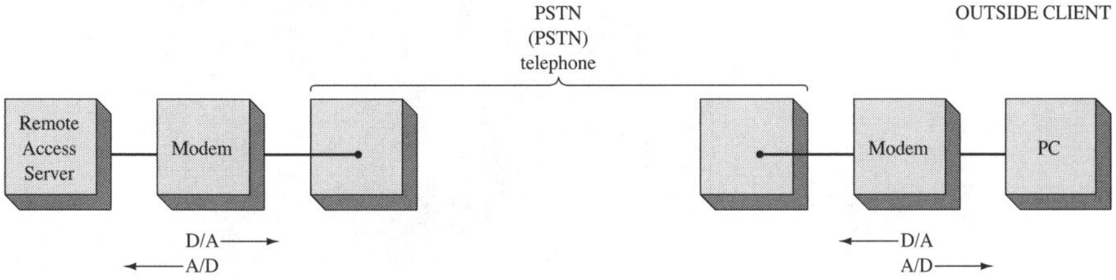

RAS
Remote access server

FIGURE 8-18   A RAS connection.

Configuring PPP Service in a Windows 2003 Server—RAS Setup   First click **Start—Programs—Control Panel—Administrative Tools—Routing and Remote Access**, as shown in Figure 8-19. The Routing and Remote Access window will come up. This is shown in Figure 8-20.

Note: There may be some minor differences displayed on your menu. When a difference occurs, follow the instructions on the menu being displayed.

To enable RAS, click **Action—Configure and Enable Routing**. The Action tab is at the upper-left of the menu. Right-click **Server Status** and **Add Server.** The This Computer option is highlighted. Click **OK**. Your computer's name will appear under Server Status. Right-click this newly created computer and select **Configure and Enable Remote Access**. This opens the Setup Wizard shown in Figure 8-21. Click **Next**. This opens the window shown in Figure 8-22. Select **Remote access server** and click **Next**.

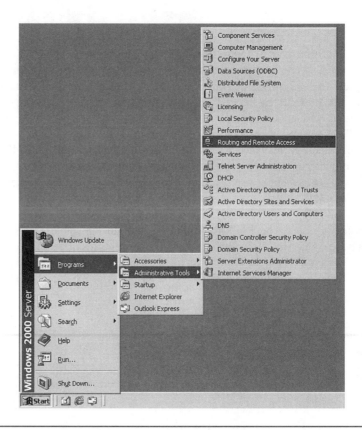

FIGURE 8-19   Starting the Remote Access Server configuration.

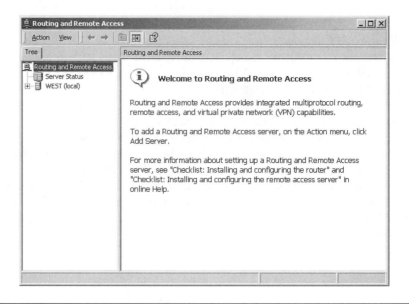

FIGURE 8-20   The Routing and Remote Access window.

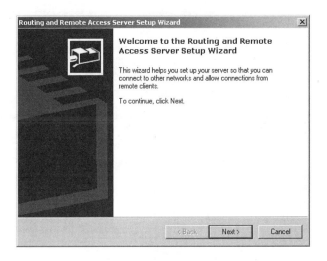

FIGURE 8-21   The Routing and Remote Access Server Setup Wizard menu.

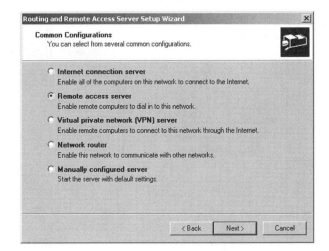

FIGURE 8-22   The window for selecting the Remote Access Server option.

The next screen (shown in Figure 8-23) is for selecting the protocols used for the remote clients. Make sure TCP/IP is selected and click **Next**. This opens the IP Address Assignment window, shown in Figure 8-24. In this example, **DHCP** (dynamic host control protocol) will be used to assign the IP address to the machine when a connection is established. Select **DHCP** and click **Next**.

DHCP
Dynamic Host Control Protocol

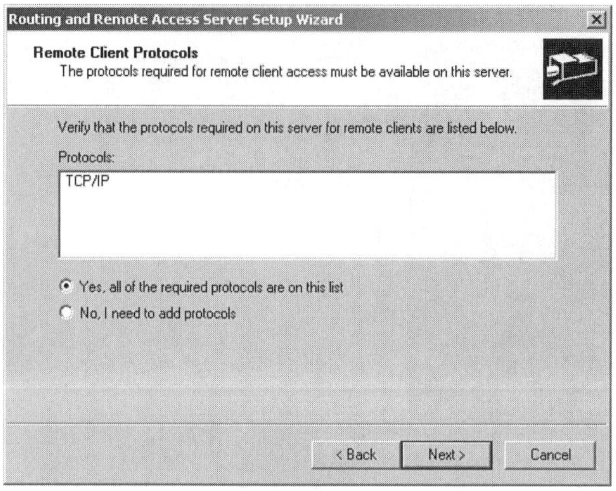

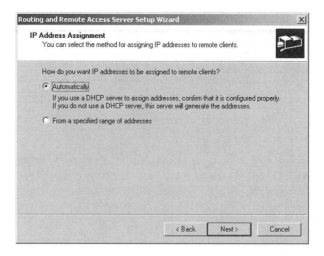

FIGURE 8-23   The window for selecting the remote client protocols.

FIGURE 8-24   The IP Address Assignment window.

The next window (Figure 8-25) is for selecting the management of multiple remote access servers. This option provides a way to centralize the RAS management. Choose the option to skip setting up a RADIUS server and click **Next**.

Windows will prompt you with a message about relaying DHCP messages. Click **OK** and the RAS server is installed.

RAS Configuration—Modem Configuration   The next steps describe the setup for the modem connection. From the main Windows 2003 screen, click **Start—Settings—Programs—Administrative Tools—Routing and Remote Access**. If the Ports window is not displayed, double-click the domain and click **Ports** on the left. The screen should look similar to Figure 8-26.

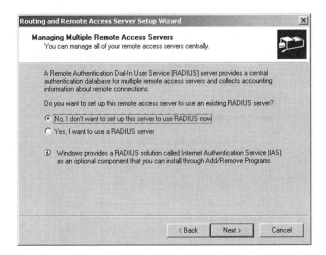

FIGURE 8-25 The Managing Multiple Remote Access Servers window.

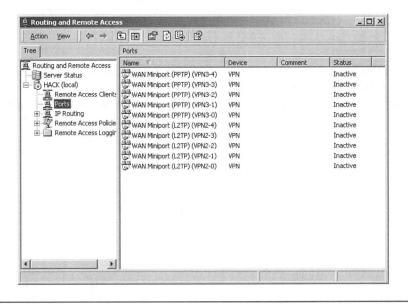

FIGURE 8-26 The Ports window.

Right-click **Ports** and click **Properties**. A list of devices should be displayed as shown in Figure 8-27. Your modem should be included in this list. Highlight the modem and click **Configure**. In this example, the Compaq Microm modem is selected.

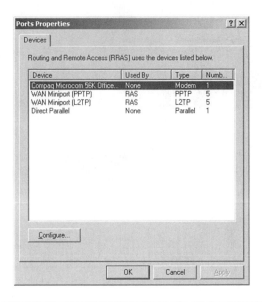

FIGURE 8-27   The Port Properties—Devices window.

Place a checkmark in the box for **Remote Access Connections**. Specify the phone number for the phone line the modem is connected to. This is shown in Figure 8-28. Click **OK** on the Configuration window and again on the Ports Properties screen to return to the Routing and Remote Access screen. Your modem should be listed among the ports. This is shown in Figure 8-29.

FIGURE 8-28   The window for specifying the phone number used by the modem.

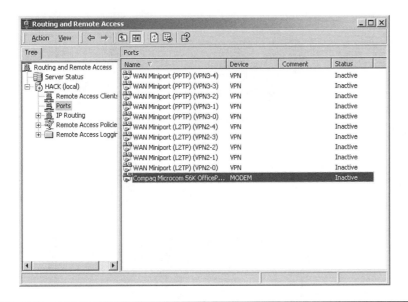

FIGURE 8-29   The addition of the modem to the Ports window.

IP Configuration   The next steps describe the setup for the IP address configuration. From the Routing and Remote Access window and under IP Configuration or IP Routing, right-click **DHCP Relay Agent** and go to **Properties**. This is shown in Figure 8-30. Type in the IP address of the DHCP server. Click **Add** and enter the IP address for the server. This is shown in Figure 8-31. In this example, the server's IP address is 10.10.20.19. Click **OK**. DHCP is now configured on the connection.

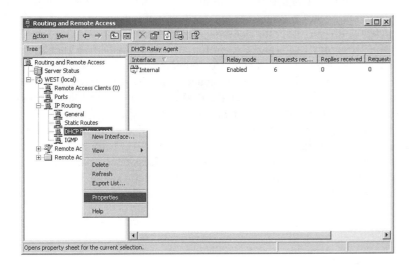

FIGURE 8-30   The steps for selecting the DHCP relay agent.

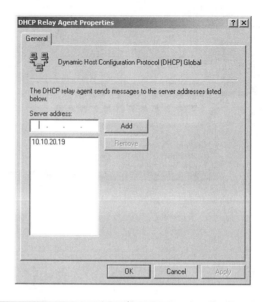

FIGURE 8-31   Specifying the IP address for the server.

Account Configuration   The next step is to establish a user account on the Windows server. (*Note:* Configuring users, computers, and groups for the Windows 2008/2003 server is examined in detail in Chapter 14.) Open the Active Directory Users and Computers window (**Start—Programs—Administrative Tools—Active Directory Users and Computers**). Click **Users** on the left of the menu. The screen will display a list of all the accounts on the system. An alternative method of doing this is to click **Start—Programs—Administrative Tools—Configure Your Server**. A configuration wizard will appear on the left side of the screen. Select **Active Directory**, scroll down to the bottom of the screen and start the wizard. You can also select **Active Directory Users and Computers** from **Adminstrative Tools**.

The Active Directory Users and Computers window is shown in Figure 8-32. We want to assign remote access permission to Administrator, so right-click **Administrator** and choose **Properties**. Click the **Dial-in** tab. Choose to **Allow Access** with **No Callback**, and click **OK**. The window is shown in Figure 8-33.

The last step in this process is to set the pool of IP addresses to be used by the remote access server. To do this, right-click the domain name (for example salsa) and click **Properties**. Next click the **IP** tab—**Static address pool—Add—Set range of IP addresses** and set the range of addresses. The Windows 2003 server will issue a default IP address in the 169.x.x.x range if this step is not completed.

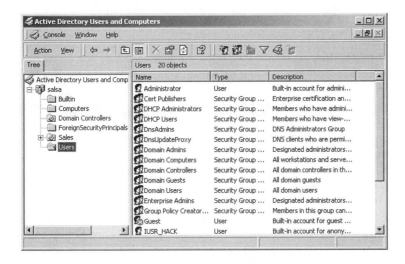

FIGURE 8-32   The Active Directory Users and Computers window.

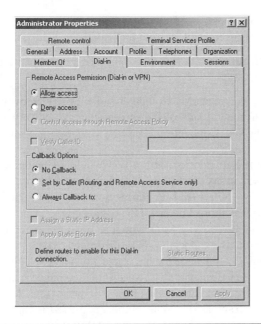

FIGURE 8-33   The Dial-in Administrator Properties window.

Client Configuration   The next step is to configuring the client-side computer for dial-up access. The steps for this vary for each operating system but the concepts are similar. The steps for client configuration in Windows Vista, Windows XP, and Mac OS X are presented.

Client Configuration in Windows Vista   To establish a dial-up network connection in Windows Vista, follow these steps:

1. Click the **Start** menu, and then select **Connect To**.
2. Select **Set-Up a Connection or network** at the bottom of the Network Connections window.
3. You are given a menu of choices for setting up the connection type, select **Set-up a dial-up connection** and click **Next**.
4. On the next screen, input the phone number for your dial-up connection, for example, 555-1212.
5. You will also need to input the username and password, and you will be asked to name the connection.
6. Click **Connect**; if your computer is connected to a phone line you should be able to establish a connection. If you are not connected, you will get a "Fail". If you are not ready to establish a phone connection, click **Set up connection anyway**. This will save your connection information.

To establish a Vista phone connection after completing the setup follow these steps:

1. Click the **Start** menu, and then select **Connect To**.
2. Select the dial-up connection from the list displayed, and then click **Connect**.

Client Configuration in Windows XP   This example is for setting up a new connection in Windows XP.

1. The first step is to open My Computer and click **My Network Places** in Windows XP. On the left side of the screen, click **View Network Connections**. Click **Create New Connection**. The New Connection Wizard will open. Click **Next** to proceed.
2. This opens the Network Connection Type window. Choose the option **Connect to the network at my workplace**, and click **Next**. This opens the network connection window. Select **Dial-up connection**. This enables a connection for use over a traditional phone line or ISDN. Click **Next**.
3. This opens the Connection Name window. Enter the name for the connection. In this example, the connection is to the server (Salsa); therefore, that is the name entered. Enter a name for the connection and click **Next**.
4. The next window displayed is for specifying the phone number being used to make the connection. Enter the phone number of the Windows 2003 RAS server. In this example, the phone number *555-2121* is entered. Click **Next**.
5. The next window is for connection availability. This option is used to restrict access to the dial-up connection or for anyone's use. Allow Windows to create the connection for **Anyone's use**. Click **Next**.
6. The next window is Completing the New Connection Wizard. The screen shows that a new connection to Salsa has been established. Click **Finish**.

The Connect window will come on the screen. Enter the administrator username and password. If you wish, you can save the username and password on the system to prevent it from prompting you each time you use the dial-up connection. Click **Dial** and the computer should connect to the server. You can then browse the network through Network Neighborhood.

Client Configuration in Mac OS X   The following are steps that can be used to establish a PPP modem connection using a Mac OS X computer.

1. Click **Apple—System Preferences—Network.** The Network menu should appear.
2. You can leave Location set to Automatic unless you plan to have more than one PPP connection.
3. Set Show to **Internal Modem**.
4. Click the **TCP/IP** tab and set configure to PPP.
5. Input the appropriate Domain Name Server (DNS) IP address.
6. Click **PPP** options and set according to your ISP's requirements.
7. Input the service provider name through which you will be connecting.
8. Input the telephone number for your modem connection. This is the phone number for your service provider.
9. Input the account name (username) and Password.
10. Verify your settings
11. Click the **Apply Now** button to save your changes.

To establish the modem connection for the Mac OS X, click **Macintosh HD—Applications—Interconnect Connect** and select **Internal Modem—Connect**. Note that the modem connection should open automatically anytime a network connection is requested.

8-6   VPN

This section introduces a technique for creating a virtual private network (**VPN**) by creating an IP tunnel on a router. An **IP tunnel** is the name given to the process of encapsulating an IP packet within another IP packet. It is used to create a virtual link from one IP end to the other. The physical interface to the VPN is through the router or through the Internet service provider. The goal of a VPN tunnel is to make the two ends of the connection appear as if they are on the same subnet. In other words, it makes the two ends behave as if they are connected via a point-to-point connection. Tunnels are sometimes used to facilitate network access for users in remote office networks or for remote users that travel a lot and need access to the network. For security and economic reasons, many network services, such as checking email, might not be accessible to clients not directly connected to the network. A tunnel makes the remote client appear as if it is directly connected to the network. In other words, the remote user becomes a virtual part of the network.

This section demonstrates how to configure a router-to-router VPN connection. The second demonstration explains how to configure a VPN tunnel from a remote PC to a VPN server. A drawing of a VPN is provided in Figure 8-34. The home network is RouterA, and RouterC is the remote user at the other end of the VPN.

VPN
Virtual private network

IP Tunnel
An IP packet encapsulated in another IP packet

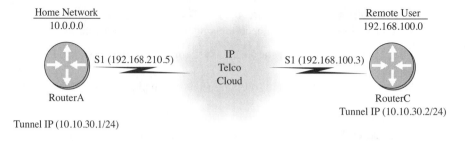

Home Network
10.0.0.0

S1 (192.168.210.5)

IP
Telco
Cloud

S1 (192.168.100.3)

Remote User
192.168.100.0

RouterA

RouterC
Tunnel IP (10.10.30.2/24)

Tunnel IP (10.10.30.1/24)

FIGURE 8-34 A virtual private network.

The objective is to establish a tunnel through the IP telco cloud to connect RouterA with RouterC. This requires that the source and destination addresses of the physical network connection be defined. In this figure, RouterA connects to the telco cloud via the router's Serial 0/1 interface. The IP address of 192.168.210.5 with a subnet mask of 255.255.255.0 has been assigned to the RouterA Serial1 interface. RouterC (the remote router) connects to the telco cloud via its Serial 0/1 interface. The IP address assigned to RouterC's Serial1 interface is 192.168.100.3 with a subnet mask of 255.255.255.0. (*Note:* Any interface that connects to the telco cloud can be used to set up the VPN interface.) A tunnel is next established on each of the routers. The tunnel is assigned an IP address that is used in the home network. For example, the home network is a 10.0.0.0 network; therefore, the tunnel between RouterA and RouterC will have a 10.x.x.x IP address. The tunnel between RouterA and RouterC is called *tunnel 0* and is assigned IP addresses of 10.10.30.1 and 10.10.30.2. After the tunnel has been created across the IP network, the two routers appear to be on the same 10.10.30.x network.

The tunnel connection makes remote users appear as if they are part of the home network. This is accomplished by encapsulating the IP packet. The first packet uses the IP address that the remote user will use after the connection has been made. The encapsulation is used to transport the data across the networks.

An example of a tunnel encapsulation is provided in Figure 8-35. Figure 8-35 (a) shows the basic IP packet. The source and destination IP address for the packet are listed. The source IP address for the remote tunnel is 10.10.30.2. The IP tunnel address for the home router interface is 10.10.30.1. This is the destination IP address. Figure 8-35 (b) shows the layer of encapsulation for the VPN tunnel. The source IP address of 192.168.100.3 is for RouterC's Serial 0/1 interface. The destination IP address of 192.168.210.5 is for the home network's RouterA Serial 0/1 interface.

The 192.168.100.3 and 192.168.210.5 IP addresses are used to deliver the VPN encapsulated data packets over a TCP/IP network. When a packet is delivered to the destination, the encapsulation layer is removed and the data packet will appear as if it came from the home 10.10.30.x network. Remember, the original packet, shown in Figure 8-35 (a), contains the IP addresses for the VPN tunnel and the encapsulation layer [Figure 8-35 (b)] includes the actual physical interface IP addresses for the VPN tunnel.

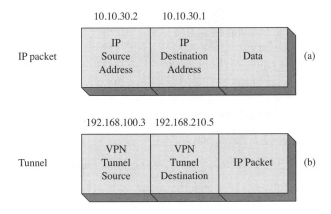

FIGURE 8-35   Data encapsulation for VPN data packets.

Configuring a VPN Virtual Interface (Router to Router)

In this example, a VPN virtual interface will be configured on two routers on two separate networks. Figure 8-36 provides an illustration of the VPN. This example simu-
lates a situation in which a VPN virtual interface is to be established between two
networks. This requires that a virtual interface be established on the home router,
RouterA, and the remote user on RouterC in Figure 8-36. The tunnels on each router
will be called *tunnel 0*. These act like a physical interface, and each has its own IP address. The difference is the tunnels require a source and destination IP address for the
tunnel. The source and destination addresses are the physical addresses (IP addresses)
for the serial interfaces on each router that connect to the telco cloud.

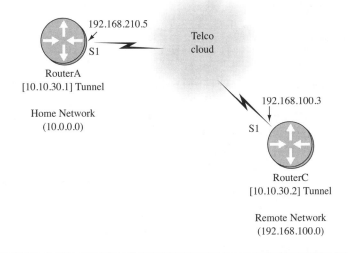

FIGURE 8-36   A virtual private network.

Make sure routing has been properly configured for each router in the network, the interfaces have been assigned an IP address, and the destination physical address from each end can be pinged prior to setting up the VPN interface and the tunnel. For example, RouterA can ping the remote network router (RouterC) using the command ***ping 192.168.100.3***. Remember, the IP address for the serial interface is being pinged, and the virtual interfaces have not yet been configured.

```
RouterA#ping 192.168.100.3
Type escape sequence to abort.
Sending 5 100-byte ICMP Echos to 192.168.100.3, timeout is 2 seconds:
!!!!!
Success rate is 100 percent (5/5), round-trip min/avg/max 52/56/72 ms
```

The successful ping indicates that there is a network connection between RouterA on the home network (192.168.210.0) and RouterC on the remote network (192.168.100.0). The next step is to configure the tunnel to establish a virtual private network between the two networks.

A tunnel is added to the router from the configuration mode **(config)#**. The command ***int tunnel0*** is entered to configure the tunnel interface. This places the router in the interface configuration mode—**(config-if)#**. The next step is to configure the virtual IP address to be used by the VPN tunnel. The IP address for the VPN tunnel must be on the same subnet as the home network IP address. For example, the home network is from the 10.0.0.0 network. In this case, the tunnel 0 interface on RouterA will be assigned an IP address of 10.10.30.1. The following shows the two steps for configuring the IP tunnel:

```
RouterA(config)#int tunnel0
RouterA(config-if)#ip 10.10.30.1 255.255.255.0
```

The next step is to define the IP destination and source address for the tunnel created on the home network router, RouterA. Referring to Figure 8-35, the source IP address for tunnel 0 from RouterA is 192.168.210.5 and the destination IP address for the remote interface on RouterC is 192.168.100.3. After configuring the tunnel source and destination IP addresses, the router prompts that the "line protocol on Interface Tunnel0" changed state to *up*:

```
RouterA(config-if)#tunnel destination 192.168.100.3
RouterA(config-if)#tunnel source 192.168.210.5
00:31:37: %LINEPROTO-5-UPDOWN: Line protocol on Interface Tunnel0,
    changed state to up
```

The command ***sh ip int brief*** can be used to check the configuration for the tunnel interface as shown. A tunnel will show status *up* and protocol *up* even if it is not actually up. In this case, the other end of the tunnel connection has not yet been configured. The only way to really test the virtual link is with a ***ping***. This will be demonstrated after the remote router (RouterC) is configured.

```
RouterA#sh ip int brief
Interface        IP-Address      OK?  Method  Status  Protocol
FastEthernet0/0  10.10.20.250    YES  NVRAM   up      up
Serial0/0        10.10.100.10    YES  NVRAM   up      down
Serial0/1        192.168.210.5   YES  NVRAM   up      up
Tunnel0          10.10.30.1      YES  manual  up      up
```

The Serial1 interface shows status *up* and protocol *up*. This is the connection to the communications carrier (telco), and this interface must be up for the tunnel to work. The command ***sh int tunnel 0*** can be used to check to see whether tunneling has been con figured on the router.

```
RouterA#sh int tunnel 0
Tunnel0 is up, line protocol is up
Hardware is Tunnel
Internet address is 10.10.30.1/24
MTU 1514 bytes, BW 9 Kbit, DLY 500000 usec, rely 255/255, load 1/255
Encapsulation TUNNEL, loopback not set, keepalive set (10 sec) Tunnel
    source 192.168.210.5, destination 192.168.100.3
Tunnel protocol/transport GRE/IP, key disabled, sequencing disabled
Checksumming of packets disabled, fast tunneling enabled
Last input never, output 00:00:01, output hang never Last clearing of
    "show interface" counters never Queueing strategy: fifo
Output queue 0/0, 0 drops; input queue 0/75, 0 drops
5 minute input rate 0 bits/sec, 0 packets/sec
5 minute output rate 0 bits/sec, 0 packets/sec
0 packets input, 0 bytes, 0 no buffer
Received 0 broadcasts, 0 runts, 0 giants, 0 throttles
0 input errors, 0 CRC, 0 frame, 0 overrun, 0 ignored, 0 abort
20 packets output, 1200 bytes, 0 underruns
0 output errors, 0 collisions, 0 interface resets
0 output buffer failures, 0 output buffers swapped out
```

The following output is a portion of the configuration file displayed using the *show run* command. This output shows that the tunnel has been configured on RouterA.

```
RouterA#sh run
.
.
!
!
interface Tunnel0
ip address 10.10.30.1 255.255.255.0
 no ip directed-broadcast tunnel source 192.168.210.5
 tunnel destination 192.168.100.3
!
!
RouterC#conf t
.
.
```

The next step is to configure the remote user on RouterC. First, enter the router's configuration mode using the *conf t* command. Remember, RouterC's connection to the telco cloud has already been established and a connection verified using the *ping* command. Recall that the IP address of 192.168.100.3 was pinged from RouterA. Next, enter the configuration for the tunnel 0 interface using the *int tunnel 0* command. At the **(config-if)#** prompt, enter the source and destination addresses for tunnel 0 as shown in the following code:

```
Enter configuration commands, one per line. End with CNTL/Z.
RouterC(config)#int tunnel 0
RouterC(config-if)#ip address 10.10.30.2 255.255.255.0
RouterC(config-if)#tunnel destination 192.168.210.5
RouterC(config-if)#tunnel source 192.168.100.3
```

The configuration for the interfaces can be checked using the *sh ip int brief* command as shown in the following. Note that the tunnel is listed as a separate interface on the router:

```
RouterC#sh ip int brief
Interface       IP-Address      OK? Method Status                Protocol
FastEthernet0/0 unassigned      YES not set administratively down down
Serial0/0       192.168.100.3   YES manual  up                    up
Serial0/1       unassigned      YES not set administratively down down
Tunnel0         10.10.30.2      YES manual  up                    up
```

The following output is a portion of the configuration file displayed using the *show run* command. This output shows that the tunnel has been configured on RouterC.

```
RouterC#sh run
.
.
!
!
interface Tunnel0
ip address 10.10.30.2 255.255.255.0
 no ip directed-broadcast tunnel source 192.168.100.3
 tunnel destination 192.168.210.5
!
!
.
.
```

Each end of the VPN has now been configured. The next step is to check the link using the *ping* command. The VPN tunnel virtual address of 10.10.30.2 is pinged from computer A as shown next:

```
RouterA#ping 10.10.30.2
Type escape sequence to abort.
Sending 5 100-byte ICMP Echos to 10.10.30.2, timeout is 2 seconds:
!!!!!
Success rate is 100 percent (5/5), round-trip min/avg/max 80/80/84 ms
```

The *ping* shows that a virtual connection has been established between the remote user and the home network router. An interesting test of the network is to compare the results of running a traceroute from the home network to the remote user using the IP address for the remote user's router interface [192.168.100.3] and then running a traceroute from the home network to the remote user's VPN tunnel address [10.10.30.2]. The results of the test are shown here:

Traceroute to the physical IP address

```
RouterA#trace 192.168.100.3
Type escape sequence to abort. Tracing the route to 192.168.100.3
1 192.168.210.5 16 msec 16 msec 16 msec
2 192.168.100.3 32 msec 32 msec *
```

Traceroute to the VPN tunnel IP address

```
RouterA#trace 10.10.30.2
Type escape sequence to abort.
Tracing the route to 10.10.30.2
1 10.10.30.2 48 msec 48 msec *
```

The results of the first trace show that it takes two hops to reach the destination. In fact, a traceroute to the physical IP address will typically show multiple router hops. The test on the VPN tunnel shows that the trace took only one hop because the remote end of the VPN tunnel is configured to be directly connected to the home "10" network. The trace route on a VPN tunnel from a home router to the remote user will show only one hop.

This section has described how to configure a VPN tunnel link. The commands for configuring and verifying the link have been discussed. The following describes steps for troubleshooting a VPN tunnel link if problems should occur.

Troubleshooting the VPN Tunnel Link

The following list are steps used to verify that the VPN tunnel is properly configured:

1. Confirm connection to the physical interface's IP address using a *ping*.
2. Check the source and destination IP addresses of the tunnel configured on the router.
3. Make sure the IP addresses on the ends of the tunnel are in the same subnet.
4. *ping* the destination from the source.
5. Use *show run* to make sure the source and destinations are properly configured.
6. If the problem is not found, try rebooting the routers.

This example has shown how a VPN tunnel can be established using two routers. This situation is appropriate for establishing a permanent VPN connection to a remote user, such as a remote office for a company. However, a remote user who travels will have to establish a VPN connection directly from his or her PC, through an ISP and the VPN server in the home network. This requires that the remote user use software that runs either the **PPTP** (Point-to-Point Tunneling Protocol) or **L2TP** (Layer 2 Tunneling Protocol). An example of the setup for a remote client's VPN connection is graphically shown in Figure 8-37.

PPTP
Point-to-Point Tunneling Protocol

L2TP
Layer 2 Tunneling Protocol

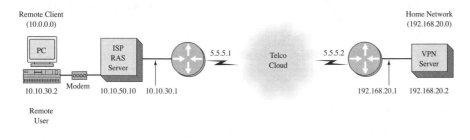

FIGURE 8-37   A remote client VPN connection.

Configuring a VPN Server

Configuring a Windows 2003 VPN server is fairly simple and only requires the routing and remote access server configuration be started by clicking **Start—Programs—Administrative Tools—Routing and Remote Access**. Right-click the server name and select **Configure and Enable Routing and Remote Access**. Follow the installation steps and choose the manually configured server option. Select **Virtual Private Network (VPN) Server** from the Common Configurations menu. The last step in this process is to set the pool of IP addresses to be used by the VPN server. To do this, right-click the server name and select **Properties**, click the **IP** tab and select **Static Address Pool—Add—Set range of IP addresses and input the desired IP address range**. The Windows 2003 server will issue a default IP address in the 169.x.x.x range if this step is not completed and your client computers will be assigned an IP address that is not valid for your network.

Configuring a Remote Client's VPN Connection

The following examples demonstrate how to configure a VPN remote client running Windows Vista, XP, or Mac OS X. These examples assume that the client has permission to connect to the VPN server on your home network.

Windows Vista—VPN Client   To start the Windows Vista VPN client configuration complete the following steps:

1. Click **Start** and select **Connect To**, then select **Set-up a connection or network**.
2. Select **Connect to a workplace** and click **Next**.
3. You may get a prompt that asks, "Do you want to use a connection that you already have?" If so, select **No, create new connection**, click **Next**, and select **Use my Internet Connection (VPN)**.
4. In the next step you will be asked to input the Internet address or the name of the VPN server.
5. In the Destination Name field, enter the name for the VPN connection (for example, salsa-vpn).
6. In the User Name field, enter the username for your VPN account. This is the account name set up on the VPN server.
7. In the Domain field, enter the name of your domain.
8. Click the **Create** and **Close** buttons to complete the setup.
9. When the setup is complete, you can establish a VPN connection by clicking **Start—Connect To**, then right-clicking the VPN connection you just created and selecting **Properties**.
10. Next, click the **Networking** tab. This gives you the option of selecting the type of VPN security. Select the type that matches the requirements for your VPN connection.

Windows XP—VPN Client

1. Click **Start—Control Panel—Network and Internet connections—Network Connections**. This opens the Network Connection window. Select **Virtual Private Network** connection. You will be asked to input a connection name for the VPN connection. This example uses the name *VPN-Remote*. Click **Next**. This opens the Public Network Connection menu. You will be asked how you are to connect to the public network. Select either **Do not dial** or **Automatically dial** based on your need. Click **Next.**
2. The next menu is for specifying the IP address of the VPN server on the home network.
3. Click **Next** and you should be notified that installation is complete. Click **Finish**.

The setup for the VPN connection is now complete for the Windows XP remote client. To start a VPN connection, click **Start—Control Panel—Network and Internet connections—Network Connections**. Select the VPN-Remote connection just created by double-clicking the icon. You will see a prompt that states that to connect to VPN-Remote you must first connect to your Internet or dial-in connection. Click **Yes**. You will be asked to input the username and password for the dial-in connection. Click the **Dial** button. After the network connection is established a new window, **Connect VPN-Remote**, will appear. Enter the username and password for the VPN connection and click **Connect**.

Mac OS X—VPN Client

1. Double-click **Mactintosh HD—Applications—Internet Connect**. This opens the Internet Connect window.
2. Click the VPN icon at the top of the Internet Connect window.
3. Make sure the settings for the tunneling are properly set to PPTP or L2TP depending on the server configuration.
4. Enter the VPN server address, your username, and password. Click **Connect** to test the connection.
5. Next, quit the Internet Connect application. You will be prompted to save the configuration and you will be asked for a name for the VPN connection. This will be the name of the VPN connection you will use to establish a VPN connection.

After completing the VPN setup, VPN connections can be established by double-clicking **Mactintosh HD—Applications—Internet Connect**. You can also establish the VPN connection by clicking the VPN icon at the top of your Mac OS X main screen. You should connect to the VPN server if your network and server are working.

The VPN connection to the home network VPN server should now be made. Remember, the remote client must have a user account and password on the Window 2008/2003 VPN server. In this example, the user's account name is *jtest*. The IP address of 192.168.20.31 is assigned to the VPN remote client by the VPN server when a connection is made. The available IP addresses were specified when the VPN server was configured. Running a ***tracert*** (traceroute) from the VPN server (192.168.20.2) to the client on the VPN network (192.168.20.31) shows a single hop. The VPN remote client appears to be on the same home network. The traceroute is shown in Figure 8-38.

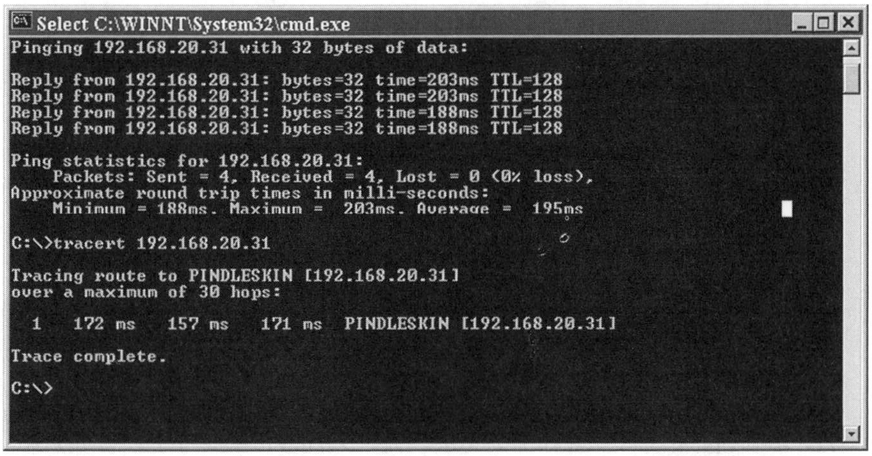

```
Select C:\WINNT\System32\cmd.exe
Pinging 192.168.20.31 with 32 bytes of data:

Reply from 192.168.20.31: bytes=32 time=203ms TTL=128
Reply from 192.168.20.31: bytes=32 time=203ms TTL=128
Reply from 192.168.20.31: bytes=32 time=188ms TTL=128
Reply from 192.168.20.31: bytes=32 time=188ms TTL=128

Ping statistics for 192.168.20.31:
    Packets: Sent = 4, Received = 4, Lost = 0 (0% loss),
Approximate round trip times in milli-seconds:
    Minimum = 188ms, Maximum = 203ms, Average =  195ms

C:\>tracert 192.168.20.31

Tracing route to PINDLESKIN [192.168.20.31]
over a maximum of 30 hops:

  1    172 ms    157 ms    171 ms  PINDLESKIN [192.168.20.31]

Trace complete.

C:\>
```

FIGURE 8-38   The traceroute from the VPN server to the VPN remote client.

IPsec
Used to encrypt data between various networking devices

Cisco VPN Client   This section examines setting up an end-to-end encrypted VPN connection using the Cisco VPN Client software. These connections can be used for both on-site and mobile (remote) users. The Cisco VPN Client uses **IPsec** with the option of two encryption modes: tunnel and transport. The tunnel mode encrypts the header and the data (payload) for each packet. The transport mode only encrypts the data (payload). IPsec can be used to encrypt data between various networking devices such as PC to server, PC to router, and router to router.

The first step for setting up the Cisco VPN Client is to install the software on the server that is to be used to establish the VPN connections. The Cisco VPN Client software must be licensed for each server installation. After the software is installed on the server, the clients connect to the server and download the Cisco VPN Client software. The individual requesting the software must have network access to the software. This usually requires that the user must have an authorized username and password. The next step is to install the client software. After the software is installed, start the Cisco VPN Client software by clicking **Start—Programs—Cisco VPN Client**.

The first window displayed after starting the VPN client is show in Figure 8-39. This window indicates that the current status is Disconnected. Click in the **Connection Entries** tab. This will list the configured connections for establishing the VPN connection. *Note:* The Cisco VPN Client software will automatically set up the connections available for the client. The available connections for the client are configured when the server software is installed. An example is shown in Figure 8-40. Select the desired link by double-clicking **Connection Entry**. The next window displayed will be the initial handshake screen as shown in Figure 8-41.

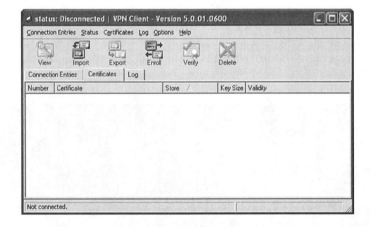

FIGURE 8-39   The first window, the VPN Client window, is displayed after starting the VPN client software. This window is showing that the current status is Disconnected.

The next window (Figure 8-42) shows that you have connected to the Virtual Private Network. It says Welcome to Chile-VPN — the Chile-Virtual Private Network.

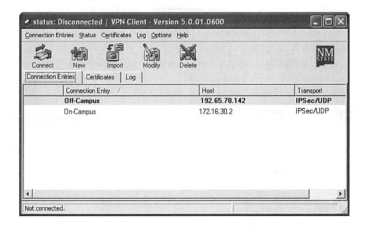

FIGURE 8-40   The listing of the available connections for establishing the VPN link.

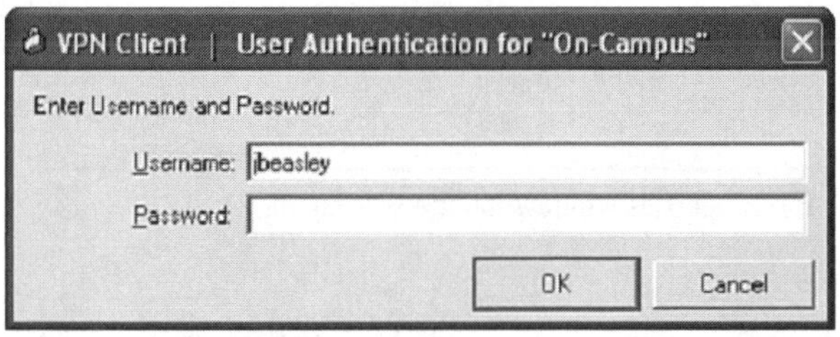

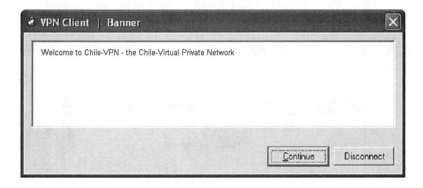

FIGURE 8-41   The initial handshake screen for the VPN client.

FIGURE 8-42   The welcome menu for Chile-VPN — the Chile Virtual Private Network.

After the VPN connection has been established you can click the VPN Client icon that should be displayed in the bottom right of your computer screen. Select the connection (for example, Chile-VPN). The properties for Chile-VPN will be displayed as shown in Figure 8-43 (a). This window shows that Group Authentication has been selected. Additionally, the group name and password are entered. In this case, all authorized users are using the same group name and password. This username and password enables the user to access the VPN but the user will have to enter an authorized username and password to actually establish a VPN connection. The certification authentication is used to verify whether the client is authorized to establish the VPN. The client must have this in their computer (installed or downloaded). This is the first step before the VPN tunnel is set up. Figure 8-43 (b) shows additional properties for the VPN connection. This window indicates that IPsec over UDP has been selected.

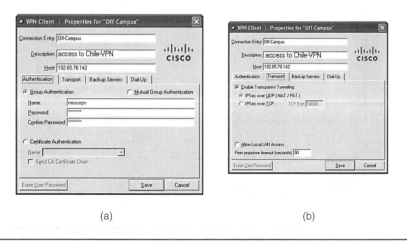

(a)   (b)

FIGURE 8-43   The Properties window for the VPN client.

The next window, shown in Figure 8-44, lists the statistics for the VPN session. The IP addresses for both the VPN server and client are listed. This screen indicates that a 168-bit 3-DES encryption is being used and the authentication type is HMAC-MD5. 3-DES is called Triple DES, and it uses the same procedure as DES except the encryption procedure is repeated three times, hence the name. HMAC-MD5 (the keyed-Hash Message Authentication Code) is a type of message authentication code (MAC) that is being used with the MD5 cryptographic function. This window also shows that UDP port 10000 is being used.

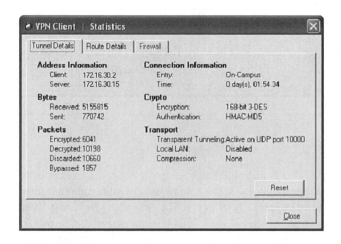

FIGURE 8-44   The Statistics window for the VPN client.

This section has demonstrated the setup and configuration of three different types of VPN connections. The first presented was a router-to-router VPN tunnel. The next was setting up a VPN link from a VPN client to a VPN server. The client configuration was demonstrated for Windows Vista/XP and Mac OS X. The last configuration was using the Cisco VPN Client software. This requires setting up the software on both a server and client computer. Each type of VPN connection has its use, and the network administrator must be familiar with each approach.

8-7   WIDE AREA NETWORK ROUTING

This section and section 8-8 examine the routing issues for wide area network (WAN) and Internet routing. Sections 8.2–8.6 examined applications of the communication technologies and making the connections to the networks being used when configuring WANs. The focus has been on the major WAN communication technologies and WAN networks currently in use.

WAN connections typically link remote sites and branch offices to the main network. These links usually have slower connection speeds than LAN connections and usually incorporate smaller and less powerful routers. It is critical that the network administrator be aware of these limited resources when choosing a routing protocol for a link to a WAN.

The easiest routing protocol for WAN links is the *static route*. At the main site you need a static route for each subnet at the remote end, as shown in Figure 8-45. At the remote site you also need a default static route. Each remote site router has a static route, attached to the network's WAN router, that goes back to the main network. No routing updates are passed across the link, and the routing table is very small and takes up very little memory in the router. This works well for single connections to the remote sites, as shown in Figure 8-45. For multiple connections you should use a dynamic routing protocol such as OSPF or EIGRP.

When choosing the routing protocol you must be cautious about the amount of routing updates traversing the link. Remember that distance vector protocols send the entire routing table at set intervals. RIP typically sends routing table updates every 30 seconds. This is an issue when large routing tables are exchanged. In some cases, the exchange of the routing table traffic could consume more than an acceptable amount of data bandwidth. OSPF and EIGRP are more desirable protocols because they send updates only when routing changes occur.

The size of the router at the remote site will also play a part in the routing protocols you implement. The amount of memory in the remote routers is usually smaller than in the LAN routers. Therefore, the size of the routing table that can be passed to the remote site might need to be smaller than the routing table at the LAN site. Access lists (see Chapter 10) can be used to filter out routes passed to the remote sites. Route filters or access lists are implemented in most modern routers, including Cisco routers. The procedures for configuring access lists are examined in Chapter 10. Some routing protocols, such as OSPF, have built-in functions to filter out routes. These are called **stubby areas** and **totally stubby areas**. Stubby areas give only interarea routes and do not accept routes from the external network, that is, routes from the Internet. Totally stubby areas use only a default route to reach destinations external to the autonomous system (AS). For a more detailed discussion of route filters and OSPF routing, you should seek out a routing reference book.

Stubby Areas
Do not accept routes from the Internet

Totally Stubby Areas
Use only a default route to reach destinations external to the autonomous system

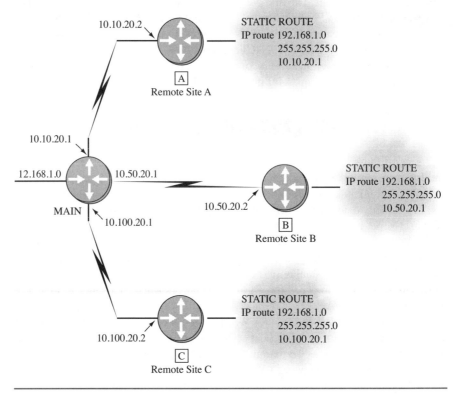

10.10.20.2

STATIC ROUTE
IP route 192.168.1.0
                255.255.255.0
                10.10.20.1

A
Remote Site A

10.10.20.1

12.168.1.0

10.50.20.1

MAIN

10.50.20.2

STATIC ROUTE
IP route 192.168.1.0
                255.255.255.0
                10.50.20.1

B
Remote Site B

10.100.20.1

10.100.20.2

STATIC ROUTE
IP route 192.168.1.0
                255.255.255.0
                10.100.20.1

C
Remote Site C

FIGURE 8-45   An example of configuring the static routes for the remote ends on a WAN.

8-8   INTERNET ROUTING

BGP
Border Gateway Protocol

Configuring an Internet connection is similar to configuring a WAN connection. The Internet connection can use the same type of link. For example, the link to the Internet could be made using a T1 connection or a high-speed link such as a DS-3 (44.7 Mbps) or OC-3 (155 Mbps). WAN connections typically connect sites that belong to the same organization, such as a branch office of a business. Internet connections are usually between an Internet service provider (ISP) and its customers. Typically, the ISP and its customers do not use routing protocols such as OSPF for the Internet connection because these protocols do not scale well to this type of implementation. Instead, the two main routing protocol options that are available for making the Internet connection to the ISP are static routes and **BGP**, the Border Gateway Protocol.

Multi-homed
This means the customer has more than one Internet connection.

Static routes are implemented in the same fashion as in the WAN routing section. The procedure for configuring static routes was presented in Chapter 7. Static routes are used only when the customer has a single Internet connection. If the customer is **multi-homed**, meaning the customer has more than one Internet connection, BGP is used. The most current version of BGP is version 4. An example of a single and multi-homed customer is provided in Figure 8-46.

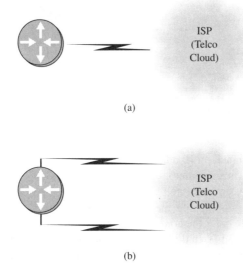

(a)

(b)

FIGURE 8-46   An example of (a) a single Internet connection and (b) a customer that is multi-homed.

BGP is considered to be an external routing protocol. This protocol is designed for routing between separate organizational networks. The BGP term for these networks is *autonomous systems*, or **AS**. An AS is assigned an AS number (**ASN**) by the same organization that assigns North American IP addresses, ARIN. The ASN has a different use than the ASN used in such IGP protocols as EIGRP and IGRP. The ASN in BGP is used to distinguish separate networks and to prevent routing loops. Each router participating in BGP must manually make a **peering** with its BGP neighbor. Peering is an agreement made for the exchange of data traffic between large and small ISPs or, as in this case, between a router and its neighbor router. The agreement on peering is how different networks are joined to form the Internet. The network administrator configuring the Internet connection must know the remote IP address and ASN to make this peering. An AS path is created when a network is connected. This is demonstrated in the next subsection. (*Note:* If BGP routers in the same AS peer with each other, that is, have the same ASN, this is called **iBGP**, or internal BGP, whereas the BGP between separate ASs is called **eBGP**, or external BGP. The protocols are collectively referred to as BGP.)

ASNs have a set of numbers reserved for private use. These numbers are 64512 through 65535 and cannot be passed into the Internet. For this section the configurations presented will use the private ASN numbers.

AS
Autonomous systems

ASN
Autonomous systems number

Peering
How an agreement is made for the exchange of data traffic between large and small ISPs or between a router and its neighbor router

iBGP
Internal Border Gateway Protocol

eBGP
External Border Gateway Protocol

Configuring BGP

This section demonstrates how to configure a router to run BGP for connecting to an ISP. Figure 8-47 illustrates the example network for this section. This is typical of the customer's connection to the ISP. In this example, the steps for configuring both the ISP router (Router-ISP) and the customer's router (RouterB) will be shown. In practice, however, the ISP router (Router-ISP) will be configured by the networking personnel with the ISP. This exercise begins with configuring the configuration of the ISP's router (Router-ISP).

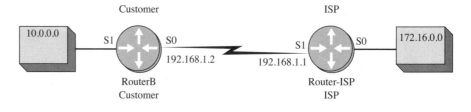

Customer   ISP

RouterB   Router-ISP
Customer   ISP

FIGURE 8-47 A BGP connection to an ISP.

The ISP has assigned an IP address of 192.168.1.1 for the interface that connects to the customer. The customer is assigned an IP address of 192.168.1.2. The ISP typically takes the .1 assignment and assigns the customer the .2 address. Enter the router's configuration mode using the ***conf t*** command from the privilege EXEC prompt as shown. Next, enter the configuration mode for the router's serial interface that connects to the customer. In this example, serial interface 1 on the ISP's router is being used for the connection; therefore, enter the command ***int ser 1***.

```
Router-ISP# conf t
Router-ISP(config)# int ser 1
```

Next enter the IP address for the connection to the customer with a subnet mask of 255.255.255.252. Recall from Chapter 5 that a subnet mask of 255.255.255.252 provides for two usable host IP addresses in the subnet. This is adequate for the connection to the customer. The command ***ip address [ip address] [subnet mask]*** is used to configure the Serial1 interface with the specified IP address and subnet mask. The ISP will typically have multiple customer connections; therefore, it is a good idea to document the IP address entry using the command ***description***. This command is used to enter a comment in the router's configuration file about an interface configuration. For example, the Serial1 interface is being configured for the connection to customer B. The router has been placed in the **(config-if)#** mode. The entry ***description Customer B*** is entered so that the network administrator of the ISP knows what the Serial1 interface is being used for. Documentation of the router's configuration file is extremely important.

```
Router-ISP(config-if)#ip address 192.168.1.1 255.255.255.252
Router-ISP(config-if)#description Customer B
```

The next step is to configure the router to run BGP. The ISP has been assigned the AS number of 65001. (*Note:* This is actually a private AS number. In practice the ISP is assigned a public AS number.) The AS number is used when entering the command for BGP. In this example, the command ***router bgp 65001*** is entered. The command ***network 172.16.0.0*** follows, which instructs the router to advertise the 172.16.0.0 network to its BGP peers. The next command is for specifying the IP address of the BGP neighbor. This is the IP address of the Serial0 interface on the customer's RouterB. The format for the command is ***neighbor [ip address] remote AS number [neighbor's AS number]***. The last command is for entering a description of the entries. The comment *neighbor 192.168.1.2 description Customer BGP* is used to document the router configuration for the neighbor IP address for the customer and that the routing protocol is BGP.

```
Router-ISP(config)#router bgp 65001
Router-ISP(config-router)#network 172.16.0.0
Router-ISP(config-router)#neighbor 192.168.1.2 remote-as 65002
Router-ISP(config-router)#neighbor 192.168.1.2 description Customer B
   BGP
```

The command *sh ip int brief* can be used to check the configuration for the interface. This shows that the ISP's router Serial1 interface has been configured and is connected.

```
Router-ISP#sh ip int brief
Interface       IP-Address    OK? Method  Status                Proto-
                                                                col
FastEthernet0/0 unassigned    YES unset   administratively down down
Serial0         unassigned    YES unset   up                    down
Serial1         192.168.1.1   YES manual  up                    up
```

The next example demonstrates the steps for configuring the customer's router (RouterB). The customer receives an IP address and subnet mask for the serial interface from the ISP when the connection is requested and after the connection is configured by the ISP. The customer will enter the configurations provided by the ISP.

The first step on the customer's router is to enter the router's configuration mode using the *conf t* command from the privilege EXEC prompt as shown. Next, enter the configuration mode for the router's serial interface that connects to the ISP. In this example, serial interface 0 is being used for the connection; therefore, enter the command *int ser 0*.

```
RouterB# conf t
Enter configuration commands, one per line. End with CNTL/Z.
RouterB(config)#int ser 0
```

Next configure the serial interface's IP address and subnet mask. In this case, the ISP assigned an IP address of 192.168.1.2 with a subnet mask of 255.255.255.252. (*Note:* It is a good idea to document your entries into the router's con figuration by using the command *description (descr)*.) The entries for the IP address and the description are shown.

```
RouterB(config-if)#ip address 192.168.1.2 255.255.255.0
RouterB(config-if)#descr ISP Connection
```

The customer has been assigned the AS number of 65002. (*Note:* This is actually a private AS number. In practice the customer is assigned a public AS number.) The AS number is used when entering the command for the BGP routing protocol. In this example, the command *router bgp 65002* is entered. The command *network 10.0.0.0* follows, which instructs the router to advertise the Border Gateway Protocol over any interfaces with an IP address in the 10.0.0.0 network. The next command is for specifying the IP address of the BGP neighbor. This is the IP address of the Serial1 interface on the ISP's RouterA. The format for the command is *neighbor [ip address] remote AS number [neighbor's AS number]*. The last command is for entering a description of the entries. The comment *neighbor 192.168.1.1 descr ISP BGP* is used to document the router configuration. The description identifies the neighbor IP address (the ISP) and comments that the routing protocol is BGP.

```
RouterB(config)#router bgp 65002
RouterB(config-router)#network 10.0.0.0
RouterB(config-router)#neighbor ?
A.B.C.D  Neighbor  address
WORD     Neighbor  tag
RouterB(config-router)#neighbor 192.168.1.1 remote-as ?
<1-65535> AS of remote neighbor
RouterB(config-router)#neighbor 192.168.1.1 remote-as 65001
RouterB(config-router)#neighbor 192.168.1.1 descr ISP BGP
```

After completing the router configuration, the next step is for the customer to ping the ISP using the IP address provided by the ISP. In this example, the ISP's IP address is 192.168.1.1.

```
RouterB#ping 192.168.1.1
Type escape sequence to abort.
Sending 5 100-byte ICMP Echos to 192.168.1.1, timeout is 2 seconds:
!!!!!
Success rate is 100 percent (5/5), round-trip min/avg/max 32/35/36 ms
```

This test verifies that the routers are connected. The command *sh ip bgp sum* can be used to see whether the routers are exchanging routes:

```
RouterB#sh ip bgp summ
BGP router identifier 192.168.1.2, local AS number 65002
BGP table version is 3, main routing table version 3
1 network entries and 1 paths using 121 bytes of memory
1 BGP path attribute entries using 92 bytes of memory
BGP activity 3/2 prefixes, 3/2 paths
0 prefixes revised.
Neighbor      V  AS     MsgRcvd MsgSent TblVer  InQ OutQ Up/Down
  State/PfxRcd
192.168.1.1  4  65001  10      12      0       0   0    00:00:09
  Idle
```

```
RouterB#sh ip bgp summ
BGP router identifier 192.168.1.2, local AS number 65002
BGP table version is 3, main routing table version 3
1 network entries and 1 paths using 121 bytes of memory
1 BGP path attribute entries using 92 bytes of memory
BGP activity 3/2 prefixes, 3/2 paths
0 prefixes revised.
Neighbor      V  AS     MsgRcvd MsgSent TblVer  InQ OutQ Up/Down
  State/PfxRcd
192.168.1.1  4  65001  10      12      0       0   0    00:00:20
  Active
```

The first screen shows a status of *Idle*. The second screen shows a status of *Active*. The screens indicate a local AS number of 65002 and a neighbor IP address of 192.168.1.1. Entering the command *sh ip bgp summ* now shows a *1* in the place where *Idle* and *Active* were present. This indicates the router is exchanging routes.

```
RouterB#sh ip bgp summ
BGP router identifier 192.168.1.2, local AS number 65002
BGP table version is 5, main routing table version 5
2 network entries and 2 paths using 242 bytes of memory
2 BGP path attribute entries using 188 bytes of memory
BGP activity 4/2 prefixes, 4/2 paths
0 prefixes revised.
Neighbor      V  AS     MsgRcvd MsgSent TblVer  InQ OutQ Up/Down
  State/PfxRcd
192.168.1.1  4  65001  24      27      5       0   0    00:05:31  1
```

The command *sh ip route* can be used to examine the customer's routing table as shown. The table shows that the Border Gateway Protocol (B) is advertising the 172.16.0.0 network via 192.168.1.1. The 172.16.0.0 network is directly attached to the ISP's router. BGP(B) is also running on the customer's 10.0.0.0 network:

```
RouterB#sh ip route
Codes: C  connected, S  static, I  IGRP, R  RIP, M  mobile, B  BGP D
   EIGRP, EX  EIGRP external, O  OSPF, IA  OSPF inter area
N1  OSPF NSSA external type 1, N2  OSPF NSSA external type 2
E1  OSPF external type 1, E2  OSPF external type 2, E  EGP
i  IS-IS, L1  IS-IS level-1, L2  IS-IS level-2, *  candidate default
```

```
U  per-user static route, o  ODR T  traffic engineered route
Gateway of last resort is not set
B 172.16.0.0/16 [20/0] via 192.168.1.1, 00:01:17
10.0.0.0/24 is subnetted, 1 subnets
D 10.0.0.0 is directly connected, Serial1
C 192.168.1.0/24 is directly connected, Serial0
```

The *show running-configuration (sh run)* command can be used to examine the changes made to the router's configuration file. A partial example of the customer's running-configuration file is shown in the following code. Don't forget to save the file to NVRAM after the changes have been verified.

```
RouterB# sh run
.
.
interface Serial0
 description ISP Connection
ip address 192.168.1.2 255.255.255.0
 no ip directed-broadcast
!
.
.
router eigrp 100
network 10.0.0.0
!
router bgp 65002
network 10.0.0.0
neighbor 192.168.1.1 remote-as 65001
neighbor 192.168.1.1 description ISP BGP
!
.
.
```

Networking Challenge—BGP

Use the Net-Challenge simulator software included with the text's companion CD-ROM to demonstrate that you can configure BGP for a router connection to an Internet service provider. The network connection is displayed on the screen when the BGP challenge is started. Place the companion CD-ROM in your computer's drive. Open the *Net-Challenge* folder, and click **net challenge.exe**. When the software is running, click the **Select Challenge** button to open a Select Router Challenge drop-down menu. Select *Chapter 8—BGP*. This opens a checkbox that can be used to verify that you have completed all the tasks. This task assumes that a connection to the Internet cloud has already been established.

1. Enter the privileged EXEC mode on the router.
2. Enter the router configuration mode [the **Router(config)#** prompt].
3. Set the hostname to *Border-Router*.
4. Configure the Fast Ethernet 0/0 interface on Border-Router with the following: IP address 10.10.1.2; subnet mask 255.255.255.0
5. Enable the router's Fast Ethernet 0/0 interface.
6. Configure the Serial0/0 interface with the following: IP address 192.168.1.2; subnet mask 255.255.255.0.
7. Enable the router's Serial0/0 interface.
8. Use the router's description command (*descr*) to indicate that this interface is the ISP Connection. (*Note:* The text ISP Connection is case-sensitive.)
9. Enable BGP on the router with an AS number of 65002.

10. Configure Border-Router's BGP neighbor with a remote AS of 65001.
11. Configure a BGP route to the 10.0.0.0 network.
12. Use the ***show ip route*** command to verify that the route from Border-Router to the ISP is configured.
13. Use the ***ping*** command to verify that the 192.168.1.1 interface is connected.
14. Use the ***sh run*** command to view the running-configuration file on Border-Router. Verify that BGP is enabled, the description *ISP Connection* has been entered, and the proper network address is specified for the ISP connection.
15. Use the ***sh ip int brief*** command to check the interface status.

8-9   ANALYZING INTERNET DATA TRAFFIC

NOC
Network operations center

Outbound Data Traffic
Data traffic leaving the network

Inbound Data Traffic
Data traffic entering the network

A campus network operations center (**NOC**) receives many emails and calls about suspected problems with the network. Many times network problems are due to operational errors by the users and possible hacker attacks. Occasionally, network equipment failure can be causing the problem. The bottom line is that the network administrator must have some expected performance measure of the network. The administrator will want to know the expected normal usage of the network, what type(s) of normal data traffic is expected, what is typical of outbound and inbound Internet data traffic, and who are the "big" data users on the network. **Outbound data traffic** is data leaving the network and **inbound data traffic** is data entering the network. This section provides an overview of the Internet data traffic patterns a NOC might monitor. These patterns are only examples of data traffic activity for a network. Data traffic patterns will vary significantly for each network, and each network will have its own typical data traffic. Also, data traffic will change during the day. Examples of this are presented in Chapter 9 in section 9-6. The data traffic images shown in this section were captured using the Finisar Surveyor Demo Portable Surveyor.

The first capture, shown in Figure 8-48, is a composite view of the data traffic activity for an Internet connection to and from a campus network. The image has four screens showing various data traffic information. This screen setup might be typical of the screen display at a network monitoring center. This does not imply that someone watches the screen continually, but the screen is looked at when a possible data traffic problem is mentioned.

Utilization/Errors Strip Chart

One of the areas NOC monitors is the typical percentage utilization of the network bandwidth. Figure 8-49 is a utilization/errors chart of an Internet feed to and from a campus network. The Utilization/Errors Strip chart shows that the network is running about 60–65 percent utilization and no errors are reported. This is a 45 Mbps network; therefore, the utilization is about 30 Mbps. Is this a good percentage of utilization? You can't answer this from the picture, but you *can* answer it if you know the expected utilization of your network. In this example, the network operations center expects an average of about 60 percent utilization of their Internet feed. The graph shows the utilization is within this range, so a quick glance at the screen indicates that the utilization is typical. This demonstrates why you need to learn and know the expected utilization of your network. The utilization chart shows stable behavior during the brief time it was monitored. There are peaks and valleys in the network utilization, but this is to be expected. Downloading large files from the Internet will temporarily increase the network utilization.

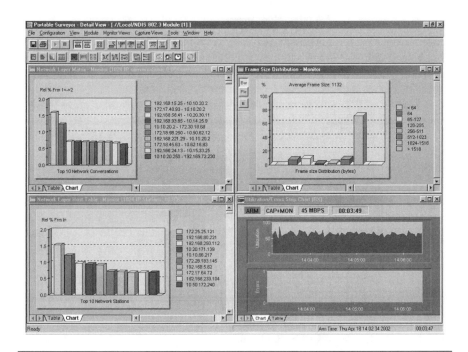

FIGURE 8-48   A composite view of network data traffic activity.

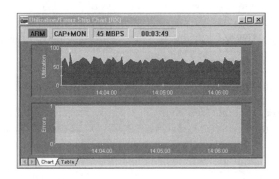

FIGURE 8-49   The Finisar-Shomiti Utilization/Errors strip chart.

Network Layer Matrix

The top 10 network layer conversations on the campus Internet feed are shown in Figure 8-50. The chart is obtained by starting the Surveyor program, starting a capture, and clicking **Capture View-Monitor Views-Network Layer Matrix**. The network layer is layer 3 in the OSI model, and this is the layer where IP addressing is defined. The monitoring software is reporting 1024 IP conversations and 8 IPX conversations. **IPX** is Novell's Internetworking Packet Exchange networking protocol. The top conversation is between the machines at IP addresses 192.168.15.25 and 10.10.20.2. The 10.10.20.2 machine is on the home 10.0.0.0 network. This one conversation is consuming more than 1.5 percent of the network's Internet bandwidth. This chart provides

IPX
Novell's Internetworking
Packet Exchange networking
protocol

the network administrator with a quick look at which host computer is tying up the network resources. It is not possible to make a reasonable guess if this is a normal network layer graph for your network by looking at only this one picture. This requires that the network administrator develop knowledge of expected behavior over a long term.

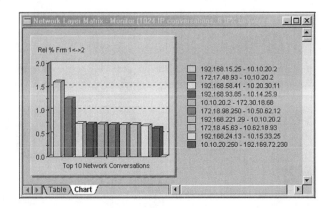

FIGURE 8-50 The Network Layer Matrix graph.

Notice that the machine with the IP address of 10.10.20.2 is listed three times in the top ten conversations. The 10.10.20.2 machine is a Web server on the 10.0.0.0 network, and it is expected that this machine will experience a fair amount of data activity.

Network Layer Host Table

The network layer host table (see Figure 8-51) provides a look at the top ten network stations. The information is plotted by the IP address of the host (computer). Notice that the IP addresses for seven of the network stations are outside the 10.0.0.0 network. Remember, the 10.0.0.0 IP address is the network address for the home network of the campus LAN discussed in this text. This indicates that the network consumes more data traffic than it exports to the Internet.

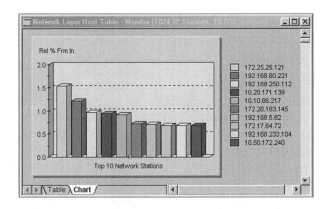

FIGURE 8-51 The Network Layer Host table.

Frame Size Distribution

Figure 8-52 shows the frame size distribution of packets in bytes being delivered to and from the campus network's Internet connection. The average frame size is 1132, which is listed at the top of the chart. The frame sizes for Ethernet packets are limited to 1500. The frame size distribution for this network has a somewhat "J" shape. The "J" in this case is skewed by the large percentage of frame size in the 1024–1518 frame size range. A "J" shape is expected because many small data frames are expected for negotiating the transfer of data over the network (frame size 65–127) and then many large frames for exchanging the data (frame size 1024–1518). There is a small peak with the 65–127 frame size, the few 128–255 and 256–511 frame size packets, and the frame sizes then begin to increase at 512–1023 and then the larger increase in the 1024–1518 region. The graph shows few data packets in the >1518 region.

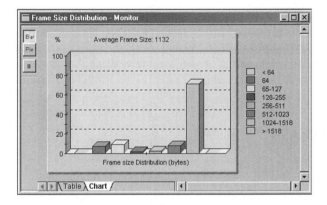

FIGURE 8-52   The Frame Size Distribution graph.

SUMMARY

This chapter presented the fundamentals of wide area networking. The student should understand and appreciate the role that the PSTN (public switched telephone net work—telco) plays in wide area networking. Many associated issues and technologies have been presented. This chapter has only introduced a fraction of the technologies and issues needed to be understood by an Internet expert such as a Cisco Certified Internet Expert (CCIE). However, the chapter has tried to address the fundamental or base knowledge needed for a networking administrator to start working in this field.

The student should understand the following:

1. The basics of a line connection to the telco
2. How Frame Relay works and the basic steps for configuring a Frame Relay inter face
3. The basics of establishing an ATM connection
4. The technologies used for establishing a dial-up connection to a network
5. How to configure a VPN connection
6. The fundamental concept of wide area networking
7. The issues for Internet routing

QUESTIONS AND PROBLEMS

Section 8-2

1. What is the data rate of a DS-3 line?
2. What is the data rate of a T1 line?
3. Define the *telco cloud*.
4. Define *fractional T1*.
5. Define *point of presence*.
6. Explain the difference between *line of demarcation* and *point of presence*.
7. A CSU/DSU has a blue alarm. What does this indicate?
8. What is *ESF*? Define the term.
9. What is the function of the 24 ESF framing bits?
10. What is *B8ZS* and how does it work?
11. The options for data encapsulation on a Cisco router can be viewed by entering what command? Show the router prompt.

Section 8-3

12. A user requests a Frame Relay T1 data service with a CIR of 768 kbps. What does this mean?
13. What is the purpose of the *dlci tag*?
14. Draw a picture of a point-to-point connection to the Frame Relay cloud.
15. Who provides the Frame Relay connection if the connection involves more than one telco?
16. What is the router command to instruct the interface for Frame Relay?

17. What does the router command ***int s0.1 point-to-point*** do?
18. A telco provides a dlci number of 150 for a Frame Relay connection. List the router command to configure the assigned dlci number.
19. A ***ping*** command is used to check a Frame Relay connection. What IP address is pinged?

Section 8-4

20. Define the *byte structure* for an ATM cell.
21. What is the *VCC* and its purpose?
22. What is VPI used for?
23. What type of encapsulation is typically specified to transport TCP/IP data traffic over ATM?

Section 8-5

24. What is the bandwidth of a voice channel in the public switched telephone network?
25. Why is the data transfer for V.92/V.90 called *asymmetric* operation?
26. What are the data speeds for V.44/V.34 and V.92/V.90?
27. Cable modems use a technique called *ranging*. Define this term.
28. What are the data rates for basic access service ISDN and the ISDN primary access channel?
29. What is *ADSL* and what are its data rates?
30. Define *discrete multitone*.
31. What is the purpose of a remote access server?
32. Define *PPP* and state its purpose.

Section 8-6

33. What is the goal of a VPN tunnel?
34. Draw a sketch of the encapsulation of a VPN data packet. Show the IP source and destination address and the VPN tunnel source and destination address encapsulated with the IP packet.
35. What is the command for adding a tunnel 0 to a router? Show the router prompt.
36. List the two router commands for specifying the tunnel destination and source IP address. Include the router prompt.
37. The command ***show ip int brief*** is used to check the configuration of a VPN tunnel on a router. The router displays the following:

```
Interface IP address OK? Method Status Protocol
Tunnel 0 10.10.20.5 YES manual up up
```

   Is the tunnel link working properly? Justify your answer.
38. What router command can be used to check to see whether tunneling has been configured on a router?
39. Explain the expected difference when running a traceroute from the home network to the remote user using the IP address for the remote user's router interface, and then running a traceroute from the home network to the remote user's VPN tunnel address.

40. List five steps for troubleshooting the VPN tunnel link.
41. Identify two tunneling protocols that can be used to configure a remote user's PC.

Section 8-7

42. What is the purpose of a wide area network connection?
43. What is the easiest routing protocol to use for WAN links? What if there are multiple connections to the remote sites?
44. Define the following:
    a. Stubby areas
    b. Totally stubby areas

Section 8-8

45. A multi-homed customer has
    a. A single internet connection
    b. More than one Internet connection
    c. Static routes
    d. None of the above
46. BGP is considered to be
    a. An external routing protocol
    b. An internal routing protocol
    c. Used for routing between the same networks
    d. Outdated
47. The router command used for entering a description is
    a. *Comment*
    b. *!*
    c. *
    d. *Description*
48. What does the router command *router bgp 65003* mean?
49. Write the router command for specifying the IP address of the BGP neighbor. Also show the router prompt.

Section 8-9

50. Define the following:
    a. Outbound data traffic
    b. Inbound data traffic
51. What is an expected percentage utilization for a network?
52. The protocol analyzer shows that the average frame size of data packets being delivered to and from the campus network's Internet connection is 1203. Is this a reasonable average? Justify your answer.

Critical Thinking

53. What is a *cloud*?

54. Your supervisor informs you that a user on the network has requested a VPN connection. Prepare a response to the supervisor discussing what is needed to provide the connection.

9

CHAPTER

Configuring and Managing the Campus Network

CHAPTER OUTLINE

9-1   Introduction

9-2   Designing the Campus Network

9-3   IP Assignment and DHCP

9-4   Network Services—DNS

9-5   Network Management

9-6   Switch/VLAN Configuration

9-7   Analyzing Campus Network Data Traffic

Summary

Questions and Problems

OBJECTIVES

- Understand the purpose of the three layers of a campus network design
- Understand the auxiliary services needed to operate a network, such as DHCP and DNS
- Understand the process of requesting an IP address using DHCP
- Understand how to use SNMP tools for network management
- Investigate how to use network data packet statistics to monitor network performance

KEY TERMS

core
distribution layer
access layer
load balancing
per-destination load balancing
per-pack load balancing
BOOTP
lease time
unicast
MT Discover
MT Offer
MT Request
MT ACK
DNS
forward domain name service

reverse domain name service
TLD
country domain
root servers
NS record
reverse DNS
SNMP
Management Information Base (MIB)
Power over Ether (PoE)
PD
PSE
endpoint PSE
midspan (mid-point) PSE
Resistive Power Discovery
PoE Plus

VLAN (Virtual LAN)
port-based VLAN
tag-based VLAN
protocol-based VLAN
static VLAN
dynamic VLAN
configure terminal (conf t)
Switch(config)#
Switch(config-line)#
Spanning-Tree Protocol
Bridge Protocol Data Unit (BPDU
Configuration BPDU
Topology Change Notification (TCN)
Topology Change Notification Acknowledgement (TCA)

9-1   INTRODUCTION

The objective of this chapter is to examine the computer networking issues that arise when planning a campus network. The term *campus network* applies to any network that has multiple LANs interconnected. The LANs are typically in multiple buildings that are close to each other and are interconnected with switches and routers.

The previous chapters introduced the fundamental issues of computer networks. These included techniques for configuring the LAN, analyzing TCP/IP data traffic, router configuration, configuring the wide area network connection, and selecting and configuring the routing protocols. This chapter looks at the planning and design of a simple campus network, including network design, IP assignment and DHCP, domain name service (DNS), network management, switch and VLAN configuration, and analyzing a campus network's data traffic.

The basics of configuring the three layers of a campus LAN (core, distribution, and access) are first examined in section 9-2. This section also addresses the important issues of data flow and selecting the network media. IP allocation and configuring DHCP service are examined in section 9-3. This includes a step-by-step description of the process of how a computer obtains an IP address manually or via DHCP in a network. Section 9-4 examines the issues of configuring DNS service for a campus network. The concepts of the root servers, the top level domains, and the subdomains are examined. The next section (9-5) addresses network management. An overview of configuring a Cisco router for SNMP operation is first presented. This section includes an example of using SNMP management software to collect router information and data statistics. This section also provides an overview of Power over Ethernet (PoE). Section 9-6 examines configuring a VLAN for use in a campus network. Basic switch commands in addition to configuring a static VLAN are presented. This section also discusses the Spanning-Tree Protocol (STP). The chapter concludes with an example of using data collected with an SNMP management program to monitor network data traffic.

9-2   DESIGNING THE CAMPUS NETWORK

Most campus networks follow a design that has core, distribution, and access layers. These layers (Figure 9-1) can be spread out into more layers or compacted into fewer depending on the size of these networks. This 3-layer network structure is incorporated in campus networks to improve data handling and routing within the network. The issues of data flow and network media are examined here.

Core Layer

Core
The backbone of the network

The network core usually contains high-end layer 3 switches or routers. The **core** is the heart or the backbone of the network. The major portion of a network's data traffic passes through the core. The core must be able to quickly forward data to other parts of the network. Data congestion should be avoided at the core if possible. This means that unnecessary route policies should be avoided. An example of a route policy is *traffic filtering,* which limits what traffic can pass from one part of a network to another. Keep in mind that it takes time for a router to examine each data packet, and unnecessary route policies can slow down the network's data traffic.

It was mentioned that high-end routers and layer 3 switches are typically selected for use in the core. Of the two, the layer 3 switch is probably the best choice. A layer 3 switch is essentially a router that uses electronic hardware instead of software to make routing decisions. The advantage of the layer 3 switch is the speed at which it can establish a network connection.

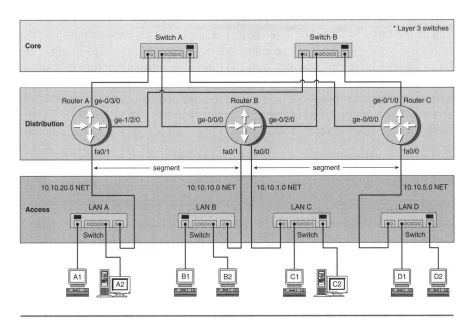

FIGURE 9-1 The core, distribution, and access layers of a campus network.

Another alternative for networking hardware in the core is a layer 2 switch. The layer 2 switch does not make any routing decisions and can quickly make network connection decisions based on the network hardware connected to its ports. The advantage to using the layer 2 switch in the core is cost. The disadvantage is that the layer 2 switch does not route data packets. High-speed layer 2 switches are more affordable than high-speed routers and layer 3 switches.

An important design issue in a campus network and the core is redundancy. *Redundancy* provides for a backup route or network connection in case of a link failure. The core hardware is typically interconnected, as shown in Figure 9-1, to all distribution network hardware. The objective is to ensure that data traffic continues for the whole network even if a core networking device or link fails.

Each layer beyond the core breaks the network into smaller networks with the final result being a group of networks that are capable of handling the amount of traffic generated. The design should thus incorporate some level of redundancy.

Distribution Layer

The **distribution layer** in the network is the point where the individual LANs connect to the campus network routers or layer 3 switches. Routing and filtering policies are more easily implemented at the distribution layer without having a negative impact on the performance of the network data traffic. Also, the speed of the network data connections at the distribution layer are typically slower than at the core. For

Distribution Layer
Point where the individual LANs connect together

example, connection speeds at the core should be the highest possible, such as 1 or 10 gigabits, where the data speed connections at the distribution layer could be 100 Mbps or 1 gigabit. Figure 9-1 shows the connections to the access and core layers via the router's Ethernet interfaces.

Access Layer

Access Layer
Where the networking devices in a LAN connect together

The **access layer** is where the networking devices in a LAN connect together. The network hardware used here is typically a layer 2 switch. Hubs can be used but are not recommended in any networks with significant amounts of data traffic. Remember, a switch is a better choice because it forwards data packets directly to destination hosts connected to its ports. Network data traffic is not forwarded to all hosts in the network. The exception to this is a broadcast that is sent to all hosts connected to the switch. Refer back to Chapter 4 for a review and a comparison of switch and hub operations.

Data Flow

An important networking issue is how data traffic flows in the core, distribution, and access layers of a campus LAN. In reference to Figure 9-1, if computer A1 in LAN A sends data to computer D1 in LAN D, the data is first sent through the switch in LAN A and then to RouterA in the distribution layer. RouterA then forwards the data to switch A or switch B. Switch A or switch B will then forward the data to RouterC. The data packet is then sent to the destination host in LAN D.

The following are some questions often asked when setting up a network that implements the core, distribution, and access layers.

- *In what layer are the campus network servers (Web, email, DHCP, DNS, etc.) located?* This varies for all campus networks and there is not a definitive answer. However, most campus network servers are located in the access layer.
- *Why not connect directly from RouterA to RouterC at the distribution layer?* There are network stability issues when routing large amounts of network data traffic if the networks are fully or even partially meshed together. This means that connecting routers together in the distribution layer should be avoided.
- *Where is the campus backbone located in the layers of a campus network?* The backbone of a campus network carries the bulk of the routed data traffic. Based on this, the backbone of the campus network connects the distribution and the core layer networking devices.

Selecting the Media

The choices for the media used to interconnect networks in a campus network are based on several criteria:

- Desired data speed
- Distance for connections
- Budget

The desired data speed for the network connection is probably the first consideration given when selecting the network media. Twisted-pair cable works well at 100 Mbps and 1 Gbps and is specified to support data speeds of 10-gigabit data traffic over twisted-pair cable. Fiber optic cable supports LAN data rates up to 10 Gbps or higher. Wireless networks support data rates up to 200+ Mbps.

The distance consideration limits the choice of media. CAT 6/5e or better have a distance limitation of 100 meters. Fiber optic cable can be run for many kilometers, depending on the electronics and optical devices used. Wireless LAN connections can also be used to interconnect networks a few kilometers apart.

The available budget is always the final deciding factor when planning the design for a campus LAN. If the budget allows, then fiber optic cable is probably the best overall choice especially in the high-speed backbone of the campus network. The cost of fiber is continually dropping, making it more competitive with lower-cost network media such as twisted-pair cable. Also fiber cable will always be able to carry a greater amount of data traffic and can easily grow with the bandwidth requirements of a network.

Twisted-pair cable is a popular choice for connecting computers in a wired LAN. The twisted-pair technologies support bandwidths suitable for most LANs, and the performance capabilities of twisted-pair cable are always improving.

Wireless LANs are being used to connect networking devices together in LANs where a wired connection is not feasible. For example, a wireless LAN could be used to connect two LANs in a building together. This is a cost-effective choice if there is not a cable duct to run the cable to interconnect the LANs or if the cost of running the cable is too high. Also wireless connections are playing an important role with mobile users within a LAN. The mobile user can make a network connection without having to use a physical connection or jack. For example, a wireless LAN could be used to enable network users to connect their mobile computers to the campus network. This topic is examined in greater detail in Chapter 11.

Load Balancing

Load balancing is the concept of distributing the network data traffic over multiple interfaces so that one interface connection is not overloaded. It is also used as a tool to control the direction of the data flow when multiple routes are available. An example of load balancing is provided in Figure 9-1. In this case, data from LAN A going to LAN B will first pass through Router A at the distribution layer. The data will next travel to core Switches A or B. The data can all be sent to Switch A or Switch B or can be split over both switches.

The selection of the data path leaving RouterA is determined by the "cost" of the data path. Remember, the "cost" of the route is typically based on the type of routing protocol and the "speed" of the connection. For example in Figure 9-1, RouterA is running OSPF for all interfaces, and the cost associated with RouterA's gigabit interface is lower than the cost of a RouterA's FastEthernet interface. The cost of a route can be programmed into the router by issuing the following command from the config-router prompt, ***ip ospf cost <number>*** where number is the cost of the network route ranging from 1 (lowest) to 65535 (highest). The lower the cost, the more preferred the route.

In this case, the cost of the route is being set by the network administrator who is using the cost metric to control the route of the data flow. For example, the command for setting the cost of the RouterA ge-0/3/0 interface to 10 is a follows. (*Note:* This example assumes that RouterA is running ospf off the ge-0/3/0 interface.)

```
RouterA<config-router># ip ospf cost 10
```

Load Balancing
Concept of distributing the network data traffic over multiple interfaces so that one interface connection is not overloaded—also used as a tool to control the direction of the data flow

RouterA is also showing a link to Switch B off the ge-1/2/0 gigabit interface. If the primary data traffic at the core should travel through Switch A, then the path to Switch B should have a higher cost. For example, setting the cost off RouterA's ge-1/2/0 interface to 20 will make the data path to Switch A ge-1/2/0 interface have a higher cost and therefore establish the ge-0/3/0 interface (cost = 10) as the primary route.

What if the cost of both RouterA's gigabit interfaces is set to 10? In this case, the routers will load balance automatically, and the data traffic will be split equally over both interfaces. Load balancing off the router can be set to work per-destination or per-packet. **Per-destination load balancing** means that the data packets coming from the router are distributed based on the destination address. This means that all data packets with the same destination are sent over the same interface. This technique preserves the order of the packets but it does not guarantee equal load balancing. Another type of load balancing is per-packet. In **per-packet load balancing**, load balance is guaranteed for all interfaces, but there is no guarantee that the packets will arrive at the destination in the proper order considering the data packet can take different routes.

Per-destination Load Balancing
Means that the data packets coming from the router are distributed based on the destination address

Per-packet Load Balancing
Load balance is guaranteed for all interfaces, but there is no guarantee that the packets will arrive at the destination in the proper order

9-3 IP ASSIGNMENT AND DHCP

IP assignment is a process where subnets are created for each subgroup or department. The IP address assignment is typically tracked by the network operations center (NOC). The IP addresses are kept in a central log file so that NOC can troubleshoot network problems. For example, a machine could be causing network problems possibly due to hacked or corrupted software. NOC needs to be able to track down the network problem(s). The NOC database will have the MAC address, the IP address, and the name of the person who uses the computer.

IP addresses are assigned by NOC based on where the subnet for the computer is located. The subnet could be in a building, a floor of the building, a department, and so on. The subnets are created by the network administrators based on the expected number of users (hosts) in a subnet (refer back to Chapter 5). For example, the 192.168.12.0 network shown in Figure 9-2 has been partitioned into four subnets. The network addresses for each of the subnets are provided in Table 9-1. Any computer in subnet B is assigned one of the 62 IP addresses from the range 192.168.12.65 to 192.168.12.126. Remember, the first IP address in the subnet is reserved for the network address, and the last is reserved for the broadcast address.

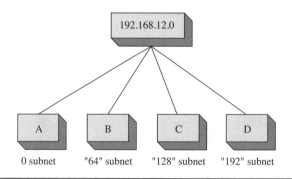

FIGURE 9-2   IP assignment of computers in a network's subnet.

TABLE 9-1 Subnet Addresses for the Subnets Shown in Figure 9-2

Subnet	Network Address	Broadcast Address
A	192.168.12.0	192.168.12.63
B	192.168.12.64	192.168.12.127
C	192.168.12.128	192.168.12.191
D	192.168.12.192	192.168.12.255

IP assignment is done either manually or dynamically. In the manual process for IP assignment within a campus network, IP addresses are entered manually for each computer in the network. This is a tedious process that requires that a file be edited with all of the necessary information about the computer, including the MAC address, the IP address, and the user (or owner) of the computer. The owner is typically the department or organizational unit within the campus LAN. This process can be automated to some extent using a program called **BOOTP** for IP assignment. BOOTP stands for *Bootstrap Protocol*, and it enables computers to discover their own IP addresses. When a client requests an IP address, it is assigned to the Ethernet address (MAC address) based on the BOOTP record. In this case, the IP and MAC addresses have a one-to-one relationship.

DHCP (Dynamic Host Configuration Protocol) simplifies the steps for IP assignment. DHCP's function is to assign IP addresses from a pool to requesting clients. DHCP is a superset of BOOTP, and runs on the same port number. DHCP requests an IP address from the DHCP server. The DHCP server retrieves an available IP address from a pool dedicated to the subnet of the requesting client. The IP address is passed to the client and the server specifies a length of time that the client can hold the address. This is called the **lease time**. This feature keeps an unused computer from unnecessarily tying up an IP address.

The process of requesting an IP address with DHCP is as follows: The client boots up and sends out a DHCP request. This is a broadcast, meaning that the message is sent to all computers in the LAN. A DHCP server listening on the LAN will take the packet, retrieve an available IP address from the address pool, and send the address to the client. The client applies the IP address to the computer and is then ready to make network connections. An example is provided in Figure 9-3.

BOOTP
Bootstrap Protocol

Lease Time
The amount of time that a client can hold an IP address

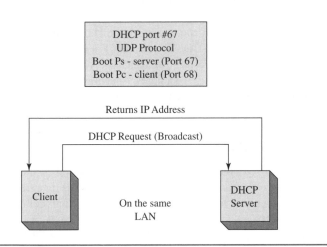

FIGURE 9-3   An example of a DHCP server and client in the same LAN.

Unicast
The packet has a fixed destination

What if a DHCP server is on the other side of the router (for example, not in the same LAN)? Remember, routers don't pass broadcast addresses, so the DHCP broadcast is not forwarded. This situation requires that a DHCP relay be used, as shown in Figure 9-4. The DHCP relay sits on the same LAN as the client. It listens for DHCP requests and then takes the broadcast packet and issues a **unicast** packet to the network DHCP server. *Unicast* means that the packet is issued a fixed destination and therefore is no longer a broadcast packet. The DHCP relay puts its LAN address in the DHCP field so the DHCP server knows the subnet the request is coming from and can properly assign an IP address. The DHCP server retrieves an available IP address for the subnet and sends the address to the DHCP relay, which forwards it to the client.

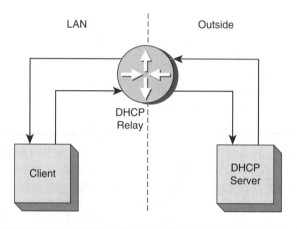

FIGURE 9-4   An example requiring the use of a DHCP relay.

Cisco routers have a DHCP relay built into their operating system. The router command to enable the DHCP relay is *Router(config-if)# ip helper [ip address of the DHCP server]*. Notice that this command is issued from the interface that connects to the LAN. In fact, the IP address for the interface is typically the gateway address for the LAN.

DHCP is a UDP protocol and uses port number 68 for the BOOTP-client and port 67 for the BOOTP-server. (BOOTP and DHCP use the same port numbers.) The BOOTP-client is the user requesting the DHCP service. The BOOTP-server is the DHCP server. The following discussion describes how these services are used in a DHCP request. The DHCP proxy on the router listens for the packets that are going to DHCP or BOOTP port numbers.

The DHCP Data Packets

The following is a discussion on the TCP packets transferred during a DHCP request. The network setup is the same as shown in Figure 9-4. The data traffic shown in this example will contain only the data packets seen by the client computer. The Finisar Surveyor Demo software was used to capture the data packets. A portion of the captured data packets is provided in Figure 9-5. Packet 10 is a DHCP request with a message type discover (**MT Discover**). This is also called the DHCP Discover packet. The destination for the packet is a broadcast. The message source has a MAC address of Dell 09B956, and the IP address is 0.0.0.0. The IP address is shown in the middle panel, and the *0.0.0.0* indicates that an IP address has not been assigned to the computer. The source and destination ports are shown in the third panel in Figure 9-5. The source port is 68, which is for the Bootstrap Protocol Client (the computer requesting the IP address). The destination port is 67, the Bootstrap Protocol Server (the DHCP server).

MT Discover
Message type discover, a DHCP Discover packet

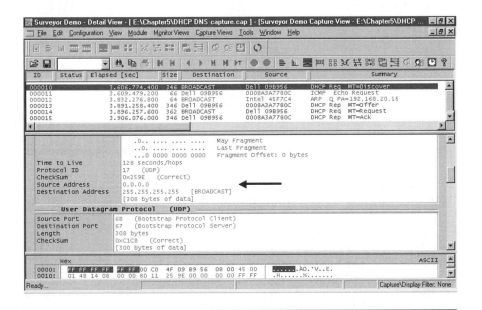

FIGURE 9-5   The captured DHCP packets.

Packet 13 is a reply from the DHCP server, an offer of the IP address to the client. This is called the DHCP Offer packet (**MT Offer**). This packet contains the domain name, the domain name server, the default gateway, other network information the client may need to connect to the network. Packet 14 has a message type of **MT Request**. This packet is sent from the client back to the server that has been selected to provide the DHCP service. (*Note*: It is possible for a campus LAN to have more than one DHCP server answering the DHCP request.) The packet is sent through the DHCP relay to the DHCP server. This means that the client is accepting the IP address offer. Packet 15 is a message type of ACK (**MT ACK**). The DHCP server is acknowledging the client's acceptance of the IP address from the DHCP server. The client computer now has an IP address assigned to it.

9-4   NETWORK SERVICES—DNS

This section examines the DNS services that are typically available in a campus network. **DNS** is the domain name service. DNS translates a human readable name to an IP address or an IP address to a domain name. The translation of a name to an IP address is called **forward domain name service**, and translation of an IP address to a domain name is called **reverse domain name service**.

MT Offer
Message type offer, a DHCP Offer packet

MT Request
Message type request, a DHCP Request packet

MT ACK
Message type acknowledgement, a DHCP ACK packet

DNS
Domain name service

Forward Domain Name Service
Translation of a name to an IP address

Reverse Domain Name Service
Translation of an IP address to a name

TLD
Top level domain

Country Domain
Usually two letters, such as
United States (.us) or
Canada (.ca), that define the
location of the domain
server for that country

The domain name service is a tree hierarchy. It starts with the top level domains and then extends to subdomains. Examples of top level domains (**TLD**) are as follows:

.com .net .org .edu .mil .gov .us .ca .info .biz .tv

Country domains are usually defined by two letters, such as .us (United States) and .ca (Canada). The primary domain server for that domain has to exist in the same country; for example, the .us primary domain server is located in the United States. Figure 9-6 shows the top level domains and their relationship to the subdomains and root servers.

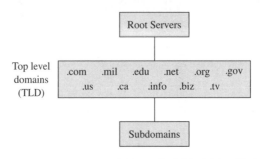

FIGURE 9-6   The domain name service tree hierarchy.

Root Servers
A group of servers that exist
using well-known IP
addresses that have been
programmed into DNS servers

The **root servers** use well-known IP addresses that have been programmed into DNS servers. When the DNS is installed on a server, the root server's IP addresses are automatically configured in the DNS. The campus DNS will query the root servers to try to find name servers of known domains.

For example, if network-A wants to know the IP address for the www server at network-B.edu, DNS queries one of the root servers and it returns the IP address for the .edu domain. Then the network-A DNS queries the .edu domain for the IP address of the network-B DNS. The network-A DNS then queries the network-B DNS to obtain the IP address for www.network-B.edu. There are many steps for obtaining the IP address via DNS. However, the DNS server keeps a cache of recent queries so this multiple-step process of obtaining an IP address does not have to be repeated unnecessarily. The *www* entry, called the *A record,* is the name for an IP address. The A record is used by a DNS server at the parent company for network-B to convert the name www.network-B.edu to an IP address.

NS Record
A record that points to a
name server

The top level domain for network-B.edu is .edu, and the subdomain is network-B.edu. At the top level of the .edu domain, and all domains, are the root servers, as shown in Figure 9-6. The .edu domain has an **NS record**, basically a record that points to a name server. They will have an NS record for network-A that points to the IP address of the network-A domain name server and the secondary DNS server's IP address and its DNS names.

The root servers have information only about the next level in the tree. Root servers know only about the top level domains (for example, .com, .gov, .mil, etc.). They will not know anything about www.network-B.edu. They only know the .edu domain server's IP address.

Campus DNS

The first step for providing DNS for a campus network is to obtain a domain name. This requires that the user seeking the domain name go to www.internic.net. Internic has a list of name registrars where a domain can be purchased. Select a company that registers domain names. When you get on the registrar's website you will be able to input a domain name. The registrar will check to see if the domain name is available. If the domain name is available, you will be prompted to complete the application for the domain name and put in the DNS servers that are to be used to host the domain. The DNS servers will be assigned an IP address and names. When the network's DNS servers are placed online, the root servers will point to the network's DNS servers.

Administering the Local DNS Server—A Campus Network Example The primary records are the A records of a campus network. These contain the host name and IP addresses for the computers. For example, network-B.edu has an assigned IP address of 172.16.12.1. When a host pings www.network-B.edu, the host computer first checks its DNS cache; assuming the DNS cache is empty, the host then sends a DNS request to the campus DNS server. Typically the host will know the IP addresses of the primary and secondary DNS server through either static input or dynamic assignment. The request is sent to the primary DNS server requesting the IP address for www.network-B.edu. The primary DNS server is the authority for network-B.edu and knows the IP address of the hosts in the network. The primary DNS server returns the IP address of www.network-B.edu, and then the ICMP process associated with a ping is started.

One might ask, "How does a PC in the campus network become part of the campus domain?" Specifically, how is an A record entered into the campus domain? Recall that the A record provides a host to IP address translation. Adding the PC to the campus domain is done either manually or dynamically.

The Steps for Manually Adding a Client to the Campus Network The steps for manually updating the DNS A records are graphically shown in Figure 9-7 and are listed as follows: A client PC updates the A record when an IP address is requested for a computer. The user obtains the PC name and the PC's MAC address. This information is sent to the network operation center (NOC). NOC issues an IP address to the client, updates the NOC database of clients on the network, and enters a new A record into the primary DNS. The entry is only made on the primary DNS. The entry will be later duplicated on the secondary DNS.

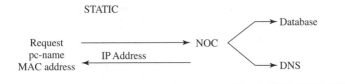

FIGURE 9-7 Manually updating the A record.

The Steps for Dynamically Adding a Client to the Campus Network A new A record can be entered dynamically when the client computer obtains an IP address through DHCP registration. This is graphically depicted in Figure 9-8. The DHCP server will issue an IP address to the client and at the same time send an updated A record to the network's primary DNS. Once again, the client name and the IP and MAC addresses are stored in the A record.

Why obtain the MAC address when entering the information into DNS? This record is used to keep track of all the machines operating on the network. The MAC address is a unique identifier for each machine. The MAC address is also used by BOOTP, which is a predecessor to DHCP. This is where a MAC address is specifically assigned to one IP address in the network.

Reverse DNS returns a hostname for an IP address. This is used for security purposes to verify that your domain is allowed to connect to a service. For example, pc-salsa1-1 (10.10.20.1) connects to an FTP server that only allows machines in the salsa domain to make the connection. When the connection is made, the FTP server knows only the IP address of the machine making the connection (10.10.20.1). The server will use the IP address to request the name assigned to that IP. A connection is made to the salsa domain server, and the salsa DNS server returns pc-salsa1-1 as the machine assigned to 10.10.20.1. The FTP server recognizes this is a salsa domain machine and authorizes the connection.

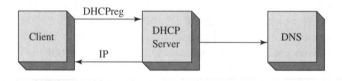

FIGURE 9-8   Dynamic updating of the A record using DHCP.

9-5   NETWORK MANAGEMENT

A campus network of moderate size has a tremendous number of data packets entering and leaving. The number of routers, switches, hubs, servers, and host computers can become staggering. Proper network management requires that all network resources be managed. This requires that proper management tools be in place.

A fundamental network management tool is **SNMP**, the Simple Network Management Protocol. SNMP, developed in 1988, is widely supported in most modern network hardware. SNMP is a connectionless protocol using the UDP (User Datagram Protocol) for the transmission of data to and from UDP port 161.

SNMP uses a **management information base (MIB)**, which is a collection of standard objects that are used to obtain configuration parameters and performance data on a networking device such as a router. For example, the MIB (ifDescr) returns a description of the router's interfaces. An example is shown in Figure 9-9. An SNMP software tool was used to collect the interface description information. The IP address of the router is 10.10.10.1, and a *get request ifDescr* was sent to port 161, the UDP port for SNMP. The descriptions of the interfaces were returned as shown.

Obtaining the SNMP data requires that SNMP be configured on the router. The following discussion demonstrates how to configure SNMP on a Cisco router.

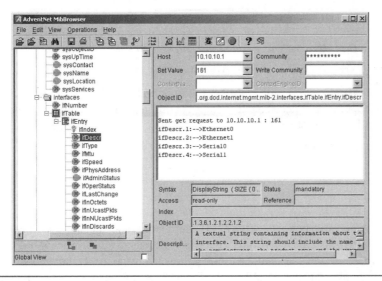

FIGURE 9-9   An example of using an SNMP software management tool to obtain descriptions of a router's interfaces using the MIB (ifDescr).

Configuring SNMP

The first step for configuring SNMP on a Cisco router is to enter the router's configuration mode using the ***conf t*** command:

```
RouterB#conf t
Enter configuration commands, one per line. End with CNTL/Z.
```

From the router's (config)# prompt enter the command ***snmp community [community string] [permissions]***. The community string can be any word. The permissions field is used to establish if the user can read only (ro), write only (wo), or both (rw). The options for configuring SNMP on the router are shown here:

```
RouterB(config)#snmp community ?
WORD SNMP community string
```

The router was connected to the computer running the SNMP management software, as shown in Figure 9-10. The router's configuration mode was entered, and the ***snmp community public ro*** command was issued. The word *public* is used as the community string. The community string is the password used by the SNMP software to access SNMP (port 161) on the router. The *ro* sets the permission to read only.

```
RouterB(config)#snmp community public ro
```

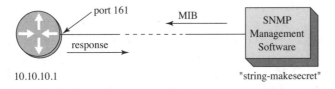

FIGURE 9-10   The setup for connecting the SNMP management software tool to the router.

In the next example, the community string password is set to *makesecret*, and the permission is set to read write (rw). Once again, the router's (config)# mode is entered and the command ***snmp community makesecret rw*** is entered:

```
RouterB(config)#snmp community makesecret rw
```

The configuration for SNMP can be verified using the ***show run*** command from the router's privileged mode prompt. A portion of the configuration file that lists the SNMP configuration for the router is shown here:

```
RouterB#sh run
.
.
snmp-server community makesecret RW
.
.
```

Figure 9-10 shows the setup of the configured router and the computer running the SNMP management software. The SNMP management software issues the MIB to the router at port 161, and the router returns the response. Figure 9-11 shows another example of using SNMP to obtain interface information about a router. The SNMP manager was configured with the host IP address of 10.10.10.1, a set value (port #) of 161 and the 10 character community string of *makesecret* shown as * * * * * * * * * *. The MIB (ifspeed) was sent to the router and a status for each of the interfaces was provided. The data displayed shows the speed settings for the router's interfaces.

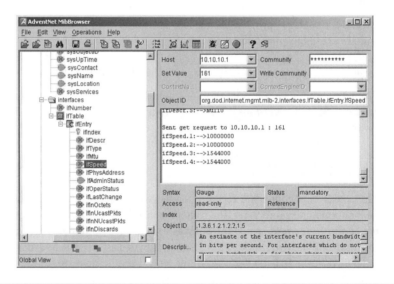

FIGURE 9-11   Using an SNMP software management tool to obtain interface speed settings.

Another important application of SNMP is for obtaining traffic data statistics. An example of this is shown in Figure 9-12. The SNMP management program issued the MIB (ifOutOctets), which returns the number of octets of data that have left the router. (The router has a counter that keeps track.) The first result shows ifOutOctets 7002270. The next result display shows that the ifOutOctets returns a value of 7002361.

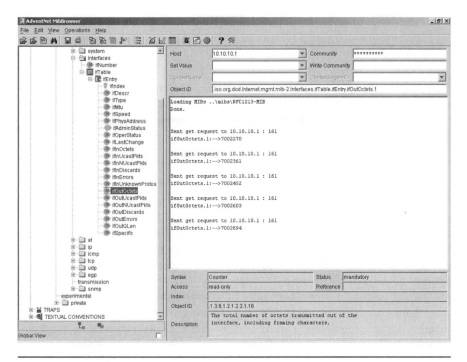

FIGURE 9-12   An example of using SNMP to collect data traffic statistics.

The SNMP management program collecting the statistics keeps track of the time interval between measurements and the number of octets that have passed. This information can be used to calculate the average traffic flow by hour, day, week, or month, depending on the information needed. An example of collecting traffic route statistics is provided in section 9-7. A final note about the router's counter: the counter does not reset unless the router is rebooted.

Power over Ethernet (PoE)

One of the challenges the network administrator faces as the campus network grows is making sure that electrical power is available for the networking devices (for example, switches, wireless access points, and IP phones). It is not always practical or affordable to run electrical power every place a networking device is needed. This challenge is met with **Power over Ethernet (PoE)**. The Power over Ethernet standard (IEEE 802.3af) was approved in 2003 for networks running 10BASE-T, 100BASE-T, and 1000BASE-T technologies. This provided a standardized technology that can be used to supply power over existing CAT5 or better network cabling (CAT5 or better) to the networking devices.

The benefits of PoE include the following:

- It is not necessary to run external power to all networking devices.
- You can run power and data over one cable.
- Monitoring of power management via SNMP.
- Networking devices can be moved easily.

Power over Ethernet (PoE)
Technology developed to supply power over the network cabling (CAT5 or better)

The power provided by PoE as defined by IEEE 802.3af is as follows:

15.4 watts per port to Ethernet devices

48 volt system

PD
Powered Device

PSE
Power Sourcing Equipment

Endpoint PSE
Example is the source port on an Ethernet switch that connects to the PD

Midspan (mid-point) PSE
Used to provide power to a PD when a powered Ethernet port is not available

There are two pieces of networking hardware defined in PoE. These are the **Powered Device (PD)** and the **Power Sourcing Equipment (PSE)**. There are three main functions provided by the PSE:

- Capability of detecting a PD
- Supplying power to the PD
- Power supply monitoring

There are two types of power sourcing equipment (PSE). These are the **endpoint PSE** and the **midspan (mid-point) PSE**. An example of an endpoint PSE is the source port on an Ethernet switch that connects, via a cable, to a PD. The power to the PD can be delivered in two ways, over the active data pairs (for example, 1–2, 3–6) or via pairs 4–5, 7–8. This is shown on Figure 9-13 (a and b). Both types of power delivery can be used for 10BASE-T, 100 BASE-T, and 1000 BASE-T. The most common way of power delivery is over pairs 1–2/3–6 as shown in Figure 9-13 (a).

A midspan or mid-point PSE is used to provide power to a PD when a powered Ethernet port is not available. This setup requires the use of a power injector and typically uses pairs 4–5/7–8, and this does not support 1000 BASE-T connections.

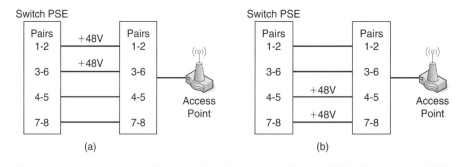

FIGURE 9-13 The two ways to deliver power to the PD: (a) pairs 1–2/3–6 and (b) 4–5/7–8

The PD is the actual device receiving power such as wireless access points and an IP phone. There are four classes of PD devices:

Class 0 (.44 to 12.95 watts)

Class 1 (.44 to 3.84 watts)

Class 2 (3.84 to 6.49 watts)

Class 3 (6.49 to 12.95 watts)

Resistive Power Discovery
Looking for devices that support PoE and have a 25kΩ resistor connected between the transmit and receive pairs

PD devices are "discovered" by the PSE by sending discovery signals on active and inactive Ethernet ports. The discovery process (called **Resistive Power Discovery**) is basically looking for devices that support PoE. Valid PDs will have a 25kΩ resistor connected between the transmit and receive pairs. Before full power is delivered to the PD, two low-voltage "discovery" signals are sent out to verify that a compatible PoE device is attached. The second of the two signals is a slightly higher voltage than the first but neither is large enough to damage an incompatible device. If the PSE detects a compatible PD, then the full 48 Volts is applied to all ports that have compatible PDs connected.

A new version of Power over Ethernet, called **PoE Plus**, based on the IEEE 802.3at standard is now available. PoE Plus provides the following features:

- supports both 802.3af (PoE) and 802.3at (PoE Plus) PDs
- support for midspan PSEs for 10000 BASE-T
- supports a minimum of 30 watts of power for the PD
- support for 10GBASE-T
- will operate with CAT5 and higher cabling

There are a limited number of problems with PoE as long as the devices support IEEE 802.3af. In cases where a vendor proprietary PoE equipment is being used, the PSEs and PDs must be compatible. Also the Network Administrator must be aware of how many PDs are connected to the PSE and that the total power requirements for the PDs does not exceed the PSEs limit. For example, a network could have 10 access point and 25 IP phone all requiring a PoE connection. The total number of devices requiring power can exceed the power output for a PSE and possibly damaging the device.

9-6 Switch/VLAN Configuration

The networking switch was introduced in Chapter 4. The basic functions and operation of a managed switch were introduced, as were the various modes of operations. This section examines the function of using a switch in a VLAN within the campus network. The terminology and steps for implementing VLANs will be first presented. The second part examines basic Cisco switch configuration and provides an introduction to the commands needed for configuring the VLAN. The third part of section 9-6 demonstrates the commands needed to set-up a static VLAN. The section concludes with a discussion on the Spanning-Tree Protocol (STP).

Virtual LAN (VLAN)

A switch can be configured as a **VLAN (Virtual LAN)** where a group of host computers and servers are configured as if they are in the same LAN even if they reside across routers in separate LANs. The advantage of using VLANs is the network administrator can group computers and servers in the same VLAN based on the organizational group (e.g. Sales, Engineering) even if they are not on the same physical segment or even the same building.

There are three types of VLANs; **port-based**, **tag-based**, and **protocol-based**. The port-based VLAN is one where the host computers connected to specific ports on a switch are assigned to a specific VLAN. For example, assume the computers connected to switch ports 2, 3, and 4 are assigned to the Sales VLAN 2 while the computers connected to switch ports 6, 7, and 8 are assigned to the Engineering VLAN 3 as shown in Figure 9-14. The switch will be configured as a port-based VLAN so that the groups of ports [2,3,4] are assigned to the sales VLAN while ports [6,7,8] belong to the Engineering VLAN. The devices assigned to the same VLAN will share broadcasts for that LAN however, computers that are connected to ports not assigned to the VLAN will not share the broadcasts. For example, the computers in VLAN 2 (Sales)

PoE Plus
A new version of PoE based on IEEE 802.3at

VLAN (Virtual LAN)
A group of host computers and servers that are configured as if they are in the same LAN even if they reside across routers in separate LANs

Port-based VLAN
Host computers connected to specific ports on a switch are assigned to a specific VLAN

Tagged-based VLAN
Used VLAN ID based on 802.1Q

Protocol-Based VLAN
Connection to ports is based on the protocol being used

share the same broadcast domain and computers in VLAN 3 (Engineering) share a different broadcast domain.

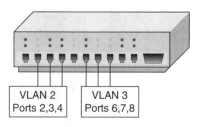

FIGURE 9-14   An example of the grouping for port-based VLANs.

In tag-based VLANs, a tag is added to the Ethernet frames. This tag contains the VLAN ID that is used to identify that a frame belongs to a specific VLAN. The addition of the VLAN ID is based on the 802.1Q specification. An advantage of an 802.1Q VLAN is it helps to contain broadcast and multicast data traffic that helps to minimize data congestion and improve throughput. This specification also provides guidelines for a switch port to belong to more than one VLAN. Additionally, the tag-based VLANs can help provide better security by logically isolating and grouping users

In a protocol-based VLANs, the data traffic is connected to specific ports based on the type of protocol being used. The packet is dropped when it enters the switch if the protocol doesn't match any of the VLANs. For example, an IP network could be set up for the Engineering VLAN on ports 6,7,8 and an IPX network for the Sales VLAN on ports 2,3, and 4. The advantage of this is the data traffic for the two networks is separated.

There are two approaches for assigning VLAN membership:

Static VLAN
Basically a port-based VLAN

Dynamic VLAN
Ports are assigned to a VLAN based on either the compuuter's MAC addrress or the username of the client logged onto the computer

- **Static VLAN:** Basically a port-based VLAN. The assignments are created when ports are assigned to a specific VLAN.
- **Dynamic VLAN:** Ports are assigned to a VLAN based on either the computer's MAC address or the username of the client logged onto the computer. This means that the system has been previously configured with the VLAN assignments for the computer or the username. The advantage of this is the username and/or the computer can move to a different location, but VLAN membership will be retained.

Switch Configuration

This section examines the basics of configuring a Cisco switch. The commands for switch configuration are similar to that of a router. Configuring a switch requires that the privileged mode be entered on the switch. The privileged EXEC mode (also called the enable mode) allows full access for configuring the switch ports and establishing a VLAN. This section focuses on general configuration steps for the switch, examining MAC address information and IP address configuration of the VLANs.

The privileged mode is entered using the command *enable* at the Switch> prompt as shown. The # sign after the switch name indicates you are in the privileged EXEC mode (Switch#).

```
Switch> enable
Password:
Switch#
```

Entry into the switch's privileged mode is typically password-protected. The exception to this is when a switch has not been configured and a password has not been assigned to it. In this case, pressing **Enter** on the keyboard from the Switch> prompt will promote the user to the privilege mode (Switch#) without requesting a password.

Use caution once you have entered the privileged mode in a switch. It is easy to make mistakes, and incorrectly entered switch configurations will adversely affect your network. This text comes with the Net-Challenge switch simulator on the companion CD-ROM to help you gain experience with switch configuration. In fact, most of the switch configuration commands presented in this section can be implemented in the switch simulator on the companion CD-ROM.

Hostname

The next commands examined require that the switch's terminal configuration mode be entered. To do this, enter the command *configure terminal* (abbreviated *conf t*) at the switch# prompt to enter the switch's configuration mode.

```
switch#conf t
Enter configuration commands, one per line. End with CNTL/Z.
switch(config)#
```

Or

```
switch#configure terminal
Enter configuration commands, one per line. End with CNTL/Z.
switch(config)#
```

Note the change in the prompt to switch(config)#. This indicates that the switch is in terminal configuration mode.

The first switch configuration option examined enables the user to assign a hostname to the switch. The generic name or the name of an unconfigured Cisco switch is *switch*, and the **hostname** command enables the user to change the name to specifically identify the switch. For example, valid hostname structures include switchA, switch-A, or switch_A, while switch A is not valid. Valid switch hostnames may not have any spaces. The word *switch* does not have to be used in the hostname.

In the privileged mode (switch#) enter the command **hostname [switch-name]** **<enter>**. This sets the hostname for the switch to *switch-name.* The following example demonstrates how the switch's hostname is changed to *SwitchA*. Notice the change with the switch's name from the first to the second line after the **hostname** command is entered.

```
switch(config)# hostname SwitchA
SwitchA#
```

Configure Terminal
(*conf t*)
Command to enter the swtch's terminal configuration mode

Enable Secret

Switch(config)#
The prompt for the switch's terminal configuration mode

Password protection for the privileged (enable) mode is configured by setting the enable secret. The steps are as follows: Enter the switch's configure terminal mode by entering *configure terminal* or *conf t* at the **Switch#** prompt. Enter the command *enable secret [your-password] <enter>*. An example is shown here:

```
SwitchA# conf t
SwitchA(config)#
SwitchA(config)# enable secret my-secret
```

This example sets the password for entering the switch's privileged EXEC mode to *my-secret*. The password for entering the switch's privileged mode must now be entered to gain access to the mode.

Setting the Line Console Passwords

Switch(config-line)#
The prompt indicating you are in the switch's line configuration mode

The switch has two line connections through which a user may gain access to the switch. The line connections available on a switch can be displayed using the *line ?* command at the **Switch(config)#** prompt. The available line connections typically are as follows:

console   Primary terminal line (console port)

vty   Virtual terminal (for a telnet connection)

The *console* (primary terminal line) is the console port, and *vty* is the virtual terminal used for telnet connections. The following steps demonstrate how to configure password protection for the console port and the virtual terminal.

The console port configuration is as follows: Enter the command *line console 0 <enter>*. Next enter the command *login,* press **Enter**, and then input the command *password [my-secret2]*, where *my-secret2* is the console port password. An example of using these commands follows.

```
SwitchA(config)# line console 0
SwitchA(config-line)# login
SwitchA(config-line)# password my-secret2
```

Note the change in the switch prompt to SwitchA(config-line)#, indicating you are in the switch's line configuration mode.

Password protection for the virtual terminal (line vty) is set from the switch's configuration mode. The virtual terminal is the method for entering the switch via a Telnet connection. The command *line vty 0 15* is first entered. This places the switch in the line configuration mode (config-line). The "0 15 " indicates that sixteen virtual terminal connections can be simultaneously made: The sixteen virtual terminal connections are identified as 0, 1, 2, 3, 4 . . . . Next enter *login*, press **Enter**, followed by entering the command *password [my-secret3]*. The entry *my-secret3* is the password for the virtual terminal connection.

```
SwitchA(config)# line vty 0 4
SwitchA(config-line)# password my-secret3
SwitchA(config-line)# login
```

Layer 3 access to the switch is set by using the following command. Note that the IP address is being set for VLAN 1. The interface for the switch is also enabled at this same point using the *no shutdown* command as shown.

```
SwitchA(config)# interface VLAN 1
SwitchA(config-if)#ip address 172.16.32.2 255.255.255.0
SwitchA(config-if) no shutdown
```

The default gateway for the switch can be set using the following command. The default gateway instructs the switch where to forward the data packet if there isn't a specified route defined in the switch.

```
SwitchA(config)# ip default-gateway 172.16.35.1
```

The configuration settings entered on the VLAN 1 interface can be viewed by entering the following command:

```
SwitchA#show interface VLAN 1
```

The running configuration for the switch is viewed using the **show running-config** command as shown. The startup configuration is displayed using the **show startup-config**, and the running-configuration file is copied to NVRAM using the **copy running-config startup-config** command as shown.

```
SwitchA#show running-configuration
SwitchA#copy running-configuration start-up configuration
```

These examples show that there is a lot of similarity between switch and router configuration at the command line interface. However, the major differences are apparent when configuring a VLAN. The next section demonstrates the steps for configuring a Static VLAN.

Static VLAN Configuration

This section demonstrates the steps for configuring a Static VLAN. In this example, the ports for VLAN 2 (Sales) and VLAN 3 (Engineering) will be defined. This requires that VLAN memberships be defined for the required ports. The steps and the commands will be demonstrated.

The first step for configuring the VLAN is to establish a terminal connection to the switch using the Cisco console cable. The console connection is used to perform the initial configurations that are needed to use the Cisco Network Assistant software.

1. Connect the Console cable to your workstation and switch.
2. Open the HyperTerminal software on your workstation.
3. Make a HyperTerminal connection to the switch. (Same steps as connecting to a router)

Now that you have made a HyperTerminal connection to the switch, the switch's initial prompt should appear as Switch>.

1. At the initial prompt type **enable** or **en**. Once this is done the prompt should change to Switch#. This allows you to enter the privileged mode of the switch.
2. Next type **configure terminal** or **conf t**. Once this is done the prompt should change to Switch(config)#. Doing this places you in the global configuration mode of the switch.
3. Now type **interface Vlan1** or **int Vlan1**. The prompt should now change to *Switch(config-if)#*. You are now able to make changes to Vlan1's interface.
4. Next enter **ip address 192.168.1.1 255.255.255.0**. This command changes the switches IP address to 192.168.1.1
5. Type **no shut**. This is needed for Vlan1 to stay up and active.

You have now set the IP address of the switch to 192.168.1.1. Notice that the subnet mask is set to 255.255.255.0 which places the switch in the 192.168.1.0 network. The IP address is set for Vlan1 because this is the default administrative VLAN for the switch, and it can never be removed. The workstation should be connected to port 1 on the switch, and the computers IP address's should be configured for 192.168.1.2. This places the computer in the same network as that defined for the VLAN1 interface. At this point, use the ***ping*** command to verify network connectivity from the computer to the switch.

The next step is to use the ***show vlan*** command to verify what ports have defined for the switch. By default, all ports are assigned to VLAN 1. An example using the ***show vlan*** command is provided next.

```
Switch# show vlan

VLAN Name                            Status      Ports
---- -------------------------------- ---------- ----------------------------
1    default                          active      Fa0/1, Fa0/2, Fa0/3, Fa0/4
                                                  Fa0/5, Fa0/6, Fa0/7, Fa0/8
                                                  Fa0/9, Fa0/10
```

This shows that all of the FastEthernet interfaces are currently assigned to VLAN 1. In the next step, two additional VLANs will be created for both the Sales and Engineering. This is accomplished modifying the VLAN database as shown in the next steps.

```
SwitchA#vlan database

Switch(vlan)#vlan 2 name Sales
VLAN 2 modified:
    Name: Sales
Switch(vlan)#vlan 3 name Engineering
VLAN 3 modified:
    Name: Engineering
```

The next step is used to verify that the new VLANs have been created.

```
Switch(vlan)# exit
Switch#show vlan

VLAN Name                            Status      Ports
---- -------------------------------- ---------- ----------------------------
1    default                          active      Fa0/1, Fa0/2, Fa0/3, Fa0/4
                                                  Fa0/5, Fa0/6, Fa0/7, Fa0/8
                                                  Fa0/9, Fa0/10
2    Sales                            active
3    Engineering                      active
```

In the next steps, ports will be assigned to the newly created VLANs. This requires that the configuration mode be entered and each FastEthernet interface (port) must be assigned to the proper VLAN. An example is presented for FastEthernet interface 0/2 being assigned to VLAN 2.

```
Switch#conf t
Enter configuration commands, one per line.  End with CNTL/Z.
Switch(config)#int fa 0/2
Switch(config-if)#switchport mode access
Switch(config-if)#switchport access vlan 2
Switch(config-if)#end
```

The next step is used to verify that FastEthernet 0/2 has been assigned to the Sales VLAN (VLAN2). This can be verified using the ***show vlan brief*** command as shown. This command only displays the interfaces assigned to each VLAN.

```
Switch#sh vlan

VLAN Name                             Status      Ports
---- -------------------------------- ---------   ----------------------------
1    default                          active      Fa0/1, Fa0/3, Fa0/4, Fa0/5
                                                  Fa0/6, Fa0/7, Fa0/8, Fa0/9
                                                  Fa0/10
2    Sales                            active      Fa0/2
```

The next steps are to assigned ports 3 and 4 to the Sales VLAN (VLAN 2) and ports 6,7,8 to Engineering (VLAN 3). Once this is completed, the port assignments can be verified using the show VLAN command as shown.

```
Switch#show vlan

VLAN Name                             Status      Ports
---- -------------------------------- ---------   ----------------------------
1    default                          active      Fa0/1, Fa0/5, Fa0/9, Fa0/10

2    Sales                            active      Fa0/2, Fa0/3, Fa0/4

3    Engineering                      active      Fa0/6, Fa0/7, Fa0/8
```

You can look specifically at the assignments for only one of the VLANs by entering the command *show vlan name <vlan-name>* where vlan-name is the name assigned to the VLAN. Please note that the name is case-sensitive. You can also use the number of the VLAN instead using the command *sh vlan id <vlan#>*. Examples of both are presented.

```
Switch#sh vlan name Engineering

VLAN Name                             Status      Ports
---- -------------------------------- ---------   ----------------------
3    Engineering                      active      Fa0/6, Fa0/7, Fa0/8


Switch#show vlan id 3

VLAN Name                             Status      Ports
---- -------------------------------- ---------   ----------------------
3    Engineering                      active      Fa0/6, Fa0/7, Fa0/8
```

The overall configuration of the switch can be viewed using the *show running-config (sh run)* command as shown. Only a part of the configuration is displayed.

```
Switch#sh run       -   -
Building configuration...

Current configuration : 1411 bytes
!
version 12.1
no service pad
service timestamps debug uptime
service timestamps log uptime
no service password-encryption
!
hostname Switch
!
ip subnet-zero
!
spanning-tree mode pvst
no spanning-tree optimize bpdu transmission
spanning-tree extend system-id
!
interface FastEthernet0/1
!-
```

```
interface FastEthernet0/2
switchport access vlan 2
switchport mode access
    .        .
    .        .
    .        .
    .        .
interface FastEthernet0/5
!
interface FastEthernet0/6
 switchport access vlan 3
 switchport mode access
!
interface FastEthernet0/9
!
interface FastEthernet0/10
!
!
interface Vlan1
 ip address 192.168.1.1 255.255.255.0
 no ip route-cache
!
ip http server
!
line con 0
line vty 0 15
 login
end
```

The running-configuration for the switch shows that the FastEthernet interfaces have been assigned to the proper VLANs. Additionally this shows that an IP address has been assigned to the default interface VLAN1.

This portion of the text has demonstrated the steps for creating a static VLAN. Both Sales and Engineering VLANs were created, and specific ports on the switch were assigned to the respective VLANs. Unassigned ports remained as part of the default VLAN 1.

Networking Challenge—Static VLAN Configuration

Use the simulator software included with the text's Companion CD-ROM to demonstrate that you can perform basic switch and static VLAN configuration. Place the CDROM in your computer's drive. Open the *Net-Challenge* folder, and click **NetChallenge.exe**. Once the software is running, click the **Select Challenge** button. This opens a Select Challenge drop-down menu. Select **Chapter 9—Static VLAN Configuration**. This opens a check box that can be used to verify that you have completed all the tasks.

1. Enter the privileged EXEC mode on the switch.
2. Enter the switch's configuration mode, **Router(config)**.
3. Set the hostname of the switch to switch-A.
4. Configure the IP address for VLAN 1 interface with the following:
   IP address: 10.10.20.250
   Subnet mask: 255.255.255.0
5. Enable the VLAN 1 interface.
6. Use the command to display the current VLAN settings for the switch.
7. Issue the command that lets you modify the VLAN database.

8. Create a VLAN called Sales
9. Verify that a new VLAN has been created.
10. Issue the command to enter the fa0/2 interface configuration mode.
11. Enter the sequence of commands that are used to assign interface fa0/2 and fa0/3 to the Sales VLAN.
12. Enter the command that enables you to display the interface assigned to each VLAN.
13. Enter the command that enables you to view specifically the assignments for the Sales VLAN.
14. Issue the command that allows you to view the switch's running-configuration.

Spanning-Tree Protocol

This last section on switches examines the **Spanning-Tree Protocol (STP)**. STP is a link management protocol that prevents looping and also controls data flow over possible redundant data paths. Looping is bad for Ethernet networks because duplicate packets can be sent over redundant paths. The switches should only send the packets over one path. The Spanning Tree Protocol is used to ensure only one data path is selected. The Spanning Tree Protocol also forces one of the redundant data paths into a stand-by mode by placing the path in a blocked state.

Switches that are participating in the Spanning-Tree Protocol exchange information with other switches in the form of **bridge protocol data units (BPDUs)**. Switches use the BPDUs for the following:

- Election of a root switch for the spanning-tree network topology.
- Removing redundant data paths.
- The shortest distance to a root switch is calculated.
- A port from each switch is selected as the best path to the root switch.
- Ports that are part of the Spanning-Tree Protocol are selected.

Switches assume they are the root switch until the BPDUs are exchanged and a root switch is elected. The root switch elected is the switch with the lowest MAC address. Part of the BPDU packet is shown. In this case a switch with the MAC address 0030194A6940 is issuing that data packet as start of the bidding process to see which switch will be elected as the "root" switch.

BPDU Config BID=0030194A6940 PID=0x801B

The "Config" indicates this is a **Configuration BPDU** and is used by the switches to elect the "root" switch. There are two other types of packets that can come from the switch. These are the **Topology Change Notification (TCN)**, which is used to indicate that a there has been a change in the switch network topology. The third is the **Topology Change Notification Acknowledgement (TCA)**. This is an acknowledgement from another switch that the TCN has been received.

An example of the contents of a BPDU is provided in Figure 9-15. This is showing that the Root ID—MAC address is 0030194A6940. The BPDUs are exchanged at regular intervals and are used to keep the switches notified of any changes in the network topology. The default notification interval is 2 seconds and is called the the "Hello Time," as shown in Figure 9-15.

Spanning-Tree Protocol
A link management protocol that prevents looping and also controls data flow over possible redundant data paths

Bridge Protocol Data Unit (BPDU)
Used by switches to share information with other switches that are participating in the Spanning-Tree Protocol.

Configuration BPDU
Used by switches to elect the "root" switch

Topology Change Notification (TCN)
Used to indicate that there has been a change in the switch

Topology Change Notification Acknowledgement (TCA)
An acknowledgement from another switch that the TCN has been received.

```
  IEEE 802.1D - Bridge
  Management Protocol
  (IEEE 802.1D)
    Protocol ID            0x0000    (Bridge PDU)
  Bridge Protocol Data
  Unit   (BPDU)
    Version                0
    Type                   0x00    (Configuration)
  Flags                    0x00
      >                    0... ....    Not Topology Change Acknowledgment
      >                    .... ...0    Not Topology Change
      >                    .000 000.    Not Used (MBZ)
    Root ID - Settable     32768
    Priority
    Root ID - MAC Address  0030194A6940    [No Vendor Name. - 4A6940]    [0030194A6940]
    Root Path Cost         0
    Bridge ID - Settable   32768
    Priority
    Bridge ID - MAC Address 0030194A6940   [No Vendor Name. - 4A6940]    [0030194A6940]
    Port Identifier        0x801B
    Message Age            0.000000 secs
    Max Age               20.000000 secs
    Hello Time             2.000000 secs
    Forward Delay         15.000000 secs
```

FIGURE 9-15   An example of a BPDU—Bridge Protocol Data Unit packet information

The switch will not begin to forward data packets when a networking device is connected to a port. Instead, during this delay, the switch will first begin to process the BPDUs to determine the topology of the switch network. This is called the forward delay, which is listed in Figure 9-15. This is showing that the forward delay is 15 seconds, which is the default value set by the root switch. During the delay period, the switch is going through the listening and learning states.

There are five Spanning-Tree Protocol states:

- **Blocking State:** In this state, the switch is not sending data out of the ports. However, the switch is receiving and monitoring the BPDUs. This state is used to prevent any possible switching loops.
- **Listening State:** BPDUs are being processed.
- **Learning State:** The switch is learning source MAC addresses from the received data packets and will add the addresses to the MAC address table.
- **Forwarding State:** The switch is now sending and receiving data packets. The BPDUs are still to be monitored for any possible change in the switch network.
- **Disabled:** This is a setting available for the network administrator to manually disable the port. This is not part of the Spanning-Tree Protocol but rather a function available on the switch.

9-7   ANALYZING CAMPUS NETWORK DATA TRAFFIC

The focus of this chapter has been on the issues of configuring and managing the campus network. A key issue in network management is network monitoring and the collection of utilization and error statistics.

Section 9-5 introduced the SNMP protocol for use in network management. An example was presented that shows how to obtain the number of octets leaving a router. This type of information can be used in a campus network to monitor the flow of data for many points in the network. Statistics can be obtained for hourly, daily, weekly, and monthly data traffic. This section discusses plots of network router utilization obtained via the router's SNMP port.

Figure 9-16 is a plot of a router's hourly data traffic. The plot shows the average number of bits coming into the router and the average number of bits out. The network administrator should become familiar with the typical hourly data traffic pattern for their network. Notice the decrease in data traffic in the early morning and the dramatic increase in data traffic around 12:00. The traffic clearly shows some type of disturbance around 12:00. The plot is showing that the bit rate significantly increases for a few minutes. This is not necessarily a problem, but it is something that a network administrator will want to watch.

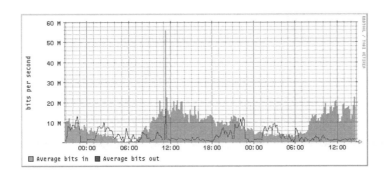

FIGURE 9-16   The hourly plot of a router's data traffic.

In this case, the network administrator looked at the daily log of network activity for the same router. This plot is shown in Figure 9-17. The cycle of the data traffic from morning to night is as expected, heavy data traffic about noon and very low data traffic in the mornings. An interesting note is the noon data traffic spikes on the first Wednesday and then repeats the following Wednesday. Whatever is causing the change in traffic appears to happen on Wednesdays. If this sudden change in data traffic turned out to be something of concern, a protocol analyzer could be set up to capture the data traffic on Wednesdays around noon so that the traffic pattern could be explained.

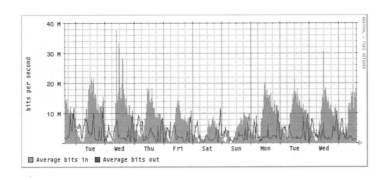

FIGURE 9-17   The daily plot of a router's data traffic.

Sometimes the graph of the network traffic over a longer period of time is needed. Figure 9-18 shows the data traffic through the router over a six-week period. The traffic shows some consistency except for a change from week 11 to week 12. Most likely this can be explained by examining the network trouble reports and maintenance logs to see if this router was briefly out of service.

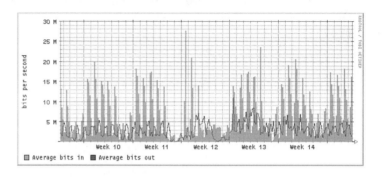

FIGURE 9-18   The weekly plot of a router's data traffic.

Justifying the expansion of a network's capability (for example, higher data rate or better core or distribution service) requires showing the manager data traffic statistics. Figure 9-19 is a plot of the router's monthly data traffic. The summer shows a significant decrease in data traffic. The plot also shows that the network was down once in the June–July period and again in January. The manager wants to know if there is justification to increase the data rate of the router to 1 gigabit (1 GB). (The router's current data rate is 100 Mbps.) Is there justification to upgrade the router to 1 GB? Probably not, at least not immediately. The maximum measured average data rate is about 16 Mbps. The router's 100 Mbps data rate does not seem to be causing any traffic congestion problems.

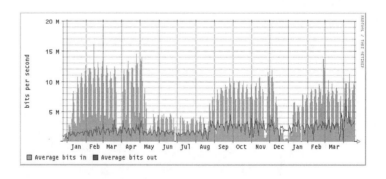

FIGURE 9-19   The monthly plot of a router's data traffic.

This section has shown how keeping logs of data traffic can be used to spot potential network problems and to help plan for possible future expansion of the network.

Summary

The fundamentals of configuring and managing a campus network have been presented in this chapter. This has been a brief overview of the campus network, and you should understand that each of the topics presented in this chapter could easily be expanded to fill an entire textbook(s). What you should understand from this reading is that configuring and managing a campus network is a major task. It is critical for the networking group to have people who truly understand the many aspects of configuring and managing the campus network. Configuring and managing a campus DNS and DHCP service is a challenging task. Planning the integration of the equipment in the layers for the campus network is also a challenging task. Monitoring the network activity requires additional networking staff resources. You should appreciate the fact that configuring and managing a campus type network requires the expertise of many people with many different networking capabilities as well as understand the following:

- The importance and function of the three layers of a campus network
- How DHCP and DNS services work
- The importance of incorporating network services such as DHCP and DNS into a campus network
- How SNMP management tools can be used to monitor the data traffic and performance within a campus network

Questions and Problems

Section 9-2

1. What networking equipment is usually found in the core of a campus network?
2. How are route policies applied in the core?
3. What is the advantage of using a layer 3 switch in the core of the campus network?
4. Can a layer 2 switch be used in the core of the campus network? Why or why not?
5. What is the function of the distribution layer in a campus network?
6. Can routing policies be implemented in the distribution layer? Why or why not?
7. What is the purpose of the access layer?
8. The campus network servers are typically located in what layer?
9. Why are routers typically not interconnected at the distribution layer?
10. What is the name for the part of the campus network that carries the bulk of the routed data traffic?
11. List three criteria for selecting the network media. Which is the final decision factor?
12. Which media is the best choice in a campus network?
13. Define load balancing in terms of data traffic flow in a computer network.
14. Define per-destination load balancing.
15. Define per-packet load balancing.

16. Referring to Figure 9-1 from the beginning of the chapter, discuss how data flows from a computer in LAN B to a computer in LAN D. Assume that the routing protocol is OSPF, the cost of RouterB's ge-0/0/0 interface has been set to 10, and the cost of RouterB's ge-0/2/0 interface has been set to 20.

Section 9-3

17. With regards to campus DHCP service, the IP address assignment is based on what?
18. What is the subnet mask for creating the four subnets illustrated in Figure 9-2 earlier in the chapter?
19. How are BOOTP and DHCP related?
20. Define *lease time*.
21. What networking function is required if the DHCP server is not on the same LAN? Why is this networking function required?
22. What command enables a DHCP relay on a Cisco router?
23. Why is packet 14 in the captured DHCP packets shown in Figure 9-5 (shown earlier in the chapter) a broadcast?
24. What are the port numbers for the DHCP protocol?

Section 9-4

25. List 11 top level domains.
26. What is the purpose of a root server in DNS?
27. A new network wants to obtain a domain name. The first step is what?
28. The hostname and IP address for a computer is stored in what for a campus DNS service?
29. How is it possible for the command *ping www.networkB.edu* to find the destination without an IP address?
30. What is the purpose of reverse DNS? Where is it used?

Section 9-5

31. What port number does SNMP use and what transport protocol?
32. The SNMP MIB get request *ifDescr* returns what information from a router?
33. What is the purpose of the MIB?
34. Write the Cisco router command for configuring SNMP on a Cisco router. Assume a community string of networking and set the permissions to read-only. Show the router prompt.
35. The command *show run* is entered on a Cisco router. Describe what the output "SNMP-server test RO" means.
36. What SNMP MIBs were most likely issued to the router discussed in section 9-7?

Use Figure 9-20 to answer questions 37 to 41.

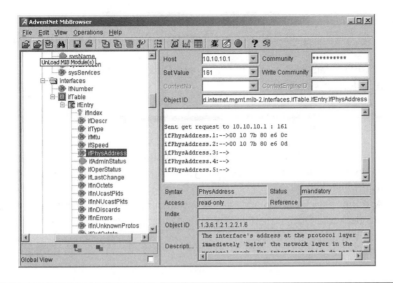

FIGURE 9-20   For problems 37–41.

37. What MIB was issued?
38. What information was returned?
39. What port number was used?
40. What protocol is being used? How do you know?
41. Who is the manufacturer of this networking device?
42. What are the two types of devices defined by PoE?
43. What should you check if you are installing a Power over Ethernet connection using computer equipment from two different manufactures?
44. Cite four benefits of Power over Ethernet.
45. What is resistive power discovery, and how does it work?
46. What wire pairs are used in PoE?
47. How much power can a class 0 PD PoE device source?
48. What are the benefits of PoE Plus?

Section 9-6

49. What is a VLAN?
50. List the three types of VLANs.
51. What type of VLAN is port-based?
52. What commands are used to assign the IP address 192.168.20.5 to VLAN1?
53. What switch command is used to display the interfaces assigned to a VLAN?
54. What is the purpose of the VLAN database?
55. List the commands used to create VLAN5 and name this VLAN Marketing group.
56. List the commands used to assign FA0/5 to the Marketing-group VLAN (VLAN5). Show the switch prompts.
57. What is the purpose of the Spanning-Tree Protocol?
58. What is a BPDU, and what its purpose?
59. Discuss how a root switch is elected.

60. What are the five STP protocol states?
61. A BPDU data packet shows that the "Hello Time" is 2.0 secs. What information does this provide?
62. A BPDU data packet lists the "Forward Delay" as 15 seconds. What information does this provide?

Critical Thinking

63. Your supervisor asks you if a layer 2 switch could be used in the core of the campus network. Prepare a response to your supervisor. Be sure to justify your recommendation.
64. A 1Gbps data link is to be set-up between building A and building B in a campus network. Does it matter if the link is fiber or microwave or some other media? Explain your answer.

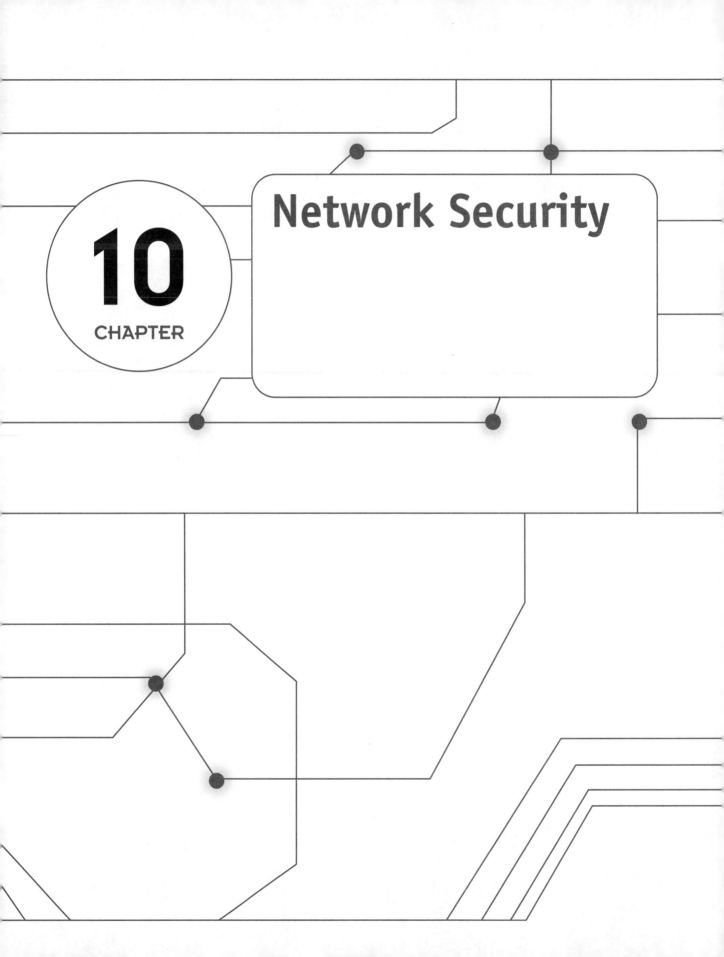

10
CHAPTER

Network Security

CHAPTER OUTLINE

10-1   Introduction
10-2   Intrusion (How an Attacker Gains Control of a Network)
10-3   Denial of Service
10-4   Firewalls and Access Lists

10-5   Intrusion Detection
10-6   Analyzing Unsecured Data Packets
Summary
Questions and Problems

OBJECTIVES

- Examine how an attacker gains control of a network
- Understand how denial of service attacks are initiated

- Examine techniques to protect the network
- Investigate how to configure access lists
- Analyze unsecured data packets

KEY TERMS

social engineering
password cracking
dictionary attack
brute force attack
packet sniffing
IPsec
buffer overflow
netstat -a -b
virus
worm

WEP (wired equivalent privacy)
WPA, WPA2
war driving
denial of service (DoS)
directed broadcast
spoof
firewall
access lists (ACLs)
packet filtering

proxy server
Stateful
SMB
permit ip any any host
intrusion detection
signatures
probing
SSH (secure shell)

10-1   INTRODUCTION

The objective of this chapter is to provide an overview of network security. A campus network is vulnerable to many types of network attacks. While network attacks can't be prevented, there are some steps that can be taken to minimize the impact an attack has on the network.

The first type of attack examined in this chapter is intrusion, an attacker gaining access to a remote network system. There are many ways by which an attacker can gain access to the network. These are social engineering, password cracking, packet sniffing, vulnerable software, viruses, and wireless connections (see Figure 10-1). These issues are examined in section 10-2. Denial of service is an attack with a goal of preventing services to a machine or to a network. This can be accomplished by flooding the network with lots of data packets or through hacking vulnerable software. For example, a certain software package might reboot if a certain sequence of data packets is sent to the host computer. This is a common problem because many software packages have this vulnerability. Denial of service and distributed denial of service attacks are examined in section 10-3.

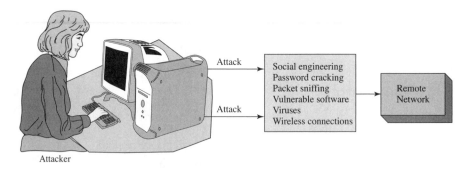

FIGURE 10-1   The ways an attacker can gain access to a remote network.

Techniques for using firewalls to protect a network are examined in section 10-4. This section discusses the role of stateful firewalls in protecting a network. In addition this section demonstrates how to configure access lists on a router. The concept of intrusion detection is briefly examined in section 10-5. The last section (10-6) uses the Surveyor Demo protocol analyzer to examine the difference in unsecured and secured data packets generated from a telnet session and an SSH (secure shell).

10-2   INTRUSION (HOW AN ATTACKER GAINS CONTROL OF A NETWORK)

Hackers use many techniques to gain control of a network. The network administrator needs to be aware of the different ways an intruder can gain network access or even control. The information presented in this chapter is an example of what the hacker already knows and what the network administrator needs to know to protect the network.

Social Engineering

The first issue of intrusion is **social engineering**. This is a way for an intruder to gain enough information from people to gain access to the network. As an example, an attacker calls a user on a network and claims he or she is from the computer support division of the network. The attacker tells the user that there is a problem with the user's account and then asks for the user's name and password. This is shown in Figure 10-2. Often a user will blindly provide the information, not realizing that the person calling is not associated with the network and is in fact an attacker. This gives the attacker an account (username and password) to attack the network from. This is just one example of social engineering. Some attackers use discarded trash to gain access to user passwords. This problem is not completely solvable because as the number of users increases, so do the possible ways to attack the network. The solution is educating users about not sharing information on how they access the network and to always require identification from support staff.

Social Engineering
A way for an intruder to obtain enough information from people to gain access to the network

FIGURE 10-2   An example of social engineering.

Password Cracking

If the attacker has access to the user's network but can't get the password from the user, the attacker can use **password cracking**. This can be done via brute force or via checking for "weak" passwords. Most networks require their users to use strong passwords.

   In password cracking, the attacker can try to guess the user's password. One method is the dictionary attack. The **dictionary attack** (Figure 10-3) uses known passwords and many variations (upper- and lowercase and combinations) to try to log in to your account. This is why many network systems prompt you not to use a dictionary word as a password. A **brute force attack** means the attacker uses every possible combination of characters for the password. (*Note:* Some attackers will use a combination brute force and dictionary attacks.)

Password Cracking
The attacker tries to guess the user's password

Dictionary Attack
Uses known passwords and many variations (upper and lowercase and combinations) to try to log in to your account

Brute Force Attack
Attacker uses every possible combination of characters for the password

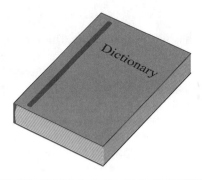

FIGURE 10-3　The dictionary attack.

Here are steps for preventing password cracking:
- Don't use passwords that are dictionary words.
- Don't use your username as your password.
- Don't use your username spelled backward as your password.
- Limit the number of login attempts.
- Make your password strong, which means it is sufficiently long (eight or more characters) and is an alphanumeric combination (for example, A b 1 & G 2 5 h).
- Change passwords often.

Packet Sniffing

Packet Sniffing
A technique where the contents of data packets are watched

IPsec
IP security

Another way attackers can obtain a password is by sniffing the network's data packets. **Packet sniffing** assumes that the attacker can see the network data packets. The attacker will have to insert a device on the network that allows him or her to see the data packets (Figure 10-4). The attacker will watch the data packets until a telnet or FTP data packet passes (or one from many of the other applications that have unencrypted logins). Many of these applications pass the username and password over the network in plain text. *Plain text* means that the information is in a human readable form. If the attacker captures all data packets from a user's computer, then the chances are good that the attacker can obtain the user's login name and password on one of the network's computers. The way to prevent this is by encrypting the user's name and password. An encrypted alternative to telnet is SSH (secure shell). The packets that pass across this SSH connection are encrypted. The reasons for securing data packets are examined in section 10-6. SSL (secure socket layer) is an encryption used by Web servers. For example, the packet transmission is encrypted when a credit card number is entered. There is also a secure version of FTP.

In these examples, the security is implemented at the application layer. Security can also be implemented at layer 3 using **IPsec** (IP security). In IPsec each packet is encrypted prior to transmission across the network link. IPsec is also a method used to encrypt VPN tunnels (see Chapter 8).

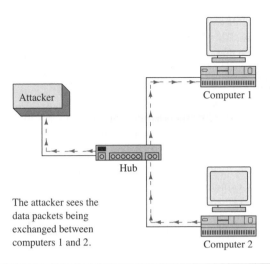

FIGURE 10-4   An example of packet sniffing.

Vulnerable Software

In the process of writing large amounts of code, errors happen that can open access to the code and to a network. The basic attack that capitalizes on these errors is the **buffer overflow**. The buffer overflow happens when a program attempts to put more data into a buffer than it was configured to hold and the overflow writes past the end of the buffer and over adjacent memory locations. The program stack contains data plus instructions that it will run. Assume, for example, that a program includes a variable size of 128 bytes. It is possible that the programmer didn't include instructions to check the maximum size of the variable to make sure it is smaller than 128 bytes. An attacker will look through pages and pages of source code and look for a vulnerability that allows the attacker to issue a buffer overflow. The attacker finds the variable and sends data to the application assigned to that variable. For example, a web application could have a vulnerability with long URLs assigned to a variable within it. If the attacker makes the URL long enough, then the buffer overflow could allow the attacker's code to be placed in the stack. When the program counter gets to the inserted code, the inserted code is run, and the attacker then has remote access to the machine. This is shown in Figure 10-5.

Buffer Overflow
Happens when a program tries to put more data into a buffer than it was configured to hold

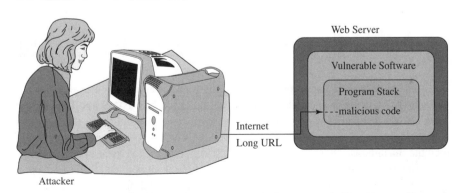

Attacker

FIGURE 10-5   An example of a buffer overflow attack.

Sometimes buffer overflows don't allow instructions to be run, but rather the application will crash. This is used in denial of service attacks, examined in section 10-4. A common code that gets run in buffer overflow attacks is setting up a *backdoor* to gain entry into the computer. What the attacker is doing is creating an application on a port and then connecting to the port. The attacker can also use this to place viruses in the computer. For example, the attacker finds a vulnerability in the source code for an operating system, such as the SSL code on a web server. The attacker downloads malicious code onto the server and then connects to the machine and instructs the code to begin attacking other machines.

Steps for Preventing Vulnerable Software Attacks
It is important to do the following to prevent vulnerable software attacks:

netstat -a -b
(-a) Command used to display the ports currently open on a Windows operating system and (-b) used to display the executable involved in creating the connection or listening port

- Keep software patches and service packs for the operating system current.
- Turn off all services and ports that are not needed on a machine. For example, if your machine does not use Web service, then turn this service off. Leaving these services on is like leaving the windows and doors open to your house. You are just inviting an attacker to come in. If you aren't using a service, shut the access. The command *netstat -a* can be used to display the ports currently open on the Windows operating system. This command shows who is connected to your machine and the port numbers. An example is provided here:

```
c: netstat -a
Active Connections
Proto Local     Address       Foreign Address      State
TCP   pcsalsa2  :1087         PC-SALSA2:0          LISTENING
TCP   pcsalsa2  :1088         PC-SALSA2:0          LISTENING
TCP   pcsalsa2  :1089         PC-SALSA2:0          LISTENING
TCP   pcsalsa2  :1090         PC-SALSA2:0          LISTENING
TCP   pcsalsa2  :135          PC-SALSA2:0          LISTENING
TCP   pcsalsa2  :1025         PC-SALSA2:0          LISTENING
TCP   pcsalsa2  :1087         salsa.chile.Edu:80   ESTABLISHED
TCP   pcsalsa2  :1088         salsa.chile.Edu:80   ESTABLISHED
TCP   pcsalsa2  :1089         salsa.chile.Edu:80   CLOSE_WAIT
TCP   pcsalsa2  :1090         salsa.chile.Edu:80   CLOSE_WAIT
TCP   pcsalsa2  :137          PC-SALSA2:0          LISTENING
TCP   pcsalsa2  :138          PC-SALSA2:0          LISTENING
TCP   pcsalsa2  :nbsession    PC-SALSA2:0          LISTENING
UDP   pcsalsa2  :nbname       *:                   *
UDP   pcsalsa2  :nbdatagram   *:                   *
```

Another useful command is **netstat -b**, which shows the executable involved creating the connection or listening port. An example is provided next that shows that Internet Explorer was used to establish the connection.

```
c: netstat - b
Active Connections

  Proto    Local Address    Foreign Address       State        PID
  TCP      pc-salsa:1152     salsa.chile.edu:http   ESTABLISHED  876
  [iexplore.exe]
```

The ports that are listening are just waiting for a connection. For example, ports 135 and 137 (shown in the *netstat –a* example) are the NETBIOS and file sharing ports for Microsoft. Every port that is established shows listening, and that port can accept a connection. For example, if your application is vulnerable and it is listening, then the machine is vulnerable to an attack. It is good idea to check to see what applications are running on your machine. And again, it is a good idea to turn off ports that are not needed. The steps for turning off ports depend on the application. For example, if port 80 (HTTP) is running, then go to the Windows services and turn off the web application.

Viruses and Worms

A **virus** is a piece of malicious computer code that when run on your machine can damage your hardware, software, or other files. Computer viruses typically are attached to executable files and can be spread when the infected program is run. The computer virus is spread by sharing infected files or sending emails with the attached files that are infected with the virus.

Problems caused by viruses include the following:

- Annoyance
- Clogging up the mail server
- Denial of service
- Data loss
- Open holes for others to access your machine

Viruses used to be a problem passed along by exchanging computer disks. Today, most viruses are exchanged via attachments to email, as shown in Figure 10-6. For example, a user receives an email that says "Look at this!" trying to coax the user into opening the attachment. By opening the attachment, the user could possibly infect his or her computer with a virus.

Virus
A piece of malicious computer code that, when opened, can damage your hardware, software, or other files.

FIGURE 10-6 An example of how computer viruses are spread.

A computer **worm** is a type of computer virus that attacks computers, typically proliferating by itself (self-replicating) and can deny service to networks. Computer worms do not need to be attached to an executable file to be distributed but can use the network to send copies of themselves to other computers. A common objective of a worm is to establish a "back door" in the infected computer, which enables an attacker access to someone's computer.

The following are steps to take to prevent viruses:

Worm
A type of virus that attacks computers, typically proliferates by itself and can deny service to networks

- Open only attachments that come from known sources. Even this can be a problem because email addresses can be spoofed, or the message can come from a known person whose computer has been infected.
- Require that the emails you receive be digitally signed so that you can verify the sender.
- Always run antivirus software on the client machines. The antivirus software is not 100% effective but will catch most viruses.
- Include email server filters to block specific types of emails or attachments.
- Keep the antivirus software up to date.
- Keep the operating system and applications software current
- Use personal firewalls when possible

Wireless Vulnerabilities

WEP (Wired Equivalent Privacy)
The goal is to provide the same security of a wireless connection that a wired connection provides

WPA, WPA2
Improved methods for securing wireless transfers

War Driving
Using wireless equipment to detect wireless management packets

With **WEP (wired equivalent privacy)**, the goal is to provide the same security for a wireless connection that a wired connection provides. The problem with WEP is that the encryption is not very strong, and an attacker can gain access through decrypting the data packets. An improvement with wireless security is provided with WPA and WPA2. **WPA** stands for WiFi Protected Access, and it supports user authentication and replaces WEP as the primary way for securing wireless transfers. **WPA2** is an improved version of WPA that enhances wireless security by incorporating authentication of the user.

War driving is a term that applies to driving with an antenna out the door connected to a mobile device running Windows or Linux (Figure 10-7). A wireless card in a PC and a software application are used to detect management packets that come from the wireless access points. Some access points allow the management packets to be turned off. All 11 channels must be cycled through to check for data (management packets). The software can also determine if wireless security is turned on, the type of access points, and so on. If wireless security is not enabled, then the attacker can attempt to break into the network. If the wireless security features are not enabled, the packets that come from the access points can be viewed.

Here are three steps to take to protecting a wireless network:

- Make sure WPA is enabled.
- Encrypt the data that is being transferred via the wireless network
- Use a wireless system with more robust security (for example, EAP-FAST).

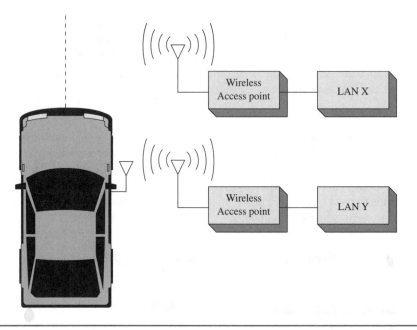

FIGURE 10-7 An example of war driving. The attacker in the car can pick up the wireless data packets' access points.

10-3   DENIAL OF SERVICE

Denial of Service (DoS) means that a service is being denied to a computer, network, or network server. Denial of service attacks can be on individual machines, on the network that connects the machines, or on all machines simultaneously.

Denial of Service (DoS)
A service is being denied to a computer, network, or server

You can initiate a denial of service attack by exploiting software vulnerabilities. For example, a software vulnerability can permit a buffer overflow, causing the machine to crash. This affects all applications, even secure applications.

The vulnerable software denial of service attack attacks the system by making it reboot repeatedly. Denial of service attacks can also be on routers via the software options that are available for connecting to a router. For example, SNMP management software is marketed by many companies and is supported by many computer platforms. Many of the SNMP packages use a similar core code that could contain the same vulnerability.

Another denial of service attack is a SYN attack. This refers to the TCP SYN (synchronizing) packet (introduced in Chapter 5). An attacker sends many TCP SYN packets to a host, opening up many TCP sessions. The host machine has limited memory set aside for open connections. If all the TCP connections are opened by the SYN attack, other users are kept from accessing services from the computer because the connection buffer is full. Most current operating systems take countermeasures against the SYN attack.

Denial of service attacks can affect the network bandwidth and the end points on the network. The classic example is the Smurf attack (Figure 10-8), which required few resources from the attacker. The attacker sent a small packet and got many packets in return. The attacker would pick a victim and an intermediate site. Figure 10-8 shows an attacker site, an intermediate site, and a victim site. The intermediate site has subnets of 10.10.1.0 and 10.10.2.0. The victim is at 10.10.1.0. The attackers send a packet to 10.10.1.255, which is a broadcast address for the 10.10.1.0 subnet. The attacker will spoof the source address information, making it look as if the packet came from the victim's network. All of the machines on the 10.10.1.0 subnet will send a reply back to the source address. Remember, the attacker has spoofed the source address so the replies will be sent to the victim's network. If this attack were increased to all of the subnets in the 10.0.0.0 network, then an enormous amount of data packets will be sent to the victim's network. This enables the attacker to generate a lot of data traffic on the victim's network without requiring the attacker to have many resources.

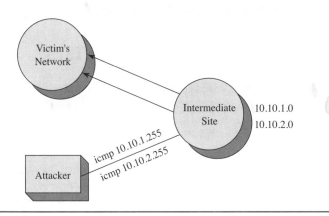

FIGURE 10-8   An example of a Smurf attack.

This type of attack is not new, and there are some steps that can be taken to stop a network from becoming an intermediate site. Cisco routers have an interface command that blocks broadcast packets to that subnet. This prevents a network from becoming an intermediate site for a network attack such as this. Make sure this command or a similar command is a default or has been enabled on the router's interface:

```
no ip directed-broadcast
```

Directed Broadcast
The broadcast is sent to a specific subnet

But aren't layer 3 devices supposed to stop broadcasts? This is true for general broadcasts (all 32 bits set to 1s or "F F F F F F F F" or 255.255.255.255). Routers will always stop these broadcasts. The type of broadcast used in this attack is a **directed broadcast**, which is passed through the router. The ***no ip directed- broadcast*** command enables only the router to reply.

Spoof
Inserting a different IP address in place of an IP packet's source address to make it appear that the packet came from another network

To prevent your network from becoming a host for an attacker, use access lists to allow only specific sources from the network to enter the router's interfaces. For example, network B connects to a router. Only packets sourced from network B are allowed to pass through the router. The downside of this is it does become a maintenance problem: keeping track of the access lists can be a challenge for the network administrator and processing access lists on the router is processor intensive and can slow the throughput of the packets. However, this does help eliminate spoofed packets. **Spoof** means the attacker doesn't use his IP address but will insert an IP address from the victim's network or another network as the source IP. There is a lot of software on the Internet that enables someone to spoof an IP address.

To prevent yourself from becoming a victim, well…there isn't a way unless you aren't connected to any network or to any other users.

Distributed Denial of Service Attacks (DDoS)

The number of packets that can be generated by a single packet as in the Smurf attack can be limited on a router. However, attackers now use worms to distribute an attack. The attacker will do a port scan and look for an open port or a software application that is vulnerable to an attack. The machine is *hacked* (attacked) and distributes the malicious software. The attacker will repeat this for many victim machines. Once the software is on the victim machines, the attacker can issue a command or instruction that starts the attack on a specific site. The attack will come from a potentially massive amount of machines that the worm has infected.

To stop DDoS attacks, stop intrusions to the network, as discussed in section 10-2. The bottom line is **PREVENT INTRUSIONS.**

10-4   FIREWALLS AND ACCESS LISTS

Firewall
Used in computer networks for protecting the network

Access Lists (ACLs)
A basic form of firewall protection

Firewalls are used in computer networks for protection against the "network elements" (for example, intrusions, denial of service attacks, etc.). **Access lists (ACLs)** are the basic form of firewall protection, although an access list is not stateful and is not by itself a firewall. Access lists can be configured on a router, on a true dedicated firewall, or on the host computer. Firewalls are examined first in this section.

Firewalls allow traffic from inside the network to exit but don't allow general traffic from the outside to enter the network. The firewall monitors the data traffic and recognizes where packets are coming from. The firewall will allow packets from the outside to enter the network if they match a request from within the network. Firewalls are based on three technologies:

- Packet filtering
- Proxy server
- Stateful packet filtering

In **packet filtering**, a limit is placed on the packets that can enter the network. Packet filtering can also limit information moving from one segment to another. ACLs are used to enable the firewall to accept or deny data packets. The disadvantages of packet filtering are

Packet Filtering
Limit is placed on the information that can enter the network

- Packets can still enter the network by fragmenting the data packets.
- It is difficult to implement complex ACLs.
- Not all network services can be filtered.

A **proxy server** is used by clients to communicate with secure systems using a proxy. The client gets access to the network via the proxy server. This step is used to authenticate the user, establish the session, and set policies. The client must connect to the proxy server to connect to resources outside the network. The disadvantages of the proxy server are

Proxy Server
Clients go through a proxy to communicate with secure systems

- The proxy server can run very slow.
- Adding services can be difficult.
- There can be a potential problem with network failure if the proxy server fails or is corrupted.

In a **stateful firewall** the inbound and outbound data packets are compared to determine if a connection should be allowed. This includes tracking the source and destination port numbers and sequence numbers as well as the source and destination IP addresses. This technique is used to protect the inside of the network from the outside world but still allow traffic to go from the inside to the outside and back. The firewall needs to be stateful to accomplish this.

Stateful
Keeps track of the data packet flow

For example, a machine called NVL is on the inside of a network. NVL establishes a connection to the outside at www.network-A.edu. The connection requires the initial TCP handshake sequence and the first SYN packet hits the firewall. The firewall has been configured to allow packets to leave the network. The firewall recognizes that a connection is being established outside the network and the firewall creates a state that includes the source and destination IP address numbers for the connection. The TCP packets arrive at www.network-A.edu (port 80) and the server at networkA.edu returns a SYN-ACK packet back through the firewall. The firewall examines the SYN-ACK packet, and matches the stored source and destination IP addresses with the packet's source/destination IP addresses and port numbers. If the information matches, the IP packets are allowed to pass. This repeats until the connection ends.

What if an attacker tries to spoof the firewall to gain access to the interior of the network? In this case, a connection already exists between NVL and www.network-A.edu. The attacker spoofs the network-A.edu domain www server's IP address and port 80 (the Web server) and tries to use this to gain access to the network. Remember, there is a sequence number associated with the data transfers in the TCP connection. The server recognizes that there is a discrepancy with the sequence and rejects the hacker's connection, preventing the attack.

But what if the campus network has a Web server? How are outside users allowed access? This requires that holes must be opened in the network that allow data packets to pass through. The three most common traffic types that require holes to be opened are Web servers, DNS, and email. The firewall must be modified so that anybody can connect to the Web server via port 80. But what if a vulnerability is discovered on port 80 for the server's operating system? When you open ports, the network administrator must continually upgrade the software so that vulnerabilities are removed. The Web server may also need to have its own firewall. Most firewalls can perform deep packet inspection. This may catch some of protocol vulnerabilities.

A big problem with firewalls is that users assume a firewall catches all possible problems. This is a wrong assumption. The user may be slow to update the patches and fixes to the software. For example, an attacker sends an email message with an attachment to a user. The user opens the attachment and unknowingly loads a Trojan horse on his or her computer that scans all of the machines on the LAN, checking for any possible open ports, compromising the entire LAN. A firewall is not the end-to-end solution.

Attack Prevention

A general rule of thumb is to place the firewall close to the machines you want to protect (for example, the network servers). Do not assume that the clients on the network will never attack your system. Clients can and will get viruses on their machines.

Create demilitarized zones for the outside servers, which means that they are moved to a place on the network so that they are isolated. If the machines are compromised, the intruder will have limited access to the inside of the network.

Firewalls are not the solution for everybody. Open networks such as a university's have limited areas where a firewall can be placed. For example, firewalls will be placed close to critical machines such as academic records. There are so many entities on a university campus network that need connections around the world. The university campus network will have multiple Web servers that can't be centrally located. If a firewall was placed on the whole university network, many holes would be required and thus negate the usefulness of the firewall. One solution is to put in server firewalls.

Access Lists   Access lists provide very basic protection for the network. The access list compares the source and destination IP address and the source and destination port numbers and sometimes might examine the packet contents above layer 4 (transport). However, access lists primarily focus on the network (layer 3) and transport (layer 4) layers. A router is often placed on the edge of a network to handle data traffic entering and exiting the network, and it is common practice to block some data traffic.

The first two steps for applying access lists on a router are

1. Identify the problem
2. Decide where to place the access list

SMB
Server message block

There can be many problems encountered on a network that require the application of an access list to a router. For example, the network administrator will block certain types of data packets from entering and exiting a network. For example, the Microsoft NetBIOS protocol for mapping drives (also called **SMB** [server message block] over TCP) is an intranet protocol and is not intended to be run over the Internet.

SMB data packets use ports 137, 138, and 139. SMB packets will be blocked from entering and exiting the network. The next issue is where to place the access list. In this case, the best place to apply the access list is the network's Internet connection.

The following discussion describes the steps for applying an access list to a router. The network management protocol SNMP (port 161) can be blocked to prevent an outside attacker from getting into your router(s). The following is an example of how to configure an edge router to block SNMP from entering a specific LAN. In this case the term "edge router" is describing the Internet connection to the campus network, and the LAN being protected is LAN B. The network topology is shown in Figure 10-9.

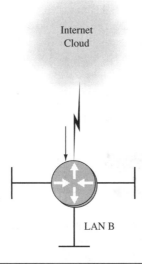

Internet Cloud

LAN B

FIGURE 10-9   An example of setting an access list on an edge router to block SNMP data packets.

The first step for configuring the access list is to enter the router's configuration mode using the ***configure terminal*** command, as shown:

```
RouterB# conf t
RouterB(config)#
```

Next, define the access list to be applied to the router interface. Access lists can be specified in two ways: They can be either a standard or extended type. A *standard* access list is used when specifying access for only IP addresses. An *extended* access list allows the addition of port numbers. For example, the access list could be defined to deny SMB data packets to enter or exit the network.

In the following example, an extended access list of 100 is being defined with the instructions to deny UDP packets from any source going to any destination equal to port 161 (SNMP). (*Note:* The 100 is just an identifier used to indicate what list is being defined.) The command ***access-list 100 deny udp any any eq 161*** is entered.

This command is used to deny all SNMP data packets from entering or exiting the network. Remember, the first step is to identify the problem. Unauthorized access to the network's router must be prevented, so the access list is being applied. SNMP uses the UDP protocol for transferring data; therefore, it is also a good idea to block UDP packets. The command **access-list 100 deny udp any any eq snmp** is used to instruct the router to deny UDP packets from any source to any destination equal to SNMP. In this example, SNMP is used instead of 161. Cisco routers allow the use of names for well-known port numbers, for example, SNMP (port 161) [see Chapter 5 for a discussion on well-known ports]. The entry of these two commands from the router's (config)# prompt is provided:

```
RouterB(config)# access-list 100 deny tcp any any eq 161
RouterB(config)# access-list 100 deny udp any any eq snmp
```

permit ip any any
The instruction added to the last line of an access list to allow all other data packets to enter and exit the router

These commands form an access list that blocks TCP and UDP data packets from any source going to any destination equal to SNMP (port 161). There is an implicit denial at the end of an access list in Cisco routers, and this statement alone will block all data packets. The access lists must be modified to permit any other data packets to enter and exit the LAN. The command **access-list permit ip any any** must be added to the last line of an access list to allow all other data packets to enter and exit the router. An example is shown here. This instruction is for access-list 100, and it instructs the router to permit IP packets from any source to any destination:

```
RouterB(config)# access-list 100 permit ip any any
```

The contents of the access list just created can be checked using the command **show access-list 100**, as demonstrated here:

```
RouterB# sh access-list 100
Extended IP access list 100
deny tcp any any eq 161
deny udp any any eq snmp
permit ip any any
```

The next step is to decide where to place the access list. Specifically, this is asking what router interface is to be used to apply the list. In this case, the access list is to be applied to the Serial0 interface and to the inbound data packets (coming from the Internet). The access list can be applied to both in and outbound data packets. The format of the command is

```
Router (config)# int s0
Router (config-if)# ip access-group 100 in
```

The **100** matches the number from the access list being applied. This access list is being applied on the *in direction* . This denies any SNMP packets from the outside. If this command was modified to **ip access-group 100 out**, this would deny any SNMP packets coming from inside the network going out. This would prevent users on the network to do SNMP queries on the Internet, but it would allow SNMP queries from the outside to come in. This is obviously the opposite of the intent of the access list. There is a limit on applying access lists to a router's interface, one access list–in per interface and one access list–out/interface. The following example demonstrates the use of an access list.

Example 10-1

Problem

Develop an access list to prevent any port 137 SMB data packets from anywhere or going anywhere to enter or exit the router's Serial0 interface.

Solution

Configure the router to use access list 120:

```
access-list 120 deny tcp any any eq 137
access-list 120 permit ip any any
```

Apply the access list to the Serial0 interface:

```
ip access-group 120
in ip access-group
120 out
```

Extended access lists identifiers are not restricted to numbers. A more convenient way to identify them is to use a name to describe the purpose of the access list. For example, in the previous example, an access list called "block-snmp" could be used. The network administrator can quickly identify the purpose of the list without having to check each entry. An example is shown:

```
LAN-B(config)#ip access-list extended block-snmp
LAN-B(config-ext-nacl)#deny tcp any any eq 161
LAN-B(config-ext-nacl)#deny udp any any eq snmp
LAN-B(config-ext-nacl)#permit ip any any
LAN-B(config-ext-nacl)# end
LAN-B#sh access-list
Extended IP access list 100
  10 deny tcp any any eq 161
  20 deny udp any any eq snmp
  30 permit ip any any
Extended IP access list block-snmp
  10 deny tcp any any eq 161
  20 deny udp any any eq snmp
  30 permit ip any any
```

Notice the *show access-list* command lists both the "100" and the "block-snmp" access lists. Both lists actually do the same thing. Next, the "block-snmp" access list is applied to the router's Serial0 interface, as shown:

```
LAN-B(config)#int s0
LAN-B(config-if)#ip access-group block-snmp in
```

Example 10-2 demonstrates an application of the named access list.

Example 10-2

Problem

Create an access list to block any UDP packets from entering the Serial1 interface on a router. Specify an extended access list of "block-udp."

Solution

From the router's **(config)#** prompt:

```
ip access-list extended block-udp
deny udp any any
permit ip any any
```

On the serial interface:

```
interface s1
ip access-group block-udp in
```

23

An interesting statistic to look at is how many times an access list has been matched. The command ***show access-list*** followed by the name or number of the list enables the statistics to be viewed. The **(# matches)** indicates how many times there has been a match to the access list. An example is shown here for the "block-snmp" access list:

```
LAN-B#sh access-list block-snmp
Extended IP access list block-snmp
    deny tcp any any eq 161
    deny udp any any eq snmp
    permit ip any any (7 matches)
LAN-B#sh access-list block-snmp
Extended IP access list block-snmp
    deny tcp any any eq 161 (6 matches)
    deny udp any any eq snmp
    permit ip any any (7 matches)
```

The first display for the ***show access-list*** indicates that no packets have been denied, but there have been seven matches for ***permit ip any any***. The second group shows that TCP data packets have been denied six times. This information can be useful for the network administrator when evaluating the effectiveness of an access list. There are times when a host with a specific IP address needs to be denied. For example, an attacker could have gained access to a host computer in the network and configured it to continually ping a server, attempting to generate a denial of service or just to slow down data traffic. Another possibility is the computer could be on a host external to the network that is continually pinging a server within the network. The network administrator examines the data traffic and determines that the IP address of the attack is from a remote computer (192.168.12.5). The computer is not in the administrator's LAN; therefore, the data traffic must be stopped in the administrator's network. Configuring an access list to deny any packets from the remote host can do this. Assume that the data traffic is entering the network via the Serial0 interface on RouterB, the Internet router, as shown in Figure 10-10. The following demonstrates how the access list could be configured:

```
LAN-B(config)#ip access-list extended block-badguy
LAN-B(config-ext-nacl)#deny ip host 192.168.12.5 any
LAN-B(config-ext-nacl)#permit ip any any      8.4

LAN-B(config-ext-nacl)#int ser0
LAN-B(config-if)#ip access-group block-badguy in
```

(24)

Host
Enables a specific host IP address to be entered in the access list

This example shows that an extended access list called "block-badguy" was created. The access list denies source packets from the host 192.168.12.5 with any destination. The **host** entry enables a specific IP address to be entered. Next the access list is applied to the router's Serial0 interface in the in direction. The *in* describes that the list is applied to any data packets coming into the interface. Example 10-3 shows the blocking of a host IP address.

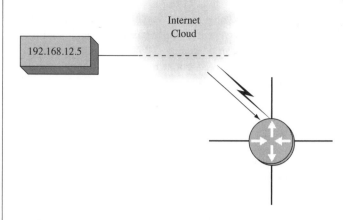

192.168.12.5

Internet
Cloud

FIGURE 10-10   An example of applying an access list to stop data traffic from a remote
host.

Example 10-3

Problem

Create an access list to block any data traffic from the IP address 192.168.12.5 to
anywhere. Specify an extended access list name of "border-router." Apply the access list to the router's Serial1 interface. Assume that the router interface is connected to the Internet, and the 192.168.12.5 host is external to the network.

Solution

```
ip access-list extended border-router
deny ip host 192.168.12.5 any
permit any any
int s1
ip access-group border-router in
```

A bad thing about access lists is that they are not stateful. This means they don't
keep track of the data packet flow. They only examine the current packet, and they
contain no information about the recent history of data traffic on that connection.
This makes it hard for access lists to allow connections to be made to the outside
world.

Access lists try to address this need for allowing a connection from the outside to
the inside if an "Established" connection exists. This requires using a flag in the
TCP header, but TCP headers can be falsified; therefore, the access list is useless
for verifying an established connection. Someone could fake an acknowledgement
flag so his or her packet could enter the network.

10-5   INTRUSION DETECTION

Intrusion Detection
Monitoring data packets passing through the network to catch potential or ongoing attacks

Intrusion detection is very similar to firewalls in the way it looks at data packets. The main idea with intrusion detection is to monitor traffic passing through your network so that potential or ongoing attacks can be detected. The intrusion box will sit on the edge of your network so that data packets entering from the Internet can be monitored, as shown in Figure 10-11.

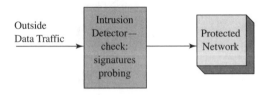

FIGURE 10-11   An example of using an intrusion box.

The following are examples of what an intrusion box looks for:

Signatures
Indicators of known attacks

Probing
Indicators of repeated attempts to make connections to certain machines

Signatures—Indicators of known attacks, for example, patterns of probes
Probing—Indicators of repeated attempts to make connections to certain machines and/or ports

Many network attacks are well-known, and the intrusion detector will know what to look for. The device must be kept up to date because there are always new attacks. For example, an attacker is probing the campus network hoping to find a vulnerable machine and scans all ports from 1 to 2048 on one machine. The intrusion box identifies that the same outside machine is attempting to connect to many ports on the same machine inside the network within a small period of time. The intrusion box will issue an alarm indicating that a host computer in the network is being probed. It is up to the network administrator to take action if this is indeed an attack. The network administrator could stop the data traffic from the attacker by using an access list *deny* command of the attacker's source IP address. The network administrator could also send a warning to the attacker computer indicating that the machine is attacking the campus network. Remember, the machine that is attacking could have been compromised by an attacker or a virus, and the owner of the machine may not be aware that the machine has been compromised.

The big problem with intrusion detection is that many common applications can falsely trigger the intrusion box into thinking an attack is taking place. It takes a lot of tweaking to configure the intrusion box so that false triggers can be avoided. It also takes a lot of labor-hours to set up the box and to monitor its alarms.

The intrusion box is resource-intensive, and some networks only use it where critical information needs to be protected. It is important for the network administrator to examine the cost–benefit ratio of placing an intrusion box on the network. The costs of protecting your asset should not be greater than the value of your asset. Why spend $100,000 to protect $1,000 in net assets?

10-6 ANALYZING UNSECURED DATA PACKETS

This chapter has examined the many ways an attacker can attack a network. It is important that the network administrator understand what needs to be done to protect the network. The administrator must also understand that many of the data packets passing across a network appear in plain text form. In other words, the attacker can see the contents of the data packets using simple networking tools.

This section examines the data packets exchanged during a telnet connection from the network administrator to a router. A router allows a telnet connection from a user on the network if the telnet service is enabled. Recall, the commands are used to enable a telnet connection to a router.

```
router(config)# line vty 0 4
router(config-line)# password Chile
router(config-line)# login
```

In this case, assume that an attacker has gained physical access to the network and can monitor network data traffic. Figure 10-12 shows the setup for this. The attacker is sitting on the network and has somehow managed to capture the data traffic on the network.

Network
Administrator

Attacker

Router

FIGURE 10-12 The setup for capturing a network's data packets.

In this example, the network administrator is telnetting to the router. The network administrator issues the command ***telnet 10.10.10.250*** as shown in Figure 10-13.

FIGURE 10-13   The steps for telnetting to another networking device.

The text *User Access Verification* is returned by the router and instructs the user to enter the telnet password as shown in Figure 10-14.

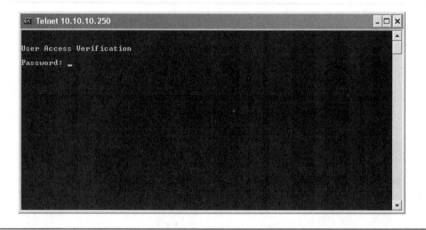

FIGURE 10-14   The User Access Verification and the password prompt from the router.

The network administrator then enters the password into the virtual terminal connection. In this example, the password is *Chile*. Telnet is a virtual terminal session, and each character is transmitted in a TCP data packet as it is typed. The administrator types the password and presses **Enter**. The next screen (Figure 10-15) shows that the network administrator has connected to the router, and the Router> prompt is displayed.

Next let's look at the information the attacker obtained. The setup for the attack is shown in Figure 10-12. In this scenario, the attacker will typically obtain many data packets and will have to search through them to find the telnet sequence. This example contains only the data packets sent to and from the network administrator's computer and the router. Figure 10-16 shows a portion of the captured network data traffic. (*Note:* This file is called [*wireless-cap4 router login.cap*], and is provided on the text's Companion CD-ROM.) Packets 1, 2, and 3 establish the TCP connection for opening a telnet session with the router. Notice the listing of port 23 (the telnet port). Packet six is highlighted; this is the first data transferred from the router. Notice that in the middle of the image under Remote Terminal Protocol (TELNET) that the data is *User Access Verification* and *Password,* the same information displayed on the network administrator's telnet screen.

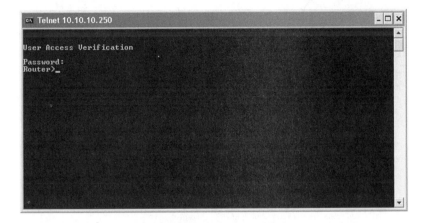

FIGURE 10-15   The screen showing that a connection has been made to the router.

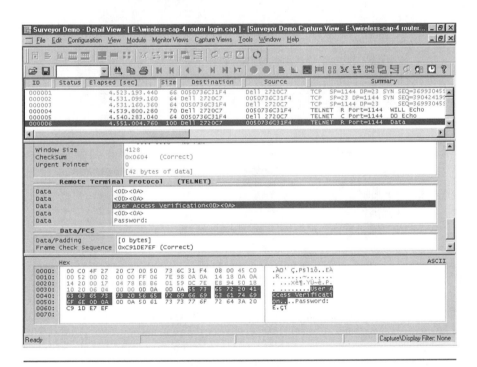

FIGURE 10-16   The first six data packets for the telnet session.

Recall that when a telnet connection is made, the keystrokes are sent one at a time. Figure 10-17 (a–e) shows that the password *Chile* can be extracted from the telnet data packets, and the attacker even sees the Router prompt, as shown in Figure 10-17 (f).

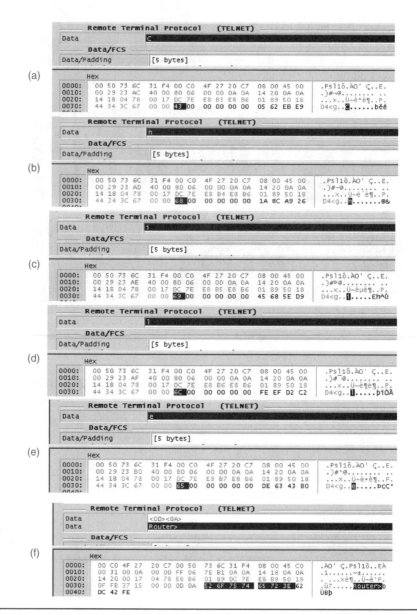

FIGURE 10-17   The captured data packets showing the password "Chile."

SSH (Secure Shell)
An encrypted version of telnet

The fact is that many applications such as telnet are not secure. The data is displayed in plain text, and an attacker can easily see the contents of network traffic. This is why unsecure applications, such as telnet, are no longer recommended and in fact should be avoided if possible. Remember, an attacker does not have to be someone from the outside—many times the biggest threat is from within the organization. What can be done to protect the contents of data packets? The use of switches instead of hubs helps to isolate data traffic and makes "eavesdropping" on network data traffic a little more difficult. Even with switches, packet contents are still viewable. There are many software applications available that enable data transfers to be encrypted. There is an encrypted version of telnet called **SSH (secure shell)**. SSH encrypts the data packets and provides secure communications over an unsecured network channel.

SUMMARY

This chapter has presented a short overview of network security. The role of the network administrator is not only to design, assemble, and maintain a good network, but also to protect the network and its users from both external and internal threats. This chapter has introduced some of the concepts critical to network security. The reader should understand the following concepts:

- The various ways an attacker can gain control of a network
- How denial of service attacks are initiated and how they can be prevented
- How firewalls work and why they are important for protecting a network
- The issues of unsecured data packets

QUESTIONS AND PROBLEMS

Section 10-1

1. List six ways an attacker gains access to a network.
2. Describe a way social engineering can be used by an attacker to gain control of a network.

Section 10-2

3. Describe how social engineering attacks can be avoided.
4. What is a *dictionary attack*?
5. Can password cracking be prevented? How?
6. How does the use of a networking switch minimize problems with packet sniffing in a LAN?
7. Describe the concept of *software vulnerabilities*.
8. What is a *buffer overflow*?
9. List two ways to prevent vulnerable software attacks.
10. What are simple ways to minimize or prevent viruses?
11. What is the purpose of WPA?

Section 10-3

12. What is a denial of service attack?
13. Describe a SYN attack.
14. Cisco routers use what command to block broadcasts to a subnet?
15. Define a directed broadcast.
16. What is the best way to keep from contributing to DDoS attacks?

Section 10-4

17. What is the purpose of a firewall?
18. Why is a stateful firewall important?

19. What is the router command for setting an access list 100 to block SNMP UDP packets from any source to any destination?
20. What command should be added to the end of an access list 150 to allow other data packets to enter and exit the router?
21. An extended IP access list 130 is to be applied to a router's Serial0 interface. The list is to be applied to inbound data packets. What command should be entered from the router's (config-if)# prompt?
22. Modify the command for Problem 21 so that the access list is applied to outbound data packets.
23. What command is used to view the number of times an access list has been matched?
24. It has been determined that a computer with an IP address of 192.168.8.4 is flooding the network with ICMP packets. Create an extended access list to stop the flood.
25. Apply the access list created in problem 24 to the inbound data traffic on the router's Serial1 interface.

Section 10-5

26. What two features of a data packet does an intrusion box examine?
27. Describe a situation that would trigger an intrusion box alarm.
28. What are some of the issues in the use of an intrusion box?

Section 10-6

29. What are the security issues in the use of telnet?
30. How can a telnet session be made secure?

Critical Thinking

31. Your network is experiencing an excessive amount of pings to your network server. The pings are from outside the network. Someone suggests that you set an access list to block ICMP packets coming into the network. How would you respond?
32. A Web server has been set up for use internal to a network (an intranet server). No outside users should be able to access the server. Describe how you would protect the server using an access list.

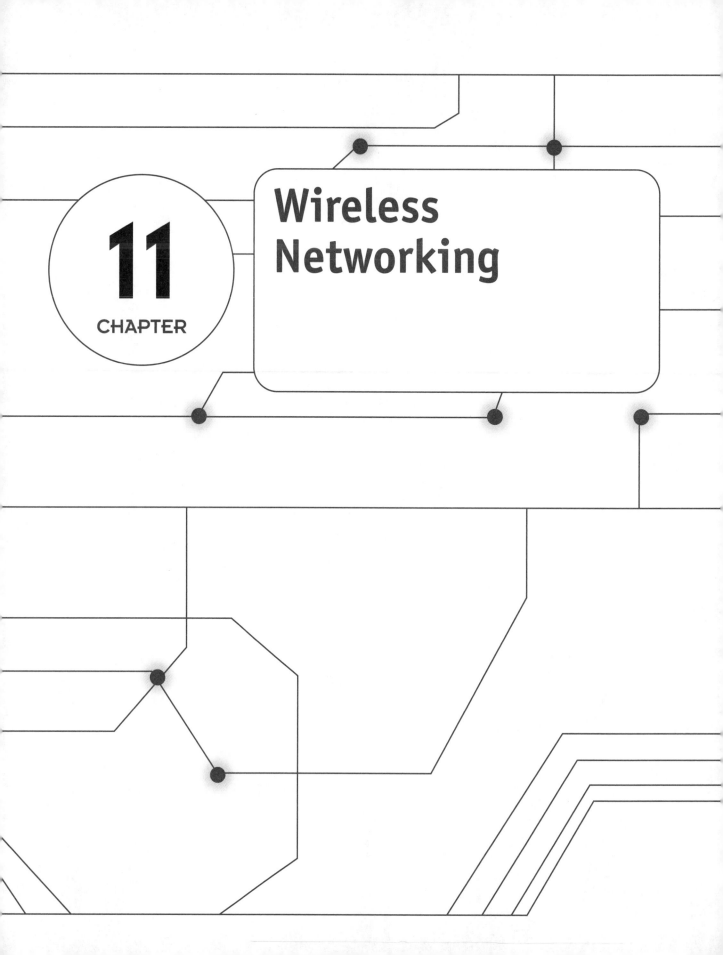

11

CHAPTER

Wireless Networking

CHAPTER OUTLINE

11-1   Introduction

11-2   The IEEE 802.11 Wireless LAN Standard

11-3   802.11 Wireless Networking

11-4   Bluetooth, WiMAX, and RFID

11-5   Securing Wireless LANs

11-6   Configuring a Point-to-Multipoint Wireless LAN: A Case Study

Summary

Questions and Problems

OBJECTIVES

- Define the features of the 802.11 wireless LAN standard
- Understand the components of the wireless LAN
- Explore how wireless LANs are configured
- Examine how site surveys are done for wireless LANs
- Investigate the issues of securing a wireless LAN
- Explore how to configure a point-to-multipoint wireless LAN

KEY TERMS

WLAN
Basic Service Set (BSS)
ad hoc
access point
transceiver
Extended Service Set (ESS)
hand-off
roaming
CSMA/CA
DSSS
ISM
FHSS

pseudorandom
hopping sequence
OFDM
U-NII
MIMO
Wi-Fi
SSID
site survey
inquiry procedure
paging procedure
piconet
pairing
Passkey

WiMAX
BWA
NLOS
last mile
Radio Frequency Identification (RFID)
backscatter
Slotted Aloha
beacon
WPA
EAP
RADIUS

11-1   INTRODUCTION

Wireless local area network

This chapter examines the features and technologies used in the wireless local area network (**WLAN**). Wireless networking is an extension of computer networks into the RF (radio frequency) world. The WLAN provides increased flexibility and mobility for connecting to a network. A properly designed WLAN for a building provides mobile access for a user from virtually any location in the building. The user doesn't have to look for a connection to plug into; also, the expense of pulling cables and installing wall plates required for wired networks can be avoided. However, a network administrator must carefully plan the wireless LAN installation and have a good understanding of the issues of using WLAN technologies to ensure the installation of a reliable and secure network.

This chapter addresses the basic issues of incorporating WLAN technologies into a network. The fundamentals of the IEEE 802.11 wireless LAN standard are examined in section 11-2. This includes an overview of wireless LAN concepts and terminology, frequency allocations, and spread spectrum communication. The applications of wireless LANs are presented in section 11-3. This includes a look at different types of wireless LAN configurations, such as point-to-point and point-to-multipoint. Other wireless networking technologies are examined in section 11-4. This section looks at Bluetooth, WiMAX, and RFID. Anytime a signal is transmitted over the air or even through a cable, there is some chance that the signal can be intercepted. Transmitting data over a wireless network introduces new security issues. Section 11-5 examines the basic issues of securing WLAN communications. The last section (11-6) presents an example of configuring a wireless LAN to provide access for users in a metropolitan area.

11-2   THE IEEE 802.11 WIRELESS LAN STANDARD

A typical computer network uses twisted-pair and fiber optic cable to interconnect LANs. Another media competing for use in higher data-rate LANs is wireless, based on the IEEE 802.11 wireless standard. The advantages of wireless include

- User mobility in the workplace
- A cost-effective networking media for use in areas that are difficult or too costly to wire

The concept of user mobility in the workplace opens the door to many opportunities to provide more flexibility. Workers can potentially access the network or their telephones (via IP telephony) from virtually any location within the workplace. Accessing information from the network is as easy as if the information were on a disk.

The benefits of wireless networks in the workplace are numerous. To provide wireless connectivity, the network administrator must be sure the network services are reliable and secure. Providing reliable network services means the administrator must have a good understanding of wireless LAN configurations and technologies. This and the following sections examine the fundamentals of wireless networking; the 802.11 standard and its family, 802.11a, 802.11b, and 802.11g and 802.11n; and how WLANs are configured.

The IEEE 802.11 wireless LAN standard defines the physical (PHY) layer, the medium access control (MAC) layer, and the MAC management protocols and services.

The PHY (physical) layer defines

- The method of transmitting the data, which may be either RF or infrared (although infrared is rarely used)

The MAC (media access control) layer defines

- The reliability of the data service
- Access control to the shared wireless medium
- Protecting the privacy of the transmitted data

The wireless management protocols and services are

- Authentication, association, data delivery, and privacy

The fundamental topology of the WLAN is the **Basic Service Set (BSS)**. This is also called the independent Basic Service Set, or **ad hoc** network. An example of an ad hoc network is provided in Figure 11-1. In this network, the wireless clients (stations) communicate directly with each other. This means the clients have recognized the other stations in the WLAN and have established a wireless data link.

Basic Service Set (BSS)
Term used to describe an independent network

Ad Hoc
Another term used to describe an independent network

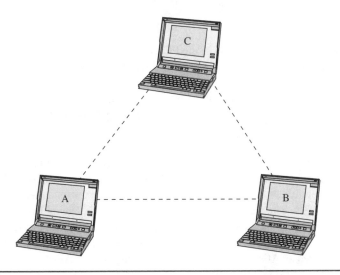

FIGURE 11-1   An example of the independent Basic Service Set or "ad hoc" network.

The performance of the Basic Service Set can be improved by including an **access point**. The access point is a transmit/receive unit (**transceiver**) that interconnects data from the wireless LAN to the wired network. Additionally, the access point provides 802.11 MAC layer functions and supports bridge protocols. The access point typically uses an RJ-45 jack for connecting to the wired network. If an access point is being used, users establish a wireless communications link through it to communicate with other users in the WLAN or the wired network, as shown in Figure 11-2.

Access Point
A transceiver used to interconnect a wireless and a wired LAN

Transceiver
A transmit/receive unit

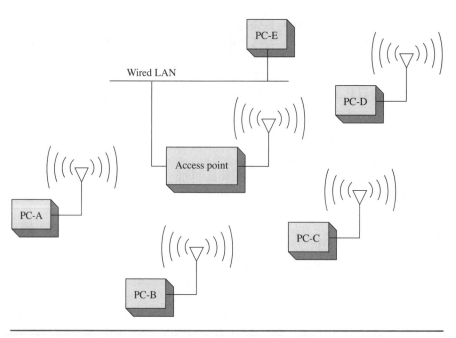

FIGURE 11-2   Adding an access point to the Basic Service Set.

If data is being sent from PC-A to PC-D, the data is first sent to the access point and then relayed to PC-D. Data sent from a wireless client to a client in the wired LAN also passes through the access point. The users (clients) in the wireless LAN can communicate with other members of the network as long as a link is established with the access point. For example, data traffic from PC-A to PC-E will first pass through the access point and then to PC-E in the wired LAN.

The problem with the Basic Service Set is that mobile users can travel outside the radio range of a station's wireless link with one access point. One solution is to add multiple access points to the network. Multiple access points extend the range of mobility of a wireless client in the LAN. This arrangement is called an **Extended Service Set (ESS)**. An example is provided in Figure 11-3. The mobile computer will establish an authorized connection with the access point that has the strongest signal level (for example, AP-1). As the user moves, the signal strength of the signal from AP-1 will decrease. At some point, the signal strength from AP-2 will exceed AP-1, and the wireless bridge will establish a new connection with AP-2. This is called a **hand-off**. This is an automatic process for the wireless client adapter in 802.11, and the term used to describe this is **roaming**.

Network access in 802.11 uses a technique called carrier sense multiple access/collision avoidance (CSMA/CA). In **CSMA/CA**, the client station listens for other users of the wireless network. If the channel is quiet (no data transmission), the client station may transmit. If the channel is busy, the station(s) must wait until transmission stops. Each client station uses a unique random back-off time. This technique prevents client stations from trying to gain access to the wireless channel as soon as it becomes quiet. There are currently four physical layer technologies being used in 802.11 wireless networking. These are direct sequence spread spectrum (DSSS), frequency hopping spread spectrum (FHSS), infrared, and orthogonal frequency division multiplexing (OFDM). DSSS is used in 802.11b/g/n wireless networks, and

Extended Service Set (ESS)
The use of multiple access points to extend user mobility

Hand-off
When the user's computer establishes an association with another access point

Roaming
The term used to describe a users' ability to maintain network connectivity as they move through the workplace

CSMA/CA
Carrier sense multiple access/collision avoidance

OFDM is used in 802.11a, 802.11g, and 802.11n. Note that 802.11g/n use both DSSS and OFDM modulation.

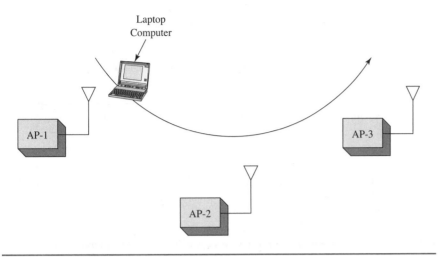

Laptop
Computer

AP-1

AP-3

AP-2

FIGURE 11-3   An example of an Extended Service Set used for increased user mobility.

802.11 **DSSS** implements 14 channels (each consuming 22 MHz) over approximately 90 MHz of RF spectrum in the 2.4 GHz **ISM** (industrial, scientific, and medical) band. The frequency channels used in North America are listed in Table 11-1. An example of the frequency spectrum for three-channel DSSS is shown in Figure 11-4.

DSSS
Direct sequence spread spectrum

ISM
Industrial, scientific, and medical

TABLE 11-1   North American DSSS Channels

Channel Number	Frequency (GHz)
1	2.412
2	2.417
3	2.422
4	2.427
5	2.432
6	2.437
7	2.442
8	2.447
9	2.452
10	2.457
11	2.462

In frequency hopping spread spectrum (**FHSS**), the transmit signal frequency changes based on a pseudorandom sequence. **Pseudorandom** means the sequence appears to be random but in fact does repeat, typically after some lengthy period of time. FHSS uses 79 channels (each 1 MHz wide) in the ISM 2.4 GHz band. FHSS requires that the transmitting and receiving units know the **hopping sequence** (the order of frequency changes) so that a communication link can be established and synchronized. FHSS data rates are typically 1 and 2 Mbps. FHSS is not commonly used anymore for wireless LANs. It's still part of the standard, but very few (if any) FHSS wireless LAN products are sold.

FHSS
Frequency hopping spread spectrum

Pseudorandom
The number sequence appears random but actually repeats

Hopping Sequence
The order of frequency changes

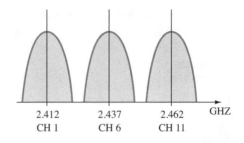

2.412   2.437   2.462   GHZ
CH 1   CH 6   CH 11

FIGURE 11-4   An example of the three channels in the DSSS spectrum.

The maximum transmit power of 802.11b wireless devices is 1000 mW; however, the nominal transmit power level is 100 mW. The 2.4 GHz frequency range used by 802.11b/g is shared by many technologies, including Bluetooth, cordless telephones, and microwave ovens.

LANs emit significant RF noise in the 2.4 GHz range that can affect wireless data. A significant improvement in wireless performance is available with the IEEE 802.11a standards. The 802.11a equipment operates in the 5 GHz range and provides significant improvement over 802.11b with respect to RF interference.

OFDM
Orthogonal frequency division multiplexing

U-NII
Unlicensed National Information Infrastructure

The 802.11a standard uses a technique called orthogonal frequency division multiplexing (**OFDM**) to transport the data over 12 possible channels in the **U-NII** (Unlicensed National Information Infrastructure). U-NII was set aside by the FCC to support short-range, high-speed wireless data communications. Table 11-2 lists the operating frequencies for 802.11a. Table 11-3 lists the transmit power levels for 802.11a.

TABLE 11-2   IEEE 802.11a Channels and Operating Frequencies

Channel	Center Frequency (GHz)	
36	5.180	
40	5.20	Lower Band
44	5.22	
48	5.24	
52	5.26	
56	5.28	Middle Band
60	5.30	
64	5.32	
149	5.745	
153	5.765	Upper Band
157	5.785	
161	5.805	

TABLE 11-3   Maximum Transmit Power Levels for 802.11a with a 6dBi Antenna Gain

Band	Power Level
Lower	40 mW
Middle	200 mW
Upper	800 mW

IEEE 802.11a equipment is not compatible with 802.11b, 802.11g, or 802.11n. The good aspect of this is that 802.11a equipment will not interfere with 802.11b, g, or n; therefore, 802.11a and 802.11b/g/n links can run next to each other without causing any interference. Figure 11-5 illustrates an example of the two links operating together.

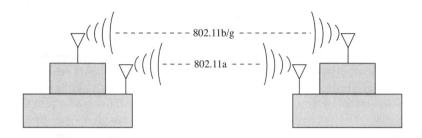

FIGURE 11-5 An example of an 802.11a installation and an 802.11b link running alongside each other.

The downside of 802.11a is the increased cost of the equipment and increased power consumption because of the OFDM technology. This is of particular concern with mobile users because of the effect it can have on battery life. However, the maximum usable distance (RF range) for 802.11a is about the same or even greater than that of 802.11b/g/n.

Another IEEE 802.11 wireless standard is IEEE 802.11g. The 802.11g standard supports the higher data transmission rates of 54 Mbps but operates in the same 2.4 GHz range as 802.11b. The 802.11g equipment is also backward compatible with 802.11b equipment. This means that 802.11b wireless clients will be able to communicate with the 802.11g access points, and the 802.11g wireless client equipment will communicate with the 802.11b access points.

The obvious advantage of this is that companies with an existing 802.11b wireless network will be able to migrate to the higher data rates provided by 802.11g without having to sacrifice network compatibility. In fact, new wireless equipment support both the 2.4 GHz and 5 GHz standards, giving it the flexibility of high speed, compatibility, and noninterference.

Another entry into wireless networks is the 802.11n. This wireless technology can operate in the same ISM frequency as 802.11b/g (2.4GHz) and can also operate in the 5 GHz band. A significant improvement with 802.11n is **MIMO** (Multiple Input Multiple Output). MIMO uses a technique called space-division multiplexing, where the data stream is split into multiple parts called *spatial streams*. The different spatial streams are transmitted using separate antennas. With MIMO, doubling the spatial streams doubles the effective data rate. The downside of this is there can be increased power consumption. The 802.11n specification includes a MIMO power-save mode. With this, 802.11n only uses multiple data paths when faster data transmission is required—thus saving power.

Table 11-4 lists the 802.11n frequency bands. This table shows frequencies in both the 2.4 GHz and 5 GHz range. The frequencies being used in the 5 GHz band are the same as those used in 802.11a, and note that there is the possibility of using both 20MHz and 40MHz channels.

MIMO
A space-division multiplexing technique where the data stream is split into multiple parts called spatial streams

TABLE 11-4   The 802.11n Frequency Bands

Frequency Band (GHz)	Independent 20 MHz Channels	Possible 40 Mhz Channels
2.40–2.485	3	1
5.15–5.25	4	2
5.25–5.35	4	2
5.47–5.75	10	5
5.75–5.85	4	2

Wi-Fi

Wi-Fi Alliance—an organization that tests and certifies wireless equipment for compliance with the 802.11x standards

Wireless networks also go by the name **Wi-Fi**, which is the abbreviated name for the Wi-Fi Alliance (Wi-Fi stands for wireless fidelity). The Wi-Fi Alliance is an organization whose function is to test and certify wireless equipment for compliance with the 802.11x standards, the group of wireless standards developed under the IEEE 802.11 standard. The following list provides a summary of the most common wireless standards:

- **802.11a (Wireless-A):** This standard can provide data transfer rates up to 54 Mbps and an operating range up to 75 feet. It operates at 5 GHz (Modulation—OFDM)
- **802.11b (Wireless-B):** This standard can provide data transfer rates up to 11 Mbps with ranges of 100 to 150 feet. It operates at 2.4 GHz. (Modulation—DSSS)
- **802.11g (Wireless-G):** This standard can provide data transfer rates up to 54 Mbps up to 150 feet. It operates at 2.4 GHz. (Modulation—DSSS or OFDM)
- **802.11n (Wireless-N):** This is the next generation of high-speed wireless connectivity promising data transfer rates over 200+ Mbps. It operates at 2.4 GHz and 5 GHz. (Modulation—DSSS or OFDM)
- **802.11i:** This standard for wireless LANs (WLANs) provides improved data encryption for networks that use the 802.11a, 802.11b, and 802.11g standards.
- **802.11r:** This standard is designed to speed handoffs between access points or cells in a wireless LAN. This standard is a critical addition to 802.11 WLANs if voice traffic is to become widely deployed.

11-3   802.11 WIRELESS NETWORKING

A wireless LAN can be configured in many ways to meet the needs of an organization. Figure 11-6 provides an example of a basic 802.11b/g/n WLAN configuration. Each PC is outfitted with a wireless LAN adapter card. The PC cards come in many styles, such as PCI, ISA, or PCMCIA, and some units are external to the computer. The wireless adapter (wireless LAN adapter) is the device that connects the client to the wireless medium. The medium is typically a radio wave channel in the 2.4 GHz ISM band. The wireless medium can also be infrared, although this is not used very often. The following services are provided by the wireless LAN adapter:

- Delivery of the data
- Authentication
- Privacy

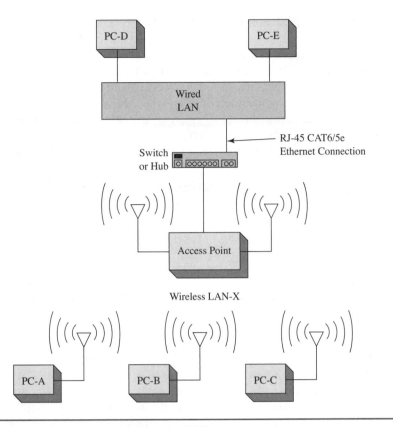

FIGURE 11-6 The setup for a basic wireless LAN.

The connection to a wired LAN is provided by a wireless access point, which provides a bridge between the wireless LAN and the wired network. A physical cable connection (typically CAT6/5e) ties the access point to the wired network's switch or hub (typically Ethernet).

For example, computer PC-A shown in Figure 11-6 sends a data packet to PC-D, a destination in the wired LAN. PC-A first sends a data packet over the wireless link. The access point recognizes the sender of the data packet as a host in the wireless LAN-X and allows the wireless data to enter the access point. At this time, the data is sent out the physical Ethernet connection to the wired LAN. The data packet is then delivered to PC-D in the wired LAN.

A question should come up at this point: "How does the access point know that the wireless data packet is being sent from a client in the wireless LAN?"

The answer is the 802.11 wireless LAN devices use an **SSID** to identify what wireless data traffic is allowed to connect to the network. The SSID is the wireless *service set identifier*, basically a password that enables the client to join the wireless network.

The access point uses the SSID to determine whether the client is to become a member of the wireless network. The term *association* is used to describe that a wireless connection has been obtained.

SSID
Service set identifier

Another common question is, "Why does the access point have two antennas?" The answer is the two antennas implement what is called "spatial diversity." This antenna arrangement improves received signal gain and performance.

Figure 11-7 provides an example of the information displayed on the wireless adapter's console port when an association is made. The text indicates that a connection has been made to a parent (access point) whose MAC address is 00-40-96-25-9d-14. The text indicates this MAC address has been "added" to the list of associations. This type of information is typically available via the wireless management software that typically comes with the wireless PC or PCMCIA adapter.

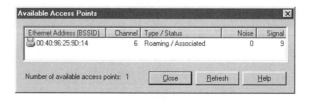

FIGURE 11-7 An example of the information displayed when an association is made by a client with an access point.

Access points use the association to build a table of users (clients) on the wireless network. Figure 11-8 provides an example of an association table. The association table lists the MAC addresses for each networking device connected to the wireless network. The access point then uses this table to forward data packets between the access point and the wireless network. The wireless client adapter will also notify the user if the client has lost an association with the access point. An example of this also is provided in Figure 11-8.

A wireless bridge is a popular choice for connecting LANs (running similar network protocols) together even if the LANs are miles apart. Examples are provided in Figure 11-9 (a) and (b). Figure 11-9 (a) shows a point-to-point wireless bridge. Each building shown in Figure 11-9 (a) has a connection from the wireless bridge to the building's LAN, as shown in Figure 11-10. The wireless bridge then connects to an antenna placed on the roof, and there must be a clear (line-of-sight) transmission path between the two buildings, or there will be signal *attenuation* (loss) or possible signal disruption. Antenna selection is also critical when configuring the connection. This issue is addressed in section 11-5. The antenna must be selected so that the signal strength at the receiving site is sufficient to meet the required received signal level.

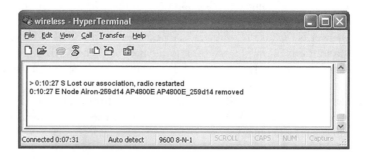

FIGURE 11-8 An example of a "lost" association.

Figure 11-9 (b) shows how a wireless bridge can be used to connect multiple remote sites to the main transmitting facility. Each building uses a bridge setup similar to that shown in Figure 11-10. The bridge connects to its respective LAN. In this case, Bld-A uses an antenna that has a wide coverage area (radiation pattern). The key objective with antenna selection is that the antenna must provide coverage for all receiving sites (in this case, Bld-B and Bld-C).

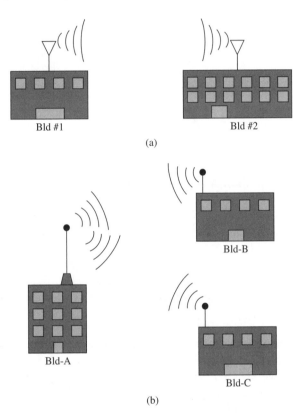

FIGURE 11-9   Examples of (a) point-to-point and (b) point-to-multipoint wireless bridge configurations.

Wireless LANs have a maximum distance the signal can be transmitted. This is a critical issue inside buildings when user mobility is required. Many obstacles can reflect and attenuate the signal, causing reception to suffer. Also the signal level for mobile users is hampered by the increased distance from the access point. Distance is also a critical issue in outdoor point-to-multipoint wireless networks.

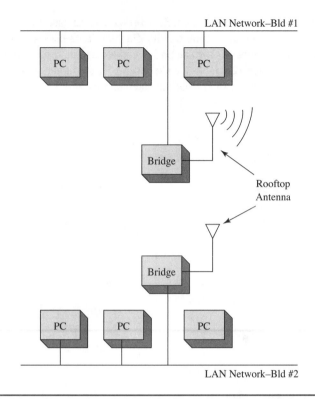

LAN Network–Bld #1

Bridge

Rooftop
Antenna

Bridge

LAN Network–Bld #2

FIGURE 11-10 The wireless bridge connection to the wired network inside the building.

A solution is to place multiple wireless access points within the facility, as shown in Figure 11-11. Mobile clients will be able to maintain a connection as they travel through the workplace because the wireless client will automatically select the access point that provides the strongest signal level. The access points can be arranged so that overlapping coverage of the workplace is provided, thus enabling seamless roaming for the client. The signal coverage is shown in the shape of circles in Figure 11-11. In actual practice, the radiation patterns are highly irregular due to reflections of the transmitted signal.

It is important to verify that sufficient RF signal level is available for the users in the WLAN. This is best accomplished by performing a **site survey**. Inside a building, a site survey is performed to determine the best location(s) for placing the access point(s) for providing maximum RF coverage for the wireless clients. Site surveys are also done with outside installations to determine the coverage area.

Site Survey
Performed to determine the best location(s) for placing the access point(s) to provide maximum RF coverage for the wireless clients

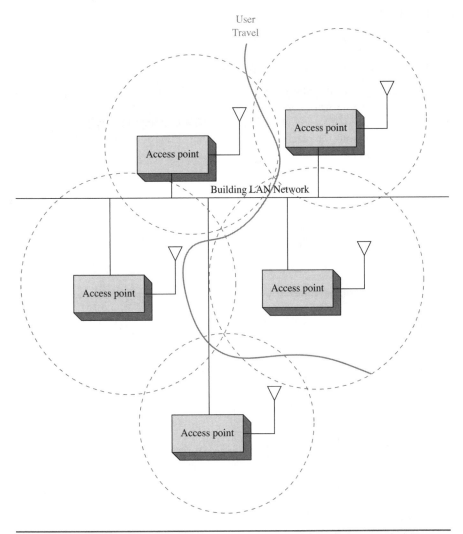

User
Travel

Access point

Access point

Access point

Access point

Building LAN Network

Access point

FIGURE 11-11 An example of configuring multiple access points to extend the range for wireless connectivity.

A site survey for indoor and outdoor installations should obtain the following key information:

Indoor

- Electrical power
- Wired network connection point(s)
- Access point placement
- RF coverage—user mobility
- Bandwidth supported
- identify any significant RF interference

Outdoor

- Electrical power (base access point)
- Connection back to the home network

- Antenna selection
- Bandwidth supported
- RF coverage
- Identify any significant RF interference

For example, a site survey was conducted to determine access point placement to provide wireless network connectivity for a building. The objective was to provide mobile client access throughout the building. The building already had two wired connections available for placing an access point. Figure 11-12 provides the floor plan for the building.

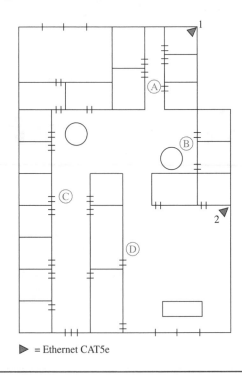

▶ = Ethernet CAT5e

FIGURE 11-12   The floor plan of the building being surveyed for a wireless LAN.

The available wired network connections are indicated in the drawing. The site survey began with placing an access point at position 1. A wireless mobile client was used to check the signal throughout the building. The wireless management software that came with the WLAN adapter was used to gather the test results.

The first measurement was taken at point A as shown in Figure 11-13. Notice that the data speed is 11 Mbps. This will change if the signal level decreases significantly. The wireless PCMCIA card also comes with a way to check the signal statistics as illustrated in Figure 11-14. This figure provides a plot of the signal quality, the missed access point (AP) beacons, transmit retries, the signal strength, and the transmit rate.

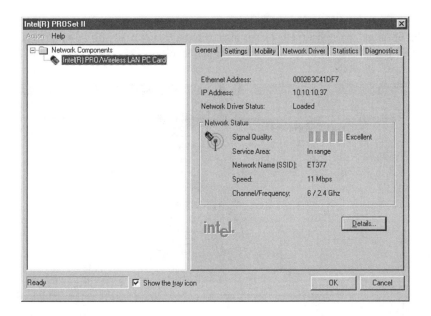

FIGURE 11-13   The RF signal level observed at point A.

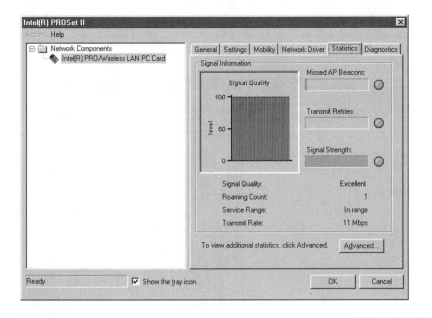

FIGURE 11-14   The signal statistics from point A.

The next observation was made at point B. A signal level of "Good" and a transmit rate of 11 Mbps was observed. The signal has decreased somewhat, but the "Good" indicates that a connection is still available. Figure 11-15 shows the observation made at point B. The signal level drops to "Fair" at point C as shown in Figure 11-16.

The mobile client was moved to point D in the building, and a signal quality of "Out of range" was observed. This is also called a *loss of association* with the access point. Figure 11-17 shows the observed signal level.

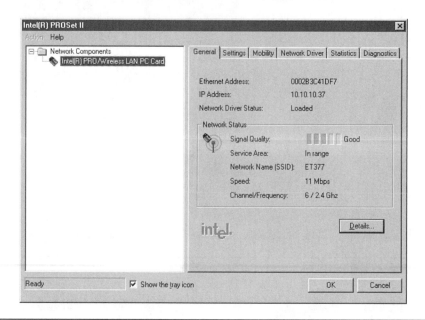

FIGURE 11-15   The signal quality of "Good" at point B.

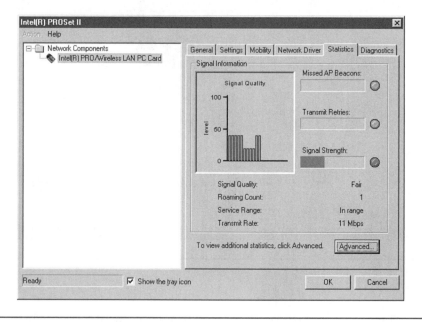

FIGURE 11-16   The drop in the signal quality to "Fair" at point C.

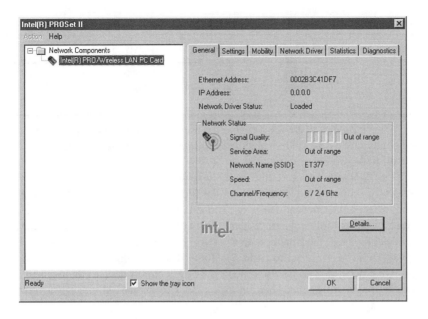

FIGURE 11-17   The "Out of range" measurement for point D.

The site survey shows that one access point placed at point 1 in the building is not sufficient to cover the building's floor plan. The survey shows that the additional cost of another access point is easily justified for providing full building wireless LAN coverage. The building has two wired network connections available for placing an access point (points 1 and 2). It was decided to place another access point at point 2. The site survey was repeated, and it showed that "Excellent" signal strength was obtained throughout the building. In some cases, a *range extender* can be used to provide additional wireless coverage. This device basically extends the reach of the wireless network.

11-4   BLUETOOTH, WiMAX, AND RFID

This section looks at three different wireless technologies: Bluetooth, WiMAX, and RFID. Each of these technologies plays important roles in the wireless networks. The sections that follow examine each of these wireless technologies, including a look at configuration and examples of the hardware being used.

Bluetooth

This section examines another wireless technology called *Bluetooth*, based on the 802.15 standard. Bluetooth was developed to replace the cable connecting computers, mobile phones, handheld devices, portable computers, and fixed electronic devices. The information normally carried by a cable is transmitted over the 2.4 GHz ISM frequency band, which is the same frequency band used by 802.11b/g/n. There are three output power classes for Bluetooth. Table 11-5 lists the maximum output power and the operating distance for each class.

TABLE 11-5 Bluetooth Output Power Classes

Power Class	Maximum Output Power	Operating Distance
1	20 dBm	~ 100 m
2	4 dBm	~ 10 m
3	0 dBm	~ 1 m

Inquiry Procedure
Used by Bluetooth to discover other Bluetooth devices or to allow itself to be discovered

Paging Procedure
Used to establish and synchronize a connection between two Bluetooth devices

Piconet
An ad hoc network of up to eight Bluetooth devices

When a Bluetooth device is enabled, it uses an **inquiry procedure** to determine whether any other Bluetooth devices are available. This procedure is also used to allow itself to be discovered.

If a Bluetooth device is discovered, it sends an inquiry reply back to the Bluetooth device initiating the inquiry. Next, the Bluetooth devices enter the paging procedure. The **paging procedure** is used to establish and synchronize a connection between two Bluetooth devices. When the procedure for establishing the connection has been completed, the Bluetooth devices will have established a **piconet**. A piconet is an ad hoc network of up to eight Bluetooth devices such as a computer, mouse, headset, earpiece, and so on. In a piconet, one Bluetooth device (the master) is responsible for providing the synchronization clock reference. All other Bluetooth devices are called slaves.

The following is an example of setting up a Bluetooth network linking a Mac OS X computer to another Bluetooth enabled device. To enable Bluetooth on the Mac OS X, click **Apple—Systems Preferences**. Under hardware, select **Bluetooth—Settings**, and the window shown in Figure 11-18 is opened. Click the **Bluetooth Power** button to turn on Bluetooth. Click **Discoverable**. This enables other Bluetooth devices to find you.

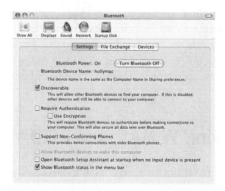

FIGURE 11-18 The window for configuring the Bluetooth settings.

Pairing
When a Bluetooth device is set up to connect to another Bluetooth device.

In the next step you will select the device with which you will be establishing a Bluetooth connection. Select **Devices—Set-up New Device—Turn Bluetooth On** if it is not already on. You will next be guided using the **Bluetooth Setup Assistant** and will be asked to select the device type. You have the choice of connecting to a mouse, keyboard, mobile phone, printer, or other device. In this case, **Other Device** is selected. This choice is selected when connecting to another computer. The **Bluetooth Device Setup** will search for another Bluetooth device. There will be a notification on the screen alerting you when another Bluetooth device is found. Select continue if this is the device you want to connect to. It is called **pairing** when another

Bluetooth device is set up to connect to another Bluetooth device. You may be asked for a Passkey. The **Passkey** is used in Bluetooth Security to limit outsider access to the pairing. Only people with the Passkey will be able to pair with your Bluetooth device.

At this point, you are now able to transfer files between the paired devices. This requires that the file exchange settings for the device have been set to allows files to come in. An example of the setup for the file transfer is shown in Figure 11-19.

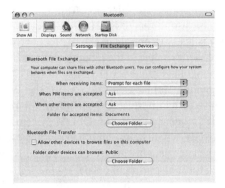

FIGURE 11-19   The window showing the settings for a file transfer.

The screen shown in Figure 11-20 shows an incoming text file. The File Transfer menu enables the user to select where received files are saved. In this case, the incoming files are being saved to the desktop.

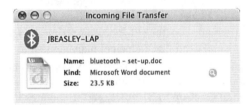

FIGURE 11-20   The window showing that a text file is coming in from another Bluetooth device.

This example has demonstrated setting up Bluetooth on a Mac OS X. The steps for setting up Bluetooth on a Windows XP or Vista computer or even a Blackberry differ slightly, but the basic steps are the same. The following are the basic steps you need to complete to pair with another Bluetooth device:

1. Enable the Bluetooth radio.
2. Enable Discoverability (this enables other Bluetooth devices to find you).
3. Select the device for pairing.

WiMAX

WiMAX
A broadband wireless system based on the IEEE 802.16e standard

BWA
Broadband wireless access

NLOS
Non line-of-sight

WiMAX (**W**orldwide **I**nteroperability for **M**icrowave **Acc**ess) is a broadband wireless system that has been developed for use as broadband wireless access (**BWA**) for fixed and mobile stations and can provide a wireless alternative for last mile broadband access in the 2 GHz to 66 GHz frequency range. BWA access for fixed stations can be up to 30 miles, whereas mobile BWA access is 3–10 miles. Internationally, the WiMAX frequency standard is 3.5 GHz while the United States uses both the unlicensed 5.8 GHz and the licensed 2.5 GHz spectrum. There are also investigations with adapting WiMAX for use in the 700 MHz frequency range. Information transmitted at this frequency is less susceptible to signal blockage due to trees. The disadvantage of the lower frequency range is the reduction in the bandwidth.

WiMAX uses Orthogonal Frequency Division Multiplexing (OFDM) as its signaling format. This signaling format was selected for the WiMAX standard IEEE 802.16a standard because of its improved **NLOS** (non line-of-sight) characteristics in the 2 GHz to 11 GHz frequency range. An OFDM system uses multiple frequencies for transporting the data, which helps minimize multipath interference problems. Some frequencies may be experiencing interference problems, but the system can select the best frequencies for transporting the data.

WiMAX also provides flexible channel sizes (for example, 3.5 MHz, 5 MHz, and 10 MHz), which provides adaptability to standards for WiMAX worldwide. This also helps ensure that the maximum data transfer rate is being supported. For example, the allocated channel bandwidth could be 6 MHz, and the adaptability of the WiMAX channel size allows it to adjust to use the entire allocated bandwidth.

Additionally, the WiMAX (IEEE 802.16e) media access control (MAC) layer differs from the IEEE 802.11 Wi-Fi MAC layer in that the WiMAX system has to compete only once to gain entry into the network. When a WiMAX unit has gained access, it is allocated a time slot by the base station, thereby providing the WiMAX with scheduled access to the network. The WiMAX system uses time division multiplexing (TDM) data streams on the downlink and time-division multiple access (TDMA) on the uplink and centralized channel management to make sure time-sensitive data is delivered on time. Additionally, WiMAX operates in a collision-free environment, which improves channel throughput.

WiMAX has a range of up to 31 miles, and it operates in both point-to-point and point-to-multipoint configurations. This can be useful in situations where DSL or cable network connectivity is not available. WiMAX is also useful for providing the last mile connection. The **last mile** is basically the last part of the connection from the telecommunications provider to the customer. The cost of the last mile connection can be expensive, which makes a wireless alternative attractive to the customer.

Last Mile
The last part of the connection from the telecommunications provider to the customer

Radio Frequency Identification (RFID)
A technique that uses radio waves to track and identify people, animals, objects, and shipments

Backscatter
Refers to the reflection of the radio waves striking the RFID tag and reflecting back to the transmitter source

The 802.16e WiMAX standard holds a lot of promise for use as a mobile air interface. Another standard, 802.20, is a mobile air interface being developed for consumer use. This standard plans to support data rates over 1 Mbps, which is comparable to DSL and cable connections. Additional 802.20 is being developed to support high-speed mobility. In other words, the user could be in a fast car or train and still have network connectivity.

RFID (Radio Frequency Identification)

Radio Frequency Identification (RFID) is a technique that uses radio waves to track and identify people, animal, objects, and shipments. This is done by the principle of modulated **backscatter**. The term "backscatter" is referring to the reflection of the radio waves striking the RFID tag and reflecting back to the transmitter source with its stored unique identification information.

Figure 11-21 illustrates the basic block for an RFID system.

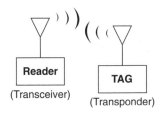

Reader
(Transceiver)

TAG
(Transponder)

FIGURE 11-21 Basic block diagram of an RFID system.

The RFID system consists of two things:

- An RFID tag (also called the RF transponder) includes an integrated antenna and radio electronics.
- A reader (also called a transceiver) consists of a transceiver and an antenna. A transceiver is the combination of a transmitter and receiver.

The reader (transceiver) transmits radio waves, which activates (turns on) an RFID tag. The tag then transmits modulated data, containing its unique identification information stored in the tag, back to the reader. The reader then extracts the data stored on the RFID tag.

The RFID idea dates back to 1948, when the concept of using reflected power as a means of communication was first proposed. The 1970s saw further development in RFID technology, in particular, a UHF scheme that incorporates rectification of the RF signal for providing power to the tag. Development of RFID technology significantly increased in the 1990s. Applications included toll collection that allowed vehicles to pass through tollbooths at highway speeds while still being able to record data from the tag.

Today, RFID technology is being used to track inventory shipments for major commercial retailers, the transportation industries, and the Department of Defense. Additionally, RFID applications are being used in Homeland Security in tracking container shipments at border crossings. Additionally, RFID is being incorporated into wireless LAN (WLAN) computer networks to keep better track of inventory. Wireless technologies are becoming more important for the enterprise. RFID technology is being used as a wireless means for asset tracking and as a result is placing more importance on its role in the network. The tracking technology is even being extended to tracking WiFi devices within the WLAN infrastructure.

There are three parameters that define an RFID system. These include the following:

- Means of powering the tag
- Frequency of operation
- Communications protocol (also called the air interface protocol)

Powering the Tag   RFID tags are classified in three ways based on how they obtain their operating power. The three different classifications are passive, semi-active, and active.

- **Passive:** Power is provided to the tag by rectifying the RF energy, transmitted from the reader, that strikes the RF tag antenna. The rectified power level is sufficient to power the ICs on the tags and also provides sufficient power for the tag to transmit a signal back to the reader. Figure 11-22 shows an example of a passive RFID tag (also called an inlay).
  The tag inlays include both the RFID chip and the antenna mounted on a substrate.
- **Semi-active:** The tags use a battery to power the electronics on the tag but use the property of backscatter to transmit information back to the reader.
- **Active:** Use a battery to power the tag and transmit a signal back to the reader. Basically this is a radio transmitter. New active RFID tags are incorporating wireless Ethernet, the 802.11b–WiFi connectivity. An example is the G2C501 Active RFID tag from G2 Microsystems shown in Figure 11-23. The power consumption of the G2C501 is 10μA in the sleep mode and uses two AA batteries with an expected lifetime of five years. The G2C501 also works in the standard 915 MHz range. The G2C501 also has location capability. This is accomplished by making Receive Signal Strength Indicator (RSSI) measurements from three separate access points. The three measurements provide sufficient information to make a triangulation measurement for use in locating the object.

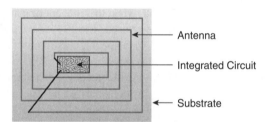

FIGURE 11-22   Examples of an RFID inlay.

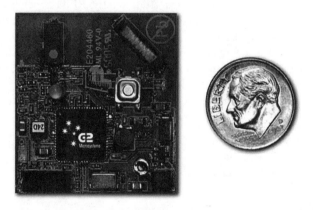

FIGURE 11-23   The G2C501 Active RFID tag from G2Microsystems (courtesy of G2Microsystems).

Frequency of Operation   The RFID tags must be tuned to the reader's transmit frequency to turn on. RFID systems typically use three frequency bands for operation, LF, HF, and UHF as shown in Figure 11-24:

- **Low-frequency (LF)** tags typically use frequency-shift keying (FSK) between the 125/134 kHz frequencies. The data rates from these tags is low (~12 kbps) and they are not appropriate for any applications requiring fast data transfers. However, the low-frequency tags are suitable for animal identification, such as dairy cattle and other livestock. The RFID tag information is typically obtained when the livestock are being fed. The read range for low-frequency tags is approximately .33 meters.

- **High-frequency (HF)** tags operate in the 13.56 MHz industrial band. High-frequency tags have been available commercially since 1995. It is known that the longer wavelengths of the HF radio signal are less susceptible to absorption by water or other liquids. Therefore, these tags are better suited for tagging liquids. The read range for high-frequency tags is approximately 1 meter. The short read range provides for better defined read ranges. The applications for tags in this frequency range include access control, smart cards, and shelf inventory.

- **Ultra-high frequency (UHF)** tags work at 860–960 MHz and at 2.4 GHz. The data rates for these tags can be from 50–150 kbps and greater. These tags are popular for tracking inventory. The read range for passive UHF tags is 10–20 feet, which make it a better choice for reading pallet tags. However, if an active tag is used, a read range up to 100 meters is possible.

LF	HF	UHF
125/134 kHz	13.56 MHz	860 - 960 MHz
		2.4 GHz

FIGURE 11-24   The frequency bands used by RFID tags.

Communications (Air Interface) Protocol   The air interface protocol adopted for RFID tags is **Slotted Aloha**, a network communications protocol technique similar to the Ethernet protocol. In a Slotted Aloha protocol, the tags are only allowed to transmit at predetermined times after being energized. This technique reduces the chance of data collisions between RFID tag transmissions and allows for the reading of up to 1000 tags per second. (Note: This is for high-frequency tags). The operating range for RFID tags can be up to 30 meters. This means that multiple tags can be energized at the same time, and a possible RF data collision can occur. If a collision occurs, the tag will transmit again after a random back-off time. The readers transmit continuously until there is no tag collision.

Slotted Aloha
A wireless network communications protocol technique similar to the Ethernet protocol

11-5   SECURING WIRELESS LANS

This section provides an overview of securing 802.11 wireless LANs. The network administrator must be aware of the security issues when configuring a wireless LAN. The fact is, RF (radio frequencies) will pass through walls, ceilings, and floors of a building even with low signal power. Therefore, the assumption should never be made that the wireless data is confined to only the user's area. The network administrator must assume that the wireless data can be received by an unintended user. In other words, the use of an unsecured wireless LAN is opening a potential threat to network security.

To address this threat to WLAN security, the network administrator must make sure the WLAN is protected by firewalls and intrusion detection (see Chapter 10), and most importantly the network administrator must make sure that the wireless security features are

TURNED ON!!!!!

This might seem to be a bold statement, but surprisingly enough, many WLANs are placed on a network without turning on available wireless security features. Many times the user in the WLAN assumes that no one would break into his or her computer because nothing important exists on the system. This may be true, but to an attacker, the user has one very important item, access to the wired network through an unsecured client.

Beacon
Used to verify the integrity of a wireless link

WLANs use an SSID (service set identifier) to authenticate users, but the problem is that the SSID is broadcast in radio link beacons about 10 times per second. In WLAN equipment, the **beacons** are transmitted so that a wireless user can identify an access point to connect to. The SSID can be turned off so it isn't transmitted with a beacon, but it is still possible for the SSID to be obtained by packet sniffing. As noted previously, *packet sniffing* is a technique used to scan through unencrypted data packets to extract information. In this case, an attacker uses packet sniffing to extract the SSID from data packets. Disabling SSID broadcasting will make it so that most client devices (such as Windows PCs and laptops) won't notice that the wireless LAN is present. This at least keeps "casual snoopers" off the network. Enterprise-grade access points implement multiple SSIDs, with each configured SSID having its own VLAN and wireless configuration. This allows the deployment of a common wireless LAN infrastructure that supports multiple levels of security, which is important for some venues such as airports and hospitals (where there are both public and private users).

IEEE 802.11 supports two ways to authenticate clients: open and sharekey. *Open* authentication basically means that the correct SSID is being used. In *sharekey* authentication, a packet of text is sent by the access point to the client with the instruction to encrypt the text and return it to the access point. This requires that wired equivalent privacy (WEP) be turned on. WEP is used to encrypt and decrypt wireless data packets. The exchange and the return of the encrypted text verifies that the client has the proper WEP key and is authorized to be a member of the wireless network. It is important to note that shared key authentication is extremely vulnerable. As a result, it's standard practice to avoid the use of shared key authentication. An example of the setting for WEP encryption is provided in Figure 11-25 (a and b). In Figure 11-25 (a), the user has the WEP options of disabled (No Privacy), 64-bit WEP (Privacy), and 128-bit WEP (More Privacy). Figure 11-25 (b) shows the wireless security settings in Windows Vista. There are clearly more options, and these newer wireless security settings are discussed next.

There is some concern that WEP isn't a strong enough encryption to secure a wireless network. There is published information about WEP vulnerabilities, but even with this, WEP does provide some basic security and is certainly better than operating the network with no security.

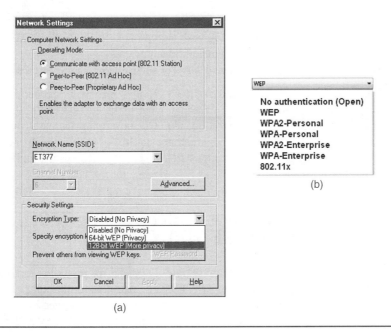

(a)

(b)

FIGURE 11-25   An example of setting WEP encryption on a wireless client.

An improvement with wireless security is provided with WPA and WPA2. **WPA** stands for Wi-Fi Protected Access, and it supports the user authentication provided by 802.1x and replaces WEP as the primary way for securing wireless transfers. WPA2 is an improved version of WPA. The 802.1x standard enhances wireless security by incorporating authentication of the user. Cisco Systems uses an 802.1x authentication system called LEAP. In Cisco LEAP, the user must enter a password to access the network. This means that if the wireless client is being used by an unauthorized user, the password requirement will keep the unauthorized user out of the network.

WPA is considered to be a higher level of security for wireless systems. In the 802.1x system, a user requests access to the wireless network via an access point. The next step is for the user to be authenticated. At this point, the user can only send EAP messages. **EAP** is the Extensible Authentication Protocol and is used in both WAP and WAP2 by the client computer and the access point. The access point sends an EAP message requesting the user's identity. The user (client computer) returns the identity information that is sent by the access point to an authentication server. The server will then accept or reject the user's request to join the network. If the client is authorized, the access point will change the user (client's) state to authorized. A Remote Authentication Dial-In User Service (**RADIUS**) service is sometimes used to provide authentication. This type of authentication helps prevent unauthorized users from connecting to the network. Additionally, this authentication helps to keep authorized users from connecting to rouge of unauthorized access points.

Another way to further protect data transmitted over a WLAN is to establish a VPN connection (see Chapter 8). In this way, the data is protected from an attacker. The following are basic guidelines for wireless security:

- Make sure the wireless security features are turned on.
- Use firewalls and intrusion detection on your WLAN.

WPA
Wi-Fi Protected Access

EAP
Extensible Authentication Protocol

RADIUS
Remote Authentication Dial-In Service

- Improve authentication of the WLAN by incorporating 802.1x features.
- Consider using third-party end-to-end encryption software to protect the data that might be intercepted by an unauthorized user.
- Whenever possible, use encrypted services such as SSH and Secure FTP.

The bottom line is that the choice of the level of security will be based on multiple factors within the network. For example, what is the cost benefit ratio of increased security? How will incorporating or not incorporating increased wireless security affect users? The network administrator and the overall management will have to make the final decision regarding wireless security before it is installed and the network becomes operational.

11-6 CONFIGURING A POINT-TO-MULTIPOINT WIRELESS LAN: A CASE STUDY

This section presents an example of preparing a proposal for providing a point-to-multipoint wireless network for a company. The administrators for the company have decided that it would be beneficial to provide a wireless network connection for their employees back to the company's network (home network). This example addresses the following issues:

1. Conducting an initial antenna site survey
2. Establishing a link from the home network to the distribution point
3. Configuring the multipoint distribution
4. Conducting an RF site survey for establishing a baseline signal level for the remote wireless user
5. Configuring the remote user's installation

The objective is to establish a point-to-multipoint wireless network that provides remote users with a wireless network connection. The remote users are to be at fixed locations within the proposed coverage area. A simple terrain profile of the proposed area is shown in Figure 11-26. The data rate for the wireless connection to remote users needs to be at least 2 Mbps.

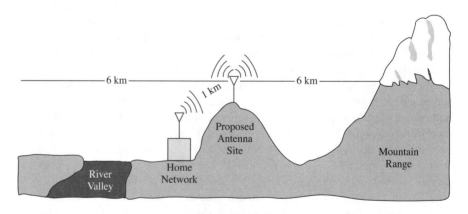

FIGURE 11-26   The terrain profile of the area to be supported by the proposed point-to-multipoint wireless network.

1. Antenna Site Survey

The proposed antenna site (see Figure 11-26) is on top of a hill approximately 1 kilometer (km) from the home network. A site survey provides the following information:

- The site has a tower that can be used to mount the wireless antenna.
- The site has a small building and available rack space for setting up the wireless networking equipment.
- There is a clear view of the surrounding area for 6 km in every direction.
- There is not an available wired network connection back to the home network. The decision is made to use the proposed antenna site and set up an 11 Mbps wireless link back to the home network.

2. Establishing a Point-to-Point Wireless Link to the Home Network

The cost is too high to put in a wired connection back to the home network; therefore, it is decided to use a point-to-point 802.11 wireless link for the interconnection. This requires that antennas be placed at both the home network and the antenna site. A wireless bridge is used at each end of the point-to-point wireless link to interconnect the networks. The bridge will connect to the wired home network and to the multipoint distribution on the antenna site. Also each antenna will be outfitted with lightning arrestors to protect the electronics from any possible lightning strikes. Figure 11-27 shows the proposed wireless connection.

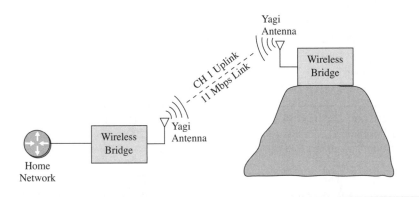

FIGURE 11-27   The proposed point-to-point wireless link from the home network to the antenna site.

There are many manufacturers of antennas that support wireless networking, and there are many types of antenna that can be used. Antenna types from many manufacturers were investigated for possible use in the interconnection. Three possible antennas were selected for the wireless network, as outlined in Table 11-6.

TABLE 11-6 Sample of 802.11b Wireless Antennas

Antenna	Type	Radiation Pattern	Range in km at 2 Mbps	Range in km at 11 Mbps	Costs
A.	Omni	Omnidirectional	7	2	Moderate
B.	Yagi	Directional	12	7.5	Moderate
C.	Dish	Highly directional	38	18	High

Antenna A has an omnidirectional radiation pattern. This means the antenna can receive and transmit signals in a 360-degree pattern. Figure 11-28 (a) shows the radiation pattern for an omnidirectional antenna. Antenna A supports a 2 Mbps data rate up to 7 km from the antenna and supports an 11 Mbps data rate at a maximum distance of 2 km. Table 11-6 also indicates that this antenna has a moderate cost.

Antenna B is a Yagi antenna with a directional radiation pattern as shown in Figure 11-28 (b). The Yagi antenna supports a 2 Mbps data rate for a maximum of 12 km.

Antenna C is a "dish" antenna or parabolic reflector. These antennas provide extremely high directional gain. In this example, the dish antenna supports 11 Mbps up to 18 km away and 2 Mbps up to 38 km away. The cost of the dish antenna can be quite high relative to the cost of the Yagi or omnidirectional antenna.

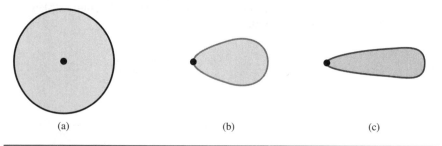

(a)   (b)   (c)

FIGURE 11-28 Antenna radiation patterns for (a) omnidirectional, (b) Yagi, and (c) dish [parabolic reflector] antenna, and supports 11 Mbps up to 7.5 km from the antenna. The cost of the Yagi antenna is comparable to the omnidirectional antenna.

Antenna B, the directional Yagi, is selected for the point-to-point link. The antenna meets the distance requirement and also meets the 11 Mbps data rate requirement. Antennas A and C were not selected for the following reasons:

- Antenna A—the omnidirectional radiation pattern is not appropriate
- Antenna C—the cost of a high gain dish antenna is not justified for the short distance

3–4. Configuring the Multipoint Distribution/Conducting an RF Site Survey

At this point, an 11 Mbps wireless data link has been established with the home network. The next task is to configure the antenna site for multipoint distribution. It was previously decided that a 2 Mbps link would be adequate for the remote users, based on the data rate to be supported for the planned coverage area.

The site survey in step 1 showed that there is a clear view of the surrounding area for 6 km in each direction. Antenna A (see Table 11-6) provides an omnidirectional radiation pattern for 7 km. This satisfies the coverage area and 2 Mbps data rate. Antenna A is mounted on the antenna site tower, connected to a lightning arrestor and then connected to the output of a wireless bridge. An RF site survey of the planned coverage area is next done to verify the signal quality provided by the antenna selected. Measurements are made from multiple locations within the planned coverage area. All remote sites within 4 km of the distribution show a signal strength of "Excellent," as shown in Figure 11-29.

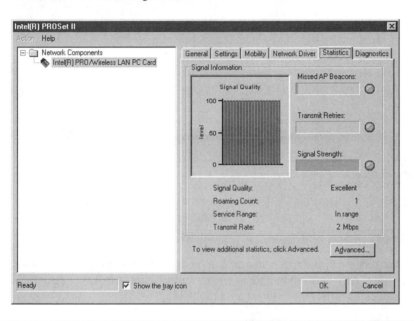

FIGURE 11-29 The signal quality of "Excellent" measured for the multipoint distribution.

The signal quality drops to "Good" at 6 km at all surveyed remote locations except for one area that shows a "Poor." The measurement for this site is provided in Figure 11-30. Apparently the signal is being affected by multipath distortion off a small lake area. A fix to this might be to move the antenna to a different height to minimize reflection problems. An antenna at a different height will receive different reflections and possibly less interference. In some cases antenna alignment can be changed to decrease the interference. A more costly solution is to add antenna "diversity." Basically this means that multiple antennas are placed on the receiving tower, and the best signal is used for the connection.

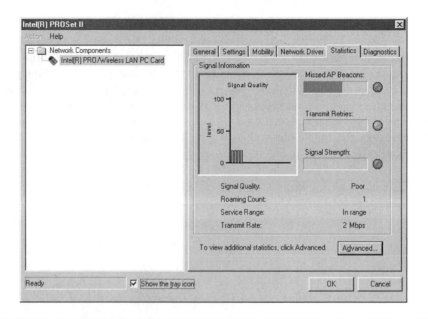

FIGURE 11-30   The signal quality of "Poor" measured at the remote site near the lake.

5. Configuring the Remote Installations

The last task is to develop a configuration for the remote users. The antenna for each remote user only needs to be able to see the multipoint distribution antenna site. The requirements for the remote client are as follows:

- 2 Mbps data rate connection
- Directional antenna (Yagi) plus mount, lightning arrestor, wireless bridge

Antenna B (see Table 11-6) is selected for the directional antenna. This antenna will provide sufficient RF signal level for the remote user. Each remote user will need a wireless bridge and a switch to connect multiple users. (Note that the bridge is set for a 2 Mbps data rate.) Figure 11-31 shows the setup for the remote user.

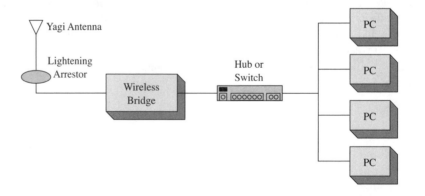

FIGURE 11-31   The setup for the remote user in the proposed point-to-multipoint wireless network.

SUMMARY

This chapter presented an overview of wireless networking. The fundamental concept and example networks were also presented. The vendors of wireless networking equipment have made them very easy to integrate into existing networks, but the reader must understand that the key objective of the network administrator is to provide a fast, reliable, and secure computer network. Carelessly integrating wireless components into the network can easily compromise this objective. Students should understand the following from reading this chapter:

- The operating characteristics of the 802.11 wireless networks
- The purpose of access points, wireless LAN adapters, and wireless bridges
- How to perform a basic site survey on a building
- How to configure the network for user mobility
- How to plan multipoint wireless distribution

A final note: The new wireless networking technologies have greatly simplified planning and installation. Anytime you are working with RF (radio frequencies) there is a chance of unexpected interference and noise. A well-planned RF installation requires a study of all known interference and a search for any possible interference. An RF study will also include signal path studies that enable the user to prepare a well-thought-out plan and allow an excellent prediction of received signal level. The bottom line is to obtain support for conducting an RF study.

QUESTIONS AND PROBLEMS

Section 11-2

1. List two advantages of wireless networking.
2. What are the three areas defined for the IEEE 802.11 standard?
3. What is an *ad hoc network*?
4. What is the purpose of an Extended Service Set?
5. What are the four physical layer technologies being used in 802.11 wireless networking?
6. Describe the frequency spectrum for the DSSS channels in 802.11b wireless networking.
7. Define a *pseudorandom sequence* as it applies to FHSS.
8. What must the FHSS transmitting and receiving units know to communicate?
9. What is the frequency range used by 802.11a, and what modulation technique is used?
10. What is the maximum data rate for the following:
    a. 802.11b
    b. 802.11a
    c. 802.11g
    d. 802.11n
11. Define MIMO as it applies to 802.11n.
12. What is the purpose of the power-save mode in 802.11n?

Section 11-3

13. What is the purpose of an access point?
14. How does the access point know if a wireless data packet is intended for its network?
15. What is an *association*, and what is its purpose?
16. Draw a picture of a point-to-point wireless connection.
17. Draw a picture of a point-to-multipoint wireless network.
18. What are the key issues to be obtained from conducting a site survey for each of the following?
    a. indoor
    b. outdoor

Section 11-4

19. In what frequency band does Bluetooth operate?
20. How many output power classes does Bluetooth have? List the power level and the operating range for each class.
21. What is a piconet?
22. What is the purpose of the inquiry procedure in Bluetooth?
23. What is the purpose of the paging procedure in Bluetooth?
24. Define the term *backscatter*.
25. What are the three parameters that define an RFID system?
26. Explain how power is provided to a passive RFID tag.
27. Cite three advantages for using an active RFID tag.
28. What are the three frequency bands typically used for RFID tags?
29. What is the WiMax frequency standard for the United States?
30. Why was OFDM selected for WiMax?
31. How does WiMax differ from Wi-Fi?

Section 11-5

32. What is the most important thing to do if using a wireless network?
33. What is the purpose of wireless beacons?
34. What information can be obtained from a wireless beacon?
35. What is the purpose of WEP?
36. List four guidelines for wireless security.
37. Describe the steps used by WPA2 to authenticate a user.
38. What is a RADIUS server?

Section 11-6

39. What type of wireless connection is used to connect the home network to a multipoint distribution site?

40. Use the Internet to find a source of omnidirectional and directional antennas for each of the following standards.
    a. 802.11b
    b. 802.11a
    c. 802.11g
    d. 802.11n

Prepare a list of three manufacturers for each antenna type. Include cost figures.

Critical Thinking

41. A wireless network receiving site is experiencing occasional loss of signal due to interference. Discuss the steps you would take to correct this problem.
42. Prepare a memo to your supervisor explaining why it is important to run encryption on your wireless network.

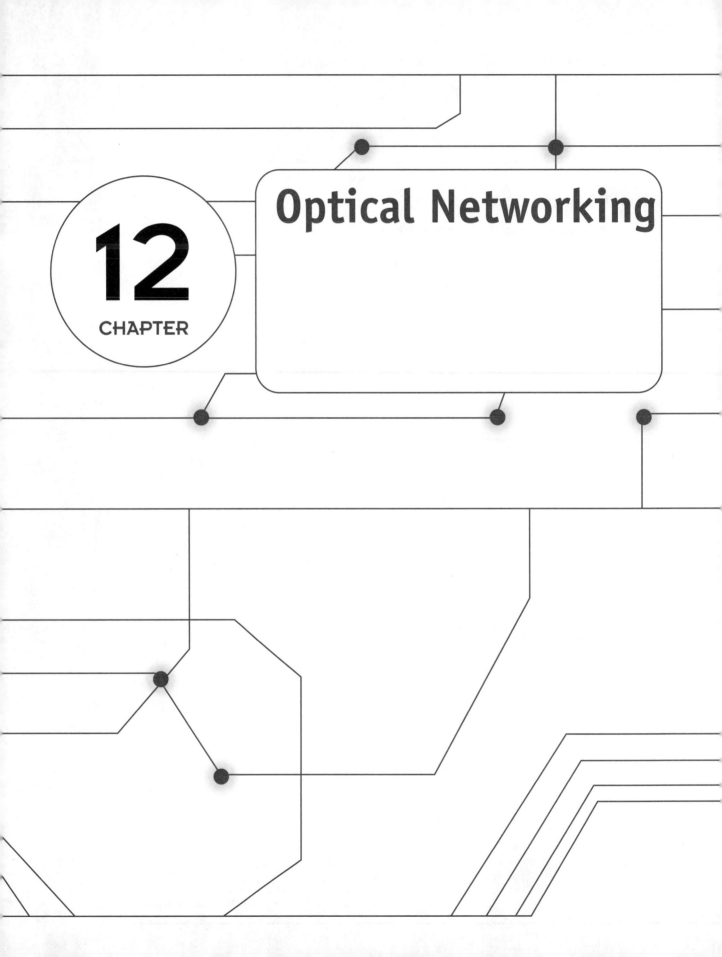

12

CHAPTER

Optical Networking

12-1 Introduction
12-2 The Nature of Light
12-3 Fiber Attenuation and Dispersion
12-4 Optical Components
12-5 Optical Networking Architectures
12-6 System Design and Operational Issues

12-7 Safety
12-8 Troubleshooting Computer Networks (The OTDR)
Summary
Questions and Problems

OBJECTIVES

- Describe the advantages of glass fiber over copper conductors
- Describe the differences in how light travels in single and multimode fiber
- Define *attenuation* and *dispersion* in fiber optic cabling
- Describe the components of a fiber optic system
- Describe the issues of optical networking, including fiber-to-the-business and fiber to-the-home

- Describe the new networking developments associated with optical Ethernet
- Calculate a complete power budget analysis for a fiber optic system
- Understand the safety issues when working with fiber optics
- Describe how to use an OTDR and analyze the test data when conducting tests on a fiber optic cable

KEY TERMS

refractive index
infrared light
optical spectrum
cladding
numerical aperture
multimode fiber
pulse dispersion
graded-index fiber
single-mode fiber
step-index fiber
long haul
mode field diameter
scattering
absorption
macrobending

microbending
dispersion
modal dispersion
chromatic dispersion
polarization mode dispersion
zero-dispersion wavelength
dispersion compensating fiber
fiber Bragg grating
DL
LED
distributed feedback (DFB) laser

dense wavelength division multiplex (DWDM)
vertical cavity surface emitting lasers (VCSELs)
tunable laser
fiber, light pipe, glass
isolator
received signal level (RSL)
fusion splicing
mechanical splices
index-matching gel
SC, ST, FC, LC, MT-RJ
SONET/SDH
STS

continues

KEY TERMS continued

FTTC

FTTH

FTTB

FTTD

optical Ethernet

fiber cross-connect

GBIC

XENPAK

IDC

IC

logical fiber map

physical fiber map

mm

sm

backbone

backhoe fading

Visual Fault Locator (VFL)

OTDR

Event

12-1   INTRODUCTION

Recent advances in the development and manufacture of fiber optic systems have made them the latest frontier in the field of optical networking. They are being used extensively for both private and commercial data links and have replaced a lot of copper wire. The latest networking technologies to benefit from the development in optical networking are gigabit Ethernet and 10 gigabit Ethernet.

A fiber optic network is surprisingly simple, as shown in Figure 12-1. It is comprised of the following elements:

1. A fiber optic transmission strand can carry the signal (in the form of a modulated light beam) a few feet or even hundreds or thousands of miles. A cable may contain three or four hair-like fibers or a bundle of hundreds of such fibers.
2. A source of invisible infrared radiation—usually a light-emitting diode (LED) or a solid-state laser—that can be modulated to impress digital data or an analog signal on the light beam.
3. A photosensitive detector to convert the optical signal back into an electrical signal at the receiver.
4. Efficient optical connectors at the light source-to-cable interface and at the cable-to-photo detector interface. These connectors are also critical when splicing the optical cable due to excessive loss that can occur at connections.

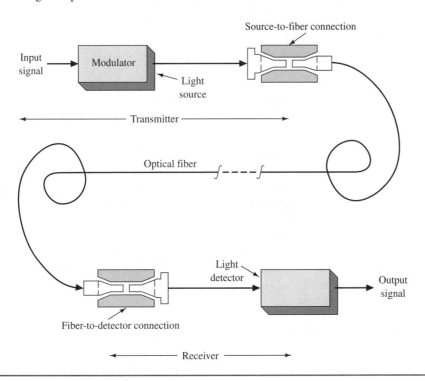

FIGURE 12-1   Fiber optic communication system. (From Modern Electronic Communication 9/e, by J.S. Beasley & G. M. Miller, 2008, p. 781. Copyright ©2002 Pearson Education, Inc. Reprinted by permission of Pearson Education, Inc., Upper Saddle River, NJ.)

The advantages of optical communication links compared to copper conductors are enormous and include the following:

1. **Extremely wide system bandwidth:** The intelligence is impressed on the light by varying the light's amplitude. Because the best LEDs have a 5 ns response time, they provide a maximum bandwidth of about 100 MHz. With laser light sources, however, data rates over 10 Gbps are possible with a single mode fiber. The amount of information multiplexed on such a system, in the hundreds of Gbps, is indeed staggering.

2. **Immunity to electrostatic interference:** External electrical noise and lightning do not affect energy in a fiber optic strand. However, this is true only for the optical strands, not the metallic cable components or connecting electronics.

3. **Elimination of crosstalk:** The light in one glass fiber does not interfere with, nor is it susceptible to, the light in an adjacent fiber. Recall that crosstalk results from the electromagnetic coupling between two adjacent copper wires.

4. **Lower signal attenuation than other propagation systems:** Typical attenuation of a 1 GHz bandwidth signal for optical fibers is 0.03 dB per 100 ft, compared to 4.0 dB for RG-58U coaxial.

5. **Lower costs:** Optical fiber costs are continuing to decline. The costs of many systems are declining with the use of fiber, and that trend is accelerating.

6. **Safety:** In many wired systems, the potential hazard of short circuits requires precautionary designs. Additionally, the dielectric nature of optic fibers eliminates the spark hazard.

7. **Corrosion:** Given that glass is basically inert, the corrosive effects of certain environments are not a problem.

8. **Security:** Due to its immunity to and from electromagnetic coupling and radiation, optical fiber can be used in most secure environments. Although it can be intercepted or tapped, it is very difficult to do so.

This chapter examines the issues of optical networking. Section 12-2 presents an overview of optical fiber fundamentals including a discussion on wavelengths and type of optical fibers. Section 12-3 examines the two distance-limiting parameters in fiber optic transmission, attenuation and dispersion. Optical components are presented in section 12-4. This includes an overview of LEDs and lasers, intermediate components used in long-haul fiber networks, and the various types of connectors currently used on fiber. Optical networking is presented in section 12-5. An overview of SONET and FDDI are presented, followed by optical Ethernet. This section includes a discussion on setting up the building and campus distribution for fiber. System design of fiber networks is presented in section 12-6. This material examines the steps for preparing a light budget for a fiber optic link. Safety is extremely important when working with fiber. A brief overview of safety is presented in section 12-7. The chapter concludes with a section on using an OTDR for troubleshooting an optical fiber link.

12-2   THE NATURE OF LIGHT

Before one can understand the propagation of light in a glass fiber, it is necessary to review some basics of light refraction and reflection. The speed of light in free space is 3×10^8 m/s but is reduced in other media, including fiber optic cables. The reduction as light passes into denser material results in refraction of the light. Refraction causes the light wave to be bent, as shown in Figure 12-2. The speed reduction and subsequent refraction is different for each wavelength, as shown in Figure 12-2 (b). The visible light striking the prism causes refraction at both air/glass interfaces and separates the light into its various frequencies (colors) as shown. This same effect produces a rainbow, with water droplets acting as prisms to split the sunlight into the visible spectrum of colors (the various frequencies).

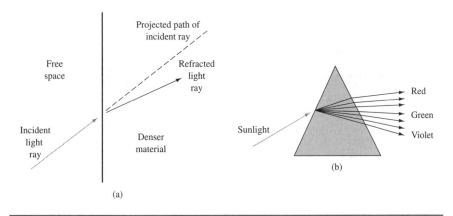

FIGURE 12-2   Refraction of light. (From Modern Electronic Communication 9/e, by J.S. Beasley & G. M. Miller, 2008, p. 782. Copyright ©2002 Pearson Education, Inc. Reprinted by permission of Pearson Education, Inc., Upper Saddle River, NJ.)

The amount of bend provided by refraction depends on the **refractive index** of the two materials involved. The refractive index, *n,* is the ratio of the speed of light in free space to the speed in a given material. It is slightly variable for different frequencies of light, but for most purposes a single value is accurate enough. The refractive index for free space (a vacuum) is 1.0, air is 1.0003, water is 1.33, and for the various glasses used in fiber optics, it varies between 1.42 and 1.50.

In the fiber optics industry, spectrum notation is stated in nanometers (nm) rather than in frequency (Hz) simply because it is easier to use, particularly in spectral-width calculations. A convenient point of commonality is that 3×10^{14} Hz, or 300 THz, is equivalent to 1 μm, or 1000 nm. This relationship is shown in Figure 12-3. The one exception to this naming convention is when discussing dense wavelength division multiplexing (DWDM), which is the transmission of several optical channels, or wavelengths, in the 1550-nm range, all on the same fiber. For DWDM systems, notations, and particularly channel separations, are stated in terahertz (THz). Wavelength division multiplexing (WDM) systems are discussed in section 12-5. An electromagnetic wavelength spectrum chart is provided in Figure 12-3. The electromagnetic light waves just below the frequencies in the visible spectrum extending

Refractive Index
Ratio of the speed of light in free space to its speed in a given material

Infrared Light
Light extending from 680 nm up to the wavelengths of the microwaves

Optical Spectrum
Light frequencies from the infrared on up

from 680 nm up are called **infrared light** waves. Whereas visible light has a wavelength from approximately 430 nm up to 680 nm, infrared light extends from 680 nm up to the microwaves. The frequency of visible light ranges from about 4.4×10^{14} Hz for red up to 7×10^{14} Hz for violet. For the frequencies above visible light, the electromagnetic spectrum includes the ultraviolet (UV) rays and X rays. The frequencies from the infrared on up are termed the **optical spectrum**.

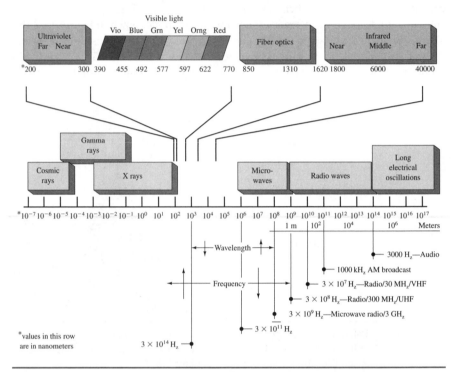

FIGURE 12-3 The electromagnetic wavelength spectrum. (From Modern Electronic Communication 9/e, by J.S. Beasley & G. M. Miller, 2008, p. 784. Copyright ©2008 Pearson Education, Inc. Reprinted by permission of Pearson Education, Inc., Upper Saddle River, NJ.)

The commonly used wavelengths in today's fiber optic systems are

- Multimode fiber: (850 and 1310) nm
- Single mode fiber: (1310 and 1550) nm
- Fiber to the home/business: 1600–1625 nm

Cladding
Material surrounding the core, which must have a lower index of refraction to keep the light in the core

Typical construction of an optical fiber is shown in Figure 12-4. The *core* is the portion of the fiber strand that carries the transmitted light. Its chemical composition is simply a very pure glass: silicon dioxide, doped with small amounts of germanium, boron, and phosphorous. The **cladding** is the material surrounding the core. It is almost always glass, although plastic cladding of a glass fiber is available but rarely used. In any event, the refraction index for the core and the cladding are different. The cladding must have a lower index of refraction to keep the light in the core. A plastic coating surrounds the cladding to provide protection. Figure 12-5 shows examples of fiber strands from a fiber bundle.

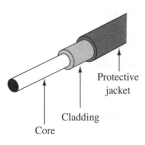

Protective
jacket

Cladding

Core

FIGURE 12-4 Single-fiber construction. (From Modern Electronic Communication 9/e, by J.S. Beasley & G. M. Miller, 2008, p. 785. Copyright ©2008 Pearson Education, Inc. Reprinted by permission of Pearson Education, Inc., Upper Saddle River, NJ.)

FIGURE 12-5 Fiber strands (courtesy of Anixter, Inc.).

Another measure of a fiber's light acceptance is **numerical aperture**. The numerical aperture is a basic specification provided by the manufacturer that indicates the fiber's ability to accept light and shows how much light can be off-axis and still propagate.

Several types of optical fibers are available, with significant differences in their characteristics. The first communication-grade fibers (early 1970s) had light carrying core diameters about equal to the wavelength of light. They could carry light in just a single waveguide mode.

The difficulty of coupling significant light into such a small fiber led to development of fibers with cores of about 20 to 100 μm. These fibers support many waveguide modes and are called **multimode fibers**. The first commercial fiber optic systems used multimode fibers with light at 800 to 900 nm wavelengths. A variation of the multimode fiber was subsequently developed, termed graded-index fiber. This afforded greater bandwidth capability.

Numerical Aperture
A measure of a fiber's ability to accept light

Multimode Fiber
A fiber that supports many optical waveguide modes

As the technology became more mature, the single-mode fibers were found to provide lower losses and even higher bandwidth. This has led to their use at 1300 nm, 1550 nm, up to 1625 nm in many telecommunication and fiber-to-the home applications. The new developments have not made old types of fiber obsolete. The application now determines the type used. The following major criteria affect the choice of fiber type:

1. Signal losses
2. Ease of light coupling and interconnection
3. Bandwidth

Pulse Dispersion
Stretching of received pulse width because of multiple paths taken by the light

A graphic of a fiber showing three different modes (that is, multimode) of propagation is presented in Figure 12-6. The lowest-order mode is seen traveling along the axis of the fiber, and the middle-order mode is reflected twice at the interface. The highest-order mode is reflected many times and makes many trips across the fiber. As a result of these variable path lengths, the light entering the fiber takes a variable length of time to reach the detector. This results in a pulse-broadening or dispersion characteristic, as shown in Figure 12-6. This effect is termed **pulse dispersion** and limits the maximum distance and rate at which data (pulses of light) can be practically transmitted. You will also note that the output pulse has reduced amplitude as well as increased width. The greater the fiber length, the worse this effect will be. As a result, manufacturers rate their fiber in bandwidth per length, such as 400 MHz/km. This means the fiber can successfully transmit pulses at the rate of 400 MHz for 1 km, 200 MHz for 2 km, and so on. In fact, current networking standards limit multimode fiber distances to 2 km. Of course, longer transmission paths are attained by locating regenerators at appropriate locations. Step-index multimode fibers are rarely used in networking due to their very high amounts of pulse dispersion and minimal bandwidth capability.

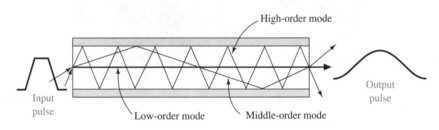

FIGURE 12-6 Modes of propagation for step-index fiber. (From Modern Electronic Communication 9/e, by J.S. Beasley & G. M. Miller, 2008, p. 787. Copyright ©2002 Pearson Education, Inc. Reprinted by permission of Pearson Education, Inc., Upper Saddle River, NJ.)

Graded-Index Fiber

Graded-index Fiber
The index of refraction is gradually varied with a parabolic profile

In an effort to overcome the pulse-dispersion problem, the **graded-index fiber** was developed. In the manufacturing process for this fiber, the index of refraction is tailored to follow the parabolic profile shown in Figure 12-7. This results in low-order modes traveling through the constant-density material in the center. High-order modes see a lower index of refraction material farther from the core, and thus the velocity of propagation increases away from the center. Therefore, all modes, even though they take various paths and travel different distances, tend to traverse the fiber length in about the same amount of time. These fibers can therefore handle higher bandwidths and/or provide longer lengths of transmission before pulse dispersion effects destroy intelligibility and introduce bit errors.

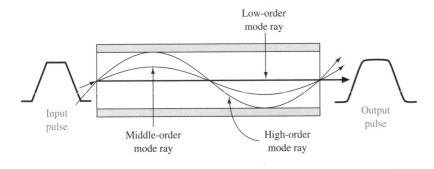

FIGURE 12-7   Modes of propagation for graded-index fiber. (From *Modern Electronic Communication* 9/e, by J.S. Beasley & G. M. Miller, 2008, p. 788. Copyright ©2008 Pearson Education, Inc. Reprinted by permission of Pearson Education, Inc., Upper Saddle River, NJ.)

Graded-index multimode fibers with 50 μm-diameter cores and 125 μm cladding are used in many telecommunication systems at up to 300 megabits per second (Mbps) over 50-km ranges without repeaters. Graded-index fiber with up to a 100 μm core is used in short-distance applications that require easy coupling from the source and high data rates, such as for video and high-speed local area networks. The larger core affords better light coupling than the 50 μm core and does not significantly degrade the bandwidth capabilities. In the telecommunications industry, there are two commonly used core sizes for graded-index fiber, these being 50 and 62.5 μm. Both have 125 μm cladding. The large core diameter and the high NA (numerical aperture) of these fibers simplify input cabling and allow the use of relatively inexpensive connectors. Fibers are specified by the diameters of their core and cladding. For example, the fibers just described would be called 50/125 fiber and 62/125 fiber.

Single-Mode Fibers

A technique used to minimize pulse dispersion effects is to make the core extremely small—on the order of a few micrometers. This type accepts only a low-order mode, thereby allowing operation in high-data-rate, long-distance systems. This fiber is typically used with high-power, highly directional modulated light sources such as a laser. Fibers of this variety are called **single-mode** (or monomode) **fibers**. Core diameters of only 7 to 10 μm are typical.

This type of fiber is termed a **step-index fiber**. Step index refers to the abrupt change in refractive index from core to cladding, as shown in Figure 12-8. The single-mode fiber, by definition, carries light in a single waveguide mode. A single-mode fiber will transmit a single mode for all wavelengths longer than the cutoff wavelength. A typical cutoff wavelength is 1260 nm. At wavelengths shorter than the cutoff, the fiber supports two or more modes and becomes multimode in operation.

Single-mode Fiber
Fiber cables with core diameters of about 7 to 10 μm; light follows a single path

Step-index Fiber
Fibers in which there is an abrupt change in the refractive index from the core to the cladding

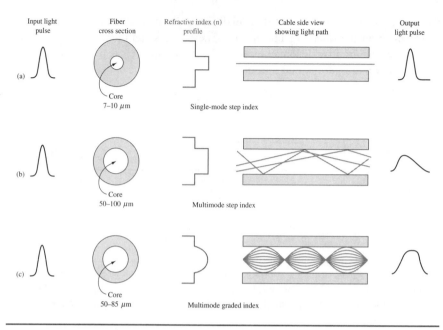

FIGURE 12-8   Types of optical fiber. (From Modern Electronic Communication 9/e, by J.S. Beasley & G. M. Miller, 2008, p. 789. Copyright ©2008 Pearson Education, Inc. Reprinted by permission of Pearson Education, Inc., Upper Saddle River, NJ.)

Long Haul
The transmission of data over hundreds or thousands of miles

Mode Field Diameter
The actual guided optical power distribution, which is typically a micron or so larger than the core diameter; single-mode fiber specifications typically list the mode field diameter

Single-mode fibers are widely used in **long-haul** and wide area network applications. They permit transmission of about 10 Gbps and a repeater spacing of up to 80 km. These bandwidth and repeater spacing capabilities are constantly being upgraded by new developments.

When describing the core size of single-mode fibers, the term **mode field diameter** is the term more commonly used. Mode field diameter is the actual guided optical power distribution diameter. In a typical single-mode fiber, the mode field diameter is 1 μm or so larger than the core diameter. The actual value depends on the wavelength being transmitted. In fiber specification sheets, the core diameter is stated for multimode fibers, but the mode field diameter is typically stated for single-mode fibers.

Figure 12-8 provides a graphical summary of the three types of fiber discussed, including typical dimensions, refractive index profiles, and pulse-dispersion effects. Table 12-1 provides a general comparison of single-mode and multimode fiber.

TABLE 12-1   Generalized Comparisons of Single-Mode and Multimode Fiber

Feature	Single-Mode	Multimode
Core size	Smaller (7.5 to 10 μm)	Larger (50 to 100 μm)
Numerical aperture	Smaller (0.1 to 0.12)	Larger (0.2 to 0.3)
Index of refraction profile	Step	Graded
Attenuation (dB/km) (a function of wavelength)	Smaller (0.25 to 0.5 dB/km)	Larger (0.5 to 4.0 dB/km)

Feature	Single-Mode	Multimode
Information-carrying capacity (a function of distance)	Very large	Small–medium
Usage	Long-haul carriers and CATV, CCTV	Short-haul LAN
Capacity	Expressed in megabits per second (Mbps)	Expressed in Mbps
Which to use (this is a judgment call)	Over 2 km	Under 2 km

Source: From Modern Electronic Communication 9/e, by J.S. Beasley & G. M. Miller, 2008, p. 790. Copyright ©2002 Pearson Education, Inc. Reprinted by permission of Pearson Education, Inc., Upper Saddle River, NJ.

12-3   FIBER ATTENUATION AND DISPERSION

There are two key distance-limiting parameters in fiber optic transmissions: attenuation and dispersion.

Attenuation

Attenuation is the loss of power introduced by the fiber. This loss accumulates as the light is propagated through the fiber strand. The loss is expressed in dB/km (decibels per kilometer) of length. The loss, or attenuation, of the signal is due to the combination of four factors: scattering, absorption, macrobending, and microbending. Two other terms for attenuation are intrinsic and extrinsic.

Scattering is the primary loss factor over the three wavelength ranges. Scattering in telecommunication systems accounts for 85 percent of the loss and is the basis of the attenuation curves and values, such as that shown in Figure 12-9, and account industry data sheets. The scattering is known as *Rayleigh scattering* and is caused by refractive index fluctuations. Rayleigh scattering decreases as wavelength increases, as shown in Figure 12-9.

Absorption is the second loss factor, a composite of light interaction with the atomic structure of the glass. It involves the conversion of optical power to heat. One portion of the absorption loss is due to the presence of OH hydroxol ions dissolved in the glass during manufacture. These cause the water attenuation or OH peaks shown in Figure 12-9 and other attenuation curves.

Macrobending is the loss caused by the light mode breaking up and escaping into the cladding when the fiber bend becomes too tight. As the wavelength increases, the loss in a bend increases. Although losses are in fractions of dB, the bend radius in small splicing trays and patching enclosures should be minimal.

Microbending is a type of loss caused by mechanical stress placed on the fiber strand, usually in terms of deformation resulting from too much pressure being applied to the cable. For example, excessively tight tie wrap or clamps will contribute to this loss. This loss is noted in fractions of a dB.

Scattering
Caused by refractive index fluctuations; accounts for 85% of attenuation loss

Absorption
Light interaction with the atomic structure of the fiber material; also involves the conversion of optical power to heat

Macrobending
Loss due to light breaking up and escaping into the cladding

Microbending
Loss caused by very small mechanical deflections and stress on the fiber

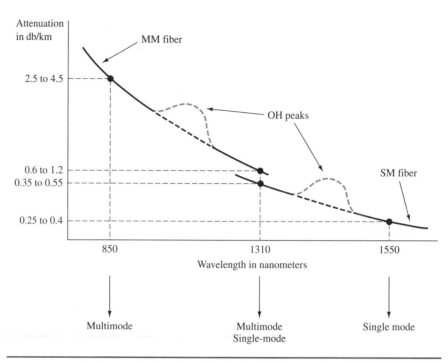

FIGURE 12-9   Typical attenuation of cabled fiber strands. (From Modern Electronic Communication 9/e, by J.S. Beasley & G. M. Miller, 2008, p. 792. Copyright ©2008 Pearson Education, Inc. Reprinted by permission of Pearson Education, Inc., Upper Saddle River, NJ.)

Dispersion

Dispersion
Broadening of a light pulse as it propagates through a fiber strand

Dispersion, or pulse broadening, is the second of the two key distance-limiting parameters in a fiber optic transmission system. It is a phenomenon in which the light pulse spreads out in time as it propagates along the fiber strand. This results in a broadening of the pulse. If the pulse broadens excessively, it can blend into the adjacent digital time slots and cause bit errors. Figure 12-10 illustrates the effects of dispersion on a light pulse. There are three types of dispersion:

Modal Dispersion
Chromatic Dispersion
Polarization Mode
Dispersion

- **Modal dispersion:** The broadening of a pulse due to different path lengths taken through the fiber by different modes.
- **Chromatic dispersion:** The broadening of a pulse due to different propagation velocities of the spectral components of the light pulse.
- **Polarization mode dispersion:** The broadening of a pulse due to the different propagation velocities of the X and Y polarization components of the light pulse.

Modal dispersion occurs predominantly in multimode fiber. From a light source, the light rays can take many paths as they propagate along the fiber. Some light rays do travel in a straight line, but most take variable-length routes. As a result, the rays arrive at the detector at different times, and the result is pulse broadening. This was shown in Figures 12-6 and 12-7. The use of graded-index fiber greatly reduces the effects of modal dispersion and therefore increases the bandwidth to about

1 GHz/km. On the other hand, single-mode fiber does not exhibit modal dispersion, given that only a single mode is transmitted.

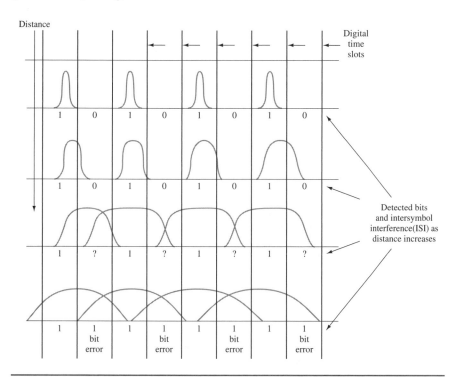

FIGURE 12-10 Pulse broadening or dispersion in optical fibers. (Adapted From Modern Electronic Communication 9/e, by J.S. Beasley & G. M. Miller, 2008, p. 793. Copyright ©2008 Pearson Education, Inc. Adapted by permission of Pearson Education, Inc., Upper Saddle River, NJ.)

A second equally important type of dispersion is chromatic. Chromatic dispersion is present in both single-mode and multimode fibers. Basically, the light source, both lasers and LEDs, produce several different wavelength light rays when generating the light pulse. Each light ray travels at a different velocity, and as a result, these rays arrive at the receiver detector at different times, causing the broadening of the pulse.

There is a point where dispersion is actually at zero, this being determined by the refractive index profile. This happens near 1310 nm and is called the **zero dispersion wavelength**. By altering the refractive index profile, this zero dispersion wavelength can be shifted to the 1550-nm region. Such fibers are called *dispersion-shifted.* This is significant because the 1550-nm region exhibits a lower attenuation than at 1310 nm. This becomes an operational advantage, particularly to long-haul carriers because with minimum attenuation and minimum dispersion in the same wavelength region, repeater and regenerator spacing can be maximized.

To further illustrate chromatic dispersion, Figure 12-11 shows a step-index single-mode fiber with different spectral components propagating directly along the core. Because they travel at different velocities, they arrive at the receiver detector at different times, causing a wider pulse to be detected than was transmitted.

Zero-dispersion Wavelength
Point where the dispersion is actually zero

Polarization mode is the type of dispersion found in single-mode systems and becomes of particular concern in long-haul and wide area network high-data-rate digital and high-bandwidth analog video systems. In a single-mode fiber, the single propagating mode has two polarizations, horizontal and vertical, or X axis and Y axis. The index of refraction can be different for the two components and this affects their relative velocity as shown in Figure 12-12.

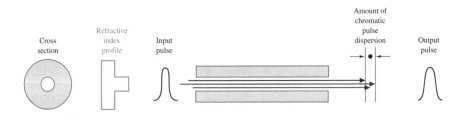

FIGURE 12-11   Spectral component propagation: single mode, step index. (From Modern Electronic Communication 9/e, by J.S. Beasley & G. M. Miller, 2008, p. 794. Copyright ©2008 Pearson Education, Inc. Reprinted by permission of Pearson Education, Inc., Upper Saddle River, NJ.)

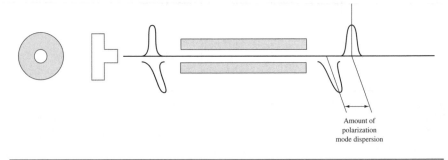

FIGURE 12-12   Polarization mode dispersion in single-mode fiber. (From Modern Electronic Communication 9/e, by J.S. Beasley & G. M. Miller, 2008, p. 794. Copyright ©2008 Pearson Education, Inc. Reprinted by permission of Pearson Education, Inc., Upper Saddle River, NJ.)

Dispersion Compensation

A considerable amount of fiber in use today was installed in the 1980s and early 1990s. This cable was called the class IVa variety. These cables were optimized to operate in the 1310-nm region, which means their zero-dispersion point was in the 1310-nm wavelength. Due to continuous network expansion needs in recent years, it is often desired to add transmission capacity to the older fiber cables by using the 1550-nm region, particularly since the attenuation at 1550 nm is less than at 1310 nm. One major problem arises at this point. The dispersion value is higher at 1550 nm (see Table 12-2), which severely limits its distance capability.

TABLE 12-2 Dispersion Values for Common Optical Wavelengths

Wavelength (nm)	Pulse Dispersion [ps/(nm—km)]
850	80 to 100
1310	2.5 to 3.5
1550	17

Source: From Modern Electronic Communication 9/e, by J.S. Beasley & G. M. Miller, 2008, p. 792. Copyright © 2008 Pearson Education, Inc. Reprinted by permission of Pearson Education, Inc., Upper Saddle River, NJ.

To overcome this problem, a fiber called **dispersion compensating fiber** was developed. This fiber acts like an equalizer, negative dispersion canceling positive dispersion. The fiber consists of a small coil normally placed in the equipment rack just prior to the optical receiver input. This does introduce some insertion loss (3 to 10 dB) and may require the addition of an optical-line amplifier.

A new device is a **fiber Bragg grating**. This technology involves etching irregularities onto a short strand of fiber, which changes the index of refraction and, in turn, reflects slower wavelengths to the output before the faster ones. This results in a compressed, or narrower, light pulse, minimizing intersymbol interference (ISI).

12-4 OPTICAL COMPONENTS

Two kinds of light sources are used in fiber optic communication systems: the diode laser (**DL**) and the high-radiance light-emitting diode (**LED**). In designing the optimum system, the special qualities of each light source should be considered. Diode lasers and LEDs bring to systems different characteristics:

1. Power levels
2. Temperature sensitivities
3. Response times
4. Lifetimes
5. Characteristics of failure

The diode laser is a preferred source for moderate-band to wideband systems. It offers a fast response time (typically less than 1 ns) and can couple high levels of useful optical power (usually several mW) into an optical fiber with a small core and a small numerical aperture. Recent advances in DL fabrication have resulted in predicted lifetimes of 10^5 to 10^6 hours at room temperature. Earlier DLs were of such limited life as to minimize their use. The DL is usually used as the source for single-mode fiber since LEDs have a low input coupling efficiency.

Some systems operate at a slower bit rate and require more modest levels of fiber-coupled optical power (50 to 250 μW). These applications allow the use of high-radiance LEDs. The LED is cheaper, requires less complex driving circuitry than a DL, and needs no thermal or optical stabilizations. In addition, LEDs have longer operating lives (10^6 to 10^7 hours) and fail in a more gradual and predictable fashion than DLs.

The light output wavelength spread, or spectrum, of the DL is much narrower than that of LEDs: about 1 nm compared with about 40 nm for an LED. Narrow spectra are advantageous in systems with high bit rates since the dispersion effects of the fiber on pulse width are reduced, and thus pulse degradation over long distances is minimized.

Dispersion Compensating Fiber
Acts like an equalizer, canceling dispersion effects and yielding close to zero dispersion in the 1550-nm region

Fiber Bragg Grating
A short strand of modified fiber that changes the index of refraction and minimizes intersymbol interference

DL
Diode laser

LED
Light-emitting diode

Distributed Feedback (DFB) Laser
A more stable laser suitable for use in DWDM systems

Dense Wavelength Division Multiplex (DWDM)
Incorporates the propagation of several wavelengths in the 1550-nm range for a single fiber

Vertical Cavity Surface Emitting Lasers (VCSELs)
Lasers with the simplicity of LEDs and the performance of lasers

Another laser device, called a **distributed feedback (DFB) laser**, uses techniques that provide optical feedback in the laser cavity. This enhances output stability, which produces a narrow and more stable spectral width. Widths are in the range of 0.01 to 0.1 nm. This allows the use of more channels in **dense wavelength division multiplex (DWDM)** systems. Another even more recent development is an entirely new class of laser semiconductors called **vertical cavity surface emitting lasers (VCSELs)**. These lasers can support a much faster signal rate than LEDs, including gigabit networks. They do not have some of the operational and stability problems of conventional lasers, however.

VCSELs have the simplicity of LEDs with the performance of lasers. Their primary wavelength of operation is in the 750 to 850-nm region, although development work is underway in the 1310-nm region. Reliabilities approaching 10^7 hours are projected. Table 12-3 provides a comparison of laser and LED optical transmitters.

TABLE 12-3   Comparison of Laser and LED Optical Transmitters

	Laser	LED
Usage	High bit rate, long haul	Low bit rate, short haul, LAN
Modulation rates	<40 Mbps to gigabits	<400 Mbps
Wavelength	Single-mode at 1310 and 1550 nm	Single-mode and multimode at 850/1310 nm
Rise time	<1 ns	10–100 ns
Spectral width	<1 nm up to 4 nm	40 to 100 nm
Spectral content	Discrete lines	Broad spectrum/continuous
Power output	0.3 to 1 mW (-5 to 0 dBm)	10 to 150 µW (-20 to -8 dBm)
Reliability	Lower	Higher
Linearity	40 dB (good)	20 dB (moderate)
Emission angle	Narrow	Wide
Coupling efficiency	Good	Poor
Temperature/humidity	Sensitive	Not sensitive
Durability/life	Medium (10^5 h)	High (> 10^6 h)
Circuit complexity	High	Low
Cost	High	Low

Note: The values shown in Table 12-3 depend, to some extent, on the associated electronic circuitry.

Source: From Modern Electronic Communication 9/e, by J.S. Beasley & G. M. Miller, 2008, p. 800. Copyright ©2002 Pearson Education, Inc. Reprinted by permission of Pearson Education, Inc., Upper Saddle River, NJ.

Tunable Laser
Laser in which the fundamental wavelength can be shifted a few nanometers, ideal for traffic routing in DWDM systems

Most lasers emit a fixed wavelength, but there is a class called **tunable lasers** in which the fundamental wavelength can be shifted a few nanometers, but not from a modulation point of view as in frequency modulation. Figure 12-13 shows an example of a tunable laser diode module. The primary market for these devices is in a network operations environment where DWDM is involved. Traffic routing is often made by wavelength, and, as such, wavelengths or transmitters must be assigned and reassigned to accommodate dynamic routing or networking, bandwidth on demand, seamless restoration (serviceability), optical packet switching, and so on. Tunable lasers are used along with either passive or tunable WDM filters.

FIGURE 12-13   A tunable laser diode module (courtesy of Fujitsu Compound Semiconductor, Inc.).

Intermediate Components

The typical fiber optic telecommunication link—as shown in Figure 12-1—is a light source or transmitter and light detector or receiver interconnected by a strand of optical **fiber**, or **light pipe**, or **glass**. An increasing number of specialized networks and system applications have various intermediate components along the span between the transmitter and the receiver. A brief review of these devices and their uses is provided.

Isolators   An **isolator** is an inline passive device that allows optical power to flow in one direction only; typical forward-direction insertion losses are less than 0.5 dB, with reverse-direction insertion losses of at least 40 to 50 dB. They are polarization independent and available for all wavelengths. One popular use of isolators is preventing reflections caused by optical span irregularities from getting back into the laser transmitter. Distributed feedback lasers are particularly sensitive to reflections, which can result in power instability, phase noise, linewidth variations, and so on.

Attenuators   Attenuators are used to reduce the **received signal level** (RSL). They are available in fixed and variable configurations. The fixed attenuators are for permanent use in point-to-point systems to reduce the RSL to a value within the receiver's dynamic range. Typical values of fixed attenuators are 3 dB, 5 dB, 10 dB, 15 dB, and 20 dB. Variable attenuators are typically for temporary use in calibration, testing, and laboratory work but more recently are being used in optical networks, where changes are frequent and require programmability.

Branching Devices   Branching devices are used in simplex systems where a single optical signal is divided and sent to several receivers, such as point-to-multipoint data or a CATV distribution system. They can also be used in duplex systems to combine or divide several inputs. The units are available for single-mode and multimode fiber.

The primary optical parameters are insertion loss and return loss, but the values for each leg may vary slightly due to differences in the device mixing region.

Splitters   Splitters are used to split, or divide, the optical signal for distribution to any number of places. The units are typically simplex and come in a variety of configurations, such as 1×4, 1×8, . . . , 1×64.

Fiber, Light Pipe, Glass
Terms used to describe a fiber optic strand

Isolator
An inline passive device that allows optical power to flow only in one direction

Received Signal Level (RSL)
The input signal level to an optical receiver

Couplers   Couplers are available in a variety of simplex or duplex configurations, such as 1×2, 2×2, 1×4, and various combinations up to 144×144. There are both passive and active couplers, the latter most often associated with data networks. Couplers can be wavelength-dependent or -independent.

Wavelength Division Multiplexers   Wavelength division multiplexers combine or divide two or more optical signals, each having a different wavelength. They are sometimes called optical beamsplitters. They use dichroic filtering, which passes light selectively by wavelength, or diffraction grating, which refracts light beams at an angle, selectively by wavelength. An additional optical parameter of importance is port-to-port crosstalk coupling, where wavelength number one leaks out of or into the port of wavelength number two. A *port* is the input or output of the device.

Optical-Line Amplifiers   Optical-line amplifiers are not digital regenerators, but analog amplifiers. Placement can be at the optical transmitter output, midspan, or near the optical receiver. They are currently used by high-density long-haul carriers, transoceanic links, and, to some extent, the CATV industry.

Detectors

The devices used to convert the transmitted light back into an electrical signal are a vital link in a fiber optic system. This important link is often overlooked in favor of the light source and fibers. However, simply changing from one photodetector to another can increase the capacity of a system by an order of magnitude.

The important characteristics of light detectors are as follows:

1. **Responsivity:** This is a measure of output current for a given light power launched into the diode. It is given in amperes per watt at a particular wavelength of light.
2. **Dark current:** This is the thermally generated reverse leakage current (under dark conditions) in the diode. In conjunction with the response current as predicted by device responsivity and incident power, it provides an indication of on–off detector output range.
3. **Response speed:** This determines the maximum data rate capability of the detector.
4. **Spectral response:** This determines the responsivity that is achieved relative to the wavelength at which responsivity is specified. Figure 12-14 provides a spectral response versus light wavelength for a typical photodiode. The curve shows that its relative response at 900 nm (0.9 μm) is about 80 percent of its peak response at 800 nm.

It should be noted that a second role exists for light detectors in fiber optic systems. Detectors are used to monitor the output of the laser diode sources. A detector is placed in proximity to the laser's light output. The generated photocurrent is used in a circuit to maintain constant light output under varying temperature and bias conditions. This is necessary to keep the laser just above its threshold forward bias current and to enhance its lifetime by not allowing the output to increase to higher levels. Additionally, the receiver does not want to see the varying light levels of a noncompensated laser. Optical fiber is made of ultrapure glass. Optical fiber makes window glass seem opaque by comparison. A window made of this pure glass 1 km thick would be as transparent as a normal pane of glass. It is therefore not surprising that the process of making connections from light source to fiber, fiber to fiber, and fiber to detector becomes critical in a system. The low-loss capability of the glass fiber can be severely compromised if these connections are not accomplished in exacting fashion.

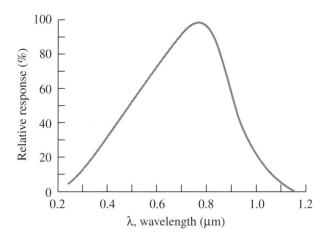

FIGURE 12-14   Spectral response of a *p-i-n* diode. (From Modern Electronic Communication 9/e, by J.S. Beasley & G. M. Miller, 2008, p. 803. Copyright ©2008 Pearson Education, Inc. Reprinted by permission of Pearson Education, Inc., Upper Saddle River, NJ.)

Optical fibers are joined either in a permanent fusion splice or with a mechanical splice (for example, connectors and camsplices). The connector allows repeated matings and unmatings. Above all, these connections must lose as little light as possible. Low loss depends on correct alignment of the core of one fiber to another, or to a source or detector. Losses for properly terminated fusion and mechanical splices is typically 0.2 dB or less. Signal loss in fibers occurs when two fibers are not perfectly aligned within a connector. Axial misalignment typically causes the greatest loss—about 0.5 dB for a 10 percent displacement. Figure 12-15 illustrates this condition as well as other loss sources. Angular misalignment [Figure 12-15(b)] can usually be well controlled in a connector. Most connectors leave an air gap, as shown in Figure 12-15(c). The amount of gap affects loss since light leaving the transmitting fiber spreads conically.

The losses due to rough end surfaces shown in Figure 12-15 (d) are often caused by a poor cut, or "cleave," but can be minimized by polishing or using pre-polished connectors. Polishing typically takes place after a fiber has been placed in a connector. The source of connection losses shown in Figure 12-15(d) can, for the most part, be controlled by a skillful cable splicer. There are four other situations that can cause additional connector or splice loss, although in smaller values. These are shown in Figure 12-15 (e), (f), (g), and (h). These are related to the nature of the fiber strand at the point of connection and are beyond the control of the cable splicer. The effect of these losses can be minimized somewhat by the use of a rotary mechanical splice, which by the joint rotation will get a better core alignment.

With regard to connectorization and splicing, there are two techniques to consider for splicing. **Fusion splicing** is a long-term method, in which two fibers are fused or welded together. The two ends are stripped of their coating, cut or cleaved, and inserted into the splicer. The ends of the fiber are aligned, and an electric arc is fired across the ends, melting the glass and fusing the two ends together. There are both manual and automatic fusion splicers; the choice usually depends on the number of splices to be done on a given job, technician skill levels available, and, of course, the budget. Typical insertion losses of less than 0.1 dB—frequently in the 0.05 dB range—can be consistently achieved.

Fusion Splicing
A long-term method where two fibers are fused or welded together

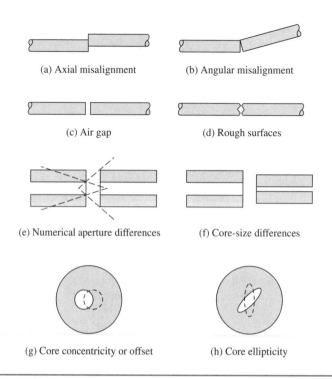

(a) Axial misalignment

(b) Angular misalignment

(c) Air gap

(d) Rough surfaces

(e) Numerical aperture differences

(f) Core-size differences

(g) Core concentricity or offset

(h) Core ellipticity

FIGURE 12-15   Sources of connection loss. (From Modern Electronic Communication 9/e, by J.S. Beasley & G. M. Miller, 2008, p. 806. Copyright © 2008 Pearson Education, Inc. Reprinted by permission of Pearson Education, Inc., Upper Saddle River, NJ.)

Mechanical splices can be permanent and an economical choice for certain fiber-splicing applications. Mechanical splices also join two fibers together, but they differ from fusion splices in that an air gap exists between the two fibers. This results in a glass-air-glass interface, causing a severe double change in the index of refraction. This change results in an increase in insertion loss and reflected power. The condition can be minimized by applying an **index-matching gel** to the joint. The gel is a jellylike substance that has an index of refraction much closer to the glass than air. Therefore, the index change is much less severe. Mechanical splices have been universally popular for repair and for temporary or laboratory work. They are quick, cheap, easy, and quite appropriate for small jobs. The best method for splicing depends on the application, including the expected future bandwidth (that is, gigabit), traffic, the job size, and economics. The loss in a mechanical splice can be minimized by using an OTDR to properly align the fiber when you are making the splice.

Fiber Connectorization

For fiber connectorization, there are several choices on the market such as SC, ST, FC, LC, MT-RJ, and others. The choice of the connector is typically dictated by the hardware being used and the fiber application. Figure 12-16 (a–e) provides some examples of SC, ST, FC, LC, and MTRJ connectors.

Mechanical Splices
Two fibers joined together with an air gap, thereby requiring an index-matching gel to provide a good splice

Index-matching Gel
A jellylike substance that has an index of refraction much closer to glass than to air

SC, ST, FC, LC, MT-RJ
Typical fiber connectors on the market

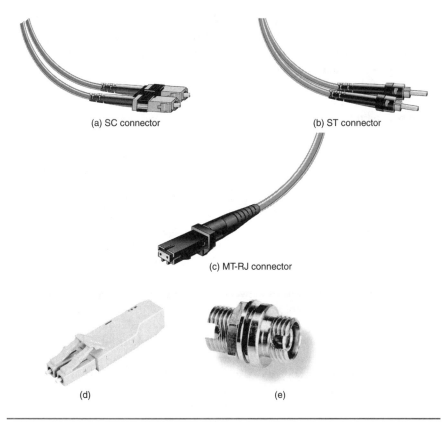

(a) SC connector

(b) ST connector

(c) MT-RJ connector

(d)

(e)

FIGURE 12-16   Typical fiber connections. [(a), (b), and (c) From Modern Electronic Communication 9/e, by J.S. Beasley & G. M. Miller, 2008, p. 808. Copyright ©2008 Pearson Education, Inc. Reprinted by permission of Pearson Education, Inc., Upper Saddle River, NJ. (d) and (e) from Black Box Corporation.]

Some general requirements for fiber connectors are as follows:

- Easy and quick to install
- Low insertion loss—a properly installed connector will have as little as 0.25 dB insertion loss
- High return loss greater than 50 dB—this is increasingly important in gigabit networks, DWDM systems, high-bandwidth video, etc.
- Repeatability
- Economical

In preparing the fiber for splicing or connectorization, only the coating is removed from the fiber strand. The core and the cladding are not separable. The 125m cladding diameter is the portion that fits into the splice or connector, and therefore most devices can handle both single and multimode fiber.

Sometimes the issue arises as to the advisability of splicing together fibers of different core sizes. The one absolute rule is, do *not* splice single and multimode fiber together! Similarly, good professional work does not allow different sizes of multimode fiber to be spliced together. However, in an emergency, different sizes can be spliced together if the following is considered:

When transmitting from a small to large-core diameter, there will be minimal, if any, increase in insertion loss. However, when the transmission is from a larger to a smaller core size, there will be added insertion loss, and a considerable increase in reflected power should be expected.

Industrial practice has confirmed the acceptability of different core size interchangeability for emergency repairs in the field, mainly as the result of tests with 50 m and 62.5 m multimode fiber for a local area network.

12-5 OPTICAL NETWORKING ARCHITECTURES

The need for increased bandwidth is pushing the fiber optic community into optical networking solutions that are almost beyond the imagination of even the most advanced networking person. Optical solutions for long-haul, wide area, metropolitan, campus and local area networks are available. Cable companies are already using the high-bandwidth capability of fiber to distribute cable programming as well as data throughout their service areas.

The capital cost differences between a fiber system and a copper-based system are diminishing, and the choice of networking technology for new networks is no longer just budgetary. Fiber has the capacity to carry more bandwidth, and as the fiber infrastructure cost decreases, then fiber will be chosen to carry the data. Of course, the copper infrastructure is already in place, and new developments are providing increases in data speed over copper (for example, CAT6 and CAT7). However, optical fiber is smaller and easier to install in already crowded ducts and conduits. Additionally, security is enhanced because it is difficult to tap optical fiber without detection. Will fiber replace copper in computer networks? For many years, a hybrid solution of fiber and copper is expected.

Defining Optical Networking

Optical networks are becoming a major part of data delivery in homes, in businesses, and for long-haul carriers. The telecommunications industry has been using fiber to carry long-haul traffic for many years. Some major carriers are merging with cable companies so that they are poised to provide high-bandwidth capabilities to the home. Developments in optical technologies are reshaping the way we will use fiber in future optical networks.

But there is a new slant with optical networks. Dense wave division multiplexing and tunable lasers have changed the way optical networks can be implemented. It is now possible to transport many wavelengths over a single fiber. Lab tests at AT&T have successfully demonstrated the transmission of 1,022 wavelengths over a single fiber. Such transport of multiple wavelengths opens up the possibilities to routing or switching many different data protocols over the same fiber but on different wavelengths. The development of cross-connects that allow data to arrive on one wavelength and leave on another opens other possibilities.

Synchronous optical network (**SONET**) and **SDH** were the North American and international standards for the long-haul optical transport of telecommunication for many years. SONET/SDH defined a standard for the following:

- Increase in network reliability
- Network management

SONET/SDH

Synchronous optical network; protocol standard for optical transmission in long-haul communication/synchronous digital hierarchy

- Defining methods for the synchronous multiplexing of digital signals such as DS-1 (1.544 Mbps) and DS-3 (44.736 Mbps)
- Defining a set of generic operating/equipment standards
- Flexible architecture

SONET/SDH specifies the various optical carrier (OC) levels and the equivalent electrical synchronous transport signals (**STS**) used for transporting data in a fiber optic transmission system. Optical network data rates are typically specified in terms of the SONET hierarchy. Table 12-4 lists the more common data rates.

STS
Synchronous transport signals

TABLE 12-4   SONET Hierarchy Data Rates

Signal	Bit Rate	Capacity
OC-1 (STS-1)	51,840 Mbps	28DS-Is or 1 DS-3
OC-3 (STS-3)	155.52 Mbps	84DS-Is or 3 DS-3s
OC-12 (STS-12)	622.080 Mbps	336 DS-1s or 12 DS-3s
OC-48 (STS-48)	2.48832 Gbps	1344 DS-1s or 48 DS-3s
OC-192 (STS-192)	9.95328 Gbps	5376 DS-Is or 192 DS-3s

OC: Optical carrier—DS-1: 1.544 Mbps

STS: Synchronous transport signal—DS-3: 44.736 Mbps

Source: From Modern Electronic Communication 9/e, by J.S. Beasley & G. M. Miller, 2008, p. 818. Copyright © 2008 Pearson Education, Inc. Reprinted by permission of Pearson Education, Inc., Upper Saddle River, NJ.

The architectures of fiber networks for the home include providing fiber to the curb (**FTTC**) and fiber to the home (**FTTH**). FTTC is being deployed today. It provides high bandwidth to a location with proximity to the home and provides a high-speed data link, via copper (twisted-pair), using VDSL (very high-data digital subscriber line). This is a cost-effective way to provide large-bandwidth capabilities to a home. FTTH will provide unlimited bandwidth to the home; however, the key to its success is the development of a low-cost optical-to-electronic converter in the home and laser transmitters that are tunable to any desired channel.

FTTC
Fiber to the curb

FTTH
Fiber to the home

Another architecture in place is fiber to the business (**FTTB**). A fiber connection to a business provides for the delivery of all current communication technologies including data, voice, video, conferencing, and so on. An additional type is fiber to the desktop (**FTTD**). This setup requires that the computer has a fiber network interface card (NIC). FTTD is useful in applications such as computer animation work that has high-bandwidth requirements.

FTTB
Fiber to the business

FTTD
Fiber to the desktop

Conventional high-speed Ethernet networks are operating over fiber. This is called **optical Ethernet** and uses the numerics listed in Table 12-5 for describing the type of network configuration. Fiber helps to eliminate the 100-m distance limit associated with unshielded twisted-pair (UTP) copper cable. This is possible because fiber has a lower attenuation loss. In a star network, the computer and the switch are directly connected. If the fiber is used in a star network, an internal or external media converter is required. The media converter converts the electronic signal to an optical signal, and vice versa. A media converter is required at both ends, as shown in Figure 12-17. The media converter is typically built into the network interface card.

Optical Ethernet
Ethernet data running over a fiber link

TABLE 12-5 Optical Ethernet Numerics

Numeric	Description
10BASE-F	10 Mbps Ethernet over fiber—generic specification for fiber
10BASE-FB	10 Mbps Ethernet over fiber—part of the IEEE 10BaseF specification; segments can be up to 2 km in length
10BASE-FL	10 Mbps Ethernet over fiber—segments can be up to 2 km in length; it replaces the FOIRL specification.
10BASE-FP	A passive fiber star network; segments can be up to 500 m in length
100BASE-FX	A 100 Mbps fast Ethernet standard that uses two fiber strands
1000BASE-LX	Gigabit Ethernet standard that uses fiber strands using longwavelength transmitters
1000BASE-SX	Gigabit Ethernet standard using short-wavelength transmitters
10GBASE-R	10 gigabit (10.325 Gbps) Ethernet for LANs
10GBASE-W	10 gigabit (9.95328 Gbps) Ethernet for WANs using OC-192 and Sonet Framing

Multimode fiber—2 km length single mode—10 km length

Source: Adapted From Modern Electronic Communication 9/e, by J.S. Beasley & G. M. Miller, 2008, p. 819. Copyright © 2008 Pearson Education, Inc. Adapted by permission of Pearson Education, Inc., Upper Saddle River, NJ.

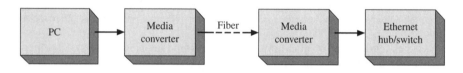

FIGURE 12-17 An example of connecting a PC to an Ethernet hub or switch via fiber. (From Modern Electronic Communication 9/e, by J.S. Beasley & G. M. Miller, 2008, p. 820. Copyright © 2008 Pearson Education, Inc. Reprinted by permission of Pearson Education, Inc., Upper Saddle River, NJ.)

Two important issues to be considered when designing a fiber network are the guidelines for the following:

Building distribution

Campus distribution

The following subsections discuss techniques for planning the fiber plant, the distribution of the fiber, and the equipment and connections used to interconnect the fiber. The first example is for a building distribution, the second for a campus distribution.

Building Distribution

Figure 12-18 shows an example of a simple fiber network for a building. Fiber lines consist of a minimum of two fibers, one for transmitting and one for receiving. Fiber networks work in the full-duplex mode, meaning that the links must be able to simultaneously transmit and receive; hence, the need for two fibers on each link.

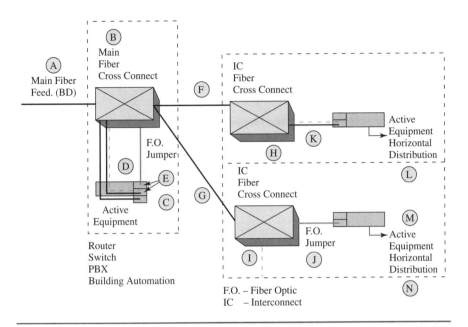

FIGURE 12-18 A simple fiber distribution in a building.

Item A is the main fiber feed for the building. This is called a *building distribution* (BD) fiber. The two fibers for the BD link terminate into a main fiber cross-connect (item B). A **fiber cross-connect** is the optical patch panel used to connect the fiber cables to the next link. The fiber cross-connect typically uses mechanical splices to make the fiber connections.

Items C and E represent the active equipment in the main distribution closet in the building. The active equipment could be a router, switch, or telephone PBX (private branch exchange). Item D shows the jumpers connecting the main fiber cross-connect (item B) to the active equipment (item C).

The active equipment will need some type of optical interface for the optical–electrical signal conversion, such as a **GBIC** (pronounced "gee-bick"). This interface is also called a SFP (Small Form factor Pluggable). GBIC is the gigabit interface converter used for transmitting and receiving higher-speed signals over fiber optic lines. The optical-to-fiber interface used at ten gigabits (10 G) is called **XENPAK**. GBIC and XENPAK modules are designed to plug into interfaces such as routers and switches. These modules are used to connect to other fiber optic systems such as 1000Base-SX and 1000Base-LX and 10GBASE, and the XENPAK module supports 850, 1310, and 1550 fiber wavelengths. The choice of the interface depends on the data rate selected and the type of active equipment being used. Figure 12-19 shows an example of a XENPAK module.

Items F and G in Figure 12-18 show the two fiber pairs patched into the main fiber cross-connect connecting to the intermediate distribution closet (**IDC**). These fibers (F and G) are called the interconnect (**IC**) fibers. The fibers terminate into the IDC fiber cross-connects (items H and I).

Items J and K are fiber jumpers that connect the fiber cross-connect to the IDC active equipment. Once again, the active equipment must have a GBIC or some other interface for the optical–electrical signal conversion.

Fiber Cross-connect
Optical patch panel used to interconnect fiber cables

GBIC
Gigabit interface converter

XENPAK
The ten gigabit interface adapter

IDC
Intermediate distribution closet

IC
Interconnect fibers branch exchange—item D shows the jumpers connecting the main fiber cross-connect (item B) to the active equipment (item C)

(a)   (b)

FIGURE 12-19   The Cisco (a) GBIC and (b) 10GBASE XENPAK module (courtesy of Cisco).

A general rule for fiber is that the distribution in a building should be limited to "2 deep." This means that a building should only have the main distribution and the intermediate distribution that feeds the horizontal distribution to the work area.

Figure 12-20 (a) and (b) illustrate an example of the "2-deep" rule. Figure 12-20 (a) shows an example of a building distribution that meets the "2-deep" rule. The IDC (intermediate distribution closet) is at the first layer, and the horizontal distribution (HD) is at the second layer. An example of a fiber distribution that does not meet the "2-deep" rule is shown in Figure 12-20 (b). In this example, the horizontal distribution (HD) and work area are 3-deep, or 3 layers from the building's main distribution.

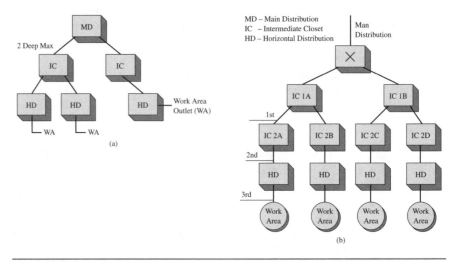

FIGURE 12-20   Examples of the "2-deep" rule: (a) the distribution meeting the requirement; (b) the distribution not meeting the requirement.

Logical Fiber Map
Shows how the fiber is interconnected and data is distributed throughout a campus

Campus Distribution

Figure 12-21 shows a map of the fiber distribution for a campus network. This map shows how the fiber is interconnected and data is distributed throughout the campus and is called a **logical fiber map**. Another style of map often used to show the fiber distribution is a **physical fiber map** as shown in Figure 12-22. This map shows the routing of the fiber but also shows detail about the terrain, underground conduit, and entries into buildings. Both map styles are important and necessary for documentation and planning of the fiber network. This material focuses on the documentation provided in the logical fiber map.

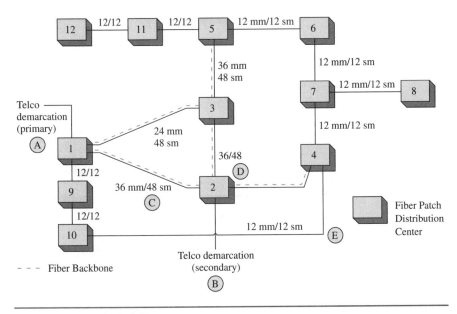

FIGURE 12-21   A logical fiber map.

Referring to the logical fiber map in Figure 12-21, this campus network has two connections to the Telco, the primary Telco demarcation (item A) in building 1 and the secondary Telco demarcation (item B) in building 2. These two Telco connections provide for redundant Internet and wide area network data services. If something happens in building 1 that shuts down the external data services, then Internet and WAN data traffic can be switched to building 2. Also data traffic can be distributed over both connections to prevent bottlenecking. Buildings 1 and 2 are interconnected with 36 multimode (**mm**) and 48 single-mode (**sm**) fibers. This is documented on the line interconnecting buildings 1 and 2 (item C) and written as 36/48 (item D). The green dotted line between buildings 1 and 2 indicates the **backbone** or main fiber distribution for the campus network. The bulk of the campus network data traffic travels over these fibers. The campus backbone (green dotted line) also extends from building 2 to building 4 and from building 3 to building 5.

This setup enables the data to be distributed over the campus. For example, data traffic from the primary Telco demarcation (item A) reaches building 12 by traveling via fiber through buildings 1-3-5-11-12. If the building 3 connection is down, then data traffic from the primary Telco demarcation can be routed through buildings 1-2-4-7-6-5-11-12. What happens to the data traffic for building 12 if building 5 is out of operation? In this case, data traffic to/from buildings 11 and 12 is lost.

Item E shows a fiber connection to/from buildings 4 and 10. This fiber bundle provides an alternative data path from the primary Telco demarcation to the other side of the campus network.

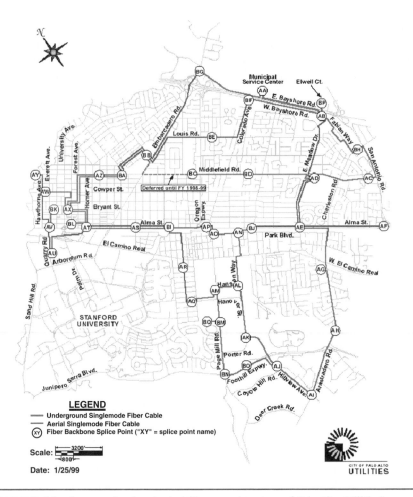

FIGURE 12-22   An example of a physical fiber map (courtesy of Palo Alto Utilities).

The cabling between buildings is a mix of multimode and single-mode fiber. The older fiber runs a 12/12 cable (12 multimode/12 single-mode). Fiber cables are bundled in groups of 12 fibers. For example, a 12/12 fiber will have two bundles, one bundle of multimode and one bundle of single mode fiber. A 36/48 cable will have 3 bundles of multimode and 4 bundles of single mode fiber. Each bundle of fibers is color-coded as listed in Table 12-6. For example, in a 36/48 fiber cable, the 3 bundles of multimode are in loose tubes that are color coded Blue/Orange/Green. The four bundles of single mode are in loose tubes that are color coded Brown/Slate/White/Red.

TABLE 12-6   The Fiber Color Code for the Twelve Fibers in a Bundle

Pair	Color
1/2	Blue/Orange
3/4	Green/Brown
5/6	Slate/White

Pair	Color
7/8	Red/Black
9/10	Yellow/Violet
11/12	Rose/Aqua Marine

In this example, the newer fiber cabling installations were run with a 36/48 and 24/48 mix. Why the difference? The main reason is economics. The cost per foot (meter) of the new fiber is cheaper, so more fiber can be placed in a cable for the same cost per foot.

The fiber connecting the buildings is typically run either in PVC conduit, which makes it easy to add or remove fiber cables, or in trenches or tunnels. Running fiber in trenches is very expensive and significantly increases the installation cost. (*Note:* Network administrators need to be aware of any trenches being dug on campus.) Even if the budget doesn't allow for buying fiber at the time, at least have a conduit and pull line installed.

Fiber provides substantially increased bandwidth for building and campus networks and can easily handle the combined traffic of PCs, switches, routers, video, and voice services. Fiber has greater capacity, which enables faster transfer of data, minimizes congestion problems, and provides tremendous growth potential for each of the fiber runs.

Another important application of optical Ethernet is extending the reach of the Ethernet network from the local and campus network out to the metropolitan and wide area networks. Essentially, optical networking is introducing Ethernet as a viable WAN (wide area network) technology. Extending Ethernet into a wide area network is a seamless integration of the technologies. The Ethernet extension into the WAN simply requires optical adapters such as a GBIC (gigabit interface converter) and two fiber strands, one for transmitting and one for receiving. Conventional high-speed Ethernet local area networks operating over fiber use the numerics listed in Table 12-6 for describing the network configuration.

12-6 SYSTEM DESIGN AND OPERATIONAL ISSUES

When designing a fiber optic transmission link, the primary performance issue is the bit error rate (BER) for digital systems and the carrier-to-noise ratio (C/N) for analog systems. In either case, performance will degrade as the link length increases. As stated in section 12-3, attenuation and dispersion are the two distance-limiting factors in optical transmissions. The distance limit is the span length at which the BER or *C/N* degrades below some specified point.

From an engineering point of view, there are two different types of environments for fiber links. These are long-haul and local area networks (LANs). A *long-haul system* is the intercity or interoffice class of system used by telephone companies and long-distance carriers. These systems typically have high channel density and high bit rate, are highly reliable, incorporate redundant equipment, and involve extensive engineering studies. LANS take a less strict position on the issues stated under long-haul applications. They typically have lower channel capacity and minimal redundance and are restricted to building-to-building or campus environments. Some LANs are becoming very large, including metropolitan area and wide area networks; as such, they usually rely on long-haul carriers for their connectivity.

From a design standpoint, those involved in long-haul work actually perform the studies on a per-link basis. LANs typically are prespecified and preengineered as to length, bit-rate capability, performance, and so on. The following is an example of a system designed for an installation typical of a LAN or a short-distance communication link.

In this example, each of the many factors that make up the link calculation, power budget, or light budget is discussed along with its typical contribution. A minimal received signal level (RSL) must be obtained to ensure that the required BER be satisfied. For example, if the minimum RSL is -40 dBm for a BER of 10^{-9}, then this value is the required received optical power. If after the initial calculations are completed the projected performance is not as expected, then go back and adjust any of the parameters, recognizing that there are tradeoff issues.

Refer to the system design shown in Figures 12-23 and 12-24 for the list that follows:

1. **Transmitter power output:** A value usually obtained from the manufacturer's specification or marketing sheet. *Caution:* Be sure the value is taken from the output port of the transmit module or rack. This is point 1 on Figure 12-24. This is the point where the user can access the module for measurement and testing. Otherwise the levels can be off as much as 1 dB due to pigtail or coupling losses in between the laser or LED and the actual module output.

2. **Cable losses:** The loss in dB/km obtained from the cable manufacturer's sheet. This value is multiplied by the length of the cable run to obtain the total loss. An example of this calculation is provided in Example 12-1.

    Note that the actual fiber length can exceed the cable run length by 0.5 percent to 3 percent due to the construction of the fiber cable (in plastic buffer tubes). Fiber cables are loosely enclosed in buffer tubes to isolate the fiber from construction stress when the cable is pulled.

3. **Splice losses:** Values dependent on the method used for splicing as well as the quality of splicing provided by the technician. Losses can vary from 0.2 dB to 0.5 dB per splice.

4. **Connector losses:** A value depending on the type and quality of the connector used as well as the skill level of the installer. Losses can vary from 0.25 dB to 0.5 dB.

5. **Extra losses:** A category used for miscellaneous losses in passive devices such as splitters, couplers, WDM devices, optical patch panels, and so on.

6. **Operational margin:** Accounts for system degradation due to equipment aging, temperature extremes, power supply noise and instability, timing errors in regenerators, and so on.

Backhoe Fading
Splice loss introduced by repairing a fiber cable dug up by a backhoe

7. **Maintenance margin:** Accounts for system degradation due to the addition of link splices, added losses to wear and misalignment of patch cords and connectors, and so on. This includes the loss generated from repairing cables that have been dug up by a backhoe. The term **backhoe fading** is used to indicate that the system has had total loss of data flow because the fiber cable has been dug up by a backhoe.

8. **Design receive signal power:** A value obtained from summing the gains and losses in items 1–7. This value should exceed the specified received signal level (RSL), as specified in item 10.

ATTENUATION OR LINK LOSS
Sample system

1	Transmitter power output (module, not LD or LED)		−15 dBm
2	Losses: Cable, 18.6 Mi/30 km @ 0.4 dB/km	12.0	
3	8 splices @ 0.2 dB ea	1.6	
4	2 connectors @ 0.5 dB ea	1.0	
5	Extra for two pigtails and inside cable	2.0	
	Total losses	16.6	16.6 dB
	Received signal power		−31.6 dBm
6	Operational margin	3.0	
7	Maintenance margin	3.0	
	Total margin	6.0	6.0 dB
8	Design receive signal power		−37.6 dBm
9	Minimum receiver sensitivity(RSL) for 10^{-9} BER (module, not APD or PIN)		−40.0 dBm
10	Extra margin		2.4 dB

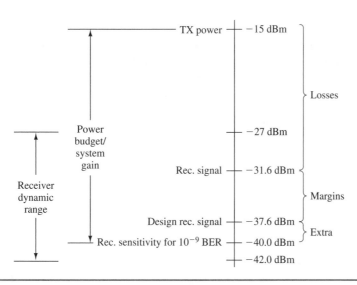

FIGURE 12-23 System design. (From Modern Electronic Communication 9/e, by J.S. Beasley & G. M. Miller, 2008, p. 810. Copyright © 2008 Pearson Education, Inc. Reprinted by permission of Pearson Education, Inc., Upper Saddle River, NJ.)

9. **Receiver sensitivity for a 10 -9 BER:** The minimum RSL for the receiver to perform at the specified BER. If the design receive signal power (item 8) does not meet this requirement, then adjustments must be made. For example, transmit power could be increased, splice loss estimates reduced, a more optimistic maintenance margin could occur, and so on. Also the receiver may have a maximum RSL, so a system may require attenuators to decrease the RSL so that it falls within a specified operating range (receiver dynamic range).

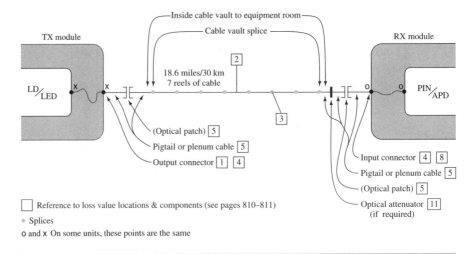

TX module   RX module

LD/LED   x   x   18.6 miles/30 km   2   PIN/APD
                   7 reels of cable
                                           3

(Optical patch) 5
Pigtail or plenum cable 5   Input connector 4 8
Output connector 1 4   Pigtail or plenum cable 5
                                                      (Optical patch) 5
                                                      Optical attenuator 11
                                                      (if required)

☐ Reference to loss value locations & components (see pages 810–811)

● Splices

o and x On some units, these points are the same

FIGURE 12-24   A graphical view of the system design problem shown in Figure 12-23. (From Modern Electronic Communication 9/e, by J.S. Beasley & G. M. Miller, 2008, p. 812. Copyright © 2008 Pearson Education, Inc. Reprinted by permission of Pearson Education, Inc., Upper Saddle River, NJ.)

10. **Extra margin:** The difference between the design receive signal power (item 8) and the receiver sensitivity (item 9). Item 8 should be greater than item 9; for example, -37.6 dBm is larger than -40 dBm. One or two dB is a good figure.
11. **Optional optical attenuator:** A place where an optional attenuator can be installed and later removed as aging losses begin to increase.

Example 12-1

Determine the loss in dB for a 30-km fiber cable run that has a loss of 0.4 dB/km.

Solution

total cable loss = 30 km × 0.4 dB/km = 12 dB

A graphical view of the previous system design problem is shown in Figure 12-21. Figure 12-25 provides another way to graphically describe the system design problem. Notice that the values are placed along the distance covered by the fiber. This provides the maintenance staff and the designer with a clear picture of how the system was put in place.

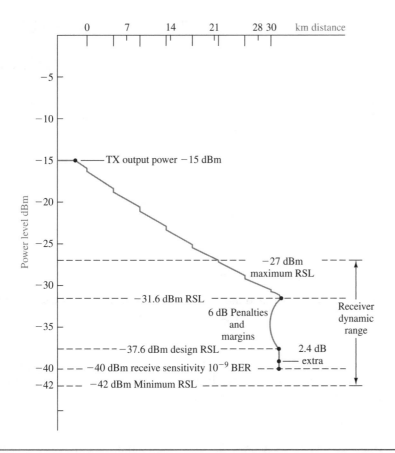

FIGURE 12-25   An alternative view of the system design problem. (From Modern Electronic Communication 9/e, by J.S. Beasley & G. M. Miller, 2008, p. 812. Copyright © 2008 Pearson Education, Inc. Reprinted by permission of Pearson Education, Inc., Upper Saddle River, NJ.)

12-7   SAFETY

Any discussion of fiber optics or optical networking is not complete unless it addresses safety issues, even if only briefly. As the light propagates through a fiber, two factors will further attenuate the light if there is an open circuit:

1. A light beam will disperse or fan out from an open connector.
2. If a damaged fiber is exposed on a broken cable, the end will likely be shattered, which will considerably disperse the light. In addition, there would be a small amount of attenuation from the strand within the cable, plus any connections or splices along the way.

However, there are two factors that can increase the optical power at an exposed fiber end.

1. There could be a lens in a pigtail that could focus more optical rays down the cable.
2. In the newer DWDM systems, there will be several optical signals in the same fiber; although separate, they will be relatively close together in wavelength. The optical power incident on the eye will then be multiplied.

There are two factors to be aware of:

1. The eye can't see fiber optic communication wavelength, so there is no pain or awareness of exposure. However, the retina can still be exposed and damaged. (Refer to Figure 12-3, the electromagnetic spectrum.)
2. Eye damage is a function of the optical power, wavelengths, source or spot diameter, and the duration of exposure.

So for those working on fiber optic equipment:

1. *DO NOT EVER* look into the output connector of energized test equipment. Such equipment can have higher powers than the communication equipment itself, particularly OTDRs.
2. If you need to view the end of a fiber, *ALWAYS turn off the transmitter,* particularly if you don't know whether the transmitter is a laser or LED, given that lasers are higher-power sources. If you are using a microscope to inspect a fiber, the optical power will be multiplied.

From a mechanical point of view:

1. Good work practices are detailed in safety, training, and installation manuals. READ AND HEED.
2. Be careful with machinery, cutters, chemical solvents, and epoxies.
3. Fiber ends are brittle and will break off easily, including the ends cut off from splicing and connectorization. These ends are extremely difficult to see and can become "lost" and/or easily embedded in your finger. You won't know until your finger becomes infected. Always account for all scraps.
4. Use safety glasses specifically designed to protect the eye when working with fiber optic systems.
5. Obtain and *USE* an optical safety kit.
6. Keep a *CLEAN* and orderly work area.

In all cases, be sure the craft personnel have the proper training for the job!

12-8 TROUBLESHOOTING COMPUTER NETWORKS (THE OTDR)

There are several techniques to measure and troubleshoot fiber links. A common technique is to use an optical power meter to determine power loss. Another tool used is a **Visual Fault Locator (VFL)**, which is a device that shines light down the fiber to help locate broken glass. Figure 12-26 (a) and (b) are traces obtained from an optical time-domain reflectometer (**OTDR**) for two different sets of multimode fibers. In field terms, this is called "shooting" the fiber. The OTDR sends a light pulse down the fiber and measures the reflected light. The OTDR enables the installer or maintenance crew to verify the quality of each fiber span and obtain some measure of performance. The X axis on the traces indicates the distance, whereas the Y axis indicates the measured optical power value in dB. Both OTDR traces are for 850-nm multimode fiber.

In regard to Figure 12-26 (a), point A is a "dead" zone or a point too close to the OTDR for a measurement to be made. The measured value begins at about 25 dB and decreases in value as the distance traveled increases. An **event**, or a disturbance in the light propagating down the fiber, occurs at point B. This is an example of what a poor-quality splice looks like (in regard to reflection as well as insertion loss). Most likely, this is a mechanical splice. The same type of event occurs at points C and D. These are also most likely mechanical splices. Points F and G are most likely the jumpers and patch-panel connections at the fiber end. The steep drop at point H is actually the end of the fiber. Point I is typical noise that occurs at the end of an "unterminated" fiber. Notice at point G that the overall value of the trace has dropped to about 17 dB. There has been about 8 dB of optical power loss in the cable in a 1.7 km run.

An OTDR trace for another multimode fiber is shown in Figure 12-23 (b); the hump at point A is basically a "dead" zone. The OTDR cannot typically return accurate measurement values in this region. This is common for most OTDRs, and the dead zone will vary for each OTDR. The useful trace information begins at point B with a measured value of 20 dB. Point C shows a different type of event. This type of event is typical of coiled fiber, or fiber that has been tightly bound, possibly with a tie-wrap, or that has had some other disturbance affecting the integrity of the fiber. Points D and F are actually the end of the fiber. At point D the trace level is about 19 dB for a loss of about 1 dB over the 150-m run. Point G is just the noise that occurs at the end of a "terminated" fiber.

Visual Fault Locator (VFL)
Device that shines light down the fiber to help locate broken glass

OTDR
Sends a light pulse down the fiber and measures the reflected light, which provides a measure of performance for the fiber

Event
A disturbance in the light propagating down a fiber span that results in a disturbance on the OTDR trace

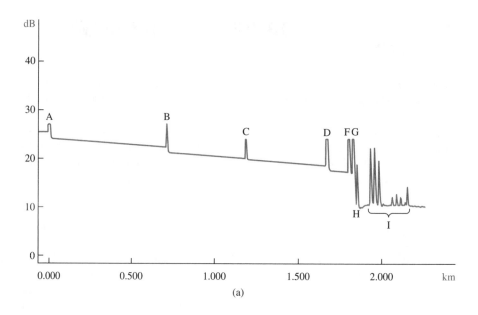

(a)

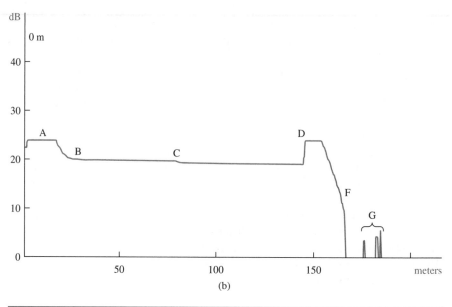

(b)

FIGURE 12-26   An OTDR trace of an 850-nm fiber. (From Modern Electronic Communication 9/e, by J.S. Beasley & G. M. Miller, 2008, p. 814. Copyright © 2008 Pearson Education, Inc. Reprinted by permission of Pearson Education, Inc., Upper Saddle River, NJ.)

SUMMARY

Chapter 12 has introduced the field of fiber optics and optical networking. The chapter has provided examples using fiber to interconnect LANs in both a building and a campus network. The major topics that the student should understand include the following:

- The advantages offered by optical networking
- The properties of light waves
- The physical and optical characteristics of optical fibers
- Attenuation and dispersion effects in fiber
- The description of the common techniques used to connect fiber
- The usage of fiber optics in local area networks (LANs), campus networks, and wide area networks (WANs)
- System design of optical networks
- Safety considerations when working with fiber
- Analysis of OTDR waveforms

QUESTIONS AND PROBLEMS

Section 12-1

1. List the basic elements of a fiber optic communication system.
2. List five advantages of an optical communications link.

Section 12-2

3. Define refractive index.
4. What are the commonly used wavelengths in fiber optic systems?
5. What part of an optical fiber carries the light?
6. A measure of a fiber's light acceptance is _____.
7. Define pulse dispersion.
8. What are the typical core/cladding sizes (in microns) for multimode fiber?
9. What is the typical core size for single-mode fiber?
10. Define mode field diameter.

Section 12-3

11. What are the two key distance-limiting parameters in fiber optic transmissions?
12. What are the four factors that contribute to attenuation?
13. Define *dispersion.*
14. What are three types of dispersion?
15. What is meant by the *zero-dispersion wavelength*?
16. What is a dispersion compensating fiber?

Section 12-4

17. What are the two kinds of light sources used in fiber optic communication systems?
18. Why is a narrower spectra advantageous in optical systems?
19. Why is a tunable laser of importance in optical networking?
20. What is the purpose of an optical attenuator?
21. List two purposes of optical detectors.
22. What is the advantage of fusion splicing over mechanical splicing?

Section 12-5

23. Define: (a) FTTC; (b) FTTH; (c) FTTB; (d) FTTD.
24. What is the purpose of a GBIC?
25. What is the "2-deep" rule?
26. What is the purpose of a logical fiber map?
27. What are the typical maximum lengths for (a) multimode and (b) single-mode fiber?
28. What is FDDI?

Section 12-6

29. What is the primary performance issue in a fiber optic transmission link?
30. What are the two different types of environments for fiber links?
31. Define *RSL*.
32. What steps can be taken if the designed receive signal power does not meet the minimum RSL requirement?
33. What should be done if the receive signal level exceeds the maximum RSL?
34. What is a receiver dynamic range?

Section 12-7

35. Why is safety an important issue in optical networking?

Section 12-8

36. Examine the OTDR trace provided in Figure 12-27. Explain the trace behavior of points *A*, *B*, *C*, *D*, and *E*.

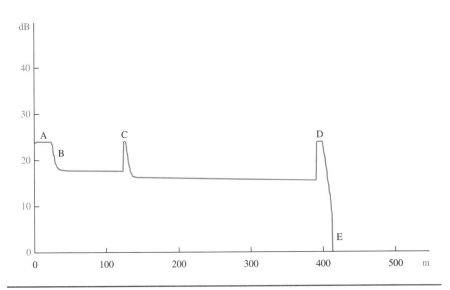

FIGURE 12-27 Figure for Problem 36. (From Modern Electronic Communication 9/e, by J.S. Beasley & G. M. Miller, 2008, p. 833. Copyright © 2008 Pearson Education, Inc. Reprinted by permission of Pearson Education, Inc., Upper Saddle River, NJ.)

Critical Thinking

37. A campus network is planning to put fiber optic cables in to replace outdated coaxial cables. They have the choice of putting in single-mode, multimode, or a combination of single–multimode fibers in the ground. Which fiber type should they select? Why?
38. The networking cables for a new building are being installed. You are asked to prepare a study about which cable type(s) should be used. Discuss the issues related to the cable selection.

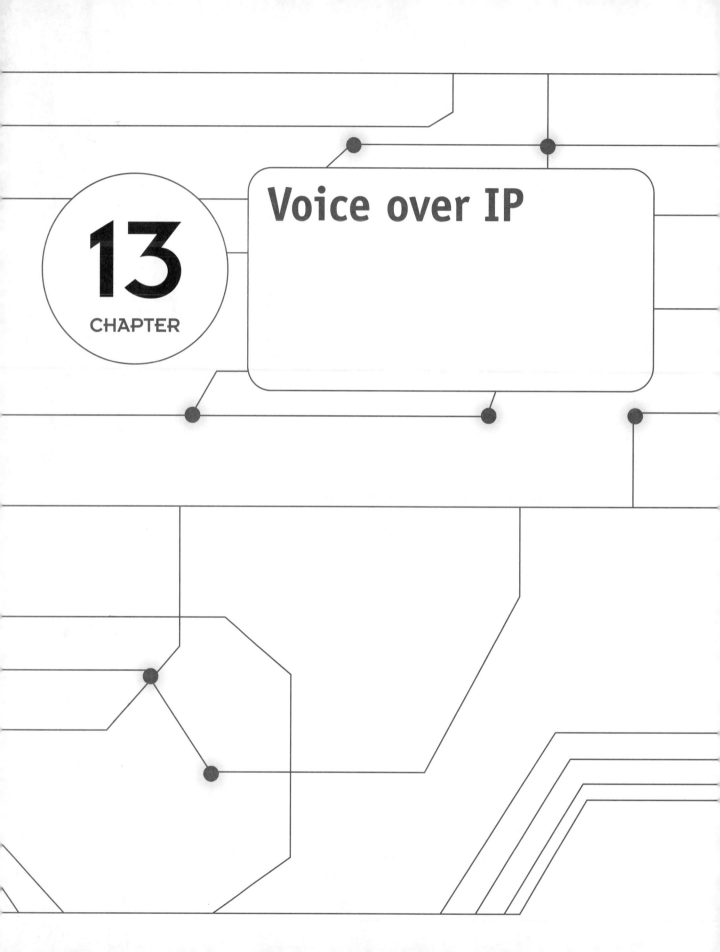

13

CHAPTER

Voice over IP

CHAPTER OUTLINE

13-1   Introduction
13-2   The Basics of Voice over IP
13-3   Voice over IP Networks
13-4   Quality of Service

13-5   Analyzing VoIP Data Packets
Summary
Questions and Problems

OBJECTIVES

- Examine the technologies used in the generation, management, and transport of voice over IP calls
- Investigate the ways voice over IP telephony can be incorporated into a network
- Develop an understanding of the key quality of service issues associated with voice over IP telephony
- Examine the data packets generated in a voice over IP call

KEY TERMS

VoIP
PBX
PSTN
signaling
SS7
H.323
SIP
SSIP
virtual tie line
PCM
CODEC
RTP

RTCP
packet sequence number
timestamp
tie line
TDM
VoIP gateway
VoIP relay
QoS
jitter
buffer
network latency

weighted random early discard (WRED)
queuing
first queued
FIFO
weighted fair queuing (WFQ)
CBWFQ
PQ
CQ
spit

13-1   INTRODUCTION

VoIP
Voice over IP telephony

Voice over IP (**VoIP**), or IP telephony, is the transport of phone conversations over packet networks. Many companies and individuals are taking advantage of the development of new technologies that support the convergence of voice and data over their existing packet networks. The network administrator can also see an additional benefit with the cost savings using a converge voice/data network. This has created a new role for the network administrator, that of a telecommunications manager. The network administrator must not only be aware of the issues of data transport within and external to the network, but also the issues of incorporating voice data traffic into the network.

This chapter examines the basics of building voice over IP networks. The technologies, the data transport, and the quality of service issues are examined. The mechanics of transporting voice data traffic over an IP network are presented in section 13-2. This includes encoding the voice signal, transporting the digitized voice data, and interfacing the data via a gateway to another IP network. Section 13-3 presents an overview of assembling voice over IP networks. This section examines three different techniques for incorporating an IP telephony solution.

Many quality-of-service issues arise with the deployment of a voice over IP network. For example, the packet arrival time is not guaranteed in an IP network; therefore, a noise problem called *jitter* is introduced. This and other quality-of-service issues are examined in section 13-4. Voice over IP data packets are examined in section 13-5. This section examines the data packets generated when an IP call is placed and how codes are used to identify the different types of data packets being transported.

13-2   THE BASICS OF VOICE OVER IP

The objective of this section is to present an overview of the technologies used in the generation, management, and transport of voice over IP (VoIP) calls. The basic VoIP system begins with a telephone. IP telephones are available as standalone units or as software running on a PC. The PC requires a microphone and a speaker to support the telephone call.

PBX ①
Private branch exchange—the user's own telephone system

PSTN ②
Public switched telephone network—the telephone company

Signaling
Used to establish and terminate telephone calls

SS7
Signaling technique used by the PSTN

Standard telephones can also be used in IP telephony if the telephones connect to a private branch exchange (**PBX**) that supports IP telephony. The PBX is a user's own telephone system. It manages the internal switching of telephone calls and also interfaces the user's phone to the **PSTN** (public switched telephone network—the telephone company or Telco). The interface of the IP telephone system to the PSTN is called a *gateway*.

③ The gateway's function is to provide an interface for IP telephony calls to the PSTN or to interface one IP telephone system with another. This requires that the voice data be packaged for transport over the IP network or the PSTN. The gateway also makes sure that the proper signaling is included for the voice data packet transport. ⑤ Signaling is used to establish and terminate telephone calls and to manage many of the advanced features available with telephones.

The PSTN uses a signaling technique called **SS7** that provides enhanced features:

④
- Toll-free services
- Worldwide telecommunications

- Enhanced call features (for example, call forwarding and three-way calling)
- Local number portability

IP telephony uses different signaling techniques. These are H.323, SIP, and virtual tie lines. **H.323** is a suite of protocols that define how voice and video are transported over IP networks. H.323 works with delay-sensitive traffic (for example, voice and video) to help establish a priority for timely packet delivery, critical for real-time applications. The bottom line is that the packets must arrive in a timely manner to ensure quality reproduction of the voice or video.

The Session Initiation Protocol (**SIP**) was developed by the Internet Engineering Task Force (IETF) to manage multimedia packet transfers over IP networks. SIP runs in the application layer of the OSI model and uses the connectionless protocol UDP for packet transport. SIP is responsible for establishing and terminating IP telephony calls and is responsible for transferring the call. A secure version of SIP has been developed called **SSIP**. SSIP provides for end-to-end secure communications by requiring user authentication.

3COM has introduced a technique called **virtual tie line** for its NBX network telephony. Virtual tie lines simplify the interconnection between the IP-PBX and the PSTN. The advantage of the NBX virtual tie line is its simplicity compared to the H.323. The disadvantage is that the NBX virtual tie line is unique to 3COM, although there is talk that other companies will start offering similar solutions.

The next part of this section addresses the issues of transporting voice (telephone call) over an IP network. It was previously mentioned that VoIP telephone calls can be made from phone to phone, PC to phone, and PC to PC. This is shown in Figure 13-1. The telephones connect to the VoIP gateway, and the computers connect directly to the IP network (intranet or Internet). A popular choice for Internet telephony is Skype. This service offers free global telephony service via the Internet to another Skype user.

H.323
Suite of protocols that defines how voice and video are transported over IP networks

SIP
Session Initiation Protocol

SSIP
Secure Session Initiation Protocol

Virtual Tie Line
Simplifies the interconnection between the IP-PBX and the PSTN

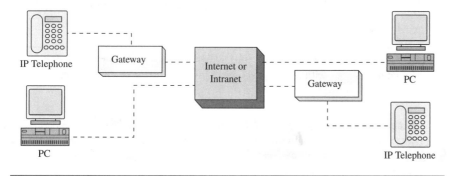

FIGURE 13-1   The various ways of placing voice over IP telephone calls.

The first step for preparing the VoIP signal for transport is to digitize the analog voice to a **PCM** (pulse code modulation) digital signal (the PCM data stream). This conversion is taken care of inside the digital telephone, computer, or PBX. Processors are used to examine the PCM data stream to remove any silent spaces. Transporting data packets that contain no information (that is, silence) is a waste of bandwidth; therefore, any digitized silence is removed. The remaining PCM data is then sent to a CODEC.

PCM
Pulse code modulation

CODEC
Encodes, compresses, and decodes the data

RTP
Real-Time Protocol

RTCP
Real-Time Control Protocol

Packet Sequence Number
Used to keep track of the order of the data packets

The purpose of the coder/decoder (**CODEC**) is to structure the PCM data for inputting into frames. This involves encoding, compressing, and decoding the data.

The frames are then placed into one packet. A Real-Time Protocol (**RTP**) header is added to each frame. The RTP header provides the following:

- Packet sequence number
- Timestamp

A companion protocol to RTP is **RTCP**, the Real-Time Control Protocol. The purpose of RTCP is to manage packet synchronization and identification and the transport of the data.

The **packet sequence number** is used to keep track of the order of the data packets and to detect any lost packets. RTP uses UDP for transporting the data. There is always a chance that packets could be lost in a congested network or the packets could arrive out of order. The RTP packet sequence number enables a processor to re-assemble the data packets. Lost digital voice data packets will cause annoying pops and clicks when converted back to analog at the receiver. One technique is to fill in the blanks with a previously received data packet. An example of this is shown in Figure 13-2. This technique helps minimize annoying pops and clicks. The substituted data packets are sometimes played back at a reduced volume to help smooth the transition.

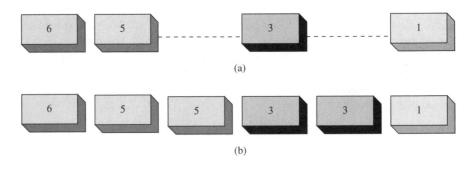

FIGURE 13-2   Reconstructing the data stream at the receiver if packets are missing: (a) the received data stream with missing packets; (b) the reconstructed data stream.

Timestamp
Reproduces playback of the voice packets with the same time interval as they were recorded

Timestamps are assigned to the voice packets by RTP to provide the correct time intervals for a packet. The receivers use the timestamps to reproduce the playback of the voice packets in the same time interval sequence as recorded.

This section has examined the fundamental issues of voice over IP telephony, including the technologies needed for transporting voice calls. The next section examines the steps for assembling a voice over IP network.

13-3   VOICE OVER IP NETWORKS

The advantages of converging voice traffic with existing data traffic are obvious. A company can have a considerable investment in routing data traffic both internally and externally to the home network. Internally, the company will have a substantial investment in installed twisted-pair cable and wall plates for computer networks.

Externally, a company might have network connections to remote sites via leased communication lines. It is a reasonable next step for the company to investigate combining voice traffic with the existing data traffic for connecting to external sites. However, best practices dictate that voice and data traffic should remain separated within the LAN. This can be accomplished by establishing VLANs to support the voice traffic. (Refer to Chapter 9 for a discussion on VLANs.)

This section examines three ways a company can implement voice over IP (VoIP) telephony into its network:

1. Replace an existing PBX voice tie line (for example, a T1 circuit) with a VoIP gateway.
2. Upgrade the company's existing PBX to support IP telephony.
3. Switch the company over to a complete IP telephone system.

Replacing an Existing PBX Tie Line

It is common practice for companies to use a PBX tie line to interconnect phone systems at different locations. The location of the PBXs could be across town from each other, or across the country or the world. The same company could also have leased data lines to interconnect the same facilities. This is shown in Figure 13-3 (a). The PBXs at each site are interconnected with a T1 tie line for the purpose of transporting telephone calls between sites. In Figure 13-3 (b), the networks are configured as a wide area data network. The company must examine the following issues:

- The company is having to lease separate lines for voice (phone) and data.
- There are times when the telephone traffic is minimal and the data traffic movement could be improved if more bandwidth was occasionally available.

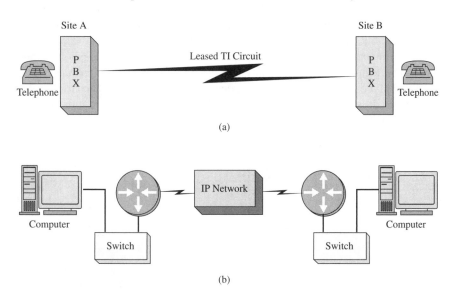

FIGURE 13-3   (a) The traditional interconnection of PBXs between sites; (b) the interconnection of data networks between sites.

A standard solution for combining voice and data networks is to multiplex the voice and data traffic over the same **tie line** (for example, a T1 connection). An example is shown in Figure 13-4. In this example, a technique called time division multiplexing (**TDM**) is used to divide the available bandwidth of the line interconnecting the two networks to carry both data and voice. The problem with this is the voice bandwidth is reserved for a required number of phone calls even if the calls are not being made. Combining the two networks simplifies the transport, but it doesn't necessarily improve the overall network performance.

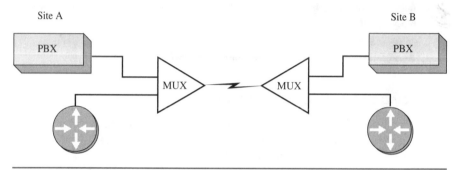

FIGURE 13-4   The use of multiplexing to combine the voice and data traffic for transport over a common T1 line.

A VoIP solution addresses the limitations of the traditional TDM arrangement. Figure 13-5 shows the modified network. The PBXs are now connected to a **VoIP gateway** (also called a **VoIP relay**). The VoIP gateway is responsible for providing the proper signaling of the digitized voice data and encapsulating the data packets for transport over the IP network. The advantage of this arrangement is the networks can more efficiently use the available bandwidth.

It is important to note that each site (see Figure 13-5) has a telephone connection to the local telephone company via the public switched telephone network (PSTN). This connection is necessary so that the phone traffic can reach users outside the network. It is also important to note that this connection serves as a backup if the Internet connection goes down.

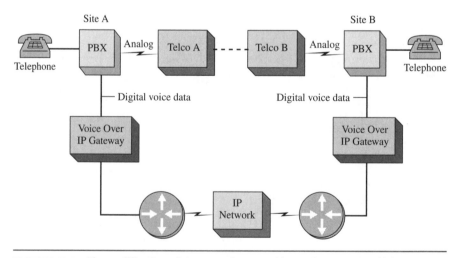

FIGURE 13-5   The modification of the network to provide a voice over IP solution.

The advantages of this arrangement are as follows:

- The voice and data traffic are combined for more efficient use of the network's available bandwidth.
- The sites can still use the existing PBX, telephones, and connections to the local PSTN.

The potential disadvantage is that growth in data or voice bandwidth requirements can impact the telephone (voice) quality of service. Few companies will be willing to sacrifice *any* quality associated with telephone calls just to implement a VoIP solution. (Note: Quality of service issues are examined in section 13-4.)

Upgrading Existing PBXs to Support IP Telephony

A company might decide that IP telephony should be used, but gradual steps should be taken toward IP telephony deployment. A solution would be for the company to upgrade its existing PBXs to support IP telephony. This enables the existing telephones to act like IP telephones and enable the IP telephones to place calls over the PSTN. Figure 13-6 illustrates an example of this voice over IP solution.

Figure 13-6 shows that the company's PBX has been replaced or upgraded to a PBX capable of supporting IP telephony. In this example, the company is running both conventional and IP telephones. Either of these phones can place telephone calls over the IP network or via the PSTN. The conventional telephones connect to the PBX in the traditional manner. The IP telephones connect to the PBX via a network switch. The PBX will have an IP call manager for placing and receiving calls. The gateway enables both IP and conventional phone calls to exit or enter the IP network. The PBX will have a connection to the PSTN to support traditional call traffic from conventional telephones. Table 13-1 outlines the advantages and disadvantages of upgrading the PBX.

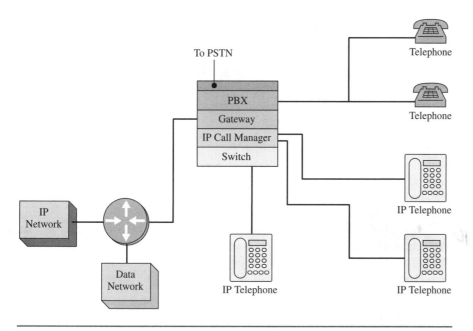

FIGURE 13-6   An example of modifying the PBX to provide a voice over IP solution.

TABLE 13-1 Advantages and Disadvantages of Upgrading the PBX

Advantages	Disadvantages
Conventional telephones will now work with IP telephony, so existing telephone hardware doesn't need to be replaced.	The cost of upgrading the PBX must justify the potential benefit.
Both PSTN and IP network voice traffic are supported.	Quality of service issues still exist.
Data traffic is easily integrated with the telephone system.	
The IP telephones can use existing computer network twisted-pair cable and RJ-45 wall plates to connect the new IP telephones.	

Switching to a Complete IP Telephony Solution

A company also has the option of switching completely to an IP telephone system. This requires the company to replace all its conventional telephones with IP telephones and/or PC telephones. The company's PBX is replaced with an IP-based PBX, and a gateway is required for connecting the IP-PBX to the PSTN. Figure 13-7 shows this IP solution.

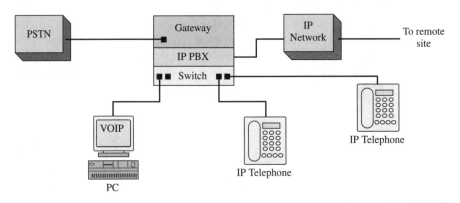

FIGURE 13-7 A complete IP telephony solution.

Figure 13-7 shows the IP telephones connecting to the IP-PBX in much the same way computers connect to a switch in computer networking. The company's IP-PBX connects to the remote site's IP telephone network. The IP-PBX also contains a gateway that connects the IP-PBX to the PSTN.

The advantage of a complete IP telephony solution is that the company can use the IP network for delivery of telephone calls within the company and to any remote site connected to the Internet or that supports VoIP.

The disadvantages of a complete IP telephony solution are as follows:

- There is a startup cost of replacing old telephones with IP hardware and/or software-based telephones.
- Quality of service issues still exist.
- The addition of new IP phones means there are new networked devices to manage, meaning more work for the network administrator.

13-4 QUALITY OF SERVICE

An important issue in the delivery of real-time data over a network (for example, voice over IP) is quality of service (**QoS**). The following are QoS issues for a VoIP network:

- Jitter
- Network latency and packet loss
- Queuing

This section examines each of these issues and how each affects the quality of real-time voice data delivery.

QoS
Quality of service

Jitter

Digitized voice data requires a fixed time interval between data packets for the signal to be properly converted back to an audible analog signal. However, there is a delay problem with transported voice data over a packet network. Variability in data packet arrival introduces **jitter** in the signal, which produces a poorly reconstructed signal at the receiver. For example, assume that a 1000 Hz tone is sent over a VoIP network. The tone is digitized at regular time intervals, assembled into frames and packets, and sent out as an RTP packet. Random delays in the packets' travel to the destination result in their arriving at irregular time intervals. The reproduced 1000 Hz analog tone will contain jitter because the arrival times for each data packet will vary.

Figure 13-8 (a) shows an accurately reconstructed sine wave, and Figure 13-8 (b) shows an unstable sine wave. This signal will contain significant distortion and may not even sound like a 1000-Hz tone at all. (Note: The bandwidth of a typical telephone call is 300–3000 Hz. The 1000 Hz tone was selected because it falls in the typical bandwidth for voice.)

Jitter
Produces a poorly reconstructed signal at the receiver due to variability in data packet arrival

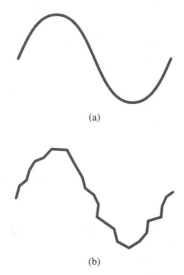

(a)

(b)

FIGURE 13-8 An example of (a) an accurately reproduced sine wave and (b) a sine wave with jitter.

⑲
Buffering the data packets long enough for the next data packet to arrive can minimize the effects of jitter. A **buffer** is temporary storage for holding data packets until it is time for them to be sent. The buffer enables the data packets to be output at regular time intervals, thereby removing most of the jitter problem. Buffering works as long as the arrival time of the next packet is not too long. If the arrival time is too late, the data packet might have to be considered "lost" because the real-time data packets can't wait too long for the buffered packet without affecting the quality of the reconstructed signal. Another issue is that the buffering stage introduces delay, and having to wait additional time only introduces more delay.

Buffer
Temporary storage for holding data packets until it is time for them to be sent

⑳

Network Latency

Network Latency
The time it takes for data packets to travel from source to destination
㉑

It takes time for a data packet to travel from the source to the destination. This is called **network latency**, and it becomes an important issue in VoIP data traffic. Telephones (both traditional and IP) feed a portion of the user's voice into the earpiece. If the round-trip delay of the voice data is too lengthy (> 50 ms), then the user will begin to hear an annoying echo in the earpiece.

Delay issues can be minimized by making sure the network routers and switches are optimized for VoIP data traffic. The VoIP network can be configured so that high-priority data packets (for example, voice packets) are transported first over the IP network. Nonsensitive data packets are given a low-priority status and are transmitted only after the high-priority packets are sent.

Another source of packet delay is network congestion. This can have a negative effect on any type of data traffic but is very disruptive to VoIP telephony. The network administrator must make sure that congestion problems are avoided or at least minimized and could have the option of configuring the routers to optimize routes for IP telephony.

Weighted Random Early Discard (WRED)
Network routers and switches are configured to intelligently discard lower priority packets
㉓

One technique used to minimize congestion problems is to configure the network routers and switches to intelligently discard lower-priority packets. This technique is called **weighted random early discard (WRED)**. This is done to maintain acceptable data traffic performance of an integrated data and VoIP network. A dropped TCP/IP data packet will typically cause the TCP data packet flow to slow down. Recall from Chapter 5 that TCP issues a window size value to the number of data packets that the receiver can accept without acknowledgement. If a packet is lost, the window size decreases until an acceptable window size is obtained that doesn't produce lost data packets. As a result, the intentionally dropped data results in a slow-down in data traffic and a less congested network.

Queuing
Provides control of the data packet transfer

Queuing

First Queued
Describing when the data packet arrives
㉔

FIFO
First in, first out

Weighted Fair Queuing (WFQ)
Used to determine what data traffic gets priority for transmission

Queuing is another technique the network administrator can use to improve the quality of service of data traffic by controlling the transfer of data packets. The administrator must identify the data traffic that must be given priority for transport. The queuing decision is made when the data packet arrives, is **first queued**, and placed in a buffer. There are many types of queuing arrangements, with the most basic being **FIFO** (first in, first out). In this case, the data packets are placed in the queue on arrival and transmitted when the channel is available.

A technique called **weighted fair queuing (WFQ)** is available on many routers and is used to determine what data traffic gets priority for transmission. This technique applies only if the buffer is full, and a decision must be made as to which data packet goes first. WFQ can be modified to provide a class-based weighted fair queuing (**CBWFQ**). This improvement enables the network administrator to define the amount of data traffic allocated to a class of data traffic (for example, VoIP).

Other queuing techniques are PQ and CQ. Priority queuing (**PQ**) is used to make sure the important data traffic gets handled first. Custom queuing (**CQ**) reserves a portion of the channel bandwidth for selected data traffic (for example, VoIP traffic). This is a decision made by the network administrator based on experience with the network. The problem with CQ is it doesn't make allowances for other traffic management when the channel is full; therefore, queuing techniques such as WFQ or WRED can't be used to manage the data flow. Table 13-1 lists the queuing techniques available to the network administrator.

CBWFQ
Class-based weighted fair queuing

PQ
Priority queuing

CQ
Custom queuing

TABLE 13-2 Queuing Techniques

FIFO	First in, first out
WFQ	Weighted fair queuing
CBWFW	Class-based weighted fair queuing
PQ	Priority queuing
CQ	Custom queuing

Two additional areas for consideration in regards to quality of service for VoIP are incorporating the use of VLANs within your network to separate voice and data traffic and securing your voice traffic:

- **VLANs for VoIP:** When deploying VoIP on LANs, it is recommended that a separate VLAN be created on your network for IP telephony. The advantage of this is the voice and data networks are kept separate. Network slowdowns or security threats to the data network will not affect the VoIP network or are at least kept to a minimum.
- **Securing the VoIP network:** The traditional PBX used in telephony is not typically vulnerable to the security threats that occur on data networks. However, VoIP networks are vulnerable to similar security threats. The most serious threat to VoIP traffic is denial of service (DoS) attacks. DoS attacks work by flooding the network with server requests or excessive data traffic. The result is a severe degradation in the quality of service available for VoIP telephony. Another threat to the quality of service is **spam over Internet telephony (spit)**. In this case, the VoIP network can be saturated with unsolicited bulk messages broadcast over the VoIP network.

Spit
Spam over Internet telephony

This section has presented the key quality of service issues in the delivery of real-time data (VoIP). The network administrator must be aware of these techniques and how each can be used to improve the VoIP quality of service. The administrator must also be aware of the tradeoff that optimizing an IP network for VoIP traffic can have on the data network.

13-5   ANALYZING VoIP DATA PACKETS

This section examines the packets exchanged during VoIP calls using both voice over Ethernet and voice over IP. The VoIP data collected for the voice over Ethernet discussion were generated from an IP telephone network that contained two IP telephones and a 3COM NBX call processor. Figure 13-9 shows a block diagram of the setup for the circuit. The communications used for these phones is running at Layer 2, the data link layer. The IP phones and the call processor were configured with IP addresses, but the phones are in the same LAN, and IP routing was not necessary. This setup is similar to the phone setup in an office or a small business. The MAC addresses for the networking equipment are listed in Table 13-3.

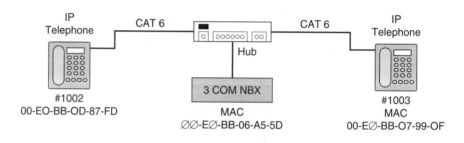

FIGURE 13-9   The setup used to collect the VoIP telephone call data packets.

TABLE 13-3   MAC Addresses for Networking Equipment Used When Gathering VoIP Data Packets

Networking Device	MAC Address
Phone (#1002)	00-E0-BB-0D-87-FD
Phone (#1003)	00-E0-BB-07-99-0F
NBX call processor	00-E0-BB-06-A5-5D

There are some basic codes used by the NBX call processor to identify the packet running over the Ethernet network. These codes identify the type of message that is being issued, such as voice data packets, request packets, and acknowledgements. These codes, listed and described in Table 13-4, will be used when analyzing the VoIP data traffic.

TABLE 13-4   IP Telephone Call Packet Codes for the NBX Call Processor

Code	Letter	Description
0x41	A	Voice data packets
0x48	H	Acknowledgement
0x52	R	Request packet, issued when a button is pressed
0x55	U	Update

The following discussion is for a set of voice call data packets obtained using the setup shown in Figure 13-9. This file is provided on the Companion CD-ROM and is named *voip-6.cap*. The first packet examined is number 7. This packet is from the NBX call processor (MAC 00-E0-BB-06-A5-5D). It is acknowledging that the #1003 phone has been picked up. Phone #1003 has a MAC address of 00-E0-BB-07-99-0F. The data in Figure 13-10 indicates Extension:1003 has picked up. The code for the call is the hexadecimal numbers (0x48 52). The code is shown boxed in Figure 13-10. This code indicates that the packet includes an acknowledgement (48) and a request (52). In the next data sequence, the #1003 phone begins to dial #1002. The following data packets show the call processor's acknowledgement (code 48) of the buttons as they are pushed. Only the contents of the data packet will be displayed. The sequence is provided in Figure 13-11 (a–d).

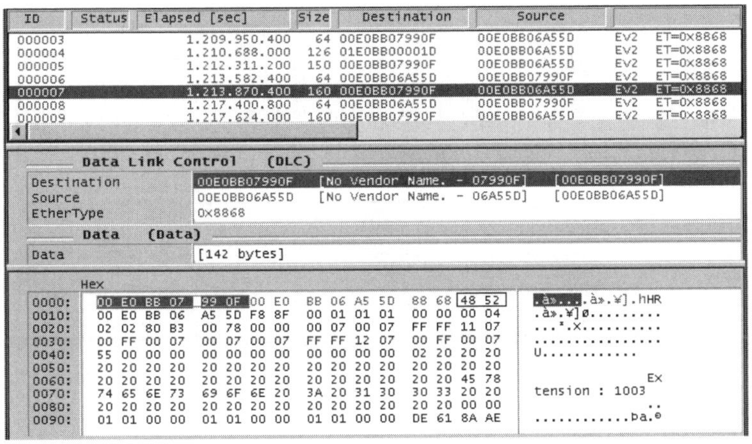

FIGURE 13-10   The acknowledgement that phone #1003 has been picked up.

The next sequence first shows the call processor notifying phone #1003 that it is dialing #1002 in Figure 13-12. Figure 13-13 shows phone #1002 acknowledging the call from the call processor, basically coming online. The codes (48 48) are acknowledgements that the request was received.

Phone #1002 has acknowledged the call, and now the call processor will go through multiple management steps to complete the call. This is shown in Figure 13-14. Notice in Figure 13-14 that the UDP data packets are being used with a source IP address of 192.168.12.6. This is the IP address of the NBX call processor. The destination IP address for the highlighted data packet is 224.0.1.59. This is a multicast address used by the call processor to manage the call setup and functions. This is used only for call setup. Once the call is set up, the IP phones will begin transferring the voice data. This is shown in Figure 13-15. The code for the data packets has changed to (41), which is for "voice" data packets. Notice that the source and destination MAC addresses are alternating during the conversation. The IP phones are communicating directly without further need of the call processor. The data shown at the bottom of Figure 13-15 is the PCM voice data.

This section has demonstrated the call setup and signaling for establishing an IP telephone call within a local area network. The transfer of the voice data packets between IP phones has also been shown. The reader should understand how the basic call was established and how to identify the type of message using the call codes (Table 13-3). The reader should also understand that the call processor uses multicast addresses to set up the call before handing it over to the IP phones.

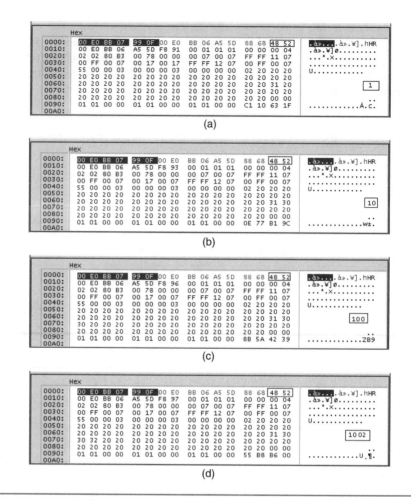

FIGURE 13-11 (a) The acknowledgement that phone #1003 has pressed number "1"; (b) the acknowledgement that phone #1003 has pressed number "1 0"; (c) the acknowledgement that phone #1003 has pressed number "1 0 0"; (d) the acknowledgement that phone #1003 has pressed number "1 0 0 2".

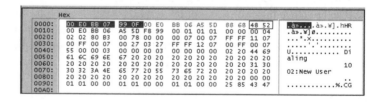

FIGURE 13-12 The message from the call processor that it is dialing #1002.

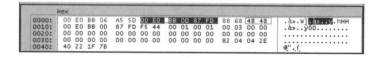

FIGURE 13-13 The acknowledgement of the call from phone #1002 back to the call processor.

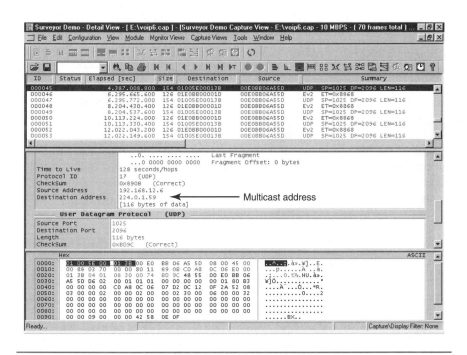

FIGURE 13-14 The call processor's management steps to set up the phones so that voice data transfer can begin.

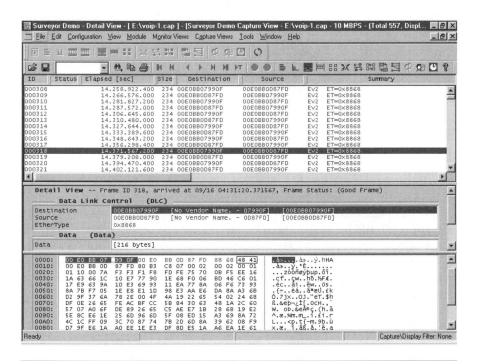

FIGURE 13-15 The exchange of voice packets (code 41) between the two IP phones.

Analyzing VoIP Telephone Call Data Packets

This section examines the data packets that are being exchanged in a VoIP telephone call. The test setup for the VoIP telephone call is shown in Figure 13-16. This picture shows that the network consists of two VoIP telephones, two NBX 3000 Call Processors, and two routers. The data packets were captured using the Finisar Surveyor Demo software provided with the text. The computer running the Surveyor Demo software and two NBX call processors were connected to a networking hub so that each share the Ethernet data link. This was done so that all the VoIP data packets being exchanged between the telephones, the call processors, and the routers could be captured at the same time with one protocol analyzer. The VoIP captures are provided on the textbook CD-ROM in the *Finisar* folder (filename *VoIP-cap2.cap*)

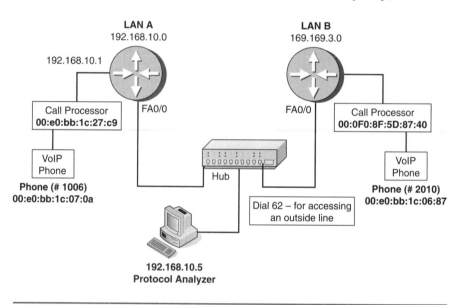

FIGURE 13-16   The test setup for the VoIP telephone call.

In the following example, a telephone call is being placed from extension 1006 to the 62-2010 extension. The first packet examined is number 5, shown in Figure 13-17. This packet source is from the LANA NBX call processor with the MAC address of 00:E0:BB:1C:27:C9. The HR text (indicated by the arrow) is an acknowledgment that extension 1006 (00:e0:bb:1c:07:0a) was picked up to dial the call. The call packet codes for the NBX call processor are listed in Table 13-4. H (0x48) is an acknowledgement, and R (0x52) is a request packet that is issued when a button is pushed.

Packet number 19 (see Figure 13-18) shows the call processor (00:E0:BB:1C:27:C9) acknowledging back to extension 1006 (00:e0:bb:1c:07:0a) dialing the number 62 to go outside the network (LANA) to talk to the destination phone in LANB. The 62 is the number used by the call processor to get an outside telephone line. This is defined in the call processors call plan. Once again, the HR code is listed at the beginning of the data packet. The HR codes will repeat throughout the call setup, Figure 13-19 (a–d).

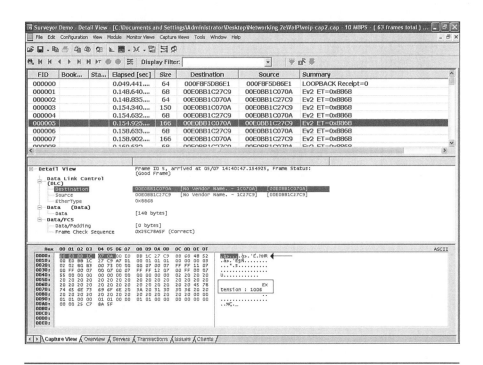

FIGURE 13-17   The acknowledgement that extension 1006 was picked up.

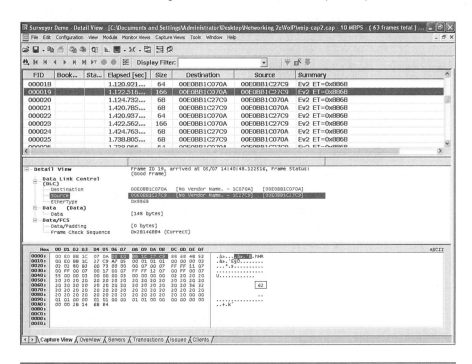

FIGURE 13-18   Dialing "62" for an outside line.

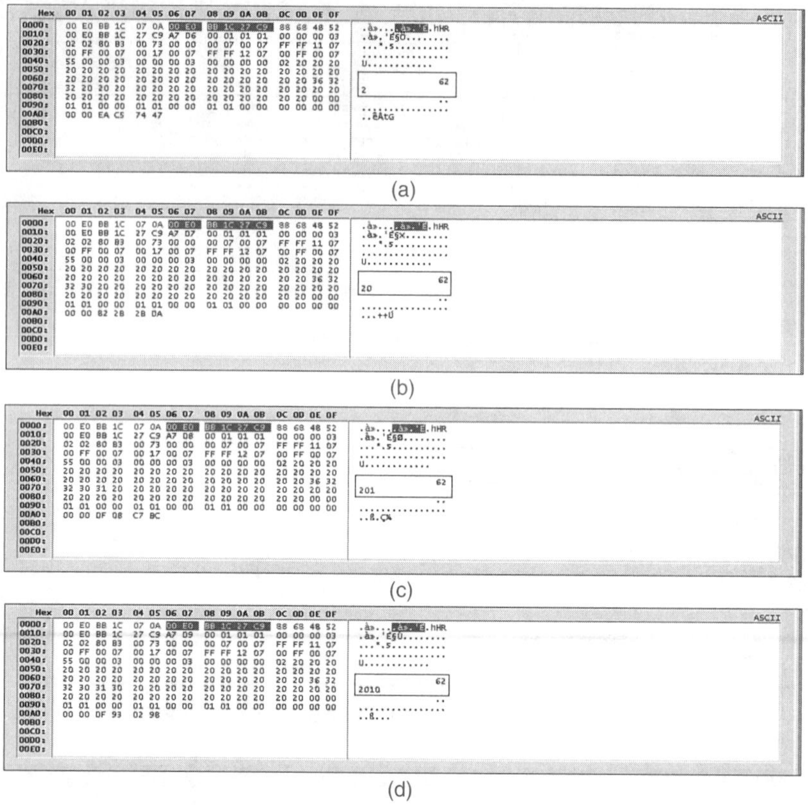

(a)

(b)

(c)

(d)

FIGURE 13-19   Dialing the outside line at 62–2010.

Packet number 23 (Figure 13-19 [a]) is showing ext. 1006 dialing the first number "2" in the corresponding phone number on LANB.

Packet number 27 (Figure 13-19 [b]) is showing ext. 1006 dialing the second number in the corresponding phone number on LANB.

Packet number 33 (Figure 13-19 [c]) is showing ext. 1006 dialing the third number in the corresponding phone number on LANB.

Packet number 39 (Figure 13-19 [d]) is showing ext. 1006 dialing the forth number in the corresponding phone number on LANB.

Packets 41–52 (Figure 13-19) are showing the handshaking between the two networks. Notice that the source and destination have changed to the IP addresses for the VoIP telephone call.

Finally, Figure 13-20 shows the packets been exchanged between the two IP phones.

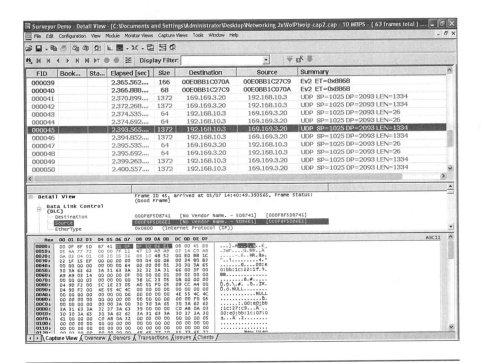

FIGURE 13-20   The handshaking between the two IP networks and the start of the VoIP telephone call.

This section has demonstrated the call setup and signaling for establishing a VoIP telephone call within two networks. The student should understand how the basic call was established (same as voice over Ethernet) and that dialing "62" was required to get an access line.

Summary

This chapter presented an introduction to voice over IP telephony. The network administrator must be aware of the impact of integrating VoIP into the network. Advancements in technology are making the integration of voice and data easier, but along with the simplification comes the requirement that the network administrator fully comprehend the capabilities and limitations of the technologies. The student should understand the following concepts:

- How IP telephony interfaces with the PSTN
- The signaling techniques used by IP telephony
- The steps for preparing the VoIP signal for transport
- How VoIP can be integrated into a company's network
- The quality of service (QoS) issues for VoIP
- The importance of using VLANs with for VoIP traffic within the LAN
- The potential security threats for VoIP
- The types of data packets issued when setting up a VoIP call

Questions and Problems

Section 13-2

1. Define *PBX*.
2. Define *PSTN*.
3. What is the purpose of a *gateway*?
4. List four enhanced features of SS7.
5. What are the signaling techniques used in IP telephony?
6. What are RTP and RTCP used for in VoIP?
7. What does a processor in a VoIP receiver do if a voice data packet is lost?
8. How is the timestamp on VoIP data packets used?

Section 13-3

9. What are three ways a company can implement VoIP into their network?
10. What is a standard solution for combining voice and data traffic?
11. What is the purpose of a VoIP gateway?
12. What is another term for a VoIP gateway?
13. What are two advantages of replacing an existing PBX tie line with a VoIP/Data network?
14. What is the disadvantage of replacing an existing PBX tie line with a VoIP network?
15. List two advantages of upgrading the PBX to support VoIP.
16. What does it mean for a company to switch to a complete IP solution?

Section 13-4

17. What are three QoS issues for a VoIP network?
18. What causes jitter in the received signal?
19. How can the effects of jitter be minimized?
20. When does buffering the received data packets not v
21. What is *network latency*?
22. What causes network data traffic congestion?
23. What is *WRED*, and what is its purpose?
24. What is the basic form of queuing?
25. What is *WFQ*, and what is its purpose?
26. What is the purpose of priority queuing?
27. Which queuing technique reserves channel bandwidt

Section 13-5

28. What is the purpose of the basic codes used by the NBX c
29. Which code identifies voice data packets?
30. What does the code 0x52 identify?
31. What is the purpose of multicasting in IP telephony?

Critical Thinking

32. Prepare a technical memo to your supervisor that explains how VoIP can be implemented on your local network.
33. Use the Internet to find out what queuing systems are currently recommended for data traffic.

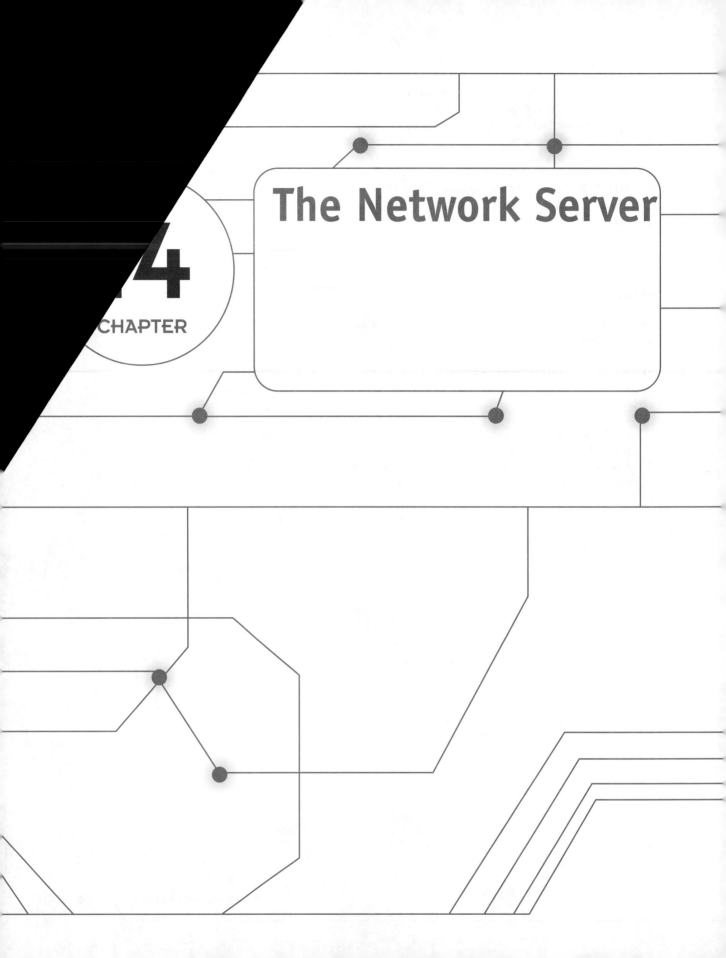

The Network Server

CHAPTER

14

CHAPTER OUTLINE

14-1 Introduction
14-2 Installing and Configuring the Network Server
14-3 Adding Computers, Users, and Groups
14-4 Setting Group Permissions and Policies

14-5 Verifying "Network" and "My Network Places" in Windows-based PCs
14-6 Configuring the Network Server's Account Lockout Policy
Summary
Questions and Problems

OBJECTIVES

- Define the concept of a peer-to-peer network
- Define the concept of a client-server network
- Describe the function of a server in a network
- Discuss the issues of installing the network operating software
- Describe the issues of installing, configuring, and administering Windows 2008/2003 servers
- Describe the procedures for setting group permissions and policies
- Describe the procedures for setting up an organizational unit
- Describing the procedures for verifying "My Network Places" on Windows-based PCs
- Describe the options for configuring a user's account lockout policy
- Describe how to identify the users connected to a Windows 2008/2003 server
- Describe how to send a message to a user connected to the server

KEY TERMS

network server
client
peer
peer-to-peer network
client/server network
Active Directory
domain controller

tree
child
forest
NetBIOS
workstation
container
community computer

organizational unit
group
authenticated
applet
net session
net send

14-1   INTRODUCTION

Network Server
Provides access to services on the network

The concept of assembling a simple office LAN was introduced in Chapter 1. This chapter introduces the next piece for the LAN, the **network server**. The network server is an integral part of today's high-performance networks. Its function is to provide access to resources such as file sharing, printing, and services such as email, security, and Internet web page services. This chapter introduces the network server from the point of view of the person or persons responsible for installing, configuring, and maintaining the server and all of the computers that connect to it, in other words, the system administrator for the LAN. The chapter begins with an overview of the basic network types and server functions used in LANs. In section 14-2, the procedures for configuring a Windows 2008/2003 server for a small LAN are presented. A network server is useless without computers, users, and groups, so the procedures for setting these up in a network are introduced in section 14-3. Section 14-4 examines setting permissions and policies for the groups. Steps for using "My Network Places" to connect to the computers on the domain follows in section 14-5. ("Network" is Windows Vista's new name for "My Network Places" and "Network Neighborhood.") The chapter concludes with a look at configuring the users account lockout policy on the network server.

Network Definitions

There are many hardware and software choices available today for configuring a computer network. This chapter introduces the fundamental concepts a LAN network administrator must know to perform his or her job and what issues must be addressed to properly select the network server software and hardware. The Windows 2008/2003 server software demonstrated in this chapter is typical of the network server software available.

There are many issues to be addressed. A small office LAN may need minimal server support. In fact, in some cases the only server function required by the small LAN is for shared printer access, something easily accomplished with a shared network printer. A larger LAN might need to share files and data. Another LAN might need to control access to data. These and other issues must be addressed when configuring the LAN. The network configuration selected depends on many factors:

- Network application
- Number of users
- Type of remote access needed
- Availability of network support
- Budget
- Level of security required

Client
Computer connected to the network that accesses services from the server

Peer
Computer that uses and provides resources to the network

Peer-to-peer Network
All computers in the network provide similar services including server functions

Network Types

The following information defines the advantages and disadvantages of two network types, a peer-to-peer and a client/server network. A **client** is a computer connected to the network that uses services from the server. A **peer** is a computer that uses and provides resources to the network. In a **peer-to-peer network**, all computers connected in the network use and provide similar services. The client computer can also function as a server for the network. The small office LAN introduced in Chapter 1 and shown in Figure 14-1 is an example of a peer-to-peer network.

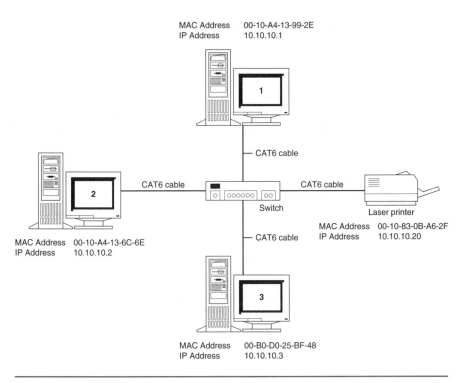

MAC Address   00-10-A4-13-99-2E
IP Address   10.10.10.1

CAT6 cable

CAT6 cable

CAT6 cable

Switch

Laser printer

MAC Address   00-10-83-0B-A6-2F
IP Address   10.10.10.20

MAC Address   00-10-A4-13-6C-6E
IP Address   10.10.10.2

CAT6 cable

MAC Address   00-B0-D0-25-BF-48
IP Address   10.10.10.3

FIGURE 14-1   An example of a peer-to-peer network.

In a **client/server network** the server handles multiple requests from multiple clients for multiple services. The network shown in Figure 14-2 is a client/server network.

It isn't practical to say which network choice, peer-to-peer or client/server, is best for all applications. Both types are used, and it is up to the users and the administrator for the LAN to make the choice. There are definite advantages and disadvantages for each, as outlined in Tables 14-1 and 14-2.

Client/Server Network
The server handles multiple requests from multiple clients for multiple services

TABLE 14-1   Advantages and Disadvantages of a Peer-to-Peer Network

Advantages	Disadvantages
Easy to set up the network	Resource sharing can affect the performance of the computers.
No centralized network administration	Poor security.
Low cost	Users must administer their own computer.
Users control the resource sharing	No central file server.
	No centralized administration of the computer's resources.

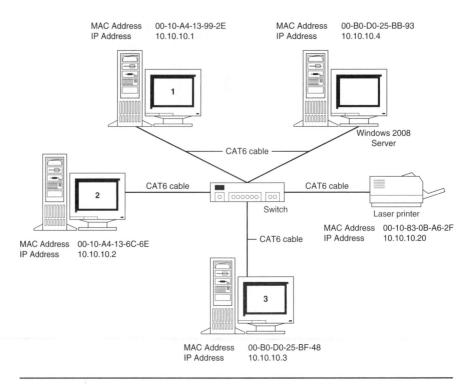

FIGURE 14-2   An example of a client/server network.

TABLE 14-2   Advantages and Disadvantages of the Client/Server Network

Advantages	Disadvantages
Centralized file storage	Client/server software and licenses can be expensive.
Centralized network security	Server hardware can be expensive.
Easy sharing of the network resources	Requires a network administrator.
	Network bandwidth/resource requirements.

Server Types

There are many types of servers used in modern computer networks. It is important to note that one server can provide many server functions. In fact, a server is typically configured to provide multiple network services. The following information defines many of the available server types:

- **Application and Information Server:** Contains the applications and technologies needed to provide and process information and interact with the client.
- **Web Server:** Exchanges files related to Web information, documents, activities, and applications.
- **Email Server:** Manages both local and Internet email service.

- **DHCP Server:** Dynamically assigns IP addresses to machines as needed. This means that a host on the network can have a different IP address assigned to it each time it connects to the network. As stated previously, an Internet service provider (ISP) dynamically assigns an IP address to your computer when you log on to the network. You keep this IP address as long as you remain connected to the network. The number expires when you log off the ISP's network. It is also important to note that network devices such as routers can also function as DHCP servers.
- **DNS Server:** Provides the name translations for the host name to an IP address. Enables the users in the network to use common names to identify the hosts rather than knowing the IP address. This is especially important in a network where the IP address is dynamically assigned.
- **Fax Server:** Manages the electronic delivery and reception of faxes.
- **FTP Server:** Provides the network administrator with the ability to control who can connect to a file server and what files can be shared. FTP service typically is integrated into all network servers. It is important to note that there are more secure ways of sharing files such as using SCP and SFTP that both use TCP port 22. SCP is used to securely transfer computer files between hosts, using the Secure Shell (SSH) protocol. SFTP uses the SSH-2 protocol to provide secure file transfers.
- **Proxy Server:** Services information requests from clients. The information requested can be from within or external to the network (such as from the Internet). The information passes through the proxy server, which can control what information passes to and from the client. The proxy server rebuilds the information received so that all packets appear to originate from the proxy server and not the original requester. Additionally, the proxy server can also be used for firewall protection by establishing rules that only allow the proxy server to connect to the Internet for any services that it is configured to support.
- **Firewall:** Manages the security of the information being transferred to and from a network. The firewall can be used to allow or deny requests for information from the network and delivery to and from hosts outside the network. Firewalls can be placed on the network edge or internal to the network or both.
- **Print Server:** Manages requests from clients for the network printer.

Adding the Network Server

Figure 14-2 shows the addition of a network server to the simple office LAN. The network still includes three computers and a laser printer. The added server has been configured to run the Microsoft Windows 2008 server operating system. The MAC and assigned IP addresses for the server are listed, and the computer has been given the name W2008 Server. Note that the cabling for the network has been upgraded to CAT6. This provides an improvement in the data-handling capability of the cable. CAT6 cable provides the ability to upgrade the network data rate to 1 gigabit. The networking devices are interconnected through a switch. Remember, the switch isolates the data traffic, which improves the performance of the data transfers in the LAN.

14-2 INSTALLING AND CONFIGURING THE NETWORK SERVER

The objective of this section is to investigate and demonstrate the procedures for installing and configuring a network server for a small LAN. The server is an integral part of making the computer network both powerful and resourceful. The networking technologies used for transporting information within your network are very important, and equally important is the access control of information afforded by the server. We introduce and discuss here the technical issues associated with configuring, maintaining, and troubleshooting the Windows 2008 server. There are many layers to the server, and it is not feasible to present a thorough discussion in one chapter or even in one text. The bottom line is that the Windows 2008/2003 server is very powerful and also very complicated. The steps presented in this chapter guide you through the procedure for setting up both the Windows 2008 and 2003 server. The steps are grouped into the following categories:

- Section 14-2 Installing and Configuring the Network Server
- Section 14-3 Adding Computers, Users, and Groups
- Section 14-4 Setting Group Permissions and Policies

Each step is well-documented with images obtained from the Windows 2008/2003 server configuration menus.

The first part of this section examines the steps for creating a server domain in Windows 2003 server using the configure Your Server Wizard. This is followed by an overview of the steps for configuring a Windows 2008 server.

Creating a Server Domain (Windows 2003 Server)

1. To install a server domain with 2003 Server, click **Start—Programs—Administrative Tools—Configure Server Wizard**.

   Active Directory is a centralized system that automates the network management of user data, security, and distributed services (computing resources are spread out over the network on more than one computer).

   You will be taken to the Active Directory Installation Wizard menu shown in Figure 14-3.

Active Directory
A centralized system that automates the management of user data, security, and distributed services

FIGURE 14-3   The Welcome screen of the Active Directory Installation Wizard menu.

2. In the Welcome screen, click **Next**. This opens the Domain Controller Type window. Select **Domain controller for a new domain**. The menu for selecting the domain controller type is shown in Figure 14-4. A **domain controller** provides authentication, stores directory information, and provides directory services.

Domain Controller
Provides authentication, stores directory information, and provides directory services

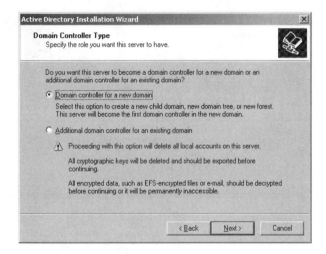

FIGURE 14-4   The menu for selecting the domain controller type.

3. In the Domain Controller Type window click **Next**. This opens the Create Tree or Child Domain window shown in Figure 14-5. Select **Create a new domain tree** in this window and click **Next.**

Tree
A domain

Child
A subset domain of the main domain

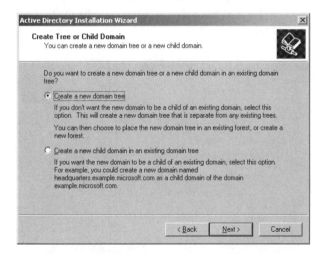

FIGURE 14-5   The menu to create a child domain in an existing tree or create a new domain tree.

Forest
A collection of groups of
domains

4. This opens the Create or Join Forest window shown in Figure 14-6. In this window, you are being asked whether you want to create a new **forest** (collection of domains) or join an existing one. The server we are adding to the LAN is the first server and is independent of any existing forests. For this exercise you will click **Create a new forest of domain trees** and click **Next.**

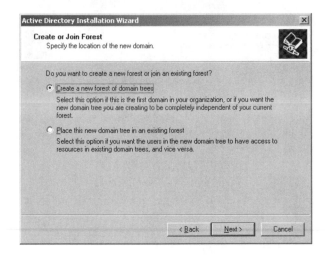

FIGURE 14-6   The menu to create or to join a forest.

5. The next window opened is New Domain Name, which allows you to specify a name for the domain. The window is shown in Figure 14-7. In the full DNS name box type the domain name exactly as you want it to appear; for this example we will use *salsa.* You can also specify a full name, such as *salsa.nmsu.edu.* For this example, we have kept the DNS name simple. After entering the name click **Next**.

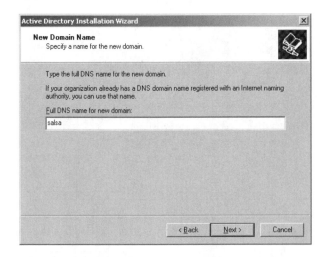

FIGURE 14-7   The window for specifying the domain name.

6. This opens the **NetBIOS** Domain Name window, which shows the name that earlier users of Windows will use to identify the new domain. The window is shown in Figure 14-8. Click **Next** to proceed to the next window.

NetBIOS
Computer naming convention that can be understood by the user and maps the NetBIOS name to an IP address.

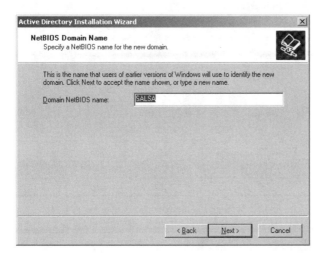

FIGURE 14-8   The NetBIOS Name window.

7. The next window is for specifying the file directory locations for the database and the active directory log (Figure 14-9). In this example the file locations used are the default file paths. After entering the correct information click **Next**.

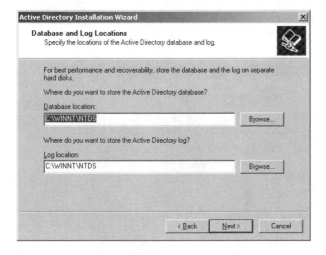

FIGURE 14-9   The window for specifying the database and log locations.

8. The next window is the Shared System Volume. The default folder location is listed in Figure 14-10. Click **Next** to proceed to the next window. In our example the warning message shown in Figure 14-11 is displayed, which advises you that a DNS server handling *salsa* could not be contacted. This is expected since you are just beginning to set up the services provided by the server.

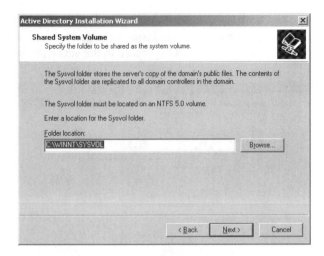

FIGURE 14-10   The Shared System Volume window.

FIGURE 14-11   The warning about DNS services.

9. Click **OK** on the DNS warning to advance to the next window and then **Configure DNS** (Figure 14-12). Select **YES, install and configure DNS on this computer** and click **Next**.

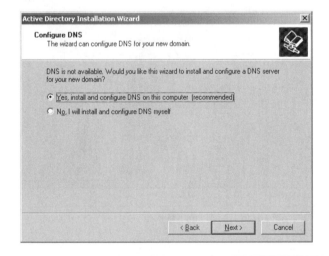

FIGURE 14-12   The Configure DNS window.

10. The next window, shown in Figure 14-13, is for setting default permissions for users and groups. Select **Permissions compatible only with Windows 2000 servers** and click **Next**.

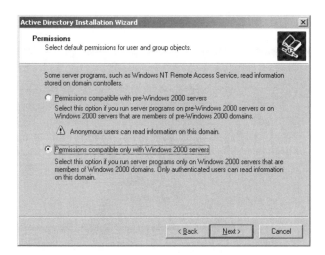

FIGURE 14-13   The Permissions window.

11. The next window is for you to specify an administrator password when starting the computer in the Directory Services Restore Mode (Figure 14-14). Enter your password where shown and enter the same password in the **Confirm password** line. In this example, the password is *chile*. Click **Next**.

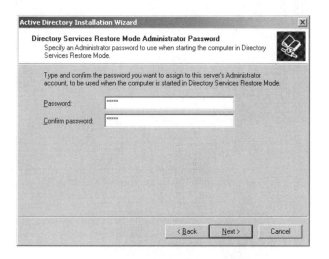

FIGURE 14-14   The window for entering the administrator password.

12. The next window, shown in Figure 14-15, displays a summary of the options selected in this installation. Check the options carefully and click **Back** if you need to make a correction. Otherwise, click **Next**.

The next window (Figure 14-16) informs you that the *salsa* active directory is installed on this computer. Click **Finish**. After clicking **Finish** you will be instructed to restart to activate the changes made to the Active Directory, as shown in Figure 14-17.

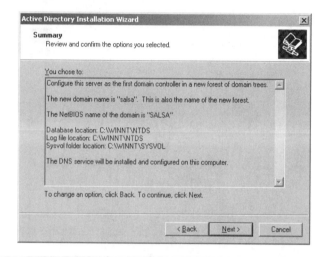

FIGURE 14-15   The window displaying a summary of the server options selected.

FIGURE 14-16   The window confirming the installation of the *salsa* active directory.

FIGURE 14-17   Restarting Windows to activate the changes made to the Active Directory.

Configuring Windows 2008 Server

The steps for configuring the 2008 server vary depending on the current status of the operating system installed on the server. This section assumes the current operating system is Windows 2003 server.

To install the 2008 server, click **Start—Administrative Tools—Server Manager** and then go to **Roles Summary—Add Roles**. This menu allows you to select the services desired (for example, Active Directory, file server, print server, mail server, and so on). For the Active Directory, select **Active Directory Domain Services**, follow the steps, and **Install**.

Configuring the IP Address

The next step is to configure the IP address for the network server. The network administrator typically selects the IP address. Make sure that you have a confirmed IP address prior to placing the server on the network. If two computers connected to the network have an IP address conflict, neither computer will function properly on the network.

On the 2008 Server, click **Start—Control Panel—Network and Sharing Center—Manage Network Connections** and then right-click **Properties** and **select TCP/IP4**. This opens the properties menu for setting the IP address, and so on.

On 2003 Server, right-click **My Network Places—Properties** and then right-click **Local Area Connection—Properties**, or (Windows 2003 Server) click **Start—Control Panel—Network Connections**—right-click **Local Area Connection Properties**

At this point you should be placed in the Local Area Connection Properties menu as shown in Figure 14-18. Double-click **Internet Protocol TCP/IP**. This places you in the Internet Protocol (TCP/IP) Properties menu shown in Figure 14-19.

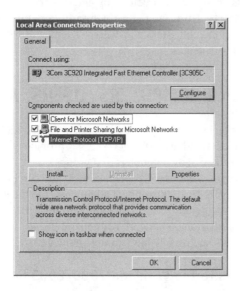

FIGURE 14-18 The Local Area Connections Properties menu with "Internet Protocol (TCP/IP)" highlighted.

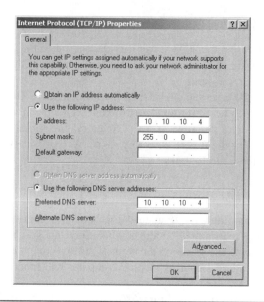

FIGURE 14-19 The Internet Protocol (TCP/IP) Properties menu.

Click **Use the following IP address** and set the address specified for your network. In this example, the private IP address 10.10.10.4 has been selected, and a subnet mask of 255.0.0.0 is being used. The other option, **Obtain an IP address automatically**, is used when the IP addresses are assigned dynamically and when a dynamic host control (DHCP) server is used. Click **OK** once this step is complete.

At this point you want to verify that the 2008 or 2003 server has accepted the requested IP address change, which you do by entering the command prompt in the **Start** menu. Click **Start—Run**, enter either **command** or **cmd**, and at the command prompt enter **ipconfig**, then hit **Return** or **Enter**. The new IP address 10.10.10.4 for the computer should be listed.

14-3 ADDING COMPUTERS, USERS, AND GROUPS

This section presents techniques for adding computers, users, and groups to the Windows 2008/2003 server. Windows 2008/2003 server provides the power to not only limit access by users but also by computers and groups.

This section begins with a discussion on how to add computers to the Windows 2008/2003 server domain. Next, the topic of adding users to the domain is examined. The section concludes with an overview of adding groups to the network server. The material includes a discussion on network administration, such as name assignments for computers and users and establishing groups in the network.

Adding Computers to the Windows 2008/2003 Server Domain

Windows 2008/2003 server recognizes all Windows operating systems, but security from the server can only be applied to computers operating Windows NT, Windows 2000 Professional, Windows XP, and Windows Vista. The type of operating system being used by a computer also determines the manner in which the computer is added to the server domain. The bottom line is the operating system must be formatted under NTFS rather than FAT file system for the computer and user to obtain secured access to the server.

Adding a Windows Vista or XP Computer   The most efficient way for a network administrator to add a computer running Windows Vista or XP is to enroll the host or computer **workstation** from the server. *Workstation* is another name for the computer. The procedure for adding a Vista or XP workstation is as follows:

Workstation
Another name for the computer

Step 1   Log on to the workstation as administrator and enter the administrator password.

Step 2   Right-click **Computer** and then select **Properties**. In the systems properties menu select the **Computer Name** tab. Click **Change**. This opens the Computer Name Changes menu shown in Figure 14-20. Enter the name of the computer (for example, Computer-3) and click **Member of Domain**. You will need to specify the name of the domain created on the Windows server. (Note also that there is only one domain per server.) After completing the entries, click **OK**. (*Note:* The name of the domain created in section 14-2 is *salsa.*)

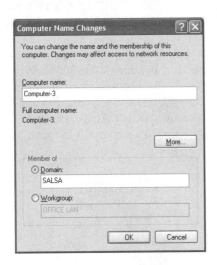

FIGURE 14-20   The Vista/XP Computer Name Changes menu.

A new Computer Name Changes menu, shown in Figure 14-21, will be opened. This menu instructs you to enter the name and password of an account with permission to join the domain. The account with this permission is the administrator. Input **administrator** as the user name and enter the password for the administrator. The administrator password was set during installation and configuration of the server.

FIGURE 14-21   The menu for entering the administrator name and password.

Step 3   After entering **administrator** and the password, click **OK**. You will be instructed to reboot the computer to complete the installation. (*Note:* The first time a newly enrolled computer logs on to the network, it can take two to three minutes to reconfigure itself and link up with the server.) This completes the step for enrolling the computer onto the Windows 2008/2003 *salsa* domain.

Container
Windows 2008/2003 server
name for a folder

Step 4   Place the enrolled computer into the proper container in the Active Directory. A **container** is a Windows 2008/2003 server name for a folder. The icons for the 2008 and 2003 containers are shown in Figure 14-22. Return to the Active Directory Users and Computers menu by clicking Start—Programs—Administrative Tools—Active Directory Users and Computers. Place the newly enrolled computer (Computer-3) into the "Computers" container.

Container

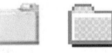

2008   2003

FIGURE 14-22   The icon for a container in Windows 2008 and 2003.

Community Computer
A computer that has no
security attached to it

Adding Windows Computers   If the computer is running Windows 9x or any operating system configured with FAT, then domain access can only be acquired by adding the computer to the domain. However, there is no security—any user will have access to the domain to print and to file share. In other words, the computer is considered a **community computer**, meaning that it has no security attached to it. The steps to add a Windows 9x computer to the Windows 2008/2003 server domain are given here.

To begin, click **Start—Programs—Administrative Tools—Active Directory Users** and then right-click the **Active Directory Domain** (for example, *salsa*) and select **New—Computer** as shown in Figure 14-23.

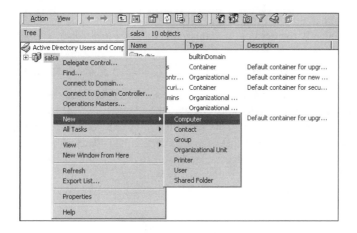

FIGURE 14-23   The Active Directory Users menu for adding a new computer.

Click **Computer**, which opens the **New Object-Computer** menu, as shown in Figure 14-24. Enter the requested information in the **New Object-Computer** menu and press **OK** when done. You will need to click the box, **Allow pre-Windows 2008/2003 computers to use this account**. (*Note:* For now, it is okay to leave the **User or group** line at the default setting *Default Domain Admins.* The computers and users will be grouped in a later section.

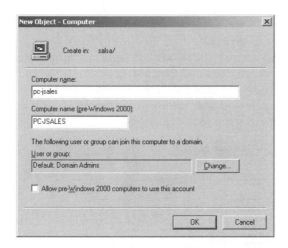

FIGURE 14-24   The New Object-Computer menu for adding a computer to the Windows 2008/2003 server domain.

A good way to specify computer names so that the computers can be later identified is by using their physical location in the LAN or by using the name of the person or the group that is using the computer. For example, the computer enrolled is named *pc-jsales*, indicating that this is a personal computer belonging to Mr. J. Sales. Another example is *pc-depot*, which indicates that this is a personal computer residing in depot maintenance. Naming conventions such as this make it easier for the network administrator to know where the computer is located or to whom the computer belongs. There are many possibilities for selecting computer names, and the final decision is ultimately the network administrator's and the supervisor's.

Adding Users to the Windows 2008/2003 Server Domain

Users are grouped according to the security permissions you want them to have. To establish group types, it is best to think of the users and what privileges they will need. The network administrator, along with the supervisors, typically define user rights and privileges. Certain users will need to have more privileges than others. Some will have different printer needs or different access levels to privileged information in the network. Accessibility for all users in all groups is set in Windows 2008/2003 server. Accessibility is defined by the network server policies. The icon for a user is provided in Figure 14-25.

user icon

2008   2003

FIGURE 14-25   The user icon.

Individual users are added to the Windows 2008/2003 server domain using the following steps:

Step 1   *(For 2008 Server)* Click Start—Administrative Tools—Active Directory Users and Computers
(For 2003 Server) Click **Start—Programs—Administrative Tools—Active Directory Users and Computers**.
Now in both right-click the Active Directory Domain (for example, *salsa*) and select **New—User**, as shown in Figure 14-26. This opens the New Object-User menu shown in Figure 14-27.

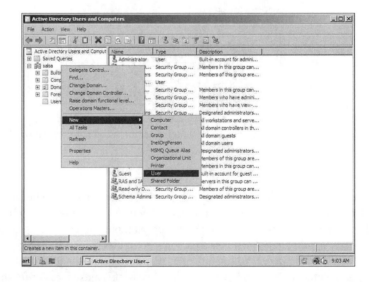

FIGURE 14-26   Adding a new user to the *salsa* domain.

FIGURE 14-27   The New Object-User menu for adding a new user to the *salsa* domain.

Step 2   Enter the first, last, and full name of the user and enter a logon name. There is also a panel that shows the user logon name for pre-Windows 2000 computers. Click **Next** after entering the necessary information.

Step 3   The next menu, shown in Figure 14-28, is for entering the user's password. Policies regarding the settings for the password type are established by the network administrator and supervisors. Click Next when complete.

FIGURE 14-28   The New Object-User menu for setting the user's password.

The next menu is a summary of the settings for the new user added to the domain (Figure 14-29). Figure 14-30 shows that the new user has been added to the Windows 2008/2003 server's *salsa* domain.

FIGURE 14-29   The New Object-User summary of the setting for the added user.

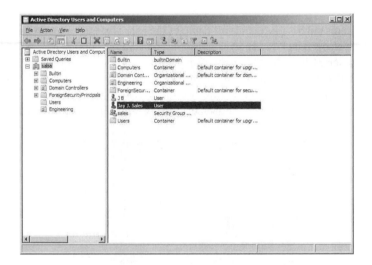

FIGURE 14-30   The Active Directory Users and Computers screen showing the addition of the new user *jsales*.

Organizational Unit
Specialized container that allows group policies to be set

Group
Collection of users and computers that can be used to set policy at the domain or organizational unit level—groups of users will have various levels of rights.

Adding Organizational Units and Groups to the Windows 2008/2003 Server Domain

This section presents the background information and the steps for adding organizational units and groups to the Windows 2008/2003 server domain. You can set policies to individual users, but if your network has many users, it is not practical to set policies to each individual. This is also true for setting policies for individual computers. The solution is to place the users and computers in groups and organizational units where permissions are set according to each group's need. An **organizational unit** is a specialized container that allows group policies to be set. A **group** is a collection of users or computers that can be used to set policy at the domain level or at the organizational unit level. Group names are typically defined by their function or position in the organization. For example, one group could be for supervisors, another for secretaries, and another for accounting. Figure 14-31 shows the icons for the group and the organizational unit.

FIGURE 14-31   The icons for a group and an organizational unit.

In regard to access of the groups and organizational units, a network administrator will need full access to the complete domain structure; however, users need access only to limited network resources such as the network printer, file sharing, and their own folders. Also not all users will have the same access rights, so different groups of users will have various levels of rights. The steps for setting group permissions and policies are outlined in section 14-4.

To add a group to the server, click **Start—Administrative Tools—Active Directory Users and Computers** and right-click the **Active Directory Domain** (for example, *salsa*). Select **New—Group** as shown in Figure 14-32. This opens the New Object-Group menu as shown in Figure 14-33. Input the required information and click **OK**. In this example, a new group called *sales* is added. The new *sales* group is shown in Figure 14-34.

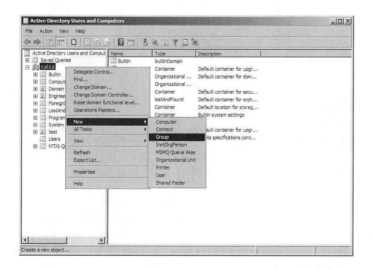

FIGURE 14-32   The screen display for adding a new organizational unit or group.

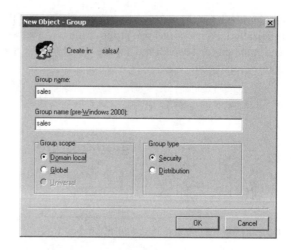

FIGURE 14-33 The menu for adding a new group.

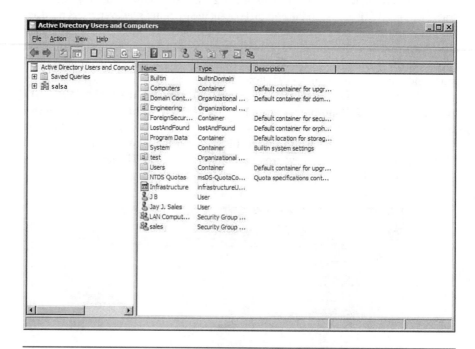

FIGURE 14-34 The addition of the *sales* group to the *salsa* domain.

The procedure for adding an organizational unit to the server is similar to adding a group. To add an organizational unit to the server, click **Start—Administrative Tools—Active Directory Users and Computers** and right-click the **Active Directory Domain** (for example, *salsa*). Select **New—Organizational Unit** as shown in Figure 14-35. This opens the **New Object-Organizational Unit** menu, shown in Figure 14-36. Input the required information and click **OK**. In this example, a new group called *sales* is added. The new *sales* group is shown in Figure 14-37.

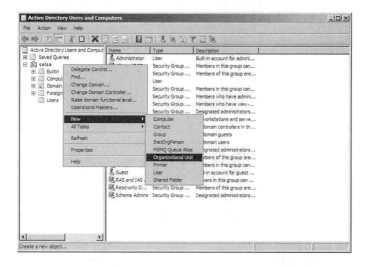

FIGURE 14-35   The screen display for adding a new organizational unit.

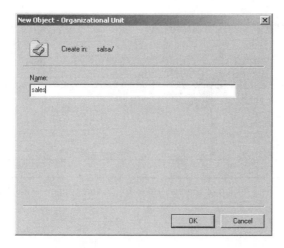

FIGURE 14-36   The menu for adding a new organizational unit.

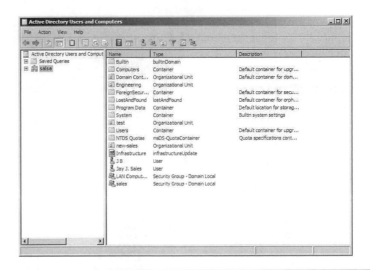

FIGURE 14-37   The addition of the new-sales organizational unit to the *salsa* domain.

The next step is to place the user *jsales* in the organizational unit *sales.* This is shown in Figure 14-38. Double-clicking the user will open a properties menu for that user, as shown in Figure 14-39.

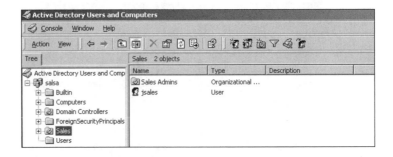

FIGURE 14-38   The addition of the user *jsales* to the *sales* organizational unit.

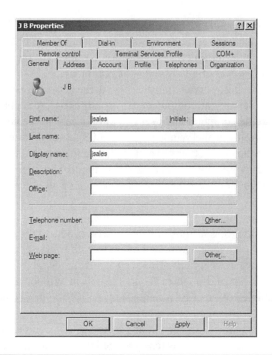

FIGURE 14-39   The Properties menu for the user *jsales*.

14-4   SETTING GROUP PERMISSIONS AND POLICIES

Permissions and policies enable the network administrator to tailor the features of the server to best complement the needs of the users in the network. Permissions and policies are not typically placed on a server to limit users' capability to do their work but rather to protect their computer environment. Network administrators do not want to impose unnecessary permissions and policies on the users of the network. If too many restrictions are placed, then the network administrator will be continually called to help fix problems that may be created by permission and policy settings. For example, the administrator can set the number of password attempts a user has: If the user fails to enter the correct password after x number of attempts, then the user can be locked out. The network administrator must carefully select the allowed number of password attempts. If too many attempts are allowed, a hacker could get into the computer. Allowing too few attempts will likely lead to excessive locked-out computers and numerous calls to the administrator to have the user accounts unlocked.

The restrictions placed on the network are there to protect the user, the server, and the network. Some policies are put in place to enhance productivity, protect the network resources, and allow users to share resources without loss of security. In computer clusters that have multiple users using multiple computers, certain restrictions, such as modifying the wallpaper settings, can be necessary so that each computer looks the same to every user.

Access to the computer's control panel can also be limited. This is useful when there is a concern that configuration options can be changed. This is undesirable in computer clusters with multiple users. You don't want to allow one user to make changes in the computer configuration that affects many.

A benefit of having a server control access to the network resources is each time a user logs on, the user and the computer are **authenticated**. Authenticated means the server verifies that the computer and user can have access to the network.

The administrator of the Windows 2008/2003 server determines the group or organizational unit the user belongs to and applies computer and user policies to that group. Computer and user policies can be set on the local machine or on the server. The server's policies take precedence if the policies on the local machine and the server conflict.

One of the most desirable features of a network is to have the capability to set permissions and policies, and thus enhance users' productivity and protect the resources of the network. Not every user will agree with every server policy, but individual users can request exceptions. This section illustrates establishing a new group and setting permissions and policies for that group in Windows 2008/2003 server. Specifically, examples of creating a new group policy are presented for both computers and users.

Setting policies affects all current and future user accounts, but it does not affect users and computers that are currently logged on. The new policies will apply to all users the next time they log on to the server. In Windows 2008/2003 server, policies for computers and users are set generally at the server, not at the workstation. The steps for setting domain policies differs for 2008 and 2003 servers. Examples of setting both are demonstrated.

2008 Server: Setting Domain Policies

To set domain policies for users and computers for Windows 2008 Server, click **Start—Administrative Tools—Group Policy Management**, as shown in Figure 14-40. This opens the Group Policy Management menu shown in Figure 14-41. Select the group for which you will be setting the policies. In this case, the LAN Computers group has been selected. Right-click the selected group and select **Edit**. This opens the Group Policy Management Editor menu shown in Figure 14-42. This menu shows folders for Computer Configuration and User Configuration. The computer policies apply first, and then the user's policies are applied.

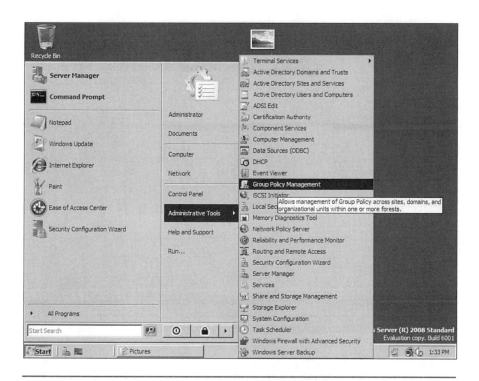

FIGURE 14-40   The steps for selecting the Group Policy Management menu.

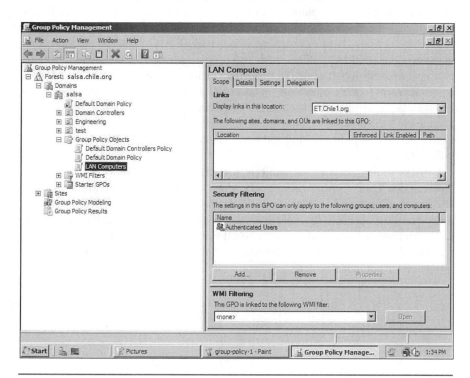

FIGURE 14-41   The Group Policy Management menu.

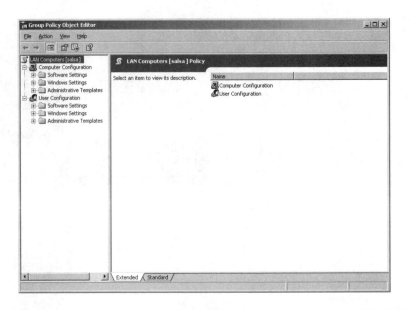

FIGURE 14-42   The Group Policy menu for the LAN Computers group.

Double-click **Computer Configuration** and select **Policies—Windows Settings—Security Settings—Local Policies—Security Options**. This opens the list of policy options for the computers in the LAN Computers group shown in Figure 14-43. Select the desired group policy that needs to be enabled. In this example, the policy *"Do not display last user name at logon screen"* is to be enabled. First highlight the policy, as shown in Figure 14-43. This policy forces the computer to not display the last user's logon name. This is beneficial for security reasons because it does not allow users to view others' logon names. If another user knows someone else's logon name, he or she only has to guess a password to gain access to the account. Double-click the policy to display the security policy setting shown in Figure 14-44. Check **Define this policy setting** and select **Enabled**. Press **OK**, and the highlighted policy should be enabled.

After setting the computer policies, the next task is to set policies for the users. Double-click **User Configuration —Policies—Administrative Template—Control Panel—Display**. The menu shown in Figure 14-45 is displayed. In this example, the policy *"Prevent changing wallpaper"* has been highlighted. Double-click the policy, select **Enabled**, and click **OK** to enable the policy as shown in Figure 14-46. This sets the policy so that a user of the computer cannot change the wallpaper settings displayed on the computer screen.

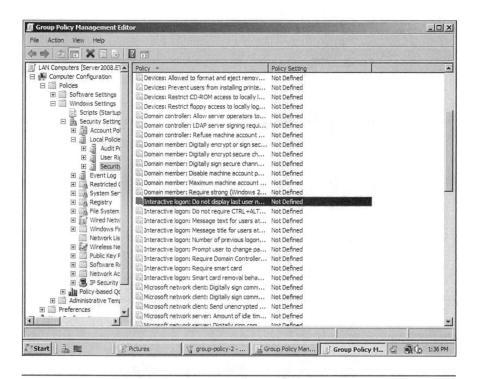

FIGURE 14-43   The list of the policies for computers in the LAN Computers group.

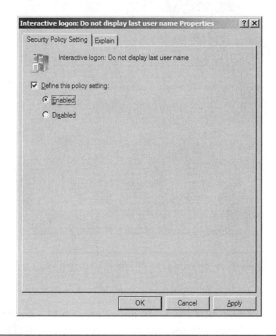

FIGURE 14-44   Enabling the "Do not display last user name in logon screen" policy.

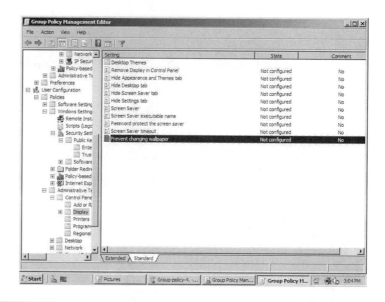

FIGURE 14-45 The Group Policy Management Editor menu with the "Prevent Changing Wallpaper" policy highlighted.

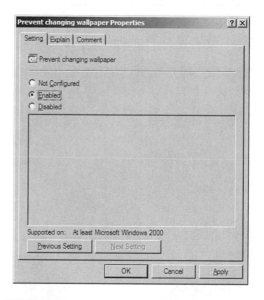

FIGURE 14-46 The menu for enabling the "Prevent Changing Wallpaper" policy.

You can also make sure that when a user logs on to a computer, the control panel is not displayed. You can use this policy (see Figure 14-47) to prevent users from changing operating parameters on the computer. This is of critical importance when you have multiple users for one computer. However, use caution if you do this because you can disable some computer features that the user needs, such as access to printing. Test the requirements of your software before arbitrarily setting policies.

The omission of the printer **applet** (small, limited-function application) from the control panel would make it so the documents could not be printed.

Applet
Small, limited-function application often used in control panels and on web pages

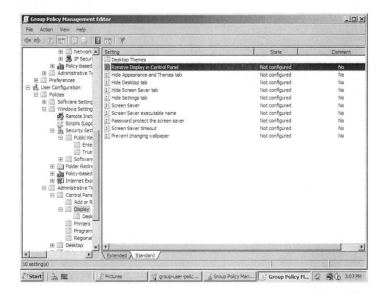

FIGURE 14-47   Selecting the policy "Remove Display in the Control Panel."

2003 Server: Setting Domain Policies

To set the policies, click **Start—Programs—Administrative Tools—Active Directory Users and Computers**. Policies can be set for organizational units or for the domain. The policies for the organizational units are set separately if the policies differ from the domain. Organizational unit policies provide stricter access than domain policies. This allows the network administrator to set different policies for different groups based on their need and function.

To set domain policies for users and computers for Windows 2003 Server, right-click the domain name (for example, *salsa*) and select **Properties** as shown in Figure 14-48. Click the **Group Policy** tab, and the *salsa* Properties menu shown in Figure 14-49 should be displayed. To add a group, click **New Group Policy Object** and enter the name of the new group. Click **OK** when done. The name of the new group should appear and be highlighted. In this case, the new group, *LAN Computers,* has been created, as shown in Figure 14-50.

While still in the *salsa* Properties menu, highlight the *LAN Computers* group name and click **Edit**. This opens the Group Policy menu shown on the left side of Figure 14-51. This menu shows folders for Computer Configuration and User Configuration. The computer policies apply first, and then the user's policies are applied.

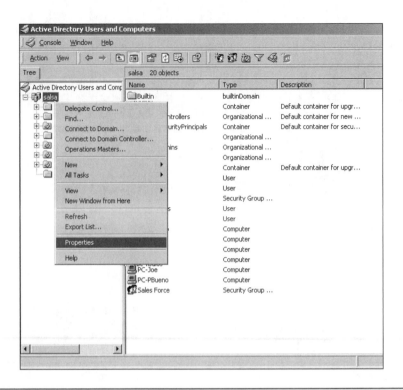

FIGURE 14-48   Selecting the Properties option for the *salsa* domain.

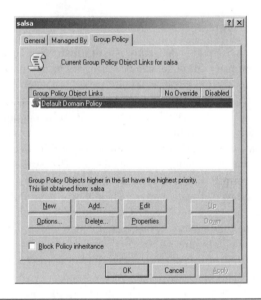

FIGURE 14-49   The Group Policy menu for adding a group policy to the domain.

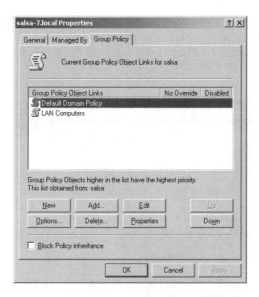

FIGURE 14-50   The LAN Computers group in the salsa domain.

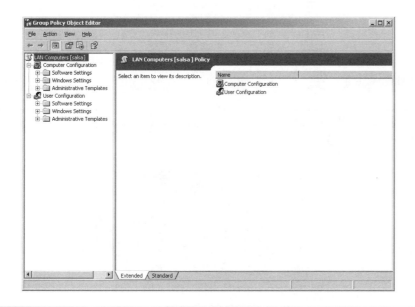

FIGURE 14-51   The Group Policy menu for the *LAN Computers* group.

Under **Computer Configuration**, click **Windows Settings—Security Settings—Local Policies—Security Options**. When in the Group Policy menu, select the desired group policy that needs to be enabled. In this example, the policy *"Do not display last user name at logon screen"* is to be enabled. First highlight the policy, as shown in Figure 14-52. This policy forces the computer to not display the last user's logon name. This is beneficial for security reasons because it does not allow other users to view your logon name. If another user knows your logon name, they only have to guess your password to gain access to your account. Double-click the policy to enable the security policy settings as shown in Figure 14-53. Check **Define this policy setting** and select **Enabled**. Press **OK**, and the highlighted policy should be enabled, as shown in Figure 14-54.

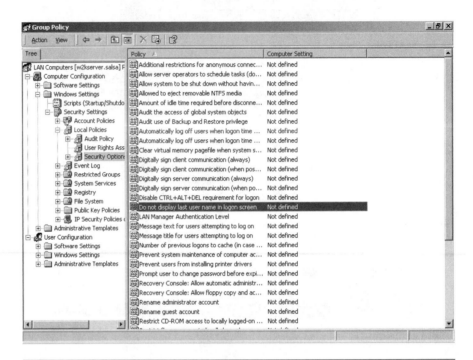

FIGURE 14-52   The Security Options—Group Policy menu for setting the policies for the *LAN Computers* group.

FIGURE 14-53   Enabling the "Do not display last user in logon screen" policy.

The next example demonstrates how to set policies for the computer's control panel. The computer's control panel enables a user to custom configure computer settings. Open access to the control panel is not desirable in a computer cluster environment with multiple users.

After setting the computer policies, the next task is to set policies for the users. Double-click **User Configuration**, double-click **Administrative Template**, double-click **Control Panel**, then double-click **Display** and the menu shown in Figure 14-55 is displayed. In this example, the policy *"Disable changing wallpaper"* has been highlighted. Double-click the policy, select **Enabled**, and click **OK** to enable the policy. This sets the policy so that a user of the computer cannot change the wallpaper settings displayed on the computer screen.

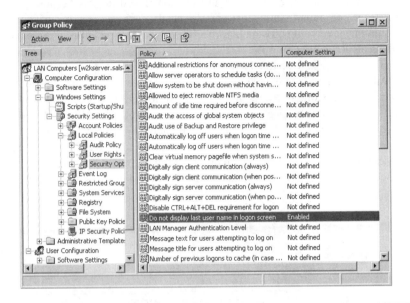

FIGURE 14-54   The "Do not display last user in logon screen" policy enabled.

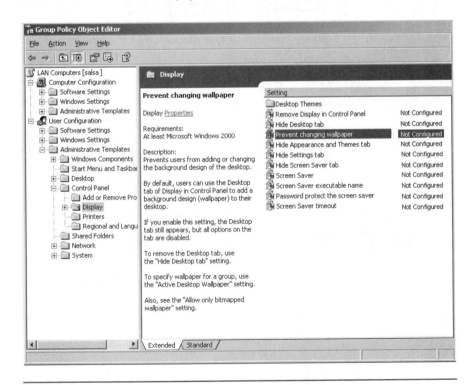

FIGURE 14-55   Setting a user policy in Windows 2003 server.

You can also make sure that when a user logs on to a computer, the control panel is not displayed. You can use this policy to prevent users from changing operating parameters on the computer. This is of critical importance when you have multiple users for a computer. However, use caution if you do this because you can disable some computer features that the user needs, such as access to printing. Test the requirements of your software before arbitrarily setting policies. In this example, the omission of the printer **applet** (small, limited-function application) from the control panel would make it so the documents could not be printed.

Another option is to enable only certain properties in the control panel. To do this, double-click **Control Panel** in the Group Policy menu shown in Figure 14-56. Double-click **Show only specified control panel applets**. Click **Enabled** on the Policy menu and then click the **Show** button highlighted in the policy list in the center of the screen (Figure 14-57). Click **Add** in the Show Contents menu. This opens the Add Item menu shown in Figure 14-58. Enter the text **printers** as shown in Figure 14-59 and click **OK**. The Show Contents menu now shows "printers" as an allowed control panel applet.

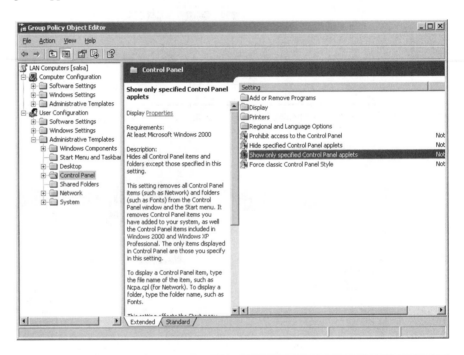

FIGURE 14-56   The Control Panel options for the user in the Group Policy menu.

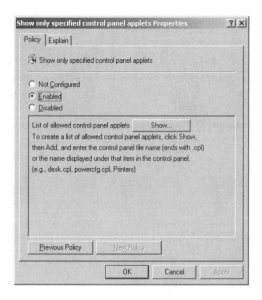

FIGURE 14-57   The Show button in the Show only specified control panel applets Properties menu.

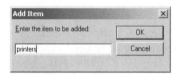

FIGURE 14-58   The Add Item menu.

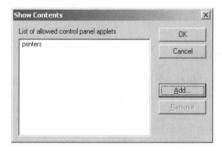

FIGURE 14-59   The menu for listing "printers" as an allowed control panel applet.

Now when a user in the *LAN Computers* group logs on to a computer, the only applet that appears in the control panel is for the printer, as shown in Figure 14-60. The only thing you need to do is make sure you have the proper printers installed in the printer folder.

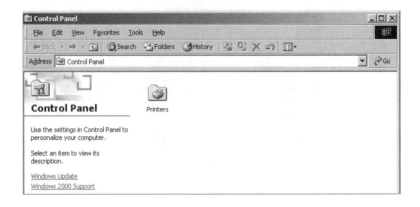

FIGURE 14-60   The modified control panel showing only the printers applet.

14-5   VERIFYING "NETWORK" AND "MY NETWORK PLACES" IN WINDOWS-BASED PCS

In this section, the procedures for verifying the "Network" and "My Network Places" connection on Windows-based PCs are presented. "Network" and "My Network Places" allow a user to determine what computers are connected to a network. It also provides a way that other computers on the network can be accessed and their resources shared. (*Note:* Windows 98 and NT call "My Network Places" "Network Neighborhood.")

The techniques for accessing "Network" and "My Network Places" are divided into specific operating systems. Techniques for Windows Vista, Windows XP, Windows 2K, and Windows NT and 98 are presented.

"Network," Windows Vista

Click **Start—Control Panel—Network and Sharing Center—view computers and devices**. This places you in the Vista equivalent of "My Network Places."

"My Network Places" on Windows XP

1. Go to the **Start** menu and select **My Computer** as shown in Figure 14-61.
2. This opens the My Computer window shown in Figure 14-62. Click **My Network Places.**

FIGURE 14-61   Selecting My Computer from the Start menu in Windows XP.

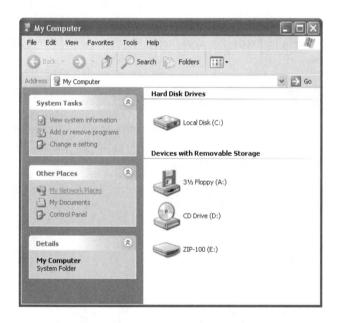

FIGURE 14-62   Selecting My Network Places in the My Computer window.

3. This opens the My Network Places window shown in Figure 14-63. Click **Entire Network.**

FIGURE 14-63   The My Network Places menu.

4. You will now see the Microsoft Windows Network icon in Figure 14-64 on the right side of the Entire Network menu. Double-click **Microsoft Windows Network.**

FIGURE 14-64   The Microsoft Windows Network icon in the Entire Network menu.

5. This opens the Microsoft Windows Network menu shown in Figure 14-65. You should now see your domain or workgroup in the menu on the right.

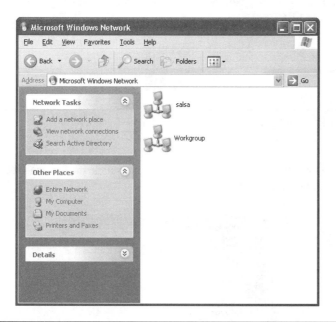

FIGURE 14-65   The Microsoft Windows Network menu showing the domains or workgroups.

6. Double-click your domain name (for example, *salsa*) to see all of the computers in your domain. An example is provided in Figure 14-66. Double-click the computer you want to connect to.

FIGURE 14-66   The computers in the *salsa* domain.

"My Network Places" on Windows 2000

1. Double-click the **My Network Places** icon on your desktop. The icon is shown in Figure 14-67.

FIGURE 14-67   The My Network Places icon in Windows 2000.

2. In the My Network Places window, double-click the **Entire Network** icon shown in Figure 14-68.

FIGURE 14-68   The Entire Network icon.

3. In the Entire Network menu shown in Figure 14-69, click **entire contents** to view the entire contents of the network.

FIGURE 14-69   The Entire Network window.

4. Now double-click the **Microsoft Windows Network** icon shown in Figure 14-70.

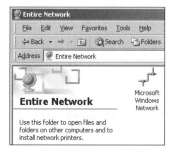

FIGURE 14-70 The Microsoft Windows Network icon.

5. In the Microsoft Windows Network window (shown in Figure 14-71), double-click your domain name (for example, *salsa*).

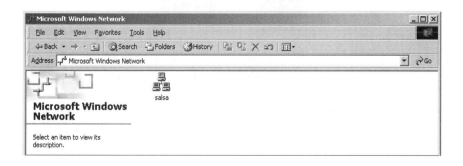

FIGURE 14-71 The Microsoft Windows Network window.

6. A window will appear with the title of your domain (*salsa*). All of your network's computers will be visible in this menu. An example is provided in Figure 14-72.

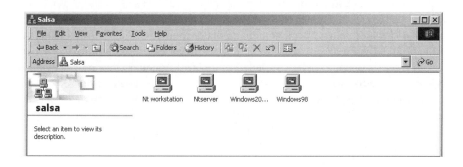

FIGURE 14-72 The *salsa* domain menu.

"Network Neighborhood" for Windows NT and 98

1. On your desktop, double-click the **Network Neighborhood** icon, shown in Figure 14-73.

FIGURE 14-73   The Network Neighborhood icon in Windows NT and 98.

2. A window will appear with the title Network Neighborhood. Here all of your network's computers will be visible. An example is provided in Figure 14-74.

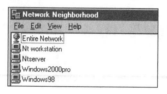

FIGURE 14-74   The display of the computers in the Network Neighborhood.

14-6 CONFIGURING THE NETWORK SERVER'S ACCOUNT LOCKOUT POLICY

A typical problem an administrator of a network server encounters is that a user in the network forgets his or her password, and the administrator must recover the lost password. This usually requires that the administrator delete the old password and activate a new one. (*Note:* The administrator cannot see the user's password once the user has configured his or her own password at login.)

Another problem network administrators encounter is when a user attempts to log in with an incorrect password or an unauthorized user is attempting to gain access to a user's account. After a limited number of attempts, that user account is locked out. The following discussion provides an example of setting the server's account lockout policy, how to identify a locked-out account, and how to reactivate the account.

The screen image shown in Figure 14-75 is for setting group policies.

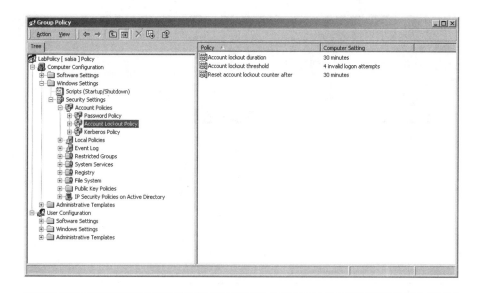

FIGURE 14-75   The account lockout policy menu.

In this example, the **Account Lockout Policy** is selected. There are three policies listed:

Account lockout duration	30 minutes
Account lockout threshold	4 invalid logon attempts
Reset account lockout counter after	30 minutes

These policies set the account lockout threshold to four invalid logon attempts. This prevents an unauthorized user from attempting repeated logons. The user's account will have a red *X* placed on it, as shown in Figure 14-76, to indicate the user is locked out. Once the number of invalid logon attempts has been exceeded, the account is locked out for 30 minutes. After 30 minutes the account is automatically reset, or the network administrator can manually reset the account by double-clicking the locked-out user's account name and clicking **Enable Account**, as shown in Figure 14-77. A prompt will appear (Figure 14-78) that indicates the user's account has been enabled.

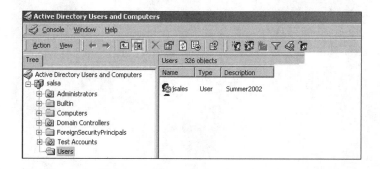

FIGURE 14-76   The red *X* indicating a locked out user's account.

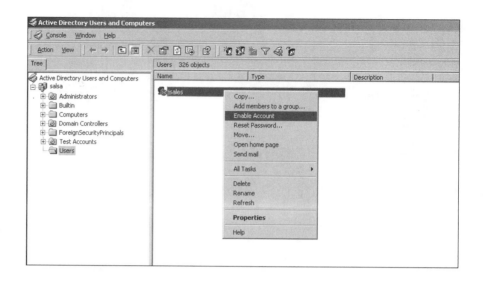

FIGURE 14-77   The menu for enabling a user's account.

FIGURE 14-78   The prompt indicating that a user's account has been enabled.

net session
Command that displays the current users connected to the server

net send
Command that allows a message to be sent over the network to a user

Another network administrator task is advising the users on the network that the server needs to be taken offline for maintenance. In Windows server, the administrator can identify the users on the network using the command *net session* at the server's command line prompt. An example of the information displayed with this command is shown in Figure 14-79. The *net session* command identifies the user's name and the IP address of each computer currently logged on to the server.

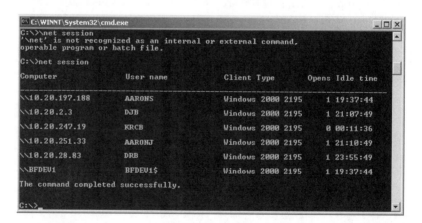

FIGURE 14-79   An example of using the *net session* command to display the users connected to the server.

Occasionally a message needs to be sent to a user or a group of users connected to the server. In Windows 2003 server, a message can be sent using the command *net send*, as shown in Figure 14-80. The user(s) will receive a prompt on their screen with the message from the server administrator. An example is provided in Figure 14-81. The structure of the *net send* command is as follows:

net send /salsa sends the message to all computers currently connected to the salsa domain

net send <*username*> sends the message only to the user currently connected to the server

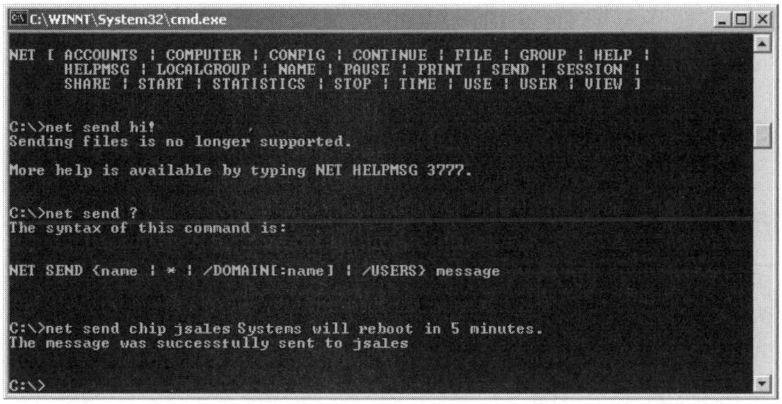

FIGURE 14-80   An example of using the *net send* command to notify the user "chip" that the system will reboot in five minutes.

FIGURE 14-81   An example of a message received by a user from the server.

This section has provided an example of setting password policies and sending messages to users on the network. These aren't the only issues a network administrator must address but are two of the more common tasks.

Summary

This chapter has presented an overview for configuring a Windows 2003/2000 server for use in a LAN. The major topics the student should understand include the following:

- The different type of network servers
- The procedures for adding computers, users, and groups to Windows 2003/2000 server
- The procedures and issues for setting network server policies
- How to verify "My Network Places" on various Windows operating systems
- How to configure the server's account lockout policy

Questions and Problems

Section 14-1

1. What is the function of a network server?
2. List five factors to be considered when configuring a LAN
3. What is a *client/server* network?
4. What is a *peer-to-peer* network?
5. Which one of the following is a disadvantage of a peer-to-peer network?
    a. No centralized administration
    b. Does not depend on other networks
    c. A central file server
    d. Requires a network administrator
6. List three advantages of the client/server network.
7. Define an *FTP* server.
8. Define a *DNS* server.
9. Define a *DHCP* server.

Section 14-2

10. Define Active Directory.
11. What is the purpose of a domain controller?
12. What is a forest?
13. What is a tree?

Section 14-3

14. What is the most efficient way for a network administrator to add a computer running Windows XP?
15. What is the purpose of a container in Windows 2008/2003?
16. A computer that has no security attached to it is called what?
17. Define *organizational unit.*
18. What is a *group* in Windows 2008/2003 server?

Section 14-4

19. What does it mean for a user to be *authenticated?*
20. How does setting a policy affect a user currently logged on to the network?
21. Discuss the issues of setting permissions and polices on a server.

Section 14-5

22. List two purposes of clicking "My Network Places" on a Windows-based PC.
23. How do "Network," "My Network Places," and "Network Neighborhood" differ?

Section 14-6

24. Why should a network administrator limit the number of logon attempts to a server?
25. What must a network administrator do if a user in the network forgets his or her password?
26. The command *net session* enables the network administrator to
    a. Determine the number of FTP sessions in progress
    b. Identify the users currently connected to the server
    c. Identify all user accounts on the server
    d. Notify the users the server is going down
27. The command for sending a notice to all users on the *chile* network is
    a. *net send all*
    b. *net send users*
    c. *net send chile users*
    d. *net send / chile*

Critical Thinking

28. Assuming you are the administrator of a LAN server, what server policies would you implement?
29. An authorized user on the network can't log on. What would you check?

15

CHAPTER

Linux Networking

CHAPTER OUTLINE

15-1   Introduction
15-2   Logging on to Linux
15-3   Linux File Structure and File
       Commands
15-4   Linux Administration Commands
15-5   Adding Applications to Linux

15-6   Linux Networking
15-7   Troubleshooting System and Net-
       work Problems with Linux
15-8   Managing the Linux System
Summary
Questions and Problems

OBJECTIVES

- Demonstrate the logon/logoff process for Linux
- Examine how to add user accounts
- Develop an understanding of the Linux file structure and related file commands
- Understand how to use key Linux administration commands

- Explore the procedures for adding applications to the Linux system
- Demonstrate the use of Linux networking commands
- Investigate how to use Linux tools to troubleshoot Linux systems and networks

KEY TERMS

root access	PID	lo
command line	kill [PID], kill -9 [PID]	ifdown, ifup
ls	su	network stop
ls -l	mount	network start
hidden files	fstab	route add default gw
ls -la	umount	openssh
bash	shutdown -h now	ncftp
more	up arrow	wu -ftpd
cat	history	daemon
cd	Konqueror	resolv.conf
pwd	telnet	dmesg
mkdir	grep	reboot
rmdir	pipe	last
rm	rpm -qf	who
mv	rpm -e	w
cp	rpm -i	nmap
chmod	httpd	chkconfig
executable (x) permission	Mozilla	netstat -ap
chown	httpd.conf	system-config- <tool-name>
chgrp	eth0, eth1, eth2, …	
man	ifconfig	ls system-config-*
ps	net mask	

15-1   INTRODUCTION

The objective of this chapter is to provide an overview of Linux networking from the point of view of an entry-level network administrator. This chapter guides the reader through many of the administrative procedures in Linux that the successful administrator must understand.

Section 15-2 discusses the process of logging on to Linux and adding a user account using a Linux user manager. The issues of setting up accounts, establishing a home directory, specifying a user ID, and creating private groups are addressed. Section 15-3 examines the Linux file structure and the basic file commands needed to successfully navigate the system. Examples of file commands are presented. The Linux administration commands, in particular the operating details of the Red Hat Package Manager, are examined in section 15-4. Key issues examined are how to kill processes, shutting down the system, and mounting external drives. The steps for installing applications such as telnet, telnet-server, SSH, and the Apache Web server are examined in section 15-5. An overview of Linux networking is presented in section 15-6. This section demonstrates the use of the commands *ifconfig*, *net mask*, *ifup*, *ifdown*, and *route* and the steps for starting and stopping network processes. Techniques for troubleshooting Linux systems are presented in section 15-7. The chapter concludes with an overview of the Red Hat Linux management tools in section 15-8. This section introduces the various GUIs that can be used to manage and configure the system.

Most of the examples presented in this chapter examine the use of Linux commands as entered from the terminal emulation mode (command line). Many of the commands presented are also available to the user via the Linux GUI (graphical user interface); however, most network administrators prefer using the command line.

The question often arises: What are the differences between Linux and Unix? The two systems have many similarities, but they are also quite different. There are many variants of Unix, and even though they are similar, many of the tasks performed on the system such as the installation of applications and devices and handling backups are unique to that version of Unix. This means that many administrators often have to specialize with a particular brand of Unix.

Linux, on the other hand, is a standardized operating system and is receiving considerable vendor support. The Linux GUI has many improvements over standard Unix systems, and in fact the Linux approach is becoming the standard. While the Linux and Unix operating systems are unique, the commands and file structure are very similar. This means that the basic commands presented in this chapter are transportable to Unix machines. It should be noted that the examples presented in this chapter are based on the Red Hat distribution. Other distributions of Linux have many similarities, but they will also have a different set of administrative tools.

15-2   LOGGING ON TO LINUX

Root Access
The user has the rights to make changes to operating and user parameters

This section demonstrates how to log in to Linux, add a new user account, and log out. This section assumes that Linux has already been installed on the user's computer and the user has root privileges. (*Note:* Many of the examples presented in this chapter require **root access**. Root access is the administrator mode for Linux—the *root user* has the rights to make changes to operating and user parameters.)

The first example demonstrates how to log in to the system. The Linux computer is first powered up, the system initializes, and the system logon screen is displayed. This screen will prompt for the username and password. If this is a new installation of Linux, log on as *root* and complete the following steps to create a user account.

A window will open for user login when Linux is running in a GUI (the default installation). This screen is where you enter the user account name and password. (If a user account has not been established, the administrator would log in as *root* to establish the user account name.) Linux will prompt for the password or the default password if the system is just being set up.

```
user account: root password: *******
```

Once logged into Linux (using the GUI interface), you will get a window similar to that shown in Figure 15-1. This is just one of the many possible Linux screens that can be displayed. The screens vary for each distribution for Linux. (*Note:* The root account should only be used for administration duties such as installing software, establishing user accounts, installing drivers, and so on. Major changes to the Linux machine system are possible with the root account access.)

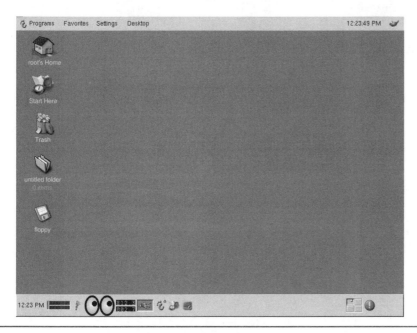

FIGURE 15-1   The main Linux GUI window.

Adding a User Account

The easiest way to add a user to the Linux operating system is from the Linux main GUI. This is accomplished by clicking **Program—System** and then selecting the **Users and Groups**, as shown in Figure 15-2. This opens the Red Hat User Manager window shown in Figure 15-3. This window is used to add and delete users as well as modify user properties. The window shows there are no current users on the system. Click the **New User** icon, and this opens the Create New User window, shown in Figure 15-4.

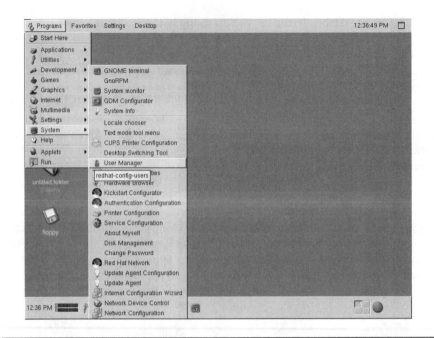

FIGURE 15-2 Selecting the Red Hat User Manager.

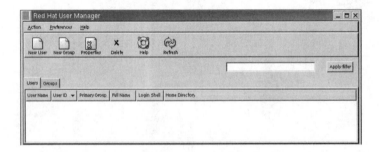

FIGURE 15-3 The Red Hat User Manager window.

FIGURE 15-4 The Create New User Window.

A new user called *usera* will be created in this step, with the username being entered on the first line (see Figure 15-4). The username must be one continuous text entry containing no spaces. The full name is next entered followed by the password. The full name is used to map the username to a person. For example, *usera* doesn't identify the name of the user on the account. The full name provides this information. The password entered is displayed with asterisks (*). This protects the privacy of the password. The next field requires that the password be reentered, to confirm that the password was correctly entered. The fifth line is for the login shell. The entry */bin/bash* is pointing to the default Linux login shell. The *login shell* is used to set up the user's initial operating environment.

The check on **Create home directory** means that a home directory called */home/usera* is being established, and this is where *usera* will be placed after logging in. The line **Create a private group for the user** is also checked. Any user being added to the Linux system can belong to an existing group or a new group can be created. In this case, a new group (*usera*) is being created. The concept of *groups* was explained in Chapter 14. The last line is used to **Specify user ID manually**. If this option is not checked, the system will select the next available user ID number. The concept of a *user ID* is explained in section 15-3. Click **OK** to complete this step and close the Create New User menu.

The user account for *usera* has now been established, as shown in the Red Hat User Manager window (Figure 15-5). Notice the entries for the User ID (500), the Primary Group (User A), the Login Shell (*/bin/bash*), and the Home Directory (*/home/usera*). The next step is to log out as *root* and log in as *usera*. You can log out by clicking **Desktop—Log Out** in the Linux GUI screen, as shown in Figure 15-6. Once logged out, the login screen for Linux is displayed, except this time, the user can log on as *usera*. The user can also log out by entering the *exit* command from the command line.

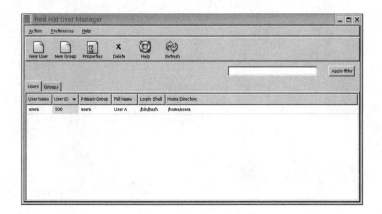

FIGURE 15-5   The addition of the *usera* account displayed by the Red Hat User Manager.

Network and system administrators typically use the **command line** for entering most Linux commands. The command line is a text entry level for commands and is accessed from the main GUI window by clicking the **Terminal emulation program** icon shown in Figure 15-7. This will place you in the Linux command line, as shown in Figure 15-8. Notice the prompt is **[usera@localhost usera]**. This indicates that we are in *usera*'s home directory. The hostname of the Linux machine is *localhost*.

Command Line
A text entry level for commands

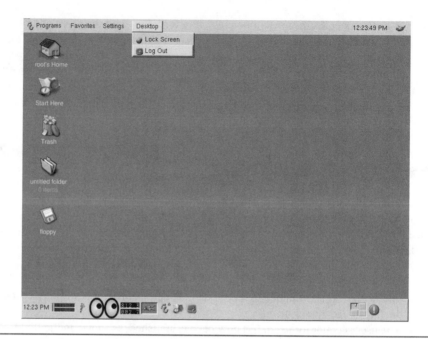

FIGURE 15-6   Selecting the logout option for Linux.

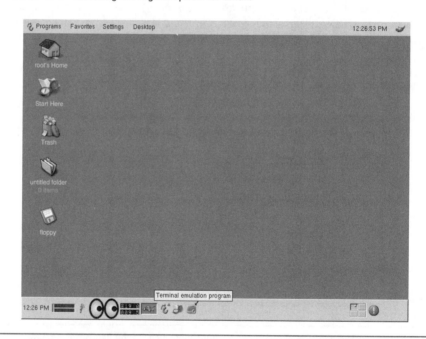

FIGURE 15-7   Selecting the Terminal emulation program from the Linux GUI.

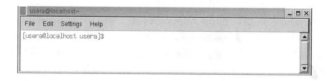

FIGURE 15-8   The Linux command line showing the prompt usera@localhost *usera*.

15-3   LINUX FILE STRUCTURE AND FILE COMMANDS

The objective of this section is for the reader to learn both the Linux file structure and how to use Linux commands to view files, file contents, and directory contents. The following Linux commands are presented in this section:

Listing Files: *ls*, *ls -l*, *ls -la*
Displaying File Contents: *more*, *cat*
Directory Operations: *cd*, *pwd*, *mkdir*, *rmdir*
File Operations: *rm*, *mv*, *cp*
Permissions and Ownership: *chmod*, *chown*, *chgrp*

The file structure in Linux is fairly complex, especially for users who are used to a Windows graphical user interface. There will be some inclination for the new Linux user to try to use the Linux GUI for all command operations. You should avoid doing this because not all Linux GUIs are the same, and the command line operations are much faster and more flexible. This section demonstrates how to successfully navigate the Linux file structure and to use the commands listed. (*Note:* Readers who wish to learn Linux in more depth should see http://www.linux.org/docs.)

Listing Files

The ls Command   The first command examined is *ls*. This command is used to display the basic files in the directory and is executed from the command line, as shown in Figure 15-9. In this example, the user is *root*, and the files examined are located in *root*'s home directory.

ls
List the basic files in the directory

FIGURE 15-9   The results of inputting the *ls* command from the command line.

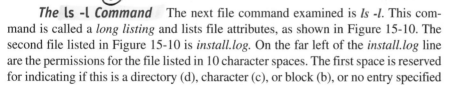

The ls -l Command   The next file command examined is *ls -l*. This command is called a *long listing* and lists file attributes, as shown in Figure 15-10. The second file listed in Figure 15-10 is *install.log*. On the far left of the *install.log* line are the permissions for the file listed in 10 character spaces. The first space is reserved for indicating if this is a directory (d), character (c), or block (b), or no entry specified ( ). In this case, no entry is specified for the *install.log* file ( ).

ls -l
Lists file attributes

FIGURE 15-10　The results of inputting the *ls -l* command.

The remaining nine character positions define three groups: the owner, the group, and everybody. Each group has three attribute settings—read, write, and executable. The attributes are turned on by setting the place value to "1." The concept of *file attributes* is further explained under the **chmod** command later in this section. The attributes for the *install.log* file shown in Figure 15-10 are listed in Table 15-1. A summary of the file attributes is provided in Table 15-2.

TABLE 15-1　File Attributes for the install.log File (starting from the left)

first character	(-)	means no attribute specified
characters 2–4	owner (rw-)	the owner has read/write privileges
charcters 5–7	group (r--)	the group has read privileges only
characters 8–10	Everyone else (r--)	everyone has read privileges only
owner of the file is *root*		
the group is *root*		
file size = 15,200 bytes		
file created July 10, 2002		

TABLE 15-2　Summary of the Attribute Abbreviations Used in the File Permissions Block

d	directory		c	Character
b	block		r	Read
w	write		x	Executable
-	not defined ⑦			

Hidden Files
Files that start with a period and that can only be viewed with the **ls -la** or **ls -al** command

ls -la
Allows you to see hidden files in addition to the file attributes

Bash
Bourne again shell

The **ls -la** *Command*　The long listing command *ls -l* can be modified to allow **hidden files** to be viewed by entering *ls -la*. The *a* extension instructs Linux to display all hidden files. Hidden files start with a period, such as . *(home directory)* and . *(parent directory)* and *.bash_history* and *.bash_logout*. The result of entering the *ls-la* command is provided in Figure 15-11. The *ls -la* command can also be entered as *ls -al*. The ordering of the extension doesn't matter. (*Note:* The *bash* files are applied to the shell that defines the environment the user works under. **Bash** stands for *Bourne again shell.*)

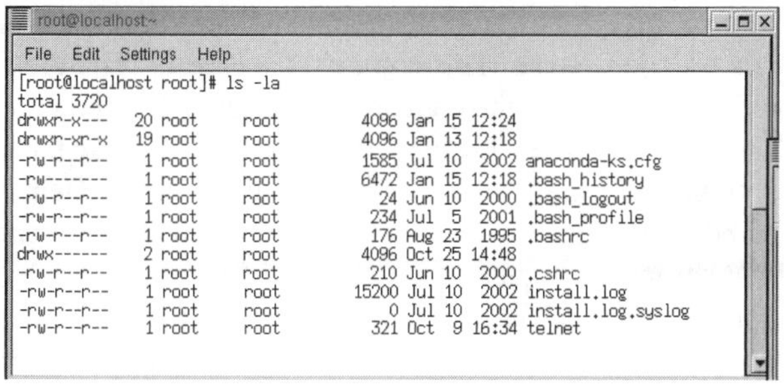

FIGURE 15-11 The results of entering the *ls -la* command.

Displaying File Contents

The more Command The next file command demonstrated is *more*. This command is used in Linux to display the contents of a text file at a pace the user controls using the spacebar. An example of using the *more* command is provided in Figure 15-12. This example uses the command to display the contents of the *install.log* file. If the information in the file exceeds one screen, a prompt is displayed indicating how much of the file contents have been displayed. In this example (Figure 15-12) 5 percent of the file contents has been displayed. Pressing the spacebar will display the next page of contents of the *install.log* file contents, and the prompt at the bottom of the screen will display the new percentage that has been viewed. Press the spacebar to keep displaying the file contents until they have all been displayed or press **Control C** to exit the *more* command.

more
Command used in Linux to display the contents of a text file

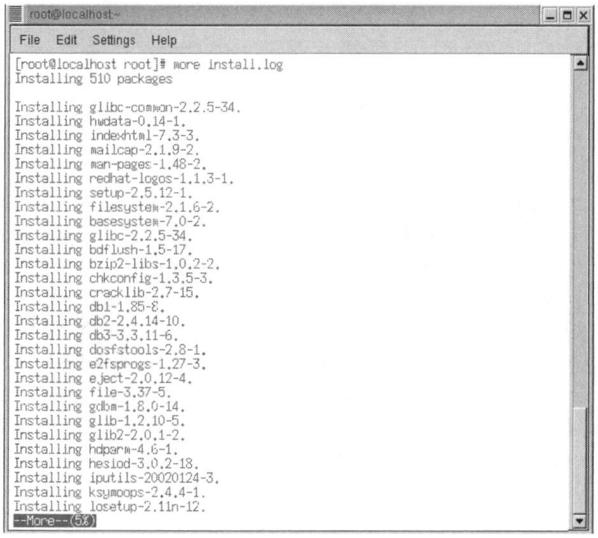

FIGURE 15-12 An example of using the *more* command.

cat **9.B**

Command used to print the file text to the screen

The cat *Command* The next file command used to display file contents is *cat*, which stands for concatenate. This command is used to print the file text to the screen and works fine as long as the contents of the file will fit on one screen. If the file is larger than one screen, then the text will quickly scroll by. In the case of a large file, it is probably best to use the *more* command so that the contents of each page can be viewed. The advantage of *cat* is that it can be tied to other programs. This will be demonstrated later in the chapter.

An example of using the *cat* command is provided in Figure 15-13. In this example, *cat* is being used to view the contents of the password file in the */etc* directory.

The command *cat /etc/passwd* is being used, as shown in Figure 15-13. Notice that the command prompt is displayed at both the top and the bottom of the screen, indicating that the entire contents of the password file are displayed.

FIGURE 15-13 An example of using the *cat* command.

The password file contains the accounts of users and processes that can log on to the Linux operating system. The contents of each entry in the password file are divided into seven fields, and each file is divided by a colon (:). For example, the first line displayed is *root:x:0:0:root:/root:/bin/bash*. The first field specifies that the account is *root*. The root user can delete, modify, or do anything with the file. This entry is followed by an *x*. The *x* (in Unix) is where the encrypted password would be. In Linux, the encrypted passwords have been moved for security purposes to a file called *shadow*. During installation the option to shadow passwords is normally presented. If the person doing the installation decides not to shadow passwords, then the *passwd* file will contain the passwords. Some versions of Linux will also let you store the password in an unencrypted format. After *x* comes a colon followed by a zero. The zero is the user ID. This is a unique ID assigned to each account. This identifier is used throughout the Linux operating system to identify users and their files. Another zero follows the user ID. This is the group ID. Notice at the very bottom of Figure 15-13 that the entry in the field for the *usera* user ID is *500*. Refer back to Figure 15-5 to see where this ID was assigned. The *root* account belongs to the zero ID. Any user that belongs to the zero group belongs to the same group as *root*. After the second zero is *:root*. This *root* is the account description for the account. After this field is *:/root,* which is the home directory for the account. The user is placed into this account when logged on to the system. The last field is *:/bin/bash*. This defines the executable program that is used during user logon. In this case, **bash** is the command shell that will run.

Directory Operations

The* cd *Command The command to change directories in Linux is *cd*. The structure for the **cd** command is ***cd [destination-directory]***. The command **cd** was used to change to the root directory */* as shown in Figure 15-14. At that point, the command **ls -l** was entered. This produces the results shown in Figure 15-14. This provides a long listing of the components of the root directory. The following are the directories normally encountered in the Linux file system that will always be there:

cd
Command for changing directories

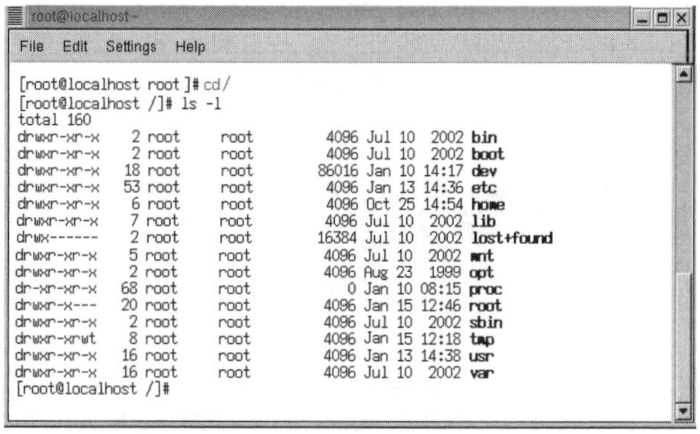

FIGURE 15-14   The long listing of the components in the root directory.

- ***/bin*:** This contains all of the binary programs and executables.
- ***/boot*:** This is where the Linux kernel resides. A *kernel* is the actual operating system image that boots up when the computer is turned on. If the kernel is not there, Linux does not boot.
- ***/dev*:** This is where the device files reside. Examples of device files are drivers for the monitor, keyboard, modem, and hard drive.
- ***/etc*:** This is where Linux holds the majority of its configuration files. For example, a program running under Linux will have its configuration files located in */etc*.
- ***/home*:** This is the directory where all user directories are located. Home directories for new user accounts are placed in this directory.
- ***/lib*:** The location for libraries that Linux uses, such as static and shared libraries.
- ***/lost+found*:** This directory is used to place files that have lost their identity, possibly due to hard drive errors.
- ***/mnt*:** The location where mounted directories are located. For example, an external drive will be mounted through this directory. *Mount* means that a file system has been made available to the user.

- **/proc:** The status of the operating system is kept in this directory—for memory, hard drive, device drivers, memory usage, uptime (how long the computer has been running), and user IDs.
- **/root:** This is the root user ID home directory and is where the root user is placed at login.
- **/sbin:** This is the system binary directory, the location where Linux keeps its system and executable program files.
- **/tmp:** This directory is used as a temporary holding area for applications. This directory is available to all users logged onto the machine. The */tmp* directory gets cleared out when the machine boots up.
- **/usr:** This is the location for the user files that are related to the user programs.
- **/var:** The files in this directory change over time. For example, system log files and mail folders appear here. From time to time, the system administrator will delete files in */var* to clean up the drive.

pwd
Command to print the working (current) directory

(14) *The* **pwd** *Command*   The next command examined is *pwd* (print working directory). The Linux directory path is complicated, and this command is available for the user to find where he or she is currently located. This is very useful when files are being moved or deleted. The user uses the *pwd* command to verify the current working directory. An example is shown in Figure 15-15.

FIGURE 15-15   An example of the text displayed when entering the *pwd* command.

In this example, *pwd* returns */home/usera/*, indicating we are in *usera*'s directory. The following information is returned by the *pwd* command:

usera	account name
@localhost	the name of the Linux machine
usera	the name of the current directory

The second part of Figure 15-15 demonstrates that the name of the current directory changes if the directory changes. The third line shows that the command *cd tmp* (change directory tmp) is used to change the working directory to *tmp*. The prompt now displays **[usera@localhost tmp]**, indicating that the current directory is *tmp*.

mkdir
Command to make a directory

rmdir
Command to remove a directory

(15) *The* **mkdir** *and* **rmdir** *Commands*   This part demonstrates the Linux command for creating or making a directory. The command is *mkdir*, for *make directory*. The structure for the command is *mkdir [directory-name]*. In this example (shown in Figure 15-16), *mkdir files* is used to create a directory called *files*. The command *ls* is used to display the *usera* home directory contents and *files* is listed. The long listing of the directory using the *ls -la* command shows that *files* is indeed a directory, indicated by a *d* in the leftmost field of the attributes. The command to remove a directory is *rmdir*. The structure for the command is *rmdir [directory-name]*. This command requires that the directory being removed is empty.

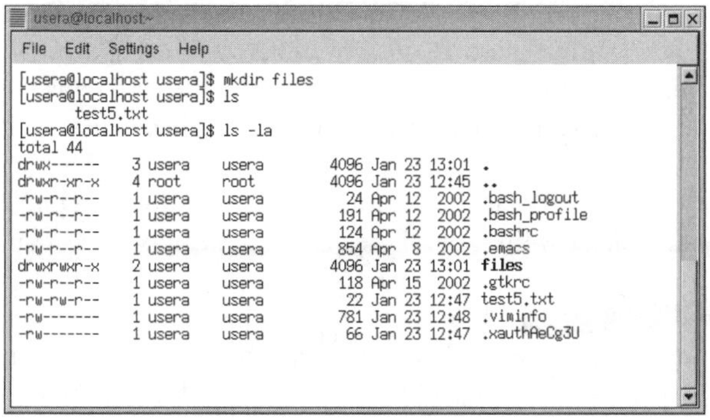

```
usera@localhost~
File  Edit  Settings  Help
[usera@localhost usera]$ mkdir files
[usera@localhost usera]$ ls
      test5.txt
[usera@localhost usera]$ ls -la
total 44
drwx------    3 usera    usera        4096 Jan 23 13:01 .
drwxr-xr-x    4 root     root         4096 Jan 23 12:45 ..
-rw-r--r--    1 usera    usera          24 Apr 12  2002 .bash_logout
-rw-r--r--    1 usera    usera         191 Apr 12  2002 .bash_profile
-rw-r--r--    1 usera    usera         124 Apr 12  2002 .bashrc
-rw-r--r--    1 usera    usera         854 Apr  8  2002 .emacs
drwxrwxr-x    2 usera    usera        4096 Jan 23 13:01 files
-rw-r--r--    1 usera    usera         118 Apr 15  2002 .gtkrc
-rw-rw-r--    1 usera    usera          22 Jan 23 12:47 test5.txt
-rw-------    1 usera    usera         781 Jan 23 12:48 .viminfo
-rw-------    1 usera    usera          66 Jan 23 12:47 .xauthAeCg3U
```

FIGURE 15-16 An example of creating a directory using the *mkdir* command.

File Operations

The* rm *Command The purpose of a basic operating system is to create, modify, and delete files. The next example shows how to delete files in Linux. The command to delete a file is *rm*, short for *remove*. The command structure is ***rm [filename]***. The command ***ls -al*** has been entered to display a long listing of files and hidden files in the directory (Figure 15-17).

rm
Command to delete a file

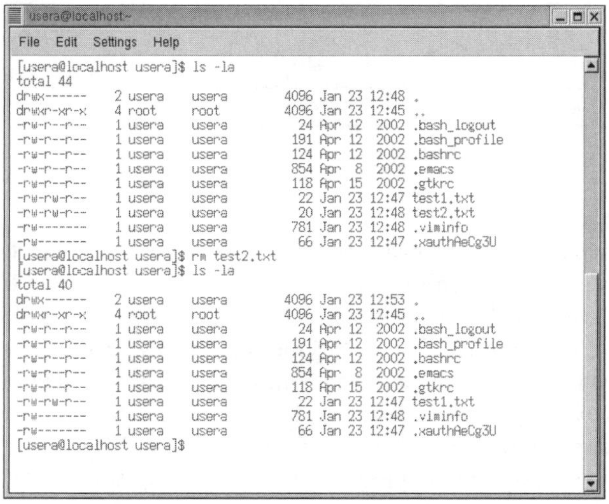

```
usera@localhost~
File  Edit  Settings  Help
[usera@localhost usera]$ ls -la
total 44
drwx------    2 usera    usera        4096 Jan 23 12:48 .
drwxr-xr-x    4 root     root         4096 Jan 23 12:45 ..
-rw-r--r--    1 usera    usera          24 Apr 12  2002 .bash_logout
-rw-r--r--    1 usera    usera         191 Apr 12  2002 .bash_profile
-rw-r--r--    1 usera    usera         124 Apr 12  2002 .bashrc
-rw-r--r--    1 usera    usera         854 Apr  8  2002 .emacs
-rw-r--r--    1 usera    usera         118 Apr 15  2002 .gtkrc
-rw-rw-r--    1 usera    usera          22 Jan 23 12:47 test1.txt
-rw-rw-r--    1 usera    usera          20 Jan 23 12:48 test2.txt
-rw-------    1 usera    usera         781 Jan 23 12:48 .viminfo
-rw-------    1 usera    usera          66 Jan 23 12:47 .xauthAeCg3U
[usera@localhost usera]$ rm test2.txt
[usera@localhost usera]$ ls -la
total 40
drwx------    2 usera    usera        4096 Jan 23 12:53 .
drwxr-xr-x    4 root     root         4096 Jan 23 12:45 ..
-rw-r--r--    1 usera    usera          24 Apr 12  2002 .bash_logout
-rw-r--r--    1 usera    usera         191 Apr 12  2002 .bash_profile
-rw-r--r--    1 usera    usera         124 Apr 12  2002 .bashrc
-rw-r--r--    1 usera    usera         854 Apr  8  2002 .emacs
-rw-r--r--    1 usera    usera         118 Apr 15  2002 .gtkrc
-rw-rw-r--    1 usera    usera          22 Jan 23 12:47 test1.txt
-rw-------    1 usera    usera         781 Jan 23 12:48 .viminfo
-rw-------    1 usera    usera          66 Jan 23 12:47 .xauthAeCg3U
[usera@localhost usera]$
```

FIGURE 15-17 Using the *rm* command to remove a file in Linux.

Notice that the directory contains two text files called *test1.txt* and *test2.txt*. The attributes for these files are listed on the left. These are read/write (rw) for the user, read/write (rw) for the group, and read only (r) for others. This means that any user in the group usera can also change the *usera* file. The owner of the file is *usera,* and the group is also *usera.* The next number is the file size, followed by the date and time the file was created and, lastly, the file name.

In this example, the file *test2.txt* will be removed using the command ***rm test2.txt***. This is shown in Figure 15-17. The *test2.txt* file is shown in the top of the screen. The command ***rm test2.txt*** is entered, and the files are redisplayed using ***ls -la***, and the *text2.txt* file is no longer listed. The file has been deleted. It is important to note that in the Linux file system there is *not* an undo option. This means that once a file is deleted, it is gone. What about a trash bin? Linux does not provide a trash bin to temporarily hold deleted files, but there are certain Linux GUIs that do apply this concept.

The mv Command   The next example demonstrates how to move a file in Linux. The command to move a file is *mv,* short for *move.* The ***mv*** command serves two purposes. It is used to rename a file, and it is used to move the file to a different directory. The command structure is ***mv [filename] [new-filename]***.

In this example, the *mv* command is used to rename the file *text1.txt* to *text5.txt.* The steps for doing this are shown in Figure 15-18. In this example, the ***cat*** command is used to display the contents of the *test1.txt* file. This is being done so that the contents of the files can be compared after the move. The ***mv*** command is next used to rename *text1.txt* to *test5.txt.* The contents of the *test5.txt* file are displayed using the ***cat*** command, showing that the contents of *test1.txt* and *test5.txt* are the same and only the filename has changed.

mv
Command for moving or renaming a file

FIGURE 15-18   An example of using the *mv* command to rename a file.

The next step is to show that files can be moved from one directory to another using the ***mv*** command. In this case, the *test5.txt* file will be moved from the *usera* directory to the *usera/files* subdirectory. The command for doing this is ***mv test5.txt files/,*** as shown in Figure 15-19. This specifies that the *test5.txt* file is to be moved to the *files* directory using the directory path *files/.* A logical next step is to verify that the file was moved to the *files* directory. The command ***cd files*** is entered, changing the working directory to *files,* as shown in Figure 15-19. The prompt now displays [usera@localhost files]. The command ***pwd*** (print working directory) also shows that the working directory is now */home/usera/files.* The information for the prompt and for print working directory is slightly different, but both indicate that the working directory is *files.* The ***ls*** command shows that the *test5.txt* file has indeed been moved to the *files* directory. The long listing ***ls -la*** shows that the file properties have not changed. The owner of the file and group assignment have not changed.

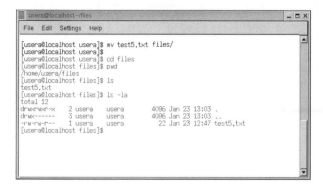

FIGURE 15-19 An example of moving a file using the *mv* command.

The cp Command The command to copy files in Linux is *cp.* The structure of the command is ***cp [source filename] [destination filename].*** In this example, a file called *test5.txt* will be copied to a new file called *test6.txt.* The *ls* command is first used to display the files in the *usera@localhost* files directory as shown in Figure 15-20. The only file listed is *test5.txt.* The *cp* command is next used to copy the file to *test6.txt,* as shown in Figure 15-20. The *ls* command is used again to display the directory contents, and both files *test5.txt* and *test6.txt* are now displayed. The file was successfully copied.

cp
Command to copy files

FIGURE 15-20 An example of using the *cp* command.

Permissions and Ownership

The chmod Command The *chmod* command is used in Linux to change permissions on files and directories. The structure of the command is ***chmod [permissions setting] [filename].*** For example, this command lets you specify if the file is readable (r), writable (w), or executable (x). A long list of the files in the *usera* account (Figure 15-21) shows that the file *test5.txt* has *rw* in the attributes in the owner's space. File *test6.txt* shows that the user has read (r)/write (w) privileges, the group has read (r)/write (w) privileges, and the outside world has read (r) privileges (-rw-rw-r--).

chmod
Command used in Linux to change permissions on files and directories

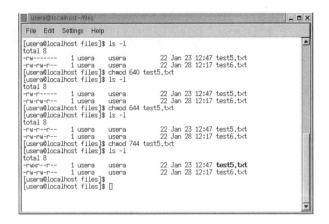

FIGURE 15-21   Using the *chmod* command to set file permissions.

Chmod uses a value to turn a privilege on or off. The value is specified for the owner, the group, and others. Table 15-3 shows how the place values are established for the owner, group, and outside user. For example, a value of 4 0 0 turns on bit position 2, the read attribute for the owner (-r). A value of 6 0 0 turns on bit positions 2 and 3, read and write for the owner (-rw) and a value of 7 0 0 turns on bits 2, 3, and 4, setting read, write, and executable permissions for the owner (-rwx). A value of 6 4 0 turns on bits 2, 3, and 5, setting read and write permissions for the owner and read permission for the group (-rw -r- ---).

TABLE 15-3   Attribute Settings for File Permissions

Bit position	1	2	3	4	5	6	7	8	9	10
	directory	owner			group			others		
Bit Values		4	2	1	4	2	1	4	2	1
	*	r	w	x	r	w	X	r	w	x

The directory bit can display the following attributes:
d—directory
b—block
c—character
—no entry specified

Another way to determine the permission settings for each permission field (owner, group, others) is to assign the following values to each permission:

read—4

write—2

executable—1

To turn on the read permission for the owner simply requires that a four (4) be placed in the first permission field. For example, *chmod 4 0 0 [filename]* sets read only permissions for the owner.

Turning on more than one permission requires that the sum of the permission values be entered. For example, turning on read/write privileges for the owner requires entering a six (6) in the proper permission field. The value is determined as follows:

read	4
write	2
executable	0
	6

The zero is assigned to the executable because this permission is not desired. The command to enable read/write privileges for the owner is **chmod 6 0 0 [filename]**.

The same steps can be applied to assigning permissions to all fields. For example, assume that the following permissions are specified:

owner	read, write, executable
group	read, executable
everyone	read, executable

The numeric entry for each permission field in the **chmod** command can be determined as follows:

	owner	group	others
read	4	4	4
write	2	0	0
executable	1	1	1
	7	5	5

Therefore, the command **chmod 7 5 5 [filename]** is used to set the permissions for the owner, group, and others.

In the example shown in Figure 15-21, read permission is to be given to the group for the *test5.txt* file. The command **chmod 640 test5.txt** is entered. The 6 sets the read/write privilege for the owner, the 4 sets the permission to read for the group, and the 0 clears any attributes for others. The **ls** command is next used to provide a long listing of the files in the *usera* account. The attributes for the *test5.txt* file have changed to (r w - r - - - - -), indicating that group now has read privileges.

In the next step, the world will be given the privilege to read the *test5.txt* file. The command **chmod 644 test5.txt** is entered. Once again, the 6 sets the read/write privilege for the owner, the 4 sets the permission to read for the group, and the next 4 sets the permission for others to read the file. The attributes for the *test5.txt* file have now changed to (r w - r - - r - -), indicating that outside users have read privileges.

The last example using **chmod** shows how to set the **executable (x) permission** for a file. An executable permission allows the program or script to run. The command **chmod 744 test5.txt** is entered. This instruction gives the owner read/write and executable privileges on the file and also grants the group and everyone else read permission. The **ls** command is used to display a long listing. The attributes for the file *test5.txt* now show (r w x r - - r - -). This confirms that the permissions have been properly set. The result is shown in Figure 15-21.

Executable (x) Permission
Allows the program or script to run

The executable setting is used by Linux to distinguish files that can be executed (run) on the system. Files that do not have an *x* attribute are considered to be data files, libraries, and so on. The *x* is also used by Linux when the system searches for executable files on the hard drive.

chown
Command used in Linux to change ownership of a file

The* chown *Command The next Linux command examined is *chown*, which is used to change the ownership of the file. The structure of the command is ***chown [new owner] [filename].*** This command can only be applied to files the user owns. The exception to this is *root* (the superuser), who can change permissions on any files. In this example, the ownership of the *test5.txt* file is going to be changed to a user called *network*. (*Note:* The new owner will be *network*, a user on this same Linux machine. In fact, changing ownership can only be done using existing users.) The long list of *usera's* files directory shows two files, *test5.txt* and *test6.txt* (Figure 15-22). The owner of *test5.txt* is *usera.* The objective of this exercise is to change ownership of the *test5.txt* file to *network.* The command ***chown network text5.txt*** is entered. A long list of the directory now shows that the ownership of *test5.txt* now resides with *network.* The steps for changing file ownership are shown in Figure 15-22.

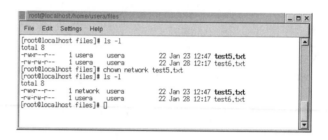

FIGURE 15-22   An example of using the *chown* command to change file ownership.

The file is still in *usera*'s directory, but the ownership has changed to *network.* The group attributes (permissions) will now have to be set by *network* if *usera* is to have permission to read, write, or execute this file, even though *usera* was the past owner and the file is in *usera*'s space. In fact, if *usera* tries to change permission on this file (*test5.txt*), Linux will prompt *usera* with the message *changing permissions of 'test5.txt': Operation not permitted*

This is shown in Figure 15-23.

FIGURE 15-23   The prompt displayed when an unauthorized user attempts to change file permissions.

chgrp
Command used in Linux to change group ownership of a file

The* chgrp *Command The Linux command *chgrp* is used to change group ownership of files. The structure of the command is ***chgrp [new group] [filename].*** This example demonstrates how to change the group ownership of a file. In this example, the group for file *test5.txt* will be changed. The steps for this are shown in Figure 15-24. A long listing of the *usera* files directory shows that the group associated with *test5.txt* is *usera.* The command ***chgrp mail test5.txt*** is next used to change group ownership of the file to *mail.* The long listing command is used again to list the file in the *usera* files directory. The screen shows that the owner is *network* and the group ownership of *test5.txt* has changed from *usera* to *mail*. This means that any members of the group *mail* now have read (r -) privileges.

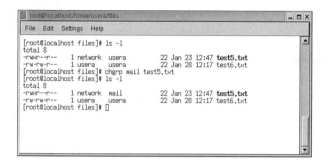

FIGURE 15-24   An example of changing the group ownership of a file.

15-4   LINUX ADMINISTRATION COMMANDS

The objective of this section is for the reader to gain an understanding of the key Linux administration commands. The commands presented focus on those most often used by the network administrator:

> *man*: Used to display the online text manual
>
> *ps*: Used to examine processes running on the machine
>
> *su*: Used to become another user on the system
>
> *mount*: Used in Linux to mount an external drive
>
> *shutdown*: Used to shut the Linux system down gracefully

This section concludes with an overview of some basic Linux shortcuts that will help simplify the administrator's job.

The *man* (manual) Command

The first command examined is *man*, used to display the online text manual for Linux. Manual pages for most Linux commands and features are available by simply entering the command *man* followed by the name of the option. For example, if the user wants to know how to use the *ps* command, entering *man ps* (Figure 15-25) will display the contents of the manual lists for *ps* (Figure 15-26).

The manual pages provide extensive information about how to invoke the command, what options are available, what the fields mean that are displayed by the command—basically everything the user needs to know about the *ps* command.

There are many *man* pages on the Linux system, for utility programs, programming files, networking commands, and others. Adding the *-k* extension to the *man* command (for example, *man -k network*) instructs Linux to list all of the *man* pages that mention the specified topic. An example is provided (Figure 15-27) that demonstrates how to use the *man -k* command to view all network-related *man* pages.

man
Command used to display the online text manual for Linux

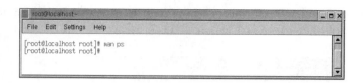

FIGURE 15-25   An example of using the *man* command.

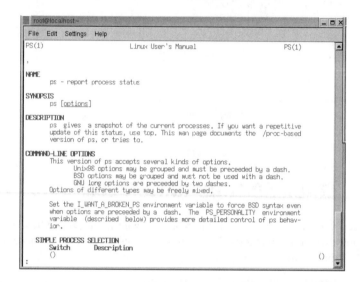

FIGURE 15-26   The manual pages displayed by entering the command *man ps*.

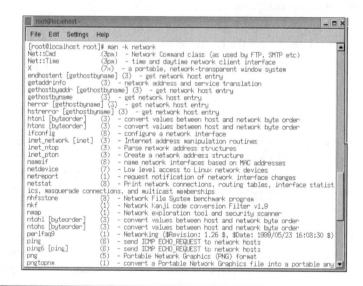

FIGURE 15-27   Using the *man* command to display all pages related to *network*.

The *ps* (processes) Command

The *ps* command lists the processes (or programs) running on the machine. The command ***ps ux*** lists all of the processes running, as shown in Figure 15-28. Each of the fields returned by the *ps* command is listed from left to right in Table 15-4.

ps
Command used to list processes running on the machine

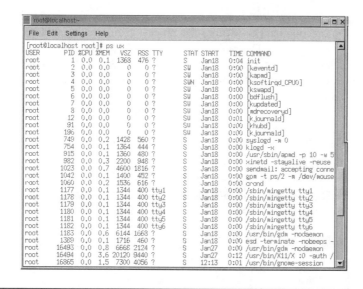

FIGURE 15-28 An example of using the *ps* command to list the processes currently running on a Linux machine.

TABLE 15-4 Fields Returned by Inputting the ps Command

User	Identifies the owner of the process.
PID	Identifies the process ID, which is a number assigned to a process when it starts. For example, if PID1, then this is the first process started on the machine.
%CPU	Shows the % utilization of the CPU for that process.
%MEM	Specifies the % of memory being used by that process.
VSZ	The virtual size of the program.
RSS	Shows how much of the program (resident set size) is in memory.
TTY	Indicates if the process is interfacing with a terminal or a serial port.
STAT	The STAT (state field) indicates the status of the process: r—running z—zombie s—sleeping t—stopped
START	Indicates when the process started. This could list a time of minutes, hours, and/or days. It is not uncommon to have a process running for an extended period on Linux.
Time	Indicates the time the process has actually spent running.
Command	Lists the actual command that was invoked to start the process.

PID
Process ID

The reason to examine running processes is to determine what processes are using the most machine resources. If a machine is running slowly, the *ps* command can be used to determine what process is using the majority of the CPU time. In some cases, it becomes necessary to *terminate* (shut down) a process to free up the machine's resources. The following are steps that should be followed to shut down a process.

1. Use the *ps* command to identify the process using the computer's resources (CPU and memory). Determine the PID for the process. For example, it has been determined that a process with a PID of 1023 must be shut down.
2. The network administrator should next contact the user of the process and inform him or her to shut down (kill) the process.

kill [PID], kill -9 [PID]
Commands used to kill a process

3. The command for killing the process is *kill [PID]*. An example is shown in Figure 15-29 for killing the process 1023. This command notifies the process to terminate. The process then begins closing files and libraries and shuts down immediately. Some processes are difficult to kill, so the command *kill -9 [PID]* can be used. An example is shown in Figure 15-29. This is the last-resort step for killing a process. The *kill -9* command is somewhat messy in that the process is stopped without properly closing any open files, libraries, and so on.

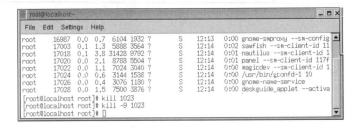

FIGURE 15-29   An example of using the *kill* and *kill -9* commands.

The *su* (substitute user) Command

su
Command used to become another user on the system

The *su* (substitute user) command is used to become another user on the system. This command assumes that the user has a valid account on the system and the password is known. The command structure is *su [username]*. An example of using this command is provided in Figure 15-30. In this example, *root* is using the *su* command to log in as *usera*. This command is quite useful for administration. The administrator can be logged in as *root* to make some changes to the system that affect *usera,* such as checking ftp options or Web access. The administrator can then use the *su* command to become *usera* and check to see if the changes worked. In fact, root user can use the su command and become any user on the system without knowing that user's password. Any authorized user can use the *su* command as long as another valid user account and password are known.

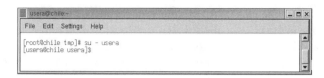

FIGURE 15-30   An example of using the *su* command to become another user.

The *mount* Command

The next command examined is *mount*, which is used to join an external file system such as that found on a CDROM or floppy, to the Linux file system to allow the files to be accessed. The external drives (for example, USB and CD-ROM) don't mount automatically unless the system has been previously configured to mount these drives. This means that a directory has to be provided to the Linux file system for the external device to mount to.

Linux lists files in the *fstab* file (*/etc* directory) that contain the arguments used when the mount command for a specific drive is requested. Figure 15-31 shows a listing of the *fstab* file in the */etc* directory.

mount
Command used to access external drives

fstab
The file that contains the arguments used when the mount command for a drive has been requested

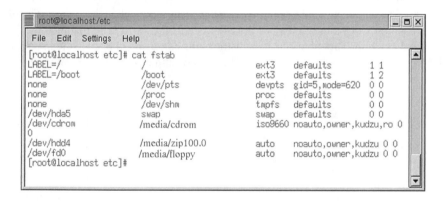

FIGURE 15-31   Listing of contents for the *fstab* file.

This is a text file, and each line refers to a file system. The first field refers to / (the root file system). The second field is the mount location (/). In this case / will mount under /. The third field is for the file system type. The entry *ext3* refers to the Linux files system. This field will change depending on the mount. For example, a Windows file might be listed as *MSDOS*. The fourth field instructs Linux to use the default settings for file system. The last two fields show a *1 1*. The first *1* is the instruction to check the integrity of the file system at boot (1 = on 0 = off). The last field refers to the Linux backup utilities (1 = backup, 0 = don't back up) (a ***man*** on *fstab* or *mount* will provide more details about this field).

This file is created when the Linux system is installed and is used if a new hard drive is added to the system. The file for the CD-ROM is shown in Figure 15-31. The first field is */dev/cdrom*. The second field, */media/cdrom,* is the mount point. (*Note:* The mount point has changed from /mnt/ for older releases of Linux to /media/.)

When a CD is placed in the CD-ROM, Linux mounts the CD and the files on the CD will be available in the */media/cdrom* directory. The third field is the file system type. The field shows that this is an ISO9660 disc, the common file format for a CD-ROM. The fourth field indicates *noauto* indicating that this drive is not to be automatically mounted. The fifth field also indicates that the owner has privileges. This means that if a regular user places a CD in the drive, the owner will inherit the CDROM files. The entry *kudzu* is a utility that Linux uses to detect new hardware on the machine. The fifth field indicates this is a read only (ro) device. The last two fields show *0 0,* which means don't check the file system at boot time and don't back it up. Another line in the *fstab* file is for the ZIP drive. The first field of this listing shows */dev/hdd4.* This is for the ZIP drive. This drive will mount in the directory */mediat/zip100.0.* The next field shows *auto,* indicating the Linux system will try to automatically detect what type of file system is being mounted. Most of the time this is a Windows-based file system. The rest of the field parameters are the same as for the CD-ROM except there isn't a *ro* declaration. Leaving off the *ro* declaration allows the contents of the ZIP files to be changed.

The **mount** command enables a drive, file, and so on, to be mounted (refer to the **man** page for the mount options). There are two ways to mount a drive. In this case, the command will be issued to mount the computer's CD-ROM.

Newly mounted files will overlay existing files in the *mount* directory. However, this is a virtual mount. No files are actually being written onto the *mount* file directory. The command **df -kh** will display the devices mounted on the system. The **df** command provides a breakdown of the file systems that have been mounted on the operating system. The **-kh** extensions instructs the command to display the listing in k—kilobytes and h—human readable form. An example of using this command is provided in Figure 15-32.

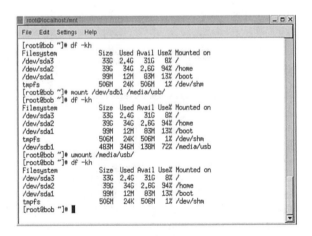

FIGURE 15-32 An example of using the *mount* and *umount* commands to mount and umount a USB drive.

The command **mount /dev/sdb1 media/usb** is next used to mount the USB drive. Notice that the USB drive is called *sdb1.* The **df -kh** command can be used to verify the drive has been mounted. The listing now shows that the USB drive has been mounted.

It is important to understand that a drive must be unmounted before the media can be removed. The USB drive can be unmounted by using the command *umount* */media/usb* as shown in Figure 15-32. It is important to note that you cannot unmount a device that has open files or directories. Entering the *df -kh* command now shows that the USB drive is no longer mounted. At this point, the USB drive can be removed.

umount
Command used to unmount a drive

The *shutdown* Command

The *shutdown* command is used to shut the Linux system down gracefully. This means that all open files and libraries are closed before the system turns off. The command in Linux to gracefully shut the system down is *shutdown -h now*. This command shuts down the operating system effective immediately. An example of using this command is provided in Figure 15-33.

shutdown -h now
Command used to gracefully shut down Linux

FIGURE 15-33   An example of using the *shutdown -h now* command.

Linux Tips

Many of the tasks performed by the network or system administrator require repeated used of the same commands or require that lengthy file names be entered. This section presents some shortcuts available in Linux that help speed up the administrator's job. The first shortcut examined is the **up arrow**. The up arrow can be used to display the previous command entered on the command line in Linux. Pressing the up arrow again displays the next previous command. This is a very useful way to recall the history of commands entered on the command line. When you find the command that you need, simply press **Enter** to execute the command. Repeatedly pressing the up arrow will allow you to find a command previously executed. The *history* command can be used to display the commands stored in the Linux system buffer. The history buffer can store thousands of entered commands. (*Note:* The history buffer can also be used to determine if someone has been using your computer. Simply entering the *history* command will display all commands executed on the system. You will be able to identify the commands that you did not execute.)

Up Arrow
Used to display the previously entered commands stored in the Linux history buffer

history
Command that displays the commands entered on the command line in Linux

Another shortcut is the Tab key. This can be used to complete entries on the command line. For example, *cd ho[tab]* displays *cd home*. Linux searches for options that begin with *ho* to complete the entry. This is very useful when long or complicated entries are used. In the case where there are multiple entries that satisfy the entry, the Tab key can be used to step through the options. Entering *f [tab]* will generate multiple possibilities. Pressing the Tab key will cycle you through each option. Pressing the Tab key twice will display all available Linux commands.

A useful program that comes with most Linux distributions is **Konqueror**, a windows type file manager. To start the fedora-Konqueror browser, click the **Konqueror** icon as shown in Figure 15-34 (a). This opens the Konqueror screen shown in Figure 15-34 (b). Files can be opened and/or moved from this screen.

Konqueror
A windows type file manager for Linux

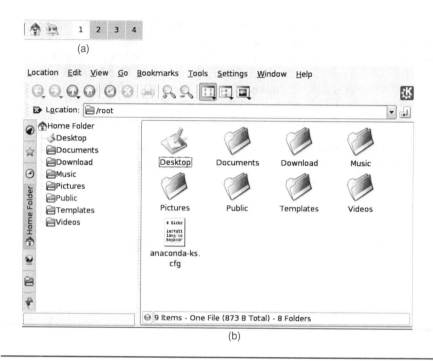

(a)

(b)

FIGURE 15-34 The (a) location of the Konqueror icon and (b) an example of the Konqueror screen.

15-5 ADDING APPLICATIONS TO LINUX

The objective of this section is to demonstrate the use of the Red Hat Package Manager (RPM) to install and uninstall applications and to query the system's database. RPM uses a database to keep track of the software installed on the system. This database is updated anytime new software is installed or software is removed. RPM keeps track of the name of the application, the version installed, and any associated files. The term *RPM* describes the entire package application and management system used in Red Hat Linux. It is also the command to start the package manager: you obtain the manual listing for RPM by entering the command ***man rpm***. The text shown in Figure 15-35 will be displayed. The *man* page shows that there are many options for the command. Although RPM is a Red Hat program, it has been adopted by many other Linux distributions as an easy and efficient way to manage applications.

The first example of using RPM is a query all. When entered, the command ***rpm -qa*** displays all of the applications installed on the system. The ***rpm -qa*** command is often used to search for an application on the Linux system. In this example, the command will be used to search for telnet. This can be done by *piping (pipe)* the results of the ***rpm -qa*** to the ***grep*** command, as shown in Figure 15-36. The command for doing this is ***rpm -qa | grep telnet***. In this case, **telnet** (a terminal emulation application for TCP/IP networks) is on the system, and in fact there is a *telnet-server-0.17-20* and a *telnet-client-0.17-20*.

Telnet
Terminal emulation application for TCP/IP networks

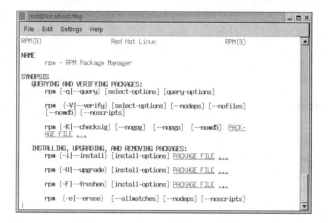

FIGURE 15-35 The *man* page for RPM.

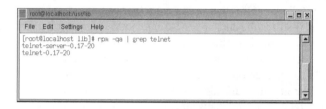

FIGURE 15-36 Using the *rpm -qa | grep telnet* command to search for files in the Linux system.

The *grep* command is similar to the Windows **search** or **find** command. **Grep** is used to search for strings in a text file or a filename. In the previous example, **grep** was used to search for telnet. Two filenames were returned. The **grep** command can also be used to return occurrences of a string within a file. All sentences with the string in them will be displayed. The *pipe* command (l) is used to take the output of one command and redirect it as an input to another command. In the example shown in Figure 15-36, the output of the **rpm** command was redirected to the input of the **grep** command. The output displayed came from the **grep** command.

Another useful tool to find out where a file came from is the command *rpm -qf [filename]* (*q* is for query, *f* is for file). This command searches the system's *rpm* database and returns the name of the file that matches the query. An example of using this command is shown in Figure 15-37.

grep
Command used to search for strings in a text file

pipe
Used to take the output of one command and redirect it as an input to another command

rpm -qf
Searches the *rpm* database and returns the name of the file that matches the query

FIGURE 15-37 An example of using the *rpm -qf [filename]* command.

The command *rpm -qf libkmedia2_idl.so* was entered, and the name *arts-1.0.0-4* was returned. This indicates that the file *libkmedia2_idl.so* belongs to the *arts-1.0.0-4* package. The command *rpm -qf* requires that a directory path be specified for file searches outside the current directory. The next section demonstrates how to uninstall a package from the database. Uninstalling removes all files associated with that package. A prompt is displayed if a file is being removed that is also being used by another application. For example, assume that the telnet-server application is to be removed. It was shown in Figure 15-36 that the command *rpm -qa | grep telnet* command is used to search for telnet.

Every instance of telnet in the database is listed. In this case, the name *telnet-server-0.17.20* and *telnet-0.17-20* (client) are listed.

rpm -e
Command for uninstalling the applications

The command for uninstalling the telnet applications is *rpm -e [filename]*. An example is shown uninstalling both the telnet-server and telnet-client applications in Figure 15-38. The telnet-server application is uninstalled using the command *rpm -e telnet-server-0.17.20*. The telnet-client application is removed using the command *rpm -e telnet-0.17.20*. There isn't a prompt that notifies the user that the application has been uninstalled, but the *rpm -qa | grep telnet* command can be used to check if the application is still in the database. Also *rpm* notifies the user if a configuration file is going to be uninstalled, as shown in Figure 15-38. It is difficult (time-consuming) to reconfigure certain applications, so the Red Hat Packet Manager will save the configuration file to another file name. This is shown in Figure 15-38 at the warning prompt. The warning message alerts the users that the *xinetd.d* configuration file is being saved as *telnet.rpmsave*. This allows the user to retain a copy of the configuration file for future use.

FIGURE 15-38   The steps for uninstalling the telnet-server and telnet-client applications and verifying that the applications are no longer in the database.

rpm -i
Command for installing an application in Linux

The next step demonstrates how to install a Red Hat application (called *RPMS*) from the distribution CD-ROM. The packages are found in the *RedHat/RPMS* directory on the distribution CD-ROM. All Red Hat CDs will contain the same file directory but the contents of the directory vary for each distribution. The command *ls tel** is used to display all files that contain the *tel* letters in the filename. This is shown in Figure 15-39. The command returns the filename *telnet-0.17-23.i386.rpm*. This is the telnet-client application, which allows this computer to establish a connection with another computer on the network A telnet-server application can also be installed on this machine. This would allow other computers to establish a network connection (telnet) to this machine. The command structure for installing an application is *rpm -i [application]*. Normally the command *rpm -ihv* would be used so that the package is verified and a hash indicator is displayed as the installation progresses. The telnet package can be installed using the command *rpm -i telnet-0.17-23.i386.rpm*. This installs all of the telnet-client files onto the Linux operating system. This includes any library, documentation (*man* pages), and any necessary links for the application to be executed on the system.

FIGURE 15-39   An example of locating and installing an RPM from the Red Hat distribution CD-ROM.

The steps for installing the telnet-server are the same as the telnet-client except the package name changes. The command is modified to ***rpm -i telnet-server-0.17.20.rpm*** to install the telnet-server. Any server on Linux will have a script (program) that starts and stops it. This requires that the script must be modified to start the program. In Red Hat Linux, the control for starting and stopping services all reside in the same directory (*/etc/rc.d/xinetd.d*). This directory contains most of the scripts for the Linux server applications. The ***ls*** command is used to display the servers installed. Scripts for every server application are found in the *xinetd.d* directory. The scripts are regular text files that can be edited to start the service. A text editor is used to modify the script. In this case, the text editor vi was used. The command ***vi telnet*** opens the telnet script for editing. The script is shown in Figure 15-40. At the very bottom of the script is **disable**. The setting for this should say **no**, as shown. Setting this setting to **no** and saving the edited script will enable the telnet-server application to run. (*Note:* The telnet-server application will only run when a remote connection is trying to be made to the computer.)

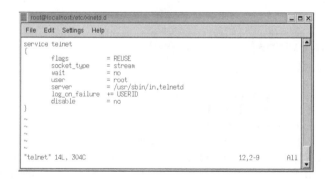

FIGURE 15-40   The script for the telnet-server application.

An expected task performed by network and system administrators is to add Web service to the network. This section presents the steps for adding the Apache Web service to the Linux operating system. Apache is the standard Web service for Linux, similar to MIIS for Microsoft Windows.

The command for installing the Apache Web service is *rpm -i apache-1.3.27-1.7.2.i386.rpm,* as shown in Figure 15-41. On occasion, a prompt will be displayed that a certain application is missing. In this case, the missing software packages can be found either with the Red Hat distribution disks or on the Internet. Once the software is installed, change directories to */etc/rc.d/init.d.* This directory contains the script (**httpd**) that starts the Web server. The command is *./httpd start,* as shown in Figure 15-42. This file was installed when the *rpm* was issued to install Apache. The *./* in front of the *httpd* is used for security reasons. This instructs the software to only look for this command in the current working directory (*/etc/rc.d/init.d*) first. This prevents the use of the command from another location. Another program of the same name could have been placed on the system and could contain malicious code. The screen displays the statement *Starting httpd: [OK],* which indicates that the service was successfully started.

FIGURE 15-41   The steps for installing the Apache Web service.

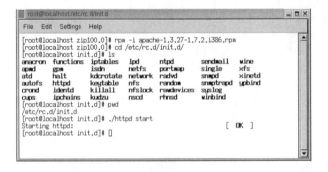

FIGURE 15-42   The steps for installing and starting the Apache Web service.

Linux uses **Mozilla** for an Internet web browser. The command for starting Mozilla is *mozilla.* The URL can be changed to the Linux machine simply by entering http://localhost/. Remember, the default name for the Linux machine is *localhost.* If the Web service is working properly, the test page shown in Figure 15-43 should be displayed. This test page provides the administrator with information about the configuration files. Linux provides this as a default page for setting the Web service.

There are two directories and files that are important relative to the Apache installation. The first is the *index.html* file, located in the */var/www/html* directory, shown in Figure 15-44. This is the root directory for the Web service. The test page actually resides in *index.html.* Users can build their web pages off this file and linked files.

FIGURE 15-43   Using the Mozilla Internet web browser to test the Web installation.

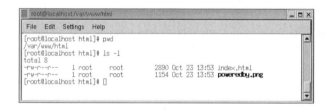

FIGURE 15-44   The location of the *index.html* file.

The second important directory and file is the *httpd.conf* file located in the */etc/httpd/conf* directory. This is shown in Figure 15-45. This is the configuration file for the Apache Web server that is read every time the service is started. The *httpd.conf* file is a text file and can be edited; however, the Apache server must be restarted for the changes to take effect, using the command *./httpd restart*, as shown in Figure 15-46. Notice that the command is issued from the */etc/rc.d/init.d* directory, and the command line displays the prompts:

httpd.conf
The configuration file for the Apache Web server

```
Stopping httpd: [ OK ] Starting httpd: [ OK ]
```

indicating the Apache Web server has stopped and restarted. The Apache web server can be stopped using the command *./httpd stop*. This provides an orderly (scripted) shutdown. The following output will be displayed on the terminal screen:

```
Stopping httpd: [ OK ]
```

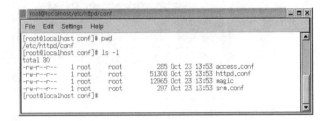

FIGURE 15-45   The location of configuration file (httpd.conf) for the Apache Web server.

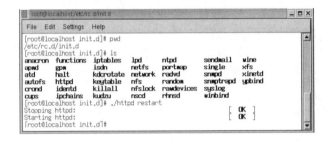

FIGURE 15-46   The steps for restarting the Apache server so that changes made to the httpd.conf configuration file can take effect.

15-6   LINUX NETWORKING

The objective of this section is to demonstrate how to configure a Linux machine to run on the network. This section assumes that the Linux machine already has a network interface card (NIC) installed. Red Hat Linux 8.0 is very good at detecting all major brands of network interface cards and also contains drivers for the NICs. Linux will automatically detect the card and may prompt you for the IP address, net mask, and gateway address during the installation of the operating system. Hardware installed after the initial system installation will still be detected by the autodetect feature running in Linux.

Ethernet cards in Linux are identified as **eth0, eth1, eth2**, and so on. The command *ifconfig* is used to report all of the network devices recognized and running on the system. This command lists all of the interfaces and the configurations for each interface. The configurations include the IP address, the **net mask** (subnet mask), the broadcast address, and the gateway. The *ifconfig* command also reports back on the status of the loopback (**lo**), as shown in Figure 15-47.

The *ifconfig* command can also be used in Linux to change the IP address configuration for the network interface. The following examples will demonstrate configuring eth0, the default interface device on most Linux machines. The command *ifconfig* displayed the eth0 and lo as shown in Figure 15-47. The IP address for the machine is currently 192.168.12.1. This example demonstrates how to change the IP address of the eth0 interface. The command *ifconfig eth0 192.168.20.5* is entered on the command line, and the *ifconfig* command is used to display the interface settings

eth0, eth1, eth2, . . .
The way Linux identifies the Ethernet interface cards

ifconfig
Reports all of the network devices recognized and running on the system, listing all of the interfaces and the configuration for each

Net Mask
Linux name for the subnet mask

lo
The Linux symbol representing the loopback

(shown in Figure 15-48). This applies the IP address to the network interface. The default values for the broadcast and subnet masks are used if no value is specified. In this case, the Bcast (broadcast) address is automatically updated to 192.168.20.255, the broadcast address for this class of network. The Mask (subnet mask) entry is automatically updated to the class C subnet mask 255.255.255.0.

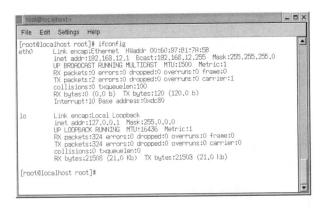

FIGURE 15-47 An example of using the *ifconfig* command to display the network interfaces and their configuration.

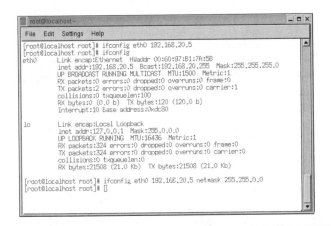

FIGURE 15-48 Using the *ifconfig* command to change the network interface IP address.

A different subnet mask can be applied to the network interface by appending the subnet mask value to the *ifconfig* command. An example of this is shown at the bottom of Figure 15-48 using the command ***ifconfig Eth0 192.168.20.5 netmask 255.255.0.0.***

Another set of commands used for controlling the network interfaces are ***ifdown [interface]*** and ***ifup [interface]***. These commands enable the administrator to shut down and bring back up the network interface. This is useful when a machine is being subjected to a network attack and the network connection needs to be shut down quickly. The ***ifdown eth0*** command brings down the Ethernet0 interface. The ***ifconfig*** command no longer displays the eth0 interface. The interface can be brought back online by issuing the ***ifup eth0*** command. The ***ifconfig*** command now shows that the

ifdown, ifup
Commands used to shut down and bring back up the network interface

eth0 interface is available. The steps for shutting down and bringing up a network interface are shown in Figure 15-49.

FIGURE 15-49   Examples of using the *ifdown* and *ifup* commands.

network stop
Shuts down all network interfaces

network start
Brings up the network interfaces

route add default gw
Command used to specify the gateway address

In some cases it is necessary to shut down all network interfaces. The command for doing this is *network stop*. Linux will echo a response of the interfaces that are shutting down. Entering the *ifconfig* command will now display that no network interfaces are active. An example of using stopping the network on Linux is shown in Figure 15-50 (a). The command for starting the network is *network start*, shown in Figure 15-50 (b). Linux prompts that it is bringing up interfaces. Issuing the *ifconfig* command now displays that eth0 and lo are both available.

The next step is to provide a gateway address for the Linux network interface. This is accomplished using the *route add default gw [ip address]* command. Entering the *route* command without any arguments displays the different routes. This is shown in Figure 15-51 (a). The display shows that the default gateway is 192.168.12.254. This can be changed to 192.168.12.1 by issuing the command *route add default gw 192.168.12.1*, as shown in Figure 15-51 (b). Linux will prompt you if an unreachable gateway address has been specified, as shown in Figure 15-51 (c). Linux will display this message if a gateway address outside the network address is specified. For example, the entry *route add default gw 192.168.20.5* displays that the address is unreachable. This is because 192.168.20.0 is a different class C network.

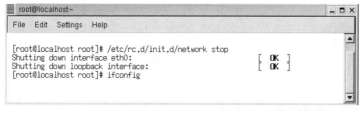

(a)

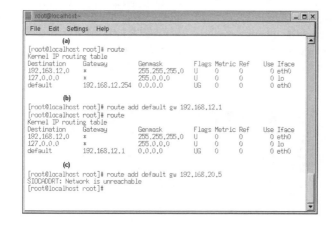

(b)

FIGURE 15-50 (a) Using the command *network stop* for shutting down all network interfaces; (b) using the command *network start* for bringing up all network interfaces.

FIGURE 15-51 (a) Using the *route* command to display the network routes available on the machine; (b) changing the network's default gateway address; (c) the Linux prompt for an unreachable gateway address.

The Linux network programs take their cue from a set of scripts in the *etc/sysconfig/network-scripts* directory. These scripts contain the values assigned to all network devices in the Linux operating system. This example looks at the contents of the *ifcfg-eth0* script, which is the file associated with the Ethernet0 network interface. The *cat* command is used to display the file, as shown in Figure 15-52. These contents identify how eth0 will be configured when booting or when the network is started. The root user can modify this file as needed.

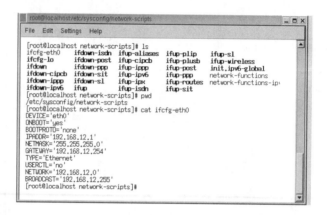

FIGURE 15-52 The steps for examining the contents of the *ifcfg-eth0* script.

Installing SSH

openssh
The secure shell application for Linux

This section demonstrates how to install SSH (the secure shell), which is similar to telnet except SSH encrypts the data traffic between the two hosts. SSH is a better tool for remote administration or remote work. The **openssh** applications, openssh-clients and openssh-server, are provided with the Red Hat distribution of Linux. Installing the openssh-client application requires that four RPMS be installed. These applications are found in the *rpm* directory as shown in Figure 15-53. (*Please note:* The files names change with each distribution, but steps for locating and installing the files are the same.)

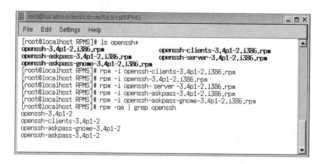

FIGURE 15-53 The listing of the openshh rpms.

Five *openssh** files are listed in the *rpm* directory. The first four files are used in the client installation; the last file is used to install the openssh-server:

- **openssh client files**
  openssh-clients-3.4pl-2.i386.rpm
  openssh-askpass-3.4pl-2.i386.rpm
  openssh-3.4pl-2.i386.rpm
- **openssh server file**
  openssh-server-3.4pl-2.i386.rpm

The openssh client is installed on the Linux machine by entering the command ***rpm -i [filename]***. This is repeated for each of the three client files, as shown in Figure 15-53. Once the files are installed, the database can be queried using the command ***rpm -qa | grep openssh***. The openssh files installed are then listed as shown in Figure 15-53.

The command ***ssh [destination]*** can be used to establish an SSH connection. This assumes that the destination has an SSH server running. In this case, the destination is user@machine.edu. An example is shown in Figure 15-54.

FIGURE 15-54 Establishing an SSH connection.

The installation of the SSH server is very similar to the installation of the SSH client. The command ***rpm -i openssh-server-3.4p1-2.i386.rpm*** is used to install the openssh-server. The installation can be verified in the same way that the installation was verified for the client.

The ftp Client

There are many ftp client applications for Linux. This section demonstrates the use of the ftp application called **ncftp**. This application is popular with network administrators because of its ease with putting files on and getting files from the command line. The command used to start the application is ***ncftp [server-name]***. An example is shown in Figure 15-55. An ftp server session with 192.168.12.2 is being requested. The screen prompts that a connection is being established, and then the prompt **salsa Microsoft FTP service (Version 5.0)** is displayed. (*Note: salsa* is our example Windows 2003 server machine.) The screen next prompts **Logging in. . . | Anonymous user logged in**. The anonymous login is listed because a user was not specified with the ***ncftp*** command. The command ***ncftp -u [server-name]*** can be used to instruct the ftp server to prompt you for the user's password. (See the *man* page for ncftp for more instructions.) The Linux box then replies **Logged in to 192.168.12.2**, indicating that a connection has been established. The prompt on the Linux machine now shows **ncftp / —**.

ncftp
An ftp application for Linux

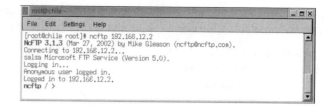

FIGURE 15-55   Using ncftp to start an application.

The ftp Server

wu-ftpd
Washington University's ftp server

daemon
Linux name for the server package

One of the most popular ftp servers is Washington University's (**wu-ftpd**). The *wuftpd* server package is found in the Fedora Core 8.0 Distribution disk #3 in the */etc/xinetd.d* directory. The files in this directory are shown in Figure 15-56. The *d* on the end of *wu-ftpd* is a common way in Linux to indicate that this file is a **daemon**, or server. The command ***rpm -i wu-ftpd*** is used to install the ftp server. The next step is to make the service available to the outside world by modifying the configuration file. This requires that the *wu-ftpd* configuration file located in the */etc/xinetd.d* directory be edited using a Linux text editor. A portion of the configuration file is shown in Figure 15-57. At the end of the file is the word **disable**. Next to this word is an option for entering **yes** or **no**. **Yes** disables the server; **no** enables it. In this case, the configuration shows that the *wu-ftpd* server application is enabled *(disable = no)*.

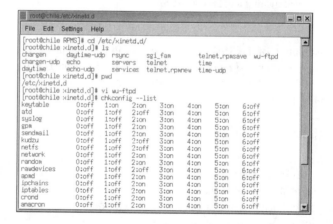

FIGURE 15-56   The location of the *wu-ftpd* package in Linux.

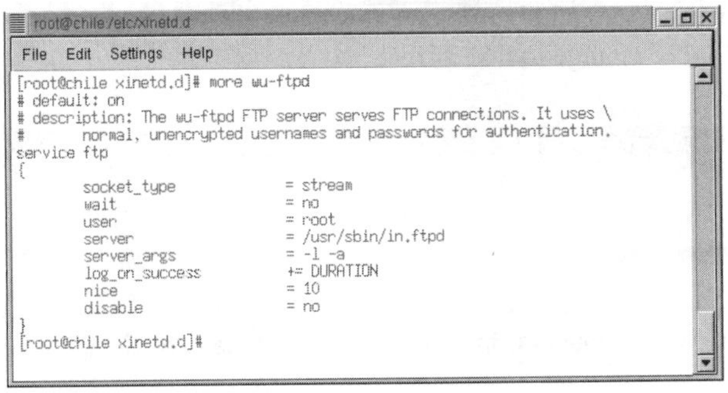

FIGURE 15-57 The *wu-ftp* configuration file.

DNS Service on Linux

DNS is used for name resolution (see Chapter 5). In Linux, the list of information for the DNS service is found in a file in the */etc* directory called ***resolv.conf***. This is shown in Figure 15-58. This file contains the list of the IP addresses for the DNS servers. The contents of an example *resolv.conf* file are listed in Figure 15-59. Two entries are shown for this file. The first is ***search localdomain***, and the second entry is ***nameserver 192.168.12.1***. This listing shows the search sequence for resolving names to an IP address. Multiple name services can appear in this list, but remember, this is a search order. Linux will not perform any name resolution if this file is empty.

resolv.conf
Contains the list of DNS servers for the Linux machine

FIGURE 15-58 The location of the DNS *resolv.conf* file in Linux.

FIGURE 15-59 The contents of the example *resolv.conf* file.

Changing the Hostname

This section demonstrates how to change the hostname of a Linux machine. The name of the Linux machine is located in the */etc* directory. The root user can be changed using the command ***hostname [name]***. In this case the example is showing that the hostname is being changed to *chile-one* as shown in Figure 15-60. You must log off and back on for the change to take place.

FIGURE 15-60   An example of using the *hostname* command to change the name of the Linux machine.

15-7   TROUBLESHOOTING SYSTEM AND NETWORK PROBLEMS WITH LINUX

Linux has many options available for troubleshooting hardware and software problems. This section presents some of the options available to the administrator and the user. The following Linux troubleshooting commands are presented in this section:

> *dmesg*
>
> *reboot*
>
> *last*
>
> *who*
>
> *w nmap*
>
> *chkconfig*
>
> *netstat -ap*

Troubleshooting Boot Processes

dmesg
Command used to display the boot processes for Linux, used to identify why certain processes failed

The dmesg *Command*   The first command examined is *dmesg*, used to display the boot process for Linux. This command is useful if a certain application fails to be recognized or boot properly. This file will display errors that can be used to better understand why a process failed. This command is available to any user on the system, but remember, only *root* will be able to fix the problems. This file can contain a large amount of text, so the command can be piped to *more* using the command *dmesg | more* as shown in Figure 15-61. This screen shows the text from the last Linux boot process. This provides information on the system devices detected, how memory is configured, hard drive information, and any errors coming from the software.

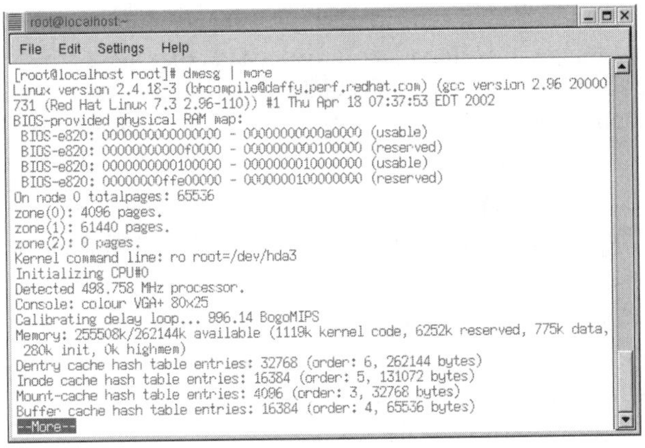

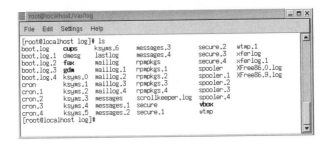

FIGURE 15-61   An example of using the *dmesg* command piped to *more*.

The reboot Command   A useful Linux command to use when the system is not operating correctly due to either hardware or software problems is *reboot*. This command gracefully shuts down the system so that it is properly configured on reboot. If a Linux machine needs to be rebooted, use the ***reboot*** command; *do not press the Reset button on the PC.* The ***reboot*** command is shown in Figure 15-62. The best directory to look for troubleshooting information is the */var/log* directory. A listing of the *var/log* directory is provided in Figure 15-63. Many of the files have a .1, .2, .3, and so on following the file name. For example:

> **reboot**
> Command used to gracefully shut down the Linux machine and reboot

boot.log
boot.log.1
boot.log.2
boot.log.3

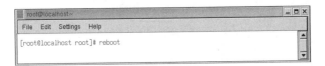

FIGURE 15-62   Entering the *reboot* command.

FIGURE 15-63   The listing of the */var/log* directory.

These files are renamed at regular intervals (hence the .1, .2, .3, ... extensions) and are kept in storage. It is important to understand that these are rolling log files. The 1 becomes 2, pushing 2 to 3, 3 to 4, and so on. Eventually, the file is deleted and replaced. A summary of the useful troubleshooting files in the *var/log* directory follows:

boot.log—Keeps track of the boot processes.

lastlog—Keeps track of user login; requires the use of the *last* command to display its contents.

maillog—Keeps a log of mail activity.

messages—Contains most of the system messages that report any software or hardware errors. This is an important troubleshooting file.

secure—Keeps track of any users entering or exiting the system and keeps track of security violations such as unauthorized users attempting login.

spooler—File for mail management.

Listing Users on the System

last
Command used to display logins to the Linux system

The* last *Command   The *last* command is extremely useful in security. This command accesses the login file and reports of logins to the Linux system. An example of using the command is provided in Figure 15-64. This command lists all users that have logged on to the system since the last reboot or for the past month. The login information displayed includes the account name, day, date, and time. This command is useful if the administrator suspects that someone has gained unauthorized access to the Linux machine. The information displayed by the *last* command shows that there are two users on the system. The first listed is *usera,* who logged in from *localhost* on Feb. 11 at 12:48 and is still logged in. The other account, *root,* is currently logged in and has logged into and out of the system many times.

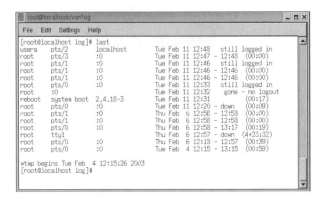

FIGURE 15-64   Using the *last* command to display the Linux login activity.

The* who *or* w *Command Two other ways to check for users on the system are to enter either the command ***who*** or ***w***. The ***who*** command displays the names of the users presently logged into the system. The ***w*** command provides similar information and provides additional details on each user, such as the following:

who
Command that displays the names of the users presently logged into the system

w
Command that displays the names of the users presently logged into the system plus additional details on each user

from: Specifies the domain where the user is logging in from

login time: Indicates when the user logged in

idle: Indicates if the user has been busy on the system

what: Displays the last command entered by the user

Figure 15-65 provides examples of the text displayed by using ***w*** and ***who*** commands.

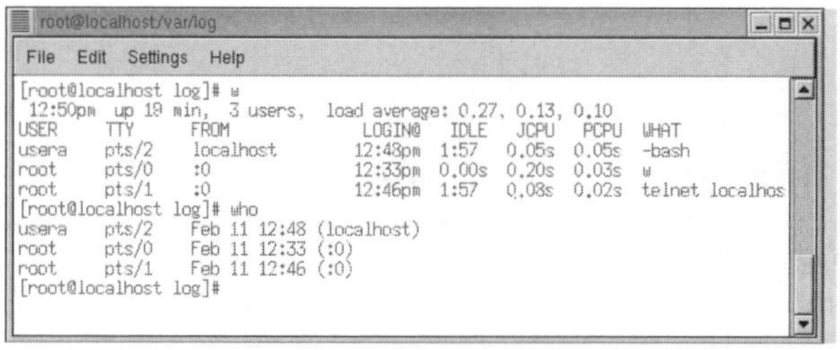

root@localhost/var/log
File Edit Settings Help
[root@localhost log]# w
12:50pm up 19 min, 3 users, load average: 0.27, 0.13, 0.10
USER TTY FROM LOGIN@ IDLE JCPU PCPU WHAT
usera pts/2 localhost 12:48pm 1:57 0.05s 0.05s -bash
root pts/0 :0 12:33pm 0.00s 0.20s 0.03s w
root pts/1 :0 12:46pm 1:57 0.08s 0.02s telnet localhos
[root@localhost log]# who
usera pts/2 Feb 11 12:48 (localhost)
root pts/0 Feb 11 12:33 (:0)
root pts/1 Feb 11 12:46 (:0)
[root@localhost log]#

FIGURE 15-65 Examples of the text displayed by the *w* and *who* commands.

Network Security

The* nmap *Command An excellent security tool that runs on Linux is ***nmap***. This is a port scanner that is used by the network administrator to scan a local computer or other computers internal to the network to determine what network ports and services are being made available to users. For example, the command ***nmap localhost*** was entered to scan the Linux machine named *localhost*. Figure 15-66 shows the results of the scan. The scan shows that the ftp, telnet, smtp (email server), sunrpc (network file server), and X11 (the GUI for Linux) are all available. Notice that each service has a port number assigned to it. (The concept of *port number* was presented in Chapter 5.) For example, ftp is on port 21 and is running TCP. Telnet is running on port 23 and is also running TCP. The network administrator may decide that the ftp or nonsecure telnet service is a security threat and that it needs to be disabled. Note that this command can also be used to scan machines outside your network by simply substituting an IP address for the machine name. For example, ***nmap 192.168.12.5*** can be used to scan the machine at IP address 192.168.12.5. (*Note:* You should only use the nmap port scanning utility on your own machines!)

nmap
A Linux port scanner

FIGURE 15-66   The results of using the *nmap* command to scan the Linux machine named *localhost*.

Enabling and Disabling Boot Services

The chkconfig *Command*   The next command examined is chkconFigure, which allows the administrator to enable and disable services at boot time. The options for the *chkconfig* command are shown in Figure 15-67.

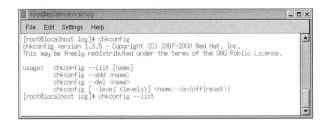

FIGURE 15-67   The options for the *chkconfig* command.

The administrator used the ***nmap*** command to check to see what network services were running. It was found that the ftp service was running (see Figure 15-66). The network administrator decided to disable the ftp service. The network administrator can use the ***chkconfig --list*** command to view the services running on the system. The command is shown at the bottom of Figure 15-67. The results of entering the ***chkconfig --list*** command are provided in Figure 15-68. The last line displayed shows **wu-ftpd: on**. This indicates that the ftp server is on. The ftp service can be disabled by using the command ***chkconfig wu-ftpd off*** as shown in Figure 15-69. The ***chkconfig --list*** command can be used again to verify the service is off. The verification that *wuftpd* is off is provided in Figure 15-70.

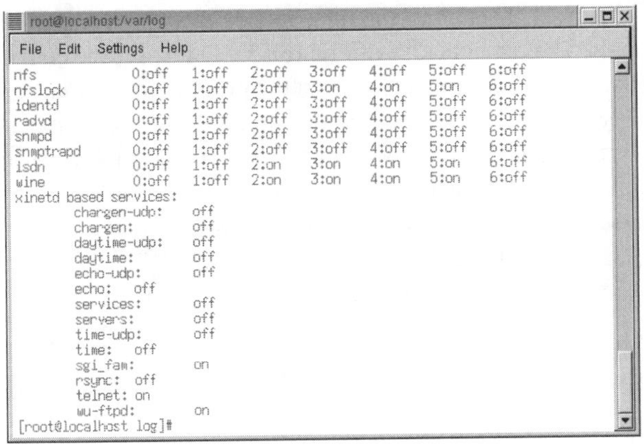

FIGURE 15-68　The results of entering the *chkconfig --list* command.

FIGURE 15-69　Using the *chkconfig wu-ftpd off* command to disable the ftp service.

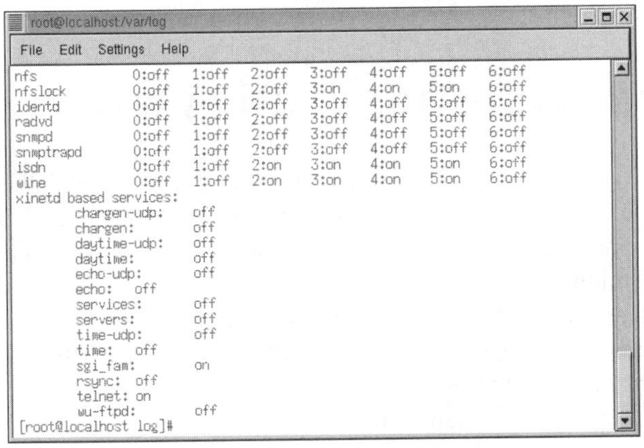

FIGURE 15-70　Using the *chkconfig --list* command to verify the service has been disabled.

The netstat -ap *Command*　Another command used by the network administrator is *netstat -ap*. This command provides information about the network connections that exist on the system. This includes internal programs and connections to the outside world. This command is very useful when the network administrator wants to determine if a machine is being used by unauthorized users, for example, as a music server for the Internet. The *netstat* command will list the connection, and it also will list the name of the program that is allowing the connection to be made. An example of using this command is provided in Figure 15-71. In this example, the *netstat -ap* |

netstat -ap
Provides information about
the network connections

more command is used. This pipes the file contents to *more* to make it easier to view the entire contents. The far right side of Figure 15-71 shows if the connection is in the listen or established mode. *Listen* means that the program is waiting for a connection to be started. *Established* means that a connection has already been made. For example, a TCP connection is established at port 3102, and the name of the program is *in.telnetd,* which is the telnet-server.

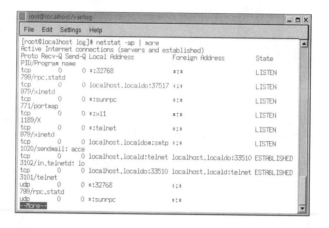

FIGURE 15-71   An example of using the *netstat -ap* command to view the network connections running on the machine.

15-8   MANAGING THE LINUX SYSTEM

This section examines some of the management tools available with the Fedora Core 8.0 distribution. The previous sections in this chapter examined the Linux command structure as input from the command line interface. While it is true that the network and system administrators insist that any member of the network management staff fully understand Linux operation from the command line, they also understand the benefits of using the well-developed GUIs available for Linux such as those available with the Red Hat 8.0 distribution. The obvious benefits of using the GUI management tools are time savings, and additionally, the dependencies for any software installation/deletion are automatically checked for you.

system-config- <tool-name>
Command for displaying the system configuration GUI for a specified tool

In Fedora Core 8.0, the **System Config** tools, which are the system administration tools, are all prefixed with *system-config* followed by the name of the tool. In order to get to the tools, log in as *root*, and at the command line enter *system-config-<tool-name>*. The menu for the tool being requested will be displayed.

ls system-config- *
Command for listing the system configuration tools

The list of system configuration tools can be displayed by changing the directory to /usr/bin and entering the following command from the prompt [**root@bob bin**] **ls system-config-***. The list generated by this command is provided in Figure 15-72. There are many configuration options available for the user and the administrator. A few of the menus are discussed next. The GUIs are fairly intuitive and typically don't need a lot of discussion to understand how they work. Examples of the system-config GUIs are provided next.

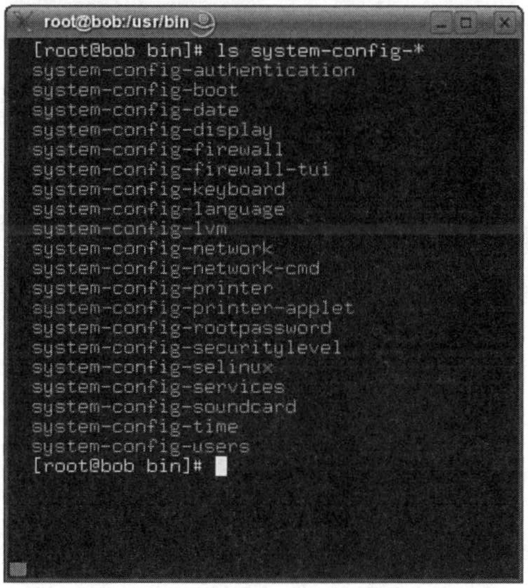

FIGURE 15-72 The list of the *system-config-* files.

For example, ***system-config-date*** is the GUI that allows you to change the time and date for the computer. Entering the command ***system-config-date*** will display the menu shown in Figure 15-73. This menu also allows you to set the time zone and also enables you to point this menu (via an IP address) to a time server for obtaining the current time for your location.

The next GUI menu displayed (Figure 15-74) is for the firewall. The firewall menu settings can be displayed by entering ***system-config-firewall*** at the command line. You can disable a firewall, configure additional settings, or modify the firewall configurations. This allows you to open ports and block ports, and all the settings are GUI based, which simplifies the tasks. For example, if you want to block port 80 (HTTP), simply click the check box for **WWW(HTTP)** and click **Disable**. On the left side of the menu are other options such as selecting other ports that are not defined on the main menu screen. You also have settings for trusted services, masquerading (network address translation), and a place for setting custom rules for your firewall.

There are many important issues that the network/system administrator faces, but security should be the top concern. When you first go out to install a new service or are maintaining existing systems, the most important issue is the system security and preventing outside threats. You want to fully understand the implications of installing the software and how the installation can possibly affect the overall network. The following is a list of some of the questions that should be asked:

- Who will be the users of the software, and what applications are they going to be running?
- Will they need special permissions?
- Will the software being installed require a firewall?
- Does the software introduce any security threats?

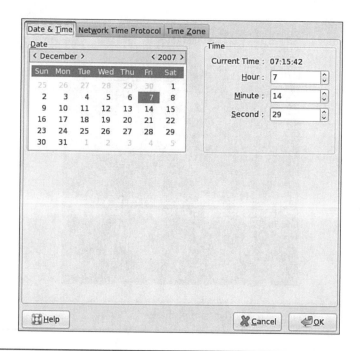

FIGURE 15-73   The system-config-date menu.

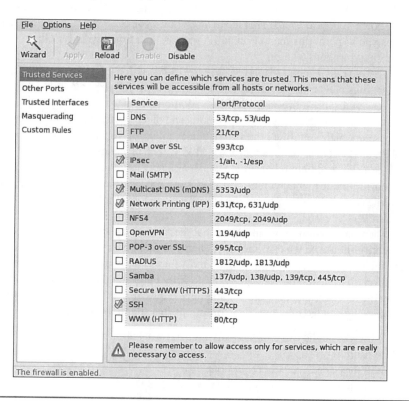

FIGURE 15-74   The system-config-firewall menu.

Regardless of the installation, you will have to set limits for security reasons. You don't want your system to get hacked, and firewall protection is a very good start.

Figure 15-75 shows the menu for the network settings. This menu is displayed by entering the *system-config-network* command when logged in as root. This is a good place to start when setting up your computer on a network for the first time. This tool allows you to set the IP address, subnet mask, host name, and DNS server address. You can also activate or deactivate the networking devices (for example, NICs) from this menu by selecting the check box for device and clicking the **activate** or **deactivate** button.

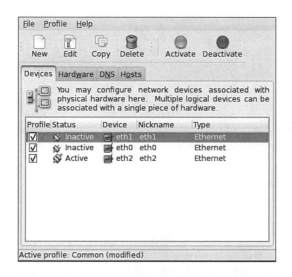

FIGURE 15-75 The system-config-network menu.

The next menu (see Figure 15-76) is for *system-config-packages.* This menu is a convenient way to add/remove software on your computer. There are tabs for Browse, Search, and List that are used to find software packages and also for installing/removing various software packages. This menu provides the same function as the *rpm -i* command used to install RPMs from the command line. The advantage of using the GUI is that the dependencies for the various software packages that are being installed or deleted are automatically checked. This helps keep the database of software applications cleaner.

The next menu, shown in Figure 15-77, is for *system-config-printer.* This menu is used for adding various types of printers to the system. The Red Hat software will have most of the commonly used printer drivers installed with the software; however, not all drivers will be there. In the case of a missing printer driver, the system administrator will have to download the driver from a CD or from the Internet. The best locations to locate a printer driver are the manufacturer's web site. In some cases you might have to do an Internet search for the driver, but make sure you download the driver from a trusted site.

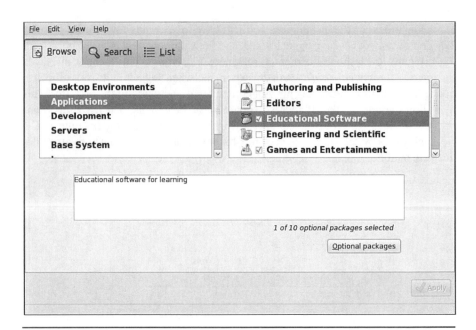

FIGURE 15-76   The system-config-packages menu.

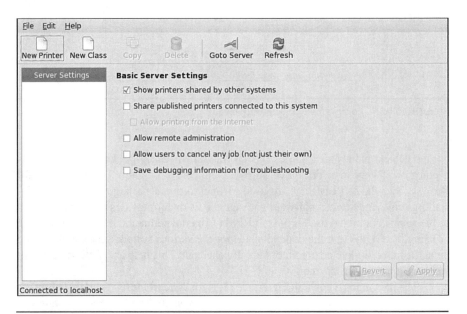

FIGURE 15-77   The system-config-printer menu.

The next menu is for ***system-config-users.*** This menu (Figure 15-78) is used for the management of the users. You can add/modify/delete users and groups from this menu. Examples of users with their Username, User ID, Primary Group, Full Name, Login Shell, and Home Directory are displayed.

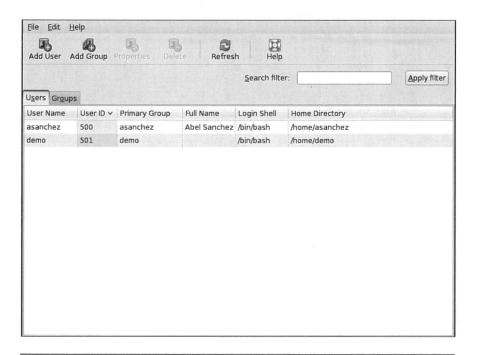

FIGURE 15-78   The system-config-users menu.

The next menu, shown in Figure 15-79, is for ***systems-config-services.*** This GUI is used to start/stop/restart services. For example, the network services can be stopped by clicking the **Network** button and clicking **Stop**. For example, the ssh service can be stopped from the GUI by clicking **sshd** and then **Stop**. This is equivalent to entering the command ***service sshd start*** command.

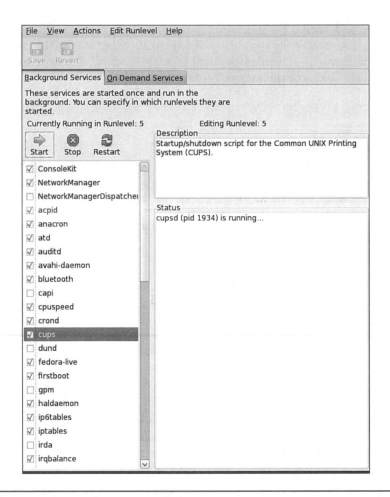

FIGURE 15-79   The system-config-services menu.

This section has presented a look at using the GUI in the Red Hat distribution for managing the various functions. The GUI greatly simplifies the management tasks, but never overlook the importance of using the command line interface.

SUMMARY

This chapter has presented numerous examples of using commands to administer the Linux operating system. The student should appreciate the complexity of configuring the Linux network server and the fact that administering a computer network requires the input of personnel with varied skills. The student should also understand that this has only been an introduction to the Linux operating system. The chapter demonstrated how to use many commands, one of the most important of which is how to read the online text *man* pages. There is a wealth of information about Linux on the Internet. The online distributions for Linux can be found at http://www.biblio.org. The Linux concepts students should understand from this chapter include the following:

- The logon/logoff procedures for Linux
- The steps for adding users to a Linux machine
- The Linux file structure and related file commands
- The use of key Linux administration commands
- How to add applications to Linux
- How to place a Linux machine on the network
- How to configure Web services for Linux
- The procedures and tools for using Linux to troubleshoot Linux systems and networks

The following are sites where you can download a bootable version of Linux running off *one CD*. This means you don't have to create dual-boot partitions on your computer or set up a separate machine running Linux. These bootable versions are available from both Red Hat and Knoppix. The latest "Live" version from Fedora is available at http://fedoraproject.org/get-fedora (698 MB) and will fit on one CD.

Knoppix is available from www.knoppix.org or from a mirror site such as http://cs.wisc.edu/pub/mirrors/linux/knoppix/. As of this writing Knoppix is at version 5.3. The file size is approximately 698 MB and will fit on a CD.

The files for Red Hat "Live" and Knoppix are ISO images, and the ISO image is a disk image of an ISO 9660 file system. The file needs to be converted into a functional file system before using. This is done when the file is written to a CD using software capable of writing ISOs to CD and making the CD bootable. Most CD burning software for Windows, Mac OS, and Linux will have this capability. Once you write the ISO file to CD, the CD can be used to boot the computer, and you will have Linux running on your computer after the boot process is complete.

QUESTIONS AND PROBLEMS

Section 15-2

1. What are the steps for entering the menu to add a user in Linux?
2. What is the purpose of the Linux login shell?
3. How can Linux be closed from the Linux GUI?
4. How is the command line accessed in Linux?
5. What is the Linux command to list only files?

6. What Linux command provides a long file listing that includes file attributes?
7. What Linux command lists hidden files and file attributes?
8. What two Linux commands can be used to display file contents?
9. How do the *more* and *cat* commands differ?
10. What is the user ID for *root*? O zero
11. What directory are the binary process and executables located in Linux?
12. What is typically placed in the */etc* directory?
13. Match the following directories to their contents:
   1. */boot* D   a) location of all user directories
   2. */dev* E   b) system log files, email folders
   3. */home* A   c) location of user files related to user programs
   4. */mnt* H   d) location of the Linux kernel
   5. */root* F   e) drivers for monitors
   6. */tmp* G   f) the home directory for *root*
   7. */usr* C   g) temporary holding area for applications
   8. */var* B   h) the location of mounted directories
14. What is the Linux command for displaying a working directory?
15. What is the Linux command for creating a directory named *chile*?
16. List the command for removing a file named *aaron*.
17. List the command to rename a file named *aaron.txt* to *bueno.txt*.
18. The command *chmod 411 drb.txt* is entered. What does this do?
19. The command *chmod 644 djb.txt* is entered. What does this do?
20. The command *chmod 755 krcb.txt* is entered. What does this do?
21. The permissions for the file *hbmbb.txt* need to be set so that only the owner has permission to read and write the file. List the command that does this.
22. List the command to set the permissions on the text file *dapab.txt* to the following:

    Owner: read/write
    Group: read
    Outside: no access
23. List the commands for setting the permissions on *bc.txt* to the following:

    Owner: read/write/executable
    Group: read/write
    Outside: read
24. The new owner of the file *CQ.txt* is *dd*. Enter the command to change ownership.
25. The new group for the *jc.txt* is *heaven*. Enter the command to change ownership.

Section 15-4

26. What command displays the online text manual for Linux?
27. List the command that returns all *man* pages that mention the topic *Apache*.
28. Why is the *ps -a* command used?
29. How is a program with a PID of 1020 shut down?
30. What command can be used as a last resort to kill a process?
31. *Root* is logged onto a Linux machine and needs to become another user to verify the changes made to the user's account. What command is used for *root* to become the user?

32. *Usera* is logged into Linux and wants to become *userb*. What is the command, and what are the steps required to make this happen?
33. What information is contained in the *fstab* file?
34. What is *kudzu*?
35. List the command for mounting a USB drive.
36. List the Linux command that is used to verify a drive has been mounted.
37. What command must be entered before the media can be removed from a drive that has been mounted?
38. List the command to gracefully shut down the Linux system.
39. The last command entered from the command line in Linux can be repeated by pressing what key?
40. What command can be entered in Linux to display previously entered commands?
41. What is the keystroke that can be used to complete entries on the command line?

Section 15-5

42. List the command to search for installed applications on Linux. Use the *pipe* command to display only results with *wu-ftpd* in them.
43. What command is used to find out where a file comes from?
44. What is the Linux command to uninstall an application?
45. What is the Linux command for installing an application?
46. How is a service controlled by *xinetd* enabled after installation?
47. What command starts the Apache Web server?
48. The script for starting the Apache Web server is found in what directory?
49. The *index.html* file is found in what directory in Linux?
50. The *httpd.conf* file is located in what directory in Linux?
51. The Apache Web server can be restarted using what command?
52. What is the Linux command for listing all network interfaces running on the system?
53. What is the subnet mask called in Linux?
54. How is the Ethernet1 network interface card identified in Linux?
55. The *ifconfig* command is entered and lo is displayed. What is this?
56. List the command to change the IP address of the Ethernet0 network interface to 10.10.20.5 with a subnet mask of 255.255.255.0.
57. List the command to shut down the Ethernet1 network interface.
58. What command can be used to verify that a network interface is down?
59. What is the command to bring a network interface back online?
60. What command shuts down all network interfaces?
61. List the Linux command for starting the network interfaces.
62. What command can be used to verify that the network has started?
63. List the command for adding a gateway address for the Linux network interface.
64. The Linux network programs use a set of scripts found in what directory?
65. What is the command to install the openssh-server in Linux?
66. FTP is being used to connect to another machine. List the command that instructs the FTP server to prompt for a user's password.

67. The Washington University FTP server is to be installed on a Linux machine. Provide the command and steps required to install the server and make the services available.
68. The list of information for the DNS service is found in what directory in Linux?
69. List the command for changing the hostname of the Linux machine to *chip*.

Section 15-7

70. Why is the ***dmesg*** command used?
71. What is the Linux command to reboot?
72. Match the following Linux troubleshooting files with their contents.

    1. *boot.log*   a) keeps track of user login
    2. *lastlog*   b) log of mail activity
    3. *maillog*   c) keeps track of the boot process
    4. *messages*   d) tracks users entering or exiting the system
    5. *secure*   e) report on hardware or software errors
    6. *spooler*   f) mail management
73. List two commands to check for users that have logged onto the system since the last reboot.
74. Which command lists all users that have logged onto the system since the last reboot?
75. What is the command to scan a computer to determine what network ports and services are being made available to users?
76. List the command used to enable and disable services at boot time.
77. The services running on a Linux machine can be listed by entering what command?
78. Write the command to disable the wu-ftpd service.
79. Identify the command that provides information about network connections that exist on the system.

Critical Thinking

80. You suspect that someone has broken into a computer. Discuss the steps you might take to correct the problem.
81. You are attempting to install the Apache Web server, and a prompt is displayed that states a certain application is missing. Describe how this problem can be corrected.
82. What questions should you ask when installing new software on any machines attached to your network?
83. What steps can you take to find a printer driver that isn't included with a Linux distribution?

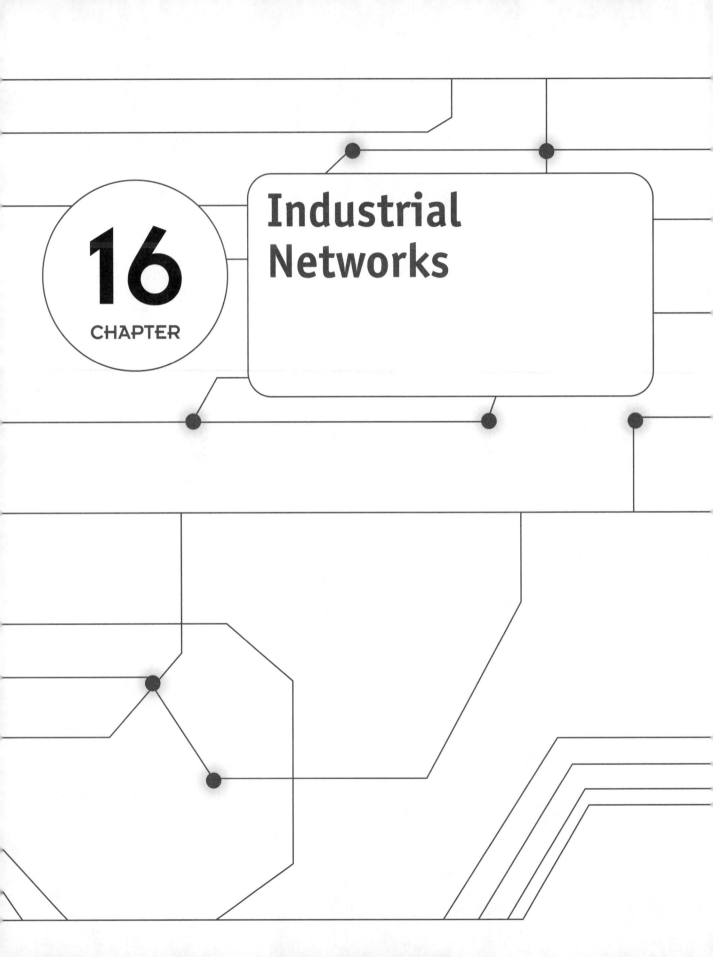

16
CHAPTER

Industrial Networks

CHAPTER OUTLINE

16-1 Introduction
16-2 Overview of Industrial Networks
16-3 Industrial Ethernet
16-4 Industrial Ethernet Protocols

16-5 Legacy Device and Controller Level Buses
Summary
Questions and Problems

OBJECTIVES

- Learn the key issues associated with industrial networks
- Examine the key characteristics of industrial networks
- Understand the role of Ethernet in industrial networks
- Became familiar with the various industrial Ethernet protocols used in industrial networks
- Examine legacy device and controller level buses

KEY TERMS

industrial networking	PLC	CIP
hierarchy	single point-of-failure	UDP/IP
redundancy	hot standby	implicit messages
determinism	shadowing	objects
CAN	legacy protocol	Foundation Fieldbus
information level	industrial Ethernet	HSE
statistical data	Just-in-time and Lean	Profinet
control data	linear network topology	IDA
COTS	Ethernet ring	RTPS
device level	light duty	MMS
intelligent (smart) devices	heavy duty	Modbus TCP
controller level	armored	
interoperability	Ethernet/IP	

16-1   INTRODUCTION

A minirevolution has started in plant automation in the past few years. Industrial networks are moving away from proprietary fieldbus protocols and adopting open network standards such as Ethernet and TCP/IP. (*Fieldbus* is an open standard developed in the late 1990s for networks that require guaranteed message delivery.) This evolution in industrial networks will enable manufacturing floor and process industry enterprises to be fully interconnected, from the factory floor to the business office and out to other factories or the corporate headquarters. There are many advantages for adopting an open industrial network standard:

- A standardized network interface for all floor equipment
- A potential decrease in network equipment cost through the use of standardized equipment
- Flexibility of interconnecting the equipment

The adoption of an open industrial networking standard means there will be increased compatibility between different equipment manufacturers and an increased capability to obtain and share manufacturing data. It is generally agreed that the basis for the industrial networks will be industrial Ethernet, although there is still much variation among industrial Ethernet standards. It is important to understand that Ethernet will not immediately replace the legacy networks already in place on the manufacturing floor. Industry tends to move conservatively because of the enormous costs involved with networking the plant and the much higher standards the equipment and systems must maintain.

This chapter presents an overview of the issues and protocols associated with industrial networks. A basic overview is presented in section 16-2. Here the reader will gain an understanding of the key issues associated with industrial networks. Industrial networks have distinct requirements that differ greatly from the commercial data network. Section 16-3 examines industrial Ethernet, considered to be the strongest contender for a universal standard in industrial networks. The key issues examined in this section are determinism and topology of the industrial network. The Ethernet protocols used in industrial Ethernet are examined in section 16-4. Section 16-5 presents a brief overview of legacy device and controller level buses.

There are many protocols competing for use on the manufacturing and processing floor. Recent technology developments in the architecture of network hardware have made it possible for industry to begin integrating conventional networking methodologies into the plant. The advantage of doing this is the ease of sharing of the data from the floor with other parts of the enterprise with the move to an open networking standard such as Ethernet.

16-2   OVERVIEW OF INDUSTRIAL NETWORKS

Industrial Networking
The process of networking the manufacturing floor with the enterprise

Computer networks are changing today's enterprises. Businesses are interconnected with high-bandwidth data lines that enable the transfer of data, voice, and video at astonishing rates. Computer networks are also changing the manufacturing floor and process industries. The generic term for this network development is **industrial networking.**

The network requirements for industrial and manufacturing processes differ greatly from the typical campus network (for example, commercial, university, and business complex systems). The components used in industrial equipment are exposed to harsh environments, high levels of electrical noise, poor power quality, and extended hours of operation. Industrial network systems must have higher reliability than conventional computer networks because the hazardous nature of industrial processes makes outages both dangerous and expensive. Many industrial and manufacturing processes deal with large amounts of energy (temperatures, currents, masses, etc.), and accidents due to the loss of network control tend to do far more damage than do similar outages in commercial systems. Even without damage, stopping an industrial process due to network downtime is expensive. For example, downtime for a paper mill is usually measured in tens of thousands of dollars per hour.

The three major differences between industrial and commercial networks are

1. **Hierarchy:** Used to divide the industrial network by function. These functions are divided into three levels: the information level, the controller level, and the device level.

2. **Redundancy:** Incorporated into industrial networks to eliminate downtime due to single points-of-failure. Industrial network topologies tend either to be inherently redundant using ring topologies or to have dual, independent operating networks.

3. **Determinism:** The ability of a network to have a guaranteed worst-case packet delivery time. Some levels of the industrial network require that data must be delivered at much tighter tolerances. A good example of this is the **CAN** (controller area network), which was designed to allow microcontrollers to communicate with each other. In fact, this network is being used to replace wiring harnesses in cars. When the driver steps on the brakes, a data packet will be sent over the CAN to the car's master cylinder, instructing it to apply the brakes. Its delivery must be reliable and deterministic.

Characteristics of Industrial Networks

Many areas of industrial networking overlap commercial networks in their use of components, topology, and protocols. However, industrial networks have unique needs requiring the use of specialized networking equipment and techniques. There are eight characteristics of industrial networks (shown in Figure 16-1) that will be discussed in this section:

- Hierarchy
- Timing considerations
- Efficiency
- Topology and redundancy
- Distance and number of devices
- Interoperability
- Message length
- Vendor support

Hierarchy
Used to divide the industrial network by function

Redundancy
Added to networks to eliminate single points-of-failure

Determinism
The ability of a network to have a guaranteed worst-case packet delivery time

CAN
Controller area network, allows microcontrollers to communicate with each other and was originally used in automotive applications

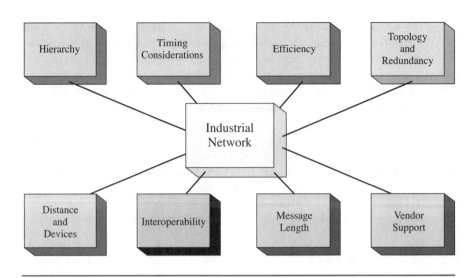

FIGURE 16-1 The eight characteristics of industrial networks.

Hierarchy Most industrial networks break down into the three hierarchical levels shown in Figure 16-2. These three levels are the information level, the controller level, and the device level. The type of information transmitted characterizes each level. The **information level** contains mostly **statistical data** such as that used in quality reports, database information for trending and statistical analysis, accounting, and job control information. Statistical data can tolerate some uncertainty in delivery times and can also tolerate delays on the order of seconds. The information level may also transmit low priority control data. **Control data** is usually intolerant of transmission uncertainty, but some control data such as alarm sharing, machine status, and utility systems status can tolerate uncertainty.

The physical location of the equipment in the information level is usually better protected from the harsh plant floor environment (for example, high levels of electrical noise, poor power quality, and extended hours of operation). This level is often implemented with commercial-off-the-shelf (**COTS**) equipment and standard Ethernet/TCP/IP implementations if the equipment is protected and the control data can tolerate uncertainty in delivery time.

At the other end of the spectrum is the **device level**, where the network interfaces with the machines on the floor (for example, robots, motors, drives, and sensors). The device level has proven to be most difficult to implement in Ethernet. The challenge is that most industrial systems run on older buses that are not compatible with Ethernet. However, industrial Ethernet (see section 16-3) is being used to transport embedded packets for these older buses. The following are common older buses on the device level:

- **ProfibusPA:** This bus allows I/O devices to be connected on one common bus line.
- **Foundation Fieldbus:** This bus is an open standard that is owned by a consortium of manufacturers and industry groups. The Foundation protocol uses layers 1, 2, and 7 (physical, data link, and application layers). It is similar to Profibus except for signaling methods and encoding.

- **DeviceNet:** This bus was developed by Allen Bradley and interfaces very well with programmable controllers. It is a local, device-level network, operating typically with up to 64 points within about 1,000 feet.

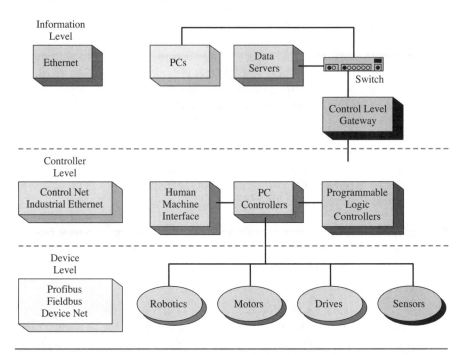

FIGURE 16-2   The three hierarchical levels of an industrial network.

At the device level, response time becomes critical. Data must be delivered on the order of milliseconds with no uncertainty in delivery time. In other words, the data *must* arrive when expected. Until recently, this inflexibility led to most systems being wired point-to-point. Each sensor, switch, and output device was wired directly to the controller using a separate pair of wires.

The ultimate goal of industrial networks may be for each discrete level device to have its own IP address. Presently, most discrete level devices are connected to remote I/O (input/output) cabinets that have networking capability. Each I/O cabinet can have several hundred discrete input or output devices connected to it. Some of the hardware devices at the device level such as motor drives and pressure transducers have networking capability. These devices are usually referred to as **intelligent** or **smart devices**. These devices can communicate directly to a controller using point-to-point wiring or over a multidrop bus such as DeviceNet or ProfibusDP.

The **controller level** is located between the information level and the device level (see Figure 16-2). The controllers provide constant communication with other controllers, the device level machinery, and the information level. The recent focus of much of the development of industrial Ethernet is at this level. Until about 1995, most of the buses at this level were proprietary buses developed by the controller manufacturer. Examples of these types of buses are Allen Bradley's DataHighway, Texas Instruments' TiWay, and Modicon's Modbus. These proprietary buses presented major problems to the end user because of the lack in **interoperability**: The

Intelligent (Smart) Devices
Devices that can communicate directly to a controller using point-to-point or multidrop wiring

Controller Level
Provides constant communication with other controllers and the device and information levels

Interoperability
Ability for the equipment to work together

buses didn't work together. User dissatisfaction with these problems led to the development of open systems such as ControlNet, Fieldbus, and others. Industrial Ethernet is rapidly replacing both the proprietary and open buses. Unfortunately there is no single industrial Ethernet protocol to replace them. The key industrial Ethernet protocols are examined in section 16-4.

Timing Considerations   The major obstacle barring the industrial adoption of Ethernet into the controller level is that Ethernet is nondeterministic. As noted, *determinism* is a guaranteed maximum worst-case delivery time that is required for real-time data transmission. The ability of multiple devices to contend for the transmission media simultaneously (CSMA/CD) guarantees data collisions and retransmissions. Improvements in Ethernet speeds and the use of layer 2 switches to isolate collision domains and other factors have produced a sufficiently deterministic network to work in most slow-speed process control applications, but the requirements of higher speed applications such as machine control are still not satisfied. Techniques for achieving determinism are examined in section 16-3.

Efficiency   The issue of efficiency examines the amount of work that must be done to send data in the network. Specifically, the key issues are the message overhead, the quantity of messages, and CPU utilization.

Message Overhead

Ethernet's minimum packet length is 64 bytes. To send one byte of data requires 64 bytes to be transmitted. In the information level, data is rarely one byte long; more often it is kilobytes long. This makes a 64-byte overhead reasonable. But at the device level, most data sizes are less than two bytes. The most common analog data word size is 12 bits. It is very inefficient to require 64 bytes of overhead to send 1.5 bytes of data.

Message Quantity

At low traffic levels, some inefficiency can be tolerated. However, industrial systems normally have hundreds or thousands of devices. An automotive assembly plant can have 250,000 switches alone. Because these switches are usually transmitted in groups of 16 (two bytes), reading each switch over an Ethernet system would require $250,000 \times 64 = 4$ MB of packets. If each switch is to be read every 10 ms, this produces 400 Mbps. Networks begin to degrade at 40–50 percent of capacity, and it becomes apparent that efficiency is a major stumbling block to moving Ethernet into the device level.

At the controller level, the picture is somewhat brighter. Controllers tend to transmit information in blocks, which is much more efficient. Now instead of using 64 bytes to transmit 16 switch states, they use 1024 bytes to transmit 500 states.

CPU Utilization

PLC
Programmable logic
controller

The important issue is how much of the computer's processing time is required for communicating with the robotics, motors, sensors, and **PLCs** (programmable logic controllers). Not all industrial interfaces provide a communications controller. This means that the computer connected to the device must manage all aspects of communication with the device. Therefore, the computer's CPU will be very busy processing the data transfers to and from the device. In the case where a communications interface is included, the computer only has to read and write data. This requires significantly less CPU processor time and yields a much more efficient system.

Topology and Redundancy   In the information level, issues of topology and re-dundancy are essentially the same for a commercial network and need not be dis-cussed here. But at the controller level, conditions mandate extra concern because industrial networks *cannot* tolerate downtime due to a **single point-of-failure**. A sin-gle point-of-failure is where a point-of-failure could shut down part of the network. Within a commercial network there are topologies that introduce single points-of-failure because network outages in these areas do not justify the additional cost of providing redundancy. However, industrial networks have such high outage costs that it is cost effective to eliminate some or all of the single points-of-failure.

Single Point-of-failure
A single failure of any device, component, cable, or software entity that can shut down part of the network

Redundant Power Supplies

It is possible to purchase key components such as switches with redundant power in-puts. This allows two independent power supplies to be connected in a **hot standby** configuration. Both supplies are operating all the time, but only one is providing power (the primary unit). Should the primary unit fail, the standby supply is already up and running, and the equipment can switch to it in microseconds and stay online.

Hot Standby
Both supplies are operating all the time, one online and the other operating as a backup ready to be switched online in case of a failure with the primary power supply

Ring Topology

Many manufacturers provide ring controllers that remove the media as a single point-of-failure. Token ring networks have problems with devices "swallowing the token" and having to use complicated protocols to recover it. In industrial rings this problem is avoided by having the network operate as a bus with one of the connections to the ring controller being idle except for a watchdog packet that circulates around the ring. When this packet is not received, the ring controller activates the standby connection, and the system operates as two buses connected by a switch. In order to remove the ring controller as a single point-of-failure, some networks interconnect two rings with standby links so that if one controller fails, the other controller "absorbs" the first controller's ring. This results in some system degradation, but at least there is not an outage.

Redundant Stars

This is a cost-effective solution for adding redundancy that requires each device to have two network interface ports. Each port connects to a dual switch. The dual switch maintains two independent switches, with the standby switch **shadowing** the active switch. Shadowing consists of maintaining identical address tables and other data structures to allow "seamless" transfer between the switches if a failure should occur. An example of a redundant star topology is provided in Figure 16-3.

Shadowing
Switches with identical address tables that allow seamless transfer between the switches if a failure should occur

Distance and Number of Devices   The relationship between distance and net-work speed is well-documented: The longer the distance, the greater the delay. At the controller level of an industrial network, these issues become critical. Industrial dis-tances may be very long compared to commercial applications. In process industries, applications tend to span large areas with thousands of devices. Even in manufactur-ing industries, cell and production line-sized networks are still large compared to commercial and campus networks.

Interoperability   It is necessary for protocols to communicate with other proto-cols at each of the three hierarchical levels of an industrial network. At the informa-tion level, this is not a major problem because most protocols at this level were designed with interoperability in mind.

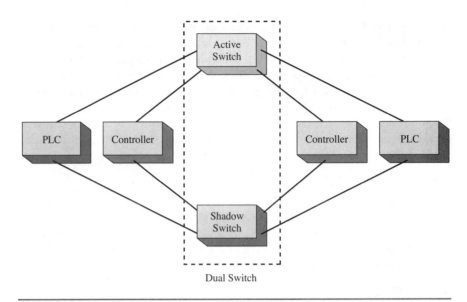

Dual Switch

FIGURE 16-3   An example of the redundant star topology.

A protocol that is in place
and cannot be replaced
primarily for operational and
economic reasons

It is a very different picture at the device level. Most **legacy protocols** are proprietary, and no effort was made by manufacturers to allow their protocol to communicate with competitor protocols. A legacy protocol is one that is in place at design time and that cannot be replaced for operational, economic, or political reasons. Upgrades and changes tend to be done much less often and are more expensive. Because of the expense and danger involved, industrial users tend to be very conservative about change. The bottom line is that the newer system must operate with the older one.

The following are examples of legacy protocols at the device and controller levels:

- **RS232, RS422, or RS485:** These are still very popular serial protocols, with the RS485 standard being most frequently used.
- **DeviceNet, Modbus, and DataHighway Plus (DH):** These are examples of proprietary buses. Many of them have been replaced by their manufacturer with open buses. For example, DH is a proprietary Allen Bradley standard that Allen Bradley has replaced with IndustrialIP.
- **Profibus, Fieldbus, and others:** Examples of open buses in the sense that the details are public but are still tied to specific manufacturers.
- **Ethernet devices restricted to operate only at 10 Mbps.**

Message Length   At the information level, a few messages are transmitted that are generally several hundred to several million bytes in length. At the device level, however, many more messages must be transmitted that are much smaller. As mentioned in the subsection on efficiency, there is a network overhead (packet headers, error detection, etc.) associated with each packet. Because of the wide variance in message length, it is impossible to build a system with optimized performance for all levels.

Vendor Support   Manufacturing and industry demand, pay for, and receive much better support for their networks. At the highest level of support are plants that have vendor field technicians and engineers onsite 24/7 (24 hours per day, 7 days per week). Most vendors maintain 24-hour hotlines with highly trained support personnel answering the phones and with engineers and senior personnel on call. Customers can purchase support contracts that guarantee onsite support within a specified time, usually within hours. Many vendors have equipment that allow offsite experts to access, troubleshoot, and configure the equipment.

This section has presented an overview of the key issues in industrial networks. The reader should now have developed an understanding of the three hierarchical levels of an industrial network (information, controller, and device) and the eight characteristics of industrial networks.

16-3   INDUSTRIAL ETHERNET

The objective of this section is to develop an understanding of the role of Ethernet in industrial networks. This is called **industrial Ethernet** and is the strongest contender for a universal industrial network for three major reasons:

- The Ethernet open-standard infrastructure has allowed bridges between previously closed areas such as controller buses, device buses, and others.
- Maintaining a competitive edge involves rapid configuration and data access in a seamless manner. Management wants "real-time" status reports. Customers, driven by methods such as **Just-in-time** and **Lean** ordering methods, demand order status information. Just-in-time and Lean are management strategies where the manufacturing materials are delivered right before they are needed.
- Decreasing costs and increasing power. The cost of developing "faster, cheaper, and better" Ethernet networking equipment is being absorbed by the commercial equipment manufacturers.

The major obstacle barring the industrial adoption of earlier Ethernet is that it used a bus topology and was nondeterministic. The fact that multiple devices could contend for the transmission media simultaneously (CSMA/CD) guaranteed data collisions and retransmissions. This made it impossible to guarantee a maximum worst-case delivery time, as required for real-time data transmission. When this was added to the 5 to 20 milliseconds data scan rates of many controllers, early Ethernet was just too slow and unreliable.

Achieving Determinism

Improvements have been made in Ethernet in four major areas in order to achieve determinism: network topology, bus management, speed, and redundancy. Examples of network topology and bus improvements include the use of switched media and using full duplex operation to obtain determinism. The switches enable a virtual point-to-point Ethernet network connection between two networking devices. The direct (switched) connection means there is not a contention problem for the network bus. Speeds have increased from 10 Mbps to 100 Mbps to 1 Gbps and to 10 Gbps. The slower data speeds work for the factory floor networks (device level) and the higher data speeds are used to link the floor networks to the enterprise (information level).

Industrial Ethernet
The strongest contender for a universal standard in industrial networks

Just-in-time and Lean
Management strategies where the manufacturing materials are delivered right before they are needed

This also permits redundancy to be built into an industrial implementation of Ethernet. The redundancy components are high speed when compared to commercial devices and switch in less than 250 msec.

Topology

Linear Network Topology
A backbone network is looped to the switches that connect to device level equipment

Ethernet Ring
Uses a switch as the ring manager to provide an alternate data path in case of a failure

The most common network topologies used in industrial Ethernet networks are **linear** and **Ethernet ring**. Figure 16-4 shows the linear network topology. In this topology, a backbone network is extended to each of the switches. The switches are used to connect the overall network to the device level network equipment (for example, PLCs).

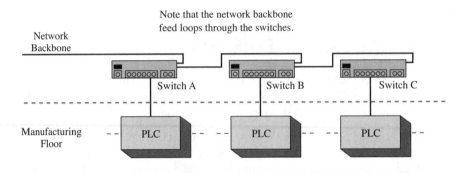

FIGURE 16-4   An example of a linear network topology.

A big concern with this type of network is that a failed switch or cable problem will cause the plant equipment to become isolated from the network, and communications will stop. This deficiency in the linear network can be overcome by adding redundancy to the Ethernet network.

Redundancy can be added by incorporating an Ethernet ring topology. This type of network is not actually a true circular ring but uses a switch as the ring manager to provide an alternate path for the data to travel to each switch as illustrated in Figure 16-5.

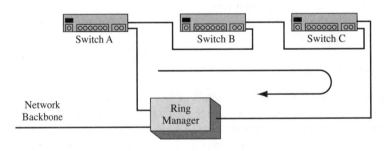

FIGURE 16-5   An example of an Ethernet ring.

The network backbone data feed connects through the ring manager. The data circulates in a clockwise direction in the network. The ring manager uses link tests to make sure that data can reach all switches in the immediate network. For example, assume that there is a break between switch A and switch B (see Figure 16-5). The ring manager determines there must be a break in the line connecting switch A and B because it detects switch A but not switch B or C. Remember, the primary data flows clockwise. The ring manager switches the data flow from the backbone so that data now flows counterclockwise. This allows data from switch A through switch C to reach switch B even with the break in the primary data path.

Switching

Perhaps the biggest step forward in the development of industrial Ethernet has been the use of switches (also known as *switching hubs* or *layer 2 switches*) to isolate collision domains. These switches build and maintain address tables and can switch a packet from the input port to the output port in microseconds (refer back to Chapter 4 for a review of network switches). They can be configured so that ports are subdivided into groups in which all packets received on one port of a group will only be transmitted to another port within the group. By overlapping these groups, one port can appear in several groups. This allows devices in logically functional units to be placed in the same group and thus further reduces collisions.

Cabling and Components

The network components used for the campus model are rated at commercial quality. Industrial networks are much harsher on cabling and components than is the campus/office environment. Industrial network areas are generally divided into **light duty** and **heavy duty** areas. Light duty areas are located inside protective cabinets. These cabinets are located either on the plant floor or in protected rooms such as motor control centers. The cabinets located on the plant floor are protected from some environmental conditions such as physical damage, electrical noise, and dust but are not protected from other conditions such as humidity and temperature. Cabinets located in motor control centers are better protected and usually air conditioned. Light duty components may be either commercial grade or industrial grade depending on the application.

Heavy duty areas have no protection. Cabling and components are exposed to the plant floor environment including dust, humidity, physical damage, electrical noise, water, and chemicals. These components should be industrial grade.

Ethernet components are normally available as either commercial grade or industrial grade. The differences are shown in Table 16-1.

Light Duty
Refers to areas located in protected cabinets

Heavy Duty
Equipment placed in areas of no protection in an industrial setting

TABLE 16-1   Differences in Specifications for Commercial and Industrial Grade Ethernet Components

Specification	Commercial	Industrial
Temperature	0 to 40° C	0 to 70° C
Shock and vibration	Not tested	Meets industrial standards such as IEC 68 or NSTA Project 1
NEC hazardous locations	Unclassified	Typically Class 1 Div II
Mounting	Not specified	Din Rail
Power	120VAC	120VAC or 18–24VDC with redundant inputs

Armored
A nondestructible covering

Cabling The UTP CAT6/5e cable used in most commercial applications is unsuitable for some industrial environments. It has a very low pull strength (< 25 lbs.) and is not crush proof. Commercial CAT5e cable is adequate for light duty areas but not for heavy duty areas. The low pull strength makes it difficult to run in conduit, and running it in cable trays may crush it. The U in UTP stands for *unshielded,* which increases the noise susceptibility of the cable. Problems with shield terminations make STP (shielded twisted-pair) only marginally better. **Armored** fiber optic is rapidly becoming the standard in heavy duty industrial network areas. The fiber cable is not susceptible to corrosion, and the armor on the cable means that it is protected from being crushed. Basically, the armored fiber has a nondestructible covering. Following are some of the advantages of fiber:

- Immunity to interference from manufacturing or process machinery.
- Corrosion effects from the manufacturing or process are not an issue.
- Safety is a big issue because fiber is a dielectric and does not conduct electricity.

Connectors An important reason for moving to Ethernet components is the availability of cost effective COTS (commercial-off-the-shelf) components. The standard connector for Ethernet in office/campus networks is the RJ-45, which is derived from telephone connectors. It is marginally adequate for office environments and unsuitable for both light and heavy duty areas in industrial environments. There are several reasons for this:

- **Waterproofing:** There is not a successful, cost-effective way to waterproof these connectors.
- **Ruggedness:** Industrial connectors are subject to multi-axis stress and to shock. Plastic connectors cannot handle this.
- **Vibration:** Researchers have found that vibration erodes the gold plating on RJ-45 connectors very quickly. There are connectors available with thicker gold plating.

Three groups, Woodhead Connectivity, Agilent (HP), and a consortium of Rockwell/Belden/Panduit/Commscope/Anixter, have developed designs for connectors based on combining the RJ-45 with an M style connector. The standard industrial Ethernet connector should come from one of these designs.

Power Most modern field devices are *loop powered.* This means that power to the field device is provided with the same cable that provides the data (control) connection. In this case, the power to the device and the data connection occupy the same physical pair of wires, giving us the typical two-wire control loops found in most applications. If Ethernet is going to move to the device level, it will have to provide power. The IEEE 802.3af standard has been developed to solve this problem. They are considering using one of the unused wire pairs in the standard CAT5e cable to provide the loop power:

16-4 INDUSTRIAL ETHERNET PROTOCOLS

The objective of this section is for the reader to gain an understanding of the various Ethernet protocols being used in industrial Ethernet. The protocols presented are based on either TCP or UDP. Recall that TCP (Transport Control Protocol) is a connection-oriented protocol. UDP (User Datagram Protocol) is also being used in industrial Ethernet and is a connectionless protocol. TCP is the dominant transport layer protocol used in commercial applications and also stands to dominate industrial Ethernet. Both protocols support the use of port numbers (refer back to Chapter 5 for a discussion on ports). These port numbers can be assigned, registered, or dynamic. Assigned numbers range from 0 to 1023 and are allocated to programs such as telnet and ftp. Numbers between 1024 and 49151 can be registered to specific products. An example of a registered port is 44818, which belongs to DeviceNet and ControlNet, industrial network protocols.

Ethernet/IP

The first protocol examined is **Ethernet/IP**, also called the Ethernet Industrial Protocol. Ethernet/IP is an open network based on the following:

1. IEEE 802.3 physical and data link standard
2. Ethernet TCP/IP protocol suite
3. Control and Information Protocol (**CIP**), which is an earlier protocol used by DeviceNet and ControlNet systems. Ethernet/IP works by inserting CIP into the application layer.

    This standard is proposed by the Open DeviceNet Vendor Association (ODVA) and was developed by Allen Bradley as an extension of their DeviceNet device level protocol. It focuses on the information and control network for discrete manufacturing plants in industries such as automotive, forest products, and electronics. Ethernet/IP has the backing of four industrial network associations—ODVA, ControlNet International, the Industrial Automation Open Networking Alliance, and the Industrial Ethernet Association.

    Ethernet/IP uses CIP to encapsulate DeviceNet and ControlNet messages inside the data field of a TCP/IP packet. TCP/IP then transmits the message to the data link layer. *Explicit messages* in the data field contain both protocol information and instructions for service performance. These types of messages are commonly used for node configuration and diagnostics. Ethernet/IP uses the simpler and faster User Datagram Protocol/Internet Protocol (**UDP/IP**) for real-time messages. UDP/IP handles both multicast and implicit messages. In **implicit messages**, the data field contains only real-time I/O data. Because the data format is predefined, these messages have low overhead and short processing times.

    On the user side of the protocol, Ethernet/IP presents itself as a set (or library) of objects. These **objects** are programs that enable Ethernet/IP to be configured for a particular machine or interface, thus making the protocol very flexible and relatively easy to integrate into an existing industrial network.

Foundation Fieldbus High-Speed Ethernet (HSE)

Foundation Fieldbus HSE was developed by the Fieldbus Foundation and focuses on process industries such as electricity, oil, and pharmaceuticals. It includes an existing industrial network protocol (called H1) that is used for device level communications. H1 has a modest market share and industry support. HSE supports the 100-Mbps Ethernet protocol and uses both TCP/IP and UDP/IP. TCP/IP is used for unscheduled messages and for large data transfers; UDP/IP is used for alarms, scheduled data transfers, and synchronizing the inputs and outputs during data transfers.

Ethernet/IP
An open networking protocol based on IEEE 802.3, TCP/IP, and CIP

CIP
Control and Information Protocol

UDP/IP
User Datagram Protocol/Internet Protocol

Implicit Messages
The data field contains only real-time I/O data

Objects
Programs that enable the Ethernet/IP protocol to be configured for a particular machine or interface

Foundation Fieldbus HSE
High-speed Ethernet protocol that focuses on support for process industries

Profinet

Profinet
Ethernet protocol that works
with the older Profibus
device level protocol

Profinet was developed by Profibus International and is an Ethernet-based protocol that works with the older Profibus device level protocol. The main industrial supporter of this standard is Siemens. The Profibus standard had a very good market share and was well accepted in European process industry. The Profinet protocol uses TCP/IP for reliable connectivity but also supports the option to use UDP/IP.

Interface for Distributed Automation (IDA)

IDA
Interface for Distributed
Automation

RTPS
Real-Time Publish-Subscribe
Protocol, provides time-
stamped data and control
packets

MMS
Manufacturing Message
Specification

Modbus TCP
Allows industrial network
connections to be made via
the Internet Protocol

This is an industrial Ethernet specification that is based on all levels of the automation hierarchy. **IDA** promises real-time data speeds to support networks operating robotics, packaging, and motion control. IDA is a UDP/IP protocol using the **RTPS** (Real-Time Publish-Subscribe) Protocol. RTPS provides time-stamped data and control packets.

Manufacturing Message Specification (MMS)

MMS is a TCP/IP protocol running over Ethernet. This protocol is a byproduct of General Motor's Manufacturing Application Protocol (MAP).

Modbus TCP

This is an industrial protocol based on TCP/IP that has been developed to allow industrial network connections to be made via the Internet. **Modbus TCP** is essentially the legacy industrial network protocol Modbus encapsulated in a TCP/IP packet.

16-5 LEGACY DEVICE AND CONTROLLER LEVEL BUSES

Most current buses may soon be replaced by protocols based on the Ethernet standard. However, the following buses will almost certainly be encountered either as legacy systems or in new systems specified by conservative adopters.

Open Buses

Profibus   This bus was developed in Germany in the late 1980s. It is based on the earlier RS485 standard and used either a 9-pin D-shell or 12 mm connectors. A baud rate up to 12 Mbps is used by this protocol with a message size of 244 bytes per message. This bus is very popular in Europe and in European equipment imported into the United States. Its DP and FMS formats allow it to be at the device and controller levels, respectively. ProfiBusDP is a polling (deterministic) network that is commonly used for I/O data. ProfiBusFMS is often used to communicate among controllers, PCs, and HMI equipment. It has both twisted-pair and fiber optic capability.

Foundation Fieldbus   In the late 1990s, the Instruments, Systems and Automation Society (ISA) developed this bus to be an open standard for mission critical, process control, and intrinsically safe environments. This bus is not tied to a specific manufacturer and has multiple vendors. It is popular with users of high-end controllers such as the Distributive Control System (DCS) used in the process industry. It uses a scheduler in each segment of the network to guarantee message delivery, so issues of determinism and repeatability are solidly addressed.

DeviceNet   This bus was developed by Allen Bradley in the mid 1990s. It is an open standard managed by the Open DeviceNet Vendor Association (ODVA). It has a software layer added to the earlier standard, CAN (controller area network). It is relatively slow, with a maximum data rate of 500 Kb/s, but supports extensive handshaking and message formats. The CAN technology was designed to be used in automotive products (specifically Mercedes). Expensive and difficult to maintain wiring harnesses were to be replaced with networks carrying control packets to devices. The CAN technology is designed to be highly reliable.

DeviceNet's maximum message size of 8 bytes makes it designed for the device and controller level.

Proprietary Buses

DataHighwayPlus   This protocol is owned by Allen Bradley for communications between PLC5 controllers and was dominant in the 1990s. It is billed as an industrial local area network. It uses twisted-pair cable (commonly called "blue hose") and can transmit up to 230 Kbps, although slower speeds are more common. It is a token-passing network. PCs could access the DataHighway network only through proprietary cards and software.

ModBus   This bus was introduced by Modicon in the late 1970s and is still popular. It is a relatively slow serial network designed to support analog control data and discrete I/O data between devices and controllers or devices and devices, often using ASCII code. Because of this and a royalty-free license, it was a very open network and became popular with a great deal of third-party support.

Modbus could either be RS-232, which is a point-to-point standard, or RS-485, which is a multinode standard. It could attain speeds of 1 Mbps, but data rates of 9600 bps were more common.

HART   This standard was developed to work over standard point-to-point instrumentation wiring sending two-way digital information simultaneously with the 4–20 mA analog control signal. This allowed "smart" devices to be configured across the existing instrumentation wiring. It did this by sending tones representing 1 and 0 across the wiring, where $0 = 2.2$ kHz and $1 = 1.2$ kHz. Many companies, chiefly Rosemont and Honeywell, began developing instruments such as pressure transmitters that used the HART technology. HART has since been moved to an open protocol supported by the HART Communications Foundation.

SUMMARY

The objective of this chapter has been to introduce the reader to industrial networks, in particular industrial Ethernet. Industrial networks are not new. Manufacturing has been successfully using proprietary network protocols for many years for controlling the manufacturing floor. The difference now is industry wants to unite the enterprise under one large, highly flexible, and fully integrated network. This means that the administration will be networked to the information, controller, and device level networks via a common Ethernet network. This also means that the manufacturing floor can be extended out onto the Internet. The concepts the reader should understand include the following:

- The key issues associated with industrial networks
- The key characteristics of an industrial network
- The role Ethernet is playing in industrial networks
- The basic industrial Ethernet protocols and the legacy protocols already in use

QUESTIONS AND PROBLEMS

Section 16-2

1. Explain how the network requirements for industrial/manufacturing differ from those for commercial networks.
2. List the three major differences between industrial and commercial networks.
3. What are the three hierarchical levels of an industrial network?
4. At what level of an industrial network is the job control information found?
5. At what level can COTS equipment be used in an industrial network?
6. Which level of an industrial network is the most difficult to implement in Ethernet and why?
7. List three common older buses used on the device level of the manufacturing floor.
8. Why is response time critical at the device level?
9. What is the purpose of controllers at the controller level?
10. Why is determinism a major obstacle to industry adopting Ethernet at the controller level?
11. How can a single point-of-failure be avoided in industrial networks?
12. Why is interoperability an important issue at the device level?

Section 16-3

13. What standard is the strongest contender for a universal industrial network?
14. List four improvements made in Ethernet that have helped provide determinism.
15. What is the big concern with a linear network topology?
16. How does the Ethernet ring topology provide redundancy?

17. Can CAT6/5e twisted-pair cable be used in an industrial Ethernet network? Justify your answer.
18. Are commercial RJ-45 connectors suitable for use in industrial networks? Justify your answer.

Section 16-4

19. What is the registered port number for DeviceNet and ControlNet?
20. In general, how does Ethernet/IP work? Why is this important?
21. What protocol is used for real-time messages in Ethernet/IP?
22. What is the data rate for Foundation Fieldbus HSE, and what protocol is used to send unscheduled messages?
23. Identify whether the following protocols use TCP/IP, UDP/IP, or both:
    a. Ethernet/IP
    b. Foundation Fieldbus HSE
    c. Profinet
    d. IDA
    e. Modbus TCP

Critical Thinking

24. What command can be used in an industrial Ethernet network to determine whether a machine on the manufacturing floor is connected to the network?
25. Could the IP address 10.20.250.1 be assigned to a device in an industrial network if the device must be accessible from the Internet? Justify your answer.

Glossary

? the help command that can be used at any prompt in the command line interface for the Cisco IOS software

10Base2 10 Mbps-Baseband-200 meters (185 meters)

10GBASE-T 10 gigabit over twisted-pair copper

absorption light interaction with the atomic structure of the fiber material; also involves the conversion of optical power to heat

access layer where the networking devices in a campus LAN connect together

access lists (ACLs) a basic form of firewall protection

access point a transceiver used to interconnect a wireless and a wired LAN

ACK acknowledgement packet

ACR combined measurement of attenuation and crosstalk; a larger ACR indicates greater data capacity

Active Directory a centralized system that automates the management of user data, security, and distributed services

ad hoc another term used to describe an independent network

administrative distance a number assigned to a protocol or route to declare its reliability

administratively down indicates that the router interface has been shut off by the administrator

ADSL (asymmetric DSL) service providing up to 1.544 Mbps from the user to the service provider and up to 8 Mbps back to the user from the service provider

advertise the sharing of route information

aging time the length of time a MAC address remains assigned to a port

AGP Accelerated Graphics Port

AMI alternate mark inversion

applet small, limited-function application often used in control panels and on Web pages

application layer provides support for applications, processes requests from hosts, and makes sure a connection is made to an appropriate port

area 0 in OSPF this is the root area and is the backbone for the network

areas partition of a large OSPF network into smaller OSPF networks

ARIN American Registry for Internet Numbers

armored a nondestructive covering

ARP Address Resolution Protocol; used to map an IP address to its MAC address

ARP cache temporary storage of MAC addresses recently contacted

ARP reply protocol where the MAC address is returned

ARP request a query asking which network interface has a specified IP address

ARP table another name for the ARP cache

ARPAnet Advanced Research Projects Agency network

AS autonomous systems

ASN autonomous systems number

association indicates that the destination address is for a networking device connected to one of the ports on the bridge; indicates that a link has been established between an access point and a client

asymmetric operation describes the modem operation when the data-transfer rates to and from the service provider differ

ATM asynchronous transfer mode

attenuation the amount of loss in the signal strength or power as the signal propagates down a wire or fiber strand

AUI port a router's 10 Mbps Ethernet port

authenticated the server verifies that the computer and user are authorized to access the network

auto-negotiation protocol used by interconnected electronic devices to negotiate a link speed

autonomous system (AS) a number assigned to a routing protocol to define which networks exchange routes

auxiliary input an alternate way to access the router, using a dial-in modem

B8ZS bipolar 8 zero substitution

backbone primary path for data traffic to and from destinations and sources in the campus network

backbone main fiber distribution

backbone cabling cabling that interconnects telecommunication closets, equipment rooms, and cabling entrances in the same building and between buildings

backhoe fading splice loss introduced by repairing a fiber cable dug up by a backhoe

balanced mode neither wire in the wire pairs connects to ground

bandwidth the data capacity of the networking link

baseband information is in a digital form

bash bourne again shell

Basic Service Set (BSS) a term used to describe an independent network

beacon used to verify the integrity of a wireless link

BGP Border Gateway Protocol

BIOS (Basic Input Output System) contains the basic instructions needed by the computer to operate

bipolar coding successive 1s are represented by pulses in the opposite voltage direction

bipolar violation the pulse is in the same voltage direction as the previous pulse

boot sequence the order in which the computer selects a drive for loading the computer's boot instructions

BOOTP Bootstrap Protocol

bottlenecking another term for network congestion

bridge a networking device that uses the MAC address to forward data and interconnect two LANs

bridging table list of MAC addresses and port locations for hosts connected to the bridge ports

broadcast transmission of data to all devices

broadcast domain any broadcast sent out on the network is seen by all hosts in this domain

broadcast storm excessive amounts of broadcasts

brute force attack attacker uses every possible combination of characters for the password

buffer temporary storage for holding data packets until it is time for them to be sent

buffer overflow happens when a program tries to put more data into a buffer than it was configured to hold

building entrance the point where the outdoor cabling interconnects with the internal building cabling

bursty data rates can momentarily exceed the leased data rate of the service

bus mastering provides a performances boost of the computer's CPU bus

bus topology the computers share the media (coaxial cable) for data transmission

cable modem modem that can use the high bandwidth of a cable television system to deliver high-speed data to and from the service provider

campus network a collection of two or more interconnected LANs in a limited geographic area

CAN controller area network, used to replace wiring harnesses in cars

cat Linux command used to print the file text to the screen

CAT5 (category 5) twisted-pair cables capable of carrying 100 Mbps of data up to a length of 100 meters

CAT5/e enhanced version of CAT5

CAT6 the current standard in high-performance twistedpair cable

CBWFQ class-based weighted fair queuing

CCIE Cisco Certified Internet Expert

CCNA Cisco Certified Network Associate

CCNP Cisco Certified Network Professional

cd Linux command for changing directories

chgrp command used in Linux to change group ownership of a file

child a subset domain of the main tree

chkconfig Linux command used by administrators to enable and disable services at boot time

chmod command used in Linux to change permissions on files and directories

chown command used in Linux to change ownership of a file

chromatic dispersion broadening of a pulse due to different propagation rates of the spectral components of the light

CIDR classless interdomain routing

CIDR block the grouping of two or more class networks together; also called supernetting

CIP Control and Information Protocol

Cisco IOS Cisco Internet Operating System, the operating software used in all Cisco routers

cladding material surrounding the core of the optical waveguide, which must have a lower index of refraction to keep the light in the core

Class A, B, C, D, and E the five classes of IPv4

class network address the network portion of the IP address based on the class of the network

classful the IP and subnet addresses are within the same network

classful addressing the network portion of a particular network address

classful network same as a class network

client computer connected to the network that accesses services from the server

client/server network the server handles multiple requests from multiple clients for multiple services

clusters storage area for files and directories

CODEC encodes, compresses, and decodes the data

color map the specification of what wire color connects to what pin on the connector

COM1, COM2, . . . the computer's serial communication ports

combo terminations the interface supports multiple types of media connections

command line a text entry level for commands

command line interface (CLI) interface type used for inputting commands and for configuring devices such as routers

committed burst information rate (CBIR) enables subscribers to exceed the committed information rate (CIR) during times of heavy traffic

committed information rate (CIR) guaranteed data rate or bandwidth to be used in the frame relay connection

community computer a computer that has no security attached to it

configure terminal (conf t) command to enter the router's terminal configuration mode

connection oriented protocol establishes a network connection, manages the delivery of data, and terminates the connection

console cable cable that connects a router's console port to a computer's serial port

console input provides an RS-232 serial communications link into the router

container Windows 2003/2000 server name for a folder

control data not usually tolerant of data time delivery but can include some control data such as alarm sharing, machine status, and utility systems status that can tolerate some variability in data time delivery

controller level provides constant communication with other controllers and the device and information levels

convergence the time it takes for the router to obtain a clear view of the routes in a network

copy run start command for copying the running-configuration to the startup-configuration

core the backbone of the network; the portion of the fiber strand that carries the light

cost measure that takes into account bandwidth and expense

COTS commercial off the shelf

country domain usually two letters, .us (United States) or .ca (Canada), that define the location of the domain server for that country

cp Linux command to copy files

CQ custom queuing

cross-connected transmit and receive signal pairs are crossed to properly align each for data communication

crossover cable transmit and receiver wire pairs are crossed

crosstalk signal coupling in a cable

CSMA/CA carrier sense multiple access/collision avoidance

CSMA/CD the Ethernet LAN protocol, carrier sense multiple access with collision detection

CSU/DSU channel service unit/data service unit

D4 framing the original data framing used in T1 circuits

daemon Linux name for the server package

data link layer provides for the flow of data

DB-25 25-pin connector

DB-9 9-pin connector

DCE Data Communications Equipment (the serial connection responsible for clocking)

DDR SDRAM double data-rate SDRAM

default gateway address the IP address of the networking device used to forward data that needs to leave the LAN

delay the time it takes a data packet to travel from source to destination

delay skew measure of the difference in arrival time between the fastest and slowest signal in the UTP wire pair

denial of service (DoS) a service is being denied to a computer, network, or server

dense wave division multiplex (DWDM) incorporates the propagation of several wavelengths in the 1550-nm range for a single fiber

determinism the ability of a network to have a guaranteed worst-case packet delivery time

deterministic access to the network is provided at fixed time intervals

device drivers interface the operating system to the hardware

device level where the network interfaces to the manufacturing or process machinery

DHCP Dynamic Host Configuration Protocol; IP addresses are assigned dynamically

dictionary attack uses known passwords and many variations (upperand lowercase and combinations) to try to log in to your account

DIMM dual in-line memory module

directed broadcast the broadcast is sent to a specific subnet

discrete mulitone (DMT) a multicarrier technique used for transporting digital data over copper telephone lines

dispersion broadening of a light pulse as it propagates through a fiber strand

dispersion compensating fiber acts like an equalizer, canceling dispersion effects and yielding close to zero dispersion in the 1550-nm region

distance vector protocol a routing algorithm that periodically sends the entire routing table to its neighboring or adjacent router

distributed feedback (DFB) laser a more stable laser suitable for use in DWDM systems

distribution layer point where the individual LANs connect together

DL diode laser

dlci tag the data link connection identifier assigned by Telco for use within the Telco cloud; the tag associates which PVC is coming through and where it is coming from

dmesg command used to display the boot processes for Linux, used to identify why certain processes failed

DNS domain name service

domain controller provides authentication, stores directory information, and provides directory services

DRAM dynamic random access memory

DRD RAM (RDRAM) Direct RAMBUS DRAM

DS digital signal

DS-0 to DS-3 common telecommunication data rates

DSL digital subscriber line

DSSS direct sequence spread spectrum

DTE Data Terminal Equipment

dynamic assignment MAC addresses are assigned to a port when a host is connected

dynamic routing protocols routing table is dynamically updated to account for loss or changes in routes or changes in data traffic

eBGP external Border Gateway Protocol

echo request part of the ICMP protocol that requests a reply from a computer

EDO RAM extended data-out RAM

EIA Electronics Industries Alliance

EIA/TIA 568B the standard that defines the six subsystems of a structured cabling system

EIGRP Enhanced Interior Gateway Routing Protocol

EISA Extended Industry Standard Architecture

EMI electromagnetic interference

enable command used to enter the router's privileged mode

enterprise network term used to describe the network used by a large company

entrance facilities another term for the building entrance

equal level FEXT (ELFEXT) calculation obtained by subtracting the attenuation value from the far-end crosstalk

equipment room a room set aside for complex electronic equipment such as the network servers and telephone equipment

ESF extended superframe framing

eth0, eth1, eth2, . . . the way Linux identifies the Ethernet interface cards

Ethernet/IP an open networking protocol based on IEEE 802.3, TCP/IP, and CIP

Ethernet, physical, hardware, or adapter address other names for the MAC address

Ethernet port (E0, E1, E2, . . .) naming of the Ethernet ports on the router

Ethernet ring uses a switch as the ring manager to provide an alternate data path in case of a failure

event a disturbance of the light propagating down the fiber span that results in a disturbance on the OTDR trace

executable (x) permission allows the program or script to run

Extended Service Set (ESS) the use of multiple access points to extend user mobility

Fast Ethernet an Ethernet system operating at 100 Mbps

fast link pulse (FLP) carries the configuration information between each end of a data link

FAT file allocation table

FAT16 uses a 16-bit file allocation table

FAT32 uses a 32-bit file allocation table

FHSS frequency hopping spread spectrum

fiber Bragg grating a short strand of modified fiber that changes the index of refraction and minimizes intersymbol interference

fiber cross-connect optical patch panel used to interconnect fiber cables

fiber, light pipe, glass synonymous terms for a fiber optic strand

FIFO first in, first out

firewall used in computer networks for protecting the network

first queued describing when the data packet arrives

flat network a network where the LANs share the same broadcast domain

forest a collection of domains

forward domain service translation of name to an IP address

Foundation Fieldbus HSE high-speed Ethernet protocol that focuses on support for process industries

fractional T1 indicates that only a portion of the T1 bandwidth is being used

frame relay cloud provides all of the required switches for routing the data to the destination network, usually provided by your local Telco

frame relay network a packet switching network designed to carry data traffic over a public data network

fstab the file that contains the arguments used when the mount command for a drive has been requested

FTP File Transfer Protocol

FTTB fiber to the business

FTTC fiber to the curb

FTTH fiber to the home

full channel consists of all the link elements from the wall plate to the hub or switch

full duplex computer system can transmit and receive at the same time

full IPv6 address all 32 hexadecimal positions contain a value other than 0

fusion splicing a long-term method where two fibers are fused or welded together

gateway describes the networking device that enables hosts in a LAN to connect to networks (and hosts) outside the LAN; the IP telephone system interface to the PSTN

GBIC gigabit interface converter

gigabit Ethernet 1000 Mbps Ethernet

graded-index fiber the index of refraction is gradually varied with a parabolic profile

grep Linux command used to search for strings in a text file

group collection of users that can be used to set policy at the domain or organizational unit level

H.323 suite of protocols that defines how voice and video are transported over IP networks

half duplex the communications device can transmit or receive but not at the same time

HDLC high-level data link control, a synchronous proprietary protocol

hand-off when the user associates itself with another access point

heavy duty equipment placed in areas of no protection in an industrial setting

hello interval time between "Hello" packets

"Hello" packets used in the OSPF protocol to verify that the links are still communicating

hex hexadecimal, base 16

hidden files files that start with a period that can only be viewed with the *ls -la* or *ls -al* command

hierarchy used to divide the industrial network by function

history displays the commands entered on the command line in Linux

holddowns prevent bad routes from being reinstated

hop count the number of routers a data packet must pass through to reach the destination

hopping sequence the order of frequency changes

horizontal cabling cabling that extends out from the telecommunications closet into the LAN work area

host enables a specific host IP address to be entered in the access list

host address same as the host number

host number the portion of the IP address that defines the location of the networking device connected to the network; also called the host address

hostname the name assigned to a networking device; the command used to change the name of a Linux machine or a router

hot standby both supplies are operating all the time, one online and the other operating as a backup ready to be switched online in case of a failure with the primary power supply

HSSI high-speed serial interface

httpd the script that starts the Web server

httpd.conf the configuration file for the Apache Web server

hub broadcasts the data it receives to all devices connected to its ports

HyperTerminal Microsoft serial communications software package

IANA the agency that assigns IP addresses to computer networks

iBGP internal Border Gateway Protocol

IC interconnect fibers

ICANN Internet Corporation for Assigned Names and Numbers

ICMP Internet Control Message Protocol

IDA Interface for Distributed Automation

IDC intermediate distribution closet

IDE Integrated Drive Electronics

IEEE Institute of Electrical and Electronic Engineers, one of the major standards-setting bodies for technological development

IEEE 1394 (Firewire, i-Link) a high-speed, low-cost serial connection

IETF Internet Engineering Task Force

ifconfig reports all of the network devices recognized and running on the system, listing all of the interfaces and the configuration for each

ifdown, ifup Linux commands used to shut down and bring back up the network interface

IGMP Internet Group Message Protocol

IGP Interior Gateway Protocol

IGRP Interior Gateway Routing Protocol

implicit messages the data field contains only real-time I/O data

inbound data traffic data traffic entering the network

index-matching gel a jellylike substance that has an index of refraction much closer to glass than to air

industrial Ethernet the strongest contender for a universal standard in industrial networks

industrial networking the process of networking the manufacturing floor with the enterprise

information level the hierarchical level of industrial networks that contains mostly statistical data

infrared light light extending from 680 nm up to the wavelengths of the microwaves

intelligent (smart) devices devices that can communicate directly to a controller using point-to-point or multidrop wiring

Internet layer defines the protocols used for addressing and routing data packets

interoperability ability for the equipment to work together

interrupt request (IRQ) determines where a computer's CPU should look for a hardware interrupt request

intranet an internal network that provides file and resource sharing but is not accessed from the Internet

intrusion detection monitoring data packets passing through the network to catch potential or ongoing attacks

IP address unique 32-bit address that identifies on which network the computer is located

IP (Internet Protocol) defines the addressing used for identifying the source and destination addresses of data packets being delivered over an IP network

IP network a network that uses IP addressing for identifying devices connected to the network

ip route router configuration command for manually setting the next hop IP address

IP tunnel an IP packet encapsulated in another IP packet

ipconfig command used to display the computer's IP address; reports all of the network devices recognized and running on the system; lists all of the interfaces and configurations for each interface

ipconfig /all enables the MAC address information to be displayed from the command prompt

IPng next generation IP

IPsec IP security

IPv4 the IP version currently being used on the Internet

IPv6 IP version 6

IPX Novell's Internetworking Packet Exchange networking protocol

ISA Industry Standard Architecture

ISDN integrated services digital network

ISM industrial, scientific, and medical

isolator an in-line passive device that allows optical power to flow only in one direction

ISP Internet service provider

jitter produces a poorly reconstructed signal at the receiver due to variability in data packet arrival

Just-in-time and Lean management strategies where the manufacturing materials are delivered right before they are needed

Keepalive packet indicates that the Ethernet interface is connected to another networking device such as a hub, switch, or router

kill [PID], kill -9 [PID] Linux commands used to kill a process

L2TP Layer 2 Tunneling Protocol

last command used to display logins to the Linux system

layer 2 switch an improved network technology that provides a direct data connection for network devices in a LAN

layer 3 network another name for a routed network

lease time the amount of time that a client can hold an IP address

LED light-emitting diode

legacy in computer networking, means that the technology is outdated

legacy protocol a protocol that is in place and cannot be replaced primarily for operational and economic reasons

light duty refers to areas located in protected cabinets

line of demarcation point where ownership of the communications equipment changes from the communications carrier to the user

linear network topology the backbone network is looped through the switches that connect to device level equipment

link point from one cable termination to another

link integrity test protocol used to verify that a communication link between two Ethernet devices has been established

link light indicates that the transmit and receive pairs are properly aligned

link pulses sent by each of the connected devices via the twisted-pair cables to indicate that the link is up

link state advertisement (LSA) the exchange of updated link state information when routes change

link state protocol establishes a relationship with a neighboring router and uses route advertisements to build routing tables

lo Linux symbol representing the loopback

load network activity of a link or router

load balancing a protocol procedure that enables the router to use any one of multiple data paths to reach the destination

local area network (LAN) network of users that share computer resources in a limited area

logical address describes the IP address location of the network and the address location of the host in the network

logical fiber map shows how the fiber is interconnected and data is distributed throughout a campus

long haul the transmission of data over hundreds or thousands of miles

loopback the data is routed directly back to the source

ls lists the basic files in the directory in Linux

ls -l lists file attributes in Linux

ls -la allows you to see hidden files in addition to the file attributes in Linux

MAC address a unique 6-byte address assigned by the vendor of the network interface card

macrobending loss due to light breaking up and escaping into the cladding

man the command used to display the online text manual for Linux

managed switch allows the network administrator to monitor, configure, and manage select network features

Management Information Base (MIB) a collection of standard objects that are used to obtain configuration parameters and performance data on a networking device

Mbps mega (million) bits per second

MCA Micro Channel Architecture

mechanical splices two fibers joined together with an air gap, thereby requiring an index-matching gel to provide a good splice

media converter used to adapt a layer 1 (physical layer) technology to another layer 1 technology

mesh topology all networking devices are directly connected to each other

metric a numeric measure assigned to routes for ranking

microbending loss caused by very small mechanical deflections and stress on the fiber

Midnight Commander a cursor-based file manager for Linux

minimum ones density a pulse is intentionally sent in the data stream even if the data being transmitted is a series of all 0's

mkdir Linux command to make a directory

mm multimode

MMS Manufacturing Message Specification

modal dispersion broadening of a pulse due to different path lengths taken through the fiber by different modes **Modbus TCP** allows industrial network connections to be made via the Internet

mode field diameter the actual guided optical power distribution, which is typically a micron or so larger than the core diameter; single-mode fiber specifications typically list the mode field diameter

more command used in Linux to display the contents of a text file

mount Linux command used to access external drives

Mozilla the Linux Web browser

MT ACK message type acknowledgement, a DHCP ACK packet

MT Discover message type discover, a DHCP Discover packet

MT Offer message type offer, a DHCP Offer packet

MT Request message type request, a DHCPRequest packet

multicast messages are sent to a specific group of hosts on the network

multicast address the addresses used to send a multicast data packet

multicasting when one host sends data to many destination hosts

multi-homed the customer has more than one Internet connection

multimode fiber a fiber that supports many optical waveguide modes

multiplexed the combining of data packets for transport

multiport bridge another name for a layer 2 switch

multiport repeater another name for a hub

mv Linux command for moving or renaming a file

ncftp an ftp application for Linux

NCP Network Control Protocol

near-end crosstalk (NEXT) a measure of the level of crosstalk or signal coupling within the cable, with a high NEXT (dB) value being desirable

net mask Linux name for the subnet mask

net send command that allows a message to be sent over the network to a user

net session command that displays the current users connected to the server

NetBIOS computer naming convention that can be understood by the user

netstat -a command used to display the ports currently open on a Windows operating system

netstat -ap provides information about the network connections

netstat -r command used to obtain the routing table for a host PC computer

network address another name for the layer 3 address

network congestion a slowdown on network data traffic movement

network interface card (NIC) the electronic hardware used to interface the computer to the network

network interface layer defines how the host connects to the network

network latency the time it takes for data packets to travel from source to destination

network layer provides routing decisions

network mask 32 bits in four octets used to allow selected addresses to pass

network number another name for the IP subnet; the portion of the IP address that defines which network the IP packet is originating from or being delivered to

network server provides access to services on the network

network slowdown degraded network performance

network start brings up the network interfaces in Linux

network stop shuts down all network interfaces in Linux

next hop address the IP address of the next networking device that can be used to forward the data packet to its destination

nmap a Linux port scanner

no shutdown (no shut) enables a router's interface

NOC network operations center

nominal velocity of propagation (NVP) some percentage of the velocity of light; dependent on the type of cable being tested

non-Internet routable IP addresses IP addresses not routed on the Internet

NS record a record that points to a name server

NTFS New Technology File System

numerical aperture a measure of a fiber's ability to accept light

numerics a numerical representation

objects programs that enable the Ethernet/IP protocol to be configured for a particular machine or interface

OC optical carrier

OFDM orthogonal frequency division multiplexing

openssh the secure shell application for Linux

optical Ethernet Ethernet data running over a fiber link

optical spectrum light frequencies from the infrared on up

organizational unit specialized container that allows group policies to be set

origanizationally unique identifier (OUI) The first 3 bytes of the MAC address that identifies the manufacturer of the network hardware

OSI open system interconnect

OSI model the seven layers describing network functions

OSPF Open Shortest Path First routing protocol

OSPFIGP Open Shortest Path First Interior Gateway Protocol

OTDR sends a light pulse down the fiber and measures the reflected light, which provides a measure of performance for the fiber

outbound data traffic data traffic leaving the network

packet provides grouping of the information for transmission

packet sequence number used to keep track of the order of the data packets

packet sniffing a technique where the contents of data packets are watched

packet switching packets are processed at switching centers and directed to the best network for delivery

pair data data collected on the UTP wire pairs

password cracking the attacker tries to guess the user's password

patch cable cabling (often twisted-pair) used to make the physical connection between networking equipment

path determination protocol procedure used to determine the best route

payload another name for the data being transported

PBX private branch exchange—the user's own telephone system

PCI Peripheral Component Interconnect

PCM pulse code modulation

peer computer that uses and provides resources to the network

peering how an agreement is made for the exchange of data traffic between large and small ISPs or between a router and its neighbor router

peer-to-peer network all computers in the network provide similar services including server functions

permit ip any any the instruction added to the last line of an access list to allow all other data packets to enter and exit the router

physical fiber map shows the routing of the fiber but also shows detail about the terrain, underground conduit, and entries into buildings

physical layer describes the media that interconnects networking devices

PID process ID

ping (**packet Internet groper**) command used to test that a device on the network is reachable

pipe Linux command used to take the output of one command and redirect it as an input to another command

PLC programmable logic controller

point of presence (POP) point where the customer connects network data traffic to the communications carrier

polarization mode dispersion broadening of a pulse due to different propagation velocities of the X and Y polarization components

port number an address used to direct data to the proper destination application

ports the interface for the networking devices

power on/off turns on/off electrical power to the router

power sum NEXT (PSNEXT) measures the total crosstalk of all cable pairs ensuring that the cable can carry data traffic on all four wire pairs at the same time with minimal interference

PPP Point-to-Point Protocol

PPTP Point-to-Point Tunneling Protocol

PQ priority queuing

presentation layer protocol conversion, data translation

private addresses IP addresses set aside for use in private intranets

privileged mode allows the router ports and routing features to be configured

probing indicators of repeated attempts to make connections to certain machines

Profinet Ethernet protocol that works with the older Profibus device level protocol

propagation delay amount of time it takes for a signal to propagate from one end of the cable to the other

protocol set of rules established for users to gain control of the network to exchange information

ps Linux command used to list processes running on the machine

PSAACRF Power Sum Alien Attenuation to Crosstalk Ratio

PSACR all four wire pairs are used to obtain an attenuation–crosstalk ratio measurement

PSANEXT Power Sum Alien Near-End Cross-Talk

PSELFEXT all four wire pairs are used to obtain a combined ELFEXT performance measurement

pseudorandom the number sequence appears random but actually repeats

PSTN public switched telephone network—the telephone company

public data network a local telephone company or a communications carrier

pulse dispersion stretching of received pulse width because of multiple paths taken by the light

PVCs permanent virtual connections

pwd Linux command to print the working (current) directory

QoS quality of service

queuing provides control of the data packet transfer

ranging technique used by cable modems to determine the time it takes for data to travel to the cable head end

RAS remote access server

reboot command used to gracefully shut down the Linux machine and reboot

received signal level (RSL) the input signal level to an optical receiver

redundancy added to networks to eliminate single pointsof-failure

refractive index ratio of the speed of light in free space to its speed in a given material

reliability a measure of a link's reliability in terms of the amount of errors generated

resolv.conf contains the list of DNS servers for the Linux machine

return loss a measure of the ratio of power transmitted into a cable to the amount of power returned or reflected

reverse DNS returns a hostname for an IP address

reverse domain service translation of an IP address to a name

RID router ID

RIP Routing Information Protocol

RJ-45 the 8-pin modular connector used with CAT5 cable

rm Linux command to delete a file

rmdir Linux command to remove a directory

roaming the term used to describe a users ability to maintain network connectivity as they move through the work place

rollover cable a cable with the signals reversed at each end

root access the user has the rights to make changes to operating and user parameters

root servers a group of servers that exist using well-known IP addresses that have been programmed into DNS servers

route add default gw Linux command used to specify the gateway address

route flapping intermittent routes going up and down creating excessive LSA updates

route print produces same displayed result as *netstat -r*

routed network uses layer 3 addressing for selecting routes to forward data packets

Router# the pound sign indicates that the user is in the router's privileged EXEC mode

Router(config)# the prompt for the router's terminal configuration mode

Router(config-if)# indicates you are in the router's interface configuration mode

Router(config-line)# the prompt indicating you are in the router's line configuration mode

Router(config-router)# prompt indicating the router is in the mode to accept routing commands

router dead interval the length of time a router neighbor is quiet before assuming the neighbor is dead

router igrp [AS number] the router command for specifying IGRP

router interface the physical connection where the router connects to the network

router ospf [number] command used to enable OSPF routing

router rip the router command used to enable the RIP routing protocol

router uptime the amount of time that the router has been running

routing loop data is forwarded back to the router that sent the data packets

routing table keeps track of the routes to use for forwarding data to its destination; a list of the possible networks that can be used to route the data packets

routing table code C router code for specifying a directly connected network

routing table code S router code for static route

rpm -e Linux command for uninstalling the applications

rpm -i Linux command for installing an application

rpm -qf searches the rpm database and returns the name of the file that matches the query in Linux

RS-232 serial communications port

RTCP Real-time Control Protocol

RTP Real-time Protocol

RTPS Real-Time Publish-Subscribe Protocol; provides time-stamped data and control packets

RX abbreviation for "receive"

SC, ST, FC, LC, MT-RJ typical fiber connectors on the market

scattering caused by refractive index fluctuations; accounts for 85% of attenuation loss

SCSI Small Computer System Interface

SDRAM synchronous DRAM

segment a way to configure the network cabling so that the data traffic for a group of computers is isolated from other segments; section of a network separated by bridges, switches, and routers; defines the physical link the routers use for forwarding data among internetworking devices

serial ports a router's serial data communication link

serial ports (S0, S1, S2 , . . .) naming of the serial ports on the router

session layer establishes, manages, and terminates sessions

shadowing switches with identical address tables that allow seamless transfer between the switches if a failure should occur

show flash lists the details on the router's flash memory

show ip interface brief (sh ip int brief) command used to verify the status of the router's interfaces

show ip protocol (sh ip protocol) command that displays the routing protocol running on the router

show ip route igrp (sh ip route igrp) command that displays only the IGRP routes

show ip route (sh ip route) command that displays the routes and the routing address entry into the routing table

show ip route static (sh ip route static) command that limits the routes displayed to only static

show running-configuration (sh run) command that displays the router's running-configuration

show startup-configuration (sh start) command that displays the router's startup-configuration

show version lists the version of the Cisco IOS software running on the router

shutdown -h now command used to gracefully shut down Linux

signaling used to establish and terminate telephone calls

signatures indicators of known attacks

SIMM single in-line memory module

single-mode fiber fiber cables with core diameters of about 7 to 10 ∞m; light follows a single path

single point-of-failure a single failure of any device, component, cable, or software entity that can shut down part of the network

SIP Session Initiation Protocol

site survey performed to determine the best location(s) for placing the access point(s) for providing maximum RF coverage for the wireless clients

sm single mode

SMB server message block

SNMP Simple Network Management Protocol

social engineering a way for an intruder to obtain enough information to gain access to the network

SONET/SDH synchronous optical network/synchronous digital hierarchy; protocol standard for optical transmission in long-haul communication

spit spam over internet telephony. A threat to quality of service in which the VoIP network can be saturated with unsolicited bulk messages broadcast over the VoIP network.

split horizons prevents routing loops

spoof inserting an IP address in place of an IP packet's source address to make it appear that the packet came from another network

SS7 the signaling technique used by the PSTN

SSH (secure shell) an encrypted version of telnet

SSID service set identifier

SSIP Secure Session Initiation Protocol provides for end-to-end secure communications by requiring user authentication

star topology the most common networking topology in today's LANs where all networking devices connect to a central hub or switch

stateful keeps track of the data packet flow

static route a data traffic route that has been manually entered into either a router's or computer's routing table

statistical data data that can tolerate delays in data delivery such as that used for quality reports, database information, accounting, and job control information

step-index fiber fibers in which there is an abrupt change in the refractive index from the core to the cladding

STP shielded twisted-pair

straight-through transmit and receive signals are aligned

straight-through cable the wire pairs in the cable connect to the same pin numbers on each end

STS synchronous transport signals

stubby areas do not accept routes from the Internet

su Linux command used to become another user (substitute user) on the system

subnet mask identifies the network/subnet portion of an IP address

subnet, NET other terms for the segment

supernets the grouping of two or more class networks together; also called CIDR blocks

supernetting allows multiple networks to be specified by one subnet mask

SVC switched virtual circuit

switch forwards the data it receives directly to its destination address

switch-56 a 56 kbps dial-up data connection

switching hub another name for a switch

SYN synchronizing packet

SYN + ACK synchronizing plus acknowledgement packet

T1 to T3 common telecommunication data rates

T568A wire color guidelines specified under the EIA/TIA568B standard

T568B wire color guidelines specified under the EIA/TIA568B standard

TCO the wall plate where the twisted-pair cable terminates in the room

TCP Transport Control Protocol

TCP/IP Transmission Control Protocol/Internet Protocol, part of the protocol suite used for internetworks such as the Internet

TCTL Transverse Conversion Transfer Loss is the loss from a balanced signal at the near-end to the unbalanced signal at the far-end.

TDM time division multiplexing

Telco the local telephone company

Telco cloud telecommunications carrier's switched network used to transport data to its destination; also used to describe the interconnected networks on the Internet

telecommunications closet location of the cabling termination points that includes the mechanical terminations and the distribution frames

telnet terminal emulation application for TCP/IP networks

terminated describes where the cable connects to a jack or a patch panel

termination required at the ends of a ThinNet network to minimize reflection problems with the data; point where the cable is connected to terminals in either a modular plug, jack, or patch panel

ThinNet a type of coaxial cable used for connecting LANs configured with a bus topology

ThinNet hub another name for a multiport repeater

TIA Telecommunications Industry Association

ticks measured delay time, where 1 tick is approximately 55 ms (1/18 second)

tie line line used to interconnect PBXs

timestamp reproduces playback of the voice packets with the same time interval as they were recorded

TLD top level domain

token passing a technique where an electrical token circulates around a network. Possession of the token enables the user to gain access to the network

token-ring hub a hub that also manages the passing of the token in a token-ring network

token-ring topology a network topology configured in a ring that complements the token passing protocol

topology architecture of a network

totally stubby areas use only a default route to reach destinations external to the autonomous system

TR telecommunications room

transceiver a transmit/receive unit

translation bridge Use to interconnect two LANs that are operating two different networking protocols

transparent bridge interconnects two LANs running the same type of protocol

transport layer ensures error-free packets

transport layer protocols define the type of connection established between hosts and how acknowledgements are sent

tree a domain

tunable laser laser in which the fundamental wavelength can be shifted a few nanometers, ideal for traffic routing in DWDM systems

TX abbreviation for "transmit"

UDP User Datagram Protocol

UDP/IP User Datagram Protocol/Internet Protocol

umount Linux command used to unmount a drive

unicast the packet has a fixed destination

U-NII Unlicensed National Information Infrastructure

up arrow used to display the previously entered commands stored in the Linux history buffer

uplink port allows the connection of hub to hub or switch without having to use a special cable

USB Universal Serial Bus

user EXEC mode used by a user to check the router status

user mode same as the user EXEC mode

UTP unshielded twisted-pair

V.44/V.34 the standard for all analog modem connections with a maximum data rate of up to 34 kbps; V.44 provides improved data compression, smaller file sizes that provide faster file transfers and improved Web browsing

V.92/V.90 the standard for a combination analog and digital modem connection with a maximum data rate of 56 kbps; V.92 provides a quick connect feature that cuts down on negotiation and handshake time as compared to V.90

variable length subnet masking routes can be configured using different subnet masks

variable length subnet masks (VLSMs) allow the use of subnet masks to better fit the needs of the network, thereby minimizing the waste of IP addresses when interconnecting subnets

VCI virtual channel identifier

vertical cavity surface emitting lasers (VCSELs) lasers with the simplicity of LEDs and the performance of lasers

virtual channel connection (VCC) carriers the ATM cell from user to user

virtual path connection (VPC) used to connect the end users

virtual tie line simplifies the interconnection between the IP-PBX and the PSTN

virus a piece of malicious computer code that when opened, starts a programs that attacks a computer and/or the network

VLB VESA Local Bus

VoIP voice over IP telephony

VoIP gateway provides the proper signaling of digitized voice data for transport over the IP network

VoIP relay another name for a VoIP gateway

VPI virtual path identifier

VPN virtual private network

w displays the names of the users presently logged into the system plus provides additional details on each user in Linux

war driving using wireless equipment to detect wireless management packets

weighted fair queuing (WFQ) used to determine what data traffic gets priority for transmission

weighted random early discard (WRED) network routers and switches are configured to intelligently discard lower-priority packets

well-known ports ports reserved by ICANN

WEP (wired equivalent privacy) the goal is to provide the same security of a wireless connection that a wired connection provides

who displays the names of the users presently logged into the system in Linux

wide area network (WAN) uses the telecommunication network to interconnect sites that are geographically distributed throughout a region, the country, or the world

wild card bits used to match network IP addresses (A.B.C.D format) to interface IPs

Windows 2K server another name for Microsoft Windows 2000 server

winipcfg command for displaying Ethernet adapter information on some Windows operating systems

wire-map a graphical or text description of the wire connections from pin to pin

WLAN wireless local area network

work area the location of the computers and printers, patch cables, jacks, computer adapter cables, and fiber jumpers

workstation another name for the computer

worm a type of computer virus that typically proliferates by itself

WPA, WPA2 WiFi Protected Access, WiFi Protected Access version 2. Improvements to wireless security that support user authentication

and replace WEP as the primary ways for securing wireless transfers

write memory (wr m) command that saves your configuration changes to memory

wu-ftpd Washington University's ftp server

X.25 a packet-switched protocol designed for data transmission over analog lines

xDSL a generic representation of the various DSL technologies that are available

zero-dispersion wavelength point where the dispersion is actually zero

Index

NUMBERS

6to4 Prefix, 184

8P8C. *See* **RJ-45 modular connectors**

10 Gigabit Interface Adapters. *See* **XENPAKs**

10GBASE-T, 59

  AXT, 83-84

  signal balance, 84

  signal transmission, 85-86

  standard, 83

802.11 WLANs, 414

  configuring, 420

    access points, 422

    bridges, 422

    lost associations, 422

    range, extending, 424

    signals, 423

    site survey, 424-428

    SSIDs, 421

  MAC layer, 415

  OFDM, 418-419

  physical layer, 415

802.11a WLANs, 420

802.11b WLANs, 419-420

802.11g WLANs, 419-420

802.11i WLANs, 420

802.11n WLANs, 419-420

802.11r WLANs, 420

8P8C. *See* **RJ-45 modular connectors**

SYMBOLS

? (help) command, 207

A

absorption, defined, 457

Accelerated Graphics Port. *See* **AGP**

access layer (campus networks), 356

access list permit ip any any command, 400

access lists. *See* **ACLs**

access points

  home networks, 20

  WLANs, 415, 422

account lockout policies (network servers), configuring, 552

  connected users, viewing, 554

  enabling user accounts, 554

  locked out accounts, 553

  messages to users, 555

ACLs (access control lists), 396-398

  blocking host IP addresses example, 403

  blocking SMB data packets example, 400-401

  extended, 399

  named access list example, 401-402

  routers, applying to, 399-400

  standard, 399

ACR (attenuation-crosstalk), 74, 79

Active Directory, 514

ad hoc networks. *See* BSS

adapter addresses. *See* MAC addresses

adapters

    home networks, 19

    PC Card, 20

    Wireless-N, 20

adaptive cut-through switching, 137

adding

    clients to campus networks, 363

    computers to Windows 2003/2008 server domain, 522-526

    groups to Windows 2003/2008 server domain, 528-532

    network servers, 513

    organizational units to Windows 2003/2008 server domain, 528-529, 531-532

    users to

        Linux, 561-564

        Windows 2003/2008 server domain, 526-527

Address Resolution Protocol. *See* ARP

addresses

    anycast, 184

    class network, 240

    default gateway, 196

    IP

        assigning, 15, 173, 268

        campus network assignments, 358, 360

        CIDR blocks, 181-182

        classes, 15, 170

        defined, 15

        format, 15

        gateway of last resort, 233

        groups. See private addresses

        home networks, 29-30

        host numbers, 16

        IPv4, 15

        IPv6, 182-185

        lease time, 359

        Linux configuration, 590

        name translation, 361

        network numbers, 16

        network servers, configuring, 521-522

        next hop, configuring, 231

        non-internet routable, 173

        octets, 172

        office-type LANs, 34

        OSPF "Hello" packets, 275

        private, 173

        RAS configuration, 321

        structure, 171

        verifying, 36

    logical, 138

    MAC

        aging time, 134

        bridge tables, 126

        defined, 11

        dynamic, 134

        filtering, 28

        OUIs, 11

        retrieving, 12-13

        samples, 14

        secure, 134

        static, 134

        viewing, 12

    multicast, 164, 184

    network, 138

    next hop, 199

    private, defined, 16

    unicast, 184

administration commands (Linux)

    man, 577

    mount, 581-582

    ps, 579-580

    shortcuts, 583

    shutdown, 583

    shutdown -h now, 583

    su, 580

    unmount, 583

administrative distance, 245

administratively down, defined, 220

ADSL (asymmetric DSL), 313

Advanced Research Projects Agency (ARPAnet), 156

advertising, 240

aging time, 134

AGP (Accelerated Graphics Port), 106-107

Alien Crosstalk. *See* AXT

American Registry for Internet Numbers. *See* ARIN

AMI (alternate mark inversion), 295

analog modem technologies, 309-310

analyzing

   campus data traffic, 378

      daily, 379

      hourly, 379

      weekly, 380

   Internet data traffic

      frame size distribution, 347

      network layer host tables, 346

      network layer matrix, 345-346

      utilization/errors strip chart, 344

   unsecured data packets

      captured packets, 405-407

      router connections, 406

      telnet session packets, 407

      telnetting to routers, 405

      user verification, 406

   VoIP data packets, 497

      acknowledgement, 499, 502

      call processor message, 499

      call processors call plans, 502

      collecting data packets, 498

      IP network handshaking, 504

      NBX call processor codes, 498

      PCM voice data, 499

      test setup, 502

anycast addresses, 184

Apache Web service installation (Linux), 588-589

applets, defined, 539

application layer

   OSI model, 123

   TCP/IP, 157-158

application servers, 512

architectures (optical networking)

   building distribution, 470-472

   campus distribution, 472-475

   data rates, 469

   defining optical networking, 468-470

   fiber to the business, 469

   fiber to the curb, 469

   fiber to the desktop, 469

   fiber to the home, 469

   optical Ethernet, 469-470

   standards, 468

area 0, 254

areas (OSPF), 251

ARIN (American Registry for Internet Numbers), 173

armored fiber optics, 628

ARP (Address Resolution Protocol), 39, 162

arp -a command, 127

ARP caches, 126

ARP replies, 39

ARP tables. *See* **ARP caches**

ARPAnet (Advanced Research Projects Agency), 156

AS (autonomous systems), 246, 339

ASNs (AS numbers), 339

associations, 421

   checking, 125

   WLANs, 422

asymmetric DSL. *See* **ADSL**

asymmetric operations, 309

ATA connections, 107

ATM (Asynchronous Transfer Mode), 305

   classes, 306

   connections, creating, 308

   interfaces, viewing, 308

   PVC interface, 306

   router configuration, 307

   router subinterface configuration, 307

   VCI, 306

   virtual channels, viewing, 308

   VPI, 306

attacks (security)

   DDoS, 396

   DoS, 395-396

   firewalls, 398

   intrusions

      detecting, 404

      packet sniffing, 390

      password cracking, 389-390

      social engineering, 389

      viruses, 393

      vulnerable software, 391-393

      wireless vulnerabilities, 394

      worms, 393

attenuation, 71-72, 457

attenuation-crosstalk. *See* **ACR**

attenuators, 463

authentication, 436, 534

auto-negotiation protocol, 145
    advantages/disadvantages, 148
    FLPs, 146
    full/half duplex, 146-147
    process, 146
autonomous systems. *See* AS
available bit-rate class, 306
AXT (Alien Crosstalk), 83-84

B

B8ZS (bipolar 8 zero substitution) encoding, 296
backbone cabling structured cabling subsystem, 52
backbones, 251, 473
backdoors, 392
backhoe fading, 476
backscatter, 432
balanced mode, UTP, 58
bash (bourne again shell), 566
Basic Input Output System. *See* BIOS
Basic Service Set. *See* BSS
beacons, 436
BGP (Border Gateway Protocol), 338
    configuring, 339-343
    Net-Challenge configuration, 343-344
bin directory (Linux), 569
binary-decimal number conversions, 165-166
binary-hexadecimal number conversions, 170
BIOS (Basic Input Output System), 116
bipolar 8 zero substitution (B8ZS) encoding, 296
bipolar coding, 296
bipolar violations, 296
Blocking state (STP), 378
Bluetooth, 429
    configuring, 430-431
    inquiry procedure, 430
    paging procedure, 430
    piconets, 430
boot directory (Linux), 569
boot processes (Linux), troubleshooting, 598-600
boot sequence
    BIOS, configuring, 116
    defined, 116

boot services (Linux), troubleshooting, 602-603
BOOTP (Bootstrap Protocol), 359
Bootstrap Protocol. *See* BOOTP
Border Gateway Protocol. *See* BGP
bottlenecking, 59
bourne again shell. *See* bash
BPDUs (Bridge Protocol Data Units), 377
branching devices, 463
bridges, 124
    advantages/disadvantages, 128
    ARP caches, 126
    associations, checking, 125
    broadcasts, handling, 125
    data traffic, isolating, 126
    Ethernet LANs, 125
    MAC address entries, 126
    multiport. *See* layer 2 switches
    translation, 127
    transparent, 127
    wireless, 127
    WLAN configurations, 422
bridging tables, defined, 124
broadband connections, 17
broadband modems/gateways, home networks, 23
broadband wireless access (BWA), 432
broadcast domains, 137, 195
broadcasts
    bridges, 125
    defined, 8
    directed, 396
    storms, 126
brute force attacks, 389
BSS (Basic Service Set), 415-416
buffer overflow attacks, 391
buffers, defined, 496
building distribution (optical networking), 470-472
building entrance structured cabling subsystem, 52
bursty data transmissions, 299
bus connections
    AGP video card, 107
    ATA, 107
    Firewire, 106
    ISA, 104
    motherboard, 103-106

overview, 102

PCI, 104

USB, 105

bus topologies, 6-8

BWA (broadband wireless access), 432

C

cable modems, 23, 310

cables

CAT3, 58

CAT5 straight-through patch cables, configuring

crimping RJ-45 plug, 71

inserting wires into RJ-45 plug, 70

jacket stripping, 69

separating wire pairs, 70

CAT5e, 57

configuring straight-through patch cables, 69-71

four wire pairs, 61

test examples, 88, 92-93

CAT6, 32, 57

four wire pairs, 61

terminating horizontal links, 65-68

testing, 75

CAT6a, 57

CAT7, 59

color maps, 60

console, 201

crossovers, 33, 64

full channels, 71

industrial Ethernet, 627-628

link pulses, 34

links, 71

office-type LANs, 32-34

patch

configuring CAT5/5e straight-through, 69-71

defined, 56

horizontal cabling, 56

rollover, 201

STP, 51, 60

straight-through, 64, 69-71

structured

campus hierarchical topology, 53

EIA/TIA 568-B, 51

horizontal cabling, 54-56

standards, 51

subsystems, 52

telecommunications architecture, 52-53

TIA/EIA 568-A, 51

terminated, 55

testing, 71

ACR, 74

attenuation, 72

CAT6 links, 75-82

channel specifications, 72

delay skew, 74

ELFEXT, 74

NEXT, 72

propagation delay, 74

PSACR, 74

PSELFEXT, 74

PSNEXT, 73

return loss, 74

ThinNet, 6

transmit/receive pairs, aligning, 62-63

troubleshooting

cable stretching, 87

CAT5e test examples, 88, 92-93

failing to meet manufacturer specifications, 87

installation, 86

UTP, 51

balanced mode, 58

bottlenecking, 59

categories, 58-59

F/UTP, 84

full duplex gigabit Ethernet support, 59

high-performance, terminating, 60-61

RJ-45 modular plug example, 57

standards, 57

wire maps, 64

caches (ARP), 126

CAM (Content Addressable Memory), 136

campus area networks. *See* **CANs**

campus networks

data traffic analysis, 378

daily, 379

hourly, 379

weekly, 380

defined, 51, 122

designing

    access layer, 356

    core layer, 354-355

    data flow, 356

    distribution layer, 355

    load balancing, 357-358

    media selection, 356-357

DNS, 361

    adding clients, 363

    hierarchy, 362

    local server administration, 363

    NS records, 362

    obtaining domain names, 363

    reverse, 364

    root servers, 362

fiber optics distribution, 472-475

IP assignment with DHCP, 358-360

Power over Ethernet (PoE)

    benefits, 367

    networking hardware defined, 368

    PDs, 368

    PoE Plus, 369

    PSE, 368

SNMP, managing with, 365-367

structured cabling hierarchical topology, 53

switch configuration, 370

    hostnames, 371

    line console, 372-373

    password protection, 372

    privileged mode, 371

    STP, 377-378

VLANs

    membership assignments, 370

    Network Challenge software, 376-377

    static configuration, 373-377

    types, 369

CAN (controller area network), 619

CANs (campus area networks), 5

carrier sense multiple access with collision detection.
    See **CSMA/CD protocol**

carrier sense multiple access/collision avoidance. *See*
    CSMA/CA

cat command (Linux), 568

CAT3 (category 3) cables, 58

**CAT5 (category 5) cables, configuring straight-
through patch cables**

jackets, stripping, 69-70

RJ-45 plugs, crimping, 71

wire pairs, separating, 70

CAT5e (category 5 enhanced) cables, 57

four wire pairs, 61

straight-through patch cables, configuring

    inserting wires into RJ-45 plug, 70

    jacket, stripping, 69

    RJ-45 plug, crimping, 71

    wire pairs, separating, 70

test examples, 92-93

    certification report, 91

    FAIL result, 88

    PASS result, 88

CAT6 (category 6) cables, 32, 57

four wire pairs, 61

horizontal link, terminating

    bend-limiting strain relief boot, 65, 68

    jacket stripping, 66

    lacing tool, 66

    RJ-45 jack and lacing tool alignment, 67

testing

    ACR results, 79

    certification report, 82

    ELFEXT results, 80

    insertion loss, 77

    NEXT results, 78

    pair data, 76

    Power Sum NEXT results, 79

    PSACR results, 79

    PSELFTEXT results, 80

    return loss, 81

    setup, 75

    summary menu, 75

    wire-map test results, 75

CAT6a (category 6a) cables, 57

CAT7 (category 7) cables, 59

CBIR (committed burst information rate), 299

CBWFQ (class-based weighted fair queuing), 497

CCIE (Cisco Certified Internet Expert), 194

CCNA (Cisco Certified Network Associate), 194

CCNP (Cisco Certified Network Professional), 194

cd command (Linux), 569

channel service unit/data service unit. *See* CSU/DSU

chgrp command (Linux), 576

chkconfig command (Linux), 602

chmod command (Linux), 573-575

chown command (Linux), 576

chromatic dispersion, 458

CIDR blocks (classless interdomain routing), 180
  applying, 181
  example, 181-182

CIP (Control and Information Protocol), 629

CIR (committed information rate), 298

Cisco 2500 series, 140-141

Cisco 2600 series, 140

Cisco 2800 series, 139

Cisco Catalyst 2960, 133

Cisco Certified Internet Expert. *See* CCIE

Cisco Certified Network Associate. *See* CCNA

Cisco Certified Network Professional. *See* CCNP

Cisco IOS (Internet Operating System). *See* IOS

Cisco Network Assistant. *See* CNA

Cisco VPN Client software, 337
  Chile-VPN welcome menu, 334
  connections, 335
  handshake screen, 335
  installing, 334
  properties, 336
  session statistics, 336
  status, 334

cladding, 452

class D IP address ranges, 275

class network addresses, 240

class-based weighted fair queuing. *See* CBWFQ

classes
  ATM, 306
  IP addresses, 15, 170

classful addressing, 240

classful networks, 180, 246

classless interdomain routing. *See* CIDR blocks

CLI (command line interface), 194

client/server networks, defined, 511-512

clients
  campus networks, adding to, 363
  defined, 510
  ftp, Linux, 595

RAS, configuring, 323-325

VPN remote, configuring
  Cisco VPN Client software, 334-337
  Mac OS X, 333
  Windows Vista, 332
  Windows XP, 332-333

clock rate command, 216

clusters, defined, 114

CNA (Cisco Network Assistant), 133

CODEC (coder/decoder), 490

collision domains, isolating, 136

color maps, 60

combo terminations, 102

command line (Linux), 563

command line interface. *See* CLI

command window, opening, 12

commands
  access list permit ip any any, 400
  arp -a, 127
  clock rate, 216
  commit, 269
  commit and- quit, 270
  configure, Juniper router hostnames, 268
  configure terminal, 212, 371
  copy run start, 235, 303
  deny, 404
  edit protocols, 269
  edit routing-options static, 268
  enable, 211
  enable secret, 213, 372
  encapsulation (encap), 297
  encapsulation frame-relay, 302
  frame-relay interface-dlci, 200, 302
  help (?), 207
  hostname, 212
  int s0/0.1 point-to-pint, 302
  int tunnel0, 328
  ip route, 231
  ipconfig, IP address verification, 36
  ipconfig /all, MAC addresses, 12
  line ?, 213
  Linux
    chkconfig, 602
    directory operations, 569-570
    dmesg, 598

file operations, 571-573
grep, 585
httpd restart, 589
httpd stop, 589
ifdown, 591
ifup, 591
ipconfig, 590
la system-config, 604
last, 600
listing files, 565-566
man, 577
mount, 581-582
netstat, 603
network start, 592
network stop, 592
nmap, 601
permissions/ownership, 573-577
pipe, 585
ps, 579-580
reboot, 599
route add default gw, 592
rpm -e, 586
rpm -i, 586-587
rpm -qa, 584
rpm -qf, 585-586
shortcuts, 583
shutdown, 583
shutdown -h now, 583
su, 580
system-config, 604
system-config-date, 605
system-config-firewall, 605
system-config-network, 607
system-config-packages, 607
system-config-printer, 607
system-config-services, 609
system-config-users, 609
unmount, 583
viewing file contents, 567-569
who, 601
net send, 554
net session, 554
netstat -a, 392
netstat -b, 392
netstat -r, 228
network, 253

no ip directed-broadcast, 396
no shutdown (no shut), 214
ping
hub-switch comparison, 131-132
LANs, testing, 35-36
Surveyor protocol analyzer, 39-40
route print, 228
router eigrp, 259
router igrp, 246
router ospf, 253
router RIP, 240, 242
routers, troubleshooting, 218-220
set protocols, 270
show, options, 207
show access-list, 402
show atm vc, 308
show controllers, 216
show controllers serial, 216
show flash, 208
show frame-relay PVC, 304
show interfaces brief, Juniper routers, 267
show ip interface brief, 218-220
show ip interface brief (sh ip int brief), 214, 218-220, 242
show ip protocol (sh ip protocol), 242
show ip route (sh ip route), 231-232
show ip route igrp (sh ip route igrp), 249
show ip route static (sh ip route static), 234
show running config (sh run), 235, 303
show startup config (sh start), 235
show version, 208
snmp community public ro, 365
winipcfg, MAC addresses, 13
write memory (wr m), 235
commercial networks versus industrial networks, 619
commercial-off-the-shelf (COTS), 620
commit and- quit command, 270
commit command, 269
committed burst information rate (CBIR), 299
committed information rate. See CIR
computers
BIOS boot sequence, configuring, 116
bus connections
AGP video card, 107
ATA, 107
Firewire, 106

ISA, *104*

motherboard, 103-106

overview, 102

PCI, 104

SCSI, 106

USB, 105

device drivers, 107

Mac OS X, 110-111

Windows Vista/XP, 108-109

FAT, 114-115

FAT32, 115

memory, 112-113

NTFS, 115

routers

Cisco 2500 series, 140-141

Cisco 2600 series, 140

Cisco 2800 series, 139

gateways, 145

interface, 138

LANs, interconnecting, 138, 143-145

segments, 145

Windows 2003/2008 server domains, adding to, 522-526

Configuration BPDUs, 377

configuration mode (Juniper routers), 266-267

configure command, Juniper router hostnames, 268

configure terminal (conf t) command, 212, 371

configuring

ACLs, 399-400

ATM routers, 307

BGP, 339-343

BIOS boot sequence, 116

Bluetooth, 430-431

CAT5/5e straight-through patch cables

crimping RJ-45 plugs, 71

inserting wires into RJ-45 plug, 70

jacket stripping, 69

separating wire pairs, 70

Fast Ethernet interfaces, 214

Frame Relay networks, 299, 305

HyperTerminal serial communications software, 203-204

Juniper routers

hostnames, 268

IP address assignments, 268

OSPF, 270-271

RIP, 269-270

static routing, 268

Linux networks

DNS, 597

etc/sysconfig/network-scripts, 594

Ethernet cards, 590

ftp clients, 595

ftp servers, 596

gateway addresses, 592

hostnames, 597

interface control, 591

IP address configuration, 590

loopbacks, 590

shutting down/starting interfaces, 592

SSH installations, 594-595

viewing interface configurations, 590

network server account lockout policies, 552

connected users, viewing, 554

enabling user accounts, 554

locked out accounts, 553

messages to users, 555

network server IP addresses, 521-522

network servers, 514

next hop IP addresses, 231

office-type LANs

cabling, 32-34

devices, documenting, 30

IP addresses, 34

star topology connections, 32

permissions, 533

Windows 2003, 539, 542-544

Windows 2008, 534-536, 539

point-to-multipoint WLANs, 438

antenna site survey, 439

multipoint distribution, 440

point-to-point wireless links, 439-440

remote installations, 442

point-to-point Frame Relay router connections, 302-304

policies, 533

Windows 2003, 539, 542-544

Windows 2008, 534-536, 539

RAS clients, 323-325

RAS for Windows 2003 servers, 315-322

enabling RAS, 315

IP configuration, 321

managing multiple servers, 318

modem configuration, 318, 320

protocol selection, 317

Routing and Remote Access Server Setup Wizard
    menu, 315

Routing and Remote Access window, 315

user accounts, 322

router serial interfaces, 214-216

routes

EIGRP, 257, 259-261

IGRP, 246-247, 249

OSPF, 252, 254-256

RIP, 242-244

static routes, 234-235

SNMP, 365-367

static routes, 234-235

static VLANs, 373-377

switches

campus networks, 370-371

hostnames, 371

line console, 372-373

password protection, 372

privileged mode, 371

STP, 377-378

TFTP, 271-273

VPNs

remote clients, 332-337

router-to-router connections, 327-331

servers, 331

Windows 2008 server, 521

wireless networks, 27

Z-Term serial communications software, 205

connection oriented protocol, 158

connections

analog modem technologies, 309-310

ATM, creating, 308

broadband, 17

bus

AGP video card, 107

ATA, 107

Firewire, 106

ISA, 104

motherboard, 103-106

overview, 102

PCI, 104

SCSI, 106

USB, 105

cable modems, 310

Cisco VPN Client software, 335

fiber connectorization, 466-467

Frame Relay networks

creating, 301-302

point-to-point router, 302-304

high-speed, 292

ISDN, 310-312

last miles, 432

layer 3 network routers, 200

office-type LAN star topology, 32

point-to-point, Frame Relay clouds, 300

PVCs (permanent virtual connections), 299

remote access servers

client configuration, 323-325

Windows 2003 server configuration, 315-322

router console ports, 201-202

switch-56, 293

VPN

remote clients, 332-337

router-to-router, 326-331

tunnel, 326

WAN lines

data channels, 292-293

encoding formats, 295-298

POP, 294

T1 framing, 294-295

wireless networks, 27

xDSL modems, 312-314

connectors (industrial networks), 628

console cables, 201

console port connections (routers)

console cables, 201

connectors, 201

HyperTerminal serial communications software, con-
    figuring, 203-204

rollover cables, 201

RS-232 serial communications ports, 201

settings, 202

Z-Term serial communications software, configuring,
    205

constant bit-rate class, 306

containers, defined, 524

Content Addressable Memory. *See* CAM

contiguous networks, 241

Control and Information Protocol. *See* CIP

control data, 620

controller area network. *See* CAN

controller level (industrial network hierarchy), 621

convergence, dynamic routing protocols, 237

converting

    IPv4 addresses to IPv6, 184-185

    numbers

        binary to decimal, 165-166

        binary to hexadecimal, 170

        decimal to binary, 166-168

        hexadecimal, 168-170

        hexadecimal to binary, 169

copy run start command, 235, 303

core layer (campus networks), 354-355

COTS (commercial-off-the-shelf), 620

country domains, 362

couplers, 464

cp command (Linux), 573

CPU utilization (industrial networks), 622

CQ (custom queuing), 497

cross connected devices, 33

cross-connects

    defined, 53

    horizontal, 53

    intermediate, 52

    main, 52

crossover cables, 64

crossovers, 33

crosstalk, 72

CSMA/CA (carrier sense multiple access/collision avoidance), WLANs, 416

CSMA/CD (carrier sense multiple access with collision detection) protocol, 10

CSU/DSU (channel service unit/data service unit), 294

custom queuing (CQ), 497

cut-through switching, 137

D

D4 framing, 294

daemons, 596

data channels, WANs, 292-293

Data Communications Equipment. *See* DCE

data encapsulation, 297-298

data flow, campus networks, 356

data link layer, OSI model, 123

data link negotiations, auto-negotiation protocol, 145

    advantages/disadvantages, 148

    full/half duplex, 146-147

    process, 146

data packets

    filtering, firewalls, 397

    FTP, 185

    "Hello" packets

        capturing, 276-277

        IP address ranges, 275

        parameters, 275

        RIDs, 276

        viewing, 277

    keepalive, 218

    layer 3 network exchange, 199

    OSPF "Hello" packets, 251

    sniffing, 436

    switching, 305

    unicast, 360

    unsecured

        captured packets, 407

        capturing packets setup, 405

        protecting, 408

        router connections, 406

        telnet session packets, 407

        telnetting to routers, 405

        user verification, 406

    VoIP, analyzing, 497

        acknowledgement, 499, 502

        call processor message, 499

        call processors call plans, 502

        collecting data packets, 498

        IP network handshaking, 504

        NBX call processor codes, 498

        PCM voice data, 499

        test setup, 502

Data Terminal Equipment. *See* DTE

data traffic, campus networks

    daily, 379

    hourly, 379

    weekly, 380

DataHighwayPlus protocol, 631

date/time, Linux, 605

DB-9 connectors, 201

DB-25 connectors, 201

DCE (Data Communications Equipment), 214

DDoS (Distributed Denial of Service) attacks, 396

DDR SDRAM (double-data-rate SDRAM), 113

DDR2 SDRAM (double-data-rate two SDRAM), 113

decimal-binary number conversions, 166-168

default gateways

  addresses, 196

  static routing, 227

delay skew, 74

Denial of Service attacks. *See* DoS

dense wavelength division multiplexing. *See* DWDM

deny command, 404

determinism, 6

  industrial Ethernet, 625

  industrial networks, 619

dev directory (Linux), 569

device drivers, 107

  Mac OS X, 110-111

  Windows Vista/XP, 108-109

device level (industrial network hierarchy), 620-621

Device Manager window, 108-109

device numbers, industrial networks, 623

Device Properties menu (Vista), 109

DeviceNet bus, 631

devices

  auto-negotiation, FLPs, 146

  cross connected, 33

  intelligent, 621

  interconnected link speeds. *See* auto-negotiation protocol

  LANs, interconnecting, 129

DFBs (distributed feedback) lasers, 462

DHCP (Dynamic Host Configuration Protocol), 317, 359

  IP assignment, campus networks, 358, 360

  servers, 513

  TCP packet transfers, 360-361

DHCP Offer packets. *See* MT Offer

dial-in access

  analog modem technologies, 309-310

  cable modems, 310

  ISDN, 310-312

  remote access servers

    client configuration, 323-325

    Windows 2003 server configuration, 315-322

  xDSL modems, 312-314

dictionary attacks, 389

digital signal (DS), 292

digital subscriber lines. *See* DSL

DIMM (dual in-line memory), 113

diode lasers. *See* DLs

Direct RAMBUS DRAM. *See* DRDRAM

direct sequence spread spectrum. *See* DSSS

directed broadcasts, 396

directory operations commands (Linux)

  cd, 569

  mkdir, 570

  pwd, 570

  rmdir, 570

Disabled state (STP), 378

discrete multitone (DMT) modulation, 313

dispersion

  compensation, 460-461

  dispersion compensating fiber, 461

  types, 458

  zero-dispersion wavelength, 459

distance (industrial networks), 623

distance vector protocols, 238-239

Distributed Denial of Service Attacks. *See* DDoS

distributed feedback lasers. *See* DFBs

distribution layer (campus networks), 355

dlci tags, 300

DLs (diode lasers), 461-462

dmesg command (Linux), 598

DMT (discrete multitone) modulation, 313

DNS (Domain Name Service). *See also* domains; names

  campus networks, 361

    clients, adding, 363

    domain names, obtaining, 363

    hierarchy, 362

    local server administration, 363

    NS records, 362

reverse, 364

root servers, 362

Linux configuration, 597

servers, 513

domain controllers, defined, 515

domains. *See also* **DNS**

broadcast, 137, 195

country, 362

top level, 362

DoS (Denial of Service) attacks, 395-396

dotted-decimal format, 171

double-data-rate SDRAM. *See* **DDR SDRAM**

double-data-rate two SDRAM. *See* **DDR2 SDRAM**

DRAM (dynamic random access memory), 113

DRDRAM (Direct RAMBUS DRAM), 113

DS (digital signal), 292

DS-0 to DS-3 data rates, 292

DSL (digital subscriber lines), 312

DSL modems, home networks, 25

DSSS (direct sequence spread spectrum), 417

DTE (Data Terminal Equipment), 214

DUAL finite state machine, 257

dual in-line memory. *See* **DIMM**

DWDM (dense wavelength division multiplexing), 451, 462

Dynamic Host Configuration Protocol. *See* **DHCP**

dynamic MAC address assignments, 134

dynamic random access memory. *See* **DRAM**

dynamic routing protocols, 236

convergence, 237

distance vector, 238-239

features, 237

link state, 239

load balancing, 237

metrics, 237

path determination, 237

dynamic VLANs (virtual local area networks), 370

E

EAP (Extensible Authentication Protocol), 437

eBGP (external BGP), 339

ECC RAM (error-correcting code random access memory), 113

echo requests, 40

edit protocols command, 269

edit routing-options static command, 268

EDO RAM (Extended data-out RAM), 113

EF (entrance facilities). *See* **building entrance structured cabling subsystem**

efficiency (industrial networks), 622

EIA (Electronic Industries Alliance), 51

EIA/TIA 568-B, 51

defined, 51

structured cabling subsystems, 52

wiring guidelines, 60

EIGRP (Enhanced Interior Gateway Routing Protocol)

DUAL finite state machine, 257

neighbor discovery recovery, 257

Network Challenge software, 262

protocol dependent modules, 257

reliable transport protocol, 257

route configuration, 257-261

EISA (Extended Industry Standard Architeture), 104

electromagnetic interference. *See* **EMI**

Electronic Industries Alliance. *See* **EIA**

ELFEXT (Equal Level FEXT), 74

ELTCTL (Equal Level Transverse Conversion Transfer Loss), 84

email servers, 512

EMI (electromagnetic interference), 60

enable command, 211

enable secret command, 213, 372

encapsulation (encap) command, 297

encapsulation frame-relay command, 302

encoding

multilevel, 85

WAN line connections

AMI, 295

B8ZS, 296

data encapsulation, 297-298

encryption, home networks, 28

endpoint PSE, 368

Enhanced Interior Gateway Routing Protocol. *See* **EIGRP**

Enterprise networks, defined, 143

entrance facilities (EF). *See* **building entrance structured cabling subsystem**

Equal Level FEXT. *See* **ELFEXT**

Equal Level Transverse Conversion Transfer Loss. *See* **ELTCTL**

ER (equipment room) structured cabling subsystem, 52

error thresholds, 137

error-correcting code random access memory. *See* **ECC RAM**

ESF (extended superframe framing), 295

ESS (Extended Service Set), 416

etc directory (Linux), 569

Ethernet
  10GBASE-T
    AXT, 83-84
    signal balance, 84
    signal transmission, 85-86
    standard, 83
  bridges, 125
  CSMA/CD protocol, 10
  Fast Ethernet, 59, 214
  full duplex gigabit support, 59
  gigabit, 59
  industrial
    cabling, 627-628
    components, 627-628
    determinism, 625
    protocols, 628-630
    switching, 627
    topologies, 626-627
  IP addresses
    assigning, 15
    classes, 15
    format, 15
    groups. See private addresses
    host numbers, 16
    IPv4, 15
    network numbers, 16
  Linux Ethernet cards, 590
  MAC addresses, 11
    retrieving, 12-13
    samples, 14
    viewing, 12
  optical, 469-470

packets, 10-11

PoE
  benefits, 367
  campus networks, 367-369
  networking hardware defined, 368
  PDs, 368
  PoE Plus, 369
  PSE, 368

Ethernet addresses. *See* **MAC addresses**

Ethernet rings, 626

Ethernet/IP protocol, 629

events, 481

executable (x) permission (Linux), 575

extended ACLs, 399

Extended data-out RAM. *See* **EDO RAM**

Extended Industry Standard Architecture. *See* **EISA**

Extended Service Set. *See* **ESS**

extended superframe framing. *See* **ESF**

Extensible Authentication Protocol. *See* **EAP**

external BGP. *See* **eBGP**

F

F/UTP (foil over twisted-pair cabling), 84

far-end crosstalk. *See* **FEXT**

fast link pulses. *See* **FLPs**

fast-forward switching, 137

FastEthernet, 59
  interface configuration, 214
  port naming, 143

FAT (file allocation table), 114-115

FAT32, 115

fax servers, 513

FC fiber connectors, 466

FEXT (far-end crosstalk), 74

FHSS (frequency hopping spread spectrum), 417

fiber Bragg grating, 461

fiber cross-connects, 471

fiber optic networks, wavelengths, 452

fiber optics
  advantages, 450
  architectures
    building distribution, 470-472
    campus distribution, 472-475

data rates, 469
    defining optical networking, 468-470
    fiber to the business, 469
    fiber to the curb, 469
    fiber to the desktop, 469
    fiber to the home, 469
    optical Ethernet, 469-470
    standards, 468
armored, 628
attenuators, 463, 478
branching devices, 463
cable loss example, 478
cable losses, 476
color code for 12 fibers in a bundle, 474
components, 449
connections and splicing, 465-466
connector losses, 476
connectorization, 466-467
construction, 452
couplers, 464
designing, 475-478
diode lasers, 461
distance-limiting parameters
    attenuation, 457
    dispersion, 458-460
    dispersion compensation, 460-461
distributed feedback lasers, 462
DLs versus LEDs, 462
environments, 475
extra losses, 476
extra margins, 478
fiber strands, 453
fibers, 463
graded-index fibers, 454-455
isolators, 463
LEDs, 461
light detectors, 464
light reflection, 451
light refraction, 451-452
maintenance margins, 476
mode field diameter, 456
multimode fibers, 453
numerical aperture, 453
operational margins, 476
optical fiber types, 453-454
optical-line amplifiers, 464

receive signal power, 476
receiver sensitivity, 477
safety, 479-480
single-mode fibers, 455-457
single-mode/multimode, compared, 456
spectrum notation, 451
splice losses, 476
splitters, 463
transmitter power output, 476
troubleshooting, 481
tunable lasers, 462
types of fiber, 456
vertical cavity emitting lasers, 462
wavelength division multiplexers, 464
fiber to the business (FTTB), 469
fiber to the curb. *See* FTTC
fiber to the desktop. *See* FTTD
fiber to the home. *See* FTTH
fibers, 463
fieldbus protocols, 618
FIFO (first in, first out), 496
file allocation table. *See* FAT
file structure (Linux)
directory operations, 569-570
    cd, 569
    mkdir, 570
    pwd, 570
    rmdir, 570
file operation commands
    cp, 573
    mv, 572
    rm, 571
listing files
    file permissions block attributes, 566
    install.log file attributes, 566
    ls, 565
    ls -l, 565-566
    ls -la, 566-567
permissions/ownership, 577
    chgrp, 576
    chmod, 573-575
    chown, 576
viewing file contents, 569
    cat, 568
    more, 567

file system formats
  FAT, 114-115
  FAT32, 115
  NTFS, 115
File Transfer Protocol. *See* **FTP**
filtering
  MAC addresses, 28
  packets, firewalls, 397
  traffic, 354
Finisar Surveyor Demo protocol analyzer, 37
  installing, 38
  packets, captured, 38-42
  pinging computers, 39-40
Finisar-Shomiti utilization/errors strip chart, 344
firewalls, 396, 513
  ACLs, 398
    applying to routers, 399-400
    blocking host IP addresses example, 403
    blocking SMB data packets example, 400-401
    extended, 399
    named access list example, 401-402
    standard, 399
  attack prevention, 398
  defined, 28
  home networks, 28
  Linux, 605
  packet filtering, 397
  proxy servers, 397
  stateful, 397
Firewire connections, 106
first in, first out. *See* **FIFO**
flat networks, defined, 195
flooding, 137
FLPs (fast link pulses), 146
flyers, 456
foil over twisted-pair cabling. *See* **F/UTP**
forests, defined, 516
formatting
  file systems
    FAT, 114-115
    FAT32, 115
    NTFS, 115
  IP addresses, 15
  IPv6 addresses, 183

  WAN line data encoding
    AMI, 295
    B9ZS, 296
    data encapsulation, 297-298
forward domain name service, 361
forwarding frames, 137
Forwarding state (STP), 378
Foundation Fieldbus, 630
Foundation Fieldbus HSE protocol, 629
fractional T1 data rates, 293
fragment-collisions, 137
fragment-free switching, 137
Frame Relay clouds, 299
Frame Relay networks, 298
  configuring, 299, 305
  connections, creating, 301-302
  point-to-point connections, 300-304
  PVCs, 300
  subinterfaces, 300
Frame Relay PVCs, 299
frame-relay interface-dlci 200 command, 302
frames, forwarding, 137
frequency hopping spread spectrum. *See* **FHSS**
frequency of operation (RFID), 435
fstab file (Linux), 581
FTP (File Transfer Protocol), 185
  clients, Linux, 595
  data packets, 185
  servers, 513, 596
FTTB (fiber to the business), 469
FTTC (fiber to the curb), 469
FTTD (fiber to the desktop), 469
FTTH (fiber to the home), 469
full channels, cables, 71
full duplex, 59, 146-147
full duplex gigabit Ethernet support, 59
full IPv6 addresses, 182
fusion splicing, 465

G – H

gateway of last resort, 233
gateways, 145
  default, static routing, 227
  defined, 145

layer 3 networks, 197

VoIP, 488, 492

GBICs (Gigabit Interface Converters), 471

gigabit Ethernet, 59

glass. *See* **fibers**

graded-index fibers, 454-455

grep command (Linux), 585

grouping IP addresses. *See* **private addresses**

groups, adding to Windows 2003/2008 server domains, 528-532

GUI window (Linux), 561

H.323 protocols, 489

half duplex, 146-147

hand-offs, 416

hardware addresses. *See* **MAC addresses**

HART bus, 631

HCs (horizontal cross-connects), 53

HDLC (high-level data link control), 296

heavy duty industrial network areas, 627

"Hello" packets, 251

capturing, 276-277

Hello intervals, 275

IP address ranges, 275

parameters, 275

RIDs, 276

viewing, 277

help (?) command, 207

hexadecimal numbers, 168-170

HF (high-frequency), 435

hierarchies

DNS, 362

industrial networks, 619, 622

controller level, 621

device level, 620-621

information level, 620

high-frequency (HF), 435

high-level data link control. *See* **HDLC**

high-speed connections, 292

high-speed serial interfaces. *See* **HSSIs**

history command (Linux), 583

holddowns, 245

home directory (Linux), 569

home networks

appearance, 25

costs, 25

data speed, 25

equipment, 17

access points, 20

broadband modems/gateways, 23

cable modems, 23

DSL modems, 25

hubs, 18

network adapters, 19

routers, 20

switches, 19

wireless routers, 21

home access, 26

implementation ease, 25

IP addressing, 29-30

planning, 25

public access, 26

routers, 17

security, 27-28

troubleshooting, 26

wired, advantages/disadvantages of, 17

wireless

advantages, 17

configuring, 27

connections, 27

hotspots, 27

range extenders, 27

routers, 17

standards, 17

Wi-Fi Alliance, 17

hopping sequences, 417

horizontal cabling, 54

patch cables, 56

structured cabling subsystem, 52

terminated, 55

horizontal cross-connects. *See* **HCs**

host numbers, 16

hostname command, 212

hostnames

Juniper router configuration, 268

Linux configuration, 597

routers, 212

switch configuration, 371

hosts

defined, 402

LANs, interconnecting, 129

hot standby configurations, 623

hotspots, defined, 27

HSSIs (high-speed serial interfaces), 292

httpd restart command (Linux), 589

httpd script, 588

httpd stop command (Linux), 589

httpd.conf file (Linux), 589

hubs

broadcasting, 8

defined, 8

home networks, 18

link lights, 33

switches, compared, 130-132

hybrid echo cancellation circuits, 85

HyperTerminal serial communications software, configuring, 203-204

I

IANA (Internet Assigned Numbers Authority), 15

IANA website, 15

iBGP (internal BGP), 339

ICANN (Internet Corporation for Assigned Names and Numbers), 157

ICMP (Internet Control Message Protocol), 35, 163

ICs (Interconnect Fibers), 471

ICs (intermediate cross-connects), 52

IDA (Interface for Distributed Automation) protocol, 630

IDCs (Intermediate Distribution Closets), 471

IDE (Integrated Drive Electronics), 105

IEEE (Institute of Electrical and Electronics Engineers), 6

IEEE 1394, 105

IEEE OUI and company ID assignment database website, 14

IETF (Internet Engineering Task Force), 250

ifdown command (Linux), 591

ifup command (Linux), 591

IGMP (Internet Group Message Protocol), 164

IGP (Interior Gateway Protocol), 277

IGRP (Interior Gateway Routing Protocol)

administrative distance, 245

autonomous systems, 246

classful networks, 246

enabling, 246

enhanced. *See* EIGRP

holddowns, 245

metrics, 245

Network Challenge software, 250

OSPF, compared, 251

routes, configuring, 246-249

split horizons, 245

implicit messages, 629

inbound data traffic, 344

index-matching gel, 466

industrial Ethernet

cabling, 627-628

components, 627-628

determinism, 625

protocols, 628

Ethernet/IP, 629

Foundation Fieldbus HSE, 629

IDA, 630

MMS, 630

Modbus TCP, 630

Profinet, 630

switching, 627

topologies, 626-627

industrial networks

characteristics, 619

commercial networks, compared, 619

determinism, 619

distance/number of devices, 623

efficiency, 622

Ethernet

cabling, 627-628

components, 627-628

determinism, 625

protocols, 628-630

switching, 627

topologies, 626-627

hierarchy, 619, 622

controller level, 621

device level, 620-621

information level, 620

interoperability, 623-624

message length, 624

open buses, 630-631

open industrial networking standard, 618

overview, 618-619

proprietary buses, 631

redundancy, 619

timing considerations, 622

topology/redundancy, 623

vendor support, 625

industrial, scientific, and medical (ISM), 417

Industry Standard Architecture. *See* **ISA**

information level (industrial network hierarchy), 620

information servers, 512

infrared lights, defined, 452

input ports, 33

inquiry procedure (Bluetooth), 430

insertion loss. *See* **attenuation**

install.log file attributes (Linux), 566

installing

cables, troubleshooting, 86

Cisco VPN Client software, 334

network servers, 514

SSH, 594-595

Surveyor protocol analyzer, 38

Institute of Electrical and Electronics Engineers. *See* **IEEE**

int s0/0.1 point-to-point command, 302

int tunnel0 command, 328

Integrated Drive Electronics. *See* **IDE**

Integrated Services Digital Network. *See* **ISDN**

intelligent devices, 621

Interconnect Fibers. *See* **ICs**

interconnecting LANs

bridges, 124-128

layer 3 networks, 196

OSI model, 122-124

routers, 138, 143-145

switches, 128-129

Interface for Distributed Automation. *See* **IDA protocol**

Interior Gateway Protocol. *See* **IGP**

Interior Gateway Routing Protocol. *See* **IGRP**

intermediate cross-connects. *See* **ICs**

Intermediate Distribution Closets. *See* **IDCs**

internal BGP. *See* **iBGP**

Internal Ethernet interface, 267

Internet Assigned Numbers Authority. *See* **IANA**

Internet Control Message Protocol. *See* **ICMP**

Internet Corporation for Assigned Names and Numbers. *See* **ICANN**

Internet data traffic, analyzing

frame size distribution, 347

network layer host tables, 346

network layer matrix, 345-346

utilization/errors strip chart, 344

Internet Engineering Task Force. *See* **IETF**

Internet Group Message Protocol. *See* **IGMP**

Internet layer (TCP/IP)

ARP, 162

ICMP, 163

IGMP, 164

IP, 162

Internet Operating System. *See* **IOS**

Internet Protocol. *See* **IP**

Internet routing, 338

autonomous systems, 339

BGP, configuring, 339-343

Net-Challenge BGP configuration, 343-344

Internet Service Providers. *See* **ISPs**

Internetworking Packet Exchange. *See* **IPX**

interoperability, 621-624

Interrupt Request. *See* **IRQ**

intranets, defined, 16

intrusions (security)

detecting, 404

packet sniffing, 390

password cracking, 389-390

social engineering, 389

viruses, 393

vulnerable software, 391-393

wireless vulnerabilities, 394

worms, 393

inverse mask bits. *See* **wild card bits**

IOS (Internet Operating System), 194

console connection confirmation, 206

help command, 207

show command options, 207

show flash command, 208

show version command, 208

User EXEC mode, entering, 206

IP (Internet Protocol), 162

addressing

assigning, 15, 173

campus network assignments, 358-360

CIDR blocks, 181-182

classes, 15, 170

defined, 15

experimental ranges, 275

format, 15

gateway of last resort, 233

groups. See private addresses

home networks, 29-30

host numbers, 16

IPv4, 15

IPv6, 182-185

Juniper interface assignments, 268

lease time, 359

Linux configuration, 590

name translation, 361

network numbers, 16

network server configuration, 521-522

next hop configuration, 231

non-internet routable, 173

octets, 172

office-type LANs configuration, 34

OSPF "Hello" packets, 275

private, 173

RAS configuration, 321

structure, 171

verifying, 36

internetwork, defined, 16

security. *See* IPsec

telephony. *See* VoIP

tunnels, 325

ip route command, 231

ipconfig /all command, MAC addresses, 12

ipconfig command

IP address verification, 36

Linux, 590

IPng. *See* **IPv6**

IPsec (IP security), 334, 390

IPv4 (IP version 4) addressing, 15

assigning, 173

classes, 170

octets, 172

private IP addresses, 173

structure, 171

IPv6 (IP version 6) addressing

format, 183

full, 182

IPv4 conversions, 183-185

types, 184

IPX (Internetworking Packet Exchange), 345

IRQ (Interrupt Request), 106

ISA (Industry Standard Architecture), 104

ISDN (Integrated Services Digital Network), 310, 312

ISM (industrial, scientific, and medical), 417

isolating collision domains, 136

isolators, 463

ISPs (Internet Service Providers), 16

J

jitter, VoIP, 495-496

Juniper routers

configuration mode, 266-267

hostname configuration, 268

interfaces

assigning IP addresses, 268

types, 266

viewing, 267-268

JUNOS CLI User Guide website, 271

operating system (JUNOS), 262

operational mode

command completion, 264

help command (?), 263

{master} mode, 263

network connectivity, 266

PICs, 266

prompts, 263

router configuration, viewing, 265

routing engines, 265

version information, 264

OSPF configuration, 270-271

RIP configuration, 269-270

static route configuration, 268

JUNOS (Juniper router operating system), 262

configuration mode, 266-267

hostname configuration, 268

interfaces, viewing, 267-268

IP addresses, assigning to interfaces, 268

JUNOS CLI User Guide website, 271

operational mode

    command completion, 264

    help command (?), 263

    {master mode}, 263

    network connectivity, 266

    PICs, 266

    prompts, 263

    router configuration, viewing, 265

    routing engines, 265

    version information, 264

OSPF configuration, 270-271

RIP configuration, 269-270

static route configuration, 268

just-in-time strategies, 625

K - L

keepalive packets, 218

kill/kill -9 commands (Linux), 580

Konqueror program (Linux), 583

L2TP (Layer 2 Tunneling Protocol), 331

LANs (local area networks)

campus

    access layer, 356

    core layer, 354-355

    data flow, 356

    data traffic analysis, 378-380

    daily, 379

    distribution layer, 355

    DNS, 361-364

    hourly, 379

    IP assignment with DHCP, 358-360

    load balancing, 357-358

    managing with SNMP, 365-367

    media selection, 356-357

    Power over Ethernet (PoE), 367-369

    static VLAN configuration, 373-377

    switch configuration, 370-373, 377-378

    VLANs, 369-370

    weekly, 380

defined, 5

Ethernet, 10

    bridges, 125

    CSMA/CD protocol, 10

    industrial Ethernet, 625-630

    IP addresses, 15-16

    *MAC addresses. **See** Ethernet; MAC addresses*

    optical, 469-470

    packets, 10-11

fiber optics, 475

interconnecting

    bridges, 124-128

    layer 3 networks, 196

    OSI model, 122-124

    routers, 138, 143-145

    switches, 128-129

IP addresses, verifying, 36

office-type

    cabling, 32-34

    devices, documenting, 30

    IP addresses, 34

    star topology connections, 32

sizes, 194

testing, 35-36

topologies, 5

    bus, 6-8

    mesh, 9

    star, 8

    token-ring, 6

VLANs

    dynamic, 370

    membership assignments, 370

    *static. **See** static VLANs*

    types, 369

last command (Linux), 600

last miles, 432

latency

switches, 137

VoIP, 496

layer 2 switches, 128

Layer 2 Tunneling Protocol. *See* L2TP

layer 3 networks, 195, 201

components, 200

data flow to/from gateways, 197

data packet exchange, 199

default gateway addresses, 196

    finding destination networks with subnet masks, 198

    LANs, interconnecting, 196

    next hop addresses, 199

    router connections, 200

    segments, 199

layers

    campus networks

        access, 356

        core, 354-355

        distribution, 355

    OSI model, 123

    TCP/IP, 156

        application, 157-158

        Internet, 162-164

        network interface, 164

        transport, 158-162

LC fiber connectors, 466

LCL (Longitudinal Conversion Loss), 84

lean strategies, 625

Learning state (STP), 378

lease time, 359

LEDs (light-emitting diodes), 461-462

legacy protocols, 624

LF (low-frequency), 435

lib directory (Linux), 569

light detectors, 464

light duty industrial network areas, 627

light pipes. *See* **fibers**

light reflection, 451

light refraction, 451-452

light-emitting diodes. *See* **LEDs**

line ? command, 213

line connections, WANs

    data channels, 292-293

    encoding formats, 295-298

    POP, 294

    T1 framing, 294-295

line of demarcation, 294

linear network topology, industrial Ethernet, 626

link integrity tests, 33

link lights, 33

link pulses, 34

link state advertisements. *See* **LSAs**

link state protocols, 239

links, cables, 71

Linux

    administration commands

        man, 577

        mount, 581-582

        ps, 579-580

        shortcuts, 583

        shutdown, 583

        shutdown -h now, 583

        su, 580

        unmount, 583

    application management

        Apache Web service installation, 588-589

        file searches, 585-586

        installed applications, viewing, 584

        installing Red Hat applications, 586-587

        Mozilla, 588

        RPM man page, 584

        uninstalling telnet applications, 586

    bash, 566

    command line, 563

    directories, 569

    file structure

        directory operations, 569-570

        file operations, 571-573

        listing files, 565-566

        permissions/ownership, 573-577

        viewing file contents, 567-569

    fstab file, 581

    Konqueror, 583

    logging on, 560-561

    main GUI window, 561

    managing, 604

    net masks, 590

    network configuration

        DNS, 597

        etc/sysconfig/network-scripts, 594

        Ethernet cards, 590

        ftp clients, 595

        ftp servers, 596

        gateway addresses, 592

        hostnames, 597

        interface control, 591

        IP address configuration, 590

        loopbacks, 590

shutting down/starting interfaces, 592

SSH installations, 594-595

viewing interface configurations, 590

root access, 560

system config tools

date/time, 605

firewalls, 605

network menu, 607

printers, 607

services, 609

software management, 607

users, 609

viewing, 604

troubleshooting

boot processes, 598-600

boot services, 602-603

security, 601

users, 600-601

users, adding, 561-563

Create New User window, 562

logout option, 564

Red Hat User Manager window, 562

website, 565

Listening state (STP), 378

listing files commands (Linux)

file permissions block attributes, 566

install.log file attributes, 566

ls, 565

ls -l, 565-566

ls -la, 566-567

lo (loopback), 590

load balancing

campus networks, 357-358

dynamic routing protocols, 237

per-destination, 358

per-packet, 358

local area networks. *See* LANs

logical addresses, 138

logical fiber maps, 472-473

long haul applications, 456

long-haul fiber optic systems, 475

Longitudinal Conversion Loss. *See* LCL

loopbacks

defined, 228

Linux, 590

lost+found directory (Linux), 569

low-frequency (LF), 435

ls command (Linux), 565

ls -l command (Linux), 565-566

ls -la command (Linux), 566-567

LSAs (link state advertisements), 251

M

MAC addresses (media acess control)

aging time, 134

bridge tables, 126

defined, 11

dynamic, 134

filtering, 28

OUIs, 11

retrieving, 12-13

samples, 14

secure, 134

static, 134

viewing, 12

Mac OS X

device drivers, 110-111

memory requirements, 112

RAS client configuration, 325

VPN client configuration, 333

Z-Term serial communications software configuration, 205

macrobending, 457

main cross-connects. *See* MCs

man command (Linux), 577

managed switches

aging time, 134

benefits, 136

broadcast domains, 137

CAM, 136

Cisco Catalyst 2960, 133

flooding, 137

frames, forwarding, 137

IP addresses, configuring, 136

isolating the collision domains, 136

MAC address assignments, 134

Management Ethernet interface, 266

management information base. *See* MIB

managing

    campus networks

        Power over Ethernet (PoE), 367-369

        SNMP, 365-367

    Linux applications, 584

        Apache Web service installation, 588-589

        file searches, 585-586

        installed applications, viewing, 584

        installing Red Hat applications, 586-587

        Mozilla, 588

        RPM man page, 584

        system config tools, 604-609

        uninstalling telnet applications, 586

MANs (metropolitan area networks), 5

manufacturer specifications for cables, 87

Manufacturing Message Specification. *See* **MMS**

masks (subnet)

    8 subnet division example, 177-178

    binary/decimal equivalents, 176

    CIDR notation, 180

    creating, 173-175

    prefix length notation, 180

    router-to-router link example, 179-180

{master} mode (JUNOS), 263

Mbps (megabits per second), 32

MCs (main cross-connects), 52

mechanical splices, 466

media access control. *See* **MAC addresses**

megabits per second. *See* **Mbps**

membership, VLANs, 370

memory

    amount installed, verifying, 113

    operating system requirements, 112

    types, 113

mesh topologies, LANs, 9

message length (industrial networks), 624

message overhead (industrial networks), 622

message quantity (industrial networks), 622

message type ACK. *See* **MT ACK**

message type discover. *See* **MT Discover**

message type request. *See* **MT Request**

messages (multicast), defined, 129

metrics

    dynamic routing protocols, 237

    IGRP, 245

metropolitan area networks. *See* **MANs**

MIB (management information base), 364

microbending, 457

midspan PSE, 368

MIMO (Multiple Input Multiple Output), 419

minimum ones density, 296

mkdir command (Linux), 570

mm (multimode) fibers, 473

MMS (Manufacutring Message Specification), 630

mnt directory (Linux), 569

modal dispersion, 458

ModBus, 631

Modbus TCP protocol, 630

mode field diameter (fibers), 456

modems

    broadband, 23

    cable, 23, 310

    DSL, 25

    RAS configuration, 318-320

    xDSL, 312-314

more command (Linux), 567

motherboard bus connections, 103-106

mount command (Linux), 581-582

Mozilla, 588

MT ACK (message type ACK), 361

MT Discover (message type discover), 361

MT Offer (DHCP Offer packets), 361

MT Request (message type request), 361

MT-RJ fiber connectors, 466

multi-homed users, 338

multicast addresses, 164, 184

multicast messages, defined, 129

multilayer switches, 137-138

multilevel encoding, 85

multimode (mm) fibers, 453, 473

Multiple Input Multiple Output. *See* **MIMO**

multiplexing, 293

multiport bridges. *See* **layer 2 switches**

multiport repeaters. *See* **hubs**

mv command (Linux), **572**

My Network Places connection

    Windows 2000, 550-551

    Windows XP, 546-549

N

name server records. *See* **NS records**

names. *See also* **DNS**

    FastEthernet ports, 143

    hostnames

        Juniper router configuration, 268

        Linux configuration, 597

        routers, 212

        switch configuration, 371

    IP address translation, 361

    serial ports, 143

nanometers (nm), 451

NAT (Network Address Translation), 29

ncftp (Linux), 595

NCP (network control protocol), 156

near end crosstalk. *See* **NEXT**

near-end testing, 72

neighbor discovery recovery (EIGRP), 257

net masks, 590

net send command, 554

net session commmand, 554

Net-Challenge software

    BGP configuration, 343-344

    router configuration privileged EXEC mode, 216-217

    router configuration User EXEC mode, 209-211

NetBIOS, defined, 517

netstat command (Linux), 603

netstat -a command, 392

netstat -b command, 392

netstat -r command, 228

"Network," 546

network adapters, home networks, 19

Network Address Translation. *See* **NAT**

network addresses, 138

Network Challenge software

    EIGRP, 262

    Frame Relay networks, 305

    IGRP, 250

    OSPF, 256-257

    static routes, 236

    static VLANs, 376-377

    TFTP, 274-275

network command, 253

network congestion. *See* **bottlenecking**

Network connection (Windows Vista), verifying, 546

network control protocol (NCP), 156

network interface cards. *See* **NICs**

network interface layer (TCP/IP), 164

network latency, VoIP, 496

network layer, OSI model, 123

network mask parameter ("Hello" packets), 275

Network Neighborhood connection (Windows NT/98), verifying, 552

network numbers, defined, 16, 253

network operations centers. *See* **NOCs**

network servers

    account lockout policies, configuring, 552

        enabling user accounts, 554

        locked out accounts, 553

        messages to users, 555

        viewing connected users, 554

    adding, 513

    computers, adding, 522-526

    configuring, 514

    groups, adding, 528-532

    installing, 514

    IP addresses, configuring, 521-522

    My Network Places connection

        Windows 2000, 550-551

        Windows XP, 546-549

    Network connection (Windows Vista), verifying, 546

    Network Neighborhood connection (Windows NT/98), verifying, 552

    network types

        client/server, 511-512

        peer-to-peer, 510-511

    organizational units, adding, 528-532

    permissions, 533-534

    policies, 533-534

        Windows 2003, 539, 542-544

        Windows 2008, 534-536, 539

    server types, 512-513

users, adding, 526-527

Windows 2003 servers, creating, 514

    Configure DNS window, 519

    Create or Join Forest window, 516

    DNS warning, 518

    domain controller types, 515

    file directory locations, 517

    NetBIOS Domain Name window, 517

    New Domain Name window, 516

    options summary, 520

    Permissions window, 519

    Shared System Volume window, 517

    Welcome screen, 515

Windows 2008, configuring, 521

network slowdowns, 126

network start command (Linux), 592

network stop command (Linux), 592

network types

client/server, 511-512

peer-to-peer, 510-511

Networking Challenge software, RIP, 244-245

New Technology File System. *See* **NTFS**

NEXT (near end crosstalk), 71-72

next hop addresses, 199, 231

NICs (network interface cards)

combo terminations, 102

defined, 11

Ethernets, 11

NLOS (non line-of-sight), 432

nm (nanometers), 451

nmap command (Linux), 601

no ip directed-broadcast command, 396

no shutdown (no shut) command, 214

NOCs (network operations centers), 344

nominal velocity of propagation (NVP), 74

non line-of-sight. *See* **NLOS**

non-internet routable IP addresses, 173

NS (name service) records, 362

NTFS (New Technology File System), 115

numbering systems

binary-decimal conversions, 165-166

binary-hexadecimal, 170

decimal-binary conversions, 166-168

hexadecimal, 168-170

numerical aperture, 453

numerics

office-type LANs, 32-33

optical Ethernet, 470

NVP (nominal velocity of propagation), 74

O

OCs (optical carriers), 292

OFDM (orthogonal frequency division multiplexing), 802.11 WLANs, 418

office-type LANs, configuring

cabling, 32-34

devices, documenting, 30

IP addresses, 34

star topology connections, 32

open authentication, 436

open buses, industrial networks, 630-631

Open Shortest Path First. *See* **OSPF**

Open Shortest Path First Interior Gateway Protocol. *See* **OSPFIGP**

open system interconnect. *See* **OSI**

openssh applications, 594

operating systems (OS), MAC address retrieval, 13

operational mode (Juniper routers)

command completion, 264

help command (?), 263

{master} mode, 263

network connectivity, 266

PICs, 266

prompts, 263

router configuration, viewing, 265

routing engines, 265

version information, 264

optical carriers. *See* **OCs**

optical Ethernet, 469-470

optical networking

advantages, 450

architectures

    building distribution, 470-472

    campus distribution, 472-475

    data rates, 469

    defining optical networking, 468-470

    fiber to the business, 469

    fiber to the curb, 469

fiber to the desktop, 469

fiber to the home, 469

optical Ethernet, 469-470

standards, 468

armored fiber optics, 628

attenuators, 463, 478

branching devices, 463

cable losses, 476-478

connections and splicing, 465-466

connector losses, 476

construction, 452

couplers, 464

designing, 475-478

diode lasers, 461

distance-limiting parameters

attenuation, 457

dispersion, 458-460

dispersion compensation, 460-461

distributed feedback lasers, 462

DLs versus LEDs, 462

environments, 475

extra losses, 476

extra margins, 478

fiber color code for 12 fibers in a bundle, 474

fiber connectorization, 466-467

fiber optic components, 449

fiber strands, 453

fibers, 463

graded-index fibers, 454-455

isolators, 463

LEDs, 461

light detectors, 464

light reflection, 451

light refraction, 451-452

maintenance margins, 476

mode field diameter, 456

multimode fibers, 453

numerical aperture, 453

operational margins, 476

optical fiber types, 453-454

optical-line amplifiers, 464

receive signal power, 476

receiver sensitivity, 477

safety, 479-480

single-mode fibers, 455-457

single-mode/multimode, compared, 456

spectrum notation, 451

splice losses, 476

splitters, 463

step-index fibers, 455

transmitter power output, 476

troubleshooting, 481

tunable lasers, 462

types of fiber, 456

vertical cavity emitting lasers, 462

wavelength division multiplexers, 464

wavelengths, 452

optical spectrums, defined, 452

optical time-domain reflectometers. *See* OTDRs

optical-line amplifiers, 464

organizational units, adding to Windows 2003/2008 server domains, 528-532

organizationally unique idenitifers. *See* OUIs

orthogonal frequency division multiplexing. *See* OFDM

OSI (open system interconnect) model

defined, 122

layers, 123

network problems, isolating, 124

OSPF (Open Shortest Path First), 250

advantages/disadvantages, 252

area 0, 254

areas, 251

"Hello" packets, 251

capturing, 276-277

IP address ranges, 275

parameters, 275

RIDs, 276

viewing, 277

Juniper routers configuration, 270-271

LSAs, 251

Network Challenge software, 256-257

RIP/IGRP, compared, 251

routes, configuring, 252-256

VLSMs, 251

wild card bits, 253

OSPFIGP (Open Shortest Path First Interior Gateway Protocol), 277

OTDRs (optical time-domain reflectometers), 481

OUIs (organizationally unique idenitifers), 11

outbound data traffic, 344

overloading, 29

ownership commands (Linux), 577
  chgrp, 576
  chmod, 573-575
  chown, 576

P

Packet Internet Groper. *See* ping command

packets
  captured, 38-42
  defined, 10
  Ethernets, 10-11
  filtering, firewalls, 397
  sequence numbers, 490
  sniffing, 390, 436
  switching, 305
  SPI, 28

paging procedure (Bluetooth), 430

pair data, CAT6 link tests, 76

passwords
  cracking, 389-390
  home networks, 27
  line console, 372-373
  protection, routers privileged EXEC mode, 213
  routers line console, 213
  switches, 372

PAT (Port Address Translation), 29

patch cables
  CAT5/5e straight-through, configuring
    inserting wires into RJ-45 plug, 70
    jacket, stripping, 69
    RJ-45 plug, crimping, 71
    wire pairs, separating, 70
  defined, 56
  horizontal cabling, 56

path determination, dynamic routing protocols, 237

payloads, 306

PBX (private branch exchange), 488
  tie lines, replacing, 491-493
  upgrading, 493-494

PC Card adapters, 20

PCI (Peripheral Component Interconnect), 103

PCM (pulse code modulation), 489

PDNs (public data networks), 298

PDs (Powered Devices), 368

peer-to-peer networks, defined, 510-511

peering, 339

per-destination load balancing, 358

per-packet load balancing, 358

performance bottlenecks, 59

Peripheral Component Interconnect. *See* PCI

permanent interfaces, 266

permanent virtual connections. *See* PVCs

permissions, configuring, 533-534

permissions commands (Linux), 573-577

physical addresses. *See* MAC addresses

physical fiber maps, 473-474

physical interface cards. *See* PICs

physical layer (OSI model), 123

physical layer cabling
  10GBASE-T
    AXT, 83-84
    signal balance, 84
    signal transmission, 85-86
    standard, 83
  CAT5e/5 straight-through patch cables, configuring
    crimping RJ-45 plugs, 71
    four wire pairs, 61
    inserting wires into RJ-45 plug, 70
    jacket stripping, 69
    separating wire pairs, 70
  CAT6 horizontal link cables, terminating, 65
    bend-limiting strain relief boot, 65, 68
    four wire pairs, 61
    jacket stripping, 66
    lacing tool, 66
    RJ-45 jack and lacing tool alignment, 67
  crossover cables, 64
  defined, 51
  STP, 60
  straight-through, 64
  structured
    campus hierarchical topology, 53
    EIA/TIA 568-B, 51
    horizontal cabling, 54-56
    standards, 51
    subsystems, 52
    telecommunications architecture, 52-53
    TIA/EIA 568-A, 51

testing, 71
   ACR, 74
   attenuation, 72
   CAT6 links, 75-82
   channel specifications, 72
   delay skew, 74
   ELFEXT, 74
   NEXT, 72
   propagation delay, 74
   PSACR, 74
   PSELFEXT, 74
   PSNEXT, 73
   return loss, 74
transmit/receive pairs, aligning, 62-63
troubleshooting
   cable stretching, 87
   CAT5e test examples, 88, 92-93
   failing to meet manufacturer specifications, 87
   installation, 86
UTP
   balanced mode, 58
   bottlenecking, 59
   categories, 58-59
   full duplex gigabit Ethernet support, 59
   high-performance, 60-61
   RJ-45 modular plug example, 57
   standards, 57
piconets, 430
PICs (physical interface cards), 266
ping (Packet Internet Groper), 35
ping command
   hub-switch comparison, 131-132
   LANs, testing, 35-36
   Surveyor protocol analyzer, 39-40
pipe command (Linux), 585
planning home networks, 25
PLCs (programmable logic controllers), 622
PoE (Power over Ethernet)
   benefits, 367
   campus networks, 367-369
   networking hardware defined, 368
   PDs, 368
   PoE Plus, 369
   PSE, 368
point of presence. *See* POP

point-to-multipoint WLAN configuration, 438
   antenna site survey, 439
   multipoint distribution, 440
   point-to-point wireless links, 439-440
   remote installations, 442
point-to-point connections, Frame Relay clouds, 300
point-to-point Frame Relay router connections, configuring, 302-304
point-to-point physical interfaces, 301
Point-to-Point protocol. *See* PPP
Point-to-Point Tunneling Protocol. *See* PPTP
polarization mode dispersion, 458
policies
   account lockout policies, configuring, 552
      enabling user accounts, 554
      locked out accounts, 553
      messages to users, 555
      viewing connected users, 554
   configuring, 533
      Windows 2003, 539, 542-544
      Windows 2008, 534-536, 539
POP (point of presence), 294
Port Address Translation. *See* PAT
port-based VLANs, 369
ports
   assignment website, 158
   defined, 8
   FastEthernet, naming, 143
   input, 33
   serial, naming, 143
   straight through, 33
   uplink, 33
   well-known, 157
Power Sourcing Equipment. *See* PSE
Power Sum Alien Attenuation to Crosstalk Ratio. *See* PSAACRF
Power Sum Alien Near-End Cross-Talk. *See* PSANEXT
Power Sum NEXT. *See* PSNEXT
power-sum attenuation-crosstalk. *See* PSACR
Powered Devices. *See* PDs
PPP (Point-to-Point protocol), 296
PPTP (Point-to-Point Tunneling Protocol), 331
PQ (priority queueing), 497
prefix length notation, 180

presentation layer (OSI model), 123

print servers, 513

printers, Linux, 607

priority queuing (PQ), 497

private addresses, defined, 16

private branch exchange. *See* PBX

private IP addresses, 173

privileged EXEC mode (routers)

   entering, 211

   Fast Ethernet interface configuration, 214

   hostname, 212

   line console passwordes, 213

   Net-Challenge software, 216-217

   password protection, 213

   serial interface configuration, 214-216

privileged mode

   defined, 211

   switches, 371

probing, 404

proc directory (Linux), 570

Profibus, 630

Profinet protocol, 630

programmable logic controllers. *See* PLCs

propagation delay, 74

proprietary buses, industrial networks, 631

protocol analyzer (Surveyor), 37

   captured packets, 38-42

   installing, 38

   pinging computers, 39-40

protocol-based VLANs, 370

protocols

   ARP, 39, 162

   auto-negotiation, 145

     advantages/disadvantages, 148

     FLPs, 146

     full/half duplex, 146-147

     process, 146

   BGP, 338

     configuring, 339-343

     Net-Challenge configuration, 343-344

   connection oriented, 158

   CSMA/CD, 10

   DataHighwayPlus, 631

   defined, 5

DHCP, 317

   IP assignment for campus networks, 358-360

   TCP packet transfers, 360-361

distance vector, 238-239

dynamic routing, 236

   convergence, 237

   distance vector, 238-239

   features, 237

   link state, 239

   load balancing, 237

   metrics, 237

   path determination, 237

EAP, 437

EIGRP

   DUAL finite state machine, 257

   neighbor discovery recovery, 257

   Network Challenge software, 262

   protocol dependent modules, 257

   reliable transport protocol, 257

   route configuration, 257-261

fieldbus, 618

FTP, data packets, 185

H.323, 489

HDLC, 296

ICMP, 35

IGP, 277

IGRP

   administrative distance, 245

   autonomous systems, 246

   classful networks, 246

   enabling, 246

   enhanced. See EIGRP

   holddowns, 245

   metrics, 245

   Network Challenge software, 250

   OSPF, compared, 251

   route configuration, 246-249

   split horizons, 245

industrial Ethernet, 628

   Ethernet/IP, 629

   Foundation Fieldbus HSE, 629

   IDA, 630

   MMS, 630

   Modbus TCP, 630

   Profinet, 630

IP, 162

IPX, 345

L2TP, 331

legacy, 624

link integrity tests, 33

link state, 239

OSPF, 250

  advantages/disadvantages, 252

  area 0, 254

  areas, 251

  Hello packets, 251, 275-277

  Juniper router configuration, 270-271

  LSAs, 251

  Network Challenge software, 256-257

  RIP/IGRP, compared, 251

  routes, configuring, 252-256

  VLSMs, 251

  wild card bits, 253

OSPFIGP, 277

PPP, 296

PPTP, 331

RAS, selecting, 317

RIP

  classful addressing, 240

  enabling, 240

  initializing, 241

  Juniper router configuration, 269-270

  network advertising, 240

  Networking Challenge software, 244-245

  OSPF versus, 251

  route configuration, 242-244

  routing loops, 239

RTCP, 490

RTP, 490

RTPS, 630

SIP, 489

Slotted Aloha, 435

SNMP

  configuring, 365-367

  managing campus networks via, 365-367

  MIB, 364

SSIP, 489

static routing

  configuring, 234-235

  data packet flow between LANs, 231

  default gateways, 227

  gateway of last resort, 233

  host PC routing tables, 228

  loopbacks, 228

  Network Challenge software, 236

  next hop IP addresses, 231

  routing table codes, 232

  three-router campus network, 228, 232

  two-router network, 229

  variable length subnet masking, 231

STP

  BPDUs, 377

  states, 378

Surveyor protocol analyzer, 37

  captured packets, examining, 38-39

  installing, 38

  packets, capturing, 40-42

  pinging computers, 39-40

TCP/IP, 16

  application layer, 157-158

  development, 156

  Internet layer, 162-164

  layers, 156

  network interface layer, 164

  transport layer, 158-162

TFTP

  configuring, 271-273

  Network Challenge software, 274-275

UDP, 161-162

WAN routing, 337

X.25, 298

proxy servers, 397, 513

ps command (Linux), 579-580

PSAACRF (Power Sum Alien Attenuation to Crosstalk Ratio), 83

PSACR (power-sum attenuation-crosstalk), 74, 79

PSANEXT (Power Sum Alien Near-End Cross-Talk), 83

PSE (Power Sourcing Equipment), 368

PSELFEXT (Power Sum Equal Level Far-End Cross-Talk), 74

pseudorandom, 417

PSNEXT (Power Sum NEXT), 73

PSTN (public switched telephone network), 488

public data networks. *See* PDNs

public switched telephone network. *See* PSTN

pulse code modulation. *See* PCM

pulse dispersion, 454

PVCs (permanent virtual connections), 299

ATM, 306

Frame Relay networks, 300

pwd command (Linux), 570

Q - R

QoS (Quality of Service), VoIP

jitter, 495-496

network latency, 496

queuing, 496-497

queuing

CQ, 497

PQ, 497

VoIP, 496-497

Radio Frequency Identification. *See* RFID

RADIUS (Remote Authentication Dial-In User Service), 437

RAM (Random Access Memory). *See* memory

range extenders, defined, 27

ranging, 310

RAS (remote access server)

client configurations, 323-325

Windows 2003 server configurations

enabling RAS, 315

IP configuration, 321

modem configuration, 318, 320

multiple servers, managing, 318

protocol selection, 317

Routing and Remote Access Server Setup Wizard menu, 315

Routing and Remote Access window, 315

user accounts, 322

Real-Time Control Protocol. *See* RTCP

Real-Time Protocol. *See* RTP

Real-Time Publish-Subscribe Protocol. *See* RTPS

reboot command (Linux), 599

receive (RX), 62

receive cable pairs, aligning, 62-63

received signal levels. *See* RSLs

Red Hat Package Manager. *See* RPM

redundancy (industrial networks), 619, 623

refractive indexes, 451

remote access servers. *See* RAS

Remote Authentication Dial-In User Service. *See* RADIUS

Resistive Power Discovery, 368

resolv.conf file (Linux), 597

return loss, 74

reverse DNS

campus networks, 364

defined, 361

RFID (Radio Frequency Identification), 432-433

air interface protocol, 435

backscatter, 432

frequency of operation, 435

tags, powering, 434

RIDs (router IDs), 276

ring topologies, industrial networks, 623

RIP (Routing Information Protocol), 239

classful addressing, 240

enabling, 240

initializing, 241

Juniper routers configuration, 269-270

network advertising, 240

Networking Challenge software, 244-245

OSPF versus, 251

route configuration, 242-244

routing loops, 239

RJ-45 modular connectors, 32, 57

rm command (Linux), 571

rmdir command (Linux), 570

roaming, 416

rollover cables, 201

root access, 560

root directory (Linux), 570

root servers, DNS, 362

route add default gw command (Linux), 592

route flapping, 252

route print command, 228

routed networks. *See* layer 3 networks

router dead intervals ("Hello" packets), 275

router eigrp command, 259

router IDs. *See* RIDs

router igrp command, 246

router ospf command, 253

router RIP command, 240-242

Router#, 211

Router(config)#, 213

Router(config-if)#, 214

Router(config-line)#, 213

Router(config-router)# prompt, 247

router-to-router VPN connections, 326-331

routers, 138

  ACLs, applying, 399-400

  ATM configuration, 307

  Cisco 2500 series, 140-141

  Cisco 2600 series, 140

  Cisco 2800 series, 139

  console port connections

    connectors, 201

    console cables, 201

    HyperTerminal serial communications software, 203-204

    rollover cables, 201

    RS-232 serial communications ports, 201

    settings, 202

    Z-Term serial communications software, 205

  Frame Relay point-to-point connection configuration, 302-304

  gateways, 145

  home networks, 17, 20

  interface, 138, 242

  Juniper

    assigning IP addresses to interfaces, 268

    configuration mode, 266-267

    hostname configuration, 268

    interfaces, 266

    JUNOS CLI User Guide website, 271

    operating system (JUNOS), 262

    operational mode, 263-266

    OSPF configuration, 270-271

    RIP configuration, 269-270

    static route configuration, 268

    viewing interfaces, 267-268

  LANs, interconnecting, 138, 143-145

  layer 3 networks

    components, 200

    data flow to/from gateways, 197

    data packet exchange, 199

    default gateway addresses, 196

    finding destination networks with subnet masks, 198

    interconnecting LANs, 196

    next hop addresses, 199

    router connections, 200

    segments, 199

  privileged EXEC mode

    entering, 211

    Fast Ethernet interface configuration, 214

    hostname, 212

    line console passwords, 213

    Net-Challenge software, 216-217

    password protection, 213

    serial interface configuration, 214-216

  segments, 145

  terminal configuration mode, 212

  troubleshooting, 217-220

  uptime, 208

  User EXEC mode

    console connection confirmation, 206

    entering, 206

    help command, 207

    Net-Challenge software, 209-211

    show command options, 207

    show flash command, 208

    show version command, 208

  wireless, 17, 21

routing

  Internet, 338

    autonomous systems, 339

    BGP, configuring, 339-343

    Net-Challenge BGP configuration, 343-344

  static, Juniper routers, 268

  WANs, 337

Routing and Remote Access Server Setup Wizard, 315

Routing and Remote Access window, 315

Routing Information Protocol. *See* RIP

routing loops, 239

routing protocols

  dynamic, 236

    convergence, 237

    distance vector, 238-239

    features, 237

    link state, 239

    load balancing, 237

    metrics, 237

    path determination, 237

EIGRP
   DUAL finite state machine, 257
   neighbor discovery recovery, 257
   Network Challenge software, 262
   protocol depenedent modules, 257
   reliable transport protocol, 257
   routes, configuring, 257-261
IGRP
   administrative distance, 245
   autonomous systems, 246
   classful networks, 246
   enabling, 246
   *enhanced. **See** EIGRP*
   holddowns, 245
   metrics, 245
   Network Challenge software, 250
   OSPF, compared, 251
   routes, configuring, 246-249
   split horizons, 245
OSFPIGP, 277
OSPF, 250
   advantages/disadvantages, 252
   area 0, 254
   areas, 251
   "Hello" packets, 251, 275-277
   Juniper router configuration, 270-271
   LSAs, 251
   Network Challenge software, 256-257
   RIP/IGRP, compared, 251
   routes, configuring, 252-256
   VLSMs, 251
   wild card bits, 253
RIP
   classful addressing, 240
   enabling, 240
   initializing, 241
   Juniper router configuration, 269-270
   network advertising, 240
   Networking Challenge software, 244-245
   OSPF, compared, 251
   route configuration, 242-244
   routing loops, 239
static, 227
   configuring, 234-235
   data packet flow between LANs, 231
   default gateways, 227
   gateway of last resort, 233
   host PC routing tables, 228
   loopbacks, 228
   Network Challenge software, 236
   next hop IP addresses, 231
   routing table codes, 232
   three-router campus network, 228, 232
   two-router network, 229
   variable length subnet masking, 231
TFTP
   configuring, 271-273
   Network Challenge software, 274-275
viewing, 242
routing tables, 144, 228
RPM (Red Hat Package Manager), application management
Apache Web service installation, 588-589
file searches, 585-586
installed applications, viewing, 584
installing Red Hat applications, 586-587
man page, 584
Mozilla, 588
uninstalling telnet applications, 586
rpm -e command (Linux), 586
rpm -i command (Linux), 586-587
rpm -qa command (Linux), 584
rpm -qf command (Linux), 585-586
RS-232 serial communications ports, 201
RSLs (received signal levels), 463
RTCP (Real-Time Control Protocol), 490
RTP (Real-Time Protocol), 490
RTPS (Real-Time Publish-Subscribe Protocol), 630
RX (receive), 62

S

safety, optical networking, 479-480
SATA (Serial Advanced Technology Attachment), 106
sbin directory (Linux), 570
SC fiber connectors, 466
scattering, 457
SCSI (Small Computer System Interface), 105-106
SDH (Synchronous Digital Hierarchy), 468
SDRAM (Synchronous DRAM), 113

secure MAC address assignments, **134**

secure session initiation protocol. *See* SSIP

Secure Shell. *See* **SSH**

security

  ACLs, 396-398

    blocking host IP addresses example, 403

    blocking SMB data packets example, 400-401

    extended, 399

    named access list example, 401-402

    routers, applying to, 399-400

    standard, 399

  DDoS attacks, 396

  DoS attacks, 395-396

  firewalls, 396

    ACLs, 398-403

    attack prevention, 398

    home networks, 28

    Linux, 605

    packet filtering, 397

    proxy servers, 397

    stateful, 397

  home networks, 27-28

  intrusions

    detecting, 404

    packet sniffing, 390

    password cracking, 389-390

    social engineering, 389

    viruses, 393

    vulnerable software, 391-393

    wireless vulnerabilities, 394

    worms, 393

  IPsec, 334, 390

  Linux, troubleshooting, 601

  passwords

    cracking, 389-390

    line console, 372-373

    switches, 372

  unsecured data packets

    captured packets, 407

    capturing packets setup, 405

    protecting, 408

    router connections, 406

    telnet session packets, 407

    telnetting to routers, 405

    user verification, 406

  VoIP, 497

  WLANs, 435-438

segments

  defined, 124, 145

  layer 3 networks, 199

Serial Advanced Technology Attachment. *See* **SATA**

serial ports, naming, 143

server message block. *See* **SMB**

servers

  application, 512

  DHCP, 513

  DNS, 513

  email, 512

  fax, 513

  FTP, 513, 596

  information, 512

  network. *See* network servers

  print, 513

  proxy, 397, 513

  remote access

    client configuration, 323-325

    Windows 2003 server configuration, 315-322

  root, DNS, 362

  types, 512-513

  VPN configuration, 331

  Web, 512

service set identifiers. *See* **SSIDs**

Session Initiation Protocol. *See* **SIP**

session layer (OSI model), 123

set protocols command, 270

sh ip int brief command, 218-220

sh ip route command, 232

sh run command, 303

shadowing, 623

sharekey authentication, 436

shielded twisted-pair. *See* **STP**

shortcuts (Linux administration commands), 583

show access-list command, 402

show atm vc command, 308

show command, options, 207

show controllers command, 216

show controllers serial command, 216

show flash command, 208

show frame-relay PVC command, 304

show interfaces brief command, Juniper routers, 267

show ip interface brief (sh ip int brief) command, 214, 218-220, 242

show ip protocol (sh ip protocol) command, 242

show ip route (sh ip route) command, 231

show ip route igrp (sh ip route igrp) command, 249

show ip route static (sh ip route static) command, 234

show running config (sh run) command, 235

show startup config (sh start) command, 235

show version command, 208

shutdown command (Linux), 583

shutdown -h now command (Linux), 583

signal transmission, 10GBASE-T, 85-86

signal transport (VoIP), 489

signaling, VoIP, 488-489

signatures, 404

Simple Network Management Protocol. See SNMP

single mode (sm) fibers, 455-457, 473

single points-of-failure, 623

SIP (Session Initiation Protocol), 489

site surveys, WLANs, 424, 426, 428

Slotted Aloha protocol, 435

slowdowns, 126

sm (single mode) fibers, 473

Small Computer System Interface. See SCSI

smart devices, 621

SMB (server message block), 398

Smurf attacks, 395

SNMP (Simple Network Management Protocol)
    campus networks, 365-367
    configuring, 365-367
    MIB, 364

snmp community public ro command, 365

social engineering, 389

SONETs (Synchronous Optical Networks), 468

spam over Internet telephony. See spit

Spanning-Tree Protocol. See STP

spatial streams, 419

spectrum notation, 451

SPI (Stateful Packet Inspection), 28

spit (spam over Internet telephony), 497

split horizons, 245

splitters, 463

spoofs, 396

SS7, 488

SSH (Secure Shell), 408, 594-595

SSIDs (service set identifiers)
    802.11 WLAN configuration, 421
    home networks, 28

SSIP (secure session initiation protocol), 489

ST fiber connectors, 466

standard ACLs, 399

star topologies
    defined, 8
    LANs, 8
    office-type LANs, 32

stateful firewalls, 397

Stateful Packet Inspection. See SPI

static, 134

static MAC address assignments, 134

static routing
    defined, 227
    Juniper routers, 268
    protocols
        configuring, 234-235
        data packet flow between LANs, 231
        default gateways, 227
        gateway of last resort, 233
        host PC routing tables, 228
        loopbacks, 228
        Network Challenge software, 236
        next hop IP addresses, 231
        routing table codes, 232
        three-router campus network, 228, 232
        two-router network, 229
        variable length subnet masking, 231
    WANs, 337

static VLANs
    configuring, 373-377
    defined, 370
    Network Challenge software, 376-377

statistical data, 620

step-index fibers, 455

store-and-forward switching, 137

STP (shielded-twisted pair) cables, 51, 60

STP (Spanning-Tree Protocol)
    BPDUs, 377
    states, 378

straight-through cables, CAT5/5e patch cable configuration, **64**
  jacket stripping, 69
  RJ-45 plugs
    crimping, 71
    inserting wires into, 70
  wire pairs, separating, 70
straight-through ports, 33
streaming data, 164
stretching cables, 87
structured cabling
  campus hierarchical topology, 53
  EIA/TIA 568-B, defined, 51
  horizontal cabling, 54
    patch cables, 56
    terminated, 55
  standards, 51
  subsystems, 52
  telecommunications architecture, 52-53
  TIA/EIA 568-A, 51
STS (Synchronous Transport Signals), 469
stubby areas, 337
su command (Linux), 580
subinterfaces
  ATM routers, configuring, 307
  Frame Relay networks, 300
subnet masks
  8 subnet division example, 177-178
  binary/decimal equivalents, 176
  CIDR notation, 180
  creating, 173-175
  destination networks, finding, 198
  prefix length notation, 180
  router-to-router link example, 179-180
  VLSM, 231, 251
subsystems, structured cabling, 52
supernetting, 180. *See also* **CIDR blocks**
SVCs (switched virtual circuits), 306
Switch(config)# prompt, 372
Switch(config-line)# prompt, 372
switch-56 connections, 293
switches
  configuring
    campus networks, 370-371
    hostnames, 371

    line console, 372-373
    password protection, 372
    privileged mode, 371
    STP, 377-378
  defined, 8
  home networks, 19
  industrial Ethernet, 627
  LANs, interconnecting, 128
    hosts, 129
    hub comparison, 130-132
    isolating the collision domains, 136
    managed switches, 133-137
    multilayer switches, 137-138
    networking devices, 129
  latency, 137
  layer 2, 128
  link lights, 33
  managed
    aging time, 134
    benefits, 136
    broadcast domains, 137
    CAM, 136
    Cisco Catalyst 2960, 133
    flooding, 137
    frames, forwarding, 137
    IP addresses, configuring, 136
    isolating the collision domains, 136
    MAC address assignments, 134
  multilayer, 137-138
  star topologies, 8
SYN attacks, 395
Synchronous Digital Hiearchy. *See* **SDH**
Synchronous DRAM. *See* **SDRAM**
Synchronous Optical Networks. *See* **SONETs**
Synchronous Transport Signals. *See* **STS**
system config tools (Linux)
  date/time, 605
  firewalls, 605
  network menu, 607
  printers, 607
  services, 609
  software management, 607
  users, 609
  viewing, 604

System Properties menu (Vista), 108

system-config commands (Linux)

date/time, 605

firewalls, 605

network menu, 607

printers, 607

services, 609

software management, 607

tools, viewing, 604

users, 609

T

T1 framing, 294-295

T1 to T3 data rates, 292

T568A wiring guideline, 60

T568B wiring guideline, 60

tables

bridging, defined, 124

routing, 144, 228

tag-based VLANs, 370

tags

dlci, 300

RFID, powering, 434

TCA (Topology Change Notification Acknowledgement), 377

TCL (Transverse Conversion Loss), 84

TCN (Topology Change Notification), 377

TCOs (telecommunications outlets), 52

TCP (Transport Control Protocol), 158, 360-361

TCP/IP (Transmission Control Protocol/Internet Protocol), 16

development, 156

layers, 156

application, 157-158

Internet, 162-164

network interface, 164

transport, 158-162

TCTL (Transverse Conversion Transfer Loss), 84

TDM (time division multiplexing), 492

TE (telecommunications enclosure). See telecommunications closet structured cabling subsystem

Telco clouds, 293

telecommunications cabling architecture, 52-53

telecommunications closet structured cabling subsystem, 52

Telecommunications Industry Association. See TIA

telecommunications outlets. See TCOs

telecommunications room (TR). See telecommunications closet structured cabling subsystem

Telnet, defined, 584

terminal configuration mode (routers), 212

terminated cables, 55

terminating

CAT6 horizontal link cables

bend-limiting strain relief boot, 65, 68

jacket stripping, 66

lacing tool, 66

RJ-45 jack and lacing tool alignment, 67

high-performance UTP, 60-61

testing

cables, 71

ACR, 74

attenuation, 72

CAT6 links, 75-82

channel specifications, 72

delay skew, 74

ELFEXT, 74

NEXT, 72

propagation delay, 74

PSACR, 74

PSELFEXT, 74

PSNEXT, 73

return loss, 74

LANs, 35-36

router interface configurations, 242

TFTP (Trivial File Transfer Protocol)

configuring, 271

data transfer, 273

port 69 write request, 273

port assignment write request, 273

Network Challenge software, 274-275

ThinNet, 6

TIA (Telecommunications Industry Association), 51

TIA/EIA 568-A, 51

tie lines, defined, 492

time division multiplexing. See TDM

timestamps, 490

timing considerations, industrial networks, 622

TLDs (top level domains), 362

tmp directory (Linux), 570

token passing, 6

token-ring hubs, 6

token-ring topologies, 6

top level domains, 362

topologies

    bus topologies, 6, 8

    defined, 5

    industrial Ethernet, 626-627

    LANs, 5-9

    mesh topologies, 9

    ring topologies (industrial networks), 623

    star topologies, 8, 32

    token-ring topologies, 6

Topology Change Notification. *See* TCN

Topology Change Notification Acknowledgement. *See* TCA

totally stubby areas, 337

TR (telecommunications room). *See* telecommunications closet structured cabling subsystem

traffic (Internet)

    analyzing, 344

        frame size distribution, 347

        network layer host tables, 346

        network layer matrix, 345-346

        utilization/errors strip chart, 344

    data traffic, campus networks

        daily, 379

        hourly, 379

        weekly, 380

    filtering, 354

transceivers, 415

transient interfaces, 267

translation bridges, 127

Transmission Control Protocol/Internet Protocol. *See* TCP/IP

transmit (TX), 62

transmit cable pairs, aligning, 62-63

transparent bridges, 127

Transport Control Protocol. *See* TCP

transport layer (OSI model), 123

transport layer protocols

    data packet sequence, 159

    TCP, 158

TCP handshake, 160

    terminating the TCP, 160-161

    UDP, 161-162

Transverse Conversion Loss. *See* TCL

Transverse Conversion Transfer Loss. *See* TCTL

trees, defined, 515

Trivial File Transfer Protocol. *See* TFTP

troubleshooting

    cables

        CAT5e test examples, 88, 92-93

        failing to meet manufacturer specifications, 87

        installation, 86

        stretching, 87

    home networks, 26

    Linux

        boot processes, 598-600

        boot services, 602-603

        security, 601

        users, 600-601

    optical networking, 481

    routers, 217-220

    VPN tunnels, 331

tunable lasers, 462

TX (transmit), 62

U

U-NII (Unlicensed National Information Infrastructure), 418

UDP (User Datagram Protocol), 161-162

UDP/IP (User Datagram Protocol/Internet Protocol), 629

UHF (ultra-high frequency), 435

unicast addresses, 184

unicast packets, 360

Universal Serial Bus 1.1. *See* USB 1.1

Universal Serial Bus 2.0. *See* USB 2.0

unmount command (Linux), 583

unsecured data packets

    captured packets, 407

    capturing packets setup, 405

    protecting, 408

    router connections, 406

    telnet session packets, 407

telnetting to routers, 405

user verification, 406

unshielded twisted-pair. *See* **UTP cables**

unspecified bit-rate class, 306

up arrow (Linux), 583

upgrading PBXs, 493-494

uplink ports, 33

uptime, routers, 208

USB 1.1 (Universal Serial Bus 1.1), 104

USB 2.0 (Universal Serial Bus 2.0), 104

USB connections, 105

user accounts, RAS configuration, 322

User Datagram Protocol. *See* **UDP**

User Datagram Protocol/Internet Protocol. *See* **UDP/IP**

User EXEC mode (routers)

entering, 206

help command, 207

Net-Challenge software, 209-211

show command options, 207

show flash command, 208

show version command, 208

users

Linux

adding to, 561-563

managing, 609

troubleshooting, 600-601

multi-homed, 338

Windows 2003/2008 server domains, adding to, 526-527

usr directory (Linux), 570

UTP (unshielded twisted-pair) cables, 51

balanced mode, 58

bottlenecking, 59

categories, 58-59

F/UTP, 84

full duplex gigabit Ethernet support, 59

high-performance, terminating, 60-61

RJ-45 modular plug example, 57

standards, 57

V

V.44/V.34 analog modem connection standard, 309

V.92/V.90 analog modem connection standard, 309

var directory (Linux), 570

var/log directory (Linux), 600

variable bit-rate real time class, 306

variable bit-rate/non–real time class, 306

variable length subnet masks. *See* **VLSMs**

VCCs (virtual channel connections), 306

VCIs (virtual channel identifiers), 306

VCs (virtual channels), 308

VCSELs (vertical cavity surface emitting lasers), 462

vendor support, industrial networks, 625

verifying

device drivers

Mac OS X, 110-111

Windows Vista/XP, 108-109

memory amounts installed, 113

My Network Places connection

Windows 2000, 550-551

Windows XP, 546-549

Network connection (Windows Vista), 546

Network Neighborhood connection (Windows NT/98), 552

vertical cavity surface emitting lasers. *See* **VCSELs**

VFLs (Visual Fault Locators), 481

viewing

ATM interfaces, 308

ATM virtual channels, 308

file contents commands (Linux), 569

cat, 568

more, 567

"Hello" packets, 277

installed applications (Linux), 584

Juniper router

configuring, 265

interfaces, 267-268

Linux system-config tools, ls system-config, 604

MAC addresses, 12

routing protocols, 242

virtual channel connections. *See* **VCCs**

virtual channel identifiers. *See* **VCIs**

virtual channels. *See* **VCs**

Virtual LANs. *See* **VLANs**

virtual path connections. *See* **VPCs**

virtual path identifiers. *See* **VPIs**

Virtual Private Networks. *See* **VPNs**

virtual tie lines, 489

viruses, 393

Visual Fault Locators (VFLs), 481

VLANs (Virtual LANs), 369

dynamic, 370

membership assignments, 370

static

configuring, 373-377

defined, 370

Network Challenge software, 376-377

types, 369

VoIP, 497

VLSMs (variable length subnet masks), 231, 251

VoIP (Voice over IP)

data packet analysis, 497

acknowledgement, 499, 502

call processor call plans, 502

call processor messages, 499

collecting data packets, 498

IP network handshaking, 504

NBX call processor codes, 498

PCM voice data, 499

test setup, 502

gateways, 488, 492

implementing

replacing PBX tie lines, 491-493

switching to IP telephony solutions, 494

upgrading PBXs, 493-494

overview, 488

packet sequence numbers, 490

PBX, 488

QoS

jitter, 495-496

network latency, 496

queuing, 496-497

security, 497

signal transport, 489

signaling, 488-489

SIP, 489

SSIP, 489

timestamps, 490

virtual tie lines, 489

VLANs, 497

VPCs (virtual path connections), 306

VPIs (virtual path identifiers), 306

VPNs (virtual private networks), 28, 325

remote client configurations

Cisco VPN Client software, 334-337

Mac OS X, 333

Windows Vista, 332

Windows XP, 332-333

router-to-router connections, 326-331

server configuration, 331

tunnel connections, 326

tunnels, troubleshooting, 331

vulnerable software attacks, 391-393

W

WANs (wide area networks), 5, 291

ATM, 305

classes, 306

connections, creating, 308

interfaces, viewing, 308

PVC interface, 306

router configuration, 307

router subinterface configuration, 307

VCI, 306

virtual channels, viewing, 308

VPI, 306

dial-in access

analog modem technologies, 309-310

cable modems, 310

ISDN, 310-312

remote access servers. See RAS

xDSL modems, 312-314

Frame Relay networks, 298

configuring, 299, 305

creating connections, 301-302

point-to-point connections, 300

point-to-point router connections, 302-304

PVCs, 300

subinterfaces, 300

Internet data traffic analyzation

frame size distribution, 347

network layer host tables, 346

network layer matrix, 345-346

utilization/errors strip chart, 344

Internet routing, 338
   autonomous systems, 339
   BGP, configuring, 339-343
   Net-Challenge BGP configuration, 343-344
line connections
   data channels, 292-293
   encoding formats, 295-298
   POP, 294
   T1 framing, 294-295
routing, 337
VPNs, 325
   Cisco VPN Client software, 334-337
   Mac OS X clients, 333
   router-to-router connections, 326-331
   server configuration, 331
   tunnel connections, 326
   troubleshooting tunnels, 331
   Windows Vista clients, 332
   Windows XP clients, 332-333

war driving, 394

wavelengths (optical networking), 452

WDM (wavelength division multiplexing), 451, 464

Web servers, 512

websites
   ARIN, 173
   IANA, 15
   IEEE OUI and company ID assignment database, 14
   JUNOS CLI User Guide, 271
   Linux, 565
   port assignments, 158

weighted fair queueing. *See* **WFQ**

weighted random early discard. *See* **WRED**

well-known ports, 157

WEP (wired equivalent privacy), 28, 394

WFQ (weighted fair queuing), 496

who command (Linux), 601

Wi-Fi. *See* **wireless networks; WLANs**

Wi-Fi Alliance, 17

Wi-Fi Protected Access. *See* **WPA**

wide area networks. *See* **WANs**

wild card bits, 253

WiMAX (Worldwide Interoperability for Microwave Access), 432

Windows 2000, verifying My Network Places connection, 550-551

Windows 2003 servers
   domains
      adding computers, to, 522-526
      adding groups to, 528-532
      adding organization units to, 528-532
      adding users to, 526-527
      creating, 514-519
      policy configuration, 539, 542-544
   RAS configuration
      enabling RAS, 315
      IP configuration, 321
      managing multiple servers, 318
      modem configuration, 318, 320
      protocol selection, 317
      Routing and Remote Access Server Setup Wizard menu, 315
      Routing and Remote Access window, 315
      user accounts, 322
   VPN server configuration, 331

Windows 2008 servers
   configuring, 521
   domains
      adding computer to, 522-526
      adding groups to, 528-532
      adding organizational units, 528-532
      adding users, 526-527
      domain policy configuation, 534-536, 539

Windows NT/98, verifying Network Neighborhood connection, 552

Windows Vista
   device drivers, 108-109
   Network connection, verifying, 546
   RAS client configuration, 324
   VPN client configuration, 332

Windows XP
   device drivers, 108-109
   My Network Places connection, verifying, 546-549
   RAS client configuration, 324
   VPN client configuration, 332-333

winipcfg command, MAC addresses, 13

wire maps, 64

wire speed routing, 138

wired equivalent privacy. *See* **WEP**

wired networks
   advantages, 17
   defined, 16

disadvantages, 17

troubleshooting, 26

wireless bridges, 127

wireless local area networks. *See* **WLANs**

wireless networks

advantages, 17

configuring, 27

connections, 27

defined, 16

hotspots, 27

range extenders, 27

routers, 17

security, 27-28

standards, 17

troubleshooting, 26

vulnerabilities, 394

Wi-Fi Alliance, 17

wireless routers, 17, 21

Wireless-N adapters, 20

wiring guidelines, EIA/TIA 568B, 60

WLANs (wireless local area networks)

802.11 configuration, 420

access points, 422

bridges, 422

lost associations, 422

range, extending, 424

signals, 423

site survey, 424-428

SSIDs, 421

802.11 standard, 414

MAC layer, 415

OFDM, 418-419

physical layer, 415

802.11a standard, 420

802.11b standard, 419-420

802.11g standard, 419-420

802.11i standard, 420

802.11n standard, 419-420

802.11r standard, 420

access points, 415

benefits, 414

Bluetooth, 429

configuring, 430-431

inquiry procedure, 430

paging procedure, 430

piconets, 430

BSS, 415-416

CSMA/CA, 416

DSSS, 417

ESS, 416

FHSS, 417

hand-offs, 416

point-to-multipoint configuration, 438

antenna site survey, 439

multipoint distribution, 440

point-to-point wireless links, 439-440

remote installations, 442

RFID, 433

air interface protocol, 435

backscatter, 432

frequency of operation, 435

tags, powering, 434

roaming, 416

security, 435-438

security vulnerabilities, 394

standard, 415

WiMAX, 432

Work Area Outlets. *See* **WOs**

work area structured cabling subsystem, 52

workstation, defined, 523

Worldwide Interoperability for Microwave Access. *See* **WiMAX**

worms, 393

WOs (Work Area Outlets), 53

WPA (Wi-Fi Protected Access), 28, 394, 437

WPA2, 394

WRED (weighted random early discard), 496

write memory (wr m) command, 235

wuftpd (Washington University ftp server), 596

X - Y - Z

X.25 protocol, 298

xDSL modems, 312-314

XENPAKs (10 Gigabit Interface Adapters), 471

Z-Term serial communications software, configuring, 205

zero-dispersion wavelength, 459